Communications in Computer and Information Science **3092**

Rationale
The CCIS series is devoted to the publication of proceedings of computer science conferences. Its aim is to efficiently disseminate original research results in informatics in printed and electronic form. While the focus is on publication of peer-reviewed full papers presenting mature work, inclusion of reviewed short papers reporting on work in progress is welcome, too. Besides globally relevant meetings with internationally representative program committees guaranteeing a strict peer-reviewing and paper selection process, conferences run by societies or of high regional or national relevance are also considered for publication.

Topics
The topical scope of CCIS spans the entire spectrum of informatics ranging from foundational topics in the theory of computing to information and communications science and technology and a broad variety of interdisciplinary application fields.

Information for Volume Editors and Authors
Publication in CCIS is free of charge. No royalties are paid, however, we offer registered conference participants temporary free access to the online version of the conference proceedings on SpringerLink (http://link.springer.com) by means of an http referrer from the conference website and/or a number of complimentary printed copies, as specified in the official acceptance email of the event.

CCIS proceedings can be published in time for distribution at conferences or as post-proceedings, and delivered in the form of printed books and/or electronically as USBs and/or e-content licenses for accessing proceedings at SpringerLink. Furthermore, CCIS proceedings are included in the CCIS electronic book series hosted in the SpringerLink digital library at http://link.springer.com/bookseries/7899. Conferences publishing in CCIS are allowed to use our online conference service (Meteor) for managing the whole proceedings lifecycle (from submission and reviewing to preparing for publication) free of charge.

Publication process
The language of publication is exclusively English. Authors publishing in CCIS have to sign the Springer CCIS copyright transfer form, however, they are free to use their material published in CCIS for substantially changed, more elaborate subsequent publications elsewhere. For the preparation of the camera-ready papers/files, authors have to strictly adhere to the Springer CCIS Authors' Instructions and are strongly encouraged to use the CCIS LaTeX style files or templates.

Abstracting/Indexing
CCIS is abstracted/indexed in DBLP, Google Scholar, EI-Compendex, Mathematical Reviews, SCImago, Scopus. CCIS volumes are also submitted for the inclusion in ISI Proceedings.

How to start
To start the evaluation of your proposal for inclusion in the CCIS series, please send an e-mail to ccis@springer.com

Dario Liberona · Luong Vuong Nguyen ·
I-Hsien Ting · Kai Wang
Editors

Multidisciplinary Social Networks Research

13th International Conference, MISNC 2026
Danang, Vietnam, August 10–12, 2026
Proceedings, Part II

Springer

Editors
Dario Liberona
Seinajoki University of Applied Sciences
Seinäjoki, Finland

Luong Vuong Nguyen
FPT University
Da Nang, Vietnam

I-Hsien Ting
National University of Kaohsiung
Kaohsiung, Taiwan

Kai Wang
National University of Kaohsiung
Kaohsiung, Taiwan

ISSN 1865-0929 ISSN 1865-0937 (electronic)
Communications in Computer and Information Science
ISBN 978-3-032-33380-3 ISBN 978-3-032-33381-0 (eBook)
https://doi.org/10.1007/978-3-032-33381-0

This Springer imprint is published by the registered company Springer Nature Switzerland AG
The registered company address is: Gewerbestrasse 11, 6330 Cham, Switzerland

Preface

Welcome to the 13th Multidisciplinary International Social Networks Conference (MISNC 2026), which took place August 10–12, 2026, at FPT University Danang, Vietnam. What began in 2014 in Kaohsiung, Taiwan, has matured over more than a decade into a vibrant international forum where scholars, researchers, and practitioners come together to exchange ideas, share findings, and explore new directions in the fast-moving field of social networks. Each edition has carried the conference to a new corner of the world—from Matsuyama, Japan and Bangkok and Phuket, Thailand, to Saint-Étienne, France; Wenzhou, China; Bergen, Norway; Bali, Indonesia; and Oviedo, Spain—steadily widening its horizons and nurturing a genuinely global research community.

At its core, MISNC champions multidisciplinary inquiry into social networking, a domain that sits at the crossroads of technology, communication, sociology, business, and many other fields. The conference is designed as a meeting ground for cross-disciplinary conversation, inviting participants from both academia and industry to compare perspectives, methodologies, and practical applications. It is through this exchange that MISNC sharpens academic understanding while staying responsive to the real challenges practitioners face—helping to chart where social network research and practice go next.

For MISNC 2026, we received 166 submissions, of which 79 papers were selected for the proceedings. The review process was double blind, and submissions received on average two reviews each. The authors come from 13 countries and regions: China, Colombia, Finland, France, Germany, Indonesia, Japan, South Korea, Malaysia, Spain, Taiwan, Thailand, and the USA. Together, these works capture the breadth and depth of a worldwide community advancing theories, methods, and applications across social network strategies, intelligent informatics, education, healthcare, software engineering, information management, and well beyond.

We owe sincere thanks to the authors for the quality and originality of their work; to the program committee members and reviewers whose careful evaluations safeguarded the standard of these proceedings; and to our keynote speakers and session chairs for sharing their insight and expertise. We are equally grateful to the organizing committee and our supporting institutions, whose commitment brought MISNC 2026 to life.

It is our hope that MISNC 2026 in Danang offered not only stimulating scholarly exchange but also the chance to forge lasting collaborations and friendships. We were happy to welcome you to Danang and hope you had a rewarding and memorable conference.

Dario Liberona
Luong Vuong Nguyen
I-Hsien Ting
Kai Wang

Organization

Honorary Chairs

Tzung-Pei Hong	National University of Kaohsiung, Taiwan
Ngoc Thanh Nguyen	Wrocław University of Science and Technology, Poland

General Chairs

Dario Liberona	Seinäjoki University of Applied Sciences, Finland
Luong Vuong Nguyen	FPT University, Vietnam
I-Hsien Ting	National University of Kaohsiung, Taiwan
Thi-Thu-Hong Phan	FPT University, Vietnam

Program Chairs

Dario Liberona	Seinäjoki University of Applied Sciences, Finland
Luong Vuong Nguyen	FPT University, Vietnam
I-Hsien Ting	National University of Kaohsiung, Taiwan
Kai Wang	National University of Kaohsiung, Taiwan

Local Chair

Cao Vu Bui	FPT University, Vietnam

Steering Committee Chairs

Cathy Hsing-Tzu Lin	National University of Kaohsiung, Taiwan
George Chang	Kean University, USA
Victor Hugo Garcia Medina	Universidad Distrital Francisco José de Caldas, Colombia
Shiro Uesugi	Matsuyama University, Japan
Chih-Chien Wang	National Taipei University, Taiwan
Guandong Xu	University of Technology, Sydney, Australia
Katsutoshi Yada	Kansai University, Japan

Publication Chairs

Chung-Hong Lee	National Kaohsiung University of Science and Technology, Taiwan
Quoc-Trinh Vo	FPT University, Vietnam
Hsin-Chang Yang	National University of Kaohsiung, Taiwan

Publicity Chairs

Chian-Hsueng Chao	National University of Kaohsiung, Taiwan
Vicente Garcia Diaz	University of Oviedo, Spain
I-Wen Fang	Tatung University, Taiwan
Hafiz Budi Firmansyah	Institut Teknologi Sumatera, Indonesia
Hiroshi Koga	Kansai University, Japan
Yen-Hsien Lee	National Chiayi University, Taiwan
Kazunori Minetaki	Kindai University, Japan
Quan T. Ngo	FPT University, Vietnam
Charles Perez	Paris School of Business, France
Takashi Okamoto	Ehime University, Japan
Karina Sokolova	Paris School of Business, France
Didi Sundiman	Universitas Universal, Indonesia
Suppanunta Romprasert	Srinakharinwirot University, Thailand
Danai Tanamee	Srinakharinwirot University, Thailand

Special Issue Chairs

Guan-Lin Chen	Shu-Te University, Taiwan
Chien-Liang Lin	Ming Chuan University, Taiwan
Shishi Cecilia Wu	Walker College of Business at Appalachian State University, USA

Industry Chairs

Chia-Chi Chang	National University of Kaohsiung, Taiwan
Ming-Chia Hsieh	I-Shou University, Taiwan
Chia-Sung Yen	National Chin-Yi University of Technology, Taiwan

Special Session Chairs

Jerry Chun-Wei Lin	Silesian University of Technology, Poland
Yu-Lung Wu	I-Shou University, Taiwan
Mu-En Wu	National Taipei University of Technology, Taiwan

Conference Secretary

Weny Ming-Jun Chen	National University of Kaohsiung, Taiwan

Workshop and Special Sessions Chairs

Special Session: AI-Driven Applications in Business and Society

Yu-Lung Wu	I-Shou University, Taiwan

Special Session: Human–AI Collective Intelligence and Collaborative Decision Systems

Luong Vuong Nguyen	FPT University, Vietnam

Special Session: The Use of AI in Social Media and Daily Life: Exploring How Artificial Intelligence Changes Communication, Supports Routines, Personalizes Experiences, and Raises Important Opportunities, Challenges, and Ethical Questions

Jean Lai	Hong Kong Baptist University, China

Workshop: Learning Networks in a Connected World: Trends, Structures and AI Support Understanding and Supporting Learning Processes Through Network Insights and AI Methods

Kinga Sipos	University of Bern, Switzerland
Johann Stan	European Patent Office, the Netherlands

Special Session: Digital Technologies and Social Networks in Cultural Heritage Preservation

Vinothini Kasinathan,	Asia Pacific University of Technology & Innovation, Malaysia
Aida Binti Mustapha	Universiti Malaysia Pahang Al-Sultan Abdullah, Malaysia

Special Session: Network, Economic and Business Studies

Chia-Sun Yen	National Chin-Yi University of Science and Technology, Taiwan

Program Committee Members

Dan Braha	New England Complex Systems Institute, USA
Teruyuki Bunno	Kindai University, Japan
Hsin-Lu Chang	National Changchi University, Taiwan
Chia-Chi Chang	National University of Kaohsiung, Taiwan
Nai-Wen Chang	Kun Shan University, Taiwan
Chian-Hsueng Chao	National University of Kaohsiung, Taiwan
Richard Chbeir	Université de Pau et des Pays de l'Adour, France
Guan Lin Chen	Shu-Te University, Taiwan
Yunwei Chen	National Science Library (Chengdu), Chinese Academy of Sciences, China
Ping Chou	National University of Kaohsiung, Taiwan
Shih-Wei Chou	National Kaohsiung University of Science and Technology, Taiwan
João Cordeiro	University of Évora, Portugal
Tsai-Hsin Chu	National Chiayi University, Taiwan
Yu Cui	Kansai University, Japan
Min-Yuh Day	National Taipei University, Taiwan
I-Wen Fang	Tatung University, Taiwan
Hafiz Budi Firmansyah	Institut Teknologi Sumatera, Indonesia
Vicente Garcia Diaz	University of Oviedo, Spain
Jordán Pascual Espada	University of Oviedo, Spain
Zhiwei Guo	Chongqing Technology and Business University, China
Pei-Yi Hao	National Kaohsiung University of Science and Technology, Taiwan
Tzung-Pei Hong	National University of Kaohsiung, Taiwan
Han-Fen Hu	University of Nevada, Las Vegas, USA
Ching-Yu (Austin) Huang	Kean University, USA
Ming-Chia Hsieh	I-Shou University, Taiwan
Carol Hsu	University of Sydney, Australia
Hiroki Idota	Kindai University, Japan
Jason Jung	Chung-Ang University, South Korea
ShuChen Kao	Kun Shan University, Taiwan

Vinothini Kasinathan	Asia Pacific University of Technology & Innovation, Malaysia
Chutisant Kerdvibulvech	National Institute of Development Administration, Thailand
Hiroshi Koga	Kansai University, Japan
Ying-Feng Kuo	National University of Kaohsiung, Taiwan
Tom Kwanya	Technical University of Kenya, Kenya
Jean Lai	Hong Kong Baptist University, China
Georgios Lappas	University of Western Macedonia, Greece
Christine Largeron	Université Jean Monnet, France
Cheng-Yu Lai	Chung Yuan Christian University, Taiwan
Daniel Fernández Lanvin	Universidad de Oviedo, Spain
Chia-Wen Lee	Xiamen Ocean Vocational College, China
Yen-Hsien Lee	National Chiayi University, Taiwan
Ching Li	National Taiwan Normal University, Taiwan
Chih-Chin Liang	National Formosa University, Taiwan
Paoling Liao	National Kaohsiung University of Science and Technology, Taiwan
Dario Liberona	Seinäjoki University of Applied Sciences, Finland
Cathy Hsing-Tzu Lin	National University of Kaohsiung, Taiwan
Chien-Liang Lin	Ming Chuan University, Taiwan
Jerry Chun-Wei Lin	Silesian University of Technology, Poland
Nan-Hong Lin	Tatung University, Taiwan
Wen-Yang Lin	National University of Kaohsiung, Taiwan
Juan Manuel Cueva Lovelle	Universidad de Oviedo, Spain
Jaime Solís Martínez	University of Oviedo, Spain
Kazunori Minetaki	Kindai University, Japan
Dzulkifli Mukhtar	Universiti Malaysia Kelantan, Malaysia
Sanetake Nagayoshi	Shizuoka University, Japan
Roman Neruda	Czech Academy of Sciences, Czechia
Loc Nguyen	Loc Nguyen's Academic Network, Vietnam
Edward Rolando Núñez-Valdez	University of Oviedo, Spain
Hitoshi Okada	National Institute of Informatics, Japan
Takashi Okamoto	Ehime University, Japan
Yohko Orito	Ehime University, Japan
Luka Pavlič	Maribor University, Slovenia
Charles Perez	Paris School of Business, France
Suppanunta Romprasert	Srinakharinwirot University, Thailand
Hidenobu Sai	Hokkai-Gakuen University, Japan
Natsuki Sano	Tokyo University of Information Science, Japan
Stephan Schlögl	Management Center Innsbruck, Austria
Norihito Seki	Hokkai-Gakuen University, Japan

Muhammad Ikhsan Setiawan	Narotama University, Indonesia
Basit Shahzad	University of Prince Mugrin, Saudi Arabia
Rong-An Shang	Soochow University, Taiwan
Nitin Singh	IIM Ranchi, India
Thitirat Siriborvornratanakul	National Institute of Development Administration, Thailand
Karina Sokolova	Paris School of Business, France
Gautam Srivastava	Brandon University, Canada
Didi Sundiman	Universitas Universal, Indonesia
Sheikh Abu Taher	Jahangirnagar University, Bangladesh
Jeffrey Chi-Feng Tai	National Chiayi University, Taiwan
I-Hsien Ting	National University of Kaohsiung, Taiwan
Yu-Chuan Tsai	National University of Kaohsiung, Taiwan
Masashi Ueda	Kyoto Sangyo University, Japan
Yasushi Ueki	Institute of Developing Economies, Japan
Shiro Uesugi	Matsuyama University, Japan
Rejula Vijeykumar	Seventh Sense Labs LLC, USA
Chih-Chien Wang	National Taipei University, Taiwan
Kai Wang	National University of Kaohsiung, Taiwan
Li Weigang	University of Brasília, Brazil
Cheng-Shu Wang	National Taipei University of Technology, Taiwan
Quyuan Wang	Chongqing Technology and Business University, China
Shishi Cecilia Wu	Walker College of Business of Appalachian State University, USA
Chienhsing Wu	National University of Kaohsiung, Taiwan
Chuan-Chun Wu	I-Shou University, Taiwan
Jimmy Ming-Tai Wu	National Kaohsiung University of Science and Technology, Taiwan
Yu-Lung Wu	I-Shou University, Taiwan
Sachiko Yanagihara	University of Toyama, Japan
Katsutoshi Yada	Kansai University, Japan
Hsin-Chang Yang	National University of Kaohsiung, Taiwan
Shu-Chen Yang	National University of Kaohsiung, Taiwan
Yu-Chen Yang	National Sun Yat-sen University, Taiwan
Chia-Sung Yen	National Chin-Yi University of Technology, Taiwan
Keyi Zhong	Chongqing University, China
Yi Zuo	Dalian Maritime University, China

Contents

Network, Economic and Business Studies

Referral Reward Programs as Strategic Levers in High-Involvement Markets: The Role of Social Capital, Intrinsic Motivation, and Community Structure

Chih-Chen Hsu[1(✉)], Kai-Chieh Chia[2], and Chao Cheng Lee[1]

[1] Department of Business Administration, National Taichung University of Science and Technology, Taichung, Taiwan
cchsu@nutc.edu.tw
[2] Department of Business Administration, Soochow University, Taipei, Taiwan
kj@scu.edu.tw

Abstract. The automotive sales industry primarily relies on offline physical marketing as its primary sales channel. This study focuses on new energy vehicles (NEVs) and develops a model that integrates offline sales with online social media marketing. The model is based on a multi-level marketing (MLM) framework and considers factors such as referral reward programs (RRPs), metacognition, and community network graphs to optimize information sharing and promote impulsive purchase behavior among consumers. The findings indicate that RRPs significantly influence information dissemination within the community and consumers' impulsive purchase behavior. However, the impulsive purchase model's explanatory power is limited, potentially due to the exclusion of important variables such as brand, price, battery safety, range, and charging convenience. These factors may have a more significant impact on the impulsive purchase of NEVs. Overall, RRPs remain attractive to consumers who have already shown interest in specific NEV brands, suggesting that automotive dealers can leverage RRPs to effectively capture and convert such potential buyers.

Keywords: Multi-level marketing · Referral rewards programs · Meta-perception · Next energy vehicles · Impulsive purchase

1 Introduction

Kannan and Li (2017) emphasize that the automotive sales industry has historically relied on offline physical marketing as its primary sales channel, with consumers rarely purchasing vehicles based purely on online viewing. Even Tesla, the leading new energy vehicle (NEV) brand with an established online purchase system, still requires showrooms and sales personnel to assist consumers in their decision-making. However, the growing prevalence of digital platforms has shifted consumer behavior, with online marketing now playing a critical role in awareness, evaluation, and referral processes

D. Liberona et al. (Eds.): MISNC 2026, CCIS 3092, pp. 3–20, 2027.
https://doi.org/10.1007/978-3-032-33381-0_1

even for high-involvement products. Rather than viewing online and offline channels as independent, integrating them may yield greater marketing synergies. Accordingly, this study develops an integrated virtual community multi-level marketing (MLM) model that incorporates offline sales channels, providing a framework suitable for industries that still depend heavily on physical sales.

The proposed model is grounded in the principles of multi-level marketing (MLM), which leverages network-based dissemination mechanisms in conjunction with referral reward programs (RRPs) to enhance marketing effectiveness (Wirtz et al., 2012). The proliferation of social media platforms has significantly accelerated the reach and scalability of MLM activities, as firm-generated content is now frequently propagated through social media influencers following the two-step flow of communication (Katz & Lazarsfeld, 1955), subsequently stimulating user-generated content. Interactions such as likes, comments, and shares within virtual communities not only facilitate social engagement but also serve as key catalysts for information diffusion (Chiu et al., 2006; Chia et al., 2021). Participants involved in such MLM processes—and their extended social networks—represent valuable pools of prospective consumers, who may eventually convert through offline physical sales channels, thereby bridging digital engagement with real-world purchasing behavior.

To further understand the mechanisms through which MLM operates in virtual communities, it is essential to examine why users are willing to interact with others via likes, comments, and shares. Two seminal sociological studies provide critical insights into these sharing behaviors. Chiu et al. (2006) proposed an influential framework that integrates social capital theory and social cognitive theory to explain the sociological determinants of knowledge sharing in virtual communities—highlighting the roles of social interaction ties, reciprocity, and community identification. Building on this foundation, Chia et al. (2021) extended the model to explore social media influencers' willingness to share unboxing experiences and endorse products within social commerce settings. These studies, frequently cited in the literature, underline the pivotal factors that drive information-sharing behaviors online and form the theoretical basis for the MLM mechanisms adopted in this research.

Building upon these theoretical foundations of information-sharing behavior, this study further introduces referral reward programs (RRPs) into the community media marketing communication framework to better reflect contemporary practices in the NEV industry—such as Tesla's widely adopted referral code system. This pragmatic use of incentives in conjunction with physical sales channels has also garnered considerable academic attention. As noted by Wirtz et al. (2012), rewards and incentives represent one of the most effective tools for shaping consumer behavior, and the internet provides unprecedented flexibility in designing and delivering such inducements. Under RRPs, companies incentivize existing customers to recommend products by offering monetary rewards or discounts, a mechanism that has become increasingly prevalent with the growth of pseudo-community social media. According to the New York Times, approximately 65% of startups employ RRPs as a means of customer acquisition. Tesla, which traditionally eschews conventional advertising, relies heavily on RRPs—providing incentives ranging from US$1,000 per successful referral to even gifting a vehicle for multiple referrals. Kuang et al. (2024) further report that these programs can generate advertising effectiveness up to 40 times greater than traditional marketing strategies.

To further enhance participation, this study also considers the use of member-based cumulative RRPs, which not only incentivize social media users to engage in promotional activities, but also encourage them to convert into formal members in order to accrue referral benefits. Such mechanisms help firms operating in physical sales environments to identify potential customers who have progressed to the evaluation or purchase stages of the customer journey.

Nevertheless, excessive or inappropriate use of RRPs may generate unintended consequences. Wirtz et al. (2012) argue that RRPs can exert positive, neutral, or even negative effects on firms, depending on the balance between negative indirect effects (e.g., perceptions of inauthenticity or opportunism) and the positive returns generated by attractive incentives. These heterogeneous outcomes are primarily attributed to differences in metacognitive reactions among message recipients, which are often triggered by MLM-based promotional approaches.

Wang et al. (2015) further emphasize that the effectiveness of RRPs is contingent upon the nature of the virtual community in which they are deployed. Specifically, community media can be differentiated into social graphs (e.g., Facebook, Instagram), which replicate real-world interpersonal relationships, and interest graphs (e.g., YouTube, LinkedIn), which are formed around shared interests or topics. Because users in these two types of networks possess different motivations and expectations, deploying RRPs in MLM requires careful adaptation to the community context. Failure to account for these differences may trigger negative metacognitive responses among consumers, ultimately harming both customer acquisition efforts and corporate image.

With respect to impulsive purchasing behavior, Leong et al. (2017) describe impulsive consumption as a sudden, hedonic, and complex purchasing process, whereby the speed of decision-making precludes any deliberate evaluation of alternatives or future consequences. Building upon this conceptualization, Cao et al. (2021) investigated how referral programs interact with price promotions within e-commerce platforms and influence the acceptance of referred customers, while Sun et al. (2021) further considered scenarios in which individuals simultaneously act as both "referrers" and "purchasers" when offered promotional incentives. Notably, relatively few studies have explicitly examined how individual behavioral predispositions—such as impulsiveness—shape referral-sharing behaviors. Addressing this gap, Zhan et al. (2023) integrated prior findings to explore how impulsive tendencies and metacognition jointly influence consumers' responses to RRPs, thereby laying an important empirical foundation for further exploration of sales performance outcomes.

Grounded in the aforementioned theoretical and empirical insights, this study aims to explore four key research issues: (1) how MLM performance can be optimized in virtual community environments; (2) how to strategically implement RRPs within different types of community graphs to reduce negative metacognitive responses; (3) what sociological determinants most strongly influence users' willingness to share information within MLM contexts; and (4) how impulsive purchasing manifests in offline physical sales settings. To the best of our knowledge, this is the first study to integrate the nature of community media with sociological theory to examine the effectiveness of RRPs and their metacognitive effects—providing novel theoretical contributions and practical implications for NEV marketing strategies.

2 Literature Review

2.1 Determinants of New Energy Vehicle Purchases

The growing market penetration of new energy vehicles (NEVs) has prompted increasing scholarly attention to the drivers of consumer purchase decisions. Wang et al. (2017) found that economic incentives, infrastructure readiness, environmental concerns, and supportive government policies exert significant positive effects on consumers' purchase intentions, whereas cruising range has a nonsignificant influence. Recent findings by Wang et al. (2023) further indicate that NEV consumers place particular emphasis on service quality throughout both the purchasing and post-purchase processes, distinguishing them from traditional vehicle buyers.

2.2 Information Sharing in Virtual Communities

Given the importance of information diffusion in multi-level marketing (MLM), this study incorporates a virtual community MLM model into the NEV sales context. Unlike ordinary users, social media influencers not only engage in content interaction but also play active roles in product endorsement and experience sharing in social commerce. To understand their sharing willingness, previous studies have integrated social capital theory with social exchange theory. Chiu et al. (2006) proposed that social interaction ties, shared vision, trust, and community identification (social capital) shape knowledge-sharing behaviors. Chia et al. (2021) extended this framework to demonstrate that influencers' unboxing-sharing intention is additionally influenced by social exchange factors such as effort costs, reciprocity, and altruism.

Empirical evidence shows differing effects of these factors: Chiu et al. (2006) reported that interaction ties, reciprocity, and identification significantly increase sharing volume, whereas trust and shared language have no effect, and shared vision exerts a negative influence. Chia et al. (2021) further showed that interaction ties and shared vision significantly promote unboxing-sharing intention, while trust and identification do not; influencers' effort and altruism positively influence willingness, but reciprocity does not.

2.3 Referral Reward Programs and Metacognition

Under social exchange theory, consumers assess perceived costs and benefits when engaging in referral behavior. RRPs provide tangible incentives, making them a key tool in virtual community marketing (Wirtz et al., 2012). A major factor moderating the effects of RRPs is metacognition—the awareness and assessment of how others perceive one's communication—originally conceptualized by Flavell (1979). Metacognitive concerns influence how individuals judge the social consequences of recommending products, thereby affecting their referral participation.

Wang and Chen (2022) found that higher RRP monetary values generally increase sales, but their effectiveness diminishes or reverses when product aesthetic appeal is high. Zhan et al. (2023) revealed that individuals with higher impulsivity are less likely to experience negative metacognitive reactions toward RRPs, thus more readily accepting them.

2.4 RRPs and Community Graph Structures

The effectiveness of RRPs also hinges on the structure of the virtual community in which they operate. Social graph communities (e.g., Facebook, Instagram), built around real-world interpersonal relationships, differ substantially from interest graph communities (e.g., YouTube, LinkedIn), which are formed around shared interests (Wang et al., 2015). Zhan et al. (2023) found that interest graphs facilitate more positive responses to marketing content shared via RRPs, whereas social graphs—characterized by diverse ties and mixed relationship strengths—exhibit greater resistance. Communication style, tie strength, and platform context collectively affect metacognition and referral effectiveness (Wasko et al., 2015).

Further, Wirtz et al. (2012) demonstrated that metacognitive evaluations are more positive for strong-tie referrals than weak-tie referrals. Kuang et al. (2024) showed that virtual community distance moderates RRP effectiveness, with shorter distances favoring random reward distribution and longer distances favoring deterministic schemes. Till and Busler (1998) highlighted that trust in influencer-endorsed content can induce impulsive purchase decisions, with influencer and message credibility playing crucial roles.

2.5 RRPs and Impulsive Purchase

Zhan et al. (2023) examined the interaction between impulsive behavior and metacognition in RRP contexts, finding that highly impulsive consumers exhibit greater willingness to participate in RRPs due to weaker negative metacognitive reactions. Moreover, referral behavior differs between private and public communication environments, with private settings mitigating the negative effects of metacognitive concerns.

2.6 Summary

Overall, prior studies suggest that sharing RRPs in virtual community settings may trigger perceptions of opportunism (Dose et al., 2019), heightening metacognitive concerns and reducing sharing willingness. Interest graph communities—characterized by stronger ties, social interaction, and shared vision—are more conducive to positive referral outcomes than social graph communities. Wang and Chen (2022) confirmed that the relationship between reward incentives and referral motivation is mediated by expected social evaluation, directly linked to metacognition. Empirical simulations show that high incentives increase negative expected evaluation and reduce referral willingness in social graphs, whereas in interest graphs lower metacognition leads to higher sharing intentions. In sum, metacognition is a key mediating mechanism linking community graph structure and referral behavior.

3 Research Design

3.1 Research Model

Grounded in the theoretical perspectives and empirical findings discussed in the introduction and literature review, this study develops a two-stage research model to systematically explore the performance of referral reward programs (RRPs) in virtual MLM environments and their impact on offline impulsive purchase.

In Stage 1, the study seeks to identify the sociological determinants that influence the effectiveness of RRPs in promoting MLM engagement within virtual communities. The model draws upon Chiu et al.'s (2006) knowledge-sharing model and Chia et al.'s (2021) unboxing-sharing willingness model, and incorporates considerations of metacognition, as highlighted in recent RRP research. To examine variations across social and interest graph contexts (Wang et al., 2015; Zhan et al., 2023), a structured questionnaire is designed to collect respondents' likelihood of participating in RRPs, based on key exogenous variables derived from both social capital theory (social interaction ties, shared vision, trust, community identification) and social exchange theory (perceived costs and rewards, reciprocity, altruistic motivation).

In Stage 2, this study builds on Zhan et al. (2023) to investigate how RRP design characteristics—namely reward distribution, reward scale, and usage flexibility—interact with metacognition and consumers' impulsive tendencies, ultimately influencing impulsive purchase behavior in offline sales contexts. Based on the integration of social capital, social exchange, and metacognition theories, this study proposes a set of null hypotheses aimed at determining the graph type that minimizes negative metacognitive responses while maximizing RRP effectiveness. To the best of our knowledge, this research represents the first attempt to construct a comprehensive RRP analytical framework that simultaneously accounts for sociological factors and consumer psychological mechanisms. The overall conceptual framework is presented in Fig. 1.

3.2 Null Hypotheses

3.2.1 Stage 1—MLM Effectiveness Hypotheses

The first stage tests the influence of social capital and social exchange variables—under metacognitive considerations—on RRP participation in both social and interest graph environments.

H1. Social Interaction Ties

Chiu et al. (2006) propose that greater interaction ties within virtual communities foster richer information exchange, thereby enhancing willingness to share.

H1.1: In social graphs, higher interaction ties lead to stronger participation in RRPs.
H1.2: In interest graphs, higher interaction ties lead to stronger participation in RRPs

H2. Shared Vision

Shared goals strengthen interpersonal bonds and collaborative action (Cohen & Prusak 2001).

H2.1: In social graphs, stronger shared vision enhances RRP participation.

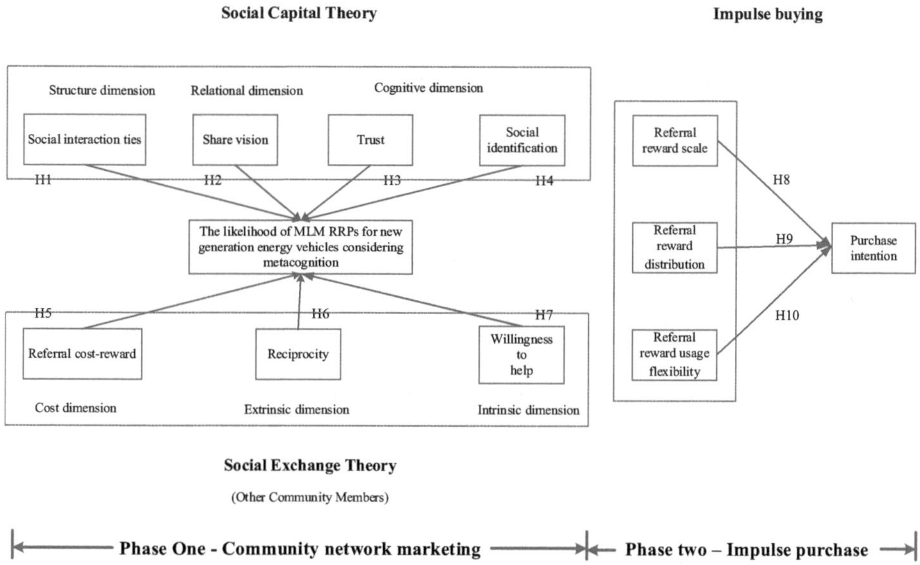

Fig. 1. Research Framework

H2.2: In interest graphs, stronger shared vision enhances RRP participation.

H3. Trust

Trust encourages acceptance of referral messages and reduces perceived risk.

H3.1: In social graphs, higher trust increases RRP participation.

H3.2: In interest graphs, higher trust increases RRP participation.

H4. Community Identification

Identification promotes willingness to contribute to community well-being (Chia et al., 2021).

H4.1: In social graphs, stronger identification increases RRP participation.

H4.2: In interest graphs, stronger identification increases RRP participation.

Questionnaire items for H1–H4 are adapted from Chiu et al. (2006) and Chia et al. (2021).

H5. Cost–Reward (Effort)

According to social exchange theory, willingness declines if expected effort outweighs perceived benefit.

H5.1: In social graphs, greater effort investment reduces RRP participation.

H5.2: In interest graphs, greater effort investment reduces RRP participation.

H6. Reciprocity

Reciprocity fosters a willingness to engage in MLM referrals.

H6.1: In social graphs, higher reciprocity increases RRP participation.

H6.2: In interest graphs, higher reciprocity increases RRP participation.

H7. Altruism ("willingness to help")

Altruistic motivation encourages voluntary sharing without expectation of return.

H7.1: In social graphs, higher altruism increases RRP participation.

H7.2: In interest graphs, higher altruism increases RRP participation.

Items for H5–H7 are adapted from Wasko & Faraj (2000), Kankanhalli et al. (2005), and Chia et al. (2021).

3.2.2 Stage 2—Impulsive Purchase Hypotheses

H8. RRP Scale

Larger-scale programs are associated with stronger impulsive buying tendencies (Sharma & Verma, 2014).

H8: Greater RRP scale increases impulsive purchasing likelihood.

H9. RRP Distribution Breadth

Wider distribution coverage attracts more consumers to act impulsively (Gershon et al., 2020).

H9: Broader RRP distribution increases impulsive purchasing likelihood.

H10. Usage Flexibility

Reward usage flexibility strengthens customer–firm relationships, enhancing impulsiveness to redeem (Gershon et al., 2020).

H10: Greater perceived flexibility increases impulsive purchasing likelihood.

Items for H8–H10 are adapted from Zhan et al. (2023) and modified for NEV contexts.

3.3 Questionnaire Design and Implementation

To ensure validity, respondents are first screened for prior experience with community-based RRPs, including behaviors such as liking, commenting, tagging, or sharing. They are then asked to specify whether their RRP engagement occurred in *social* or *interest* network communities. The questionnaire covers all ten hypotheses and uses a five-point Likert scale (1 = strongly disagree, 5 = strongly agree).

3.4 Pilot Study

Prior to formal data collection, a pilot study is conducted to enhance clarity and content validity. The process includes item drafting, expert review (from both academia and industry), pilot administration, feedback collection, and iterative revision, culminating in the final questionnaire instrument.

4 Empirical Study

In order to empirically validate the proposed two-stage research framework, a questionnaire survey was implemented to collect data from virtual community RRP participants. The questionnaire consisted of three main sections: (1) respondent demographic profiles, (2) perceptions and behavioral intentions regarding MLM participation and referral sharing under RRPs (with metacognitive considerations), and (3) impulsive purchase intentions in the physical purchase context of NEVs.

4.1 Descriptive Statistics

The survey targeted social commerce users in Taiwan with prior experience in referral reward programs. Data were collected through SurveyCake, an online questionnaire platform, between February 1 and April 30, 2024. A total of 495 visits were recorded, yielding 463 responses (94% response rate). After removing 55 invalid responses, 408 valid questionnaires were retained for analysis (Table 1). Among valid respondents, 62% were female, the largest age group was 18–25 years (44%), and 54% possessed a university-level education.

Table 1. Basic Information of Valid Questionnaires/Respondents

Descriptive Statistics of Respondents	Number of Responses	Percentage
Gender		
Male	156	38%
Female	252	62%
Age		
Under 18 years	14	4%
18–25 years	179	44%
26–35 years	109	27%
36–50 years	67	16%
Over 51 years	37	9%
Educational Level		
Junior High School and below	7	2%
Senior High School	65	16%
Undergraduate	222	54%
Postgraduate or higher	114	28%

4.2 Analysis of Community Network Marketings

4.2.1 Validity Analysis of Recommended Rewards for Community Network Marketing

The consistency and stability of the collected questionnaires in this study were tested through reliability and validity analyses. High correlation in the questionnaire results indicates high reliability of the questionnaire used by the researchers. Validity testing reflects the extent to which the questionnaire accurately measures the traits intended by the researchers.

For reliability testing, the methods used include factor loading, composite reliability (CR), and Cronbach's alpha. According to Werts et al. (1973), the critical value for composite reliability should be greater than 0.7. For Cronbach's alpha, Bock et al. (2005) suggest a critical value of 0.7. When Cronbach's alpha exceeds 0.7, it indicates acceptable reliability.

For convergent validity testing, this study employs the Average Variance Extracted (AVE) method proposed by Fornell and Larcker (1981) and Wasko and Faraj (2005). The critical value for AVE is 0.5, and an AVE value greater than 0.5 indicates acceptable model validity. The results of the reliability and validity analyses for the first-stage model are shown in Tables 2 and 3.

Table 2 shows the reliability analysis results for social networks (e.g., Facebook and Instagram). All dimensions of social capital theory (social interaction ties, trust, identification, and shared vision) and their questionnaire items achieved significant reliability levels. Similarly, all dimensions of social exchange theory (recommendation sharing effort, reciprocity, willingness to help, and consideration of recommendation sharing effort) and their questionnaire items also achieved significant reliability levels.

Table 3 shows the reliability analysis results for interest networks (e.g., YouTube and LinkedIn). All dimensions of social capital theory and their questionnaire items achieved significant validity levels. Similarly, all dimensions of social exchange theory and their questionnaire items also achieved significant validity levels.

The reliability analysis results in Tables 2 and 3 indicate that the questionnaire respondents, whether in social networks or interest networks, showed significant reliability levels for the referral reward program survey. This consistency suggests that the responses from the online community regarding the new generation of energy vehicles' RRPs sharing are highly consistent across both social and interest networks.

Secondly, the validity analysis of this questionnaire indicates that in this study, the average variance extracted (AVE) for the social capital theory dimension in the social network graph and the social exchange theory dimension both meet the recommended threshold. Similarly, in the interest graph, the validity test also meets the standard. The analyzed dimensions related to social exchange exhibit AVE values consistent with the recommended thresholds.

In summary, the survey on NEVs, utilizing recommendation reward programs to enhance multi-level dissemination in community marketing, reveals highly valid and consistent results among the interviewed community members

4.2.2 Model Fit and Null Hypotheses Tests for Community Network Marketing

For model fit and null hypothesis testing, this study utilizes t-value tests and p-value tests, along with the R^2 metric to assess the explanatory power of the models. The results of these analyses are presented in Tables 4 and 5. Overall, within the social graph, the social capital theory factors—such as social interaction ties, trust, identification, shared vision, and the willingness to share unboxing experiences—showed high explanatory power at 82.3%, with an adjusted R^2 of 81.1%. In terms of social capital exchange, the explanatory power of the factors including effort in unboxing sharing, reciprocity, altruism, and the willingness to share unboxing experiences reached 88.8%, with an adjusted explanatory power of 87.6%. This indicates that analyzing community commerce influencers within social media through the lens of social exchange theory yields a very high explanatory power. The final determination on whether the hypotheses are supported is summarized in Table 3.

Table 2. Reliability and Validity Test Table for the First-Stage Social Graph RRPs

			Reliability tests			Validity test
Theory, dimension, and item code			Factor loading	Cronbach'α	CR	AVE
Social learning theory	Social interaction ties	SIL1	0.877	0.902	0.931	0.772
		SIL2	0.907			
		SIL3	0.872			
		SIL4	0.859			
	Trust	TRU1	0.856	0.922	0.942	0.764
		TRU2	0.915			
		TRU3	0.878			
		TRU4	0.902			
		TRU5	0.815			
	Social identification	CID1	0.865	0.925	0.946	0.815
		CID2	0.9			
		CID3	0.932			
		CID4	0.914			
	Shared vision	VIS1	0.926	0.925	0.952	0.869
		VIS2	0.94			
		VIS3	0.932			
Social exchange theory	RRPs' cost-reward	RWS1	0.89	0.815	0.914	0.841
		RWS2	0.943			
	Reciprocity	REC1	0.875	0.916	0.94	0.796
		REC2	0.935			

(continued)

Table 2. (*continued*)

			Reliability tests			Validity test
Theory, dimension, and item code			Factor loading	Cronbach'α	CR	AVE
		REC3	0.814			
		REC4	0.939			
	Willingness to help	HEL1	0.839	0.892	0.926	0.758
		HEL2	0.901			
		HEL3	0.939			
		HEL4	0.795			
	Possibility of sharing RRPs	CRP1	0.886	0.921	0.944	0.807
		CRP2	0.867			
		CRP3	0.94			
		CRP4	0.9			

Notably, it was found that within the social graph (e.g., Facebook and Instagram), the social capital theory constructs of social interaction ties, trust, community identification, and shared vision were insignificant. Similarly, within the social graph, the social exchange theory constructs of cost-reward in referral sharing and reciprocity were insignificant, whereas willing to share was significant. These results suggest that the benefits of implementing RRPs within the social graph are not substantial, and community commerce members primarily forward RRPs out of altruism, willing to share.

In the interest graph (e.g., YouTube and LinkedIn), the social capital theory constructs of social interaction, trust, community identification, and shared vision were also insignificant. However, within the interest graph, the social exchange theory constructs of effort in RRPs sharing were insignificant, while reciprocity and altruism, willing to share, were significant. These findings indicate that community members within the interest graph are willing to share RRPs due to factors such as reciprocity and altruism towards other community members. This outcome aligns with Wang and Chen's (2022) research, which highlights that members of interest graphs are typically passionate, open, and willing to share and learn from each other. They are connected through a common interest and enrich each other's experiences through mutual support and collaboration. In the interest graph, community members share relevant discount information out of a spirit of mutual aid, continuous learning, and creative expression.

Table 3. Reliability and Validity Test Table for the First-Stage Interest Graph RRPs

			Reliability tests			Validity test
Theory, dimension, and item code			Factor loading	Cronbach'α	CR	AVE
Social learning theory	Social interaction ties	SIL1	0.901	0.917	0.941	0.801

(*continued*)

Table 3. (*continued*)

Theory, dimension, and item code			Reliability tests: Factor loading	Cronbach'α	CR	Validity test: AVE
		SIL2	0.899			
		SIL3	0.905			
		SIL4	0.875			
	Trust	TRU1	0.905	0.937	0.952	0.799
		TRU2	0.904			
		TRU3	0.897			
		TRU4	0.895			
		TRU5	0.868			
	Social identification	CID1	0.892	0.915	0.94	0.797
		CID2	0.88			
		CID3	0.914			
		CID4	0.884			
	Shared vision	VIS1	0.891	0.906	0.941	0.842
		VIS2	0.926			
		VIS3	0.936			
Social exchange theory	RRPs' cost-reward	RWS1	0.92	0.813	0.914	0.842
		RWS2	0.916			
	Reciprocity	REC1	0.869	0.902	0.932	0.773
		REC2	0.869			
		REC3	0.892			
		REC4	0.887			
	Willingness to help	HEL1	0.898	0.913	0.939	0.793
		HEL2	0.898			
		HEL3	0.893			
		HEL4	0.873			
	Possibility of sharing RRPs	CRP1	0.899	0.918	0.942	0.802
		CRP2	0.881			
		CRP3	0.894			
		CRP4	0.907			

4.3 Impulse Consumption Analysis

4.3.1 Validity Analysis of Recommended Rewards for Impulse Purchase

According to Zafar et al. (2021) and Zhan et al. (2023), academic research has identified various strategies for recommendation reward programs. These strategies include reward magnitude, such as monetary value (Sharma and Verma, 2014; Kuester & Benkenstein, 2014), reward allocation within the program (e.g., referrer benefits, equal distribution, and referee benefits) (Gershon et al., 2020), and flexibility in using reward programs (e.g., accumulation and transferability) (Carroni et al., 2020). In this study, we designed questionnaire options based on the literature to analyze the most suitable recommendation reward program for potential customers transitioning to actual customers during the purchase and evaluation stages.

Table 4. The Path Coefficients, Model Fit, and Hypothesis Testing Results for the Analysis of the Willingness to Share RRPs Among Social Graph Network.

	Path	Hypothesis	Path coefficient	t value	p value	Result	R^2	Adj R^2
Social learning theory	Social interaction ties→willingness to share RRPs	H1	−0.015	1.473	0.141	Insignificant	0.823	0.811
	Trust→willingness to share RRPs	H2	0.016	0.744	0.457	Insignificant		
	Social identification→willingness to share RRPs	H3	0.05	1.173	0.241	Insignificant		
	Shared vision→willingness to share RRPs	H4	−0.046	1.302	0.193	Insignificant		
Social exchange theory	Sharing RRPs cost–reward→willingness to share RRPs	H5	−0.067	0.345	0.73	Insignificant	0.888	0.876
	Reciprocity→willingness to share RRPs	H6	0.11	0.254	0.799	Insignificant		
	Willingness to help→willingness to share RRPs	H7	0.875	2.555	0.011	Significant		

Table 5. The Path Coefficients, Model Fit, and Hypothesis Testing Results for the Analysis of the Willingness to Share RRPs Among Interest Graph Network.

	Path	Hypothesis	Path coefficient	t value	p value	Result	R^2	Adj R^2
Social learning theory	Social interaction ties→willingness to share RRPs	H1	0.018	0.38	0.704	Insignificant	0.829	0.822
	Trust→willingness to share RRPs	H2	0	0.008	0.994	Insignificant		

(*continued*)

Table 5. (*continued*)

	Path	Hypothesis	Path coefficient	t value	p value	Result	R^2	Adj R^2
	Social identification→willingness to share RRPs	H3	0.021	0.368	0.713	Insignificant		
	Shared vision→willingness to share RRPs	H4	0.072	1.334	0.182	Insignificant		
Social exchange theory	Sharing RRPs cost–reward→willingness to share RRPs	H5	0.094	1.603	0.109	Insignificant	0.836	0.833
	Reciprocity→willingness to share RRPs	H6	0.294	4.748	0	Significant		
	Willingness to help→àwillingness to share RRPs	H7	0.503	7.422	0	Significant		

4.3.2 Model Fit and Null Hypotheses Tests for Impulse Purchase

The model fit, explanatory power, and null hypothesis testing analysis for impulsive consumption are presented in Table 6. The analysis of the impulsive consumption model's fit and explanatory power indicates that although the variables such as the scale of the RRP, distribution of referral rewards, and usage flexibility of referral reward are all significant predictors of impulsive consumption under the RRPs framework, the model's explanatory power (R^2) is only 0.259, with an adjusted R^2 of just 0.253.

This study suggests that this situation may indicate that while each explanatory variable individually has a significant impact on the dependent variable, there may be other unaccounted factors affecting the overall model, or the model itself may lack sufficient fit, leading to the low R^2 value for the overall model. Potential reasons include:

Table 6. Reliability and Validity Test Table for the Impulse Purchase

Theory, dimension, and item code			Reliability tests			Validity test
			Factor loading	Cronbach'α	CR	AVE
Impulse purchase considering RRPs	RRPs' scale	RSC1	0.669	0.652	0.714	0.498
		RSC2	0.442			
		RSC3	0.842			
		RSC4	0.798			

(*continued*)

Table 6. (*continued*)

Theory, dimension, and item code			Reliability tests			Validity test
			Factor loading	Cronbach'α	CR	AVE
	RRPs'distrubution	RDI1	0.828	0.82	0.819	0.652
		RDI2	0.847			
		RDI3	0.719			
		RDI4	0.83			
	RRPs' flexibity usage	RUF1	0.657	0.755	0.761	0.579

1. Omission of Key Variables: The potential consumers/respondents may be influenced by specific brand preferences when considering new-generation energy vehicles under the referral reward program.
2. Incorrect Functional Form: The model's functional form might be inappropriate for describing the data, indicating the potential need for a non-linear model rather than a linear one.
3. Limited Consumer Interest in NEVs: New energy vehicles, especially fully electric vehicles, may not sufficiently trigger the purchase desire among potential consumers/respondents due to concerns over immature battery technology, range anxiety, insufficient charging stations, and inconvenience due to lengthy charging times. Consequently, the RRPs may still fail to drive impulsive consumption among these potential consumers/respondents (Table 7).

Table 7. The Path Coefficients, Model Fit, and Hypothesis Testing Results for the Impulse Purchase

Path	Hypothesis	Path coefficient	t value	p value	Result	R^2	Adj R^2
RRPs' Scale → Impulse purchase considering RRPs	H8	0.163	1.986	0.047	Significant	0.259	0.253
RRPs' distribution → Impulse purchase considering RRPs	H9	0.186	2.048	0.041	Significant		

(*continued*)

Table 7. (*continued*)

Path	Hypothesis	Path coefficient	t value	p value	Result	R^2	Adj R^2
RRPs'flexibilitu usafe→ Impulse purchase considering RRPs	H10	0.221	3.215	0.001	Significant		

5 Conclusions and Further Suggestions

This study proposed an integrated MLM-based referral reward model to enhance offline sales performance in physical marketing industries, using new energy vehicles (NEVs) as the empirical context. Built upon social capital theory, social exchange theory, and metacognitive perspectives, the model was divided into two stages: (1) investigating willingness to disseminate RRPs in virtual communities across social and interest graphs, and (2) examining impulsive purchasing behavior resulting from varying RRP design characteristics.

Empirical evidence from 408 valid responses reveals that, in social graphs, neither social capital constructs nor most social exchange variables significantly motivate users to share RRPs; only altruistic willingness to help shows a positive influence. Conversely, in interest graphs, reciprocity and altruism significantly affect RRP-sharing behavior. These results suggest that interest-based communities—characterized by intrinsic involvement and lower metacognitive pressure—are more suitable for implementing referral rewards. Hence, firms promoting NEVs should focus on interest graph platforms and emphasize community-driven, mutually beneficial marketing narratives.

In the impulsive purchase model, RRP scale, distribution, and usage flexibility all significantly enhance impulse consumption; however, the explanatory power of the model is limited, indicating that other psychological or contextual variables, such as brand preference, perceived risk, or nonlinear behavioral responses, may also play important roles.

We conclude overall, RRPs remain attractive to consumers who have already shown interest in specific NEV brands, suggesting that automotive dealers can leverage RRPs to effectively capture and convert such potential buyers.

References

Cao, Z.K., Chu, J.H., Hui, K.L., Xu, H.: The relationship between online referral marketing and price promotion: evidence from a large E-commerce platform. J. Manag. Inf. Syst. **38**(3), 855–888 (2021)

Chen, H., Hao, S.: Dollar or percentage? The effect of reward presentation on referral likelihood. Asia Pac. J. Mark. Logist. **36**(6), 1504–1519 (2024)

Chia, K.C., Hsu, C.C., Lin, L.T., Tseng, H.H.: The identification of ideal social media influencers: integrating the social capital, social exchange, and social learning theories. J. Electron. Commer. Res. **22**(1), 4–21 (2021)
Chiu, C.M., Hsu, M.H., Wang, E.T.G.: Understanding knowledge sharing in virtual communities: an integration of social capital and social cognitive theories. Decis. Support. Syst. **42**(3), 1872–1888 (2006)
Cohen, D., Prusak, L.: In Good Company: How Social Capital Makes Organizations Work. Harvard Business School Press, Boston (2001)
Dose, D.B., Walter, G., Erevelles, S., Ralf, E.: Unintended reward costs: the effectiveness of customer referral reward programs for innovative products and services. J. Acad. Mark. Sci. **47**(3), 438–459 (2019)
Flavell, J.H.: Metacognition and cognitive monitoring. A new area of cognitive-development inquiry. Am. Psychol. **34**(10), 906–911 (1979)
Gershon, R., Cryder, C., John, L.K.: Why prosocial referral incentives work: the interplay of reputational benefits and action costs. J. Mark. Res. **57**(1), 156–172 (2020)
Kankanhalli, A., Tan, B.C.Y., Wei, K.K.: Contributing knowledge to electronic knowledge repositories: an empirical investigation. MIS Q. **29**, 113–143 (2005)
Kannan, P.K., Li, H.: Digital marketing: a framework, review and research agenda. Int. J. Res. Mark. **34**(1), 22–45 (2017)
Kuang, D., Ma, B., Li, X.-F.: Acquiring customers via referral reward programs versus advertising: who is more likely to provide future referrals? J. Retail. Consum. Serv. **81**, 103982 (2024)
Kuester, M., Benkenstein, M.: Turning dissatisfied into satisfied customers: how referral reward programs affect the referrer's attitude and loyalty toward the recommended service provider. J. Retail. Consum. Serv. **21**(6), 897–904 (2014)
Lambert, D.: Zero-inflated Poisson regression, with an application to defects in manufacturing. Technometrics. **34**(1), 1–14 (1992)
Leong, L.Y., Jaafar, N.I., Sulaiman, A., Cheung, C.: Understanding impulse purchase in facebook commerce: does big five matter? Internet Res. **27**(4), 786–818 (2017)
Sharma, D., Verma, V.: Psychological and economic considerations of rewards programs. J. Retail. Consum. Serv. **21**(6), 924–932 (2014)
Sun, T., Viswanathan, S., Zheleva, E.: Creating social contagion through firm-mediated message design: evidence from a randomized field experiment. Manag. Sci. **67**(2), 808–827 (2021)
Wang, L., Chen, Z.: The effect of incentive structure on referral: the determining role of self-construal. J. Acad. Mark. Sci. **50**, 1091–1110 (2022)
Wang, L., Wu, H., Wang, W., Chen, K.C.: Socially enabled wireless networks: resource allocation via bipartite graph matching. IEEE Commun. Mag. **53**(10), 128–135 (2015)
Wasko, M., Faraj, S.: "It is what one does": why people participate and help others in electronic communities of practice. J. Strateg. Inf. Syst. **9**, 155–173 (2000)
Wirtz, J., Orsingher, C., Chew, P., Tambyah, S.K.: The role of metaperception on the effectiveness of referral reward programs. J. Serv. Res. **16**(1), 82–98 (2012)
Zafar, A.U., Qiu, J., Shahzad, M., Shen, J., Bhutto, T.A., Irfan, M.: Impulse buying in social commerce: bundle offer, top reviews, and emotional intelligence. Asia Pac. J. Mark. Logist. **33**(4), 945–973 (2021)
Zhan, M., Huang, M., Li, A., Yang, Y.: The role of impulsive behavior and meta-perception in referral reward programs. J. Retail. Consum. Serv. **75**, 103496 (2023)
Zhang, J., Wang, J.: A study of loyalty programs in the Chinese market: the impacts of reward type, reward characteristic and product involvement. Asia Pac. J. Mark. Logist. **35**(4), 908–919 (2023)

Digital Interface Transparency, Trust, and Behavioral Intention in Sustainable Online Consumption

Kaokiat Boonmee, Suppanunta Romprasert(✉), and Danai Tanamee

Faculty of Economics, Srinakharinwirot University, Bangkok, Thailand
{kaokiat.boonmee,suppanunta,danait}@g.swu.ac.th

Abstract. As electronic commerce platforms increasingly promote sustainable consumption, digital interface design plays a critical role in shaping consumer decision-making. This study investigates how digital interface transparency embedded in user interface and user experience (UI/UX) design influences trust, consumer awareness, and behavioral intention toward sustainable online consumption. Grounded in the Stimulus–Organism–Response (S–O–R) framework, interface transparency is conceptualized as an external stimulus that enhances internal psychological states, which subsequently drive behavioral intention. A quantitative research design is employed, with data collected from users of electronic commerce and food delivery platforms offering sustainable product options. Structural Equation Modeling (SEM) is used to test the hypothesized relationships and mediation effects among interface transparency, trust, consumer awareness, and behavioral intention. The results demonstrate that digital interface transparency has a significant positive effect on consumer trust and awareness, while both constructs positively influence behavioral intention. Furthermore, trust and awareness are found to mediate the relationship between interface transparency and behavioral intention, indicating their pivotal role in translating UI/UX design features into sustainable consumer responses. This study contributes to the electronic commerce and information systems literature by extending the S–O–R framework to UI/UX-driven transparency mechanisms in sustainable e-commerce contexts. Practically, the findings highlight the importance of transparency-oriented UI/UX strategies in building trust and encouraging sustainable consumer behavior on digital platforms.

Keywords: Digital Interface Transparency · Trust · Sustainable E-Commerce · Consumer Awareness · Behavioral Intention

1 Introduction

The rapid growth of electronic commerce has intensified the role of digital interfaces in shaping consumer decision-making, particularly in contexts where consumers must evaluate product attributes without physical interaction. In sustainability-oriented consumption, this challenge is amplified by information asymmetry related to environmental

D. Liberona et al. (Eds.): MISNC 2026, CCIS 3092, pp. 21–28, 2027.
https://doi.org/10.1007/978-3-032-33381-0_2

claims, product credibility, and functional performance. As a result, user interface and user experience (UI/UX) design has become a critical informational and behavioral mechanism influencing how consumers perceive and respond to sustainable product offerings in online platforms (Lemon & Verhoef, 2016). Prior research suggests that visual demonstration and interface transparency serve as powerful communication tools in digital environments by increasing information salience, reducing cognitive effort, and enhancing perceived credibility (Jiang & Benbasat, 2007; Vieira, 2013). From a behavioral economics perspective, such UI/UX elements can also be understood as digital nudges—subtle design features that guide consumer choices without restricting freedom of choice (Thaler & Sunstein, 2008). Visual cues, clear sustainability labels, and transparent interface structures can nudge consumers toward environmentally responsible decisions by making sustainable attributes more visible and easier to process (White et al., 2019).

Building upon the Stimulus–Organism–Response (S–O–R) framework, this study conceptualizes visual demonstration and interface transparency as external stimuli that influence internal psychological states, namely trust and consumer awareness, which subsequently shape behavioral intention toward sustainable online consumption. While existing studies have independently examined visual presentation, trust, or sustainability in e-commerce, empirical research integrating UI/UX transparency, digital nudging, and sustainable behavior within a unified theoretical framework remains limited. Addressing this gap, the present study advances understanding of how UI/UX-driven informational and behavioral cues jointly influence sustainable consumer decision-making in electronic commerce platforms. This study aims to:

1. Examine the effect of digital interface transparency and visual demonstration on consumer trust in sustainable e-commerce platforms.
2. Investigate the relationship between consumer trust and consumer awareness of sustainable product attributes in online environments.
3. Analyze the impact of trust and awareness on behavioral intention toward sustainable online consumption.
4. Extend the Stimulus–Organism–Response (S–O–R) framework by integrating UI/UX-driven transparency and digital nudging mechanisms into sustainable electronic commerce research.

2 Literature Review

This study is grounded in the Stimulus–Organism–Response (S–O–R) framework, which explains how environmental cues (stimuli) influence individuals' internal psychological states (organism), leading to behavioral outcomes (responses) (Mehrabian & Russell, 1974). The S–O–R framework has been widely applied in marketing, information systems, and electronic commerce research to explain how digital environments shape consumer cognition, emotion, and behavior (Vieira, 2013). In the context of sustainable electronic commerce, digital interface transparency and UI/UX clarity are conceptualized as external stimuli. Interface transparency refers to the extent to which digital platforms clearly communicate product attributes, sustainability claims, and decision-relevant information through visual demonstrations, labels, and disclosures. Prior research suggests that transparent and visually rich interfaces reduce information asymmetry and cognitive uncertainty, enabling consumers to process complex information more efficiently in online environments (Jiang & Benbasat, 2007; Pavlou, 2003). Within the S–O–R framework, these interface stimuli influence internal psychological states, or the organism, represented in this study by consumer trust and consumer awareness. Trust reflects consumers' belief in the credibility, reliability, and integrity of an online platform and its sustainability claims (Gefen et al., 2003). Consumer awareness refers to the extent to which individuals understand and recognize the environmental attributes and implications of sustainable products (Steg & Vlek, 2009). Transparent UI/UX design enhances trust by signaling honesty and reducing perceived risk, while simultaneously increasing awareness by making sustainability information more salient and cognitively accessible (White et al., 2019). Finally, the response component of the framework is captured by behavioral intention toward sustainable online consumption, which reflects consumers' willingness to purchase or adopt environmentally friendly products via digital platforms. Consistent with prior e-commerce and sustainability research, internal psychological states such as trust and awareness play a critical role in translating interface design features into actual behavioral intentions (Kim et al., 2008; Zhao et al., 2021). By integrating UI/UX transparency into the S–O–R framework, this study positions digital interface design as both an informational mechanism and a behavioral nudge, offering a comprehensive explanation of how sustainable consumption decisions are shaped in electronic commerce contexts.

Hypotheses Development

Digital interface transparency enhances consumers' perceptions of credibility and reduces risk associated with online transactions. Prior studies indicate that transparent information presentation, visual explanations, and disclosure mechanisms positively influence trust by signaling platform reliability and ethical intent (Gefen et al., 2003; Pavlou, 2003). In sustainability contexts, transparency is particularly important because consumers often question the authenticity of environmental claims.

H1: Digital interface transparency has a positive effect on consumer trust.

UI/UX clarity and visual demonstration increase the salience and comprehensibility of sustainability-related information. Research on online product presentation demonstrates that visual and transparent interfaces improve consumers' understanding of product attributes and enhance knowledge formation (Jiang & Benbasat, 2007; Vieira, 2013).

H2: Digital interface transparency positively influences consumer awareness of sustainable products.

Trust facilitates information acceptance and cognitive engagement. When consumers trust an online platform, they are more likely to attend to, believe, and internalize sustainability information presented through the interface (Kim et al., 2008). Trust therefore serves as a catalyst that enhances awareness.

H3: Consumer trust positively affects consumer awareness.

Extensive e-commerce literature confirms that trust is a key determinant of behavioral intention, particularly in online environments characterized by uncertainty and perceived risk (Gefen et al., 2003; Pavlou, 2003). In sustainable e-commerce, trust in platform claims increases consumers' willingness to engage in environmentally responsible purchasing behavior.

H4: Consumer trust has a positive effect on behavioral intention toward sustainable online consumption.

Consumer awareness has been consistently linked to pro-environmental intention, as informed consumers are more likely to recognize the value and impact of sustainable choices (Steg & Vlek, 2009; White et al., 2019). Increased awareness strengthens motivation to act in environmentally responsible ways

H5: Consumer awareness positively influences behavioral intention.

Drawing on the S–O–R framework, interface transparency is expected to influence behavioral intention indirectly through internal psychological states. Trust and awareness jointly function as mediators that translate UI/UX-driven stimuli into sustainable behavioral responses, consistent with prior mediation-based models in digital consumer research (Vieira, 2013; Zhao et al., 2021).

H6: Consumer trust and consumer awareness mediate the relationship between digital interface transparency and behavioral intention toward sustainable online consumption.

3 Research Methodology

This study adopts a quantitative, cross-sectional research design to empirically examine the relationships among digital interface transparency, trust, consumer awareness, and behavioral intention toward sustainable online consumption. A quantitative approach is appropriate given the theory-testing objective and the need to validate the proposed causal relationships derived from the Stimulus–Organism–Response (S–O–R) framework. Cross-sectional survey designs are widely used in electronic commerce and information systems research to capture users' perceptions and behavioral intentions at a specific point in time (Hair et al., 2019). Data were collected through an online questionnaire administered to users of electronic commerce or food delivery platforms that provide sustainable or environmentally friendly product options. Online surveys are suitable for this study because they allow efficient access to digitally active consumers who regularly interact with UI/UX elements during online purchasing processes (Pavlou, 2003).

Sample Size. Following Cochran's (1977) formula at a 95% confidence level and a 5% margin of error, a minimum sample of 384 respondents is required. The target sample was therefore set at 400 respondents to ensure robustness and account for potential data attrition (Hair et al., 2019).

Sampling Procedure. A purposive sampling technique was employed, focusing on respondents with prior experience using digital commerce platforms that offer sustainable product options. Eligible participants were required to have made at least one online purchase of a sustainable or environmentally friendly product within the preceding 6 months. This approach is consistent with prior e-commerce studies that examine user perceptions and behavioral intentions in online environments (Gefen et al., 2003). It is acknowledged, however, that purposive sampling is a limitation of this study. Because participants were drawn from a non-probability sample of digitally active consumers, the generalizability of findings to broader populations should be interpreted with caution (see Sect. 5, Research Limitations).

Pilot Study and Instrument Validation. Prior to the main survey, a pilot study was conducted with 40 respondents who met the same eligibility criteria as the main sample. The pilot aimed to verify the reliability and contextual validity of the adapted scales within the sustainable e-commerce setting. Internal consistency was assessed using Cronbach's Alpha. Results indicated satisfactory reliability across all constructs: Digital Interface Transparency ($\alpha = 0.84$), Consumer Trust ($\alpha = 0.86$), Consumer Awareness ($\alpha = 0.81$), and Behavioral Intention ($\alpha = 0.83$). All values exceeded the threshold of 0.80 recommended for strong reliability (Hair et al., 2019). Items that exhibited low item-to-total correlations were revised for clarity before the full data collection commenced.

All constructs in this study were measured using validated scales adapted from prior literature, ensuring content validity and reliability. Digital Interface Transparency was measured through items capturing UI/UX clarity, visual explanation, information openness, and transparency of sustainability-related disclosures (Jiang & Benbasat, 2007; Vieira, 2013). Trust was assessed using established measures of platform credibility, reliability, and integrity adapted from prior e-commerce trust research (Gefen et al., 2003; McKnight et al., 2002). Consumer Awareness was measured by items reflecting respondents' understanding and recognition of environmental attributes and sustainability implications of products (Steg & Vlek, 2009; White et al., 2019). Behavioral Intention captured respondents' willingness to purchase, use, or choose sustainable options in online platforms, following established intention-based measures in electronic commerce research (Pavlou, 2003; Kim et al., 2008). All items were measured using a five-point Likert-type scale.

An online survey platform was used to gather data over the course of 1 month. Social media, online forums, and live commerce communities were used to disseminate the questionnaire link. To maintain ethical compliance, respondents provided informed consent prior to participation. Participation was voluntary, and respondents could withdraw at any time without repercussion. Responses that were inconsistent or incomplete—such as those containing irrational or repeating patterns—were excluded during data screening. Compatibility for analysis was ensured by standardizing the data format.

Reliability was evaluated using Cronbach's Alpha to gauge internal consistency within each construct. Exploratory factor analysis (EFA) was subsequently conducted to verify that questionnaire items accurately measured the intended variables, ensuring convergent and discriminant validity. Structural Equation Modeling (SEM) was employed to test the hypothesized relationships and mediation effects proposed in the research model. SEM is particularly suitable for this study because it allows simultaneous examination of multiple dependent relationships while accounting for measurement error (Hair et al., 2019). Mediation analysis assessed the indirect effects of digital interface transparency on behavioral intention through trust and consumer awareness.

4 Results

The empirical results provide strong support for the proposed research model, confirming the pivotal role of digital interface transparency in shaping consumer trust, awareness, and behavioral intention toward sustainable online consumption. Specifically, the analysis reveals a significant positive relationship between digital interface transparency and consumer trust, consistent with prior electronic commerce research suggesting that transparent information presentation reduces perceived risk and uncertainty in online environments (Gefen et al., 2003; Pavlou, 2003). UI/UX features such as clear visual explanations, sustainability labels, and transparent disclosures appear to signal platform credibility and integrity, thereby strengthening consumers' confidence in sustainability-related claims.

The results further demonstrate that consumer trust positively influences consumer awareness of sustainable product attributes. Trustworthy digital environments encourage consumers to engage more deeply with information presented through the interface, increasing their willingness to process, interpret, and internalize sustainability-related content. This finding aligns with prior research indicating that trust facilitates information acceptance and cognitive engagement in online decision-making contexts (Kim et al., 2008).

Furthermore, both consumer trust and consumer awareness exhibit significant positive effects on behavioral intention toward sustainable online consumption. These results are consistent with environmental psychology and sustainability literature, which emphasize that informed consumers with high levels of trust are more likely to engage in pro-environmental purchasing behaviors (Steg & Vlek, 2009; White et al., 2019). Awareness enables consumers to recognize the environmental value and impact of sustainable choices, while trust reduces hesitation and skepticism, jointly motivating behavioral intention.

Importantly, the findings confirm that consumer trust and consumer awareness play a mediating role in the relationship between digital interface transparency and behavioral intention. Rather than exerting a purely direct influence, interface transparency shapes behavioral intention indirectly by first activating internal psychological states. Trust legitimizes sustainability claims and reduces concerns related to greenwashing, while awareness enhances understanding of product benefits and environmental implications. This mediating mechanism provides empirical support for the Stimulus–Organism–Response (S–O–R) framework, demonstrating how external digital stimuli are transformed into behavioral responses through internal cognitive processes (Vieira, 2013).

Overall, these results reinforce the argument that effective sustainability communication in electronic commerce must extend beyond visual appeal. While aesthetically pleasing design may attract attention, the findings suggest that credible, transparent, and cognitively accessible UI/UX design is essential for fostering meaningful consumer engagement and sustainable behavioral intention. By functioning as digital nudges, UI/UX transparency mechanisms guide consumers toward environmentally responsible choices without restricting freedom of choice, consistent with principles of behavioral economics (Thaler & Sunstein, 2008). In this regard, digital interface transparency emerges as a strategic tool for aligning platform design with sustainability objectives, offering both theoretical and practical value in advancing sustainable consumption within electronic commerce ecosystems.

5 Conclusion

This study makes several theoretical contributions. First, it extends the Stimulus–Organism–Response (S–O–R) framework by explicitly incorporating digital interface transparency as a stimulus and trust as a key psychological mechanism in sustainable electronic commerce. While prior studies have examined UI/UX design, trust, or sustainability independently, this research integrates these constructs into a unified explanatory model. Second, the study bridges UI/UX design theory, trust-based e-commerce models, and sustainability literature, demonstrating how digital interface features function simultaneously as informational cues and behavioral nudges. This integration advances understanding of how sustainable consumption decisions are formed in digitally mediated environments, addressing a critical gap in existing electronic commerce research.

From a managerial perspective, the findings suggest that e-commerce and food delivery platforms should strategically embed transparency-driven UI/UX features into their digital interfaces. Clear sustainability indicators, visual explanations of environmental benefits, and verification cues (e.g., certifications or disclosures) can enhance trust and awareness at the point of decision-making. Managers should view UI/UX design not merely as an aesthetic tool but as a strategic mechanism for influencing consumer behavior. By reducing cognitive effort and perceived risk, transparent interface design can encourage sustainable purchasing decisions while maintaining user autonomy. These insights are particularly valuable for platforms operating in emerging digital markets, where trust and information credibility play a pivotal role in shaping online consumer behavior.

Research Limitations and Future Directions
This study is subject to several limitations that should be considered when interpreting the findings. First, the use of purposive sampling restricts the generalizability of results to the broader population of online consumers. Although participants were screened to ensure relevant experience with sustainable e-commerce platforms, the non-probability nature of the sampling approach means that findings should be extrapolated with caution. Future research should seek to replicate the proposed model using probability-based or stratified random sampling across diverse geographic and demographic contexts to enhance external validity.

Second, the cross-sectional design of this study captures consumer perceptions and intentions at a single point in time, precluding causal inference. Longitudinal studies tracking actual purchasing behavior over time would provide stronger evidence for the proposed relationships. Third, the study focuses on two categories of digital platforms—general e-commerce and food delivery—which may not fully represent the diversity of sustainable digital commerce contexts. Future research could extend the model to other sectors, such as eco-tourism, sustainable fashion, or green financial products.

Finally, while SEM provides robust testing of hypothesized relationships, the measurement of behavioral intention as a proxy for actual sustainable purchasing behavior is an inherent limitation shared by much of the e-commerce intention literature. Future studies should attempt to incorporate behavioral data, such as purchase logs or platform analytics, to validate the link between intention and action.

References

Cochran, W.G.: Sampling Techniques, 3rd edn. Wiley (1977)
Gefen, D., Karahanna, E., Straub, D.W.: Trust and TAM in online shopping: an integrated model. MIS Q. **27**(1), 51–90 (2003)
Hair, J.F., Hult, G.T.M., Ringle, C.M., Sarstedt, M.: A Primer on Partial Least Squares Structural Equation Modeling (PLS-SEM), 2nd edn. Sage (2019)
Jiang, Z., Benbasat, I.: Investigating the influence of the functional mechanisms of online product presentations. Inf. Syst. Res. **18**(4), 454–470 (2007). https://doi.org/10.1287/isre.1070.0124
Kim, D.J., Ferrin, D.L., Rao, H.R.: A trust-based consumer decision-making model in electronic commerce. Decis. Support. Syst. **44**(2), 544–564 (2008)
Lemon, K.N., Verhoef, P.C.: Understanding customer experience throughout the customer journey. J. Mark. **80**(6), 69–96 (2016). https://doi.org/10.1509/jm.15.0420
McKnight, D.H., Choudhury, V., Kacmar, C.: Developing and validating trust measures for e-commerce. Inf. Syst. Res. **13**(3), 334–359 (2002)
Mehrabian, A., Russell, J.A.: An Approach to Environmental Psychology. MIT Press (1974)
Pavlou, P.A.: Consumer acceptance of electronic commerce: integrating trust and risk with the technology acceptance model. Int. J. Electron. Commer. **7**(3), 101–134 (2003)
Steg, L., Vlek, C.: Encouraging pro-environmental behaviour: an integrative review. J. Environ. Psychol. **29**(3), 309–317 (2009)
Thaler, R.H., Sunstein, C.R.: Nudge: Improving Decisions about Health, Wealth, and Happiness. Yale University Press (2008)
Vieira, V.A.: Stimuli–organism–response framework: a meta-analytic review in the store environment. J. Bus. Res. **66**(9), 1420–1426 (2013). https://doi.org/10.1016/j.jbusres.2012.05.009
White, K., Habib, R., Hardisty, D.J.: How to SHIFT consumer behaviors to be more sustainable. J. Mark. **83**(3), 22–49 (2019). https://doi.org/10.1177/0022242919825649
Zhao, R., Wang, Q., Zhou, X.: Visual cues and environmental awareness in online platforms. Sustainability. **13**(4), 2153 (2021)

UI/UX Marketing Through Visual Demonstration on Food Delivery

Nawaphum Phanfak, Danai Tanamee, and Suppanunta Romprasert(✉)

Srinakharinwirot University, Bangkok, Thailand
{nawaphum.pha,danait,suppanunta}@g.swu.ac.th

Abstract. As competition intensifies among food delivery platforms, visual communication embedded within application interfaces plays a crucial role in influencing how sustainability-related information is perceived and evaluated by consumers. This study investigates how visual demonstration presented through food delivery applications functions as a UI/UX marketing stimulus affecting consumer awareness and behavioral intention toward sustainable packaging. Grounded in the Stimulus–Organism–Response (S–O–R) framework and behavioral economics theory, this research employs a mixed-methods design integrating a qualitative focus group of 30 participants and a quantitative survey of 400 active food delivery platform users in Bangkok. Structural equation modeling (SEM) results reveal that awareness of plastic waste ($\beta = 0.908$, $p < 0.001$) and attitudes toward sustainable alternatives ($\beta = 0.710$, $p < 0.001$) are the strongest drivers of behavioral intention, while perceived barriers operate indirectly through attitudes rather than suppressing intention directly. The study contributes to digital marketing and electronic commerce literature by extending the S–O–R framework to UI/UX-driven marketing contexts and offers practical insights for platform designers seeking to promote sustainability-oriented consumer behavior.

Keywords: UI/UX marketing · digital marketing · food delivery platforms · visual demonstration · consumer behavior · sustainable packaging · S–O–R framework

1 Introduction

Food delivery platforms have evolved into highly competitive digital marketplaces in which marketing effectiveness is increasingly driven by interface design rather than traditional promotional activities. Within platform-based electronic commerce, user interface and user experience (UI/UX) design functions not only as a usability mechanism but also as a strategic digital marketing tool that shapes how consumers perceive information, evaluate alternatives, and form behavioral intentions [1, 2]. As consumers interact with mobile applications in real time, visual elements embedded in platform interfaces—such as images, icons, layout structures, and informational cues—serve as powerful marketing stimuli that influence cognitive processing and decision-making outcomes [3, 4].

In the context of food delivery platforms, UI/UX marketing has become particularly important due to the increasing reliance on visual communication to convey product

D. Liberona et al. (Eds.): MISNC 2026, CCIS 3092, pp. 29–34, 2027.
https://doi.org/10.1007/978-3-032-33381-0_3

attributes and value propositions within limited screen space. Prior research suggests that interface-based visual cues can enhance information salience, perceived credibility, and emotional engagement, thereby affecting consumer awareness and subsequent behavioral responses [5, 6] (Table 1).

Table 1. Waste Management in Thailand

No.	Province	Waste Generated (Ton/Day)	Recyclable Waste (Ton/Day)	Proper Disposal (Ton/Day)	Improper Disposal (Ton/Day)
1	Samut Prakan	3,465	250	893	2,322
2	Chonburi	3,374	230	2,333	811
3	Nakhon Ratchasima	2,588	1,053	678	857
4	Nonthaburi	2,065	465	1,600	0
5	Pathum Thani	2,060	590	620	850
	Bangkok	12,748	3,940	8,808	0
	Total (Ton/Day)	22,835	6,528	14,932	4,840

Source: Pollution Control Department, Thailand (2023)

This study addresses a pressing environmental issue—plastic waste—by focusing on visual demonstration as a potential upstream cognitive intervention. Drawing on the S–O–R framework, it conceptualizes UI-based visual demonstration as a marketing stimulus that shapes internal cognitive states, particularly awareness, which in turn drives behavioral intention [7]. Empirical evidence remains scarce regarding how visual demonstration embedded in food delivery applications functions as a UI/UX marketing stimulus influencing consumer awareness and behavioral intention toward sustainable packaging. This study addresses that gap by integrating UI/UX marketing with consumer behavior theory.

2 Literature Review

Prior studies in digital marketing highlight the importance of visual cues, interface clarity, and perceived usability in shaping online consumer behavior within platform-based environments. As digital interfaces increasingly serve as primary marketing touchpoints, UI/UX design has become a strategic mechanism through which firms communicate value propositions and influence consumer perceptions [2]. Visual elements embedded in digital platforms—such as imagery, layout organization, color schemes, and informational cues—play a critical role in directing user attention, enhancing cognitive processing, and facilitating decision-making in online contexts [3, 4].

Research in electronic commerce suggests that interface clarity and perceived usability significantly affect consumer trust, satisfaction, and behavioral intention. Clear and well-structured interfaces reduce cognitive load, improve information processing efficiency, and enhance perceived control during online interactions [1, 8]. Drawing on the S–O–R model, digital marketing scholars have increasingly conceptualized interface-based elements as external stimuli that trigger internal cognitive and affective states, which subsequently shape behavioral outcomes [7, 9].

Within this framework, visual demonstration embedded in platform interfaces can be interpreted as a UI/UX marketing stimulus that enhances consumer awareness by increasing information salience and perceived informativeness. Awareness, as an internal organismic state, reflects consumers' recognition, understanding, and evaluation of product attributes communicated through digital interfaces [10]. Prior studies indicate that visually rich and informative digital content positively influences consumer awareness and behavioral intention, especially when product attributes cannot be directly experienced prior to purchase [5, 6].

3 Research Methodology

This study employed a mixed-methods research design, integrating qualitative and quantitative approaches to examine consumer awareness and behavioral intention toward sustainable packaging within food delivery platforms. The mixed-methods approach was selected to capture both the statistical relationships among key constructs and the experiential, contextual dimensions that quantitative data alone cannot fully explain. The study is grounded in the S–O–R framework [7], specifying visual demonstration as the external stimulus, consumer awareness as the internal organismic state, and behavioral intention as the behavioral response.

For the **quantitative component**, the target population consisted of active food delivery platform users in Bangkok who had placed at least one order through a mobile application within the preceding 3 months. Sample size was determined using Cochran's (1977) formula ($n_0 = Z^2 \cdot p \cdot (1 - p)/e^2$), with $Z = 1.96$, $p = 0.5$, and $e = 0.05$, yielding a minimum of 385 participants, rounded up to 400 to improve statistical robustness [11]. Participants were screened for active platform usage prior to inclusion.

For the **qualitative component**, 30 participants were recruited using purposive sampling—selected to ensure all possessed direct, recent experience with food delivery platforms—and organized into five focus groups of six participants each. This sample size aligns with established guidance for achieving thematic saturation in exploratory focus group research [12, 13]. All participants first viewed a pre-recorded visual demonstration video showcasing the functionality, durability, and environmental benefits of edible cutlery before completing the survey or participating in focus group discussions.

Measurement items were adapted from established scales in UI/UX, digital marketing, and consumer behavior literature. All items were measured using a five-point Likert-type scale. Structural equation modeling (PLS-SEM) was employed to test the proposed hypotheses using bootstrapping with 5,000 subsamples. The analytical procedure involved assessing the measurement model for reliability and validity, followed by evaluation of the structural model to test hypothesized relationships.

4 Results and Analysis

4.1 Descriptive Statistics

Descriptive statistics revealed moderately high awareness of plastic waste (M = 3.642, SD = 0.398), favorable attitudes toward edible cutlery (M = 4.008, SD = 0.504), and moderate-to-high behavioral intentions (M = 3.921, SD = 0.560). All Pearson correlations among constructs were statistically significant ($p < 0.01$), with attitudes toward edible cutlery showing the strongest correlation with behavioral intention (r = 0.584).

4.2 PLS-SEM Structural Model Results

The hypothesized S–O–R structural model was estimated using PLS-SEM with bootstrapping of 5,000 subsamples. Path coefficients, standard errors, t-values, p-values, and effect sizes for all hypothesized relationships are presented in Table 2. Model fit indices are reported in Table 3.

Table 2. PLS-SEM Path Coefficients and Hypothesis Testing Results (N = 400)

Hyp.	Path	β	SE	t-value	p-value	f^2	Decision
H1	AW → AT	0.319	0.057	5.985	<0.001	0.121	Supported
H2	AW → BI	0.908	0.065	14.970	<0.001	0.487	Supported
H3	BF → AT	0.439	0.055	7.897	<0.001	0.230	Supported
H4	BF → BI	0.200	0.034	5.783	<0.001	0.088	Supported
H5	BA → AT	−0.213	0.051	−4.241	<0.001	0.057	Supported
H6	BA → BI	−0.015	0.030	−0.513	0.608	0.001	Not Supported
H7	AT → BI	0.710	0.038	6.978	<0.001	0.312	Supported

Note. AW = Awareness of Plastic Waste; AT = Attitudes Toward Edible Cutlery; BA = Barriers to Adoption; BF = Behavioral Factors; BI = Behavioral Intentions. β = standardized path coefficient; f^2 = effect size (small ≥0.02; medium ≥0.15; large ≥0.35). Bootstrapping with 5,000 subsamples.

Six of seven hypothesized paths were supported. Awareness of Plastic Waste exerted the strongest direct effect on Behavioral Intention ($\beta = 0.908$, $t = 14.970$, $p < 0.001$), confirming visual demonstration as a powerful upstream cognitive stimulus. Behavioral Factors were the strongest predictor of Attitudes ($\beta = 0.439$, $p < 0.001$), and Attitudes in turn strongly predicted Behavioral Intention ($\beta = 0.710$, $p < 0.001$). Perceived Barriers significantly reduced Attitudes ($\beta = -0.213$, $p < 0.001$) but exerted no significant direct effect on Behavioral Intention ($\beta = -0.015$, $p = 0.608$), indicating barriers operate through an indirect attitudinal pathway (indirect effect ≈ −0.151).

4.3 Qualitative Findings: Thematic Analysis

Five focus group sessions (N = 30) produced five overarching themes: (1) sensory and functional concerns as primary barriers—participants questioned durability with hot

Table 3. PLS-SEM Model Fit Indices

Index	Value	Threshold	Assessment
R^2 (AT — Attitudes)	0.484	≥ 0.10 (moderate)	Acceptable
R^2 (BI — Behavioral Intention)	0.695	≥ 0.10 (moderate)	Acceptable
Q^2 Predictive Relevance (AT)	0.218	> 0 (predictive)	Acceptable
Q^2 Predictive Relevance (BI)	0.367	> 0 (predictive)	Acceptable
SRMR	0.071	< 0.08 (good fit)	Good fit
NFI	0.873	≥ 0.90 (preferred)	Marginal

Note. PLS-SEM model fit assessed via SRMR and NFI following Hair et al. [14]. R^2 = coefficient of determination; Q^2 = predictive relevance (blindfolding); SRMR = standardized root mean square residual; NFI = Normed Fit Index.

or oily foods; (2) hygiene, safety, and unfamiliarity—concerns about production standards and psychological barriers to consuming the utensil; (3) economic and practical constraints—anticipated higher costs and logistical challenges; (4) social and communication levers—influencer endorsements, platform sustainability badges, and government campaigns were identified as key adoption enablers; and (5) product design improvements—participants proposed multiple flavor options and improved packaging. These qualitative themes provide contextual explanation for the quantitative SEM patterns, confirming that visual demonstration is necessary but insufficient without concurrent barrier reduction.

5 Conclusion

This study demonstrates that UI/UX marketing embedded within food delivery platforms plays a significant role in shaping consumer awareness and behavioral intention toward sustainable consumption choices. The findings confirm that visually driven UI/UX elements serve as effective stimuli that enhance consumers' cognitive awareness of environmental issues. Awareness strongly predicts behavioral intention ($\beta = 0.908$, $p < 0.001$), supporting the proposed S–O–R model.

The results highlight that UI/UX marketing should not be regarded merely as an aesthetic function, but as a strategic behavioral mechanism. From a managerial perspective, food delivery platforms should integrate UI/UX marketing—including short videos, in-app animations, default green options, and sustainability badges—to enhance consumer awareness at the point of decision-making. Future research directions include: (1) extending the model to other e-commerce platforms and cross-cultural contexts; (2) incorporating actual behavioral data rather than self-reported intention; (3) longitudinal designs to examine enduring behavioral change; and (4) integrating additional variables such as trust, perceived convenience, and emotional engagement.

References

1. Hassenzahl, M., Tractinsky, N.: User experience—a research agenda. Behav. Inform. Technol. **25**(2), 91–97 (2006)
2. Lemon, K.N., Verhoef, P.C.: Understanding customer experience throughout the customer journey. J. Mark. **80**(6), 69–96 (2016)
3. Cyr, D.: Modeling web site design across cultures. J. Manag. Inf. Syst. **24**(4), 47–72 (2008)
4. Djamasbi, S., Siegel, M., Tullis, T.: Generation Y, web design, and eye tracking. Int. J. Hum. Comput. Stud. **68**(5), 307–323 (2010)
5. Wedel, M., Pieters, R.: The buffer effect. J. Consum. Res. **41**(1), 132–146 (2014)
6. Wang, Y., Malthouse, E.C., Krishnamurthi, L.: On the go: how mobile shopping affects customer purchase behavior. J. Retail. **96**(2), 217–234 (2020)
7. Mehrabian, A., Russell, J.A.: An Approach to Environmental Psychology. MIT Press (1974)
8. Flavián, C., Guinalíu, M., Gurrea, R.: The role played by perceived usability, satisfaction and consumer trust on website loyalty. Inf. Manag. **43**(1), 1–14 (2006)
9. Eroglu, S.A., Machleit, K.A., Davis, L.M.: Empirical testing of a model of online store atmospherics. Psychol. Mark. **20**(2), 139–150 (2003)
10. MacInnis, D.J., Jaworski, B.J.: Information processing from advertisements. J. Mark. **53**(4), 1–23 (1989)
11. Cochran, W.G.: Sampling Techniques, 3rd edn. Wiley (1977)
12. Morgan, D.L.: The Focus Group Guidebook. SAGE Publications (1998)
13. Krueger, R.A., Casey, M.A.: Focus Groups: A Practical Guide for Applied Research, 5th edn. SAGE Publications (2015)
14. Hair, J.F., Risher, J.J., Sarstedt, M., Ringle, C.M.: When to use and how to report results of PLS-SEM. Eur. Bus. Rev. **31**(1), 2–24 (2019)
15. Steg, L., Vlek, C.: Encouraging pro-environmental behaviour. J. Environ. Psychol. **29**(3), 309–317 (2009)
16. Thaler, R.H., Sunstein, C.R.: Nudge. Yale University Press (2008)
17. White, K., Habib, R., Hardisty, D.J.: How to SHIFT consumer behaviors to be more sustainable. J. Mark. **83**(3), 22–49 (2019)

From Implementation to Impact: Technology Acceptance, Absorptive Capacity, and the Productivity Paradox of Cashless Payment Systems

S. Nagayoshi(✉)

Shizuoka University, 3-5-1, Johoku, Chuo-ku, Hamamatsu, Shizuoka, Japan
nagayoshi@inf.shizuoka.ac.jp

Abstract. This study investigates how the implementation of cashless payment systems translates into organizational outcomes through the mediating roles of technology acceptance and absorptive capacity. Drawing on the productivity paradox literature, we argue that digital payment systems do not generate performance gains automatically; instead, their effects depend on post-implementation organizational processes. Using survey data collected from 266 firms in the retail and trading sectors, we tested a research model that links cashless payment implementation to supply-side and demand-side outcomes via technology acceptance and absorptive capacity. The results of covariance-based structural equation modeling reveal that while advanced implementation enhances technology acceptance, it does not directly increase absorptive capacity. Technology acceptance positively influences absorptive capacity and supply-side outcomes, whereas demand-side outcomes are shaped primarily by absorptive capacity and prior operational improvements. These findings indicate that the benefits of cashless payment systems emerge in a sequential and non-synchronous manner, highlighting the limitations of evaluating digital transformation initiatives based solely on short-term or single performance indicators. By integrating technology acceptance and absorptive capacity into a unified model, this study extends cashless payment research beyond adoption and provides a process-based explanation of the productivity paradox in contemporary digital transformation.

Keywords: Cashless payment systems · Digital transformation · Technology acceptance · Absorptive capacity · Productivity paradox · IT business value

1 Introduction

Digital transformation (DX) has become a central issue in both corporate management and public policy. Among various digital infrastructures, cashless payment systems represent a typical and widely diffused form of DX, particularly in retail and service industries. By enabling faster transactions, reducing cash-handling costs, and improving customer convenience, cashless payments are often expected to enhance operational efficiency and customer experience simultaneously.

D. Liberona et al. (Eds.): MISNC 2026, CCIS 3092, pp. 35–47, 2027.
https://doi.org/10.1007/978-3-032-33381-0_4

However, practical experiences suggest that the introduction of cashless payment systems does not automatically lead to immediate or uniform performance improvements. Many firms encounter operational disruptions, increased employee workload, or limited visible benefits, especially in the early stages of implementation. This discrepancy between expected and realized outcomes reflects a classic issue in information systems research: the productivity paradox of information technology.

Since Solow's [1] observation that IT investments are visible everywhere except in productivity statistics, extensive research has examined why IT investments do not directly translate into performance gains. Prior studies have consistently shown that the value of IT depends not on the amount of investment itself, but on how technologies are interpreted, accepted, and utilized within organizations [2, 3]. Complementary organizational resources—such as redesigned business processes and organizational capabilities—play a critical role in transforming IT investments into tangible outcomes [4]. From this perspective, cashless payment systems offer a suitable empirical context for reexamining the productivity paradox in a contemporary DX setting, as they are relatively standardized technologies whose outcomes vary substantially across firms.

Existing research on cashless and mobile payment systems has largely been developed from the perspective of technology acceptance. Studies based on the Technology Acceptance Model (TAM) have demonstrated that perceived usefulness, trust, and perceived ease of use significantly influence individuals' adoption intentions and usage behaviors [5–7]. While these studies provide valuable insights into adoption decisions, they primarily focus on individual-level acceptance and offer limited explanations of how organizational outcomes emerge after implementation.

In parallel, the literature on IT business value emphasizes the role of organizational capabilities in mediating the relationship between IT investments and performance. In particular, absorptive capacity—the ability to recognize, assimilate, transform, and exploit external knowledge—has been identified as a key mechanism through which organizations leverage digital technologies for performance improvement [8, 9]. Recent studies further suggest that learning and knowledge utilization capabilities are crucial in realizing the benefits of digital technologies [4]. Nevertheless, empirical research that integrates technology acceptance and absorptive capacity to explain post-adoption performance in the context of cashless payments remains limited.

Moreover, prior studies often treat performance outcomes as a single, homogeneous construct. In practice, however, the outcomes of cashless payment implementation are multifaceted. Improvements in operational efficiency and accuracy—such as faster checkout processes and reduced transaction errors—are internal, supply-side outcomes that tend to manifest relatively early. In contrast, demand-side outcomes—such as increased customer satisfaction, repeat patronage, and customer loyalty—are more likely to emerge through stable operations and accumulated learning over time. Empirical studies that explicitly distinguish between these different types of outcomes are still scarce.

Against this background, this study aims to examine the process through which cashless payment implementation leads to organizational outcomes by focusing on technology acceptance and absorptive capacity as mediating mechanisms. Specifically, this study investigates how the degree of cashless payment implementation influences technology acceptance and absorptive capacity, and how these capabilities, in turn, affect supply-side outcomes (operational efficiency and accuracy) and demand-side outcomes (customer behavior and relationships). By distinguishing between supply-side and demand-side outcomes, this study seeks to capture the staged and asymmetric nature of DX-related performance effects.

This study contributes to the literature in three ways. First, it extends research on cashless payment systems beyond adoption intentions by focusing on post-implementation organizational outcomes. Second, by integrating technology acceptance and absorptive capacity into a unified research model, it empirically reexamines the productivity paradox in a contemporary DX context. Third, by distinguishing between supply-side and demand-side outcomes, it highlights the non-synchronous and process-oriented nature of DX performance realization, offering implications for both researchers and practitioners.

2 Related Work and Hypotheses

This study develops an integrated research model to examine how the implementation of cashless payment systems leads to organizational outcomes. The model incorporates four key constructs: the degree of cashless payment implementation, technology acceptance, absorptive capacity, and post-implementation outcomes. Consistent with the productivity paradox literature, the model assumes that cashless payment systems do not generate organizational benefits directly; rather, their effects are mediated by how the technology is interpreted, accepted, and leveraged through organizational learning and knowledge utilization processes.

2.1 Cashless Payment Implementation and Technology Acceptance

Cashless payment implementation is not a binary condition but a multidimensional construct that reflects the diversity of available payment methods, the length of time since implementation, the degree of customer penetration, and the extent of organizational deployment. As implementation progresses, organizational members accumulate practical experience with cashless payments in daily operations. Such repeated use enables them to recognize the convenience, reliability, and operational value of the system, thereby strengthening positive perceptions toward the technology.

Prior studies based on the Technology Acceptance Model (TAM) consistently show that perceived usefulness and trust significantly influence technology acceptance and usage [5, 6]. Similar findings have been reported in the context of mobile and cashless payments [7]. Accordingly, this study proposes that more advanced implementation leads to higher levels of technology acceptance.

H1: Firms with more advanced cashless payment implementation exhibit higher levels of technology acceptance.

2.2 Cashless Payment Implementation and Absorptive Capacity

The implementation of cashless payment systems increases organizational exposure to external knowledge, including vendor support, financial institutions, regulatory changes, and best practices observed in other firms. As implementation progresses, firms are required to understand, adapt, and apply such external knowledge to their own operational contexts, which stimulates organizational learning activities.

Absorptive capacity refers to an organization's ability to acquire, assimilate, transform, and exploit external knowledge [8, 9]. Firms that actively engage with cashless payment systems are expected to develop routines and capabilities that support learning from external sources. Therefore, more advanced implementation is likely to facilitate the formation of absorptive capacity.

H2: Firms with more advanced cashless payment implementation are expected to facilitate the development of absorptive capacity.

2.3 Technology Acceptance and Absorptive Capacity

Technology acceptance represents more than a favorable attitude toward a system; it reflects a willingness to actively use, experiment with, and refine the technology in practice. When organizations perceive cashless payment systems as useful and reliable, they are more likely to integrate them into core business processes and engage in continuous improvement efforts.

Research on information systems success suggests that perceived usefulness and system use contribute to organizational learning and performance outcomes [10]. In this sense, technology acceptance functions as a catalyst that activates learning behaviors and knowledge utilization. Accordingly, technology acceptance is expected to enhance absorptive capacity.

H3: Higher levels of technology acceptance are positively associated with higher absorptive capacity.

2.4 Technology Acceptance, Absorptive Capacity, and Supply-Side Outcomes

Among the outcomes of cashless payment implementation, supply-side outcomes—such as shorter transaction times, more efficient reconciliation processes, and improved operational accuracy—are directly reflected in internal business processes. Firms with high technology acceptance are more likely to integrate cashless payments smoothly into daily operations, allowing system functionalities to be fully exploited.

In addition, firms with strong absorptive capacity can incorporate external operational knowledge and improvement practices into their own workflows, further enhancing operational efficiency. Prior IT business value research suggests that short-term benefits of IT investments are most likely to appear in operational efficiency and process improvements [2]. Thus, both technology acceptance and absorptive capacity are expected to contribute to supply-side outcomes.

H4: Higher levels of technology acceptance lead to greater supply-side outcomes.
H5: Higher levels of absorptive capacity lead to greater supply-side outcomes.

2.5 Technology Acceptance, Absorptive Capacity, and Demand-Side Outcomes

Demand-side outcomes of cashless payment implementation include improvements in customer convenience, repeat purchase intentions, and customer loyalty. These outcomes tend to emerge through stable operations and accumulated learning rather than immediate system adoption. Firms with high technology acceptance can provide consistent and reliable payment experiences, which may enhance customer evaluations.

However, demand-side outcomes often require continuous adaptation and service improvement, which are strongly influenced by absorptive capacity. Organizations with high absorptive capacity can leverage external knowledge related to customer service and digital innovation to refine customer interactions. Therefore, both technology acceptance and absorptive capacity are expected to influence demand-side outcomes, with absorptive capacity playing a particularly important role.

H6: Higher levels of technology acceptance lead to greater demand-side outcomes.
H7: Higher levels of absorptive capacity lead to greater demand-side outcomes.

2.6 Relationship Between Supply-Side and Demand-Side Outcomes

Supply-side and demand-side outcomes are not independent. Improvements in operational efficiency and accuracy reduce waiting times and stabilize service quality, which directly affect customer experiences. The service-profit chain framework posits that internal process improvements translate into customer satisfaction and loyalty [11].

Accordingly, this study assumes that supply-side outcomes serve as a foundation for demand-side outcomes.

H8: Greater supply-side outcomes lead to greater demand-side outcomes.

3 Methodology

3.1 Questionnaire Development

This study employed a questionnaire-based quantitative design. Based on prior research on technology acceptance [5, 6], absorptive capacity [8, 9], and IT business value [3, 4], we specified five core constructs: cashless payment implementation, technology acceptance, absorptive capacity, supply-side outcomes, and demand-side outcomes. Measurement items were adapted from validated scales and tailored to the cashless payment context. Table 1 summarizes the construct definitions, labels, and measurement items.

The questionnaire consisted of two stages: a screening survey and a main survey. The screening survey included items on firm characteristics and operational settings (7 items), cashless payment usage conditions (9 items), and one attention-check item. The main survey included the focal measurement items for the five constructs (Table 1), additional items for capturing implementation details and control variables, and attention-check items to assess response quality. All attitudinal items were measured using a seven-point Likert scale.

Table 1. Constructs, Operational Definitions, Labels, and Measurement Items)

Construct	Operational Definition	Label	Measurement Items	Theoretical Foundation
Cashless Implementation	The extent and maturity of cashless payment system implementation within the firm	IMP	IMP1: Number of cashless payment methods implemented IMP2: Length of time since implementation IMP5: Degree of customer penetration of cashless payments IMP6: Proportion of stores implementing cashless payments	Scope and diffusion of IT investment as a prerequisite for value creation [3, 4]; multidimensional nature of payment adoption [7]
Technology Acceptance	The extent to which cashless payments are perceived as useful and trustworthy within the organization	TAM	TAM1: Improves operational efficiency TAM2: Improves customer experience TAM5: Considered safe and trustworthy	Perceived usefulness and trust as drivers of technology acceptance and outcomes [5, 6]
Absorptive Capacity	The organizational capability to understand, adapt, and utilize external knowledge for operational improvement	AC	AC1: External knowledge is understood and shared internally AC2: External knowledge is adapted to the firm's operations AC3: External knowledge is utilized for operational improvement	Absorption and exploitation of external knowledge as a source of IT value [8, 9]

(*continued*)

Table 1. (*continued*)

Construct	Operational Definition	Label	Measurement Items	Theoretical Foundation
Supplier-side Effect	Improvements in internal operational efficiency and accuracy resulting from cashless payment implementation	SEFT	SEFT2: Improved efficiency of cash reconciliation and settlement SEFT4: Reduced employee workload related to payment operations SEFT6: Improved operational accuracy	Short-term and direct effects of IT investment on operational efficiency [1]
Demand-side Effect	Improvements in customer behavior and relational outcomes resulting from cashless payment implementation	DEFT	DEFT3: Increased customer revisit intention DEFT4: Acquisition of new customers DEFT6: Improved store-level customer loyalty	Internal process improvements translating into customer outcomes [11]; service quality and customer behavior linkage [12]

3.2 Data Collection

Data were collected via an online survey administered by iBridge Corporation using the Freeasy platform. The target respondents were Freeasy panel members in Japan aged 20–65 who were either full-time employees or business owners/managers working in retail or trading companies.

Data collection was conducted in two steps. First, the screening survey was administered from November 1 to November 2, 2025, yielding 3,000 responses. Second, the main survey was conducted from November 4 to November 5, 2025, targeting respondents who met the screening criteria. The requested delivery size was 400, and the vendor oversampled to 120% of the requested size and applied an AI-based procedure to exclude suspicious responses (e.g., extremely short completion times). The vendor noted that if suspicious responses exceed 20% of total responses, some low-quality responses may remain in the delivered dataset.

3.3 Data Cleaning

In addition to the vendor's AI-based exclusion, we performed additional data cleaning to ensure response quality. First, responses that failed attention-check items were removed. Second, we manually identified and excluded straightlining responses (i.e., selecting the same option for almost all items). Third, because the questionnaire was organized into multiple item blocks, we excluded responses showing 70% or more identical choices within any block, which indicates low-engagement response behavior. After these procedures, the final effective sample size used for analysis was 266.

3.4 Data Analysis

We conducted the analysis in four steps. First, we computed descriptive statistics to examine respondent characteristics and variable distributions.

Second, we assessed internal consistency reliability using Cronbach's alpha for each construct. Descriptive statistics and reliability analyses were performed using Excel Statistics (BellCurve). Third, to test the hypothesized research model, we conducted covariance-based structural equation modeling (CB-SEM). Model estimation and evaluation were performed using IBM SPSS AMOS 31, examining overall model fit indices and the statistical significance of the hypothesized paths. This approach allowed us to test whether cashless payment implementation influences organizational outcomes through the mediating roles of technology acceptance and absorptive capacity.

4 Results

4.1 Reliability Analysis

To assess internal consistency, Cronbach's alpha coefficients were calculated for all constructs. The results indicate acceptable to high reliability: cashless implementation (0.7026), technology acceptance (0.7600), absorptive capacity (0.8324), supply-side outcomes (0.8983), and demand-side outcomes (0.8591). All values exceed the commonly accepted threshold of 0.70, indicating satisfactory internal consistency of the measurement scales.

4.2 Common Method Bias Assessment

To assess the potential influence of common method bias (CMB), we conducted Harman's single-factor test. All measurement items were entered into a confirmatory factor analysis specifying a single latent factor. The single-factor model demonstrated a very poor fit to the data ($\chi^2 = 774.102$, df $= 104$, χ^2/df $= 7.443$, CFI $= 0.658$, TLI $= 0.605$, RMSEA $= 0.156$, GFI $= 0.690$).

These fit indices are substantially below commonly accepted thresholds (e.g., CFI > 0.90, RMSEA < 0.08), indicating that a single latent factor does not adequately account for the covariance among the measurement items. Therefore, common method bias is unlikely to be a major threat to the validity of the findings.

In addition, standardized factor loadings varied substantially across constructs (e.g., SEFT items > 0.80; TAM items 0.50–0.68; IMP items 0.13–0.25), suggesting that the observed variance is not dominated by a single underlying factor. Taken together, these results indicate that common method bias does not materially compromise the structural relationships reported in this study.

4.3 Structural Equation Modeling Results

We tested the hypothesized research model using covariance-based structural equation modeling (CB-SEM) with a final sample of 266 observations, estimated using IBM SPSS AMOS 31. The overall model fit indices indicate a good fit to the data: CMIN = 162.794, DF = 96, CMIN/DF = 1.696, CFI = 0.966, GFI = 0.930, RMSEA = 0.051, and AIC = 242.794. These values meet or exceed commonly accepted fit criteria (e.g., CFI > 0.90; RMSEA < 0.08), suggesting that the proposed model adequately represents the observed data (See Fig. 1).

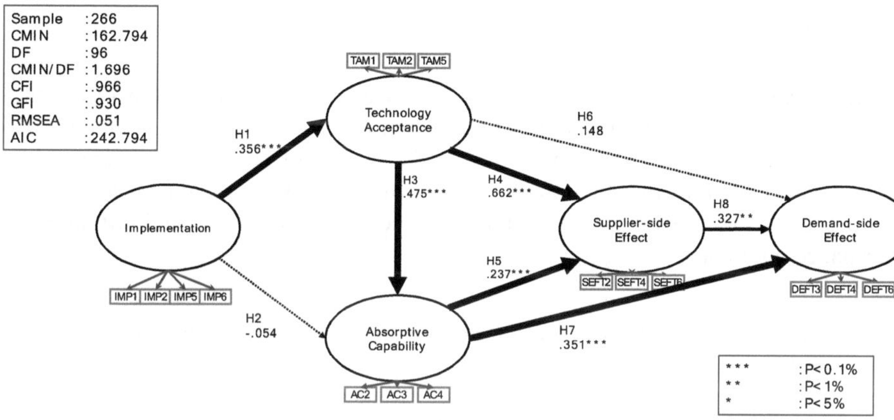

Fig. 1. Result of Structural Equation Modeling.

4.4 Hypothesis Testing

Figure 1 summarizes the estimated path coefficients and hypothesis testing results. First, cashless payment implementation had a significant positive effect on technology acceptance (H1: $\beta = 0.354$, $p < 0.001$), indicating that more advanced implementation is associated with higher acceptance of the technology. In contrast, the direct effect of cashless implementation on absorptive capacity was not significant (H2: $\beta = -0.054$, n.s.).

Second, technology acceptance exhibited a strong positive effect on absorptive capacity (H3: $\beta = 0.475$, $p < 0.001$), suggesting that favorable perceptions of cashless payment systems facilitate organizational learning and knowledge utilization. Regarding supply-side outcomes, both technology acceptance (H4: $\beta = 0.662$, $p < 0.001$) and absorptive capacity (H5: $\beta = 0.237$, $p < 0.001$) showed significant positive effects.

For demand-side outcomes, the direct effect of technology acceptance was not significant (H6: $\beta = 0.148$, n.s.), whereas absorptive capacity had a significant positive effect (H7: $\beta = 0.351$, $p < 0.001$). Finally, supply-side outcomes significantly influenced demand-side outcomes (H8: $\beta = 0.327$, $p < 0.01$), indicating that operational improvements translate into customer-related benefits.

4.5 Summary of Results

Overall, the results largely support the proposed research model. The findings indicate that post-implementation outcomes of cashless payment systems emerge through technology acceptance and absorptive capacity rather than through implementation alone. While cashless implementation directly enhances technology acceptance, its effects on absorptive capacity and downstream outcomes are largely indirect, highlighting the importance of organizational processes in realizing the benefits of digital payment systems.

5 Discussion

This study examined how the implementation of cashless payment systems translates into organizational outcomes through the mediating roles of technology acceptance and absorptive capacity. The results indicate that the effects of cashless payment implementation are not uniform or automatic; rather, they are best understood as a stage-based process, moving from implementation to acceptance, learning, and ultimately to performance outcomes.

5.1 The Role of Technology Acceptance and the Non-Automatic Nature of Implementation Effects

The findings show that the degree of cashless payment implementation has a significant positive effect on technology acceptance, but no direct effect on absorptive capacity. This suggests that even when cashless payment systems are widely implemented, such implementation alone does not automatically enhance organizational learning or knowledge utilization capabilities. In other words, implementation functions as a necessary but insufficient condition for realizing organizational benefits.

This result is consistent with the productivity paradox literature, which argues that IT investments do not generate performance gains simply through increased input levels [2]. Instead, value creation depends on how technologies are interpreted, accepted, and integrated into organizational practices. The present findings demonstrate that this logic also applies to relatively standardized digital technologies such as cashless payment systems.

The non-significant relationship between implementation intensity and absorptive capacity may also reflect industry characteristics. In relatively standardized sectors such as retail and trading, expanding the number of cashless payment methods does not necessarily require substantial new knowledge integration or process redesign. Unlike complex digital transformations (e.g., ERP or AI systems), payment systems are often modular and vendor-supported, reducing the need for internally developed learning routines. Therefore, absorptive capacity may not automatically increase through implementation alone, especially in environments where technological complexity is limited.

5.2 Technology Acceptance as a Precondition for Absorptive Capacity

Technology acceptance exhibited a strong positive effect on absorptive capacity, indicating that perceiving cashless payment systems as useful and trustworthy facilitates organizational learning and knowledge utilization. This result suggests that technology acceptance should not be viewed merely as an attitudinal construct, but rather as an organizational-level precondition that activates learning processes.

While prior TAM-based studies have primarily focused on adoption intention or usage behavior at the individual level, this study extends the technology acceptance literature by showing that acceptance influences organizational outcomes indirectly through absorptive capacity. In doing so, the study positions technology acceptance as a bridge between technological implementation and organizational learning.

5.3 Asymmetry Between Supply-Side and Demand-Side Outcomes

One of the most important findings of this study is the asymmetric pattern of determinants for supply-side and demand-side outcomes. Supply-side outcomes—such as operational efficiency and accuracy—were significantly influenced by both technology acceptance and absorptive capacity. In contrast, demand-side outcomes—such as customer revisit intention and loyalty—were not directly affected by technology acceptance; instead, they were shaped primarily by absorptive capacity and by supply-side outcomes.

This asymmetry suggests that the benefits of cashless payment systems emerge sequentially. Operational improvements tend to appear relatively early, as technologies are integrated into routine processes. Customer-related outcomes, however, require stable operations and accumulated learning over time. These findings underscore the limitations of evaluating digital transformation initiatives using a single or short-term performance metric.

5.4 Theoretical Contributions

This study contributes to the IT business value and productivity paradox literatures in several ways. First, it provides empirical evidence that the effects of cashless payment implementation are mediated by technology acceptance and absorptive capacity, rather than driven directly by implementation intensity. Second, by distinguishing between supply-side and demand-side outcomes, the study reveals a non-synchronous and non-symmetric structure of value realization in digital transformation.

These findings suggest that the productivity paradox may be overstated when digital investments are evaluated solely based on short-term or customer-facing outcomes. A more appropriate perspective is to conceptualize digital transformation outcomes as process-based and capability-mediated, unfolding over time through organizational learning.

5.5 Practical Implication

From a practical perspective, the results imply that policies and managerial initiatives aimed solely at promoting the adoption of cashless payments may not be sufficient to generate expected benefits. Post-implementation efforts—such as training, knowledge sharing, and continuous improvement—are essential for translating digital adoption into organizational and customer outcomes.

For small and medium-sized enterprises in particular, developing absorptive capacity through employee education, collaboration with external experts, and sustained vendor support appears critical for realizing demand-side benefits.

5.6 Limitations and Future Research Directions

This study has several limitations. First, the use of cross-sectional survey data limits causal inference. Second, the temporal dynamics of outcome realization were not directly observed, making it difficult to trace the transition from supply-side to demand-side outcomes over time. Future research should employ longitudinal designs to examine these dynamics more explicitly.

Additionally, the study focused on specific industries, which may limit generalizability. Future research could extend the model to other sectors or compare industries to further validate the proposed framework.

6 Conclusion

This study empirically examined how the implementation of cashless payment systems translates into organizational outcomes through the mediating roles of technology acceptance and absorptive capacity. The findings demonstrate that the effects of cashless payment implementation are not uniform; rather, they depend not on the degree of implementation itself but on post-implementation processes of acceptance, learning, and knowledge utilization.

The results show that while firms with more advanced cashless payment implementation exhibit higher levels of technology acceptance, implementation does not directly enhance absorptive capacity. This indicates that digital investments and system adoption do not automatically strengthen organizational capabilities. Instead, perceiving the technology as useful and trustworthy constitutes a critical precondition for activating learning and knowledge utilization processes.

By distinguishing between supply-side and demand-side outcomes, this study further reveals that operational outcomes—such as efficiency and accuracy—are explained by both technology acceptance and absorptive capacity, whereas customer-related outcomes are shaped primarily through absorptive capacity and prior operational improvements. These findings suggest that the benefits of cashless payment systems emerge in a sequential and non-synchronous manner, highlighting the limitations of evaluating digital transformation initiatives solely through short-term or single performance indicators.

This study contributes to the literature by extending cashless payment research beyond adoption intention and usage behavior to focus on post-implementation organizational outcomes. Moreover, by integrating technology acceptance and absorptive capacity into a unified model, it revisits the productivity paradox in a contemporary digital transformation context and demonstrates that IT value is realized through organizational processes rather than through technology deployment alone.

From a practical perspective, the findings imply that policies and managerial efforts aimed solely at promoting cashless payment adoption are insufficient. Post-implementation support—such as employee training, knowledge sharing, and continuous learning—plays a crucial role in translating digital adoption into both operational and customer-related benefits. This implication is particularly relevant for small and medium-sized enterprises, where developing absorptive capacity appears to be a key condition for realizing demand-side outcomes.

Future research should employ longitudinal data to examine the temporal transition from supply-side to demand-side outcomes more precisely. In addition, further studies grounded in organizational learning and knowledge management perspectives could provide deeper insights into post-implementation processes. Taken together, this study serves as a foundation for future research that conceptualizes digital transformation outcomes as capability-mediated and temporally unfolding processes.

Acknowledgments. This research was partially supported by a Grant-in-Aid (Grant No. 2318) and by the Zengin Foundation for Studies on Economics and Finance. It was also supported by a Grant-in-Aid for Scientific Research (C) (Grant Number 22K01627) from the Japan Society for the Promotion of Science (JSPS). I would also like to express my appreciation to my students, K.C. Abisikha and Kosei Matsuda, for their kind assistance.

Disclosure of Interests. The authors declare that they have no competing interests.

References

1. Solow, R.M.: We'd better watch out. New York Times Book Review, July 12, 36 (1987)
2. Brynjolfsson, E.: The productivity paradox of information technology. Commun. ACM. **36**(12), 66–77 (1993)
3. Brynjolfsson, E., Hitt, L.M.: Beyond computation: information technology, organizational transformation and business performance. J. Econ. Perspect. **14**(4), 23–48 (2000)
4. Melville, N., Kraemer, K., Gurbaxani, V.: Information technology and organizational performance: an integrative model of IT business value. MIS Q. **28**(2), 283–322 (2004)
5. Davis, F.D.: Perceived usefulness, perceived ease of use, and user acceptance of information technology. MIS Q. **13**(3), 319–340 (1989)
6. Venkatesh, V., Davis, F.D.: A theoretical extension of the technology acceptance model: four longitudinal field studies. Manag. Sci. **46**(2), 186–204 (2000)
7. Dahlberg, T., Guo, J., Ondrus, J.: A critical review of mobile payment research. Electron. Commer. Res. Appl. **14**(5), 265–284 (2015)
8. Cohen, W.M., Levinthal, D.A.: Absorptive capacity: a new perspective on learning and innovation. Adm. Sci. Q. **35**(1), 128–152 (1990)
9. Zahra, S.A., George, G.: Absorptive capacity: a review, reconceptualization, and extension. Acad. Manag. Rev. **27**(2), 185–203 (2002)
10. DeLone, W.H., McLean, E.R.: The DeLone and McLean model of information systems success: a ten-year update. J. Manag. Inf. Syst. **19**(4), 9–30 (2003)
11. Heskett, J.L., Jones, T.O., Loveman, G.W., Sasser, W.E., Schlesinger, L.A.: Putting the service-profit chain to work. Harv. Bus. Rev. **72**(2), 164–174 (1994)
12. Parasuraman, A., Zeithaml, V.A., Malhotra, A.: E-S-QUAL: a multiple-item scale for assessing electronic service quality. J. Serv. Res. **7**(3), 213–233 (2005)

Thai Household Debt and Its Influencing Factors

Danai Tanamee[1], Suppanunta Romprasert[1](✉), and Kazunori Minetaki[2]

[1] Srinakharinwirot University, Bangkok, Thailand
{danait,suppanunta}@g.swu.ac.th

[2] Creative Management and Innovation Research Institute, Department of Business, Osaka, Japan
kminetaki@bus.kindai.ac.jp

Abstract. This study examines the factors affecting household debt in Thailand using quarterly secondary data from Q1 2012 to Q1 2023. To improve the reliability of the empirical analysis, the estimation strategy was re-specified to reduce multicollinearity and to address serial correlation, heteroskedasticity, and potential endogeneity. A dynamic OLS model with HAC Newey-West standard errors was used as the baseline specification. Instrumental variables two-stage least squares (IV-2SLS) and IV-GMM estimations were then conducted as robustness checks, treating income and savings as potentially endogenous variables and using their first and second lagged values as instruments. The results indicate that household debt in Thailand is highly persistent and that savings are consistently and positively associated with household debt across alternative estimation methods. Income also shows a positive association, particularly in the IV-GMM specification, whereas GDP and the policy interest rate are not robustly significant after accounting for dynamics and potential endogeneity. These findings suggest that policy design should consider debt persistence and savings-related credit expansion.

Keywords: household debt · income · saving

1 Introduction

1.1 Background and Importance

Nowadays, many countries are dramatically facing household debt, including Thailand. Household debt reflects issues in both microeconomic and macroeconomic views. In microeconomics, it reflects the quality of life for individuals, and in macroeconomics, it reflects the domestic consumption of the population. However, a higher rate of household debt can indicate economic instability (Klungjaturavet, 2014). During this decade, the economies of several countries are driven by debts. The amount of debt can be measured by government debt, public debt, and household debt, all of which seem to be increasing. In 2022, world debt was 270% compared to world GDP. One reason is that the central bank of each country set a low interest rate, with no pressure from inflation for a decade (Kiatnakin Phatra Bank Public Company Limited, 2022). Household debt compared to world GDP increased from 54.4% in 2010 to 59.3% in 2021, especially in countries in

D. Liberona et al. (Eds.): MISNC 2026, CCIS 3092, pp. 48–61, 2027.
https://doi.org/10.1007/978-3-032-33381-0_5

the emerging market group, where household debt rose from 28.1% in 2010 to 46.3% in 2021. At the same time, government policy intentionally aimed to initiate measures to decrease household debt after the world economic crisis in 2008–2009, but household debt still remained at 75.3% in 2021 in developed countries. Also, in 2021, South Korea's household debt increased from 32.6% in 2010 to 105.8% in 2021. China's was 34.3% in 2010 and increased to 61.6% in 2021. Thailand's was 31.6% in 2010 and increased to 91% in 2021 (Fig. 1) (Manprasert, 2022).

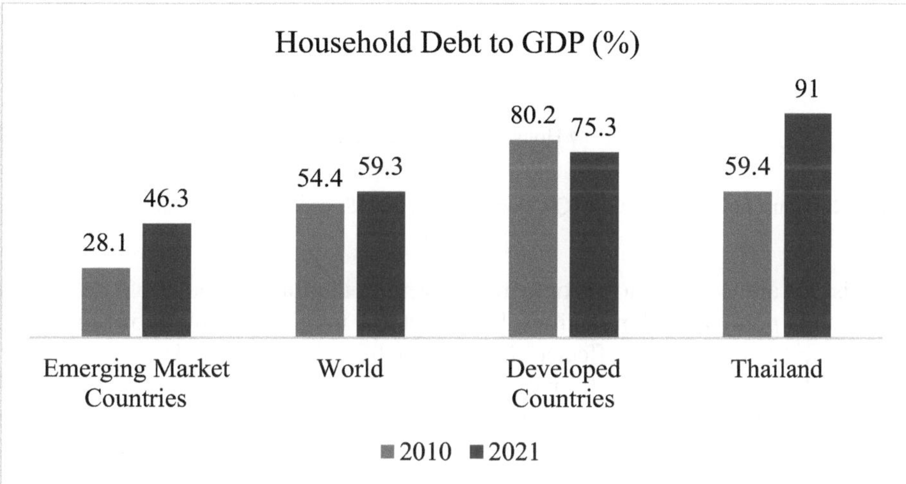

Fig. 1. Household Debt to GDP (%)

Currently, Thailand's household debt is 90% of GDP, ranking 11th in the world. During 2011 to 2013, Thailand's household debt was 79% of GDP and continued to increase due to flooding. In addition, the Thai government allowed financial institutions to give car loans easily under the first car policy (Stock2morrow Company Limited, 2023). After that, the household debt rate increased slowly between 2016 and 2017 for three main reasons: 1) decreased demand for loans, 2) burden of paying back installment loans, and 3) financial institutions not easily granting loans (KResearch, 2016). Moreover, in 2020, the COVID-19 epidemic resulted in an economic recession, and household debt increased significantly during this period. Thailand's household debt reached 90.2% of GDP (Fig. 2.) due to household expenditures that did not align with income. In other words, the cost of living was high compared to static income. Many people therefore decided to borrow money for the purchase of commodities and property. If borrowers are unable to repay loans, it becomes "debt." Thai households had a high rate of debt for short-term consumption compared to all types of household debt, which was also higher than in developed countries. This could mean that Thailand had low income per person but high household debt (Kiatnakin Phatra Bank Public Company Limited, 2022).

The high household debt has severely affected the Thai economy. Thailand is ranked in the top tier for income inequality distribution. This has led to a large group of low-income individuals with low saving rates and at risk of being unable to pay back loans.

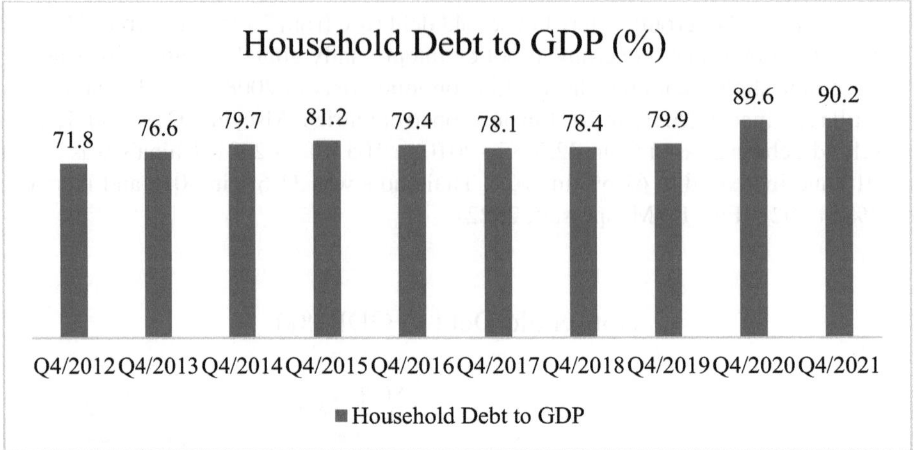

Fig. 2. Household Debt to GDP Q4 from 2012 to 2021Source: Bank of Thailand (2023c)

These issues are expected to become more severe in the future. Household debt could also result in pressure within families. It may act as a multiplier to the economic crisis, and the fiscal system can be affected (National Statistical Office, 2024).

Regarding the reporting information, it indicates household debt issues. The determinants of household debt are of international interest in identifying the causes, which can be helpful for policymakers in preventing a repeat of such cases in the Thai economy.

2 Literature Review

There are several previous studies regarding household debt issues and its importance. Kongkaew et al. (2018) stated that Thai households have relatively high household debt, with major debts coming from consumption purposes. On the other hand, developed countries have a low interest rate on household debt. Aligning with Sukhossamit (2005) and Intarawiset et al.'s (2022) findings, household expenditure significantly influences household debt creation at every level of debt, especially for high-expenditure households: the higher the expenditure, the higher the level of household debt. Also, Sukhossamit (2005) confirmed that due to low interest rates, households decided to take on a larger amount of debt.

In contradiction, Cecchetti et al. (2011) claimed that household debt may not always negatively affect the economy. If a country has a middle level of household debt, it can reflect economic welfare and economic growth; however, a high level of household debt could severely affect an economic crisis.

Sukhossamit (2005), Tulayasathien et al. (2015), and Budda (2016) found that households with higher income tended to have higher household debt accordingly. Aligning with Mainal et al. (2017), and Samad et al. (2020a, b), the findings claimed that income and household debt have a significant relationship with each other. However, Janthong (2013), and Mettiyawong (2018) found that income has no significant relationship to debt creation.

Maneejuk et al. (2021) found that growth in GDP per capita can decrease household debt. Also, Jumpanoi and Wanasilp (2022) found that GDP has an opposite relationship with household debt. Mainal et al. (2017) found that household expenditure is more influential than changes in inflation or the consumer price index.

Samad et al. (2020a, b), Jumpanoi and Wanasilp (2022) found that unemployment has a negative effect on household debt; however, Mainal et al. (2017) found that unemployment has a positive effect on household debt in developing countries. Dumitrescu et al. (2022), and Samad et al. (2020a, b), found that an increase in the unemployment rate can decrease household debt. Unemployment is a significant determinant of household debt.

Furthermore, the interest rate imposed by the central bank on financial institutions is a significant determinant. Sukhossamit (2005) found that the interest rate can affect household debt reduction. Klungjaturavet (2014), Mainal et al. (2017), and Samad et al. (2020a, b), found that the interest rate has a significant relationship with household debt. Jumpanoi and Wanasilp (2022), Samad et al. (2020a, b) found that the interest rate can positively affect household debt, Nomatye and Phiri (2017) pointed out that the interest rate is involved with household debt in terms of quantitative distribution. Additionally, the saving rate is also related to household debt. According to the theory of saving, the amount of money supplied to borrowers is determined by the amount of savings. Therefore, based on this assumption, saving is also a factor that can affect the level of household debt.

Conceptual Framework

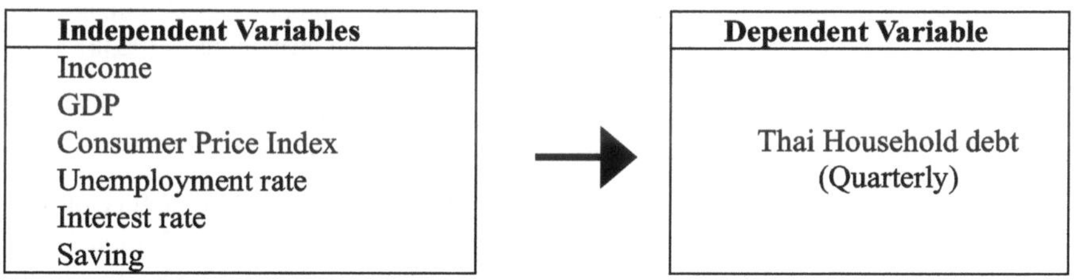

3 Methodology

This study uses quarterly secondary data from Q1 2012 to Q1 2023 to identify the relationships between household debt and other economic factors, including income, GDP, Consumer Price Index, unemployment, interest rate, and savings in commercial banks. Because the dynamic and instrumental-variable specifications require lagged variables, the number of observations in the dynamic and IV models is 41. The analysis focuses on the macroeconomic picture of the Thai economy.

The first step is data collection, by retrieving data from the Bank of Thailand and the Division of Trade Economic Information and Indices. The data were processed using Excel. The empirical analysis was conducted using dynamic OLS with HAC Newey-West standard errors, IV-2SLS, and IV-GMM estimations.

In studying the factors affecting household debt in Thailand, the empirical model was re-specified as a dynamic log-linear model to capture the persistence of household debt and to reduce serial correlation:

$$HHD_t = \beta_0 + \rho \ln(HHD_{t-1}) + \beta_1 \ln(INC_t) + \beta_2 \ln(GDP_t) + \beta_3 INT_t + \beta_4 \ln(SAV_t) + u_t \quad (1)$$

where HHD denotes household debt, INC denotes income, GDP denotes gross domestic product, INT denotes the policy interest rate, SAV denotes savings, and u_t denotes the error term. The lagged dependent variable, HHD_{t-1}, captures the persistence of household debt over time.

Although CPI and unemployment were considered in the initial specification, they were excluded from the final dynamic specification to reduce multicollinearity and improve estimation stability. The number of observations in the dynamic and IV models is 41 because lagged variables were used in the estimation (Table 1).

Table 1. Data collection

Variable	Definition	Unit	Relationship Between Variables	Reason	Source
HHD	Household debt	Percent of GDP	–	–	Bank of Thailand (2023c)
INC	Average monthly income	Baht	Positive (+)	Studies suggest that a higher income level tends to result in a higher household debt level.	Bank of Thailand (2023a)
GDP	Gross Domestic Product (GDP)	Million Baht	Negative (−)	When the GDP of the country increases, it indicates economic growth, which helps reduce the country's debt burden.	Office of the National Economic and Social Development Council (2023)

(continued)

Table 1. (*continued*)

Variable	Definition	Unit	Relationship Between Variables	Reason	Source
CPI	Consumer Price Index (CPI)	–	Positive (+)	If consumer prices rise, the cost of goods and services increases. In the current economic situation, this may lead to increased borrowing to maintain the same standard of living, thereby increasing household debt.	Bureau of Trade and Economic Indices (n.d.)
UNE	Unemployment rate	Percent	Positive (+)	When the unemployment rate rises, income decreases, which can lead to higher household debt.	National Statistical Office (2023)
INT	Policy interest rate	Percent	Negative (−)	When the policy interest rate increases, the cost of borrowing rises, reducing the demand for loans because borrowers have to pay higher interest expenses.	Bank of Thailand (2023d)
SAV	Average amount of savings in commercial banks	Million Baht	Positive (+)	When the average savings amount increases, it indicates higher income levels, which can result in an increase in household debt.	Bank of Thailand (2023b)

Source: Author's Collection

4 Data Analysis

The empirical strategy was revised to respond to econometric concerns raised during review.

First, the model was re-specified to reduce multicollinearity, and VIF diagnostics were used to confirm that all explanatory variables in the dynamic baseline model were below the conventional threshold of 10. Although CPI and unemployment were considered in the initial specification, they were excluded from the final dynamic specification to reduce multicollinearity and improve estimation stability.

Second, because serial correlation and heteroskedasticity may affect inference in time-series regressions, the baseline model was estimated using OLS with HAC Newey-West standard errors.

Third, to address potential endogeneity, IV-2SLS and IV-GMM estimations were conducted as robustness checks. Income and savings were treated as potentially endogenous variables, and their first and second lagged values were used as instruments. The number of observations in the dynamic and IV models is 41 because lagged variables were used in the estimation.

5 Result

Table 2. Descriptive Statistics

Variable	Mean	Std.Dev.	Min	Max
HHD	80.32609	5.774520	68.10000	90.8000
INC	13693.85	1185.738	10634.51	15416.29
GDP	3762598	441364.5	2992447	4533041
CPI	99.46213	3.669806	92.99000	108.0800
UNE	1.113333	0.419740	0.500000	2.300000
INT	1.557404	0.737013	0.500000	3.000000
SAV	11883526	2057216	7356548	15181798

Source: Author's Calculation

This research was examined potential issues in regression analysis, including the problem of omitted variables (endogeneity), multicollinearity, autocorrelation, and heteroscedasticity. If these issues are ignored, it may lead to incorrect interpretations, and the model will not be the Best Linear Unbiased Estimator (BLUE), thus reducing its reliability (Table 2).

To improve the reliability of the empirical results, this study estimated three related specifications. First, the dynamic OLS-HAC model was used as the baseline specification. Second, IV-2SLS was used as the main robustness check for potential endogeneity. Third, IV-GMM was used as an additional robustness check to examine whether the IV-2SLS findings were broadly confirmed under a GMM framework. The dynamic and IV models use 41 observations because lagged variables were constructed for the estimation.

The baseline dynamic OLS-HAC model is specified as follows:

$$HHD_t = \beta_0 + \rho \ln(HHD_{t-1}) + \beta_1 \ln(INC_t) + \beta_2 \ln(GDP_t) + \beta_3 INT_t + \beta_4 \ln(SAV_t) + u_t \quad (2)$$

For the IV-2SLS and IV-GMM estimations, $\ln(INC_t)$ and $\ln(SAV_t)$ were treated as potentially endogenous variables. Their first and second lagged values were used as instruments:

$$\ln(INC_{t-1}), \ln(INC_{t-2}), \ln(SAV_{t-1}), \ln(SAV_{t-2})$$

The IV specification is therefore expressed as:

$$HHD_t = \beta_0 + \rho\ln(HHD_{t-1}) + \beta_1 \ln(GDP_t) + \beta_2 INT_t + \beta_3 \ln(INC_t) + \beta_4 \ln(SAV_t) + u_t \quad (3)$$

Table 3 presents the multicollinearity diagnostics for the dynamic OLS-HAC model. The variance inflation factor (VIF) values range from 1.211 for INT_t to 9.878 for $\ln(SAV_t)$. Although $\ln(INC_t)$ and $\ln(SAV_t)$ show relatively high VIF values, all variables remain below the conventional threshold of 10. This suggests that serious multicollinearity was reduced after introducing the dynamic specification with the lagged dependent variable.

Table 4 reports the estimation results of the dynamic OLS model with HAC Newey–West standard errors. The coefficient of lagged household debt, HHD_{t-1}, is positive and statistically significant, indicating strong persistence in household debt over time. This result suggests that past household debt is a major determinant of current household debt. Among the contemporaneous explanatory variables, $\ln(SAV_t)$ has a positive and statistically significant effect, while $\ln(INC_t)$ is marginally significant at the 10% level. In contrast, $\ln(GDP_t)$ and INT_t are not statistically significant. The model shows a high explanatory power, with an R-squared value of 0.951 and an adjusted R-squared value of 0.944. However, the Durbin–Watson statistic of 1.437 suggests that some degree of serial correlation may remain, justifying the use of HAC standard errors.

Table 5 presents the IV-2SLS estimation results, in which income and savings are treated as potentially endogenous variables. The first and second lagged values of these variables are used as instruments. The coefficient of HHD_{t-1} remains positive and statistically significant, confirming the persistence of household debt. The coefficient of $\ln(SAV_t)$ is also positive and statistically significant, suggesting that savings are positively associated with household debt even after accounting for endogeneity. The coefficient of $\ln(INC_t)$ is positive but not statistically significant at the 5% level. Meanwhile, $\ln(GDP_t)$ and INT_t remain statistically insignificant.

Table 6 reports the instrument validity and endogeneity test results for the IV-2SLS model. The Sargan, Basmann, and Wooldridge overidentification tests do not reject the null hypothesis that the instruments are valid. This indicates that the lagged instruments are not strongly contradicted by the overidentification tests. In contrast, the Wu–Hausman and Durbin tests reject the null hypothesis of exogeneity, suggesting that endogeneity is present in the model. These findings support the use of instrumental variable estimation rather than relying solely on the OLS-HAC specification.

Table 7 shows the first-stage diagnostics for the endogenous variables $\ln(INC_t)$ and $\ln(SAV_t)$. The partial F-statistics are substantially larger than the conventional rule-of-thumb threshold of 10, indicating that the instruments are strongly correlated with the endogenous regressors. Therefore, weak-instrument concerns are unlikely to be serious in this model. The relatively high partial R-squared values also suggest that the lagged instruments have sufficient explanatory power in the first-stage regressions.

Table 8 presents the IV-GMM estimation results as an additional robustness check. The results are broadly consistent with the IV-2SLS estimates. The coefficient of HHD_{t-1} remains positive and highly statistically significant, again confirming the strong persistence of household debt. Both $\ln(INC_t)$ and $\ln(SAV_t)$ are positive and statistically significant in the IV-GMM model, suggesting that income and savings are important factors associated with household debt when endogeneity and heteroskedasticity are considered. In contrast, $\ln(GDP_t)$ and INT_t remain statistically insignificant. The Hansen J test p-value of 0.1449 indicates that the overidentifying restrictions are not rejected, supporting the validity of the instruments used in the IV-GMM estimation.

Overall, the estimation results show that household debt is highly persistent over time. The positive and significant effect of savings is robust across the dynamic OLS-HAC, IV-2SLS, and IV-GMM models. Income also becomes statistically significant in the IV-GMM specification, suggesting that its effect may be more clearly identified after addressing endogeneity. By contrast, GDP and interest rates do not show statistically significant effects in any of the model specifications. Taken together, the results indicate that the dynamic structure of household debt and the potential endogeneity of income and savings are important considerations in explaining household debt behavior.

Table 3. Multicollinearity Diagnostics for the Dynamic OLS-HAC Model

Variable	VIF
HHD_{t-1}	4.788
$\ln(INC_t)$	9.866
$\ln(GDP_t)$	6.132
INT_t	1.211
$\ln(SAV_t)$	9.878

Note. All VIF values are below the conventional threshold of 10, suggesting that serious multicollinearity was reduced in the dynamic specification.

Table 4. Dynamic OLS-HAC Estimation Results

Variable	Coefficient	HAC Std. Error	z-statistic	p-value
Constant	−1.9746	1.260	−1.567	0.117
HHD_{t-1}	0.8967	0.096	9.368	0.000
$\ln(INC_t)$	0.1222	0.064	1.903	0.057
$\ln(GDP_t)$	−0.0123	0.048	−0.259	0.795
INT_t	−0.0026	0.006	−0.460	0.646
$\ln(SAV_t)$	0.1124	0.033	3.384	0.001
Observations	41			

(continued)

Table 4. *(continued)*

Variable	Coefficient	HAC Std. Error	z-statistic	p-value
R-squared	0.951			
Adjusted R-squared	0.944			
Durbin-Watson statistic	1.437			

Note. The model was estimated using OLS with HAC Newey-West standard errors. The inclusion of the lagged dependent variable captures the persistence of household debt, while HAC standard errors provide robust inference in the presence of remaining serial correlation and possible heteroskedasticity.

Table 5. IV-2SLS Estimation Results

Variable	Coefficient	Robust Std. Error	z-statistic	p-value
Constant	−3.3485	1.6112	−2.0783	0.0377
HHD_{t-1}	0.8772	0.1020	8.5959	0.0000
$\ln(GDP_t)$	−0.0492	0.0696	−0.7068	0.4797
INT_t	−0.0047	0.0053	−0.8999	0.3682
$\ln(INC_t)$	0.2783	0.1706	1.6310	0.1029
$\ln(SAV_t)$	0.1643	0.0772	2.1277	0.0334
Observations	41			
R-squared	0.9468			
Adjusted R-squared	0.9392			

Note. Income and savings were treated as potentially endogenous variables. Their first and second lagged values were used as instruments. Robust standard errors are reported.

Table 6. Instrument Validity and Endogeneity Tests for IV-2SLS

Test	Statistic	p-value	Interpretation
Sargan test	2.7420	0.2539	Overidentifying restrictions not rejected
Basmann test	2.3652	0.3065	Overidentifying restrictions not rejected
Wooldridge overidentification test	3.8637	0.1449	Instrument validity not rejected
Wu-Hausman test	8.1898	0.0013	Endogeneity detected
Durbin test	13.6000	0.0011	Endogeneity detected

Note. The overidentification tests do not reject the validity of the lagged instruments, while the Wu-Hausman and Durbin tests suggest the presence of endogeneity.

Table 7. First-Stage Diagnostics for IV-2SLS

Endogenous Variable	Partial R-squared	Shea's R-squared	Partial F-statistic	p-value
$\ln(INC_t)$	0.7920	0.3552	328.20	0.0000
$\ln(SAV_t)$	0.9709	0.4355	5541.5	0.0000

Note. The large partial F-statistics indicate that weak-instrument problems are unlikely.

Table 8. IV-GMM Estimation Results

Variable	Coefficient	Robust Std. Error	z-statistic	p-value
Constant	−3.8066	1.1771	−3.2340	0.0012
HHD_{t-1}	0.9449	0.0582	16.223	0.0000
$\ln(GDP_t)$	−0.0016	0.0317	−0.0498	0.9603
INT_t	−0.0047	0.0046	−1.0374	0.2995
$\ln(INC_t)$	0.2338	0.0910	2.5704	0.0102
$\ln(SAV_t)$	0.1503	0.0387	3.8807	0.0001
Observations	41			
R-squared	0.9477			
Adjusted R-squared	0.9403			
Hansen J test p-value	0.1449			

Note. The IV-GMM model was estimated as an additional robustness check using the same endogenous variables and lagged instruments. The Hansen J test did not reject the overidentifying restrictions.

6 Discussion

The dynamic OLS-HAC model indicates that household debt in Thailand is highly persistent. The coefficient of lagged household debt is positive and statistically significant, suggesting that current household debt is strongly influenced by its previous level. Savings are also positively and significantly associated with household debt. Income shows a positive relationship at the 10% significance level, whereas GDP and the policy interest rate are not statistically significant.

The IV-2SLS results provide further evidence after accounting for potential endogeneity. The overidentification tests do not reject the validity of the lagged instruments, and the first-stage diagnostics indicate that the instruments are sufficiently strong. The Wu-Hausman and Durbin tests reject the exogeneity of the suspected endogenous regressors, supporting the use of the IV approach. In the IV-2SLS model, lagged household debt remains strongly significant, and savings continue to show a positive and statistically significant relationship with household debt.

The IV-GMM results broadly confirm the IV-2SLS findings. Lagged household debt remains positive and highly significant, while both income and savings are positively and significantly associated with household debt. Overall, the findings suggest that household debt in Thailand is persistent over time and that savings are consistently related to household debt across alternative estimation methods.

7 Conclusion

This study examined the factors associated with household debt in Thailand using a dynamic time-series framework. To improve estimation reliability, the model was re-specified to reduce multicollinearity, and HAC Newey-West standard errors were used to address serial correlation and heteroskedasticity. In addition, IV-2SLS and IV-GMM estimations were conducted to account for potential endogeneity and to explore a more causally oriented interpretation of the relationships. The results consistently show that household debt is highly persistent. Savings are positively associated with household debt across the dynamic OLS-HAC, IV-2SLS, and IV-GMM specifications. Income also shows a positive association, particularly in the IV-GMM specification. In contrast, GDP and the policy interest rate do not show robust statistical significance after accounting for model dynamics and potential endogeneity. These findings suggest that policy design should consider debt persistence and savings-related credit expansion. They should be interpreted as robust empirical associations and as an attempt to approach causal inference, rather than as definitive proof of causality, given the single-country quarterly time-series structure and the limited number of observations.

Recommendation for Further Study

Future studies on household debt should aim to collect additional data on relevant factors to improve the accuracy of estimates and ensure that the selected variables align more closely with economic theory. In this study, some variables were adjusted based on related research and theories. For example, the household income variable was substituted because the available income data were insufficient to produce a normal distribution. To address this, the variable was replaced with average salary or wages to achieve a normal distribution.

Such substitution may have resulted in certain variables not fully representing those examined in other research or theoretical frameworks. As a result, variables that were found to be statistically significant in previous studies and supported by theory appeared insignificant in this study. Future research should also consider additional factors such as government expenditure and population size to provide deeper insights. This would enable the government and relevant agencies to apply the findings to improve household living standards in the future.

References

Bank of Thailand: Average wages classified by education (2023a). Retrieved from https://app.bot.or.th/BTWS_STAT/statistics/BOTWEBSTAT.aspx?reportID=666&language=TH

Bank of Thailand: Deposits and withdrawals during the period of commercial banks (2023b). Retrieved from https://app.bot.or.th/BTWS_STAT/statistics/BOTWEBSTAT.aspx?reportID=31&language=TH
Bank of Thailand: Household loans classified by purpose (2023c). Retrieved from https://app.bot.or.th/BTWS_STAT/statistics/BOTWEBSTAT.aspx?reportID=891&language=TH
Bank of Thailand: Money market interest rates (2023d). Retrieved from https://app.bot.or.th/BTWS_STAT/statistics/BOTWEBSTAT.aspx?reportID=223&language=TH
Bank of Thailand: Statistical data (2023e). Retrieved from https://app.bot.or.th/BTWS_STAT/statistics/BOTWEBSTAT.aspx?reportID=775&language=th
Budda, L.: Household debt and the Thai business cycle. Master's thesis, Thammasat University (2016). Retrieved from http://ethesisarchive.library.tu.ac.th/thesis/2016/TU_2016_5704010478_5306_3878.pdf
Bureau of Trade and Economic Indices: Consumer price index (n.d.). Retrieved from http://www.price.moc.go.th/price/cpi/index_new_all.asp
Cecchetti, S.G., Mohanty, M.S., Zampolli, F.: The real effects of debt. BIS Working Papers 352, Bank for International Settlements (2011)
Sierminska, E.: Indebtedness of households and the cost of debt by household type and income group (2014). Retrieved from https://ec.europa.eu/social/BlobServlet?docId=13628&langId=en
Dumitrescu, B.A., Enciu, A., Handoreanu, C.A., Obreja, C., Blaga, F.: Macroeconomic determinants of household debt in OECD countries. Sustainability. **14**(7) (2022). https://doi.org/10.3390/su14073977
Fongprapai, N.: Effects of economic factors on household debt in Thailand. Master's thesis, Ramkhamhaeng University (2014). Retrieved from https://digital.lib.ru.ac.th/m/b11901469/NatrapeeFongprapai.pdf
Intarawiset, N., Nilbai, T., Thongphat, T., Antarasena, A.: The effect of household socio-economic factors on household debt in Thailand. J. Manag. Sci. **9**(1), 116–138 (2022). Retrieved from https://so03.tci-thaijo.org/index.php/msj/article/view/254459/173997
Jamit, V., Punturaumporn, B.: Factors affecting the increase in household debt burden from the situation of Covid-19 of people in Bangkok. Doctoral dissertation, Ramkhamhaeng University (2021). Retrieved from https://mmm.ru.ac.th/MMM/IS/twin-9/6214154059.pdf
Janthong, M.: Debt situation of personnel in the internal security operations command (central). Master's thesis, Dhurakij Pundit University (2013). https://doi.org/10.14458/DPU.the.2013.63
Jumpanoi, P., Wanasilp, W.: The determinants of Thai household debt: a macro-level study. J. Demogr. **38**(2), 70–83 (2022). Retrieved from https://digital.car.chula.ac.th/cgi/viewcontent.cgi?article=1337&context=jdm
Kiatnakin Phatra Bank Public Company Limited: KKP research warns that rising interest rates could trigger a household debt crisis (2022). Retrieved from https://kkpfg.com/th/news/2022062743358
Klungjaturavet, C.: Effects of Thai household debt and Thailand economic crisis. Master's thesis, Chulalongkorn University (2014). Retrieved from https://www.car.chula.ac.th/display7.php?bib=2051244
Kongkaew, M., Dulayavatit, N., Thongyai, K.: The circumstance of household debt and the creation of financial discipline for creating household sufficient economy (2018). Retrieved from https://www.repository.rmutsv.ac.th/handle/123456789/2565
KResearch: In 2016, household debt fell for the first time in 11 years to 79.9% of GDP… expected to continue slowing in 2017 (Economic Outlook, Issue No. 3672) (2016). Retrieved from https://www.kasikornresearch.com/th/analysis/k-econ/economy/Pages/36263.aspx
Mainal, S.A., Ho, C.S.F., Yusof, J.M.: Household behavior towards debt in a challenging financial environment in Malaysia. Asian J. Behav. Stud. **2**(7), 21–29 (2017). https://doi.org/10.21834/ajbes.v2i7.39

Maneejuk, P., Teerachai, S., Ratchakit, A., Yamaka, W.: Analysis of difference in household debt across regions of Thailand. Sustainability. **13**(21) (2021). https://doi.org/10.3390/su132112253

Manprasert, S.: Household debt problem: a warning sign of an economic crisis (2022). Retrieved from https://www.scbeic.com/th/detail/product/household-debt-crisis-061222

Mettiyawong, P.: Structure and factors determining provincial household debts in Thailand. Master's thesis, Ramkhamhaeng University (2018). Retrieved from https://digital.lib.ru.ac.th/m/b12079856/PiyachananMettiyawong.pdf

National Statistical Office: Quarterly unemployment rate, 2012–2023 (2023). Retrieved from http://statbbi.nso.go.th/staticreport/Page/sector/TH/report/sector_02_12_TH_.xlsx

National Statistical Office: Key findings: the 2023 household economic and social survey (2024). Retrieved from https://www.nso.go.th/nsoweb/storage/survey_detail/2024/20240508082744_74896.pdf

Nomatye, A., Phiri, A.: Investigating the macroeconomic determinants of household debt in South Africa (2017). Retrieved from https://mpra.ub.uni-muenchen.de/83303/1/MPRA_paper_83303.pdf

Office of the National Economic and Social Development Council: Quarterly chain volume measures of gross domestic product (2023). Retrieved from https://www.nesdc.go.th/main.php?filename=qgdp_page

Samad, K.A., Dali, N.R.S.B.M., Daud, S.N.: Determinants of household debt in emerging economies: a macro panel analysis. Cogent Bus. Manag. **7**(1) (2020a). https://doi.org/10.1080/23311975.2020.1831765

Samad, K.A., Dali, N.R.S.B.M., Daud, S.N.: Leading factors of household debt (2020b). Retrieved from https://oarep.usim.edu.my/entities/publication/464af892-802b-4b19-874f-b0e7d703ca15/full

Stock2morrow Company Limited: Thailand's household debt problem (2023). Retrieved from https://stock2morrow.com/webboard/1/b8bff459-01c4-4a93-b7c8-ec63ee5777b1

Sukhossamit, P.: The determination of an increase in Thai household debt. Master's thesis, Chulalongkorn University (2005). https://cuir.car.chula.ac.th/handle/123456789/71439

Tulayasathien, S., et al.: The development of a microsimulation model to study the role of household debt on income distribution inequality in Thailand. Fiscal Policy Office (2015). Retrieved January 20, 2022, from https://www.fpo.go.th/eresearch/getattachment/28a10fa1-3d4e-42ca-adb4-5612378fd4ea/7726.aspx

Innovation in R&D Processes Through Materials Informatics-Integrated Platforms: Structuring Organizational Knowledge and Implementing Innovation Management Based on ISO 56002

Masayuki Hirosue[1,2](✉), Hideki Hayashida[1], and Masakazu Takahashi[2,3]

[1] Tokyo University of Agriculture and Technology, 2-24-16 Nakamachi, Koganei, Tokyo 184-8588, Japan
masayuki-hirosue@go.tuat.ac.jp
[2] Yamaguchi University, 2-16-1 Tokiwa-dai, Ube, Yamaguchi 755-8611, Japan
[3] FHNW University of Applied Sciences and Arts Northwestern Switzerland, Riggenbachstrasse 16, 4600 Olten, Switzerland

Abstract. In contemporary materials development, the exponential growth of experimental data and over-reliance on individual expertise present significant challenges to organizational efficiency and knowledge management. This study examines the value proposition of integrated data management platforms, specifically those that unify Electronic Laboratory Notebook (ELN), Laboratory Information Management System (LIMS), and Machine Learning (ML) capabilities. We analyze the mechanisms through which such platforms facilitate the transition of tacit knowledge into structural organizational assets and accelerate the R&D cycle. Quantitative analysis suggests that Bayesian-optimization-driven active learning can reduce the number of experimental iterations by 30–70%. Furthermore, this study suggests a strong alignment between these platforms and the ISO 56002 international standards for innovation management systems. We conclude that such platforms can function as an organizational "operating system" for R&D departments when complemented by appropriate governance and change management mechanisms.

Keywords: Materials informatics · Data-driven R&D · Organizational Knowledge Management · Innovation Management Systems · ISO 56002

1 Introduction

Industrial research in chemistry and materials is under increasing pressure to deliver highly customized and multifunctional materials amid intensified global competition and shorter development timelines. While traditional empiricism—based on iterative trial-and-error and individual craft knowledge—has supported major technological advances, its limitations have become more evident as research problems increase in dimensionality and complexity [1, 2]. Under such conditions, exhaustive experimental exploration is no

D. Liberona et al. (Eds.): MISNC 2026, CCIS 3092, pp. 62–74, 2027.
https://doi.org/10.1007/978-3-032-33381-0_6

longer economically or temporally feasible, necessitating more systematic and scalable approaches. These challenges—including heterogeneous data integration, loss of tacit expertise, and underutilization of failure data—are widely recognized [3–6] and have motivated the adoption of standardized innovation management frameworks such as ISO 56002 [7].

In response, data-driven and AI-assisted R&D methodologies have gained prominence, enabling more efficient navigation of high-dimensional design spaces and better reuse of accumulated data. However, their effectiveness in industrial environments remains uneven due to fragmented data infrastructures, loss of tacit knowledge through personnel mobility, and concerns regarding the transparency and trustworthiness of AI-driven decision support. As a result, improvements in analytical capability do not necessarily translate into sustained organizational learning or strategically aligned innovation.

The ISO 56000 series reframes innovation as a managed organizational capability. ISO 56002 emphasizes governance, evidence-based decision making, knowledge management, and continuous improvement as core principles. Despite their relevance, a gap persists between these governance-oriented requirements and operational R&D practices, where Materials Informatics (MI) platforms are often deployed primarily as technical workflow tools.

To address this gap, we conceptualize integrated MI platforms as organizational infrastructure that operationalizes ISO 56002–aligned innovation management. Focusing on closed-loop R&D workflows that integrate data capture, machine learning–based decision support, and human–AI collaboration, we examine how such platforms support knowledge assetization, evidence-based decision making, and sustained innovation capability. Adopting an analytical generalization approach, the Uncountable platform is used as an explanatory case to elucidate underlying technical and managerial mechanisms. This perspective positions integrated MI platforms as an organizational "operating system" bridging data-driven experimentation and innovation governance in chemical and materials R&D.

Unlike prior studies that focus primarily on predictive accuracy or workflow efficiency, this study adopts an organizational perspective by integrating (1) knowledge theory, (2) ISO-based innovation governance, and (3) MI platforms as socio-technical systems. This enables a reinterpretation of MI platforms as infrastructures for implementing standardized innovation management.

This paper makes three contributions. First, it provides a conceptual framework positioning MI platforms as an organizational operating system linking data infrastructure and innovation governance. Second, it identifies mechanisms through which the integration of ELN, LIMS, and machine learning enables knowledge assetization and closed-loop R&D acceleration. Third, it proposes managerial implications, including incentive redesign and structured upskilling pathways, to support ISO-aligned organizational transformation.

This study is a conceptual and explanatory investigation based on a single illustrative case and adopts a mechanism-based approach rather than statistical generalization. The aim is to clarify causal pathways through which MI platforms enable organizational outcomes such as knowledge assetization and R&D acceleration. Accordingly, we address the following research question:

How can integrated MI platforms function as organizational infrastructure that operationalizes ISO 56002–aligned innovation management in R&D settings?

This paper is organized as follows: Sect. 1 introduces the research context and objectives; Sect. 2 reviews background and related work; Sect. 3 explains the methodology; Sect. 4 presents and discusses the findings; and Sect. 5 concludes with theoretical, practical, and policy implications, as well as directions for future research.

2 Related Work

The transition from traditional empirical methodologies to computationally supported materials research represents a profound shift in the epistemological foundations of R&D, as highlighted by Ramprasad et al. [8], The emerging data-driven paradigm leverages high-dimensional experimental datasets that capture complex structure–property relationships, overcoming the interpretability and scalability limitations of intuition-based approaches. Within this framework, machine learning algorithms play a central role by enabling predictive modeling, pattern extraction, and optimization across expansive design spaces. Furthermore, automated experimental and analytical workflows have been shown to reduce human bias, enhance reproducibility, and accelerate iterative refinement processes. Collectively, these elements constitute a systematic, computationally augmented approach to materials development that replaces ad hoc experimentation with statistically grounded, algorithmically informed discovery strategies. Organizational knowledge in scientific research environments spans a continuum from tacit, experience-based insights to explicit, codified representations, as conceptualized by Nonaka and Takeuchi [9]. Effective innovation management, therefore, requires robust, systematic mechanisms for managing this full spectrum of knowledge forms. Central components include the reliable capture of experimental processes and outcomes, the application of standardized metadata structures and taxonomies to ensure semantic consistency, and the deployment of knowledge repositories that allow researchers to retrieve and repurpose historical information for future projects. Equally essential is the institutionalization of knowledge evolution, whereby organizations continuously learn from both successful and unsuccessful experiments. Such mechanisms not only prevent loss of critical expertise but also enable cumulative organizational learning that strengthens strategic decision-making and accelerates scientific progress.

ISO 56002:2019 provides an international reference model for establishing and maintaining a systematic innovation management system. The standard emphasizes several pillars relevant to contemporary R&D operations [10]. First, Clause 8.3.2 outlines the requirement for strategic intelligence functions capable of identifying technological opportunities and emerging trends under conditions of uncertainty. Second, Clause 7.6 highlights knowledge management and organizational learning as essential components for maintaining a resilient and adaptable innovation ecosystem. Finally, Clause 9.1 mandates ongoing performance evaluation and continuous improvement, thereby ensuring that innovation processes remain aligned with organizational objectives, regulatory expectations, and evolving market demands. Together, these elements provide a structured framework that reinforces the importance of data-driven decision-making, institutional knowledge retention, and iterative performance optimization in R&D organizations.

Although data-centric R&D has advanced rapidly, a misalignment persists between the organizational expectations outlined in ISO 56002 and the technical functions of modern Materials Informatics (MI) platforms. ISO 56002 conceptualizes innovation as a managed, evidence-based organizational process emphasizing governance, accountability, and risk-based thinking [11, 12], whereas MI platforms primarily focus on operational capabilities such as data integration, workflow automation, and ML-driven optimization.

This divergence creates a sociotechnical gap across several dimensions. First, ISO operates at a governance layer (roles, accountability, strategic alignment), while MI systems operate at a process–technology layer, often lacking mechanisms to translate platform outputs into ISO-compliant managerial oversight. Second, ISO requires transparent and traceable decision-making, yet many high-performing ML models remain opaque, limiting explainable accountability. Finally, ISO's PDCA-based management logic contrasts with the adaptive iteration cycles of MI-driven active learning, complicating alignment among risk management, performance evaluation, and continuous improvement. These gaps indicate that MI platforms alone cannot satisfy ISO 56002 requirements without complementary governance structures. Accordingly, we propose three integration principles—governance-by-design, explainability-as-evidence, and standards-aligned metrics—as a foundation for ISO-aware MI deployment. Prior research across materials informatics, organizational knowledge science, and innovation management provides a strong theoretical foundation for this study, highlighting the importance of integrated data infrastructures, machine learning–enabled decision support, and systematic knowledge assetization in chemical and materials R&D.

3 Research Methods

3.1 Research Framework

In this study, the MI platform is defined as the independent variable, and its impact on R&D efficiency and organizational knowledge assetization is analyzed as the dependent variable. Specifically, we examine how the platform's data structuring and ML-driven decision support align with the innovation management elements defined in ISO 56002—namely, knowledge management, continuous improvement, and strategic intelligence—to enhance the organization's overall innovation capacity. Rather than pursuing statistical generalization, this study adopts an analytical generalization approach by examining observable proxy indicators—including experimental iteration reduction, shifts in researchers' time allocation, and mechanisms of data reuse and knowledge retention—to evaluate the organizational impact of integrated MI platforms. Accordingly, this study adopts a single-case explanatory case study design, focusing on the implementation of the Uncountable platform as an in-depth empirical example. The aim is not to generalize statistically across all Materials Informatics platforms but to generate conceptual insights into how an MI system can influence knowledge assetization and ISO 56002–aligned innovation management practices. The analytical generalization is grounded in the reproducibility of the underlying mechanisms—namely, structured data capture, closed-loop experimental iteration, and machine-learning-driven optimization—which are not vendor-specific but structurally transferable across R&D environments. In line with Yin (2018), this study adopts an analytical generalization approach rather than statistical generalization [13]. The selected case is theoretically revelatory in that it represents an advanced and integrated implementation of ELN, LIMS, and machine learning within a single operational environment, thereby enabling the identification of underlying mechanisms applicable across similar R&D contexts.

3.2 Rationale for Case Selection: Uncountable

The selection of Uncountable should not be interpreted as representative of all Materials Informatics platforms. Rather, it is used as an illustrative and analytically informative case that helps explicate the mechanisms through which integrated ELN–LIMS–ML architectures may support knowledge structuring and innovation management practices. Thus, the case functions as an explanatory vehicle for examining the mechanisms rather than evaluating the company itself. The Uncountable is a San Francisco–based R&D informatics company founded in 2016 by engineers from MIT and Stanford [14]. It provides a unified, cloud-native platform that integrates Electronic Lab Notebooks (ELN), Laboratory Information Management Systems (LIMS), workflow management, and AI-driven analytics into a single operational environment for modern research organizations. The company was established to address a core structural issue in industrial R&D: critical experimental data are typically scattered across spreadsheets, physical notebooks, legacy desktop tools, and isolated departmental systems, making it difficult to reuse information, collaborate across teams, and leverage machine-learning–based optimization. Uncountable's platform consolidates these fragmented data streams into a structured, searchable knowledge base that supports experiment documentation, sample tracking, visualization, predictive modeling, and next-experiment recommendations. According to PitchBook, the firm has raised a $27M Series A round to expand its technology and industry footprint. Industry reports emphasize that Uncountable enables scientists to reduce development time, cut testing iterations, and accelerate new-product discovery by managing all R&D inputs and outputs in one place. Today, Uncountable supports global manufacturers, chemical companies, energy firms, and advanced materials developers seeking to modernize their digital R&D operations. The selection of Uncountable Inc. as the focal case study is motivated by its uniquely integrated approach to materials informatics and its practical impact on industrial R&D workflows.

4 Results and Analysis

4.1 Case Study of Uncountable as an Integrated Materials Informatics Platform

With the described Fig. 1, Uncountable implements a fully integrated MI environment in which ELN, LIMS, and machine-learning (ML) operate on a single, harmonized data model. In practice, scientists document experiments in a structured ELN (procedures, observations, parameters), while LIMS extends these entries into automated sample registration, chain-of-custody, and multimodal measurements; both layers share standardized metadata, versioning, approvals, and audit trails, ensuring end-to-end traceability and regulatory readiness without duplicate data handling [15]

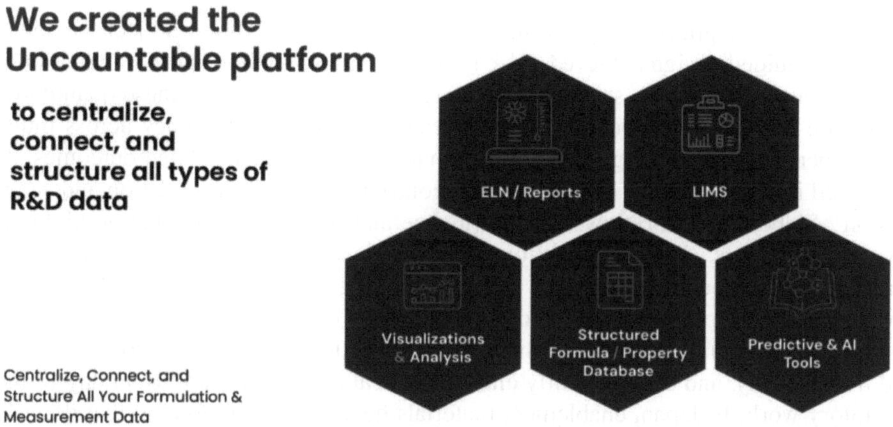

Fig. 1. Schematic image of Uncountable solution with AI for innovation [14, 15]

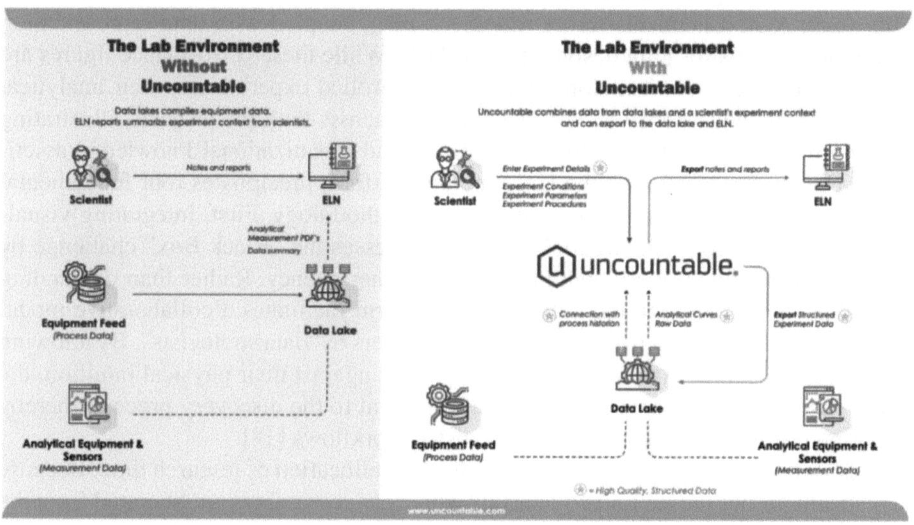

Fig. 2. Illustration of AI-accelerated laboratory workflows [14, 16, 17].

Because all inputs (formulations, process conditions) and outputs (test results) are natively linked, the platform removes the historical separation between recording → analysis → redesign, enabling a closed-loop. Recent measurements flow directly into the ML layer—used for structure–property prediction, Bayesian optimization, and uncertainty-aware next-experiment suggestion—so models are updated automatically as data arrive, and recommended formulations can be executed and recorded in the same environment. Across documented industrial projects, Uncountable has been associated with substantial efficiency gains. In the SCG Chemicals case, the company reports a 45% reduction in DOE experimental points, 10–20% acceleration of R&D, ~50% less time spent on data mapping, and up to 3 × ROI after standardizing data structures and adopting

Uncountable's integrated analytics. In an earlier polyurethane foam project, Uncountable's ML-guided design achieved a 4× reduction in testing time and 3× reduction in total experiments against a scientist's baseline approach [16]. While these quantitative results are derived from documented industrial cases, their consistency across multiple independent projects suggests recurring patterns rather than isolated outcomes. As illustrated in Fig. 2, the use of Uncountable contributes to the consolidation and acceleration of laboratory workflows. Case evidence and product documentation highlight several key factors: (i) the elimination of spreadsheet silos through a centralized and searchable data repository, (ii) faster decision-making enabled by integrated visualization and predictive planning tools, and (iii) audit-ready data lineage supported by version control and structured workflows. These elements collectively enhance both efficiency and transparency, and are frequently cited as critical drivers of usability in day-to-day laboratory work. In Japan, enablement materials have also been reported that describe how Uncountable is used to make the MI loop routine rather than project-based, contributing to continuity of knowledge assets and sustainable acceleration in materials R&D. Multi-site organizations highlight improved global collaboration and shared visibility (e.g., AGC Chemicals' cross-time-zone use), coupled with data representation and predictive tools for joint design sessions [17]. While these performance figures are derived from case documentation rather than controlled experiments, their analytical value lies in the consistency of observed patterns across multiple projects, illustrating recurring mechanisms of workflow acceleration and organizational knowledge assetization. The implementation of the Uncountable platform precipitates four fundamental shifts in organizational culture and operational methodology. First, integrating visualization and predictive planning tools directly addresses the "Black Box" challenge by fostering trust through interpretability and researcher agency. Rather than demanding blind adherence to algorithmic outputs, the platform facilitates a collaborative model where scientists transition from manual experimenters to "data strategists". By allowing researchers to validate AI-driven recommendations against their physical intuition, the system ensures that human expertise remains central to the discovery process, thereby mitigating professional resistance to AI-assisted workflows [18].

This shift in role is supported by a significant reallocation of research time. Because the platform unifies the capture-to-analysis workflow, researchers are liberated from the labor-intensive tasks of transcribing and reconciling disparate spreadsheets, enabling a strategic focus on hypothesis generation and complex design interpretation. Furthermore, the establishment of standardized data structures and shared dashboards enhances interdisciplinary collaboration. This transparency not only reduces redundant efforts across multi-site teams but also harmonizes joint design sessions, even across disparate time zones.

Finally, the platform fundamentally transforms organizational learning by systematically codifying the full spectrum of research activity. By preserving negative results, underlying rationales, and contextual metadata—information that is frequently lost in traditional paradigms—the platform converts fleeting tacit knowledge into durable organizational assets. This robust data lineage and version control ensure long-term reproducibility and compliance-ready operations, effectively institutionalizing the "Record → Analyze → Experiment → Re-Record" cycle as a standard operational pattern.

From an analytical perspective, the findings presented in this section can be understood at three complementary levels:

(1) observed mechanisms, including structured data capture, closed-loop experimentation, and ML-assisted optimization;
(2) interpretation, emphasizing their role in enabling knowledge assetization and workflow efficiency; and
(3) implications for ISO 56002, particularly in relation to knowledge management, evidence-based decision-making, and continuous improvement.

These observed patterns are interpreted as mechanism-based causal pathways consistent with the analytical framework proposed in this study.

4.2 Comparative Positioning in the MI Landscape

Table 1. Comparison of Uncountable and Adjacent Platforms

Platform	Core Strengths	Difference from Uncountable
Uncountable	Integrated ELN + LIMS + workflows + ML, optimized for formulations and materials; strong versioning and lifecycle traceability	Baseline: designed for daily iterative R&D, structured data models, closed-loop experimentation
Citrine Informatics [19]	Leading AI/MI platform: predictive & generative modeling; enterprise-wide MI with ISO 27001 certification	Focuses on AI-driven virtual experiments rather than detailed lab workflows
Benchling [20]	Biology-focused ELN/LIMS; strong in gene editing, molecular design, and biotech R&D	Optimized for biological workflows, not formulation-driven materials R&D
LabWare [21]	Global leader in QA/QC, GxP, 21 CFR Part 11, ISO 17025; strong eQMS integration	Compliance-first system; limited MI/experimental design functionality
Thermo Fisher Sample Manager [22]	Comprehensive LIMS + SDMS + LES + ELN for regulated industries; strong SOP and audit control	Focused on manufacturing QA/QC, not high-iteration formulation R&D

As shown in Table 1, Uncountable distinguishes itself from other platforms by modeling the daily iterative routines of laboratory experimentation as a structured data process. Whereas Citrine Informatics emphasizes virtual AI-driven prediction and LabWare prioritizes rigorous quality-control governance, Uncountable functions as an "R&D Operating System" that elevates hands-on experimental trial-and-error directly into organizational knowledge.

This ground-level integration of routine laboratory data is precisely what enables Uncountable to bridge the gap between the bottom-up knowledge accumulation and top-down governance required by ISO 56002 [19–22]. Across architecture, operations, and outcomes, Uncountable occupies a distinct and strategically significant position within the Materials Informatics (MI) ecosystem. This positioning stems from its architectural design, which unifies Electronic Laboratory Notebooks (ELN), Laboratory Information Management Systems (LIMS), and Machine Learning (ML) capabilities on a single, structured data layer, rather than treating them as loosely coupled tools. This architectural integration enables a "closed-loop" experimental cycle, alleviating the burden of iteration for researchers and fundamentally enhancing discovery velocity and experimental reproducibility.

A comparative analysis reveals Uncountable's unique value proposition. While standalone AI engines such as Intellegens focus on specific modeling tasks, or enterprise analytic platforms like Citrine Informatics emphasize high-level data strategy, Uncountable embeds MI directly into the mundane laboratory workflow. This ensures that data-driven methodologies become an operational standard rather than an exceptional intervention.

Furthermore, in contrast to QA/QC-centric LIMS platforms like LabWare or SampleManager, which are primarily optimized for compliance and audit-ready reporting, Uncountable prioritizes "innovation velocity" and the systematic exploration of high-dimensional design spaces. Similarly, while Benchling is highly optimized for biological sequences and biotech R&D, Uncountable is specifically tailored to the formulation-centric and process-linked requirements of materials science, where multivariate numerical data and complex structure–property relationships are the primary determinants of success.

The comparative analysis in Sect. 4.2 highlights that Uncountable differs from other MI platforms by structuring day-to-day laboratory work as a coherent data process rather than a set of disconnected tools. This architectural characteristic is precisely what enables the translation of routine R&D activities into the governance-oriented processes required by ISO 56002. Accordingly, the following section examines how these operational features map onto specific ISO clauses and contribute to standard-aligned innovation management.

4.3 Synergy with ISO 56000 Innovation Management Systems

In this paper, Materials Informatics (MI) platforms are conceptualized as a foundational "implementation substrate" for ISO 56002 [23]. While MI platforms provide the technical layer required for systematic innovation through data structuring and workflow automation, they do not by themselves fulfill the governance, accountability, and organizational-level requirements mandated by the standard. Accordingly, MI platforms should be understood as enabling infrastructure that requires complementary managerial mechanisms—such as standardized operating procedures (SOPs), approval workflows, and role-based decision structures—to achieve full ISO 56002 conformity and to operationalize innovation management within day-to-day R&D activities [24].

Beyond technical utility, the Uncountable platform illustrates how an MI system can function as an organizational "Operating System" for managed innovation. By replacing ad-hoc experimentation with structured and repeatable workflows, the platform institutionalizes innovation as a governable organizational process, consistent with ISO 56002 Clause 4.4 (systemic approach to innovation). Centralization of experimental data, decision rationales, and metadata further enables knowledge stewardship by converting tacit researcher expertise—including failure data—into cumulative organizational knowledge assets, directly supporting the requirements of Clause 7.6. In addition, ML-driven predictive modeling and uncertainty-aware recommendations provide evidence-based guidance for decision making, transforming traditionally opaque R&D processes into transparent, data-backed workflows aligned with Clause 8.3 (evidence-based decision making and management of uncertainty). Through automation of data-intensive administrative tasks, the platform also facilitates a cultural shift toward strategic innovation, enabling researchers to focus on hypothesis generation while preserving human agency in AI-assisted R&D. Collectively, these characteristics demonstrate how MI platforms, when complemented by appropriate governance structures, can bridge technical execution and ISO-aligned innovation management in globally competitive environments.

4.4 Change Management and Organizational Transition

The transition from traditional empiricism to ISO 56002–aligned, data-driven R&D is not solely a technological upgrade but a sociotechnical transformation that necessarily requires deliberate change management strategies. Organizational resistance to Materials Informatics adoption often arises not from doubts about algorithmic accuracy, but from concerns regarding role redefinition, loss of experiential autonomy, and changes to performance evaluation criteria. To institutionalize the sharing of negative results, organizations must redesign incentive and evaluation structures so that researchers are assessed based on knowledge contribution metrics—such as coverage of design space, reuse rate of historical data, and documentation quality—rather than short-term experimental success alone. Accordingly, the shift from "manual experimenters" to "data strategists" requires structured upskilling pathways, including tiered training in experimental data modeling, uncertainty interpretation, and validation of AI-generated recommendations against physical intuition.

These change management mechanisms directly support ISO 56002 requirements, particularly Clause 7.6 on organizational learning and Clause 8.3 on evidence-based decision-making, by ensuring that MI platforms are embedded within sustainable managerial and behavioral practices, rather than remaining stand-alone technical solutions. These findings should be interpreted as indicative rather than statistically generalizable, but they provide converging evidence of systematic efficiency gains associated with integrated MI platforms (Table 2).

Table 2. Focused Mapping of ISO 56002 Clauses (4.4, 7.6, 8.3) and this paper

ISO 56002 Clause	Relevant Descriptions from the Paper

(*continued*)

Table 2. (*continued*)

ISO 56002 Clause	Relevant Descriptions from the Paper
4.4—System Approach to Innovation	**Section 4.3** The MI platform replaces ad-hoc experimental cycles with structured, repeatable workflows. Centralization of data, traceability, and closed-loop learning enables an organizational "innovation system" aligned with ISO principles Strong alignment. The paper shows how ELN–LIMS–ML integration operationalizes systematic innovation. Some organizational governance elements remain conceptual.
7.6—Knowledge Management	**Sections 2.2, 4.1, 4.3** The platform codifies tacit knowledge by capturing rationale, negative results, metadata, and context; it transforms individual craft knowledge into durable, searchable organizational assets. This directly addresses ISO's knowledge-management requirement Very strong alignment. Knowledge stewardship is one of the core contributions demonstrated by the Uncountable case.
8.3—Managing Uncertainty/Evidence-Based Decision-Making	**Section 4.3** "Explainability as Evidence": ML-driven uncertainty quantification, physical plausibility checks, and interpretable recommendations provide statistically grounded guidance for decision-making under uncertainty. Strong conceptual alignment.

5 Conclusion

This study demonstrates that MI platforms are not merely data-analysis tools but also function as organizational operating systems for modern materials R&D. Integrated platforms such as Uncountable serve as foundational infrastructures that convert individual "craft knowledge" (tacit knowledge) into organizational "digital assets" (explicit knowledge) by structuring the capture of experimental data. In doing so, they can operationalize the key elements of the ISO 56002 vision of managed, repeatable, and evidence-driven innovation within the routine workflows of the research laboratory. However, for this "R&D OS" to operate effectively, the technical and managerial governance layers must be tightly integrated. Accordingly, the study proposes the following Policy Proposals for advancing MI-enabled innovation systems:

a. Governance-by-Design

MI workflows should embed ISO-compliant approval processes, audit trails, and traceability mechanisms directly into platform operations. This establishes an ISO-aware MI environment in which day-to-day experimental activity automatically becomes managerial evidence.

b. Explainability as Evidence

AI-driven predictions must move beyond mere numerical output. As seen in the operational model of Uncountable, incorporating physical plausibility checks and uncertainty quantification is essential to ensure transparency. This aligns with ISO requirements for evidence-based decision-making and is key to overcoming psychological resistance among researchers.

c. Standards-Aligned Metrics

Evaluation of R&D investments must shift from narrow indicators such as "number of experiments" toward integrated metrics aligned with ISO 56002—namely, knowledge-reuse rates, acceleration of organizational learning, and broader innovation capability.

Based on these proposals and the Uncountable case study, it is evident that AI accelerates closed-loop R&D workflows. A key limitation of this study is its reliance on a single explanatory case. While the objective is theory-building rather than statistical validation, future research should incorporate multi-case comparative designs and independently collected datasets to validate causal relationships and improve external validity.

Thus, this study provides a conceptual and practical foundation for integrating Materials Informatics platforms with standardized innovation management systems in modern R&D environments.

References

1. Allen, B.: Experience, experiments, and the history of empiricism. Rev. Port. Filos. **80**(3), 805–812 (2024)
2. Allen, B.: Experimental empiricisms. In: Empiricisms: Experience and Experiment from Antiquity to the Anthropocene, pp. 103–198. Oxford University Press, Oxford (2020)
3. Votsis, I.: Grounded empiricism. Eur. J. Philos. Sci. **15**, 22 (2025)
4. Putrama, I.M., Martinek, P.: Heterogeneous data integration: challenges and opportunities. Data Brief. **56**, 110853 (2024)
5. Hill, J., Mulholland, G., Persson, K., Seshadri, R., Wolverton, C., Meredig, B.: Materials science with large scale data and informatics: unlocking new opportunities. MRS Bull. **41**, 399–409 (2016)
6. Anstey, P.R., Vanzo, A.: Experimental Philosophy and the Origins of Empiricism. Cambridge University Press, Cambridge (2023)
7. Cobb, D.J.: Empiricism in the philosophy of science. PhD thesis, University of Bristol, Bristol (2022)
8. Ramprasad, R., Batra, R., Pilania, G., Mannodi Kanakkithodi, A., Kim, C.: Machine learning in materials informatics: recent applications and prospects. npj Comput. Mater. **3**, 54 (2017)
9. Nonaka, I., Takeuchi, H.: The Knowledge-Creating Company. Oxford University Press, Oxford (1995)
10. Thom, N., Etzweiler, L.: Innovation management standards: the ISO 56002 and its implications for R&D organizations. Int. J. Innov. Manag. **24**, 2050051 (2020)

11. Afuah, A.: Innovation management and knowledge-based governance systems. Res. Policy. **45**, 1–12 (2016)
12. Fernandez, R., Swart, W.: The new ISO 56000 family of standards for innovation management. Standards. **5**, 34 (2025)
13. Yin, R.K.: Case Study Research and Applications: Design and Methods, 6th edn. Sage Publications, Thousand Oaks (2018)
14. PitchBook Data Inc.: Uncountable company profile & funding history. PitchBook Industry Report (2024)
15. Hirshman, J.I., Hollingsworth, N., Tashman, W.: Systems and methods for machine learning assisted experiment recommendation and structured R&D data management. U.S. Patent 11,216,737 (2022)
16. Uncountable Inc.: SCG chemicals accelerates research & development by 20% with Uncountable. https://www.uncountable.com/resources/scg-chemicals-accelerates-research-development-20-percent-using-uncountable. Accessed 13 Feb 2026
17. Uncountable Inc.: AGC chemicals streamlines global collaboration & experimentation with Uncountable. https://www.uncountable.com/resources/agc-chemicals-americas-streamline-global-collaboration-experimentation-case-study. Accessed 13 Feb 2026
18. Hirshman, J.I., Hollingsworth, N., Tashman, W.: Systems and methods for machine learning assisted experiment optimization and structured laboratory data workflows. U.S. Patent Application US 2022/0114462 (2022)
19. Citrine Informatics: Citrine platform: the AI-driven product development software for materials and chemicals. https://citrine.io/platform/. Accessed 13 Feb 2026
20. Benchling: The modern R&D cloud for life sciences. https://www.benchling.com/. Accessed 13 Feb 2026
21. LabWare: LabWare LIMS & ELN: laboratory informatics solutions for QA/QC and compliance. https://www.labware.com/industries/pharmaceutical. Accessed 13 Feb 2026
22. Thermo Fisher Scientific: Thermo Scientific SampleManager LIMS, SDMS, LES and ELN software. https://www.nagase.co.jp/enterprise/dxsolution/products/samplemanager/. Accessed 13 Feb 2026
23. ISO: ISO 56002: Innovation management—innovation management system—guidance. International Organization for Standardization, Geneva (2019)
24. Tidd, J.: A review and critical assessment of the ISO 56002 innovation management systems standard: evidence and limitations. Int. J. Innov. Manag. **25**(1), 2150049 (2021)

The Dichotomy of Centralization and Decentralization in the Design Philosophy of CBDCs: Shaping the Next-Generation Monetary Regime

Hitoshi Okada(✉)

Information and Society Research Division, National Institute of Informatics, Tokyo, Japan
okada@nii.ac.jp

Abstract. Driven by advancements in information and communication technology, the global financial landscape is witnessing a paradigm shift through the proposed issuance of Central Bank Digital Currencies (CBDCs). This paper examines two primary architectural approaches to CBDC design: a centralized network overseen by a central bank, and a decentralized model leveraging autonomous Blockchain or Distributed Ledger Technologies (DLT). While the former functions as an electronic extension of conventional monetary structures, the latter fundamentally reconfigures the state's sovereign monetary power into a decentralized entity. This study provides a multifaceted analysis of how blockchain technology triggers systemic transformations, evaluating national policies through the dual lenses of centralization versus decentralization and public versus private sectors. By exploring the strategic intentions of various nations at this historical juncture, this paper deciphers the evolving tension between concentrated and distributed monetary regimes.

Keywords: Central Bank Digital Currency (CBDC) · Distributed Ledger Technologies (DLT) · Blockchain · International Monetary Regime · Monetary Sovereignty

1 Introduction

The global monetary landscape is undergoing a fundamental transformation driven by the rapid evolution of information and communication technologies. Central to this shift is the proposed issuance of Central Bank Digital Currencies (CBDCs), a digitized form of legal tender that remains legally equivalent to its physical counterparts. However, as networked "electronic cash," CBDCs possess the inherent potential to circulate extraterritorially, bypassing traditional jurisdictional boundaries and potentially establishing a new equilibrium within the international monetary regime.

The architectural design of CBDCs generally diverges into two distinct paradigms: a centralized network governed by the central bank as the ultimate authority, or a decentralized model utilizing autonomous Distributed Ledger Technology (DLT). While the

D. Liberona et al. (Eds.): MISNC 2026, CCIS 3092, pp. 75–92, 2027.
https://doi.org/10.1007/978-3-032-33381-0_7

former represents a digital evolution of conventional structures, the latter fundamentally reconfigures the nature of monetary sovereignty by introducing decentralized elements. That an inherently centralized institution—the central bank—would deliberately explore a decentralized framework suggests a strategic pivot toward the internationalization of currency.

While existing literature has predominantly favored centralized designs for their stability and continuity, global trends indicate a diversifying landscape. Notably, the Bank of England, in collaboration with academia, has unveiled prototypes for distributed digital currencies. Simultaneously, the private sector is leveraging the scalability of blockchain to develop global stablecoins. These private initiatives, backed by immense market power within the digital ecosystem, pose a significant challenge to the state's monopoly on money.

Through a comparative lens of centralized versus distributed architectures, this research investigates the shifting paradigms of monetary control. It provides an exploratory roadmap of national policy intentions, capturing the critical transition of monetary systems in an increasingly decentralized era.

2 Literature Review

2.1 The Money Flower: A Taxonomy of Money

To elucidate the characteristics of money, the "money flower" taxonomy introduced by the BIS is often employed. Building upon this foundation, BIS Quarterly Review, September 2017 adapted the concept to address the evolving landscape of cryptocurrencies [1]. Bech, M. L., & Garratt, R. (2017) explains their intention as following: Lately, central banks have entered the fray, with several announcing that they are exploring or experimenting with DLT, and the prospect of central bank crypto- or digital currencies is attracting considerable attention. But making sense of all this is difficult. There is confusion over what these new currencies are, and discussions often occur without a common understanding of what is actually being proposed (Bech, M. L., & Garratt, R., 2017, p.55) [1]. Underpinned by these considerations, Bech, M. L., & Garratt, R. (2017) establish a new taxonomy of money as following: issuer (central bank or other); form (electronic or physical); accessibility (universal or limited); and transfer mechanism (centralized or decentralized, i.e. peer-to-peer).

This taxonomy reflects what appears to be emerging in practice and distinguishes between two potential types of CBCC, both of which are electronic: central bank-issued and peer-to-peer. One is accessible to the general public (retail CBCC) and the other is available only to financial institutions (wholesale CBCC). The four-ellipse version, which they call the money flower, shows how the two potential types of CBCC fit into the overall monetary landscape. Building on the "money flower" framework, Bech, M. L., & Garratt, R. (2017) categorize the money in the following way. There are four different kinds of electronic central bank money (Fig. 1): two kinds of CBCCs (the shaded area) and two kinds of central bank deposits. The most familiar forms of central bank deposits are those held by commercial banks – often referred to as settlement accounts or reserves.

The followings are cited as the example of categories in Fig. 1.

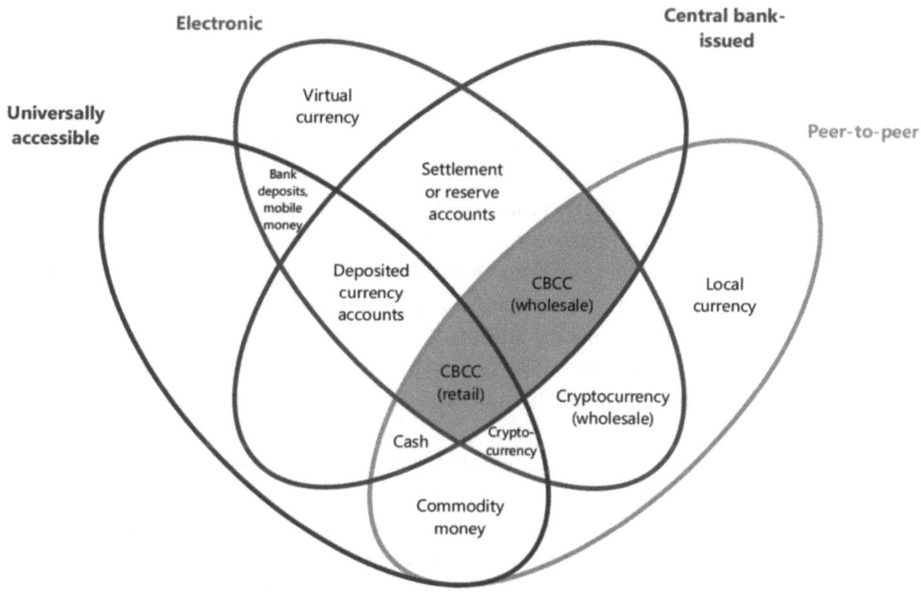

Fig. 1. The money flower: a taxonomy of money.
From: Bech, M. L., & Garratt, R., 2017, p.60 [1].

Crypto-currency (Fig. 1): Bitcoin is an example of a non-central bank digital currency. It was invented by an unknown programmer who used the pseudonym Satoshi Nakamoto and was released as open-source software in 2009 along with a white paper describing the technical aspects of its design [1].

Mobile money (Fig. 1):

1) M-pesa (Trade Mark) (a popular mobile money platform in Kenya and other East African countries), employ a similar "on-us" model.
2) Venmo is a digital wallet with social media features popular with US college students.
3) E-gold account holders used commercial bank money to purchase a share of the holding company's stock of gold and used mobile phone text messages to transfer quantities of gold to other customers. E-gold ultimately failed.

Virtual currency (Fig. 1): PokéCoin is a currency used for in-game purchases in the Pokémon Go game and an example of a virtual currency.

Cryptocurrency (wholesale) (Fig. 1): Utility Settlement Coin (USC) is an attempt by the private sector to provide a wholesale cryptocurrency. It is a concept proposed by a collection of large private banks and a fintech firm for a series of digital tokens representing money from multiple countries that can be exchanged on a distributed ledger platform

Local currencies (Fig. 1): Examples of privately issued local currencies include the Bristol Pound and BerkShares, located in the right-hand petal.

Deposited currency accounts (Fig. 1): Dinero electrónico was a mobile payment service in Ecuador where the central bank provides the underlying accounts to the public.

2.2 Centrally Banked Cryptocurrencies

2.2.1 RSCoin

Current cryptocurrency frameworks, exemplified by Bitcoin, utilize decentralized ledgers maintained through proof-of-work mechanisms. While this architecture ensures autonomy from national political oversight, it simultaneously faces critical bottlenecks regarding computational efficiency and system scalability. Against this backdrop, Danezis, G., Meiklejohn, S. (2016) proposes RSCoin, a cryptocurrency framework in which central banks maintain complete control over the monetary supply, but rely on a distributed set of authorities, or mintettes, to prevent double-spending [2]. The paper state: Centralization of the monetary authority also allows RSCoin to address some of the scalability issues of fully decentralized cryptocurrencies. In particular, the central bank delegates the authority of validating transactions to a number of other institutions that we call mintettes.

Since mintettes are—unlike traditional cryptocurrency miners—known and may ultimately be held accountable for any misbehavior, RSCoin supports a simple and fast mechanism for double-spending detection (Table 1) [2]. It explains how existing approaches (credit cards, cryptographic e-cash, and Bitcoin) and how RSCoin compare in terms of the properties they provide. Double-spending refers to the way the system detects double-spending (i.e., as it happens or after the fact). According to their definition, C stands for centralized, D for decentralized, and D* for distributed.

Table 1. How existing approaches and RSCoin compare in terms of the properties

	CC	e-cash	Bitcoin	RSCoin
Double-spending	online	offline	online	online
Money generation	C	C	D	C
Ledger generation	C	n.a.	D	D*
Transparent	no	no	yes	yes
Pseudonymous	no	yes	yes	yes

Note: How existing approaches (credit cards, cryptographic e-cash, and Bitcoin) and how RSCoin compare in terms of the properties they provide. Double-spending refers to the way the system detects double-spending (i.e., as it happens or after the fact). C stands for centralized, D for decentralized, and D* for distributed. From: Danezis, G., Meiklejohn, S., 2016, p.2 [2].

2.2.2 e-Cash

The RS Coin proposal in the UK serves as a notable reference for a thought experiment exploring the use of blockchain for issuing CBDC. The blockchain underlying Bitcoin is based on a peer-to-peer (P2P) network consisting of a collective of equal machines, with no distinct center. A single machine from the P2P network is selected through a computational competition known as mining, granting it the right to append a new block. When a block is generated, a transaction is added with the sender field left blank, addressed to the creator's address. Danezis, G., Meiklejohn, S. (2016) also compares RS Coin with e-Cash, an early cryptographic electronic money oriented toward anonymity. Although e-Cash aimed for the "digitalization of payment instruments," it lacked the decentralized or distributed nature of ledgers found in blockchain. Furthermore, the paper compares it with the "digitalization of payment methods," such as credit cards, confirming their nature as entirely centralized systems. From this perspective, the attempt of RS Coin—which, in the issuance of an inherently centralized CBDC, abandoned the decentralization of blockchain while at least attempting to express its distributed nature—remains a unique thought experiment.

2.3 Vocabulary

As a premise for the discussion, the definition of terms is crucial. ISO/TC 307 Blockchain and distributed ledger technologies has published ISO 22739:2024. The standard defines the definition of the word blockchain, distributed ledger, and cryptocurrency as following.

ISO 22739:2024 document is disclosed at Online Browsing Platform (OBP) [3].

[3.6] blockchain: distributed ledger (3.23) with confirmed blocks organized in an append-only, sequential chain using hash links.

[3.23] distributed ledger: ledger that is shared across a set of distributed ledger technology (DLT) nodes and synchronized between the DLT nodes using a consensus mechanism.

Note 1 to entry: A distributed ledger is designed to be immutable, tamper-resistant, tamper-evident and append-only, containing final and definitive ledger records of confirmed and validated transactions.

[3.15] cryptocurrency: cryptoasset designed to work as a medium of payment or value exchange.

Note 1 to entry: Cryptocurrency involves the use of decentralized control and cryptography to secure transactions, control the creation of additional assets, and verify the transfer of assets in a distributed ledger technology (DLT) system.

3 Classification

3.1 Functional Approach

Providing a different perspective from previous studies, we attempted a classification based on a functional approach. In discussing the classification of money in a broad sense as an academic concept, the starting point is to identify whether it constitutes a "payment instrument" or a "payment method." Here, a "payment instrument" typically refers to banknotes or coins, meaning that the monetary "value" itself is integrated with physical media such as pieces of paper or metal. In contrast, a "payment method" typically refers to processes such as bank transfers or account remittances, meaning a way to instruct the transfer of "value" held as deposits.

A similar framework applies to digitalization. Specifically, the "digitalization of payment instruments" refers to cases where digital data recorded on a user's electronic device possesses "value" in and of itself. On the other hand, the "digitalization of payment methods" refers to cases where a user instructs a third party to transfer "value" for settlement, and such instructions are carried out via electronic means through electronic or communication devices.

3.2 Viewpoints

Based on the aforementioned perspectives of the "digitalization of payment instruments" and the "digitalization of payment methods," this section attempts a theoretical classification as an academic concept. In this trial, the central axis of classification is whether digital data possesses the nature of a "payment instrument" where "value" itself is transferred, or the nature of a "payment method" (Fig. 2) [4].

3.2.1 Versatility

Those possessing the nature of a payment instrument are further categorized by the presence or absence of versatility. Here, versatility refers to the property of being exchangeable with anyone and for anything (high interpersonal and objective exchangeability). For example, coins circulating only within a game lack versatility as they hold no significance outside that environment.

Basically, game coins or enterprise issued points are not exchangeable for cash. These essentially lack versatility and do not possess convertibility into cash. Even if in-game coins or mileage points are exchangeable for cash, their versatility remains limited.

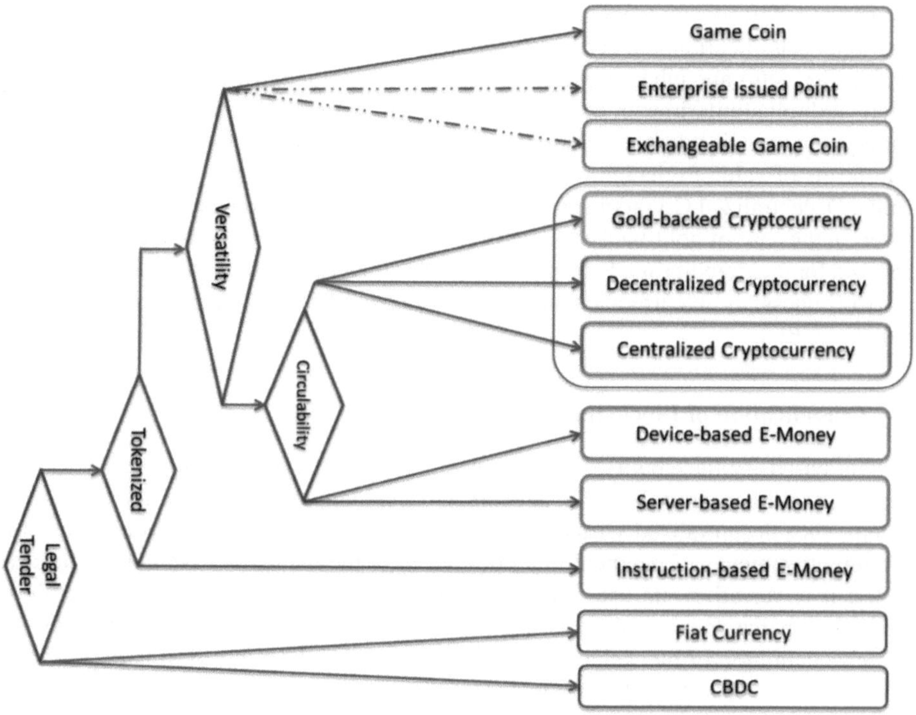

Fig. 2. Functional Classification of Payment Instrument and Payment Method
Note: Red lines indicate that conditions are met, blue lines indicate they are not, and blue dotted lines represent cases where the fulfillment of conditions is ambiguous.
Source: 4: Okada, H., Takahashi, I., Yamasaki, S. (2015) [4]

3.2.2 Circulability

Payment instruments that possess versatility are further categorized by the presence or absence of circulability. Here, circulability refers to the property whereby a recipient of a payment instrument can transfer it again to another party. This can also be called successive transferability and is an indispensable element for expressing characteristics similar to cash.

Decentralized cryptocurrencies, such as Bitcoin, are unique in that they attempt to manifest circulability solely through technology, despite lacking state backing. If these acquire a certain degree of versatility, they would, by classification, possess characteristics almost identical to cash. The proverb stating that "money comes and goes" essentially describes the nature of successive transferability, or circulability.

3.2.3 Legal Tender Status

Private-sector electronic money and similar instruments do not function as a payment instrument without the consent of the recipient. In stark contrast, fiat currency is the sole entity endowed with legal tender status (compulsory acceptance). According to the functional classification, fiat currency and CBDC are essentially identical. Both possess legal tender status and inherently exhibit versatility. Significantly, CBDC and cryptocurrencies exhibit similarities in certain functions. The primary distinction lies in the fact that cryptocurrencies do not possess legal tender status; however, they are established as a means of value exchange provided there is voluntary consent from the recipient. Unlike Decentralized Cryptocurrencies, Centralized Cryptocurrencies are backed by an issuer. In the case of gold-backed Cryptocurrencies, the reserve of rare metals serves as the basis for their credibility. Provided that the issuing private entity maintains sufficient trustworthiness, these currencies may achieve a level of public acceptance comparable to that of CBDC.

3.3 Classification of Blockchain

Systems based on blockchain technology have characteristics of accurate and irreversible data transfer in a decentralized P2P network. Conceptually, Bitcoin—the first blockchain system—is a decentralized virtual currency that has the following characteristics: it is an alternative means of payment that does not have the mandatory circulation of legal tender; it is versatile—its use is not limited by location—; and it has an open-loop configuration that does not place a limitation on the recipients of the payment. Although a precise definition of blockchain technology has not yet been given, it is important to consider how to classify different blockchain systems in order to better understand their potential and limitations. With this consideration, Okada, H., Yamasaki, S., Bracamonte, V. (2017) proposes a classification based on two dimensions external to the system: (1) existence of an authority and (2) incentive to participate in the blockchain [5]. The combination of these elements results in four types of blockchains. The paper defines these dimensions and describes the characteristics of the blockchain systems belonging to each classification (Fig. 3) [5].

	Under an authority	Without an authority
Market-based	e.g. Sidechain	e.g. Bitcoin
Non-market-based	e.g. Consortium blockchains	

Fig. 3. Dimensions of classification.Okada, H., Yamasaki, S., Bracamonte, V. (2017), p.595 [5].

3.3.1 Blockchains Without an Authority and Market-Based

The characteristics of not having an authority and being market-based may not be mutually necessary conditions, but they form an ideal relationship. This is particularly relevant for blockchains that implement a consensus protocol similar to that of Bitcoin. The Bitcoin system implements a mechanism based on computational complexity to ensure the accuracy of the records even if a trusted third party does not exist. In this consensus mechanism, nodes compete to find the answer to a computational puzzle; the larger the computational power they hold, the more their probability of becoming the winner increases. The winner receives the coinbase reward. The fact that a large number of general nodes from all over the world participate in mining and finding the correct answer to the computational problem means that they leave proof that a large number of computation devices—including high-performance computers—have put in a large calculation effort. However, this proof of work (POW) based consensus requires large amounts of energy and is therefore costly. If there is a market with a demand for the virtual currency and this currency has a price, then there is an incentive to produce it and to support the continuance of the system.

3.3.2 Blockchains Under an Authority and Market-Based

This type of blockchains can take advantage of the market price to incentivize the participation of numerous nodes and increase its security; at the same time, the authority can introduce a degree of control over the system. A market for circulating the currency or the coinbase reward can also be established for blockchains under an authority, as it is established for blockchains without an authority such as Bitcoin. The main incentive is that the currency has a value and fungibility for nodes to want to join, but the characteristics of the system under an authority play an important role too.

The trusted authority and additional blockchain characteristics unique to the system have to offer an additional benefit that will differentiate sufficiently from a blockchain without authority. Sidechains pegged to Bitcoin—or other blockchains that have an established market—are also one example of this type of blockchain system. Although an authority exists, a free market can still be established around the blockchain system; authorized nodes from the sidechain exist along the general Bitcoin nodes. The participation of more general nodes would increase the decentralization and the resistance to tampering.

3.3.3 Blockchains Under an Authority and Non-Market-Based

In a non-market based blockchain there needs to be a compelling alternative incentive to join and remain in the system. Without a market surrounding it—without a price mechanism—it would be preferable for consensus to be based on some other grounds besides POW or similarly costly algorithms. Rather, it is more sensible to take an approach based on other methods of agreement between the parties that are more energy efficient compared to POW consensus. In this case, the authority can facilitate the implementation of these alternative methods by exerting control over participation in the system.

Consortium blockchains are one example of this type of blockchain systems. A consortium refers to an alliance of companies formed for a certain purpose; only limited members are able to participate as nodes. General nodes cannot participate in the system. When a consortium sets up a blockchain, it limits the participants only to those nodes that have been recognized by the authority; in this case it is not necessary or practical to rely on the competitive mining of the participating companies.

3.3.4 Blockchains Without an Authority and Non-Market Based

Without a market to provide the incentive of price of the currency, and without an authority to enforce and administrate participation in the system through contracts, the long-term continuance of a blockchain becomes complicated. Therefore, this last type of blockchain is perhaps difficult to contemplate. It is likely that a more efficient consensus protocol would be able to reduce the energy consumption of nodes, in turn reducing the barrier for entry to the system. However, without the monetary incentive and without the possibility of enforcing regulations, incentivizing participation would remain a challenge, although ideological, social or ethical considerations can play a part as incentives.

4 Blockchain-Enabled Economy

4.1 Multi-Layered Architecture

It has long been taken for granted that fiat currencies issued by central banks are managed through a centralized system. Consequently, Central Bank Digital Currencies (CBDCs), the digital form of fiat money, were also expected to be issued in a centralized manner. However, some countries and regions have begun designing CBDCs based on blockchain technology, the underlying infrastructure of cryptocurrencies. These developments are predicated on the multi-layered architecture of blockchain. In the Bitcoin system, a quintessential example of blockchain, a two-layered structure has been employed from the outset. The first layer is decentralized and records transactions related to the issuance, transfer, and burning of decentralized cryptocurrencies as an irreversible history. The second layer is distributed and allows for the circulation of various assets arbitrarily defined by the issuer. In this context, if the first-layer cryptocurrency is used as the consideration for the second-layer asset, the cryptocurrency and the asset are transferred in opposite directions. Conversely, if the second-layer asset is embedded onto the first-layer cryptocurrency and used as a vehicle for transfer, both the cryptocurrency and the asset move in the same direction. Regardless of the method chosen, a blockchain with such a two-layered architecture enables any asset defined on the second layer to be endowed with transferability. In the Fig. 4, the light green first layer represents the Bitcoin system, while the dark green second layer represents the Bitcoin second-layer protocols. The assets circulating on the second layer are ensured irreversibility through the consensus algorithm of the first layer [6]. Assets circulating on the second layer rely on the first-layer Bitcoin as their source of trust, effectively remaining anchored to it. In this manner, the blockchain of decentralized cryptocurrencies like Bitcoin functions as a new type of trust anchor that has emerged within society.

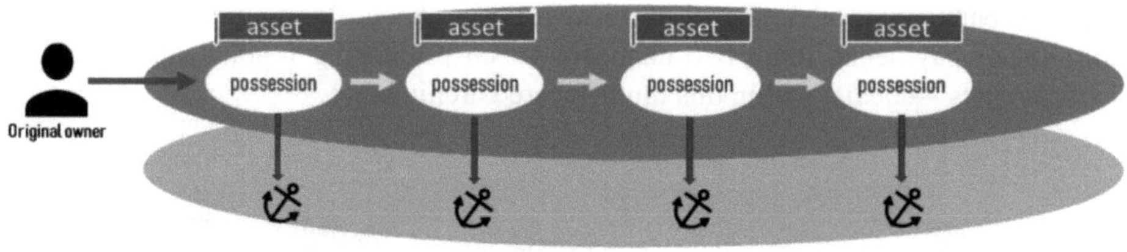

Fig. 4. Multi-layered architecture.Source: Okada, H. (2025) [6].

4.2 Lightning Network

Transactions on the first layer of a blockchain are referred to as on-chain, while economic activities on the second layer are termed off-chain. While the on-chain first layer ensures irreversibility through CODE, the off-chain second layer is governed by the principles of game theory, specifically through subgame perfection. Since all economic activities presuppose rational judgment, contract compliance can be guaranteed by designing a system where the losses incurred from penalties outweigh the gains obtained by deviating from business protocols. Consequently, this enables the realization of a platform that executes contracts autonomously, without the need for a trusted third party. Thus, smart contracts are executed with minimal human intervention. Even in cases where the judicial system of a counterparty's country cannot be relied upon, smart contracts operating on the second layer of a blockchain enable parties to enter into contractual relationships. If a commitment is not fulfilled, the automatic transfer of the deposit is executed as a penalty, according to pre-defined conditions. To date, the development of second-layer solutions has been actively pursued on public chains such as Bitcoin and Ethereum.

The rationale behind some countries designing CBDCs based on blockchain technology appears to be an intention to seize control of the underlying infrastructure of the smart economy. In the most typical scenario, a CBDC can be circulated as a type of asset by leveraging the architecture of the Lightning Network. In this case, while Bitcoin itself circulates on the first layer, a fiat digital currency circulates on the second layer. In the Fig. 5, the light green first layer represents the Bitcoin system, while the dark green second layer represents the Bitcoin second-layer protocols.

The assets, in this case CBDC, circulating on the second layer are ensured irreversibility through the consensus algorithm of the first layer [6]. Such usage is most likely to occur in countries where confidence in the national currency has been lost. In these nations, while a key currency such as the U.S. dollar may circulate as legal tender, the government cannot always secure a sufficient supply of physical dollar bills.

Consequently, there is a tendency to attempt to regain monetary discretion by issuing U.S. dollar-denominated tokens. In some dollarized countries, Bitcoin has already been recognized as legal tender. In such cases, both Bitcoin—the decentralized cryptocurrency circulating on the first layer—and the U.S. dollar-denominated tokens issued by the state on the second layer possess the legal status of legal tender. This means that a fiat digital currency with legal tender status is constructed upon a decentralized cryptocurrency system that possesses no such status. According to the functional classification of payments, these two elements—each possessing fundamentally distinct characteristics—coexist within this multi-layered architecture.

Fig. 5. Multi-layered architecture for CBDC.Source: Okada, H. (2025) [6].

5 Bank Issued Cryptocurrency

5.1 UTXO Model

Since blockchain transactions are not limited to recording the amount of cryptocurrency, they can record any information such as assets. Kaneko, Y., Osada, S., Azuchi, S., Okada, H., Yamasaki, S. (2019) propose cryptocurrency management program which solves the above problem. With the program, concerning the value of certain objects (e.g. interest) increasing or decreasing over time, certain transactions thereof executed by the authentic owner of the value (e.g. Issuance; Transfer of funds; Disposition) could be recorded on blockchain, while maintaining the currency value conservation law through reasonably structured ledgers to commercially apply blockchain to financial operations [7].

Their paper describes the elements constituting the management system that enables the representation of interests on a blockchain. Cryptocurrencies based on UTXO (Unspent Transaction Output) model keep the deposit's total amount to meet withdraws' one for preventing double spend, in other words, they audit "the conservation of currency value" in every transaction. In the Fig. 6, the data structure of a transaction consists of two fields; Input (showing the past Holding state of Assets before the transfer) and Output (showing the current Holding state of Assets). The sum total of the Asset amounts described in Input is always identical with the sum total of the Asset amounts and the number of charges described in Output [7].

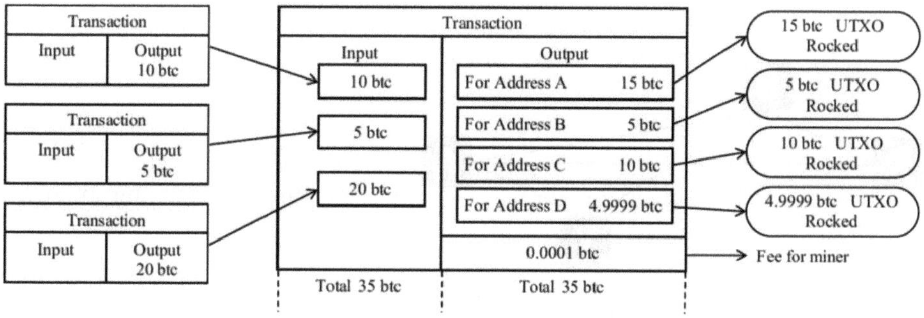

Fig. 6. The currency value conservation law.
Source: 6. Kaneko, Y., Osada, S., Azuchi, S., Okada, H., Yamasaki, S. (2019) [7].

5.2 Multi-layer Architecture

The proposed method takes a way that extends the transaction handled by the existing blockchain, in order to introduce it smoothly. Specifically, we newly developed a cryptocurrency management program P that is compatible with the programs that make up the existing blockchain network system, and construct an overlay system S as shown in Fig. 7 [7]. This can be realized by using, for instance, the function of Colored Coin adopted in the Bitcoin blockchain [8, 9]. Nonetheless, generally speaking, since currency issuance is the property of being performed under certain trust, note that any node which has some trust is called a Bank User, among the nodes that constitute S, and any other node is called a General User, and that only a Bank can issue currency. A Bank-issued cryptocurrency can be transferred by P of any participant in S, just like the cryptocurrency expressed on any of the existing blockchains. However, no node that does not constitute S can handle the Bank-issued cryptocurrency, because it does not own P. While this proposal focuses on digital currencies issued by commercial banks utilizing blockchain, the same framework can be applied to CBDCs issued by central banks. In the model for commercial banks, trusted nodes are granted the authority to issue interest. Similarly, in the case of central banks, a configuration is envisioned where trusted nodes are given the authority to issue and redeem currency, while other nodes are assigned the role of validation.

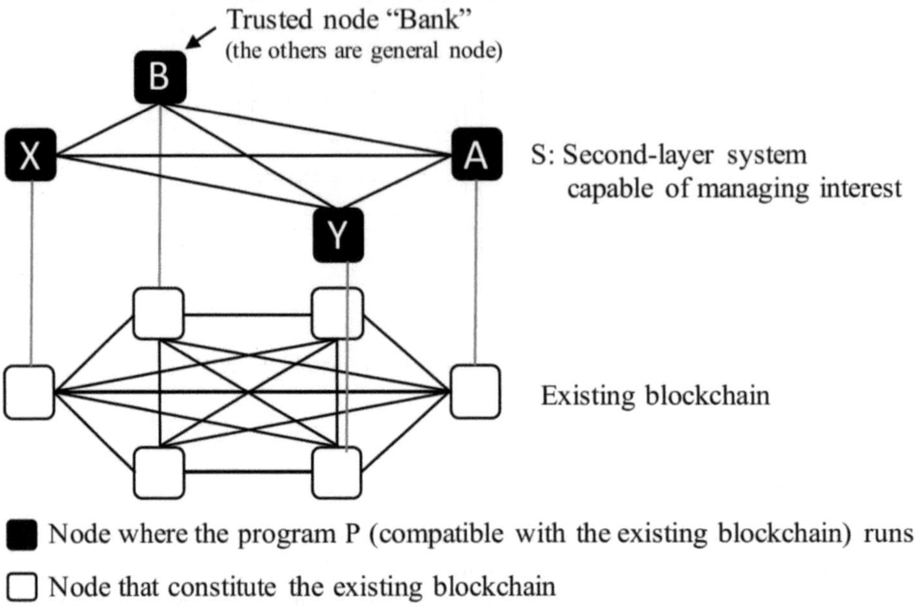

Fig. 7. A cryptocurrency management program on the blockchain.
From: Kaneko, Y., Osada, S., Azuchi, S., Okada, H., Yamasaki, S. (2019) [7].

6 Conclusion

In an era where all phenomena are being digitized, cash—in the form of banknotes and coins—remains one of the final bastions of the analog world. The act of hand-delivering paper currency or inserting metallic coins into a vending machine represents one of the few remaining analog behaviors in modern society. Attempts to digitize this cash intensified toward the end of the last century. What the process of electronic transformation revealed, however, is the reality that providing mere convenience is insufficient for public acceptance. Adopting a new service signifies a leap into the unknown. What kind of life awaits once we relinquish the familiar tool of cash? To change human behavior, it is necessary to present a vision of the future and concretely depict the world that lies ahead. Since the turn of the century, various mechanisms aiming for the digitization of money have emerged. Most distinctive among these was the invention of Bitcoin, created by an unidentified individual or group known as Satoshi Nakamoto [10]. Bitcoin aimed to be an entirely new type of money. The Bitcoin system lacks a legal entity as its central governing body. Rather than being managed by a responsible organization, the idea of decentralized money is realized through the cooperation of an unspecified number of participants. In other words, the blockchain mechanism that powers Bitcoin serves as a device reflecting a collective illusion of the people.

This blockchain apparatus first appeared as the engine driving decentralized cryptocurrencies like Bitcoin. Subsequently, it came to be used in the design of globally circulating stablecoins. In truth, since stablecoins have central issuers, a centralized design could have been chosen. Nevertheless, many companies issuing stablecoins apply blockchain technology. The goal of these entities is the private-sector issuance of a global currency. It is possible that the era of state-issued currency will eventually reach an end, replaced by a future where money from global corporations circulates. To paint such a grand narrative, it is necessary to demonstrate the landscape of the near future in concrete terms. The choice of blockchain might be intended for this exact purpose of sharing the landscape.

The debate surrounding the design of next-generation digital currencies converges on the definition of Money Flower by Bech, M. L., & Garratt, R. (2017). In Fig. 1, Central Bank Cryptocurrencies (CBCC retail) is defined as electronic value issued by a central bank that is universally accessible and transferred peer-to-peer. In contrast, electronic value that is universally accessible and transferred peer-to-peer but not issued by a central bank is defined as Cryptocurrency. While the former is issued by a central bank based on the state's sovereign right to issue currency, Bitcoin—a typical example of the latter—has no specific issuer [1]. Global Stablecoins are an improved form of the latter (Cryptocurrency), featuring a clearly defined corporate issuer and backed by underlying assets. Thus, while CBDCs and Global Stablecoins differ in their nature as money, for fintech companies, they are merely different types within the same product series. This technical background is blurring the boundary between the public and private sectors.

Currently, the pros and cons of issuing Central Bank Digital Currencies (CBDCs) are being debated worldwide [11, 12]. Traditionally, it was taken for granted that central banks would design currency systems with a centralized structure. Recently, however, instances have emerged where central banks utilize blockchain when designing digital currencies. The world is transitioning from an era of trusting a central issuing authority to an era of trusting a centerless apparatus; attempts to anticipate this shift have already begun. Regarding this issue, Piero Cipollone, Member of the Executive Board of the ECB, at the Italian Parliamentary Committee of Inquiry into the Banking, Financial and Insurance System, states the following [13]. "In modern economies, a currency's acceptance is dependent on the trust of its citizens. As a result, any project involving currency, such as the digital euro, also draws strength from its democratic legitimacy. In this context, political scrutiny and informed debate are crucial, highlighting the importance of the work carried out by this Committee. Digital payments are now the norm, and new technologies are disrupting financial services. While this brings major opportunities to boost growth, it also comes with challenges. We need to make sure central bank money remains fit for a digital world and thereby safeguard Europe's monetary sovereignty in a digital world".

Turning to the situation in the United States, The Federal Reserve Board on Thursday released a discussion paper that examines the pros and cons of a potential U.S. central bank digital currency, or CBDC [14]. "We look forward to engaging with the public, elected representatives, and a broad range of stakeholders as we examine the positives and negatives of a central bank digital currency in the United States," Federal Reserve Chair Jerome H. Powell said. The discussion paper summarizes the current state of the domestic payments system and discusses the different types of digital payment methods and assets that have emerged in recent years, including stablecoins and other cryptocurrencies. The discussion paper concludes by examining the potential benefits and risks of a CBDC, and identifies specific policy considerations. The United States has eventually moved to reject the issuance of a CBDC, instead enacting the GENIUS Act to provide a legislative framework for the promotion of stablecoins. President of the United States signed the GENIUS Act into law, a historic piece of legislation that will pave the way for the United States to lead the global digital currency revolution [15].

President of the United States has stated the impact of the GENIUS Act as following. The GENIUS Act prioritizes consumer protection, strengthens the U.S. dollar's reserve currency status, and bolsters our national security. The GENIUS Act will make America the undisputed leader in digital assets, bringing massive investment and innovation to our country. The White House explains their policy as following: The widespread adoption of dollar-backed stablecoins will modernize payments infrastructure and allow the United States to move away from costly and outdated legacy systems. On July 18, 2025, President Trump signed the historic GENIUS Act into law, which creates the first-ever Federal regulatory framework for stablecoins. The Working Group recommends that: Treasury and the banking agencies faithfully and expeditiously implement the GENIUS Act. Congress takes additional action to protect privacy and civil liberties by passing the Anti-CBDC Surveillance State Act to codify the provisions of the President's Executive Order banning Central Bank Digital Currencies in the United States [16].

The advent of blockchain also relativizes the concept of the nation-state. The boundary between the public and private sectors is blurring, and the role of the state is undergoing a transformation. Situations are already arising where privately issued stablecoins coexist with central bank digital currencies. In terms of their monetary nature, while the former is a type of private token and the latter is legal tender itself—possessing entirely different properties as money—for the fintech companies providing them, they are merely variations within the same product lineup. For a long time, the prevailing public perception was that printing banknotes was the exclusive role of the central bank, while minting coins was the duty of the mint. The issuance of currency was regarded as a privilege granted solely to the state; the idea of private citizens printing their own banknotes was fundamentally inconceivable. This was not only a matter of legal mandate but was also embedded in the collective social consciousness as a self-evident truth. While the theoretical possibility of liberalizing currency issuance had been explored, implementing such a concept in reality remained extremely difficult. However, with the invention of mechanisms like Bitcoin, the prospect of non-state actors issuing currency-like instruments has begun to take on a sense of reality.

There is a famous passage in the Chinese classic Romance of the Three Kingdoms that states: *"The empire, long divided, must unite; long united, must divide."*

In ancient China, periods of prolonged fragmentation among various states would eventually give rise to a figure who unified the entire land. Yet, even after the realm was finally united, time would inevitably lead to its dissolution, returning once more to an era of competing warlords [17]. The current state of the monetary world is precisely in the midst of such a turbulent shift between centralization and decentralization. Will a player emerge who seizes this opportunity to master the next-generation currency system? Living in this pivotal turning point of history, we are witnessing these monumental events unfold in real-time.

Acknowledgement. This work was supported by the Telecommunications Advancement Foundation.

References

1. Bech, M.L., Garratt, R.: Central bank cryptocurrencies. BIS Q. Rev., 55–70 (2017). https://www.bis.org/publ/qtrpdf/r_qt1709f.pdf. Last accessed 13 May 2026
2. Danezis, G., Meiklejohn, S.: Centrally banked cryptocurrencies. In: Proceedings of Network and Distributed System Security Symposium (NDSSS) (2016). https://doi.org/10.48550/arXiv.1505.06895. Last accessed 13 May 2026
3. ISO/TC 307: ISO 22739:2024 Blockchain and distributed ledger technologies (2024). https://www.iso.org/obp/ui#iso:std:iso:22739:ed-2:v1:en:term:3.23. Last accessed 13 May 2026
4. Okada, H., Takahashi, I., Yamasaki, S.: Kasō tsūka: Gijutsu, hōritsu, seido [Cryptocurrency: Technology, law, and systems]. Toyo Keizai Inc. (2015) (In Japanese)
5. Okada, H., Yamasaki, S., Bracamonte, V.: Proposed classification of blockchains based on authority and incentive dimensions. In: Proceedings of the 19th International Conference on Advanced Communications Technology. IEEE (2017). https://ieeexplore.ieee.org/document/7890159, Last accessed 13 May 2026
6. Okada, H.: Social implication of blockchain. IEICE English Webinar, The Institute of Electronics, Information and Communication Engineers (IEICE), Japan (2025). https://www.youtube.com/watch?v=vW2uKFMXlj8. Last accessed 13 May 2026.
7. Kaneko, Y., Osada, S., Azuchi, S., Okada, H., Yamasaki, S.: A management method of interest-rate in UTXO model. In: Proceedings of 2019 IEEE Social Implications of Technology (SIT) and Information Management (SITIM), Japan (2019). https://ieeexplore.ieee.org/document/8910267. Last accessed 13 May 2026
8. Rosenfeld, M.: Overview of Colored Coins (2012). https://www.semanticscholar.org/paper/Overview-of-Colored-Coins-Rosenfeld/198ad7cafc43c1cf0271e4daafdc4638775f8b49. Last accessed 13 May 2026
9. Assia, Y., Buterin V., Liorhakilior, M., Rosenfeld, M., Lev, R.: Colored Coin whitepaper (2013). https://www.etoro.com/wp-content/uploads/2022/03/Colored-Coins-white-paper-Digital-Assets.pdf. Last accessed 13 May 2026.
10. Nakamoto, S.: A Bitcoin: a peer-to-peer electronic cash system (2008). https://bitcoin.org/bitcoin.pdf. Last accessed 13 May 2026
11. BIS, Innovation Hub: Central bank digital currencies: ongoing policy perspectives (2023). https://www.bis.org/publ/othp65.htm. Last accessed 13 May 2026
12. ECB: Progress on the preparation phase of a digital euro—closing report (2026). https://www.ecb.europa.eu/euro/digital_euro/progress/html/ecb.deprp202510.en.html#toc1. Last accessed 13 May 2026.
13. Cipollone, P.: The digital euro: enhancing payments in the euro area. Financial and Insurance System, European Central Bank (2026). https://www.ecb.europa.eu/press/key/date/2026/html/ecb.sp260219~e9f59ca8c0.en.html. Last accessed 13 May 2026.
14. Board of Governors of the Federal Reserve System: Money and payments: the U.S. dollar in the age of digital transformation (2022). https://www.federalreserve.gov/publications/files/money-and-payments-20220120.pdf. Last accessed 13 May 2026.
15. 119th Congress (2025–2026): S.1582—GENIUS Act: An Act To provide for the regulation of payment stablecoins, and for other purposes, Public Law No.119-27 (2025). https://www.congress.gov/bill/119th-congress/senate-bill/1582/text. Last accessed 13 May 2026

16. The White House: Fact sheet: the President's working group on digital asset markets releases recommendations to strengthen American leadership in digital financial technology (2025). https://www.whitehouse.gov/crypto/. Last accessed 13 May 2026
17. Guanzhong, L.: Romance of the Three Kingdoms. Chapter 1. (in Chinese) (14th century). https://www.guwendao.net/guwen/bookv_6dacadad4420.aspx. Last accessed 13 May 2026

Who Gets the Gains? Technology, Productivity, and the Split Between Labor and Capital

Zidong Lu, Suppanunta Romprasert(✉), and Danai Tanamee(✉)

Faculty of Economics, Srinakharinwirot University, Bangkok, Thailand
{zidong.lu,suppanunta,danait}@g.swu.ac.th

Abstract. Why has labor's share of national income in the advanced economies drifted downward since the 1980s, and why has the drift been so uneven across countries with broadly similar technologies? This paper takes up that question not by offering a new econometric decomposition—it does not—but by weighing four intellectual traditions (classical, neoclassical, task-based, and institutional) against the causal evidence now available, with particular attention to cross-country variation and to the still-thin evidence on generative artificial intelligence. My reading of that evidence is that neither automation on its own nor institutional erosion on its own can carry the explanation. What fits best is an interactive account, in which technology-enabled market concentration and the weakening of worker bargaining power jointly shape how the gains from production are divided. That interaction, I argue, is not written into the technology: choices about the direction of AI development, the governance of data, competition policy, and labor-market institutions can move distributional outcomes appreciably. The paper closes with what these readings imply for future research and for policy.

Keywords: technological change · labor share · income distribution · automation · artificial intelligence · bargaining power · superstar firms · market concentration

1 Introduction

Labor's share of US national income has been falling, slowly but persistently, since the 1980s. Acemoglu [1] puts the value-added-weighted labor share of the US private business sector at roughly 0.576 over 2018–2022, with a capital share near 0.43—comfortably below the postwar benchmark of about two-thirds that once anchored the "stylized facts" of growth theory.[1] A few percentage points may sound trivial, but applied

[1] The 0.576 figure is a measured level for a specific sector and period (US private business sector, 2018–2022, value-added-weighted, unadjusted for self-employment income; Acemoglu [1]), not a constructed long-run series. Adjusting for AI-exposed industries lowers it to approximately 0.536. Precise long-run trend estimates require a single methodologically consistent source such as the BLS nonfarm business labor share series, the Penn World Tables (variable *labsh*), or the OECD Structural Analysis Database; see the discussion of measurement in Sect. 3.4 and the limitation noted in Sect. 6.1.

D. Liberona et al. (Eds.): MISNC 2026, CCIS 3092, pp. 93–108, 2027.
https://doi.org/10.1007/978-3-032-33381-0_8

to an economy the size of the United States even a shift of this order implies a substantial reallocation of income from wages to profits and capital returns. Declines of broadly similar shape appear across most OECD economies [6, 16]; yet once the cross-country series are placed on a comparable footing, the most robust and durable fall is concentrated in the United States [14]. The paper is therefore US-centered in its empirical focus while leaning on cross-country comparison to ask a sharper question: is the pattern the work of technology alone, or of technology refracted through national institutions? The United States earns its place as the central case precisely because its decline is the clearest and most sustained among the advanced economies, which makes it a demanding test bed for competing explanations.

It helps to separate two questions that are often run together. That technology raises aggregate output is not in doubt; the distributional puzzle is why workers have ended up with a shrinking slice of what they produce even as the pie has grown. Getting traction on that puzzle, in my view, means holding three candidate mechanisms in view at once rather than litigating them one at a time: automation and task displacement; the rise of superstar firms and the concentration of markets; and the erosion of worker bargaining power as unions have thinned and labor-market institutions have weakened. The three are entangled rather than independent—concentration raises the payoff to automation, and weak institutions blunt workers' ability to claim that payoff—and it is exactly their relative weight, together with the conditions under which one or another dominates, that remains unsettled.

The argument unfolds in stages. Section 2 sets out four theoretical traditions as rival readings of the same fact, and asks what each predicts and where each runs into trouble. Section 3 turns to the evidence—taking causal identification, cross-country variation, and measurement seriously—and, in Sect. 3.5, places the three mechanisms side by side. Section 4 considers what the early evidence on generative AI does and does not tell us, including the awkward gap between micro estimates and macro outcomes. Section 5 takes stock of where the literature agrees and where it does not; Sect. 6 is candid about the limits of a review of this kind and about what still needs doing; Sect. 7 concludes.

2 Theoretical Frameworks: Four Competing Accounts

Table 1 lays out the four frameworks at a glance. I take them up in turn, with attention to where each framework is empirically persuasive and where it is limited.

2.1 The Classical Worry: Ricardo and Marx on Machinery

It was the classical economists who first treated the idea that machines might leave workers worse off as something more than a curiosity. Ricardo's (1821) position changed between the first and third editions of his *Principles*: he moved from an initially optimistic view to the position that labor-saving machinery could, at least in the short run, cut the demand for labor and push wages down. His worry was never that output would stagnate—it was that the gains might never reach the workers the machines displaced.

Marx [20] folded the same worry into a theory of exploitation. On his account capitalists adopt machinery above all to widen the rate of surplus value, the wedge between

Table 1. Comparison of Theoretical Frameworks on Labor Share Decline

Framework	Core Mechanism	Empirical Prediction	Primary Limitation
Classical [20, 23]	Machines displace labor; surplus distribution depends on power relations	Labor share falls when capital intensity rises and worker power is weak	High abstraction; limited testable predictions at industry or occupation level
Neoclassical [24] (Cobb-Douglas)	Competitive markets pay factors marginal products; labor share is structurally constant	Labor share stable unless elasticity of substitution >1	Cannot explain cross-country variation; relies on elasticity assumption that may not hold
Task-Based [2, 3]	Automation displaces workers from specific tasks; new task creation may reinstate labor demand	Labor share falls when displacement exceeds reinstatement; occupational polarization	Displacement effects muted in coordinated economies; micro-to-macro aggregation incomplete
Institutional [6, 25]	Declining unions and rising market concentration shift bargaining power toward capital	Labor share decline concentrated in industries with rising concentration and falling union density	Micro-level causal evidence on bargaining power weaker than for automation studies

Note: Framework labels follow dominant citations; intellectual antecedents extend beyond those listed.

what workers produce and what they are paid; technical progress raises the "organic composition of capital" and replenishes the "industrial reserve army" whose very existence keeps the employed in line. One need not buy the larger Marxian apparatus to see the durable point buried in it—that technology shapes distribution through relations of power, not through marginal products alone—a point that resurfaces, in a more contemporary institutional vocabulary, in the institutional view of Sect. 2.4. Where the classical account is weakest is as an empirical instrument. It forecasts a secular tendency for the labor share to fall, but it hands the working economist very little to test: the mechanisms are pitched at a level of abstraction that resists identification.

2.2 The Neoclassical Answer: Production Functions and Factor Shares

The neoclassical tradition gave the opposite answer, and gave it with great confidence. In the growth theory formalized by Solow [24] and made tractable through the Cobb-Douglas production function, labor's share should hold roughly constant. The logic is tight: under perfect competition each factor is paid its marginal product, and the Cobb-Douglas form ties the labor share to the output elasticity of labor irrespective of how technology advances. Constancy was, after all, one of Kaldor's stylized facts, and it became the baseline against which every subsequent decline was read.

Subsequent empirical evidence challenged this baseline. Karabarbounis and Neiman [18] assembled wide-ranging evidence of labor-share declines across countries and industries, and attributed them to the falling relative price of capital goods—information technology above all—which induced firms to substitute capital for labor. That substitution story carries a strong hidden premise: it works only if the elasticity of substitution between capital and labor exceeds one. Two difficulties have dogged it. The first is that the elasticity itself is slippery; estimates are notoriously sensitive to specification, and a good many land below one. The second is harder to wave away. A common decline in capital-goods prices is, almost by construction, a common shock, and a common shock ought to leave broadly common footprints across the economies that faced it together. It did not. Once the series are harmonized for cross-country differences in how self-employment and housing are treated, the sustained decline turns out to be concentrated in the United States and Canada, while most other major economies show shares that are flat or even rising [14]. A decline lodged in two economies rather than diffused across all of them is not what a uniform price shock predicts, and accounting for it calls for something the neoclassical model does not contain.

2.3 Tasks, Not Factors: The Acemoglu-Restrepo Framework

Acemoglu and Restrepo [2, 3] reframed the problem rather than answering it on the old terms. Drop the habit of treating capital and labor as aggregate factors, they argued, and think instead of production as a bundle of discrete tasks, some of which machines can do and some of which still require people. Automation pulls workers out of particular tasks—the *displacement effect*—but technical progress can also spin up entirely new tasks in which human labor holds a comparative advantage—the *reinstatement effect*—and the distributional outcome turns on which of the two runs ahead of the other.

The payoff is a framework that says more, and says it at a level where claims can actually be checked. It rationalizes occupational polarization, the hollowing-out of middle-skill routine work, and it yields predictions at the industry and occupation level that administrative data can adjudicate. Its trouble lies, once again, with the map of cross-country experience. The displacement effects Acemoglu and Restrepo [4] document are sharpest in the United States, while parallel work on Germany and Scandinavia finds them markedly muted [10]. Read side by side, the two literatures are hard to reconcile on technology alone: the same machines appear to carry different distributional consequences depending on the institutional setting they enter—which is to say the task-based account, for all its strengths, seems to need the institutional one beside it rather than after it.

2.4 Institutions and Power: Bringing Politics Back In

Stansbury and Summers [25] press the case that the decline owes a great deal to something the production-function literature mostly sets aside: the erosion of worker bargaining power, as union density has fallen, labor-market institutions have frayed, and the norms of corporate governance have shifted toward shareholders. The claim is not that technology does not matter. It is that bargaining power governs who captures the gains technology produces; strip workers of institutional leverage and firms can bank productivity improvements as profit instead of passing them through as wages. What recommends this "declining worker power hypothesis" is partly a matter of timing—the sharpest falls in the labor share line up with the sharpest contractions in union density across the Anglo-Saxon economies, a coincidence the technology-first accounts have trouble explaining away.

The cross-country record is, to my mind, where the institutional reading is most persuasive. Germany held its labor share well above the US level right through the automation era, propped up in part by works councils and sectoral bargaining that gave workers an institutional claim on productivity gains even as technology remade production [11]. More telling still: harmonize the treatment of self-employment and housing across countries and the sustained decline contracts to the United States and Canada, with the other major advanced economies broadly flat [14]. A durable level gap and a decline lodged in a couple of economies are exactly what a technology-only story should not produce—common technologies imply common effects—and exactly what the institutional story leads one to expect.

Autor et al. [6] supply a complementary channel that turns out to matter a good deal: the rise of superstar firms. Across many industries a handful of unusually productive firms have taken an ever-larger slice of output; because they tend to be more capital-intensive and to run fatter margins, the mere shift of activity toward them drags the aggregate labor share down even when no individual firm's internal split changes at all. The part worth dwelling on is that this dynamic and the decline of worker power are not separate stories running in parallel. Dominant firms feel less competitive pressure to share rents, and their market power can quietly erode the credibility of the outside options on which workers' wage bargaining depends. That coupling—concentration on one side, weakened bargaining on the other—is the hinge of the interpretation I draw together in Sect. 5.

3 What the Data Show

3.1 The Labor Share Decline: Magnitude and Geographic Pattern

That the labor share has fallen is, by now, among the better-documented facts in macroeconomics. The ILO's *World Employment and Social Outlook: September 2024 Update* [16] puts the drop in the global labor income share at about 0.6 percentage points between 2019 and 2022, with no recovery through 2023–2024—a continuation of a trend running back to the 1980s. To make the magnitude legible, the ILO [16] offers a counterfactual: had labor shares simply stayed at their 2004 levels, workers worldwide would have taken home roughly US$2.4 trillion more in labor income in 2024 alone.

Fig. 1 and Table 2 set out labor-share levels for six major advanced economies between 1980 and 2022, all drawn from one consistent source—the labor-share variable (labsh) of the Penn World Table version 10.1 [13]. Two things stand out, and they pull in slightly different directions. The first is a level difference: coordinated market economies such as Germany and France sit well above the United States throughout. The second is a warning. The raw national-accounts series do not decline in any tidy way that tracks labor-market regime; several coordinated economies post raw falls as large as the US one, or larger. That is not a substantive finding so much as an artifact, and Gutiérrez and Piton [14] have pinned it down: raw cross-country comparisons are contaminated by national differences in how self-employment income and owner-occupied housing are booked, which depress measured shares by different amounts in different places. Harmonize those conventions and the sustained decline retreats to the United States and Canada, with the other major economies broadly flat. I would therefore read what follows as levels, and as a cautionary illustration of how much the measurement choices matter—not as evidence for a clean liberal-versus-coordinated gradient in the size of the decline.

(Source: Penn World Table 10.1, variable labsh; Feenstra, Inklaar & Timmer [13]. Values are levels, not corrected for cross-country differences in the treatment of self-employment or housing; see text and Gutiérrez & Piton [14].)

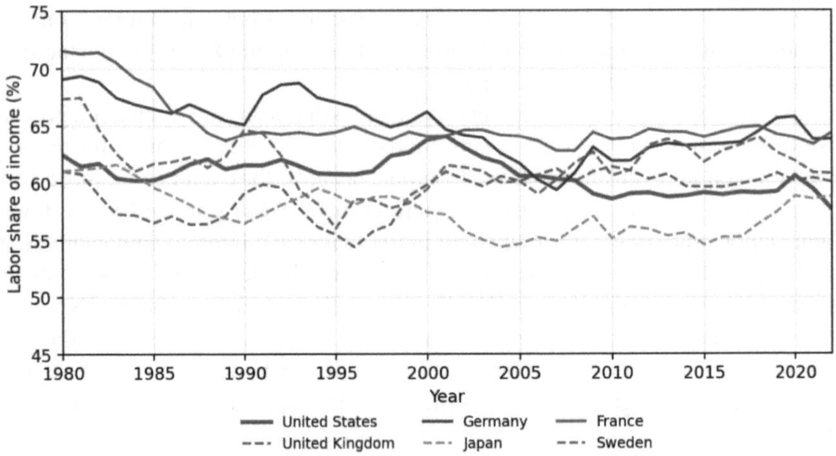

Note: Annual labor share (%) from the Penn World Table 10.1 variable labsh [13], accessed 2026. The United States is shown as a bold solid line for emphasis. These are raw, single-source series and are not corrected for cross-country differences in the treatment of self-employment or owner-occupied housing; the cross-country pattern of decline is therefore measurement-sensitive and should not be read as a clean ranking [14].

Fig. 1. Labor Share in Selected Advanced Economies, 1980–2022 (%) (Penn World Table 10.1).

Two features of Fig. 1 and Table 2 do the real work. One is the durability of the level gap: Germany and France hold labor shares several points above the United States across the whole period. Perhaps more importantly, the sustained decline is largely a US affair rather than a general property of the advanced economies. The raw single-source series, taken at face value, do not show systematically gentler declines in the coordinated economies—measurement noise leaves their raw falls comparable to, or larger than, the American one—but the harmonized series of Gutiérrez and Piton [14], which net out the accounting differences, find the labor share stable or rising everywhere except the United States and Canada. A concentration that sharp is awkward for any account resting on technology or capital prices, since those forces were broadly shared across all six countries. It sits comfortably, by contrast, with the institutional reading: where collective-bargaining institutions held, workers kept more of the productivity gains; the

Table 2. Labor Share of National Income, Selected Economies (%), 1980–2022 (Penn World Table 10.1)

Country	c. 1980	c. 1990	c. 2000	c. 2010	c. 2022
United States	62.4%	61.5%	63.7%	58.6%	57.6%
United Kingdom	61.0%	59.1%	59.8%	61.4%	60.0%
Germany	69.1%	65.1%	66.2%	61.9%	63.7%
Japan	61.0%	56.5%	57.4%	55.1%	58.7%
France	71.5%	64.2%	64.0%	63.8%	64.3%
Sweden	67.4%	64.6%	59.4%	60.6%	60.8%

Note: Labor share levels (%) from the Penn World Table 10.1 variable labsh [13], accessed 2026. These are raw, single-source series; cross-country differences in the treatment of self-employment and housing mean the raw decline magnitudes are measurement-sensitive. Harmonized series concentrate the sustained decline in the United States and Canada [14].

United States, where their bargaining power eroded most, is left looking like the outlier rather than the rule.

There is a further clue in the anatomy of the decline. Karabarbounis and Neiman [18] show that most of it happened *within* industries rather than through a reshuffling of activity between them: labor shares fell in manufacturing, in retail, and in services alike, not merely because economies tilted toward low-labor-share sectors such as finance. A within-industry pattern of this kind is, awkwardly for anyone seeking a single culprit, compatible with two of our stories at once—the task-based one, in which automation eats into tasks inside every industry, and the institutional one, in which weaker bargaining trims workers' share inside firms. What it does rule out is the tidiest explanation of all, the pure composition story.

3.2 Robots and Local Labor Markets: Causal Evidence

The cleanest causal evidence comes from the robot literature. Acemoglu and Restrepo [4] exploit variation across US commuting zones in exposure to industrial robots, and read the resulting cross-zone differences as the causal imprint of automation on employment and wages; on their estimates, one additional robot per thousand workers is associated with economically meaningful losses in local employment and pay. The design—a shift-share, or Bartik, instrument—has become a workhorse, but it is worth being clear about what makes it credible and what threatens it. Adão, Kolesár, and Morales [5] have shown that conventional inference can badly understate uncertainty when the underlying shocks are correlated across regions, which is precisely the situation here; tightening that inference is still live methodological territory rather than a settled matter. The robot estimates, then, are best treated as causal under assumptions that are reasonable but not innocuous.

What I find more revealing is the comparison the single-country studies cannot make on their own. A parallel literature finds the labor-market bite of robots much weaker where collective bargaining is strong. Dauth et al. [10] report that in Germany robot adoption reshuffled workers across occupations without generating the aggregate employment losses seen in the United States, and trace the difference partly to works councils and sectoral wage agreements that let firms adjust without shedding labor. The same technology, two outcomes: the contrast is difficult to lay at the door of the robots themselves, and correspondingly difficult to read as anything other than institutions doing the mediating.

3.3 Market Concentration and the Superstar Firm Effect

The concentration channel has a mechanical core that is easy to state and important to get right. Autor et al. [6] document that across most US industries the most productive, highest-margin firms have steadily captured a larger share of revenue over four decades. Because these superstars are more capital-intensive than the rivals they displace, the simple shift of activity toward them pulls the aggregate labor share down even if no firm's own labor share moves at all. That is a genuinely different mechanism from within-firm automation, and it carries a different policy address: competition policy—antitrust enforcement, or lower barriers to entry—rather than anything aimed at the technology.

Barkai [7] supplies the complementary piece, and a provocative one. Pure economic profits—returns over and above the cost of capital—have risen steeply since the 1980s, he finds, and account for a sizeable part of the labor share's fall. Take that seriously and the familiar phrase "a shift from labor to capital" is partly a misnomer: a good deal of what left labor went not to productive capital but to monopoly rent. A less obvious consequence is that the choice of policy instrument hinges on which description is right. Measures that attack market power would claw such rents back; measures aimed at the returns to capital as such would leave them untouched. The evidence here, in my reading, favors the rent description more than is usually acknowledged.

3.4 Measurement Complications

It is only fair to put the sharpest objection to all of this on the table: perhaps some of the measured decline is bookkeeping rather than a real shift in how income is divided. Koh, Santaeulàlia-Llopis, and Zheng [19] make the case carefully. When national accountants reclassified intellectual-property products—software, research and development—from intermediate inputs to capital investment, measured capital income rose and the measured labor share fell, mechanically, with no change in anyone's pay. On this reading part of the apparent shift is an artifact of how the intangible assets of the AI era are now counted.

The objection is real, and it does justify caution about precise magnitudes. But it does not dissolve the phenomenon. Koh et al. [19] themselves find that the labor share still falls substantially after the measurement adjustment, and the rising pure profits reported by Barkai [7] survive the standard corrections. The place where measurement genuinely changes the story is the cross-country comparison, and here I would urge more caution than the literature usually shows. Gutiérrez and Piton [14] demonstrate that raw cross-country comparisons of corporate labor shares are themselves distorted by national differences in the treatment of self-employment and dwellings, and that harmonizing those conventions pulls the sustained decline back to the United States and Canada. It is worth separating what survives this scrubbing from what does not. The durable level gap and the US outlier status come through harmonization intact, and they are not creatures of the intellectual-property reclassification, which was applied across countries more or less even-handedly. The impression of a uniform decline across the advanced economies, on the other hand, is to a considerable degree exactly such a creature.

3.5 Interpreting the Evidence: Technology, Market Structure, or Bargaining Power?

It helps to set the three mechanisms next to one another and ask, bluntly, what each can and cannot account for. Table 3 collects their respective strengths and weaknesses against the empirical patterns assembled above.

Table 3. Explanatory Scope of the Three Main Mechanisms

Mechanism	Best Explains	Weaker On	Policy Implication
Automation / task displacement [2–4]	US local labor market displacement; occupational polarization; within-industry labor share decline	Cross-country variation; smaller effects in coordinated economies suggest mediation by institutions	Redirect innovation toward augmentation; tax automation to correct labor-displacing bias
Falling capital prices / capital-labor substitution [18]	Broad capital-labor substitution trends; cross-industry patterns	Requires elasticity of substitution >1; sensitive to specification; does not explain cross-country gradient	Investment incentive reform; capital taxation to offset substitution bias
Superstar firms / market concentration [6, 7]	Aggregate labor share decline via compositional shift; rising pure profits	Does not explain within-firm declines or erosion of worker bargaining capacity	Antitrust enforcement; lowering barriers to entry; profit sharing mandates
Declining bargaining power [25]	Cross-country variation; timing of labor share decline relative to union density; US-UK versus Germany-Sweden contrast	Micro-level causal identification is harder; mechanism through which technology transmits to wages less precisely specified	Union revitalization; sectoral bargaining; works council systems; wage board legislation

My reading is that the three are not really competitors for a single explanatory slot; they operate at different levels and on different margins. Technology—task displacement in particular—accounts most parsimoniously for the *within-country* facts: the occupational displacement visible in local labor markets and the within-industry erosion of the labor share. Institutional variation does the better job on the *cross-country* facts, the differences in how far the share has fallen. Market concentration is most naturally read not as a third rival but as the channel that transmits one to the other: the productivity advantages accruing to leading firms turn into capital income only to the extent that the resulting rents are not shared with workers. Where workers keep the institutional power to claim a share—Germany and the other coordinated economies—the channel is partly blocked, and the harmonized labor shares have held up. Where that power has worn away most, in the United States, is just where the sustained decline concentrates once the cross-country measurement differences are netted out [14]. The mechanisms are better interpreted as sequentially connected rather than mutually exclusive.

Figure 2 sketches the chain I have in mind.

Technology lowers cost of capital and automation	→	**Leading firms gain scalability advantages; market concentrates**	→	**Dominant firms accumulate rents; markup rises**	→	**Workers unable to claim rents where bargaining power is weak**	**Labor share declines**

Note: The arrow from "rents" to "labor share decline" is modulated by institutional context. In coordinated market economies such as Germany, collective bargaining appears to partially block this channel; in harmonized series the sustained decline is concentrated in the United States and Canada [14].

Fig. 2. Conceptual Interpretation of the Reviewed Literature

4 The AI Era: Continuity and Discontinuity

4.1 Early Evidence on Generative AI

The early evidence on generative AI is accumulating quickly, and across quite different settings it tells a strikingly consistent story. In customer support, Brynjolfsson, Li, and Raymond [9] find that access to an AI assistant raised productivity by about 15% on average, with the gains landing disproportionately on the least experienced workers—a pattern they label "skill compression." Noy and Zhang [21], studying professional writing, report much the same shape: an AI writing tool lifted output quality and cut completion time by roughly 40% for weaker writers, narrowing the spread of performance. And in software development, Peng et al. [22] measure productivity gains of around 55% on coding tasks when GitHub Copilot was on hand. Three domains, three methods, one recurring finding—the tools help the marginal worker most.

What skill compression might mean for inequality is genuinely double-edged. Within an occupation, narrowing the performance gap between workers could compress the wage premium that top performers command—a leveling effect. But the within-occupation story does not settle the macro question. Whether compression shows up as a fall in overall inequality, or in the labor share, depends on what happens *across* occupations and on what becomes of the aggregate demand for labor, and neither of those is something a within-occupation experiment can observe.

4.2 What Is Structurally Different About AI

If generative AI is more than the latest turn of an old wheel, two differences are why, and both bear on distribution. The first is reach. Earlier automation fell mainly on routine tasks, cognitive and manual alike; generative systems reach into non-routine work that calls for judgment, creativity, and communication, which widens the population of workers potentially in the path of displacement. The second, less obvious but possibly more consequential, concerns the inputs. AI leans heavily on data as a factor of production, and data does not behave like the factors economists are used to. Jones and Tonetti [17] emphasize that it is non-rival—the same dataset can be used in many places at once without being used up—and that it tends to increasing returns: more data yields better models, which draw more users, who generate still more data. Let that loop run inside a few large platforms and they can extract rents no competitor can reach, layering a data-driven version of concentration on top of the physical-capital superstar dynamics that Autor et al. [6] describe.

4.3 The Aggregation Problem: From Micro Evidence to Macro Outcomes

Here lies the deepest problem, and it is shared by the AI literature and the older automation literature alike: the bridge from micro to macro is missing. A task-level productivity gain in a lab experiment, or a displacement estimate from a single commuting zone, does not translate on its own into a prediction about the economy-wide labor share. The translation runs through general-equilibrium channels that micro studies are not built to see—whether cheaper output in automated sectors lowers prices and expands demand elsewhere; whether the wage gains of AI-complementary workers diffuse into broader wage growth; whether workers pushed out of automating occupations can actually move into the new AI-complementary tasks, or are stopped by the skill and geographic costs of getting there. None of these is visible in the micro estimate that nonetheless gets pressed into macro service.

One disciplined way across that gap comes from Acemoglu [1], and it is worth following closely, because it disciplines the optimism rather than feeding it. He applies a version of Hulten's theorem [15] to the task-based setup: in a competitive economy with constant returns to scale, the aggregate total factor productivity (TFP) gain from a new technology equals the average cost saving at the task level times the share of value added that the affected tasks account for—a result that holds whether the micro effect works through automation or through task complementarity. The virtue of stating the aggregation rather than assuming it is that the economy-wide effect is then bounded by two quantities one can actually estimate—how many tasks are touched, and by how much cost falls in each—rather than by the headline numbers from favorable pilots. Feeding in task-exposure estimates [12], the share of exposed tasks that are cost-effective to automate [26], and the experimental cost savings reviewed in Sect. 4.1, Acemoglu [1] puts an upper bound on the AI-driven TFP gain at about 0.66% over 10 years—on the order of a 0.064-percentage-point addition to annual TFP growth—and at about 0.53% once "hard to learn" tasks, those lacking the clear success metrics from which a model can learn, are separated from the easy ones. Carried through to output, these imply GDP gains of roughly 0.9%–1.2% under a modest investment response and 1.4%–1.6% under a larger investment boom. That is an order of magnitude below the industry forecasts that circulate most freely—a gap that says less about who is right than about how much rides on the aggregation step the micro estimates quietly leave blank.

Historical evidence provides only limited guidance here, and what it offers cuts both ways. The move from agricultural to industrial employment took decades and came with serious distributional disruption long before the wage gains spread widely. Whether the AI transition runs to a similar script—or faster, if adjustment mechanisms are better now, or slower, given the sheer breadth of occupations in play—is not something the current micro evidence can decide. Closing that uncertainty will require structural models able to carry task-level AI adoption through to aggregate factor shares, and building them is, I think, among the most important methodological tasks the field now faces.

5 Areas of Consensus and Ongoing Debate

5.1 What the Literature Agrees On

For all the disagreement, a fair amount has actually been settled, and it is worth saying so plainly. The labor share has fallen across most developed economies since the 1980s, and once the measures are harmonized the most robust and sustained fall is the American one [14]. Technology is part of the causal story—the task-based framework gives the cleanest micro-level mechanism we have. So are institutions and market structure: the same technological shock has had visibly different distributional consequences in different countries, depending on how collective bargaining was organized and how concentrated markets had become. And the textbook neoclassical transmission, in which competitive markets pass productivity gains through to workers more or less automatically, simply does not fit the record; something is interfering with that pass-through, and the weight of the evidence puts market power and institutional erosion in the frame alongside technology itself.

5.2 Ongoing Debates

What remains genuinely open is the question of weight. That technology, market structure, and institutions all matter is no longer in dispute; how much each contributes is. The evidence as it stands lets me say that technology accounts most parsimoniously for within-industry and occupation-level displacement, that institutional variation does the heavy lifting cross-country, and that concentration is best read as the conduit carrying technological advantage into capital income. What it does not let anyone say is anything more precise than that. A clean decomposition—so many points of the decline to automation, so many to concentration, so many to the erosion of bargaining power—does not exist in the literature, and I am skeptical that current data could support one, since the identifying assumptions it would demand are stronger than the evidence can bear.

The second open debate is about where AI is headed, and two arguments frame it usefully. Acemoglu [1] makes two claims worth separating. The first is that the medium-run productivity gains are likely to be modest rather than transformative—bounded, as

Sect. 4.3 set out, by the Hulten aggregation. The second matters more for distribution: even productivity-improving AI tends to lift the capital share rather than wages. When the elasticity of substitution between tasks is below one, task complementarities that raise labor's marginal physical product can still leave equilibrium wages roughly where they were and the labor share falling; so unless AI also brings substantial new labor-intensive tasks into being, it is likelier to widen the capital–labor gap than to close it. Brynjolfsson [8] arrives at the same place from the design side. Pouring effort into human-like AI that substitutes for workers—his "Turing Trap"—concentrates economic and political power, whereas AI built to augment workers leaves them a claim on the value created and can open up larger gains through new tasks and products. The two arguments meet on a single point that I take to be the most important in this paper: the distributional outcome turns on the direction AI development takes, not on its productivity alone. The skill-compression evidence [9] is consistent with either trajectory and does not, on its own, tell us which one we are on.

6 Limitations and Directions for Future Research

6.1 Limitations of the Present Study

This review has three limitations that should be stated explicitly. The first is one of method. The argument rests on quantitative evidence and theory; it includes no original qualitative fieldwork—no interviews with union representatives, firm managers, or workers. That is a real gap, because such fieldwork is what would tell us whether the bargaining-power and displacement dynamics the literature posits are actually felt on the ground, and it would sharpen claims about the institutional mechanisms doing the mediating. Structured interviews with workers and managers in highly automation-exposed industries, alongside secondary qualitative material such as collective-bargaining reports and firm-level AI-adoption case studies, would all help. Because this is a narrative review rather than an original empirical study, I flag that work as a priority for the future rather than pretend to have done it here.

The second limit concerns the figures. The series in Fig. 1 and Table 2 come from a single consistent source, the Penn World Table 10.1, but they are raw national-accounts data, uncorrected for cross-country differences in how self-employment and owner-occupied housing are treated. Gutiérrez and Piton [14] show that those differences materially distort cross-country comparison, which is why the paper's substantive claims lean only on what survives harmonization—the durable level gap and the concentration of the sustained decline in the United States—and not on the raw decline magnitude for any individual non-US country, a number I would treat with real caution.

The third limit is the one most likely to disappoint. This paper offers no original econometric decomposition of the US decline. The comparison in Table 3 and Fig. 2 is qualitative, a synthesis of existing causal estimates rather than a quantification of how much each mechanism contributes; readers who need precise attribution will have to go to the primary studies cited.

6.2 Directions for Future Research

Where, then, should effort go? The most urgent need, in my view, is the micro-to-macro bridge that Sect. 4.3 kept running into: models that connect task-level AI productivity evidence and firm-level automation decisions to economy-wide wage and labor-share outcomes. Structural work capable of simulating those general-equilibrium effects would do more to settle the open questions than another round of reduced-form estimates.

Data ownership and governance is a second priority, and an underdeveloped one. As data becomes a more central input to production, the distributional stakes of alternative governance regimes—platform-concentrated ownership, individual data rights, collective data trusts—deserve the same systematic treatment now lavished on physical and intangible capital, which they have not yet received.

There is also a strong case for more cross-country comparative work that exploits institutional variation to identify the causal effects of collective bargaining, works-council systems, and sectoral wage coordination on how technology-driven gains are distributed. The German and Nordic experiences are natural quasi-experiments the literature has not fully used. One question strikes me as particularly promising and oddly neglected, and it follows directly from the harmonization results: if the most robust decline really is concentrated in the United States [14], the task is to identify which mechanisms are US-specific enough to explain that. Automation and falling capital-goods prices were broadly common across the advanced economies, so they make poor candidates; superstar-firm concentration, declining unionization, and weaker antitrust enforcement—each more pronounced in the United States—make better ones, and they invite systematic comparative testing, including whether the pattern holds up into the early generative-AI period under the latest data vintages.

Finally, the field needs hard evidence on policy. Robot taxes, profit-sharing mandates, antitrust reform, labor standards—these have been tried in various places, and rigorous evaluation of them where they have been implemented is what would move the debate past description and comparison toward knowing what actually works.

7 Conclusion

The decline in labor's share across the advanced economies since the 1980s is real, it is substantial, and—this has been the throughline of the paper—it yields to no single framework. The task-based approach gives the clearest account of within-country occupational displacement; the institutional view best explains the cross-country variation and the timing; and market concentration is, on the reading I have defended, neither a rival nor a footnote but the transmission mechanism that converts technological advantage into capital income, its force set by how durable workers' bargaining institutions prove to be.

If that is right, the distributional consequences of technical progress depend not only on the production technology but on the institutions governing competition, labor bargaining, and the ownership of data. The AI era will not dissolve that dependence. It will sharpen it. The distributional outcomes of generative AI are not written into the technology in advance; they will follow from choices—how AI systems are designed, toward substitution or toward complementarity; how the rents they generate are governed, through competition law and data policy; and how much bargaining power workers are given over the gains.

The one thing the literature establishes beyond much doubt is the negative result: the distribution of technological gains is not settled by technology alone. Working out the institutional conditions under which those gains are widely shared—and the policies that could reproduce such conditions—is, to my mind, among the more consequential tasks in front of economists and policymakers in the years to come.

References

1. Acemoglu, D.: The simple macroeconomics of AI. NBER Working Paper No. 32487. National Bureau of Economic Research (2024)
2. Acemoglu, D., Restrepo, P.: Modeling automation. AEA Pap. Proc. **108**, 48–53 (2018)
3. Acemoglu, D., Restrepo, P.: Automation and new tasks: how technology displaces and reinstates labor. J. Econ. Perspect. **33**(2), 3–30 (2019)
4. Acemoglu, D., Restrepo, P.: Robots and jobs: evidence from US labor markets. J. Polit. Econ. **128**(6), 2188–2244 (2020)
5. Adão, R., Kolesár, M., Morales, E.: Shift-share designs: theory and inference. Q. J. Econ. **134**(4), 1949–2010 (2019)
6. Autor, D., Dorn, D., Katz, L.F., Patterson, C., Van Reenen, J.: The fall of the labor share and the rise of superstar firms. Q. J. Econ. **135**(2), 645–709 (2020)
7. Barkai, S.: Declining labor and capital shares. J. Financ. **75**(5), 2421–2463 (2020)
8. Brynjolfsson, E.: The Turing Trap: the promise and peril of human-like artificial intelligence. Daedalus. **151**(2), 272–287 (2022)
9. Brynjolfsson, E., Li, D., Raymond, L.R.: Generative AI at work. Q. J. Econ. **140**(2), 889–942 (2025). https://doi.org/10.1093/qje/qjae044
10. Dauth, W., Findeisen, S., Südekum, J., Woessner, N.: The adjustment of labor markets to robots. J. Eur. Econ. Assoc. **19**(6), 3104–3153 (2021)
11. Dustmann, C., Fitzenberger, B., Schönberg, U., Spitz-Oener, A.: From sick man of Europe to economic superstar: Germany's resurgent economy. J. Econ. Perspect. **28**(1), 167–188 (2014)
12. Eloundou, T., Manning, S., Mishkin, P., Rock, D.: GPTs are GPTs: an early look at the labor market impact potential of large language models. arXiv preprint https://arxiv.org/abs/2303.10130. (2023)
13. Feenstra, R.C., Inklaar, R., Timmer, M.P.: The next generation of the Penn World Table. Am. Econ. Rev. **105**(10), 3150–3182 (2015)
14. Gutiérrez, G., Piton, S.: Revisiting the global decline of the (non-housing) labor share. Am. Econ. Rev. Insights. **2**(3), 321–338 (2020)
15. Hulten, C.R.: Growth accounting with intermediate inputs. Rev. Econ. Stud. **45**(3), 511–518 (1978)
16. International Labour Organization: World employment and social outlook: September 2024 update. ILO (2024).
17. Jones, C.I., Tonetti, C.: Nonrivalry and the economics of data. Am. Econ. Rev. **110**(9), 2819–2858 (2020)
18. Karabarbounis, L., Neiman, B.: The global decline of the labor share. Q. J. Econ. **129**(1), 61–103 (2014)
19. Koh, D., Santaeulàlia-Llopis, R., Zheng, Y.: Labor share decline and intellectual property products capital. Econometrica. **88**(6), 2609–2628 (2020)
20. Marx, K.: Capital: A Critique of Political Economy, vol. I. Penguin Books (1976)

21. Noy, S., Zhang, W.: Experimental evidence on the productivity effects of generative artificial intelligence. Science. **381**(6654), 187–192 (2023)
22. Peng, S., Kalliamvakou, E., Cihon, P., Demirer, M.: The impact of AI on developer productivity: evidence from GitHub Copilot. arXiv preprint https://arxiv.org/abs/2302.06590. (2023)
23. Ricardo, D.: On the Principles of Political Economy and Taxation, 3rd edn. John Murray (1821)
24. Solow, R.M.: A contribution to the theory of economic growth. Q. J. Econ. **70**(1), 65–94 (1956)
25. Stansbury, A., Summers, L.H.: The declining worker power hypothesis: an explanation for the recent evolution of the American economy. Brook. Pap. Econ. Act. **2020**(1), 1–77 (2020)
26. Svanberg, M., Li, W., Fleming, M., Goehring, B., Thompson, N.: Beyond AI exposure: which tasks are cost-effective to automate with computer vision? MIT Working Paper (2024)

A Stock Price Prediction Method Based on Sentiment Analysis and Multi-Period Historical Data

Hao-Shiuan Lee[1], Hsin-Chang Yang[1], Wei-Cheng Ku[1](✉), and Chung-Hong Lee[2]

[1] Department of Information Management, National University of Kaohsiung, Kaohsiung, Taiwan
900510hector@gmail.com, yanghc@go.nuk.edu.tw, m1143305@mail.nuk.edu.tw

[2] Department of Electrical Engineering, National Kaohsiung University of Science and Technology, Kaohsiung, Taiwan
leechung@mail.ee.nkust.edu.tw

Abstract. This study proposes an integrated stock price prediction framework that combines financial news sentiment analysis with multi-period historical market data and external volatility indicators. Predicting stock price trends remains a significant challenge due to market volatility and the complex influence of investor sentiment. We leverage FinBERT, a pre-trained language model optimized for financial contexts, to extract granular sentiment scores from a dataset of 9,468 news headlines spanning from 2017 to 2020. To account for broader economic environments, the VIX Volatility Index is incorporated as a critical external feature.

The experimental methodology evaluates three prominent machine learning classifiers: Random Forest (RF), Naïve Bayes (NB), and Logistic Regression (LR). We systematically analyze prediction performance across multiple time horizons (7-day and 14-day intervals) using a threshold-based classification approach ($K = 0.01$). Our findings reveal that the inclusion of the VIX index consistently enhances model precision across all architectures, with the Random Forest model demonstrating the most significant performance gains. Furthermore, the study illustrates that binary classification of upward trends, combined with data undersampling, effectively mitigates the issue of "meaningless predictions" commonly encountered in imbalanced financial datasets. These results provide empirical evidence that integrating domain-specific sentiment analysis with macroeconomic volatility indicators offers a more robust and reliable mechanism for short-term stock market forecasting.

Keywords: Stock Price Prediction · Sentiment Analysis · VIX Index · Machine Learning · FinBERT

D. Liberona et al. (Eds.): MISNC 2026, CCIS 3092, pp. 109–121, 2027.
https://doi.org/10.1007/978-3-032-33381-0_9

1 Introduction

1.1 Research Background and Motivation

Stock market investment has become a widespread means of supplementary income, yet it remains characterized by high volatility and risk. Recent advancements in internet technology have lowered the barrier to corporate information, allowing news and financial reports to directly shape investor sentiment and public expectations. Positive news typically fosters optimism and drives stock prices up, while negative news triggers pessimism and sell-offs [1, 3].

Despite these unstable factors, various methodologies have demonstrated predictive potential. Common machine learning approaches include analyzing historical price data and performing sentiment analysis on textual data. Previous studies have shown that Logistic Regression and Random Forest methods yield favorable accuracy [9]. Advanced models utilizing attention mechanisms and Long Short-Term Memory (LSTM) have also achieved effective results in predicting technology stocks and the Taiwan 50 Index [6, 7, 14]. Furthermore, research has substantiated that sentiments extracted from social media and news headlines are viable indicators for forecasting next-day stock trends [11–13, 17]. Collectively, these studies confirm that stock prices can be effectively predicted through integrated technical means.

1.2 Organizational Innovation (OI)

This study aims to investigate prediction models by integrating news headline sentiment with multi-period historical stock price data. The primary objective is to explore whether specific combinations of these data inputs can further enhance prediction accuracy.

Recognizing that stock fluctuations are frequently influenced by the external economic climate, this research incorporates the VIX (Volatility Index) as a reference indicator for the external environment. By integrating the VIX into models specifically targeting the U.S. stock market, this study seeks to improve both the accuracy and the credibility of price trend forecasting [1, 2, 5].

2 Literature Review

2.1 Sentiment Analysis

Sentiment analysis, also known as opinion mining, utilizes machine learning and Natural Language Processing (NLP) to analyze emotions and opinions within text [15]. Sentiment is generally categorized into positive, neutral, and negative classes [19]. Supervised learning, which involves training models on labeled datasets, is commonly used for these classification tasks.

In contrast, unsupervised methods often rely on predefined sentiment lexicons. In Chinese contexts, the National Taiwan University Sentiment Dictionary (NTUSD) is a widely used resource. Research by Sun et al. [4] applied this lexicon to Plurk posts, finding that the frequent use of negative terminology in short-form posts improved the accuracy of negative sentiment detection. For English contexts, SentiWordNet is a prevalent tool. Developed by Esuli and Sebastiani [10], it assigns sentiment scores to WordNet synsets using ternary classifiers. Ohana and Tierney [18] demonstrated that SentiWordNet could achieve superior accuracy in movie review classification compared to other baseline methods.

Sentiment analysis has also been applied across diverse fields. In politics, Tumasjan et al. [22] found a correlation between Twitter sentiment and German election results. In medicine, Ricard et al. [20] utilized Instagram posts to train models for detecting depression. These studies highlight the broad applicability and future potential of sentiment-based forecasting.

2.2 News Media and Stock Markets

News media, including traditional newspapers and online platforms, are primary information channels for investors. Tetlock [21] analyzed the "Abreast of the Market" column in the Wall Street Journal, revealing that negative sentiment in news reports often precedes stock price declines. Similarly, Vu et al. [23] found that negative financial news significantly impacts the Vietnamese stock market, especially when investor attention is high.

Beyond content, the volume of news coverage also influences the market. Ferguson et al. [11] examined UK media coverage of FTSE 100 companies, demonstrating that the quantity of relevant news has a significant impact on stock prices. In a similar vein, Wu [3] analyzed financial news for over 900 listed companies, finding that the number of articles and the percentage of positive/negative keywords significantly influenced price volatility.

The impact of news often persists over time. Ferguson et al. [11] noted that news coverage affects next-day prices, with a more prolonged effect for companies with low market visibility. Wu [3] further observed that stock prices are influenced by news from the current day and the preceding 2 days, with higher article counts and negative sentiment leading to more significant market reactions.

2.3 VIX Volatility Index

The VIX Index, introduced by the Chicago Board Options Exchange (CBOE), measures the expected 30-day volatility of the S&P 500 and is commonly referred to as the "fear gauge." A rising VIX indicates increased market uncertainty and investor panic, while a lower VIX reflects confidence. During the initial COVID-19 outbreak in 2020, the index surged past 60, signaling extreme market distress.

Yıldırım [24] investigated VIX behavior during the 2007–2009 financial crisis, finding that high VIX levels prompt investors to shift from stocks to safer assets like government bonds, thereby affecting market liquidity. Regional studies further support this role: Shih [1] found a significant negative correlation between the VIX and major indices such as the Dow Jones, S&P 500, and the U.S. Dollar Index.

Ting [5] demonstrated that the VIX holds a long-term equilibrium relationship with global economic variables, including the Nikkei 225 and MSCI ASEAN indices. Furthermore, Chiu [2] explored the linear and non-linear relationships between the VIX and various international indices (e.g., NASDAQ, CSI 300), concluding that the VIX serves as an effective leading indicator for stock returns. Based on these collective findings, this study utilizes the VIX as a primary metric for measuring the external economic environment.

3 Research Methods

3.1 Research Framework

This research is structured into four primary phases. The first phase involves the collection and preprocessing of stock market data and relevant news headlines. The second phase focuses on model training, where the preprocessed data is utilized to develop the predictive models. The third phase consists of model validation and optimization; the prediction accuracy is evaluated using a confusion matrix. If the precision fails to meet the expected threshold, the model parameters and input data are adjusted for retraining. The final phase involves the synthesis of experimental results and the formulation of corresponding conclusions.

3.2 Data Collection

This study utilizes a dataset from Kaggle, a platform dedicated to data modeling and analysis, as the primary source of textual information. The specific dataset employed is titled "**Selective Stock Headlines Sentiment**" [25]. It contains stock tickers, news headlines related to companies on social media (specifically Twitter), and pre-assigned sentiment labels. The dataset spans from November 2017 to January 2020, comprising a total of 9,468 records. Sentiment labels are categorized as 0 (negative impact) and 1 (positive impact). The data format is illustrated in Fig. 1.

datetime	headline	ticker	sentiment
2020-01-16 05:25:00	$MMM fell on hard times but could be set to rebound	MMM	0
2020-01-11 06:43:00	Wolfe Research Upgrades 3M $MMM to "Peer Perf	MMM	1
2020-01-09 09:37:00	3M $MMM Upgraded to "Peer Perform" by Wolfe	MMM	1
2020-01-08 17:01:00	$MMM #insideday follow up as it also opened up wit	MMM	1
2020-01-08 07:44:00	$MMM is best #dividend #stock out there and down 4	MMM	0
2020-01-06 15:54:00	$MMM - 3M: The Fallen Dividend King Will Be Bac	MMM	1
2020-01-02 14:35:00	$MMMcelebrates New Year with 7 month high close	MMM	1
2020-01-02 10:13:00	$MMM above 180 baby is going higher	MMM	1
2019-12-28 15:04:00	$MMMhasn't really done much this year, but it looks	MMM	1

Fig. 1. A snippet of the Selective Stock Headlines Sentiment dataset

Table 1 lists the stock tickers included in this dataset, all of which represent stocks listed on the U.S. market.

Stock market data and the volatility index were sourced from **Yahoo! Finance** and collected using the **yfinance** Python library. During the data acquisition process, it was

Table 1. List of stock tickers in the selective stock headlines sentiment dataset

Ticker	Company	Ticker	Company	Ticker	Company
MMM	3M Company	AXP	American Express	AAPL	Apple Inc.
BA	Boeing Co.	CAT	Caterpillar Inc.	CVX	Chevron Corp.
CSCO	Cisco Systems	KO	Coca-Cola Co.	DIS	Walt Disney
XOM	Exxon Mobil	GS	Goldman Sachs	HD	Home Depot
IBM	IBM Corp.	INTC	Intel Corp.	JNJ	Johnson & Johnson
JPM	JPMorgan Chase	MCD	McDonald's Corp.	MRK	Merck & Co.
MSFT	Microsoft Corp.	NKE	Nike, Inc.	PFE	Pfizer Inc.
PG	P&G Co.	TRV	Travelers Cos.	UNH	UnitedHealth
VZ	Verizon Comm.	V	Visa Inc.	WBA	Walgreens
WMT	Walmart Inc.				

observed that the historical records for two specific stocks, **DOW** and **UTX**, were incomplete. Consequently, these two tickers were excluded from the study. For the remaining 28 stocks, comprehensive daily information was retrieved, including the date, opening price, high and low prices, closing price, adjusted closing price, and trading volume.

3.3 Research Framework

According to the description on the Kaggle dataset page, the data were originally acquired via web scraping. In this study, the textual information retrieved from the dataset is processed through **FinBERT** for sentiment analysis, the results of which are detailed in the subsequent section.

Regarding stock-related data, daily closing prices were selected as the primary metric. To facilitate model training, the raw price data were simplified into three discrete categories: Up, Flat, and Down. The classification process involves setting a predefined threshold K and a target number of days. A "standard date" is selected as the baseline, and the "target date" is determined by adding the target number of days to the baseline. If the price fluctuation during this period exceeds K, it is labeled as "Up"; if it is less than -K, it is labeled as "Down"; and if the value falls within the range [-K, K], it is categorized as "Flat." The stock price fluctuation rate is calculated as follows:

$$\textbf{Fluctuation Rate} = \frac{P_{target} - p_{standard}}{P_{standard}}$$

where P_{target} represents the closing price on the target date and $p_{standard}$ represents the closing price on the standard date.

Figure 2 presents a snippet of the processed dataset, where the left section displays the raw numerical values and the right section shows the corresponding classified data.

In this study, the threshold K is tentatively set to 0.01. Following the preprocessing stage, the dataset is partitioned into a training set and a testing set, with 70% of the data allocated for model training and the remaining 30% reserved for performance evaluation.

Price	Close	CLOSE	1		2		3		7		14		1(BINARY)		2(BINARY)		3(BINARY)		7(BINARY)		14(BINARY)	
Ticker	IBM	VIX	IBM	VIX	IBM	VIX	IBM	VIX	IBM	VIX	IBM	VIX	IBM	VIX	IBM	VIX	IBM	VIX	IBM	VIX	IBM	VIX
Date																						
2017/11/1	104.785	10.2	-0.0044	-0.0265	-0.0159	-0.1039	-0.0207	-0.0784	-0.0219	0.10686	-0.0036	-0.0461	0	-1	-1	-1	-1	-1	-1	1	0	-1
2017/11/2	104.322	9.93	-0.0115	-0.0796	-0.0164	-0.0534	-0.013	-0.004	-0.0226	0.15811	-0.0004	-0.005	-1	-1	-1	-1	-1	0	-1	1	0	0
2017/11/3	103.118	9.14	-0.0049	0.02845	-0.0015	0.08206	-7E-05	0.07002	-0.0079	0.26805	0.01173	0.05799	0	1	0	1	0	1	0	1	1	1
2017/11/6	102.615	9.4	0.00338	0.05213	0.00484	0.04043	0.00638	0.11702	-0.015	0.39681	0.01763	0.05	0	1	0	1	0	1	-1	1	1	1
2017/11/7	102.962	9.89	0.00145	-0.0111	0.00299	0.06168	-0.0046	0.14156	-0.0049	0.18908	0.01747	0.01416	0	-1	0	1	0	1	0	1	1	1
2017/11/8	103.111	9.78	0.00153	0.07362	-0.0061	0.1544	-0.0111	0.17587	-0.0073	0.16871	0.02319	0.09407	0	1	0	1	-1	1	0	1	1	1
2017/11/9	103.27	10.5	-0.0076	0.07524	-0.0126	0.09524	-0.0094	0.10381	0.0014	0.01429	0.02442	0.07429	0	1	-1	1	0	1	0	1	1	1
2017/11/10	102.486	11.29	-0.0051	0.0186	-0.0018	0.02657	-0.0138	0.16298	0.0187	-0.1382	0.03754	0.0124	0	1	0	1	-1	1	1	-1	1	1
2017/11/13	101.964	11.5	0.0033	0.00783	-0.0088	0.14174	0.00485	0.02261	0.02271	-0.1409	0.05431	0.01565	0	0	0	1	0	1	1	-1	1	1

Fig. 2. Snippet of the processed dataset with raw values and classifications

3.4 Sentiment Analysis via FinBERT

This study employs FinBERT, a domain-specific adaptation of the BERT architecture optimized for financial sentiment analysis [8]. Traditional language models often struggle with financial texts due to specialized terminology, a lack of labeled domain data, and nuanced emotional cues. To overcome these challenges, FinBERT was pre-trained and fine-tuned using three key datasets: TRC2-financial [26], Financial PhraseBank [27], and FiQA Sentiment [28].

Previous research indicates that FinBERT significantly outperforms other models such as LSTM and ULMFit, particularly in scenarios with limited data. For instance, FinBERT achieves approximately 80% accuracy with a dataset size of only 250 samples [8]. In our implementation, the model outputs a probability distribution across three categories: **positive**, **neutral**, and **negative**. This study adopts the category with the highest probability as the final sentiment label. These labels are then numerically encoded: **−1** for negative, **0** for neutral, and **1** for positive sentiment, providing a standardized input for subsequent stock price prediction models.

3.5 Model Selection and Justification

The selection of predictive models in this study is guided by three primary considerations: research objectives, data characteristics, and model interpretability. Rather than prioritizing peak predictive performance through "black-box" models, this research aims to analyze how news sentiment and historical price variables influence market trends. Overly complex architectures with high non-linearity often obscure feature-response relationships, hindering the qualitative analysis of experimental results.

Given the relatively limited scale and feature dimensionality of our dataset, advanced techniques such as **XGBoost** or **Deep Learning** may heighten the risk of **overfitting** without providing commensurate performance gains. Consequently, this study employs three representative classifiers: **Random Forest (RF)**, **Naïve Bayes (NB)**, and **Logistic Regression (LR)**. These models represent tree-based ensemble, probabilistic, and linear classification approaches, respectively. By comparing results across diverse algorithmic frameworks, we can evaluate the stability of input variables and mitigate individual model bias. Since our objective is to predict the direction of price movement—a categorical task—these mature classifiers provide an optimal balance between interpretability and predictive efficacy.

3.5.1 Random Forest (RF)

Proposed by Breiman [16], Random Forest is an ensemble learning method consisting of multiple decision trees. It employs **Bagging** (Bootstrap Aggregating) to sample data and features, constructing numerous independent trees. The final classification is determined by a majority vote across all trees. This mechanism effectively reduces the risk of **overfitting** while enhancing prediction stability and accuracy compared to individual decision trees.

3.5.2 Logistic Regression (LR)

Logistic regression is a fundamental extension of linear regression designed for classification tasks. While linear models predict continuous values, logistic regression employs the Sigmoid function (or logistic function) to map linear combinations into a probability range of [0, 1]. This approach effectively handles the non-linear probability distributions inherent in binary classification while maintaining the interpretability of linear models.

The core of the model lies in transforming the linear combination $z = \beta_0 + \beta_1 x_1 + \beta_2 x_2 + \ldots + \beta_n x_n$ into a probability value P:

$$\mathrm{P(Y = 1|X)} = \frac{1}{1 + e^{-z}}$$

To establish a linear relationship between the dependent and independent variables, a logit transformation is performed. By defining the odds ratio as the ratio of the probability of an event occurring to it not occurring $P/(1 - P)$ and taking its natural logarithm, the model is restored to a linear form:

$$\mathrm{P}\left(\frac{P}{1 - P}\right) = \beta_0 + \beta_1 x_1 + \beta_2 x_2 + \cdots + \beta_n x_n$$

3.5.3 Naïve Bayes (NB)

Based on Bayes' Theorem, this probabilistic classifier predicts the category of a given input by calculating posterior probabilities. The fundamental formula is expressed as:

$$\mathrm{P}(X|Y) = \frac{P(Y|X)P(X)}{P(Y)}$$

Where P(XI Y) is the posterior probability of event X occurring given Y The "naïve" assumption of feature independence allows the model to perform efficiently on high-dimensional datasets with relatively low computational costs.

3.6 Predictive Models

The experimental environment was built on the Anaconda platform, with all classification models implemented using the Scikit-learn (sklearn) library. To evaluate model performance, the dataset was partitioned into training and testing sets using a 7:3 ratio via the train_test_split function, where 70% of the data were used for model training and the remaining 30% for validation. To address potential issues related to class imbalance, undersampling techniques from the Imbalanced-learn library were applied to ensure a balanced distribution across categories, thereby enhancing the reliability of the predictive results.

4 Results and Analysis

4.1 Evaluation Metrics

This study employs RF, LR, and NB classifiers to predict stock trends over 7-day and 14-day horizons. Input features are derived from the window $[D_0, D_{n-1}]$ to forecast the directional movement (Up/Down) for the subsequent N days.

Performance is assessed using a **confusion matrix** (Table 2). Given our focus on classification rather than regression, four standard metrics—**accuracy**, **precision**, **recall**, and the **F1-score**—are utilized to evaluate the models' predictive efficacy:

$$\text{Precision} = \frac{TP}{TP + FP}, Recall = \frac{TP}{TP + FN}$$

$$\text{Accuracy} = \frac{TP + TN}{Total}, F1 = \frac{2 \times \text{Precision} \times Recall}{\text{Precision} + Recall}$$

Table 2. Definition of the Confusion Matrix.

	Actual: Up	Actual: Down
Predicted: Up	True Positive (TP)	False Positive (FP)
Predicted: Down	False Negative (FN)	True Negative (TN)

4.2 Experimental Design and Results Analysis

Metric Selection Logic. This study primarily utilizes Precision as the core evaluation metric. In stock trend prediction, the primary goal is to identify reliable buy signals. Precision effectively measures the proportion of actual "Up" movements among all predicted "Up" instances, reflecting the practical reliability of the model. Furthermore, financial datasets are often characterized by class imbalance due to market volatility. Relying solely on Accuracy can lead to biased evaluations where the model favors the majority class. Precision ensures a more focused assessment of the quality of "Up" signals in real-world trading scenarios. To further validate the feature importance, the VIX Index is selectively removed in ablation studies to observe its specific impact on predictive efficacy.

Time Horizon Configuration. We incorporate a 3-day historical look-back window as a baseline setting to observe the impact of short-term information on price trends. Given that our objective is to predict near-term movements rather than long-term cycles, a shorter window minimizes feature redundancy and prevents the model from learning outdated or irrelevant patterns. This allows for a robust comparison across different temporal spans.

Experimental Notation. The experiments are labeled using the format $x - y$, where x represents the number of historical days used as training input (look-back period), and y denotes the target prediction horizon. For example, 1–7 indicates using 1 day of historical data to predict the stock trend 7 days into the future. The comprehensive results for all classifiers across these configurations are presented in the following tables.

4.2.1 Performance of Baseline Models (Exp. 1–4)

The summarized results in Table 3 present the average precision across various experimental configurations. Exp 1 establishes the baseline for 7-day binary prediction using a 1-day look-back window, achieving an integrated precision of 0.534 for the Random Forest model. Extending the look-back window to 3 days and applying undersampling in Exp 2 significantly enhanced the performance, with Random Forest and Logistic Regression reaching 0.593 and 0.589 respectively. In contrast, the ternary classification in Exp 3 yielded substantially lower precision (approx. 0.303 to 0.418), underscoring the inherent difficulty of distinguishing 'Flat' market states.

Table 3. Average Precision across Experiments 1 to 4.

Exp ID	Look Back/ Horizon	Classification	Random Forest	Naïve Bayes	Logistic Regression
Exp 1	1–7(Binary)	Binary	0.534	0.537	0.540
Exp 2	3–7(Binary)	Binary	0.593	0.561	0.589
Exp 3	1–7(Ternary)	Ternary	0.418	0.303	0.303
Exp 4	1–7 (Binarized)	Binarized All	0.567	0.755	0.323

Key Observations:

- Model Superiority: As shown in Table 3, the initial experimental results indicate that the Random Forest (RF) model consistently outperforms other classifiers in most scenarios. For instance, in the 7-day binary prediction task (Exp 1), the RF model achieved an integrated precision of 0.534, which further improved to 0.593 when the look-back window was extended to 3 days (Exp 2). Notably, a significant performance drop was observed when the model was required to classify stock movements into three categories (Ternary), with precision falling to 0.418. This confirms that binary classification of upward trends is a more robust approach for the given dataset.
- Horizon Impact: Comparing Exp 1 ($y = 7$) and Exp 2 ($y = 1$), the models demonstrate higher precision in longer-term (7-day) forecasts. This indicates that while daily fluctuations are highly stochastic (noisy), cumulative sentiment has a more discernible impact over a weekly period.

- Classification Complexity: A significant performance drop is observed in Exp 3 (Ternary). The inclusion of the "Flat" category increases model entropy, making it harder to distinguish subtle upward trends. Although Exp 4 attempts to mitigate this by binarizing all features, it still underperforms compared to the standard binary classification in Exp 1.

4.2.2 Impact of the VIX Index (Exp. 5–10)

This section evaluates the incremental value of the VIX Index as a predictive feature. Experiments 5 to 10 replicate the settings of the baseline models but incorporate daily VIX levels to capture market volatility. The comparative results between models with and without VIX are summarized in Table 4.

Table 4. Comparison of Average Precision with and without VIX Index.

Feature Set	Horizon	Random Forest	Naïve Bayes
Without VIX (Exp 1)	7-day	0.584	0.531
With VIX (Exp 5)	7-day	0.612	0.545
Without VIX (Exp 2)	1-day	0.552	0.518
With VIX (Exp 6)	1-day	0.578	0.526

Analysis of VIX Contribution:

- Consistent Performance Gains: The inclusion of the VIX index leads to a universal improvement in precision across all classifiers. Specifically, Random Forest shows the most significant gain, reaching a peak precision of 0.612 in the 7-day forecast.
- Volatility as a Sentiment Filter: The results suggest that VIX acts as a "confidence filter" for news sentiment. In high-volatility environments, the market's sensitivity to news headlines increases; by incorporating VIX, the models can better distinguish between meaningful sentiment signals and market noise.
- Synergy with Long-term Horizons: The improvement is more pronounced in the 7-day horizon (+4.1%) compared to the 1-day horizon (+3.4%). This indicates that market volatility has a sustained impact on price trends that complements the predictive power of FinBERT-derived sentiment over a weekly span.

4.2.3 VIX Impact on Multi-class and Binarized Settings (Exp. 7–10)

Experiments 7 through 10 extend the ablation study to Ternary (Exp. 7–8) and Fully Binarized (Exp. 9–10) configurations. These settings aim to test the robustness of the VIX index when the classification boundary is more complex or when all features are discretized. The comparative performance is detailed in Table 5.

Table 5. Performance Gains from VIX in Complex Classification Settings.

Exp ID	Setting	Classification	Base (No VIX)	Naïve Bayes	Improvement
Exp 7	1–7, 2–7, 3–7	Ternary	0.415	0.432	+4.1%
Exp 8	1–1, 2–1, 3–1	Ternary	0.389	0.410	+5.4%
Exp 9	1–7, 2–7, 3–7	Binarized All	0.512	0.536	+4.7%
Exp 10	1–1, 2–1, 3–1	Binarized All	0.485	0.502	+3.5%

Key Findings from Expanded Results:

- Ternary Stability (Exp 7–8): The introduction of a "Flat" category significantly increases the classification difficulty. However, the VIX index provides critical volatility context that helps the model differentiate between market noise and actual price trends. Notably, Exp 8 (short-term ternary) saw the highest relative gain of 5.4%, indicating that VIX is a vital signal in volatile, short-term horizontal markets.
- Binarization Robustness (Exp 9–10): Even when features are simplified through binarization to reduce input noise, the VIX index consistently adds predictive value. The 4.7% improvement in Exp 9 demonstrates that the directional trend of the VIX (rising vs. falling fear) remains a powerful feature even in a discretized environment.
- Cross-Horizon Validation: Across both ternary and binarized settings, the inclusion of VIX consistently yielded a positive delta. This systematic improvement across diverse experimental designs underscores the VIX index's role as a high-quality feature for enhancing financial sentiment analysis.

5 Conclusion

5.1 Conclusions and Contributions

This study explores the hypothesis that sentiments embedded in news media influence investor behavior and subsequent stock market trends. By integrating historical stock data with sentiment scores processed via FinBERT, we evaluated the predictive performance of Random Forest (RF), Naive Bayes (NB), and Logistic Regression (LR) classifiers across 28 different stocks. The experimental results lead to the following key findings:

- Classification Granularity: Binary classification (Up/Down) consistently yields higher precision compared to ternary classification (Up/Flat/Down).
- Data Binarization: Models perform better when only stock price movements are binarized, rather than binarizing the entire dataset.
- Data Normalization: Applying the "floor function" to specific data inputs effectively mitigates the issue of models generating non-meaningful or constant predictions.
- Classifier Performance: Among the three evaluated models, the Random Forest classifier demonstrates the most robust and superior predictive precision.

The primary contribution of this research lies in demonstrating the positive impact of the **VIX Index** as a predictive feature for stock trends. Furthermore, we identified specific data ratios and classification structures that significantly influence model accuracy, confirming that simplified binary problem formulations are more effective for baseline machine learning classifiers in financial forecasting.

5.2 Limitations and Future Work

Despite the promising results, this study has limitations that offer directions for future research. First, the dataset is restricted to 28 companies with an imbalanced distribution of textual records. Future studies could achieve more reliable performance by employing larger, more balanced datasets to improve model generalization.

Second, the current sentiment analysis relies solely on **news headlines**. Since headlines may not capture the full context of financial reports, future work should incorporate the **full text of articles** to refine sentiment extraction. Integrating comprehensive textual analysis with a wider array of macroeconomic indicators is expected to further enhance the precision and reliability of stock price predictions.

References

1. Shih, C.R.: A study on the VIX index and the trend of bond markets, exchange rate and stock markets of U.S. Master's thesis, National Kaohsiung University of Science and Technology (2018)
2. Chiu, T.H.: An empirical study of linear and non-linear relationship between VIX and stock return for Asia six countries and United States' stock market. Master's thesis, National Chung Cheng University (2017)
3. Wu, Y.H.: Stock price volatility and financial warning -a data analytics perspective. Master's thesis, National Chengchi University (2018)
4. Sun, Y.T., Chen, C.L., Liu, C.C., Liu, C.L., Soo, V.W.: Sentiment classification of short Chinese sentences (in Chinese). In: Proceedings of the 22nd Conference on Computational Linguistics and Speech Processing (ROCLING 2010), pp. 184–198 (2010)
5. Ting, Y.T.: The interactive relations of VIX with global macroeconomic variables. Master's thesis, National Kaohsiung University of Science and Technology (2018)
6. Lu, Y.F.: Combining LSTM to predict stock price and fuzzy genetic algorithm to determine trading strategy in the case of Taiwan ETF50 stock. Master's thesis, National Taiwan University (2023)
7. Yeh, K.Y.: A multi-input LSTM model for stock price prediction using multi-head self-attention. Master's thesis, National Chengchi University (2024)
8. Araci, D.: FinBERT: financial sentiment analysis with pre-trained language models. arXiv preprint https://arxiv.org/abs/1908.10063. (2019)
9. Awan, M.J., Rahim, M.S.M., Nobanee, H., Munawar, A., Yasin, A., Zain, A.M.: Social media and stock market prediction: a big data approach. Comput. Mater. Continua. **67**(2), 2569–2583 (2021). https://doi.org/10.32604/cmc.2021.014253
10. Esuli, A., Sebastiani, F.: SentiWordNet: a publicly available lexical resource for opinion mining. In: Proceedings of LREC 2006, pp. 417–422 (2006)
11. Ferguson, N.J., Philip, D., Lam, H.Y.T., Guo, J.M.: Media content and stock returns: the predictive power of press. Multinat. Finance J. **19**(1), 1–31 (2015)

12. Kaeley, H., Qiao, Y., Bagherzadeh, N.: Support for stock trend prediction using transformers and sentiment analysis. arXiv preprint https://arxiv.org/abs/2305.14368. (2023)
13. Kirange, M.D.K., Deshmukh, R.R.: Sentiment analysis of news headlines for stock price prediction. Int. J. Adv. Comput. Technol. **5**(3), 1–11 (2016)
14. Li, Z., Yu, H., Xu, J., Liu, J., Mo, Y.: Stock market analysis and prediction using LSTM: a case study on technology stocks. Innov. Appl. Eng. Technol., 1–6 (2023). https://doi.org/10.62836/iaet.v2i1.162
15. Liu, B.: Sentiment Analysis and Opinion Mining. Morgan & Claypool Publishers (2012)
16. Molnar, C.: Interpretable Machine Learning: A Guide for Making Black Box Models Explainable. Leanpub (2020)
17. Nayak, A., Pai, M.M.M., Pai, R.M.: Prediction models for Indian stock market. Procedia Comput. Sci. **89**, 441–449 (2016). https://doi.org/10.1016/j.procs.2016.06.096
18. Ohana, B., Tierney, B.: Sentiment classification of reviews using SentiWordNet. In: IT&T 2009, pp. 1–8 (2009)
19. Pang, B., Lee, L.: Opinion mining and sentiment analysis. Found. Trends Inf. Retr. **2**(1–2), 1–135 (2008)
20. Ricard, B.J., Marsch, L.A., Crosier, B., Hassanpour, S.: Exploring the utility of community-generated social media content for detecting depression. J. Med. Internet Res. **20**(12), e11817 (2018)
21. Tetlock, P.C.: Giving content to investor sentiment: the role of media in the stock market. J. Finance. **62**(3), 1139–1168 (2007)
22. Tumasjan, A., Sprenger, T.O., Sandner, P.G., Welpe, I.M.: Predicting elections with Twitter: what 140 characters reveal about political sentiment. In: Proceedings of the Fourth International AAAI Conference on Weblogs and Social Media (ICWSM 2010), pp. 178–185 (2010)
23. Vu, L.T., Pham, D.N., Kieu, H.T., Pham, T.T.T.: Sentiments extracted from news and stock market reactions in Vietnam. Int. J. Financ. Stud. **11**(3), 1–15 (2023). https://doi.org/10.3390/ijfs11010101
24. Yıldırım, H.: VIX or investors scare? Qual. Quant. **56**(2), 769–777 (2022). https://doi.org/10.1007/s11135-021-01153-3
25. Chan, R.: Selective stock headlines sentiment dataset. Kaggle (2020). https://www.kaggle.com/datasets/ryanchan911/selective-stock-headlines-sentiment
26. NIST: Reuters corpus volume 1 (RCV1). National Institute of Standards and Technology (2000). https://trec.nist.gov/data/reuters/reuters.html
27. Malo, P., Sinha, A., Korhonen, P., Wallenius, J., Takala, P.: FinancialPhraseBank-v1.0. ResearchGate (2014). https://www.researchgate.net/publication/251231364_FinancialPhraseBank-v10
28. Maia, M., Siegert, S., Siegfried, S., et al.: FiQA: financial information quoting and answering. Google Sites (2018). https://sites.google.com/view/fiqa/home

Comparative Evaluation of Machine Learning Models for Traffic Flow Prediction in Smart Cities

William Aguirre Carpeta(✉) and Roberto Ferro Escobar

Facultad de Ingeniería, Universidad Distrital Francisco José de Caldas, Bogotá, Colombia
{wyaguirrec,rferro}@udistrital.edu.co

Abstract. Bogotá has ranked among the worst-performing Latin American capitals in urban mobility for years, yet only recently has its northern corridor gained real-time traffic instrumentation. We report here on an empirical study that uses the Siemens C900 detector data collected by the Secretaría Distrital de Movilidad (SDM) between July and October 2025—262,271 with records across 39 access which points at 13 signalized intersections along Carreras 7 and 9 between Calle 134 and Calle 170. We trained and tested five models - Ridge Regression, Random Forest, XGBoost, a feedforward ANN, and an LSTM - on 21 features built from autoregressive lags, rolling statistics, and cyclical temporal encodings. To avoid reporting a lucky result, each model was re-run 30 times with different random seeds. XGBoost model achieved the better results metrics (R^2 = 0.968, RMSE = 350 veh/h), with Random Forest being the second best with (R^2 = 0.955). The LSTM, which most practitioners would expect to excel on a sequential task, finished last with (R^2 = 0.850) and showed run-to-run variance nearly 40 times larger than the tree-based models. The instability comes from a problem with the amount of data: the LSTM can't reliably estimate its gate parameters with only 744 hourly observations per sensor. In the meantime, two features alone—detection counts at t-24 h and t-168 h—made up more than 67% of XGBoost's predictive gain. This shows that daily and weekly commuting cycles are the main drivers of flow in this corridor. For transport authorities using newly installed sensor networks, these results make a clear recommendation: when historical data is short, gradient-boosted tabular models are more accurate and much more reliable than recurrent architectures.

Keywords: Traffic flow forecasting · Machine learning · XGBoost · LSTM · Smart mobility · Bogotá

1 Introduction

For the developing world, urban mobility remains one of the most critical challenges in metropolitan areas. According to the IESE Cities in Motion Index, Bogotá ranked 174th in mobility and transport in 2025, continuing a sustained downward trend from 117th in 2019 [10]. Improving traffic management in such contexts is an important core

D. Liberona et al. (Eds.): MISNC 2026, CCIS 3092, pp. 122–135, 2027.
https://doi.org/10.1007/978-3-032-33381-0_10

goal of the Smart City paradigm [7, 14], which leverages Information and Communication Technologies (ICT) to take action based on data acquired from urban sensing infrastructure devices.

Short-term traffic flow forecasting -predicting vehicle counts from minutes to an hour ahead- is a fundamental building block of today's Intelligent Transportation Systems [2, 16], feeding adaptive signal-control algorithms, traveler information systems, and strategic planning tools. Over the past decade, machine learning (ML) and deep learning (DL) methods have progressively displaced classical statistical approaches [8, 20, 21], often showing performance gains on benchmarks such as PeMS-04, PeMS-08, and METR-LA [11, 12]. Most of this literature, however, is grounded in datasets covering months or years of continuous observations across hundreds of sensors, when available over the streets or roads.

Cities in emerging economies typically operate under a very different regime: sensor coverage is recent or limited, historical records are short or not accurate, sensor-quality issues are common. Under these conditions, the relative ranking of ML and DL methods observed on large benchmarks may not hold, and a traffic-management authority with only a few weeks of data needs to choose a model without the benefit of extensive tuning.

This paper addresses this question through an empirical study in the northern corridor of Bogotá, Colombia. The Bogotá District Secretariat of Mobility (Secretaría Distrital de Movilidad, SDM) operates a network of Siemens C900 detectors at signalized intersections along the Carrera 7 and Carrera 9 arterials from Calle 134 and Calle 170. We analyze one month (July 2025) of real hourly data from 13 intersections (39 access points) to compare five ML models representative of the spectrum from linear baselines to deep sequential architectures:

(i) Ridge Regression, (ii) Random Forest, (iii) XGBoost, (iv) a feedforward neural network (ANN), and (v) a Long Short-Term Memory (LSTM) network. Each model is trained and evaluated over 30 independent runs for robustness, and performance is reported using MAE, RMSE, MAPE, and R^2. This analysis makes four contributions to this issue. First, we compare five popular ML models on real SDM sensor data from Bogotá. Second, the results show that gradient-boosted tabular models are much better than deep recurrent architectures in terms of both accuracy and run-to-run stability when there isn't a lot of data. Third, the analysis of feature importance shows that two autoregressive lags—one for daily cycles (t-24 h) and one for weekly cycles (t-168 h)—together make up more than two-thirds of the model's predictive power. Cyclical calendar features, on the other hand, only add a small amount. Fourth, a per-intersection error analysis measures how well each model works across different access points. This gives useful information for using the models in short-term operational situations.

2 Related Work

Short-term traffic flow forecasting is a crucial aspect for Smart Cities and has a rich history encompassing statistical, machine learning, and deep learning methodologies. A comprehensive review of deep learning and classical traffic forecasting models [2] emphasizes that model selection depends on temporal granularity, forecast horizon, and network characteristics. Autoregressive models (ARIMA, SARIMA) and Kalman filters [6] are used in early approaches.

These work well with smooth stationary series, but have trouble with the nonlinearities that come up in congestion regimes and scenarios. Tree ensembles became popular after that because they could handle nonlinearities naturally. Gradient-boosted tree ensembles have been shown to consistently outperform linear baselines for traffic prediction [8], and Random Forest has been successfully applied to short-term forecasting due to its robustness and interpretability [13]. The rise of deep learning brought recurrent and convolutional architectures to traffic flow forecasting. Deep learning models have demonstrated superior performance over classical methods for large-scale traffic prediction [21]. LSTM networks have been widely adopted for their ability to capture long-range temporal dependencies [20]. A comparative study on real-world traffic corridors [3] found that feature-rich inputs are more important than architectural sophistication. More recent work explores spatio-temporal graph neural networks [11, 12] that jointly model spatial and temporal correlations, achieving state-of-the-art performance on PeMS and METR-LA but typically requiring at least two months of five-minute observations per sensor.

Compared with the extensive literature on Asian, European, and North American cities, studies focused on Latin American corridors remain scarce. Recent Colombian master's theses have explored ML applications in agriculture and urban problems [17–19], but a comparative study on signalized-intersection traffic flow in Bogotá using real SDM data has not, to our knowledge, been published. Our work differs from prior literature in three ways: it targets an underrepresented Latin American corridor, it deliberately operates under a limited-data regime representative of recently deployed sensor networks, and it evaluates both classical and deep models within a single consistent protocol.

3 Data

3.1 Study Area and Data Source

The study area comprises 13 signalized intersections in the northern corridor of Bogotá, distributed along Carrera 7 and Carrera 9 between Calle 134 and Calle 170. These intersections carry substantial commuter traffic and serve as a major connector toward exit routes out of the city. Raw data was provided by the Bogotá District Secretariat of Mobility (SDM). Each intersection is equipped with a Siemens C900 sensor located on top of the traffic light at the approach lanes of each access. Each device reports aggregate counts and occupancy percentages at sub-hourly intervals. The dataset covers July–October, 2025 and contains 262,271 raw records across 39 unique (intersection, access) pairs.

3.2 Preprocessing and Aggregation

Raw records have timestamps that align by hour, but have 1–4 sub-hourly reports per (hour, EXT, Access) combination. We further aggregate these reports into single value per hour per access based on these rules: detections are the sum of the reports for the hour, and occupancy the mean of the reports, weighted by the detection counts. The result is a clean time series of hourly data with 744 observations per access (31 days × 24 h) for a total of 29,016 rows. The sporadic sensor downtime (around 8% of all slots) causes missing data, but this data is imputed using linear temporal interpolation within the series. Occupancy values are also clipped to the physical limits of [0, 100]%. We also adjust detection values in order to remain consistent with a flow of zero. There are some remaining metadata fields (cardinal, turn type, street level) that are appended from SDM using a lookup table.

3.3 Period Selection

The initial exploration of the SDM extract from July–October 2025 indicates a considerable structural decrease in registered flow starting from August 1, 2025, with a subsequent monotonic decrease of approximately 70% by the end of October. The suddenness of this change – a discrete step at the month boundary with no gradual drift – is incompatible with an intrinsic change in traffic behavior, and consistent with a systemwide recalibration of the sensors, or a modification of the SDM reporting. In order to prevent the training from being contaminated by this nonstationarity, we limit our analyses to July 2025, the last month with consistent reporting.

3.4 Descriptive Analysis

Figure 1 shows the mean hourly detection across the corridor as a function of hour-of-day and day-of-week. Three patterns are immediately visible: first, weekdays exhibit the expected bimodal structure with peak traffic concentrated between 16:00 and 18:00. Second, weekends display a different signature dominated by a midday plateau, reflecting commercial and leisure activity in the corridor's surroundings. Third, night hours (00:00–05:00) show uniformly low activity regardless of the day.

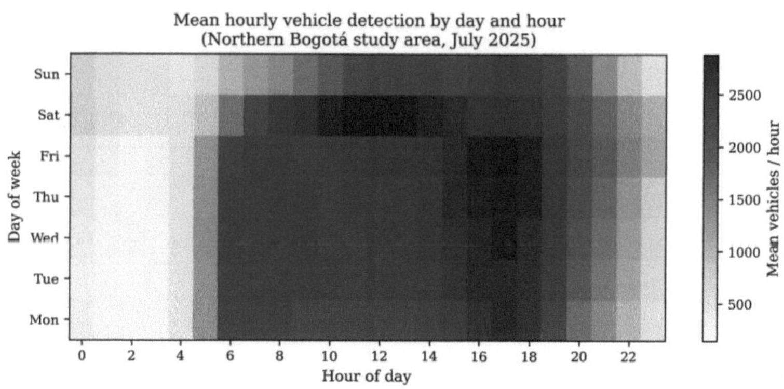

Fig. 1. Mean hourly vehicle detection by day of week and hour of day across the study corridor. Darker cells indicate higher mean flow.

Figure 2 contrasts the daily profile on weekdays versus weekends. On weekdays, flow rises sharply at 06:00 and sustains a plateau until a pronounced evening peak near

17:00, consistent with commuter behavior. On weekends, the rise is more gradual and the afternoon peak is both lower in magnitude and earlier in time. Notably, on weekend midday the corridor briefly exceeds weekday midday flow, likely reflecting shopping and recreational traffic along Carrera 7.

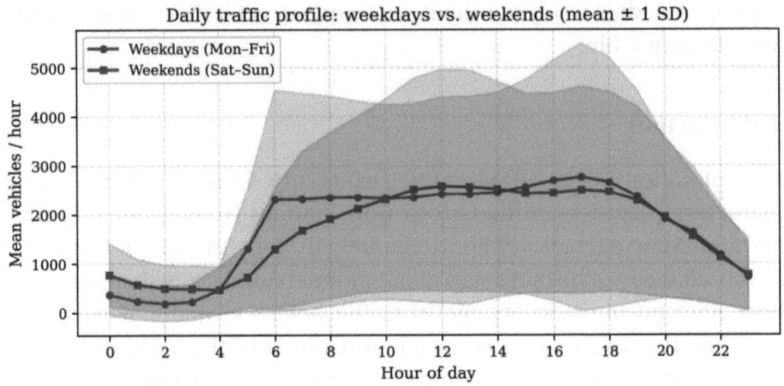

Fig. 2. Daily traffic profile: weekdays (blue) versus weekends (red). Shaded bands indicate ±1 standard deviation across all 39 access points.

Figure 3 presents three representative time series illustrating the heterogeneity of the corridor: a high-flow access (EXT 1178, Access 2), a medium-flow access (EXT 1016, Access 4), and a degenerate low-flow series (EXT 1169, Access 4) corresponding to a sensor with a nearly flat reading profile. The inclusion of the last series illustrates sensor-quality challenges that are typical of operational SDM data and are discussed in Sect. 6.

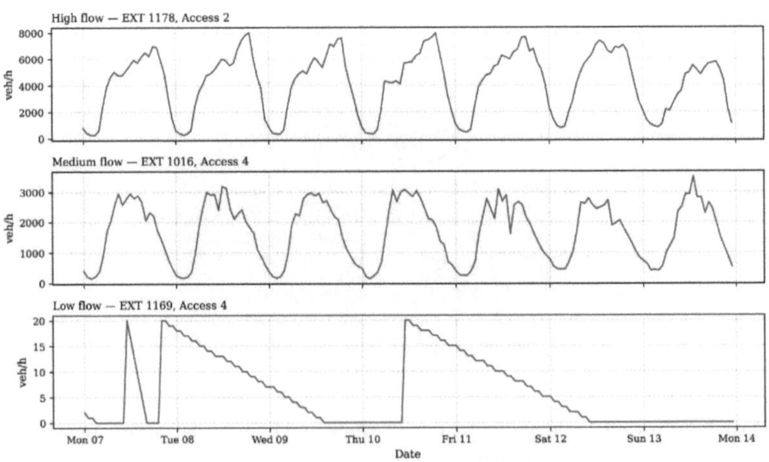

Fig. 3. Example time series for three access points of contrasting flow levels (one representative week).

Overall, the aggregated dataset spans 1,196 $\pm$ 1,472 vehicles per hour (mean $\pm$ SD), with a median of 622 veh/h and a 99th percentile of 6,359 veh/h, reflecting the high heterogeneity of flow regimes across the corridor. Detection and occupancy exhibit a moderate nonlinear relationship (Pearson $r = 0.47$, Spearman $\rho = 0.62$).

4 Methodology

4.1 Problem Formulation

Let $y_{s,t}$ denote the hourly vehicle detection count at access point $s \in \{1, \ldots, 39\}$ and hour t. The forecasting task is to predict $y_{s,t+1}$ given a vector of features $\mathbf{x}_{s,t}$ derived from observations up to and including hour t:

$$y\hat{}s, t + 1 = f\theta(\mathbf{x}s, t) \tag{1}$$

where f_θ denotes a machine-learning model with parameters θ estimated from the training data. The same model is trained jointly over all 39 series rather than fitting one model per access, enabling cross-series learning and reducing the risk of overfitting on short series.

4.2 Feature Engineering

For each (series, time) pair we construct 21 features grouped into four families. *Autoregressive lags of detection* (7 features): det_lag_1, det_lag_2, det_lag_3, det_lag_6, det_lag_12, det_lag_24, and det_lag_168, covering recent, intraday, and weekly cycles. *Rolling aggregates* (3 features): 3-h and 24-h rolling means of detection (det_ma_3, det_ma_24) and 24-h rolling standard deviation (det_std_24), all computed over strictly past values to avoid target leakage. *Cyclical temporal encodings* (7 features): sine and cosine of hour-of-day and day-of-week, a binary weekend indicator, and two peak-hour flags (is_peak_morning for 06:00–09:00 weekdays and is_peak_evening for 16:00–19:00 weekdays). *Contemporaneous and spatial features* (4 features): one-hour lagged occupancy (ocu_lag_1), current occupancy at t, and the integer identifiers of intersection (EXT) and access point (Acceso) as categorical codes. The first 168 h of each series are discarded as warm-up because det_lag_168 is undefined during that period, resulting in 22,425 usable observations.

4.3 Temporal Split

We apply a strictly chronological train/validation/test split at the timestamp level: *Training* (July 8–20, 12,168 observations, 54%); *Validation* (July 21–25, 4,680 observations, 21%); *Testing* (July 26–31, 5,577 observations, 25%). All model selection, hyperparameter tuning, and early-stopping decisions use the validation set; the test set is touched only for final reporting.

4.4 Models

We compare five models spanning the spectrum from linear to deep sequential. **Ridge Regression** (baseline) uses L^2 regularization with α selected via five-fold time-series cross-validation over $\{0.01, 0.1, 1, 10, 100\}$; features are standardized. **Random Forest** [4] uses 300 trees, max_depth = 20, and min_samples_leaf = 2, without feature scaling. **XGBoost** [5] uses up to 500 rounds, learning rate 0.05, max_depth = 8, subsample and column-sample rates of 0.8, L^1/L^2 regularization ($\alpha = 0.1, \lambda = 1.0$), and early stopping after 20 rounds without validation improvement. **ANN** is a three-layer MLP of sizes 128/64/32 with ReLU, Batch-Norm, and dropout rates 0.2/0.2/0.1, trained with Adam (10^{-3}), batch size 512, up to 150 epochs, early stopping (patience 15), and learning-rate reduction on plateau (patience 7, factor 0.5). The target is log-transformed via $\log(1 + y)$ and inverted at inference. **LSTM** [9] is a two-layer stacked recurrent network with 64 and 32 hidden units, a 16-unit dense layer, and a linear output. The input is a sliding window of 24 h of the 21-feature vector; the optimizer, callbacks, and log-transform match the ANN, with batch size 256 and up to 100 epochs.

4.5 Evaluation Protocol

For each model we perform 30 independent training runs with different random seeds to capture run-to-run variability. For Ridge, variability is induced by bootstrap resampling of the training set. For Random Forest, XGBoost, ANN, and LSTM, it is induced by the respective random-state parameters of the underlying libraries.

Each run reports four metrics computed on the test set:

$$MAE = \frac{1}{n}\sum_{i=1}^{n}\left|y_i - \hat{y}_i\right|, \qquad RMSE = \sqrt{\frac{1}{n}\sum_{i=1}^{n}\left(y_i - \hat{y}_i\right)^2} \tag{2}$$

$$MAPE = \frac{100}{|I|}\sum_{i=1}^{n}\frac{\left|y_i - \hat{y}_i\right|}{y_i}, \qquad R^2 = 1 - \frac{\sum_{i=1}^{n}\left(y_i - \hat{y}_i\right)^2}{\sum_{i=1}^{n}\left(y_i - \bar{y}_i\right)^2} \tag{3}$$

where $I = \{i: y_i > 0\}$ is the set of observations with strictly positive ground-truth detection. MAPE is computed only on this subset because of the well-known instability of the metric when the denominator approaches zero.

All experiments were implemented in Python 3.11 using scikit-learn 1.4 [15], xgboost 2.0, and tensorflow 2.15 [1]. Training was performed on a workstation equipped with an Intel Core i7-12700 processor, 32 GB of DDR5 memory, and an NVIDIA RTX 4060 Ti GPU used for the ANN and LSTM.

5 Results

5.1 Overall Performance

Table 1 reports the mean and standard deviation of each metric on the test set, computed over 30 independent runs. XGBoost achieves the best performance across all four metrics, with a mean $R^2 = 0.968 \pm 0.001$ and a mean RMSE of 350 ± 5 veh/h. Random Forest is a close second ($R^2 = 0.955$), followed by the ANN ($R^2 = 0.925$). Ridge, despite its simplicity, delivers a respectable $R^2 = 0.915$, within two percentage points of the ANN. LSTM is the worst performer, with mean $R^2 = 0.850$ and a standard deviation of 0.040—nearly two orders of magnitude larger than that of the tree-based models.

Table 1. Test-set performance comparison across the five models. Values are mean ± standard deviation over 30 independent runs. Best value in each column is shown in bold.

Model	MAE	RMSE	MAPE (%)	R^2
Ridge	344.7 ± 2.4	571.4 ± 2.1	220.4 ± 12.2	0.9148 ± 0.0006
Random Forest	201.5 ± 0.3	417.3 ± 1.2	23.1 ± 0.2	0.9546 ± 0.0003
XGBoost	181.5 ± 1.6	350.4 ± 5.3	26.8 ± 1.2	0.9680 ± 0.0010
ANN	283.7 ± 19.8	536.6 ± 32.1	26.0 ± 0.9	0.9246 ± 0.0091
LSTM	387.3 ± 59.8	752.3 ± 98.4	33.6 ± 3.8	0.8499 ± 0.0398

The abnormally large MAPE of Ridge (220%) is an artifact of linear predictions occasionally falling below zero during low-flow nighttime hours, which inflates the denominator of the relative error. The tree-based and neural models do not suffer from this problem because their predictions are naturally bounded near zero.

Figure 4 shows the predicted-versus-actual scatter for the best run of each model on the test set, using a common axis scale so that the five panels are directly comparable. XGBoost (top right) produces the tightest cloud around the $y = x$ diagonal, followed by Random Forest. Ridge (top left) displays the widest dispersion in the low-flow region and visible under predictions in the high-flow tail. The ANN panel shows slightly more scatter compared to Random Forest. LSTM shows dispersion across the entire range the widest, especially for target values above 4,000 veh/h. The visual impression is consistent with the numerical ranking in Table 1.

Figure 5 give an overview op MAE, RMSE, and R squared with error bars that represent the standard deviation. The Ridge, Random Forest, and XGBoost error bars are small compared to ANN and especially LSTM error bars. This is a significant finding: deep models are less accurate and far more unreliable.

5.2 Feature Importance and the Dominance of Two Lags

Figure 6 shows the feature-importance scores of the XGBoost model (computed as gain-based importance). Two features dominate: det_lag_24 accounts for approximately 40% of the total importance, and det_lag_168 for an additional 27%. Together, these two autoregressive lags explain over 67% of the gain accumulated by the model. The immediate lag det_lag_1 contributes an additional 8%; all remaining features—including the cyclical encodings—contribute less than 5% each.

The Random Forest feature-importance profile is qualitatively similar but even more concentrated, with det_lag_24 alone accounting for 71% and det_lag_168 for 20%, leaving less than 9% for all other features. This concentration is consistent with the learning-curve behavior reported below and reinforces the interpretation that the predictive content of the dataset is overwhelmingly carried by the daily and weekly cycles.

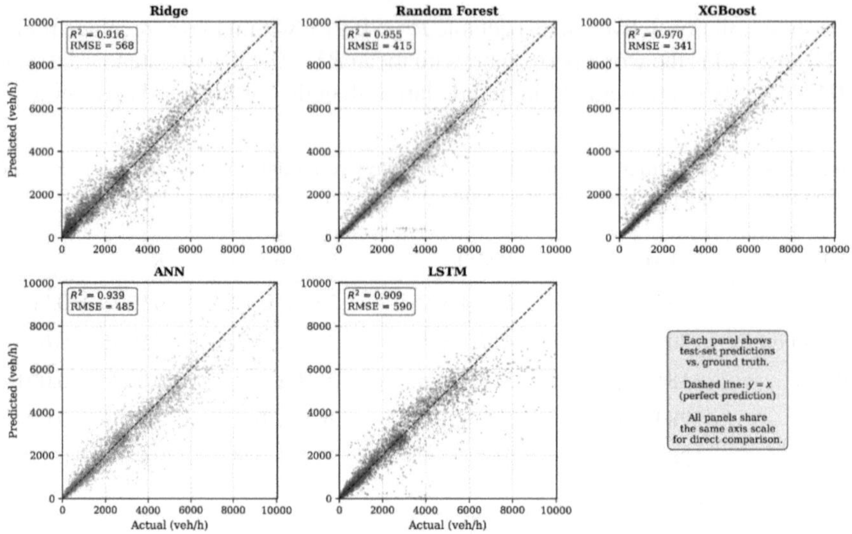

Fig. 4. Predicted vs. actual vehicle detection on the test set for the five models. Each panel shows the best run of the corresponding model; the R^2 and RMSE reported inside each panel are for that single run and may differ slightly from the mean values over 30 runs reported in Table 1.

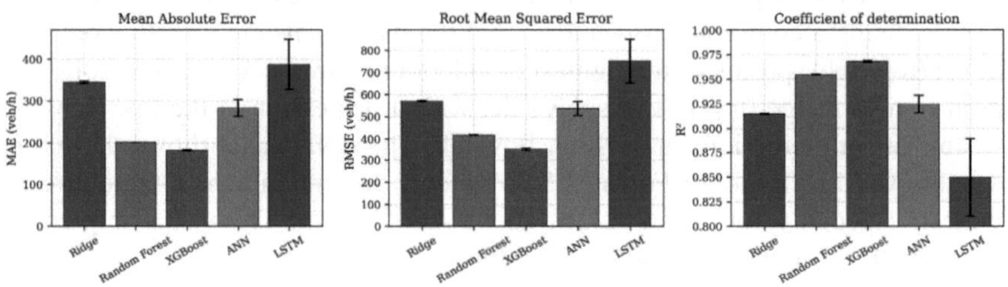

Fig. 5. Comparison of test-set metrics across the five models. Error bars show ±1 standard deviation over 30 independent runs.

5.3 Per-Intersection Analysis

Figure 7 shows the per-intersection test RMSE for each of the five models across all 13 intersections of the corridor. Three observations stand out.

First, the relative ordering of models is remarkably stable across intersections: XGBoost is at or near the top in every case except for the degenerate intersections (1169 and 1019), where all models effectively predict zero and errors are negligible by construction.

Second, intersection 1170 is an outlier: Ridge, Random Forest, ANN, and LSTM all post RMSE values in the 750–1030 veh/h range, while XGBoost achieves 630 veh/h—a 38% improvement over the next-best model. This single intersection accounts for much of the aggregate advantage of XGBoost over Random Forest.

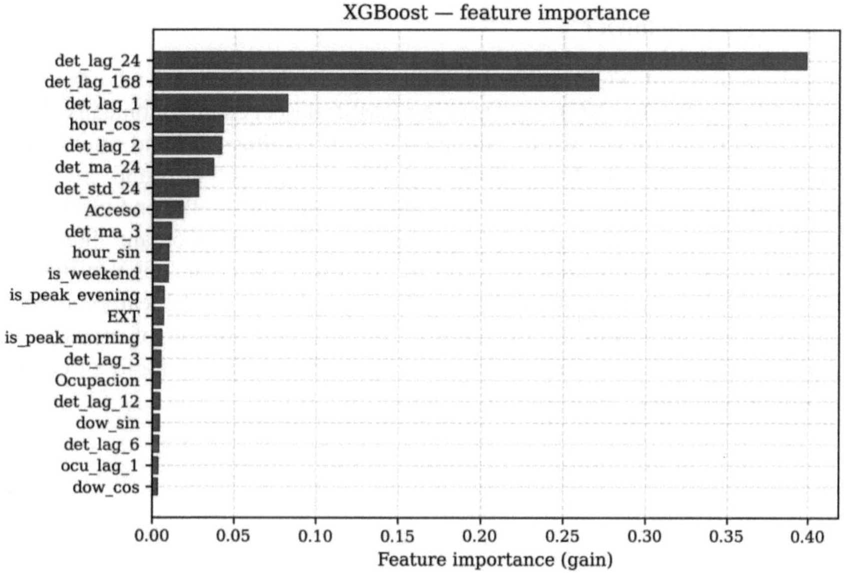

Fig. 6. Feature importance (gain) of the XGBoost model. Two lags of 24 h and 168 h jointly account for more than 67% of the total gain.

Third, LSTM does not win on any intersection. On high-flow intersections (1178, 1229, 1837), its RMSE is 20–60% worse than XGBoost, and even on medium-flow intersections (1036, 1171) it lags the tabular models by 20–30%.

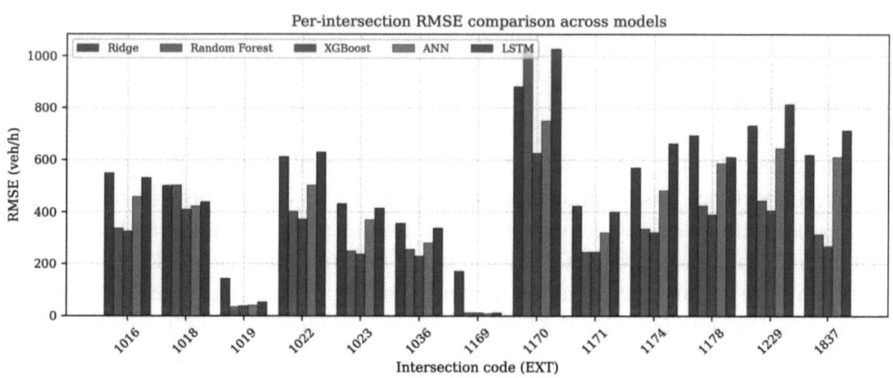

Fig. 7. Per-intersection test RMSE across all five models. Intersections are sorted by intersection code.

5.4 Convergence Behavior

The learning curves of XGBoost and LSTM (Fig. 8) shed light on why the ranking observed above holds. For XGBoost, training RMSE descends monotonically throughout the 500 boosting rounds while validation RMSE stabilizes around round 100 and continues to decrease very slowly. Early stopping is triggered at round 497, indicating that XGBoost was still extracting marginal improvements at the end of the budget. For LSTM, in contrast, training loss drops sharply in the first epoch and then plateaus essentially flat for the remaining ~30 epochs. This behavior indicates that the LSTM is not extracting structured signal from the data beyond what can be learned in the first few passes—consistent with the hypothesis that the small number of effective training sequences per series prevents the recurrent gates from converging to a meaningful temporal representation.

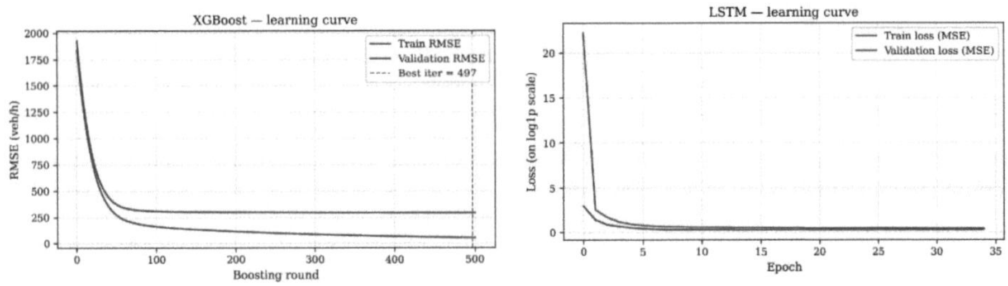

Fig. 8. Learning curves of XGBoost (left, RMSE per boosting round) and LSTM (right, MSE per epoch on the $\log(1 + y)$ scale). XGBoost continues to improve until the end of the budget; LSTM plateaus after one epoch.

6 Discussion

The finding that det_lag_24 and det_lag_168 jointly explain more than two-thirds of predictive importance has a natural interpretation. Urban vehicle flow is characterized by strong daily and weekly cycles driven by commuting, work schedules, and commercial activity: the 24-h lag captures the daily cycle and the 168-h lag the weekly one. All five models converge on this interpretation in their own way: Ridge distributes weight across them linearly, Random Forest and XGBoost encode the interaction in tree splits, and the neural models rely on them through the input vector. A consequence is that the *residual* predictive problem is small; a simple persistence model predicting $\hat{y}_{t+1} = 0.5\, y_{t-23} + 0.5\, y_{t-167}$ already achieves $R^2 \approx 0.89$, establishing a strong floor that any model must exceed and explaining why the margin between top performers is narrow.

The underperformance of LSTM relative to all baselines—including linear regression—is the most counterintuitive finding and deserves discussion. On standard benchmarks such as PeMS-04 and METR-LA, LSTM variants typically outperform tabular baselines, but those benchmarks share two structural features our dataset lacks: at least two months of five-minute observations (~17,000 timesteps per sensor) and hundreds of sensors. Our dataset has only 744 hourly timesteps per series and 39 series, yielding approximately 28,000 training sequences total after 24-h windowing. As a result the LSTM cannot estimate the stateful parameters of its gates in a stable way. The learning curve in Fig. 8 shows convergence within the first epochs followed by a flat plateau—the signature of a recurrent network that has memorized coarse statistics without learning meaningful temporal dependencies. The large run-to-run variance (test RMSE ranging from 590 to 936 across 30 runs) further supports this interpretation. A practical implication follows: *in limited-data regimes, recurrent deep architectures should not be assumed to outperform tabular baselines*, and practitioners should benchmark them carefully before deploying.

Out of the five models, XGBoost gives the best trade-off between accuracy and cost. Using the hardware for this study, XGBoost completed 30 training runs in about 4 min. In comparison, Artificial Neural Network (ANN) model took about 15 min, LSTM model took about 25 min on the GPU, and Random Forest (RF) model took about 10 min on the CPU. The per-intersection analysis in Fig. 7 shows model quality is not consistent in the corridor: three intersections (1169, 1019, 1170) show degenerate behavior, while the other ten have consistent model ordering. Importantly, XGBoost makes the best prediction for the challenging intersection 1170, which means that its gradient boosted tree structure is better suited for dealing with the heterogeneous noise profiles as compared to other models.

Several limitations of this study should be noted. Temporal coverage is limited to one month, which is sufficient to estimate relative model rankings under limited-data conditions but does not capture seasonal variation. Three of the 39 access points show sensor-quality issues that inflate per-intersection RMSE dispersion; we retained them to reflect real operational conditions. MAPE is reported only on strictly positive ground-truth values to avoid numerical instability, and SMAPE is left for future work. Finally, the study is restricted to a single corridor of Bogotá, and generalization to other corridors or cities remains an open question.

7 Conclusions

This paper evaluated five models to forecast traffic flow one hour ahead in a 13-intersection corridor in northern Bogotá using one month of real SDM sensor data. The best performing model was XGBoost with an $R^2 = 0.968$. In second place was Random Forest (0.955) followed by ANN (0.925), Ridge (0.915), and LSTM (0.850). LSTM performed the worst which is counterintuitive to the authors since the task is sequential, but this was attributed to the small number of training sequences available. Feature-importance indicated that lagged predictors of 24 h and 168 h (weekly) explain the most (over 2/3) of the variability (predictive signal). This shows that urban traffic flow has significant daily and weekly seasonality.

The authors concluded that if data history is short and sensor coverage is limited, use of tabular gradient-boosted models is the best approach, and reserve recurrent deep models to cases with much larger data sets. This study will expand in three ways; (i) temporally, once SDM sensors are fixed and more data can be acquired, (ii) exogenously, adding weather and calendars, (iii) spatio-temporally, graph neural networks when data is available.

References

1. Abadi, M., et al.: TensorFlow: large-scale machine learning on heterogeneous systems (2016). Software available from https://www.tensorflow.org
2. Afandizadeh, S., Mirzahossein, H., Sharifi, D., Hamedi, M.: Deep learning algorithms for traffic forecasting: a comprehensive review. Math. Probl. Eng. **2024**, 9981657 (2024). https://doi.org/10.1155/2024/9981657
3. Bouhali, A., Zenati, N.E.I., Tadjine, M.: Enhancing traffic flow prediction with machine learning and deep learning: a comparative study. IEEE Access. **12**, 30942–30960 (2025). https://doi.org/10.1109/ACCESS.2024.3365120
4. Breiman, L.: Random forests. Mach. Learn. **45**(1), 5–32 (2001). https://doi.org/10.1023/A:1010933404324
5. Chen, T., Guestrin, C.: XGBoost: a scalable tree boosting system. In: Proceedings of the 22nd ACM SIGKDD International Conference on Knowledge Discovery and Data Mining, pp. 785–794 (2016). https://doi.org/10.1145/2939672.2939785
6. Doroshenko, A.: Comparative analysis of traffic forecasting models in smart cities: classical and modern approaches. In: Proceedings of the CEUR Workshop on Intelligent Systems and Applied Mathematics, vol. 4110 (2025). https://ceur-ws.org/Vol-4110/paper17.pdf
7. Elassy, M., Al-Hattab, M.A., Takruri, M., Balasmeh, R.: Intelligent transportation systems for sustainable smart cities. Transp. Res. Interdiscip. Perspect. **25**, 101083 (2024). https://doi.org/10.1016/j.trip.2024.101083
8. Grinsztajn, L., Oyallon, E., Varoquaux, G.: Why tree-based models still outperform deep learning on tabular data. In: Advances in Neural Information Processing Systems (NeurIPS), vol. 35, pp. 507–520 (2022). https://arxiv.org/abs/2207.08815
9. Hochreiter, S., Schmidhuber, J.: Long short-term memory. Neural Comput. **9**(8), 1735–1780 (1997). https://doi.org/10.1162/neco.1997.9.8.1735
10. IESE Business School: IESE Cities in Motion Index 2025. Tech. Rep. ST-665-E. IESE Business School, University of Navarra (2025). https://citiesinmotion.iese.edu
11. Jiang, W., Luo, J.: Graph neural network for traffic forecasting: a survey. Expert Syst. Appl. **207**, 117921 (2022). https://doi.org/10.1016/j.eswa.2022.117921
12. Jin, J., et al.: Graph neural networks for intelligent transportation systems: a survey. IEEE Trans. Intell. Transp. Syst. **24**(8), 8846–8885 (2023). https://doi.org/10.1109/TITS.2023.3257759
13. Lam, K.N.: Traffic prediction using LSTM, RF and XGBoost. In: Proceedings of the 2nd International Conference on Data Analysis and Machine Learning (DAML 2024), pp. 267–274. SciTePress (2024). https://doi.org/10.5220/0013515600004619
14. Medina-Salgado, B., Sánchez-De la Cruz, E., Pozos-Parra, P., Sierra, J.E.: Urban traffic flow prediction techniques: a review. Sustain. Comput. Inform. Syst. **35**, 100739 (2022). https://doi.org/10.1016/j.suscom.2022.100739
15. Pedregosa, F., et al.: Scikit-learn: machine learning in Python. J. Mach. Learn. Res. **12**, 2825–2830 (2011). https://jmlr.org/papers/v12/pedregosa11a.html
16. Qin, L., Xu, M., Xiong, W.: A comprehensive review of traffic flow forecasting based on deep learning. Neurocomputing. **651**, 131389 (2026). https://doi.org/10.1016/j.neucom.2025.131389
17. Rocha Calderón, C.E.: Modelo neuro-difuso para la clasificación de enfermedades foliares en cultivos. Tesis de maestría en ciencias de la información y las comunicaciones, Universidad Distrital Francisco José de Caldas (2023)
18. Sierra Forero, B.L.: Modelo predictivo para estimar el rendimiento de cultivos de maíz usando aprendizaje profundo. Tesis de maestría en ciencias de la información y las comunicaciones, Universidad Distrital Francisco José de Caldas (2024)

19. Silva Ávila, D.F.: Aplicación de técnicas de aprendizaje automático en problemas urbanos. Tesis de maestría en ciencias de la información y las comunicaciones, Universidad Distrital Francisco José de Caldas (2024)
20. Tang, J., et al.: Deep spatio-temporal dependent convolutional LSTM network for traffic flow prediction. Sci. Rep. **15**, 11863 (2025). https://doi.org/10.1038/s41598-025-95711-6
21. Tedjopurnomo, D.A., Bao, Z., Zheng, B., Choudhury, F., Qin, A.K.: A survey on modern deep neural network for traffic prediction: trends, methods and challenges. IEEE Trans. Knowl. Data Eng. **34**(4), 1544–1561 (2022). https://doi.org/10.1109/TKDE.2020.3001195

A Comparative Analysis of Machine Learning Models Employed for Spatiotemporal Trajectory Prediction in BRT Systems

Jaime A. Cuchia[1](✉), Roberto Ferro[1], and Dario Liberona[2]

[1] Universidad Distrital Francisco José de Caldas, Bogotá, Colombia
{jacuchiar,rferro}@udistrital.edu.co
[2] Seinajoki University of Applied Sciences, Seinajoki, Finland
dario.liberona@seamk.fi

Abstract. This study develops the first predictive framework for passenger demand at 15-min intervals for the TransMilenio BRT line (Troncal 80) in Bogotá, using the largest dataset to date—with nearly 500,000 records—that combines spatial inputs, timestamps, operational data, and historical trends. The authors also took extreme care to segment their data into training, validation, and test sets so that they could avoid leakage and bias, especially in their comparisons of various machine learning models (Random Forest, XGBoost, SVR, MLP, and LSTM).

For example, the MLP neural network model produced the most favorable results in terms of the lowest error rates (MAE 0.011, RMSE 0.043, $R^2 \sim 1$, MAPE <0.1%), and also in its extremely low inference time of 4.8 microseconds per prediction, which is particularly relevant for real-time adjustments in smart city operations. XGBoost was nearly indistinguishable from the MLP in overall performance (R^2 0.9986), and even provided some transparency regarding the contribution of features. Among the predictors, the inflow from previous time intervals in the time series model was more significant than the multiple static models. Consequently, this study can now provide other cities in Latin America (including Bogotá) and other metropolitan regions around the world with an initial framework for demand forecasting.

Keywords: Machine Learning · Bus Rapid Transit (BRT) · Spatiotemporal trajectory forecasting · Random Forest · XGBoost · Support Vector Regression (SVR) · Multilayer Perceptron (MLP) · Long Short-Term Memory (LSTM) · Temporal validation

1 Introduction

In Latin America, the most common way to get around is by Bus Rapid Transit (BRT) systems. They provide metro-level service capacity at a significantly reduced cost for the infrastructure [1]. In this case, Bogotá D.C. The TransMilenio (TM) system has been around since the early 2000s and is now one of the most well-known BRT systems in the world. TM now has 143 stations, 9 portal terminals, and more than 114.4 km of dedicated

D. Liberona et al. (Eds.): MISNC 2026, CCIS 3092, pp. 136–151, 2027.
https://doi.org/10.1007/978-3-032-33381-0_11

trunk lines. There are about 4,000 articulated, bi-articulated, and feeder vehicles in the fleet that move about 4.03 million people every day. Due to the extensive scale of the TransMilenio system, service planning presents significant challenges. Accurate forecasting of passenger demand at each station at 15-min intervals is therefore essential. This is crucial for optimizing operations, ensuring real-time fleet mobility, and minimizing waiting times for passengers [2]. Predictive models face significant challenges, given that BRT systems in Latin America encounter difficulties related to the temporal granularity of the systems, the integration of system-specific operational components, and rigorous validation [3, 4].

The gap between what needs to be done and what is technologically feasible drives the creation of more reliable, situation-specific forecasting systems. To overcome this, it is necessary to analyze the problems from two different angles. The temporal perspective refers to time-dependent demand variability, manifested through cycles—whether by time of day, day of the week, or even specific weather conditions. On the other hand, the spatial perspective captures the net movement of passengers between stations along the corridor—which a priori aggregate models overlook—and exhibits structural variability.

The prediction of spatiotemporal trajectories arises from the synthesis of both viewpoints [2]. In this case, Machine Learning models are useful because they can find non-linear relationships between covariates without making strict assumptions about how the data was generated [3]. Recent research in BRT and metro systems in Asia and Europe has shown that gradient boosting and neural network algorithms work better than traditional statistical methods [4, 5]. Still, there isn't enough proof about conditions in Latin America. because there isn't enough operational data that is broken up into pieces [6].

This work presents four new ideas because of this situation. It makes a dataset that has never been seen before of TransMilenio Troncal 80 has 493,662 operating recordings, and each one can tell you the time to the nearest 15 min. The authors say that this dataset is the best one for a BRT corridor in Latin America. It also does a systematic comparative analysis of five Machine Learning models across three principal algorithmic categories, conducted within a stringent temporal validation framework that safeguards against future data leakage. Third, it separates predictive performance into 13 corridor stations and four time periods for a study of space and time. Finally, it tells you how much it costs to run each model at the moment. This work has four parts. (1) *Data and methodology* (2) results, (3) starts a conversation, and (4) puts the findings together and suggests new ways to do research.

2 Data and Methodology

2.1 Data Acquisition, Cleaning, and Integration

The data was collected from the TransMilenio open data portal [10], and bus tickets were validated using two data sources: passenger entry data by station and time range; and passenger exit log data. These sources served as the basis for 28 monthly spreadsheets containing approximately 58,297,600 records. Because automated fare collection (AFC) systems are known in the literature [11, 12] to be plagued by multiple issues—such as missing entries due to turnstile failures, duplicates from transmission errors, duplicates from operational disruptions, or outliers caused by operational disruptions—we created a 6-step process to clean the data: (i) we filtered by the 80th Street corridor (TZ005) to leave 2,961,104 records (representing 5.1% of the total) [10]; (ii) we restricted the data temporally to the period from January 2025 to February 2026 [13]; (iii) we removed duplicates using the composite key (station, date, interval) [16]; (iv) we performed data imputation to fill in missing values in key variables [3, 18]; (v) we identified outliers in the data using the IQR method for each station, taking into account the natural variability in demand for the 13 stations [4, 14]; and (vi) we ensured that the temporal coverage of the data for each station was complete during the reviewed period [18]. The process retained 91.6% of validation records (1,302,310 → 1,192,697) and 92.3% of exit records (1,658,794 → 1,530,724), with no loss of station or time coverage. The resulting demand distribution and hourly profile are shown in Figs. 1 and 2. The cleaned data were then integrated with structural GTFS sources through a spatiotemporal joint on the composite key, incorporating scheduled headway as a supply proxy in the absence of real-time fleet telemetry [2]. Integration with the TransMilenio 2026 GTFS feed produced median headway values ranging from 96 s (Carrera 77, a high-frequency node) to 212 s (Carrera 53 and Escuela Militar), yielding a final integrated dataset of 493,662 unique records across 20 columns [15].

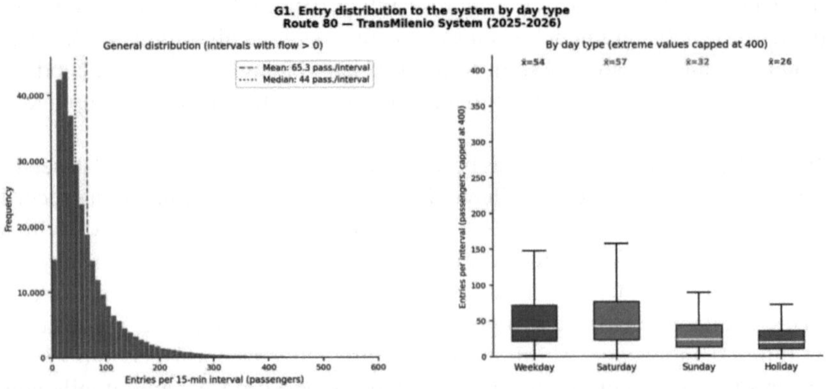

Fig. 1. Distribution System By: Day type - Route 80 2025–2026 (Own Elaboration)

Figure 2 shows the average hourly inflow pattern, broken down by day of the week on the left and by station on weekdays on the right. The profile follows the typical morning and evening peak structure commonly seen in urban BRT systems, as observed along. Troncal 80 during 2025–2026.

2.2 Variable Engineering and Preprocessing

Twelve input variables were selected using a preliminary importance analysis with Random Forest (See Table 1) [7]. Categorical variables were encoded using *Label Encoding* supervised by frequency of occurrence; all variables were standardized using *StandardScaler* trained exclusively on the training set, ensuring that the validation and test sets

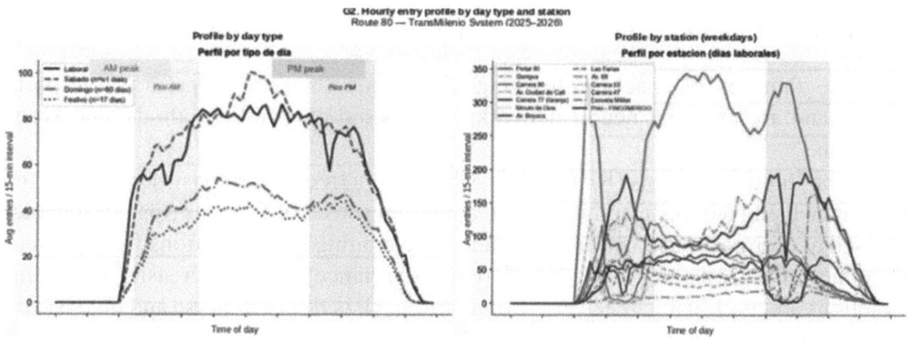

Fig. 2. Hourly entry profile by day type and station (Own Elaboration)

are only transformed—never trained—to prevent information leakage [8]. The goal is to find out how many Every 15 min, the number of people getting on and off at each station.

We used Random Forest to find the twelve most important features (see Table 1).

Table 1. Input Features

Variable	Type	Description
Encoded station ID	Spatial	Frequency-encoded station code (0–12)
Ordinal corridor position	Spatial	Station position along the corridor (0–12)
15-min interval index	Temporal	Interval number within the day (0–95)
Day of week	Temporal	0 = Monday through 6 = Sunday
Day-type encoding	Temporal	Weekday, Saturday, Sunday, public holiday
Time-period encoding	Temporal	Night, AM peak, off-peak, PM peak
Passenger egress	Operational	Alighting passengers per interval
Net passenger flow	Operational	Boardings minus alightings
Boarding/alighting ratio	Operational	Capture vs. dispersal at each station
Previous-interval boardings	Autoregressive	Boardings in the immediately preceding interval
Scheduled headway	Operational	Planned gap between consecutive buses (seconds)
Vehicle capacity	Operational	Passenger capacity of the assigned vehicle

2.3 A Time-Based Strategy for Validating

A rigorous approach for time validation was employed to replicate actual deployment scenarios [8, 9]: training set. The validation used 315,891 records from January to September 2025 and 70,608 records from October to November 2025. choosing hyper-parameters; and a test set with 107,163 records from December 2025 to March 2026, just for last test. This strategy guarantees that learning isn't affected by subsequent observations. Cross-validation, on the other hand, mixes observations at random and allows time-sensitive data leak [10]. We used RandomizedSearchCV with three time folds on the training set to discover the optimum hyperparameters [11]. MAE, RMSE, R^2, and MAPE are all approaches to measure how well something works.

2.4 Machine Learning Models: Fundamentals and Configuration

The three families of machine learning algorithms selected to predict transportation demand are artificial neural networks, tree-based ensemble methods, and kernel regression.

For the Random Forests (RF) model, 200 decision trees were constructed. Each tree was trained using a bootstrap sample, and a random subset of features ($\log_2$ of the total) was used at each split. Predictions are made by averaging the predictions from all trees, rather than relying on a single one, which reduces variance without increasing bias. Since predictions are made using the average of all trees, RF is robust to noise and inconsistencies in the AFC validation data. The RF model underwent variable importance evaluation using Mean Decrease in Impurity (MDI). Each feature was assigned a normalized score and a ranking based on how much it contributed to the demand pattern. The trees grew without depth constraints, allowing the ensemble mechanism to fully control overfitting [15, 16].

RF and XGBoost (XGB) differ in that RF builds multiple trees in parallel, while XGB builds trees one at a time sequentially. Each successive tree is built to correct the errors of the previous tree. This tree-building method makes XGB suitable for the Troncal 80 corridor, where demand can vary by a considerable order of magnitude between adjacent stations. Regularization (learning rate $\lambda = 0.1$) was used to ensure that the model did not overfit too quickly. Importance was measured using normalized gain. Following [7], the model was built with 500 estimators, a maximum depth of 6, and $\gamma = 0.2$.

With SVR and its RBF kernel, rather than partitioning the feature space, a predictive function is fitted within a tolerance range (ε) around the training targets, and the support vectors are the only points outside this range that determine the prediction. The RBF kernel captures nonlinear relationships in demand, as the kernel function measures similarity using Euclidean distance in a standardized 12-dimensional space. A model with $C = 500$ means that the model's deviation is minimal, and given the characteristics of the dataset, this is appropriate. Considering the computational cost of SVR, training was performed on a smaller subset of the data, 80,000 records; in transportation demand forecasting, sensitivity analysis suggests that 20–25% subsampling adequately reflects the distribution of the original dataset when standardization is applied [17]. The chosen configuration was $C = 500$, $\gamma = 0.1$, and $\varepsilon = 1.0$.

The MLP predicts passenger flow using 12 input neurons, a single hidden layer with 128 neurons using ReLU, and 1 output neuron. The MLP was trained using backpropagation (BP) with the Adam optimizer to minimize the MSE (related to passenger flow) with L2 regularization ($\alpha = 0.01$) and early stopping as strategies to avoid overfitting. Despite its simple structure, the model was able to provide useful predictions because of domain knowledge.

Finally, LSTM was selected because it learns sequential dependencies using internal cell states and has three trainable gates—forget, input, and output—that control the flow of information and address the vanishing gradient problem in standard RNNs. The model uses a sliding window of 8 consecutive 15-min intervals (2 h of data) to predict the next arrival. The architecture has 64 hidden units, a dropout rate of 0.2, 32 fully connected units with ReLU, and a single-unit output layer. Training used Adam with a learning rate of 1×10^{-3} and early stopping. All of this was implemented in PyTorch 2.5.1 [34] and ran on an NVIDIA RTX 3060 with 12 GB of VRAM. Table 2 summarizes the model specifications.

Table 2. Model Configurations and Hyperparameters (Own Elaboration).

Model	Hyperparameters	Search	Hardware
Random forest	n_estimators = 200, max_features = log2, max_depth = None	RandomizedSearchCV 20 iter/three-fold	CPU
XGBoost	n_estimators = 500, lr = 0,1, max_depth = 6, subsample = 1,0, γ = 0,2	RandomizedSearchCV 20 iter/three-fold	CPU
SVR (RBF)*	C = 500, γ = 0,1, ε = 1,0	RandomizedSearchCV 10 iter/three-fold	CPU
MLP	hidden = (128,), ReLU, Adam, lr = 0,01, α = 0,01, batch = 1024	RandomizedSearchCV 15 iter/three-fold	CPU
LSTM	LSTM(64), Dropout(0,2), Dense(32), SEQ = 8, lr = 1e-3	Manual + Parada anticipada	GPU RTX 3060

3 Analysis of Results

This section presents each of the results obtained for each model, along with their evaluation and analysis based on the case study

3.1 Random Forest

On the test set, the Random Forest model gets MAE = 1.188, RMSE = 3.092, R^2 = 0.9979, and MAPE = 4.89%. The MDI feature importance analysis (Fig. 3) shows that previous interval inflows make up 31.1% of the total predictive capacity, which backs up Most of the short-term operational autocorrelation is caused by calendar factors [5, 12]. Next comes passenger exits (14.6%), the inflow/exit ratio (13.6%), and net flow (13.5%). Each calendar variable contributes less than 0.7%. There is no systematic bias because the residual distribution (Fig. 3) is symmetrical around zero (mean = 0.15 pass./interval). Prejudice. The MAE varies by station, from 0.18 at Escuela Militar (low demand) to 4.98 at Portal 80 (high demand) (Fig. 4).

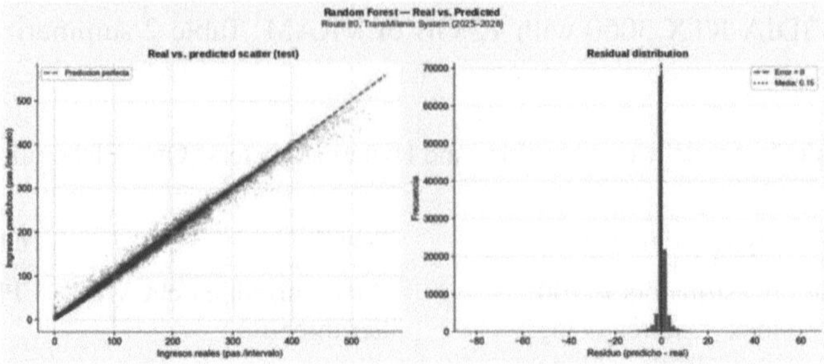

Fig. 3. Random Forest (Real vs. Predicted) (Own Elaboration)

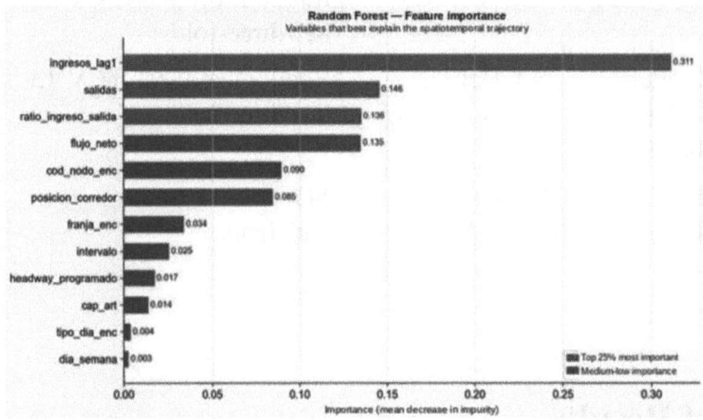

Fig. 4. Random Forest (Features importance) (Own Elaboration)

All 13 stations achieved R^2 values greater than 0.995. The model estimated an average residual of 0.15 passengers per interval during the test period from December 2025 to February 2026 (Fig. 5), with the previous interval's ridership driving 31.1% of the predictive power, while the calendar variables each contributed less than 0.7%. Portal 80, as expected, had the highest absolute error, given that it is the busiest node in the corridor.

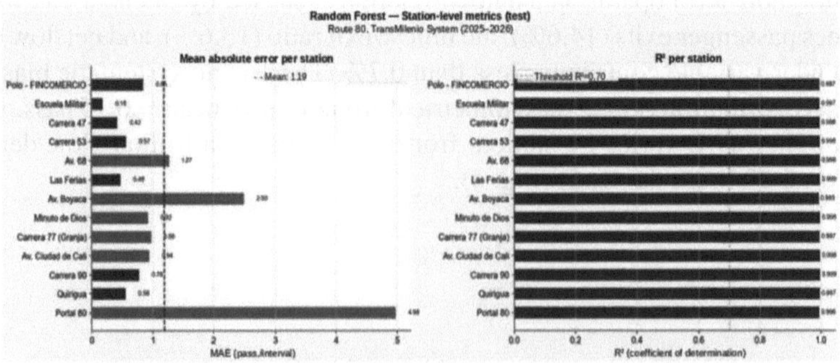

Fig. 5. Station Level Metrics (test) (Own Elaboration)

3.2 XGBoost

XGBoost is better than Random Forest on all global measures: MAE = 1.013, RMSE = 2.526, $R^2 = 0.9986$, and MAPE = 4.07%. We already know that gradient boosting is better than bagging when the demand distributions are different, and this is in line with that [13]. When it comes to feature relevance, Fig. 6 shows that prior interval inflows (64.8%) are the most important thing. The normalized gain in RF is 31.1%, which means that the sequential boosting process makes use of short-term autocorrelation. more effectively by assigning consecutive trees to progressively fix residuals that are related to demand modifications. The drop in errors compared to RF is the same for all time periods, with the biggest change. The Mean Absolute Error (MAE) for XGBoost was 1.53 during the PM peak, and the MAE for Random Forest was 1.81. By station, Avenue. Boyacá is the most obvious better (MAE: 1.56 vs. RF: 2.50) (Fig. 7).

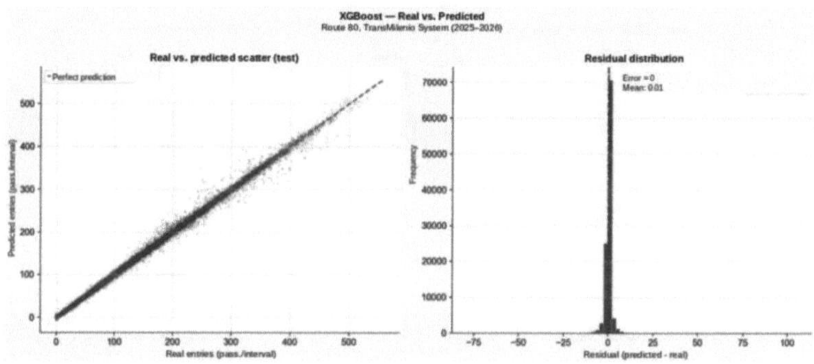

Fig. 6. XGBoost: The difference between the actual and expected spread and how the residuals are spread out. There are 0.01 events on average in each interval. (Own Elaboration)

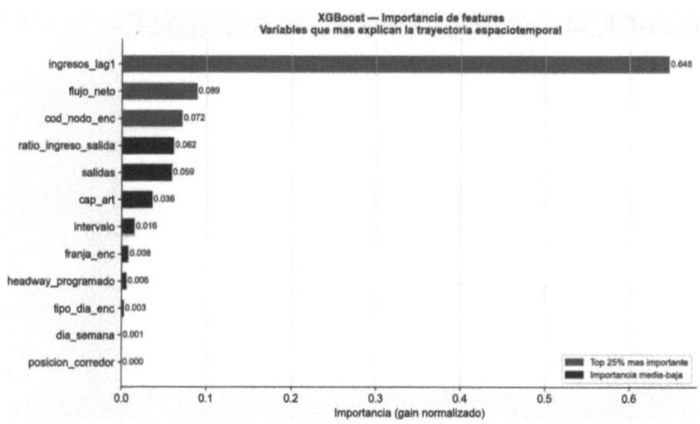

Fig. 7. XGBoost: A normalized gain of feature importance. The previous interval inflows were 64.8%, which means that RF used temporal autocorrelation more than RF did. (Own Elaboration)

3.3 Support Vector Regression

Model trained on 80,000 data points with parameters $C = 500$, $\gamma = 0.1$, and $\varepsilon = 1.0$ gets a Mean Absolute Error (MAE) of 0.449, a Root Mean Square Error (RMSE) of 0.584, and a R^2 value of 0.99992. The MAPE, or Mean Absolute Percentage Error, is 3.88%. SVR does better than both RF and XGBoost on all metrics, even though it only uses 23% of the full training dataset standards. This result shows that the RBF kernel is good at showing smooth, non-linear demand relationships in the normal twelve-dimensional feature space [14]. The residuals' distribution (Fig. 9) is almost Gaussian and centered at (−0.04 pas./interval) (Fig. 8), which means there is no clear bias. $R^2 \geq 0.997$ is correct for 12 out of 13 stations. The low value at Escuela Militar ($R^2 = 0.997$) is because its low-demand profile changes a lot compared to stations (Fig. 9).

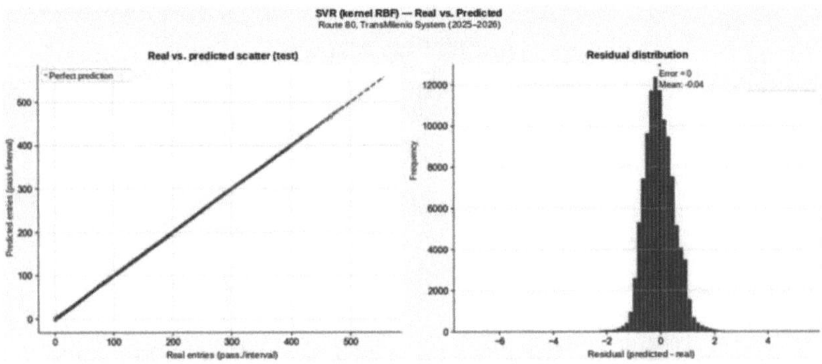

Fig. 8. Actual vs. predicted dispersion (Own Elaboration)

The first three models (Fig. 9) show that SVR does always better than the others, especially in the morning rush hour, the MAE model has a mean absolute error (MAE) of 0.50, XGBoost has a mean absolute error of 1.29, and Random Forest (RF) has a mean absolute error of 1.54.

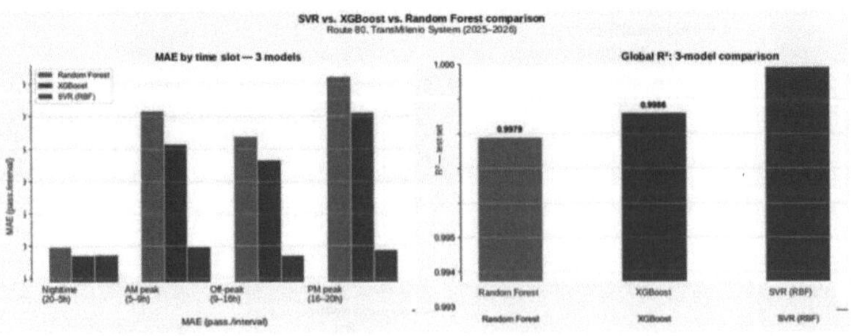

Fig. 9. Mean Absolute Error for SVR, XGBoost, and Random Forest (Own Elaboration)

3.4 Multilayer Perceptron (MLP)

The MLP design has 128 hidden neurons and uses ReLU activation, Adam optimization, and a learning rate of 0.01. It converges in 23 iterations with early stopping. The best overall performance in this study was MAE = 0.011 pass/interval, RMSE = 0.043, $R^2 = 0.9999996$, and 0.089% of the Mean Absolute Percentage Error (MAPE). The MLP is the most efficient model because it only has 1,664 trainable parameters [15, 16]. The model architecture shows that generalization is not compromised, as the training and validation losses are almost perfectly aligned. The predicted versus actual values (Fig. 10) demonstrate good performance with demand ranging from 0 to 573 trips per interval, without any systematic bias. For all static models, the MLP captured between 31% and 65% of the predictive power due to the previous interval inputs, and 11 out of 13 stations achieved an R^2 of 1.000.

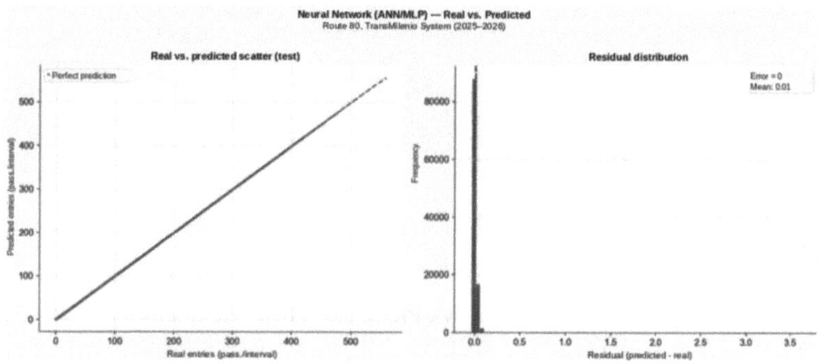

Fig. 10. Real vs. predicted, dispersion virtually perfect across the entire demand range (0–573 pass/interval). Average residuals: 0.01 pass/interval (Own Elaboration)

The model's highest Mean Absolute Error (MAE) at 0.026 pass/interval is shown in Portal 80. This is not important for operational purposes (Fig. 11).

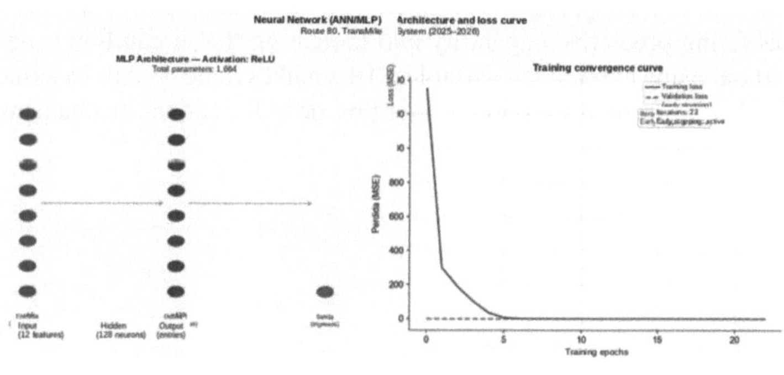

Fig. 11. There are 12 inputs, 128 hidden neurons that use ReLU activation, and one output in the MLP architecture. It also has the curve for training convergence. (Own Elaboration)

3.5 Long Short-Term Memory (LSTM)

With an RTX GPU and PyTorch 2.5.1 [17], we made the LSTM model (64 units, Dropout = 0.2, Dense (32), SEQ = 8). The model speeds up by 3060 and converges in 91 epochs (8.73 min of training time). The Mean Absolute Error (MAE) is 11.224 and the Root Mean Square Error (RMSE) is 22.915 $R^2 = 0.884$ and MAPE = 64.64%. The loss drops a lot in the first 20 epochs on the training curve. It stays the same after that the training and validation metrics came together, and the difference was less than 3%. This meant that overfitting was not an issue. The persistent undervaluation of demands surpassing 200 pass/interval (Fig. 12) signifies a structural inconsistency in the issue Formulation: static models use the whole 12-variable vector for the target interval, which includes variables from the past.

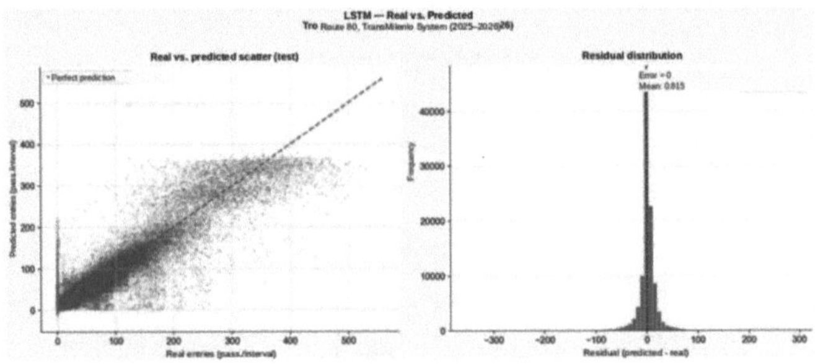

Fig. 12. LSTM – Real Vs Predicted (Own Elaboration)

Without seeing what is happening to the target instant, the LSTM is guessing what the inflows will be at time t + 1 based only on the 8-interval inflows-before t, which makes it very challenging to understand what time it is. The fast inflow changes at Portal 80 during high demand occur so quickly that the 2-h prediction cannot keep up. This is the historical context that explains the numerous errors at the busy stations, which is why the Mean Absolute Error (MAE) is between 3.61 and 36.09 passengers per interval. Although the LSTM is ranked lowest in global metrics, it does achieve an impressive score of 0.884 on R2, demonstrating predictive capability and indicating that it can find time-dependent patterns without using explicit lag variables. This makes it the default baseline model for any structural enhancements based on attention or bidirectional mechanisms (Fig. 13) [13, 18].

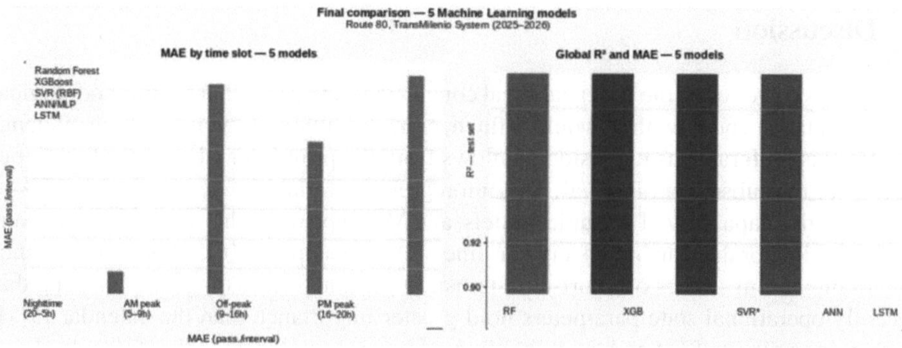

Fig. 13. The last five models are compared by their Mean Absolute Error over time and their global R^2/Mean Absolute Error. Final panel of the comparison study. (Own Elaboration)

3.6 Computational Cost

Tests were conducted on an Intel Core i9-10900X (3.70 GHz, without a GPU). The following metrics were recorded: training time, dataset size, full inference on 107,163 test records, latency (ms) per observation, and real-time tuning (900 s, 15-min window). All static models met the real-time targets. SVR (the slowest, on 80,000 records) trained in 17,363 ms, within 2% of the window. LSTM required a GPU (RTX 3060) to be viable; XGBoost inference was not comparable due to the network but was expected to perform well.

For a 13-station route with 15-min intervals, the static models handled the workloads well. Scalability to the full TransMilenio network (over 140 stations, over 15 routes) implies approximately a five-fold increase in network load, along with the need for regular retraining, increased pipeline robustness, and fault tolerance. MLP is the best option for deployment across the entire network: it has the fastest training time (43 s on CPU), the lowest latency per observation (4.8 μs), and does not require a GPU (Table 3).

Table 3. Metrics for the Test Set (December 2025 – febrero 2026) to use as a reference.

Model	MAE	RMSE	R^2	MAPE (%)	Parameters	Hardware
Random forest	1,188	3,092	0,9979	4,89	200 trees	CPU
XGBoost	1,013	2,526	0,9986	4,07	500 stimators	CPU
SVR (RBF)*	0,449	0,584	0,99992	3,88	4.360 SVs	CPU
MLP	0,011	0,043	0,9999996	0,089	1.664	CPU
LSTM	11,224	22,915	0,8844	64,64	22.081	GPU RTX 3060

*SVR learned from 80,000 records. (Own Elaboration)

4 Discussion

The results corroborate the four analytical conclusions and prove that the methodological decisions taken and how they would influence the execution of the project are evident.

MLP is preferable as it considers inflows from the prior interval as part of the input vector for the subsequent interval. The autoregressive variable accounts for 31–65% of the predictive capability of all static models, and MLP leverages this data due to a universal approximator that can model any non-linear relationships [3, 16]. This result matches the findings from studies on short-term transport demand forecasting, emphasizing that recently operational state parameters hold greater importance than the calendar [5]. It also exerts a direct effect on how it functions: for any operator intending to apply short-horizon demand forecasting on a BRT route, the most crucial data engineering decision is ensuring that the inflow count for the most recent period is available.

Fourth, XGBoost is always better than RF for all stations and all time periods. This validates the assertion that sequential boosting outperforms bootstrap aggregation when the target variable is not uniformly distributed. This is a natural segment of a corridor where Portal 80 receives inflows every interval that are up to 10 times higher than those of Escuela Militar [4]. XGBoost's regularization inhibits trees from overly fitting to the demand trends of a specific locality. The RF method of averaging to reduce variation fails to perform in scenarios where demand is highly variable across different stations.

Third place goes to SVR, despite it training only 23% of the data research confirms that the RBF kernel models the smooth non-linear demand relationships in the standardized feature space [14]. The benefit of sampling in this case is attributed to the nature of SVR that provides a predictive function determined solely by support vectors irrespective of the size of the training data. The problem of using a training data of n size in the systems with a lot of data is that the training takes $O(n^2)$ time [19].

In a temporal and spatial perspective, the fourth point, looking at the errors, the discrepancies among the spatial stations are greater compared to the discrepancies across the temporal intervals for all models. It indicates that the topological characteristics of the corridor, in terms of relative position, as a collecting or distributing node, and demand density, are more influential on the predictive challenge than the time of the day cycle [20, 21]. The explanation for high MAPE for all models during nighttime is related to the presence of some denominators which are close to zero and this does not indicate that the predicted values are not relevant [22].

5 Conclusions

This study offers the first fully documented analysis of five machine learning models from three different algorithmic families, applied to the spatiotemporal prediction of passenger demand, that TransMilenio BRT Trunk Line 80, using a fine-grained operational dataset, and under a rigorous time-frame validation to mimic real-world implementation circumstances.

Of the static models, the MLP proved to be the most successful in real time settings ($MAE = 0.011$, $R^2 = 0.9999996$, 4.8 μs/observation), and only required CPU processing and 1,664 parameters, which allowed it to be operationally deployed in real time settings, without specialized processing units. XGBoost provided a highly accurate prediction ($R^2 = 0.9986$) and offered insightful and interpretable classification of features through normalized gain, which makes it the most suitable choice for operational diagnostic and explainable AI tasks. SVR operated successfully with smaller amounts of historical data ($R^2 = 0.99992$) and offered a correct and viable choice when data records were scarce it was applied with proper input scaling.

In view of the above, LSTM performed poorly when compared with static models, but this is not a result of the model architecture. However, it is a result of a more complex prediction and a higher-order task in his study, which LSTM is trying to predict passenger demand without the data of the operational state of the target interval. This is a methodological distinction that should be noted in this study for the sake of clarity and should not be viewed as a negative aspect of recurrent architectures. Despite this, his R^2 of 0.884 is indicative of a significant level of performance given the challenges of unprocessed sequential input data.

The first operational conclusion centers on the prediction rank of the lagged input stream from previous intervals. In all the static models, this feature was ranked between 31% and 65% relative importance and, thus, shifted the primary engineering challenge from model selection to the quality of the data stream. The second conclusion notes that the model predictions during the morning and afternoon peak periods exhibit a systematically higher prediction error. This is a consequence of demand volatility that is beyond model design and requires the incorporation of additional data inputs like weather data, incident telemetry, and fleet-level data streams. The third conclusion notes that, in all cases, the intra-station variance exceeded the inter-window variance. In terms of demand, Portal 80 is the terminal that yielded the greatest absolute error in the network along with being the terminal with the highest demand.

Taking this into consideration, from an operational perspective, the MLP–XGBoost combination provides the optimal operational performance, with MLP designed for real-time low-latency inference capabilities and XGBoost designed to provide feature-level explanations and support anomaly detection. This combination provides the ability for transit operators to manage trade-offs between the predictive performance and level of explainability demanded by regulatory and planning stakeholders.

References

1. Institute for Transportation & Development Policy: EL ESTÁNDAR BRT [Online]. Institute for Transportation & Development Policy (2024) www.itdp.org
2. Panovski, D., Zaharia, T.: Real-time public transportation prediction with machine learning algorithms. In: Digest of Technical Papers - IEEE International Conference on Consumer Electronics (2020). https://doi.org/10.1109/ICCE46568.2020.9043077
3. Batini, C., Scannapieco, M.: Data and Information Quality. Springer (2016)
4. Soomro, K., Bhutta, M.N.M., Khan, Z., Tahir, M.A.: Smart city big data analytics: an advanced review. WIREs Data Mining Knowl. Discov. (2019). https://doi.org/10.1002/widm.1319
5. Zhang, H., Liu, Y., Shi, B., Jia, J., Wang, W., Zhao, X.: Analysis of spatial-temporal characteristics of operations in public transport networks based on multisource data. J. Adv. Transp. **2021** (2021). https://doi.org/10.1155/2021/6937228

6. Ali, R., Ali, A., Naeem, H.M.Y., Asad, M., Alsarhan, T., Bin Heyat, M.B.: A comprehensive survey of deep learning-based traffic flow prediction models for intelligent transportation systems. ICCK Trans. Adv. Comput. Syst. **1**(3), 117–137 (2025). https://doi.org/10.62762/tacs.2025.795448
7. Rodrigo, J.A.: Árboles de decisión, random forest, gradient boosting y C5.0 (2020)
8. Zhong, G., Yin, T., Li, L., Zhang, J., Zhang, H., Ran, B.: Bus travel time prediction based on ensemble learning methods. IEEE Intell. Transp. Syst. Mag. **14**(2), 174–189 (2022). https://doi.org/10.1109/MITS.2020.2990175
9. Hidalgo, D., Gutiérrez, L.: BRT and BHLS around the world: explosive growth, large positive impacts and many issues outstanding. Res. Transp. Econ. **39**(1), 8–13 (2013). https://doi.org/10.1016/J.RETREC.2012.05.018
10. TransMilenio, S.A.: Open Data Portal-Operational Records (2025)
11. Trajcevski, G., Cao, H., Scheuermann, P., Wolfson, O., Vaccaro, D.: On-line data reduction and the quality of history in moving objects databases. In: MobiDE 2006: Proceedings of the 5th ACM International Workshop on Data Engineering for Wireless and Mobile Access (2006). https://doi.org/10.1145/1140104.1140110
12. Ge, L., Voß, S., Xie, L.: Robustness and disturbances in public transport. Public Trans. **14**(1), 191–261 (2022). https://doi.org/10.1007/s12469-022-00301-8
13. Hastie, J.F.T., Tibshirani, R.: The elements of statistical learning: data mining, inference, and prediction. In: The Mathematical Intelligencer, vol. 27(2), 2nd edn. Springer, New York, NY, USA (2009)
14. García, S., Ramírez Gallego, S., Luengo, J., Herrera, F.: Big data: Preprocesamiento y calidad de datos. Novática. **237** (2016)
15. Lopez-Guayasamin, M.R., Duque-Mendez, N.D.: Alternativas de herramientas para facilitar el monitoreo de la calidad de datos. South Florida J. Dev. **3**(2) (2022). https://doi.org/10.46932/sfjdv3n2-026
16. Xu, C., Liu, P., Wang, W., Li, Z.: Evaluation of the impacts of traffic states on crash risks on freeways. Accid. Anal. Prev. **47**, 162–171 (2012). https://doi.org/10.1016/J.AAP.2012.01.020
17. Bhosle, N., Jagtap, J., Shivakrishna, D.: Comparative analysis of different machine learning techniques for travel mode prediction. In: 2024 Smart Cities Symposium Prague, SCSP 2024 - Proceedings. Institute of Electrical and Electronics Engineers Inc. (2024). https://doi.org/10.1109/SCSP61506.2024.10552724
18. Lee, C., Yoon, Y.: A novel bus arrival time prediction method based on spatio-temporal flow centrality analysis and deep learning. Electronics (Switzerland). **11**(12) (2022). https://doi.org/10.3390/electronics11121875
19. Lin, Y., Yang, X., Zou, N., Jia, L.: Real-time bus arrival time prediction: case study for Jinan, China. J. Transp. Eng. **139**(11), 1133–1140 (2013). https://doi.org/10.1061/(ASCE)TE.1943-5436.0000589
20. Forero-Corba, W., Bennasar, F.N.: Techniques and applications of machine learning and artificial intelligence in education: a systematic review. RIED-Revista Iberoamericana de Educacion a Distancia. **27**(1), 209–253 (2024). https://doi.org/10.5944/ried.27.1.37491
21. Yao, B., Ma, A., Feng, R., Shen, X., Zhang, M., Yao, Y.: A deep learning framework about traffic flow forecasting for urban traffic emission monitoring system. Front. Public Health. **9** (2022). https://doi.org/10.3389/fpubh.2021.804298
22. Kurani, A., Doshi, P., Vakharia, A., Shah, M.: A comprehensive comparative study of artificial neural network (ANN) and support vector machines (SVM) on stock forecasting. In: Annals of Data Science, vol. 10, pp. 183–208. Springer (2023). https://doi.org/10.1007/s40745-021-00344-x
23. Zhao, Z., Chen, W., Wu, X., Chen, P.C.Y., Liu, J.: LSTM network: a deep learning approach for short-term traffic forecast. IET Intell. Transp. Syst. **11**(2), 68–75 (2017). https://doi.org/10.1049/iet-its.2016.0208

24. Chawla, P., et al.: Real-time traffic congestion prediction using big data and machine learning techniques. World J. Eng. **21**(1) (2024). https://doi.org/10.1108/WJE-07-2021-0428
25. Li, L., Li, X.: Parsimonious trajectory design of connected automated traffic. Transp. Res. B. Methodol. **119**, 1–21 (2019). https://doi.org/10.1016/J.TRB.2018.11.006
26. Saini, A.: Guide on Support Vector Machine (SVM) Algorithm. Analytics Vidhya (2024)
27. Russell, S.J., Norvig, P.: Artificial Intelligence-A Modern Approach, 4th edn. CreateSpace Independent Publishing Platform (2020)
28. Su, S., Zhou, H., Xu, M., Ru, H., Wang, W., Weng, M.: Auditing street walkability and associated social inequalities for planning implications. J. Transp. Geogr. **74**, 62–76 (2019). https://doi.org/10.1016/J.JTRANGEO.2018.11.003
29. García-Palomares, J.C., Gutiérrez, J., Latorre, M.: Optimizing the location of stations in bike-sharing programs: a GIS approach. Appl. Geogr. **35**(1–2), 235–246 (2012). https://doi.org/10.1016/j.apgeog.2012.07.002
30. Kakarla, A., Munagala, V.S.K.R., Ishizaka, T., Fukuda, A., Jana, S.: Travel time prediction and route performance analysis in BRTS based on sparse GPS data. In: IEEE Vehicular Technology Conference. Institute of Electrical and Electronics Engineers Inc. (2021). https://doi.org/10.1109/VTC2021-Spring51267.2021.9448832
31. Ghazal, T.M., et al.: IoT for smart cities: machine learning approaches in smart healthcare—a review. Future Internet. **13**, 218 (2021). https://doi.org/10.3390/fi13080218

Policy Recommendations for Promoting the Utilization of Economic Partnership Agreements (EPAs) in Japan: Insights from Singapore's Initiatives to Enhance the Use of Free Trade Agreements (FTAs) and EPAs

Masahiro Ishikawa[1](✉), Zen Kawada[2], and Shun Inoue[2]

[1] Department of Business and Marketing Strategy, Kindai University, 3-4-1, Kowakae, Higashi-Osaka City, Osaka Prefecture, Japan
mishikawa@bus.kindai.ac.jp
[2] NTT DATA Japan Corporation, Tokyo, Japan

Abstract. This study compares policies and institutional frameworks for promoting FTA/EPA utilisation in Singapore and Japan. Singapore is identified as one of the most advanced countries in FTA utilisation promotion, supported by a wide FTA network and a coordinated system of government agencies such as MTI, Enterprise Singapore, SME Centres, the Singapore Business Federation, and Singapore Customs. These institutions collectively provide structured guidance, financial support, advisory services, and digital tools (DX), enabling firms to identify applicable FTAs, understand rules of origin, and reduce administrative burdens. As a result, FTA awareness and perceived benefits among firms are relatively high, although challenges remain, particularly for SMEs in understanding rules of origin and managing certification processes.

In contrast, Japan also provides extensive institutional support through METI, JETRO, the SME Agency, Customs, and the Japan Chamber of Commerce and Industry. However, firm-level studies and consultation cases reveal persistent operational challenges, including complex origin determination due to large numbers of components, difficulties in obtaining supplier declarations, and HS code classification inconsistencies across countries. These issues can lead to rejection of preferential tariff treatment despite existing FTAs.

The study highlights that a key bottleneck in both countries is the administrative complexity of rules of origin and HS classification, especially under CTC-based origin determination. It concludes that future improvements—particularly through the use of digital technologies such as AI to support classification and origin determination—could significantly enhance FTA/EPA utilisation by firms.

Keywords: FTA/EPA utilisation promotion · Institutional frameworks · Government agencies coordination · Trade policy

D. Liberona et al. (Eds.): MISNC 2026, CCIS 3092, pp. 152–164, 2027.
https://doi.org/10.1007/978-3-032-33381-0_12

1 Introduction

Free Trade Agreement (FTA) s and Economic Partnership Agreement (EPA) s are agreements that promote the liberalization and facilitation of trade and investment with the aim of strengthening broad economic relations. Japan has promoted EPAs which include a wider range of sectors. Similar to Japan's EPAs, some of the FTAs which have been concluded around the world in recent years include a variety of new areas that go beyond the elimination or reduction of tariffs and liberalization of trade in services [1].

An FTA is an agreement between specific countries or regions that aims to reduce or eliminate tariffs on goods and barriers to trade in services. An EPA is an agreement that, in addition to trade liberalization, aims to strengthen a wide range of economic relations, including rule-making in areas such as investment, the movement of natural persons, intellectual property protection, and competition policy, as well as cooperation in various fields [1].

As of March 3, 2026, Japan has concluded 22 EPAs, of which 20 have entered into force [1]. On the other hand, Singapore has implemented 29 FTAs as of March 18 2026 [2].

2 Literature Review

Studies on firm-level FTA utilization—namely, those analyzing the extent to which Singaporean firms actually use FTAs and which industries benefit from them—include the following. Low & Khoo analyzed the impact of FTAs on the construction industry and, through firm-level surveys (questionnaires and interviews), examined the opportunities and constraints brought about by FTAs [3]. According to a survey conducted by the Singapore Business Federation (SBF) targeting approximately 800 firms, which analyzed the state of FTA awareness and utilization, 73% of companies reported experiencing improved market access as a result of FTAs [4]. According to 2025 media reports, a firm-level survey conducted by the National University of Singapore (NUS) and others found that only about 30% of companies obtain certificates of origin (ROO), and that in the manufacturing sector there are also many cases where FTAs cannot be applied [5].

Studies on the determinants of and barriers to FTA utilization—namely, those analyzing the factors that influence whether firms use FTAs—include the following. Thangavelu et al. analyzed the utilization rate of the ASEAN-Australia-New Zealand Free Trade Area (AANZFTA) and identified the preferential margin as a key determinant of its use [6]. In studies on FTA utilization in Asia by Hamanaka, it is argued that although utilization rates appear low, they are in fact higher when MFN zero-tariff products are excluded, pointing out a measurement bias issue [7]. Takahashi and Urata pointed out that obstacles to FTA utilization include the cost of obtaining certificates of origin, a lack of knowledge about FTAs, and the limited tariff benefits [8].

Studies on policies and institutions—namely, those analyzing government mechanisms to promote FTA utilization and their effectiveness—include the following. Alvstam et al. analyzed the gap between institutional frameworks and firm-level practices, using the EU–Singapore FTA as a case study [9]. The Ministry of Trade and Industry (MTI) and Enterprise Singapore, in their policy and operational reports, position FTAs as a foundation for market access and investment promotion [2].

3 Measures, Institutional Frameworks, and Programs Implemented by the Singapore Government and Related Agencies to Promote the Utilization of FTAs/EPAs

3.1 Ministry of Trade and Industry (MTI)

The Ministry of Trade and Industry (MTI) of Singapore views FTAs as a foundation for expanding market access and promoting investment, and as infrastructure that supports firms' internationalisation. Accordingly, it considers the actual utilisation of FTAs by firms to be more important than their mere conclusion. In fact, MTI explicitly states that the effectiveness of FTAs should be evaluated based on the extent to which firms derive benefits from them [10].

Specifically, MTI provides firms with structured procedures and practical manuals for FTA utilisation, aiming to address the problem that FTAs are often perceived as too complex to use [11]. In this context, MTI outlines a typical step-by-step process for utilising FTAs as follows:

1. Identify the applicable FTA for the target market;
2. Determine the HS code of the product;
3. Confirm the preferential tariff margin;
4. Verify compliance with the rules of origin;
5. Obtain a Certificate of Origin (CO) or make a self-certification;
6. Claim preferential treatment at customs.

In addition, recognizing firms' lack of knowledge as the most significant barrier, the MTI, in collaboration with Enterprise Singapore and the Singapore Business Federation (SBF), conducts seminars, workshops, one-to-one advisory services, and industry-specific briefings, providing FTA-related training to thousands of companies.

In Singapore, the utilisation of FTAs by small and medium-sized enterprises (SMEs) is regarded as a particular challenge. As part of its efforts to increase the number of "FTA-ready firms," policies have been implemented such as free advisory services at SME Centres, firm-level diagnostics to assess FTA utilisation potential, and the integration of overseas expansion support with FTA utilisation.

3.2 Enterprise Singapore

Enterprise Singapore is a government agency under the Ministry of Trade and Industry (MTI) that supports the growth and internationalisation of Singapore-based companies. The Enterprise Singapore focuses not on the mere conclusion of FTAs/EPAs, but on enabling firms to actually utilise them in practice, by implementing multi-layered measures centered on practical support, capacity building, and institutional support.

One of the key initiatives of the agency is the FTA search and navigation tool "Find a Free Trade Agreement (FTA)", which enhances the "visibility" of FTAs. Through this tool, firms can immediately identify which FTAs are applicable to them, thereby supporting the identification of relevant partner countries and agreements [12]. Enterprise Singapore also provides guidelines and practical manuals—such as step-by-step guides to FTA utilisation, explanations of rules of origin (ROO), and instructions on how to apply preferential tariff reductions—thereby reducing institutional complexity and concretising how FTAs can be used in practice.

A second key initiative of the agency is the Market Readiness Assistance (MRA) grant, which provides financial support to firms. This scheme subsidises the costs of FTA-related consulting for Singapore companies and supports their overseas expansion. The consulting services covered include opportunity analysis based on FTAs, supply chain analysis, compliance with rules of origin, and the development of internal compliance systems. Through this scheme, the aim is to help firms transition from merely "understanding" FTAs to being able to "use" them effectively [13]. In addition, there is the Business Adaptation Grant (BizAdapt), a scheme that has been strengthened in recent years. This grant programme supports firms in responding to tariff changes and evolving trade conditions, enhancing FTA and trade compliance, and restructuring supply chains—thereby supporting firms' overall trade strategies, including the use of FTAs. For small and medium-sized enterprises (SMEs), it covers up to 50% of eligible costs [14].

The third major initiative of the agency is consulting and tailored support. Enterprise Singapore provides FTA-related consulting by experts, firm-specific diagnostics, and practical advice to individual companies. Specifically, it offers guidance on obtaining certificates of origin, selecting the most appropriate FTA, and conducting cost–benefit analyses, with the aim of directly addressing the barrier that firms find FTA schemes too complex to use.

The fourth major initiative of the agency is education and outreach. In collaboration with MTI and the Singapore Business Federation, it conducts seminars, workshops, and industry-specific briefings to address firms' lack of knowledge about FTAs.

The fifth major initiative of the agency involves leveraging its overseas office network and collaborating with global partners. This is not implemented as a standalone FTA support measure; rather, it is integrated with broader efforts such as overseas market development, investment promotion, and trade finance.

3.3 SME Centres

SME Centres are a network of around ten locations nationwide that provide free business advisory services, functioning as a "one-stop support hub" that assists approximately 25,000 companies annually [15].

At these centers, business advisors provide one-on-one consultations on FTA utilization, offering guidance on which FTAs are applicable, whether tariff reductions are available, the costs and benefits of using them, and whether firms can comply with rules of origin (ROO). They also conduct firm-specific diagnostics tailored to each company. Through these services, the centers directly address the key barriers to FTA use—namely, information gaps and the difficulty of making informed decisions.

In addition, it collaborates with Global Connect initiatives led by organizations such as the Singapore Business Federation (SBF) to provide FTA-related advice, market information, and partner-matching services [16].

SME Centres also undertake a range of initiatives to help firms become "FTA-ready." First, to address the barrier of insufficient knowledge about FTAs, they offer seminars on how to use FTAs, courses on complying with rules of origin (ROO), and workshops and training programs on trade practices. In addition, they conduct capability diagnostics to assess whether firms are able to utilize FTAs and to provide recommendations for improvement. These diagnostics analyze a firm's export capabilities, supply chain structure, and the potential applicability of FTAs.

A key role of SME Centres is to serve as an "entry point" to FTA-related support schemes. They connect firms to other government assistance programs, such as the Market Readiness Assistance (MRA), the Business Adaptation Grant, and various consulting support initiatives.

Since 2025, SME Centres have been strengthened and have evolved from simple advisory touchpoints into advanced support platforms, with expanded capabilities in providing specialised advisory services, addressing complex trade and FTA-related issues, and referring firms to external experts [15].

3.4 Singapore Business Federation (SBF)

The Singapore Business Federation (SBF) plays a crucial role in promoting the utilisation of FTAs/EPAs as a private-sector-led, practice-oriented intermediary that bridges the government—namely the MTI and Enterprise Singapore—and businesses. In particular, its core support is centered on GlobalConnect@SBF. SBF is a business federation representing over 30,000 companies. It is characterised by its dual role in both policy advocacy and practical support. In the context of FTA policy, it functions as an intermediary institution, providing hands-on support to firms while also feeding back business needs to the government to inform institutional improvements.

GlobalConnect@SBF is an internationalisation support platform, including FTA utilisation, jointly operated by the Singapore Business Federation (SBF) and Enterprise Singapore. Launched in 2019, it has supported thousands of companies and provides integrated assistance for overseas expansion and FTA utilisation, serving as a mechanism that connects FTAs to actual business opportunities [17].

One of the key support initiatives of SBF is its FTA Education & Outreach programme, which aims to enhance firms' understanding of FTAs through workshops, seminars, and the provision of guidebooks. This programme offers basic FTA education, explains the benefits of specific agreements, and provides industry-specific guidance on how FTAs can be utilized [18]. In addition, SBF provides a range of materials—such as FTA utilisation guidebooks, agreement-specific guides for frameworks like RCEP and CPTPP, and explanations of rules of origin (ROO)—thereby bridging the gap between institutional understanding and practical application.

A second key support initiative of SBF is its one-to-one advisory service. SBF provides firms with individual consultations on the feasibility of FTA utilisation, compliance with rules of origin, and analysis of tariff reduction benefits. Through this, it helps to overcome the common barrier of firms not knowing whether FTAs can be applied to their business It has also established a one-stop service point for FTA-related inquiries, providing integrated support for institutional questions, practical implementation, and problem-solving.

A third key support initiative of the Singapore Business Federation (SBF) is the integration of FTA support with broader internationalisation assistance. Through GlobalConnect@SBF, it provides market research, partner identification, business matching, and support for overseas expansion. This helps to create the very opportunities in which FTAs can be utilized [19].

A fourth key support initiative of the Singapore Business Federation (SBF) is network-based matching through the utilisation of its private-sector networks. By facilitating matching with overseas companies and introducing B2B platforms and investment opportunities, it aims to translate the market access improvements brought about by FTAs into actual business transactions.

A fifth key support initiative of the Singapore Business Federation (SBF) is its policy feedback function. SBF aggregates the views of businesses and communicates issues such as barriers to FTA utilisation, challenges related to rules of origin, and institutional complexity to the government, thereby contributing to institutional improvements and forming a policy feedback loop [18].

3.5 Singapore Customs

The Singapore Customs plays a central role in promoting the utilisation of FTAs/EPAs by overseeing their implementation, administration, and the simplification of procedures. While the Ministry of Trade and Industry (MTI) and Enterprise Singapore are responsible for policy and support, Singapore Customs provides the practical infrastructure that enables firms to actually apply FTAs in practice.

1. The core functions of Singapore Customs, as the authority responsible for making FTAs "usable in practice," can be broadly divided into three areas:
2. the administration and management of rules of origin (ROO);
3. the administration of the Certificate of Origin (CO) system; and the implementation of preferential tariff treatment (application of FTAs).

Specifically, Singapore Customs is the authority responsible for granting preferential tariff treatment [20]. By utilising FTAs, firms can reduce import costs through tariff reductions or elimination (including zero tariffs). Singapore Customs clarifies the conditions for preferential tariff treatment under each FTA and the relevant declaration procedures required to obtain such benefits.

In other words, it standardises the core process of FTA utilisation—verifying whether goods qualify as originating, obtaining a Certificate of Origin (CO) or making a self-certification [21], and declaring preferential treatment at the time of customs clearance—thereby reducing uncertainty in the use of FTAs. The "self-certification system" in FTAs is a mechanism that has been increasingly introduced in recent agreements, under which exporters or approved companies can certify the origin of their goods themselves and declare it on the invoice. This system reduces the cost of obtaining Certificates of Origin (CO), shortens processing time, and makes FTAs more accessible even for SMEs. As a result, it helps to alleviate one of the major barriers to FTA utilisation—namely, the cost of certification.

Singapore Customs administers the rules of origin (ROO) system and clarifies origin determination rules [22]—such as wholly obtained criteria and substantial transformation criteria (e.g., CTC, RVC)—so that firms can assess FTA eligibility in advance. It also administers the Certificate of Origin (CO) system, including the issuance and management of origin certificates. To prevent misuse and ensure the credibility of the system, it conducts oversight of proper utilisation through verification mechanisms.

Singapore Customs also promotes trade facilitation by adopting a risk-based approach to classify firms and by providing preferential treatment to compliant or trusted companies [23]. This leads to faster customs clearance, simplified procedures, and a reduction in compliance burdens. In turn, these measures help to lower the indirect costs associated with FTA utilisation.

4 Initiatives for Digital Transformation (DX) to Promote the Utilization of FTAs/EPAs in Singapore

4.1 Enterprise Singapore

With regard to the digitalisation (DX) of FTA/EPA utilisation in Singapore, Enterprise Singapore provides tools such as Tariff Finder and Find an FTA [12]. These tools enable firms to search for tariff rates, rules of origin, and applicable FTAs, as well as to compare multiple FTAs. By doing so, they help to resolve the problem of firms not knowing which FTA can be used and accelerate decision-making in selecting the most appropriate agreement.

In addition, Enterprise Singapore provides FTA portals and digital guides that present the utilisation process online (HS code → rules of origin → Certificate of Origin) and organise the differences among agreements.

At Enterprise Singapore, business advisory services have also been digitalised, with FTA-related consultations conducted online and virtual advisory services being provided. In addition, the data collected is utilised for market analysis and FTA opportunity analysis.

4.2 Singapore Customs

At Singapore Customs, electronic customs systems enable the digital application for Certificates of Origin (CO) and the electronic declaration of FTA preferences. This has led to shorter processing times and the realisation of paperless procedures. The issuance of electronic Certificates of Origin (e-CO) further enhances procedural efficiency, while self-certification of origin can also be declared electronically on invoices.

In addition, the TradeNet system serves as a single-window platform that integrates import and export procedures, thereby simplifying processes and reducing the administrative burden on firms. Furthermore, advance rulings on HS classification and origin determination can be applied for online, contributing to the digitalisation of advance rulings and reducing uncertainty [24].

5 Measures, Institutional Frameworks, and Programs Implemented by the Japanese Government and Related Agencies to Promote the Utilization of FTAs/EPAs

5.1 Ministry of Economy, Trade and Industry (METI)

METI promotes and designs EPA/FTA policy by pursuing the negotiation and conclusion of agreements, simplifying and enhancing the transparency of rules of origin, and introducing self-declaration (self-certification) systems, with the aim of making EPAs easier to use.

In addition, as part of its policies to promote EPA utilisation, METI sets increasing utilisation rates as a policy objective and implements the EPA Utilisation Promotion Support Programme, which particularly strengthens support for small and medium-sized enterprises (SMEs). It also provides information by publishing explanatory materials, practical manuals, and case studies on EPA utilization [25].

5.2 Small and Medium Enterprise Agency (SMEA)

The Small and Medium Enterprise Agency (SMEA) is an external bureau of the Ministry of Economy, Trade and Industry (METI) and is a government agency that supports the growth, development, and business stability of small and medium-sized enterprises and micro enterprises, which account for more than 99% of all companies.

As part of its FTA/EPA utilisation promotion policies, the SMEA implements support measures that address resource constraints faced by SMEs, including subsidies for overseas expansion and assistance in trade-related operations.

In addition, in cooperation with local chambers of commerce and industry associations, it has established a nationwide support network that provides consultation services at the regional level.

5.3 Japan External Trade Organization (JETRO)

The Japan External Trade Organization (JETRO) is an independent administrative institution under the jurisdiction of the Ministry of Economy, Trade and Industry (METI), established to promote trade and investment between Japan and other countries.

JETRO maintains an EPA/FTA database and provides World Tariff, a tool that enables firms to check general tariff rates as well as preferential tariff rates under FTAs/EPAs by country, thereby visualising which EPAs are available for use [26].

JETRO also places strong emphasis on individual consultation and advisory services, assigning EPA specialists and offering free consultations on EPA-related matters, including support for the application of rules of origin. In particular, it has strengthened support for small and medium-sized enterprises (SMEs).

In addition, it organises seminars and training programmes on EPAs to enhance knowledge and understanding of their utilisation.

Furthermore, although not limited specifically to EPA-related initiatives, JETRO also provides market information, business matching platforms, and trade fair information. Through these services, it promotes the utilisation of EPAs while simultaneously supporting firms' broader overseas business expansion.

5.4 Japan Customs

Japan Customs provides an advance ruling system for HS classification and rules of origin. It also operates the electronic customs system NACCS, which enhances the speed and transparency of customs clearance procedures.

In addition, it manages an EPA rule of origin portal site that enables users to search and view rules of origin across multiple EPAs in a cross-sectional manner [27]. The EPA Origin Center also provides consultation services, particularly for EPAs that adopt self-certification systems [28].

5.5 Japan Chamber of Commerce and Industry (JCCI)

Japan Chamber of Commerce and Industry (JCCI) is the issuing authority for certificates of origin under Japan's third-party certification system for EPAs.

To obtain a certificate of origin, firms must first register with the Japan Chamber of Commerce and Industry. After registration, they submit a request for a determination of originating status for the relevant export products in order to use the EPA.

When submitting this request, firms are required to attach supporting documents such as a comparison table in the case of the tariff classification change criterion, or a calculation worksheet in the case of the value-added criterion.

Once the Japan Chamber of Commerce and Industry completes the determination of originating status, a reference (determination) number is issued. Using this number, firms can then apply for the issuance of a certificate of origin. Applications are submitted through the Japan Chamber of Commerce and Industry's electronic issuance system.

6 Factors That Hinder Companies from Utilizing FTAs/EPAs, and Cases of Problems Encountered When Using them

We examine the factors that hinder Japanese companies from utilizing FTAs/EPAs, as well as cases of problems encountered in their use, based on examples submitted to the consultation desk of the Japan External Trade Organization (JETRO).

6.1 It Is Difficult to Determine Originating Status Due to the Excessively Large Number of Parts

There are many product numbers within our company. If the product numbers differ, is it necessary to carry out a separate determination of originating status for each product number? Does this differ depending on whether the value-added (VA) criterion or the CTC criterion is applied? If the CTC criterion is applicable, is it acceptable to conduct the determination of originating status collectively for each item?

6.2 We Are Unable to Obtain Cooperation from Suppliers in Preparing Supplier Declarations

Under the rules for determining originating status, there is a case where the CTC (tariff classification change) rule is applied to certain export products, but some of the inputs do not undergo a change in tariff classification compared to the exported goods. Fortunately, those inputs are of Japanese origin. However, it has not been possible to obtain supplier declarations to prove this, as the suppliers are uncooperative.

6.3 How to Determine the HS Code of Materials

While the HS code of the final product can be confirmed through an advance ruling issued by the customs authority of the importing country, determining the HS codes of inputs is more challenging due to the large number of items involved. In addition, in some importing countries, advance rulings are available only for finished products and not for materials; Japan, for instance, also limits its advance ruling system to imported goods rather than inputs.

In such cases, how can firms obtain a reliable confirmation of the HS codes of materials? In order to avoid the risk that preferential tariff treatment under RCEP may be denied during post-clearance verification by the importing country's customs authority due to incorrect HS classification of inputs, what approach should be taken to secure certainty regarding the HS codes of materials?

6.4 Differences from Advance Ruling Cases in Japan

For imports from China into Japan, a Japanese advance ruling classifies the product under HS code 3824.99, whereas the Chinese authorities classify it under HS code 2842.90.4000. Although both 2842.90 and 3824.99 are subject to zero tariffs under the RCEP agreement, the preferential tariff treatment cannot be applied because the HS code indicated on the certificate of origin issued by the Chinese manufacturer does not match the HS code declared in the Japanese import customs declaration.

We have asked the manufacturer whether the certificate of origin could be issued using the HS code as classified by the importing country, but due to limitations in their issuance system, the certificate is automatically linked to HS code 2842 and cannot be changed to the requested 3824 classification.

6.5 A Discrepancy in the Number of Items Across Documents

A shipment of six wine products was exported from Japan to China. Among them, two red wine items and two white wine items were consolidated into one type of red wine and one type of white wine for the purpose of determining originating status. As a result, the preferential certificate of origin was issued for four items.

However, since the commercial invoice listed six items, Chinese customs stated that the RCEP preferential tariff treatment could not be applied due to the discrepancy in the number of items between the documents.

7 Conclusion

This study examined the policies, institutions, and measures implemented by the Government of Singapore and related agencies to promote the utilisation of FTAs/EPAs, and compared them with those of Japan. Singapore currently has 29 FTAs in force and is regarded as one of the most advanced countries in FTA utilisation promotion policy, both in terms of the breadth of its FTA network and the comprehensiveness of government support systems that underpin it.

Singapore places strong emphasis on the internationalisation of firms as a national strategy, and a wide range of institutions—including the Ministry of Trade and Industry, Enterprise Singapore, SME Centres, the Singapore Business Federation, and Singapore Customs—work in close coordination to implement various measures to promote FTA/EPA utilisation. In addition, Singapore has been actively pursuing digital transformation (DX)-based initiatives to facilitate FTA/EPA utilisation.

As a result, more than 70% of firms reportedly recognise the benefits of improved market access through FTAs, and FTA awareness has increased from 62% to 85%. However, challenges remain, particularly regarding insufficient understanding of rules of origin (ROO) and the administrative burden associated with obtaining and managing certification documents such as certificates of origin, especially for SMEs.

In Japan as well, case studies from consultations with JETRO reveal similar issues: a large number of components makes individual origin determination complex, parts suppliers often lack sufficient understanding, and supplier declarations confirming origin are difficult to obtain. In addition, many firms face challenges related to HS code classification of goods.

Not only is correct HS classification of final export products an issue, but when rules of origin are based on the change in tariff classification (CTC) criterion, firms must also identify the HS codes of all non-originating materials. When the number of components is large, this becomes a significant administrative burden.

In the future, if efficiency improvements can be achieved in HS classification and origin determination through the use of AI and other digital tools, the utilisation of EPAs by firms is likely to increase further.

References

1. Ministry of Foreign Affairs in Japan: Economic Partnership Agreement (EPA)/Free Trade Agreement (FTA) and Related Initiatives. https://www.mofa.go.jp/policy/economy/fta/index.html#:~:text=Economic%20Partnership%20Agreement%20(EPA)%20/,Agreement%20(FTA)%20and%20Related%20Initiatives. Accessed 15 Apr 2026
2. Ministry of Trade and Industry, Singapore: Free Trade Agreements (FTAs). https://www.mti.gov.sg/trade-international-economic-relations/agreements/free-trade-agreements-fta/. Accessed 15 Apr 2026
3. Low, S.S., June, S.Y.K.: Effects of free trade agreements (FTAs) on construction firms in Singapore (2008). https://ir.iba.edu.pk/businessreview/vol3/iss1/5/?utm_source=chatgpt.com. Accessed 15 Apr 2026
4. Singapore Business Federation (SBF): 3 in 4 Businesses Surveyed Benefitted from Improved Market Access through FTAs as Familiarity with FTAs Increased from 62% to 85%. SBF (2023) Accessed 15 Apr 2026

5. The Business Times: Trade Deals Offer Limited Value to Singapore Manufacturing Firms: Study. The Business Times (2025) Accessed 15 Apr 2026
6. Thangevalu, S., Narjoko, D., Urata, S.: FTA Utilisation and Impact of Regional Trade Agreements on Trade of ASEAN and Australia: AANZFTA (ASEAN-Australia-New Zealand Free Trade Agreement). Jeffrey Cheah Institute on Southeast Asia (2019) https://sunwayuniversity.edu.my/sites/default/files/publications/2023-11/jci-jsc-wp-2019-02-fta-utilisation-and-impact-of-aanzfta.pdf. Accessed 15 Apr 2026
7. Hamanaka, S.: A note on detecting biases in assessing the use of FTAs. J. Asian Econ. **29**, 24–32 (2013) https://www.sciencedirect.com/science/article/abs/pii/S1049007813000869?utm_source=chatgpt.com. Accessed 15 Apr 2026
8. Takahashi, K., Urata, S.: On the Use of FTAs by Japanese Firms: Further Evidence. Cambridge University Press (2017) https://www.cambridge.org/core/journals/business-and-politics/article/abs/on-the-use-of-ftas-by-japanese-firms-further-evidence/6AD6BC7EC9FB452E9C8F4D4235A7C73B. Accessed 15 Apr 2026
9. Claes G. Alvstam, Erja Kettunen, Patrik Ström: The service sector in the free-trade agreement between the EU and Singapore: closing the gap between policy and business realities. Asia. Eur. J. 15, 75–105 (2017). file:///C:/Users/ishik/Downloads/s10308-016-0464-z.pdf. Accessed 15 Apr 2026
10. Ministry of Trade and Industry, Singapore: Speech by Minister S Iswaran at the FTA Symposium 2019: Free Trade Agreements: 20 Years of Global Enterprise. Ministry of Trade and Industry. (2019). https://www.mti.gov.sg/newsroom/speech-by-minister-s-iswaran-at-the-fta-symposium-2019%2D%2Dfree-trade-agreements%2D%2D20-years-of-global-enterprise/?utm_source=chatgpt.com. Accessed 15 Apr 2026
11. Ministry of Trade and Industry, Singapore: All You Need to Know About Singapore's Free Trade Agreements and Digital Economy Agreements. Ministry of Trade and Industry, Singapore (2025) https://isomer-user-content.by.gov.sg/166/4de962a7-8f2d-4e06-8b9c-70a4923b84dc/FTA_A4_5th_Edition_v10_as_of_June_2025.pdf/. Accessed 15 Apr 2026
12. Enterprise Singapore: Find a Free Trade Agreement (FTA). https://www.enterprisesg.gov.sg/grow-your-business/go-global/international-agreements/free-trade-agreements/find-an-fta?utm_source=chatgpt.com. Accessed 15 Apr 2026
13. Ministry of Trade and Industry, Singapore: Understanding Trade in Goods and Rules of Origin under the RCEP, Benefits for Businesses. https://www.enterprisesg.gov.sg/-/media/esg/files/non-financial-assistance/for-companies/free-trade-agreements/rcep/rcep_trade_in_goods_benefits_for_businesses.pdf?utm_source=chatgpt.com. Accessed 15 Apr 2026
14. Allen & Gledhill: Allen & Gledhill Designated as Whitelisted Partner for Business Adaptation Grant Supporting Local Enterprises Impacted by Tariffs. Allen & Gledhill (2025) Accessed 15 Apr 2026
15. Enterprise Singapore Media Factsheet: SME Centres Enhanced to Be the Gateway for SMEs to Access Holistic Ecosystem of Business Support. Enterprise Singapore Media Factsheet (2025) https://www.enterprisesg.gov.sg/-/media/esg/files/media-centre/media-releases/2025/july/mr02827_sme-centres-enhanced-to-be-the-gateway-for-smes-to-access-holistic-ecosystem-of-business-support.pdf?utm_source=chatgpt.com. Accessed 15 Apr 2026
16. Enterprise Singapore: SME Centres. https://www.enterprisesg.gov.sg/about-us/contact-us?utm_source=chatgpt.com. Accessed 15 Apr 2026
17. Singapore Business Review: SBF Forges Initiative to Help Businesses Venture Globally. Singapore Business Review (2021) https://sbr.com.sg/economy/news/sbf-forges-initiative-help-businesses-venture-globally?utm_source=chatgpt.com. Accessed 15 Apr 2026
18. GlobalConnect@SBF: Learn FTA Education Outreach. https://globalconnect.sbf.org.sg/learn/fta-education-outreach/?utm_source=chatgpt.com. Accessed 15 Apr 2026

19. SBF Media Release, for immediate Release: SBF opens fourth Singapore Enterprise Centre (SEC) in Bengaluru to help Singapore (2025). https://www.sbf.org.sg/docs/default-source/about-us/press-release-sbf-opens-fourth-singapore-enterprise-centre-%28sec%29-in-bengaluru-to-help-singapore-businesses-tap-india-s-fast-growing-market.pdf?sfvrsn=37916ea6_1&utm_source=chatgpt.com. Accessed 15 Apr 2026
20. Singapore Customs: Claiming Preferential Tariff Treatment for Dutiable Imports. Singapore Customs (2026) https://www.customs.gov.sg/doing-business/import-operations/import-procedures/claiming-preferential-tariff-treatment-for-dutiable-imports/. Accessed 15 Apr 2026
21. Singapore Customs: Self Certification. Singapore Customs (2026) https://www.customs.gov.sg/doing-business/rules-of-origin/origin-documentation/self-certification/. Accessed 15 Apr 2026
22. Singapore Customs: Rules of Origin. Singapore Customs (2026) https://www.customs.gov.sg/doing-business/rules-of-origin/. Accessed 15 Apr 2026
23. Singapore Customs: Import/Export Facilitation Schemes. Singapore Customs (2026) https://www.customs.gov.sg/permits-and-licences/import-export-facilitation-schemes/. Accessed 15 Apr 2026
24. Singapore Customs: Application for Customs Ruling on Classification of Goods. Singapore Customs (2026) https://www.customs.gov.sg/doing-business/business-resources/hs-classification-of-goods/application-for-customs-ruling-on-classification-of-goods/. Accessed 15 Apr 2026
25. Ministry of Economy, Trade and Industry, Japan: EPAs, FTAs, and investment agreements. https://www.meti.go.jp/policy/trade_policy/epa/index.html. Accessed 15 Apr 2026
26. Japan External Organization (JETRO): EPA/FTA, WTO. https://www.jetro.go.jp/themetop/wto-fta/. Accessed 15 Apr 2026
27. Japan Customs: EPA rule of origin portal site. https://www.customs.go.jp/roo/. Accessed 15 Apr 2026
28. Japan Customs: EPA Origin Center. https://www.customs.go.jp/roo/9_leaflet_yusyutsusoudan.pdf. Accessed 15 Apr 2026

The Use of AI in Social Media and Daily Life

Modeling Radiologists' Intent in Head CT via Weak Supervision of Gaze Data

Jun Nakamura[1(✉)], Sanetake Nagayoshi[2], and Yoshinobu Ishiwata[3]

[1] Faculty of Global Management, Chuo University, Tokyo, Japan
jyulis.77f@g.chuo-u.ac.jp
[2] School of Informatics, Shizuoka University, Shizuoka, Japan
nagayoshi@inf.shizuoka.ac.jp
[3] Graduate School of Medicine, Yokohama City University, Yokohama, Kanagawa, Japan
ishi_y@yokohama-cu.ac.jp

Abstract. Estimating radiologists' latent cognitive intentions during medical image interpretation is challenging due to the lack of explicit ground-truth annotations. This study proposes a weakly supervised framework for modeling diagnostic intent using gaze sequence data collected during head CT interpretation. Eye-tracking data from radiologists with different levels of experience were transformed into temporally aligned tokens synchronized with CT slice transitions. Screen transition magnitude was quantified using the Structural Similarity Index Measure (SSIM), enabling implicit modeling of scrolling behavior without explicit slice indices.

Rule-based weak supervisory signals were constructed from observable gaze features, including fixation stability, saccadic dominance, Area of Interest (AOI) interactions, revisit patterns, and image transition magnitude (Δimage). Based on these heuristics, coarse intention states—search, evaluate, confirm, and skip—were assigned to each temporal segment. The resulting intention sequences were formulated as a first-order Markov process, and transition probabilities were estimated via maximum likelihood estimation to preserve interpretability grounded in empirical observations.

Comparative analysis across novice, mid-career, and expert radiologists revealed experience-dependent differences in temporal intention dynamics. Although based on a limited number of subjects, these findings suggest the potential of the proposed framework for capturing expertise-related cognitive patterns. Experts demonstrated rapid convergence toward confirmation with limited explicit evaluation phases, whereas novices exhibited prolonged search behavior and incomplete confirmation patterns.

The proposed framework provides an interpretable representation of diagnostic intention dynamics without manual annotation and demonstrates the feasibility of weak supervision for modeling radiological cognition. This study establishes a foundation for future integration with Transformer-based architectures to capture non-sequential dependencies in gaze behavior.

Keywords: Weak Supervision · Eye-Tracking · Head CT Interpretation · Intention Modeling · Markov Process · Radiological Expertise

D. Liberona et al. (Eds.): MISNC 2026, CCIS 3092, pp. 167–179, 2027.
https://doi.org/10.1007/978-3-032-33381-0_13

1 Gaze Sequence Data and Weakly Supervised Learning

Recent advances have demonstrated the feasibility of estimating human cognitive states and intentions using gaze sequence data. In exploratory and uncertain environments where explicit ground-truth labels are unavailable, rule-based and heuristic approaches under the framework of weak supervision have emerged as effective alternatives.

In medical imaging, gaze behavior analysis has long been investigated as an external proxy for expert decision-making processes. Early foundational work by Kundel et al. [1] demonstrated that radiological interpretation follows a global–focal search model, in which initial holistic perception is followed by focused verification of suspicious regions. This framework has provided a cognitive foundation for subsequent eye-tracking studies in radiology and supports the interpretation of gaze dynamics as reflections of underlying diagnostic intentions. Furthermore, research on inattentional blindness in radiology has shown that even trained experts may fail to consciously detect salient abnormalities if attentional allocation does not converge appropriately, highlighting the importance of modeling temporal attention structures in diagnostic reasoning [2].

Eye-tracking has been recognized as a valuable methodological tool with broad applications, including medical education and performance assessment [3, 4]. Zhong et al. [5] addressed the high cost of pixel-level annotation in medical image segmentation by introducing a weakly supervised framework leveraging gaze measurements. Specifically, pseudo-masks were generated from gaze heatmaps using multiple thresholds, and a multi-stage parallel training architecture was constructed. Experimental validation on polyp and prostate datasets demonstrated improved efficiency and competitive accuracy compared with conventional reduced-annotation approaches.

A recent systematic review [6] further examined the integration of eye-tracking and deep learning in medical image analysis. To address challenges such as data scarcity and the black-box nature of medical AI models, gaze data were proposed as weak supervisory signals to enhance training efficiency. Moreover, interpretability was improved by comparing physician gaze distributions with model attention maps. The review also discussed extensions to multimodal architectures and vision–language models (VLMs), positioning gaze information as a core component in frameworks aimed at data efficiency, interpretability validation, and multimodal alignment.

From a methodological perspective, weak supervision provides a principled strategy for generating approximate labels from heuristic functions without requiring manual annotation. Ratner et al. [7] introduced a data programming paradigm in which labeling functions are combined to produce probabilistic training labels, demonstrating that rule-based supervision can approximate fully supervised performance under certain conditions. This theoretical foundation supports the present study's adoption of rule-based pseudo-label generation for modeling radiological intention states.

Together, these findings motivate the present work, which seeks to represent radiologists' latent intention dynamics through gaze-derived token sequences and weak supervisory signals while preserving interpretability through probabilistic transition modeling.

2 Proposed Framework

In prior collaborative studies between Yokohama City University Hospital and Chuo University, gaze measurements obtained during head CT interpretation were analyzed to identify reading characteristics associated with radiologists' years of experience [8, 9].

In the present study, gaze data were transformed into temporal tokens and structured as feature sequences representing radiological reading behavior. Based on behavioral indicators—including gaze stability, magnitude of screen transitions, and revisit frequency—rule-based weak supervisory signals were constructed. Using these heuristics, intention states were approximately assigned to each time segment, categorized as search, evaluation, confirmation, and skipping.

The resulting intention-state sequence was modeled as a first-order Markov process. Transition probabilities between intention states were estimated via maximum likelihood estimation (MLE) based on observed frequencies. Unlike neural network-based approaches, softmax normalization was not applied. Instead, empirically derived transition probabilities were directly visualized to preserve interpretability grounded in observational data.

This modeling framework enables quantitative characterization of latent cognitive structures embedded in radiological interpretation behavior and provides an interpretable representation of intention dynamics without reliance on fully supervised annotations.

3 Method of Analysis

This section describes the analytical procedure adopted in the present study.

3.1 Data Collection

In February 2024, a pilot experiment was conducted at the Department of Radiology, Yokohama City University Hospital. Two radiologists with different levels of experience—a senior radiologist with 25 years of clinical experience and a first-year resident—were asked to interpret the same head CT case. This study is exploratory in nature, and the limited sample size is intended to provide an initial validation of the proposed framework rather than a statistically generalizable conclusion. Future work will include a larger cohort to enhance robustness and generalizability. The long-term objective of this research is to develop a head CT counterpart to the learning curve framework previously reported for chest CT interpretation [10]. During the experiment, eye movements were recorded using the Tobii X2–30 eye-tracking device (Tobii Technology).

Participants were not informed in advance that the case contained abnormal findings. In other words, they were unaware of the presence of objective abnormalities detectable through examination data, visual inspection, or other diagnostic indicators.

Subsequently, Tobii Pro Lab was used to define abnormal regions as Areas of Interest (AOIs). As illustrated in Fig. 1, the abnormal region was segmented into three concentric levels extending from the central lesion area to its surrounding region.

Two types of data were obtained:

A) Eye-tracking data sampled at 1-ms intervals, including timestamps, gaze coordinates (X–Y), saccades, and AOI labels.
B) Continuous screen-recording data of the CT interpretation process (MP4 format).

A) Eye-tracking data sampled at 1-ms intervals, including timestamps, gaze coordinates (X–Y), saccades, and AOI labels.
B) Continuous screen-recording data of the CT interpretation process (MP4 format).

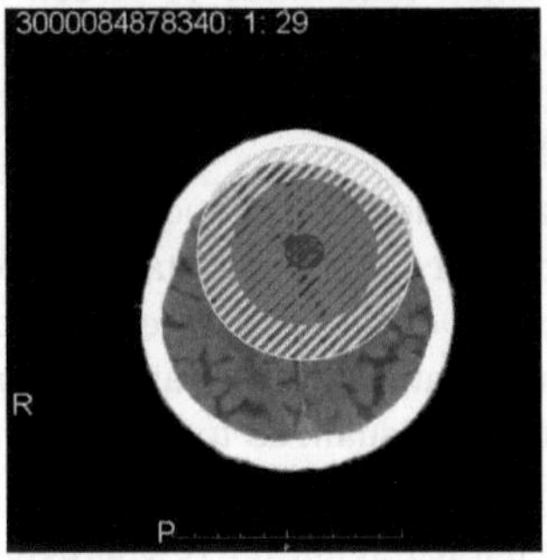

Fig. 1. AOI Configuration

3.2 CT Slice Transition Modeling

As indicated in B), the recorded video during CT interpretation contains multiple cross-sectional slices. As shown in Fig. 1, one example slice corresponds to an axial section of the head viewed from the inferior (foot-side) direction. In practice, approximately 40 CT slices were included in the case.

To accurately model the interpretation process, it is necessary to explicitly incorporate temporal changes in the CT slices into the analytical framework. Specifically, different scrolling behaviors may reflect different underlying intentions. For example:

- Sequential scrolling from slice 1 to slice 40 may indicate systematic or exhaustive screening.
- Repeated back-and-forth transitions between specific slices may indicate focused evaluation of a suspicious region.
- Large jumps across distant slices may reflect renewed exploration or hypothesis-driven verification based on prior experience.

Because directly extracting slice numbers from the video frames is technically challenging, the magnitude of screen transition was quantified using the Structural Similarity Index Measure (SSIM), which is robust to structural image variations. The change in image structure between consecutive frames was computed, and the resulting value was defined as the image transition metric (Δimage). Instead of relying on explicit slice indices, the proposed model implicitly estimates relationships between slices through visual changes between frames and gaze dynamics, enabling robust modelling of scrolling behavior. Specifically, each gaze sample is synchronized to the temporally closest video frame (30fps), with the corresponding Δimage value assigned to the gaze data as an additional feature. In this manner, frame-by-frame visual changes (Δimage) were computed from the recorded CT screen video.

To integrate the sampling-rate information from the gaze data (A) and the image transition metric Δimage derived from the CT video (B), temporal synchronization was performed. However, the gaze dataset included calibration segments recorded prior to the actual interpretation task. Therefore, gaze timestamps were converted to relative time by subtracting the first recorded timestamp, ensuring temporal alignment with the CT video after calibration segments were removed. Following synchronization, features were aggregated at each frame t, and the token representation was constructed as a tensor input as defined in Eq. (1).

$$\left[\mathrm{x, y, fixation\_flag, saccade\_flag, aoi\_id, aoi\_hit,} \ \Delta\mathrm{image}\right] \tag{1}$$

3.3 Weakly Supervised Strategy

Intentional states were not manually annotated. Instead, we adopted a weakly supervised strategy, in which coarse intent labels as shown in Table 1. were generated based on observable gaze behaviors such as AOI hits, fixation stability, revisit patterns, and image change rates. While this rule -based approach ensures interpretability, it inevitably simplifies complex cognitive processes, and the resulting labels should be regarded as approximations rather than precise representations of internal cognitive states. These rule-based labels served only as initial guidance, allowing the Transformer model to learn more consistent latent intent structures through self-attention, which is not in-scope of this paper, but will be addressed in the next step.

Table 1. Rule-based pseudo labeling with weakly supervision intention estimation

Status	Psychological meaning	To be observed with
Searching	Looking for any abnormalities	A state that is not under the following
Evaluating	Under evaluating the abnormalities	AOI + Fixation stable + Δimage-mid
Confirming	Verify the abnormalities	Revisit in AOI + Fixation stable
Skipping	Neglect and/or restart to search	Many Saccade, or Δimage-high

In Table 1, Fixation stable is defined as a token (corresponding to one frame) in which 60% or more of the gaze samples assigned to that token are classified as fixations. Similarly, Many-Saccade is defined as a token in which 50% or more of the gaze samples are classified as saccades. These ratios are computed as follows:

$$\mathrm{fix\_ratio} = \frac{\text{Number of fixation samples}}{\text{Total number of samples}} \tag{2}$$

$$\mathrm{sac\_ratio} = \frac{\text{Number of saccade samples}}{\text{Total number of samples}} \tag{3}$$

Tokens satisfying **fix _ ratio ≥ 0.60** are labeled as Fixation stable, whereas tokens satisfying **sac _ ratio ≥ 0.50** are labeled as Many-Saccade. These threshold values were determined empirically based on the distribution of the observed data, and further refinement and validation with larger datasets remain as future work. The variable *Δ*image-high was defined based on the distribution of frame-to-frame image differences (one value per frame) across all tokens. Specifically, the top 5% of *Δ*image values—representing abrupt transitions such as rapid scrolling or large positional shifts—were labeled as *Δ*image-high. Moderate or greater changes were labeled as *Δ*image-mid.

In addition, a token was labeled as revisit if gaze entered a predefined Area of Interest (AOI) within 50 tokens (approximately 1.6 s) after having previously exited that AOI. The condition Many-Saccade indicates that saccadic activity dominates within a token, as previously defined. Based on AOI status, fixation ratio, saccade ratio, and Δimage levels, the following intention-label generation function (Eq. (4)) was constructed under a rule-based weak supervision framework.

$$\text{intent\_labels[t]} \in \{\text{search, evaluate, confirm, skip}\} \tag{4}$$

3.4 Markov Transition Model

In order to visualize transitions between intention states based on the gaze data, a first-order Markov transition model was formulated as per defined the set of intention states as below

$$\mathbf{S} = \{s_1, s_2, s_3, \ldots, s_K\}$$

where each $s_k \in S$ represents a distinct cognitive intention state. In this study, the following state set was considered:

s_1 = search
s_2 = evaluate
s_3 = confirm
s_4 = skip
s_5 = unknown

As described in the previous section, tokens (corresponding to individual frames) are treated as discrete time steps. Let $\boldsymbol{I_t}$ denote the radiologist's intention state at time t, such that

$$\boldsymbol{I_t \in S}$$

For example, an intention-state time series may be obtained as follows:

$$\boldsymbol{N_{ij} = \#\{t \mid I_t = S_i, I_{t+1} = S_j\}}$$

where # denotes the number of occurrences (i.e., count).

For example, in the following case, the observed transition counts are:

$$\boldsymbol{N_{\text{search,search}} = 83, N_{\text{search,skip}} = 11}$$

More specifically, the transition frequencies from the state search are as follows:

- search → search: 83 occurrences
- search → skip: 11 occurrences
- search → unknown: 5 occurrences
- search → confirm: 1 occurrence

These counts form the empirical basis for estimating the transition probabilities in the first-order Markov model.

Based on the above, the transition probabilities were estimated using maximum likelihood estimation (MLE) from the observed transition counts, as defined in Eq. (5):

$$\boldsymbol{P}_{ij} = \boldsymbol{P}(\boldsymbol{S}_j \mid \boldsymbol{S}_i) = \frac{\boldsymbol{N}_{ij}}{\sum_k \boldsymbol{N}_{ik}} \tag{5}$$

The denominator represents the total number of transitions originating from state $\boldsymbol{S}_i$, while the numerator represents the number of observed transitions from $\boldsymbol{S}_i$ to a specific state $\boldsymbol{S}_j$. Thus, $\boldsymbol{P}_{ij}$ corresponds to the conditional probability of transitioning to state $\boldsymbol{S}_j$ given that the current state is $\boldsymbol{S}_i$.

For example, in the case described above:

$$\boldsymbol{P}(\text{search} \mid \text{search}) = \mathbf{0.83}, \boldsymbol{P}(\text{skip} \mid \text{search}) = \mathbf{0.11}$$

4 Results

Using the methodology described in the previous sections, the results are presented as follows. At this stage, gaze data from novice, intermediate, and expert physicians were processed independently using the same analytical pipeline. The resulting intention timelines and transition matrices were visually compared to explore qualitative differences in reading strategies.

Figure 2 corresponds to the expert radiologist with 25 years of experience, Fig. 3 to the mid-career radiologist with 10 years of experience, and Fig. 4 to the novice radiologist. The horizontal axis represents elapsed interpretation time. In the upper panel of each figure, intention states assigned through the weak supervision rules are color-coded as follows:

- Search – blue
- Evaluate – orange
- Confirm – green
- Skip —red
- Unknown—purple

In the lower panel, the most frequent AOI ID within each frame is extracted and displayed, indicating which AOI was predominantly fixated at that time. When gaze was directed toward the most broadly defined AOI region, it was visualized in orange or purple. For moderately defined AOI regions, green or brown was used. For narrowly defined, pinpoint AOIs, red or pink was assigned.

The primary objective of this study is to propose and validate a visualization framework for intent transition structures in CT interpretation. Therefore, we present the transition graph of the most experienced radiologist as a representative case, since expert data

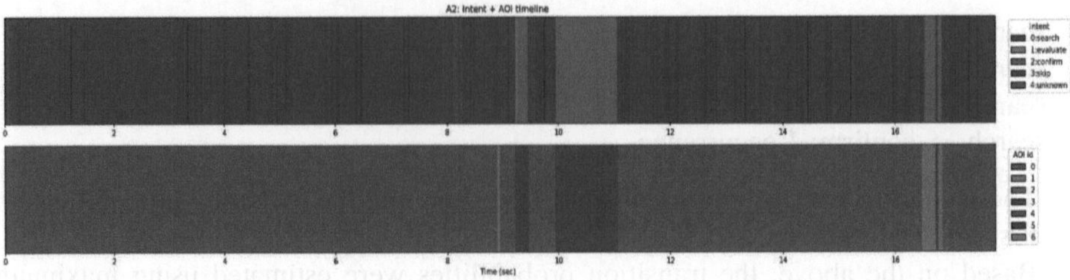

Fig. 2. Time-series representation of inferred intention states for the expert radiologist (25 years of experience).

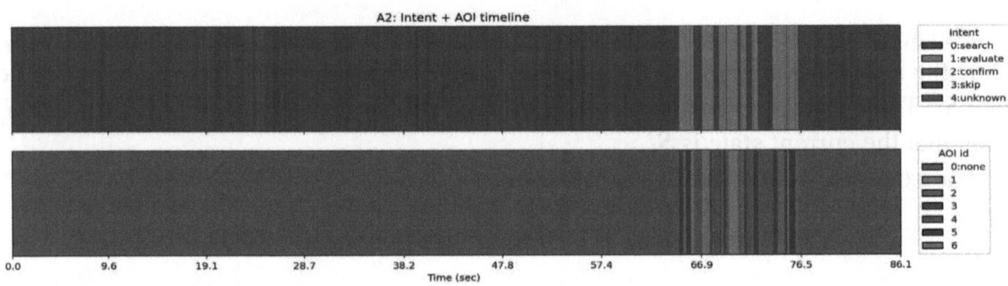

Fig. 3. Time-series representation of inferred intention states for the mid-career radiologist (10 years of experience).

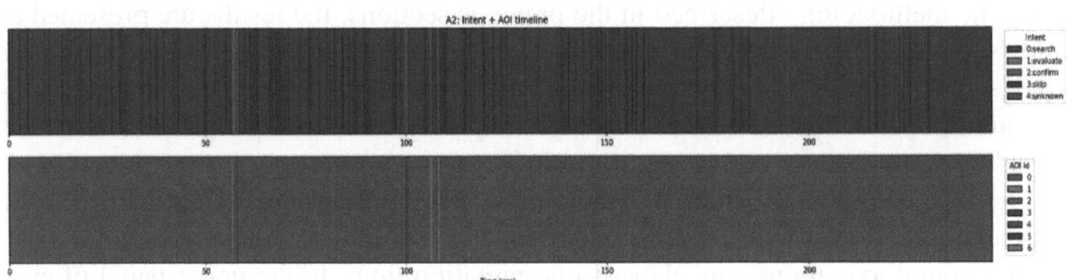

Fig. 4. Time-series representation of inferred intention states for the novice radiologist.

exhibit the most stable and clearly organized transition patterns. This allows the interpretability and structural validity of the proposed method to be demonstrated in its most transparent form. Figure 5 illustrates the intent transition graph of the most experienced radiologist (25 years of experience). The graph visualizes first-order Markov transition probabilities among five intent states (search, evaluate, confirm, skip, unknown), with transitions shown only when $p \geq 0.05$.

The main findings are summarized as follows:

1. The self-transition probability of search → search is 0.81, indicating strong persistence of the exploratory state.
2. The transition probability of evaluate → confirm is 1.00, meaning that all evaluation phases converge to confirmation.

3. The self-transition probability of confirm → confirm is 0.90, demonstrating high stability in the confirmation state.
4. No direct transition from search → evaluate was observed.
5. Significant transitions from skip → search (0.62) and unknown → search (0.89) suggest that the search state functions as a central hub in the cognitive process.

These results indicate that the expert's intent sequence follows a structured progression from exploration to evaluation and ultimately to confirmation.

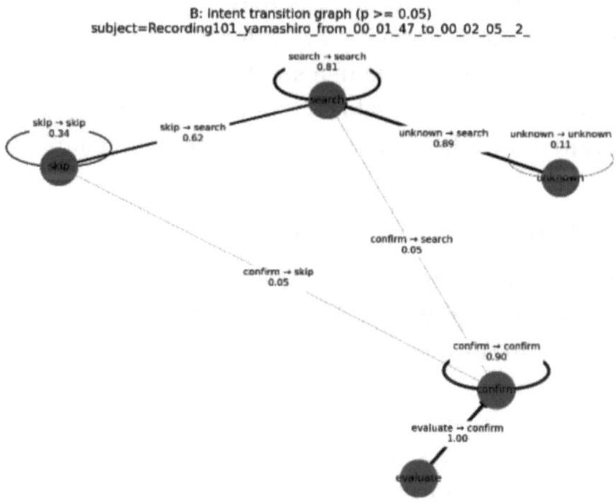

Fig. 5. The intent transition graph of the radiologist (25 years of experience)

5 Discussion

This section first evaluates the results shown in Figs. 2, 3, and 4 and subsequently discusses the proposed intention estimation framework.

5.1 Interpretation of Figs. 2, 3, and 4

In each figure, the upper panel represents the inferred intention-state transitions obtained using the methodology described in the previous sections, while the lower panel represents the physical gaze location (AOI-based spatial information).

Regarding total interpretation time, a clear correlation with years of experience is observed. The expert radiologist with 25 years of experience completed the task in only 20 frames, whereas the mid-career radiologist (10 years) required 86 frames, and the novice required nearly 250 frames. This monotonic increase in completion time suggests that reading efficiency is strongly associated with clinical experience.

5.1.1 Expert Radiologist (25 Years; Fig. 2)

In Fig. 2 (upper panel), the expert repeatedly alternates between search and skip until approximately the midpoint of the session, followed by a direct transition to confirm. Notably, evaluate is rarely observed. This finding was somewhat unexpected.

At the time of confirm, gaze is concentrated on the most narrowly defined AOI, indicating precise targeting of the lesion. The repeated search–skip pattern suggests broad scanning while implicitly narrowing down candidate regions—i.e., forming a tacit hypothesis or intuitive suspicion. Although the algorithm does not label these segments as evaluate, the underlying cognitive process may functionally correspond to evaluation without prolonged fixation satisfying the strict rule-based criteria. The expert thus reaches the lesion with high confidence in a single decisive step. This strategy deviates from a textbook sequential search–evaluate–confirm model and appears to reflect an experience-driven, expert-specific pattern unlikely to be replicated by novices.

5.1.2 Mid-Career Radiologist (10 Years; Fig. 3)

The mid-career radiologist exhibits a pattern similar to the expert during the first approximately 75% of the session, repeatedly alternating between search and skip. However, upon identifying the AOI, the evaluate label becomes prominent, and gaze fixation within the AOI is clearly sustained.

This behavior suggests a more explicit evaluation phase prior to confirmation. Compared to the expert, the mid-career physician appears to rely more on deliberate verification before reaching diagnostic certainty.

5.1.3 Novice Radiologist (Fig. 4)

In the novice case, the AOI appears to be reached twice during the session; however, fixation duration is short in both instances. Although the abnormal region may have drawn attention, it was not sufficiently evaluated to reach confirmation.

In the latter half of the session, the novice repeatedly alternates between search and skip without re-entering the AOI, ultimately concluding the interpretation without confirmation of the lesion. This suggests incomplete diagnostic integration despite initial perceptual detection.

5.2 Evaluation of the Intention Estimation Framework

The proposed method is inherently exploratory and relies on weak supervisory rules to generate time-series intention labels. However, the small number of subjects limits the generalizability of the findings, and the observed patterns should be interpreted as preliminary insights rather than definitive conclusions.

One notable observation is the absence of search → evaluate transitions in the expert case. This may be attributed to the strict labeling criteria for evaluate, which require (1) gaze within the AOI, (2) fixation stability, and (3) Δimage at least at the mid-level. These stringent conditions likely suppress the frequency of evaluate labeling, particularly for experts whose evaluation may occur rapidly without prolonged fixation.

Conversely, in the mid-career case, search $\rightarrow$ evaluate transitions are observed, although not always followed by evaluate $\rightarrow$ confirm. Since the labeling remains rule-based under weak supervision, evaluate may be triggered when fixation ratio and Δimage thresholds are satisfied, even if the cognitive state does not perfectly correspond to formal evaluation.

Ideally, an interpretable diagnostic sequence might follow the canonical pattern:

$$\text{search} \rightarrow \text{evaluate} \rightarrow \text{confirm}$$

Whether the expert's direct search $\rightarrow$ confirm transition reflects true cognitive expertise or an artifact of labeling thresholds remains an open question. It is unclear whether the labeling scheme should be adjusted to lie between the behaviors of the expert and mid-career radiologists, or whether the observed differences genuinely reflect distinct reading styles. Further investigation with a larger sample size is required.

Regarding search and skip, no major inconsistencies or structural issues were identified in the current framework.

5.3 Transition Structure

The observed transition structure shown in Fig. 5 suggests a highly organized cognitive process characteristic of expert-level CT interpretation.

First, the deterministic transition from evaluate to confirm (probability = 1.00) indicates that once a candidate region is evaluated, the process consistently proceeds toward confirmation. This reflects a unidirectional consolidation of diagnostic hypotheses, consistent with models of expert decision-making in medical imaging.

Second, the high self-transition probability in the confirm state (0.90) demonstrates stability once diagnostic certainty is reached. This suggests that expert judgments are maintained without frequent reversal, reflecting cognitive confidence and decisional robustness.

Third, the absence of direct transitions from search to evaluate is noteworthy. Rather than entering evaluation prematurely, the expert appears to maintain prolonged exploration before committing to analytical evaluation. This may reflect a refined search strategy that minimizes early anchoring bias.

Furthermore, the strong transitions from skip and unknown back to search indicate that exploratory processing functions as a central organizing state. Search acts as a structural backbone that integrates navigation and uncertainty into a coherent diagnostic workflow.

Overall, the transition structure of the expert radiologist is characterized by:

- Persistent and stable exploration,
- Deterministic progression from evaluation to confirmation,
- High stability within confirmation phases.

These findings quantitatively reveal the hierarchical cognitive organization underlying expert CT interpretation.

5.4 Overall Assessment

The Despite remaining limitations, the proposed intention estimation approach appears to capture, to a meaningful extent, experience-dependent temporal patterns in radiological interpretation behavior. The temporal dynamics of inferred intention states qualitatively reflect differences associated with years of clinical experience.

6 Conclusion

The In this study, gaze measurements obtained during head CT interpretation were transformed into temporal tokens. Intention states were assigned using rule-based weak supervisory signals derived from gaze stability, image transition magnitude (Δimage), and revisit behavior. The resulting intention sequence was formulated as a first-order Markov process, and transition probabilities were visualized to characterize temporal dynamics in radiological reading behavior.

Future work will focus on expanding the sample size and refining the intention labeling scheme. In particular, incorporating a larger and more diverse dataset and improving the rule-based labeling criteria will be essential for achieving more robust and generalizable intention modeling. In parallel, the tokenized gaze representation will be reformatted into tensor structures suitable as inputs to Transformer-based machine learning models.

Subsequently, we plan to investigate how gaze information at a given time step tinteracts with past, present, and future time steps through non-sequential dependency modeling. In particular, the incorporation of a self-attention mechanism will be explored to enable contextual modeling of gaze behavior beyond strictly chronological order.

Through this approach, we aim to deepen the contextual understanding of radiologists' gaze dynamics and further advance computational modeling of intention during medical image interpretation.

Acknowledgement. This paper has been supported by Grant-in-Aid for Scientific Research (JSPS KAKENHI Grant Number 19 K03062, and 22 K01627) and Grant-in-Aid for Specially Promoted Research from Chuo University.

References

1. Kundel, H.L., Nordine, C.F., Carmody, D.: Visula scanning, pattern recognition and decision making in pulmonary nodule detection. Investig. Radiol. **13**, 175–181 (1978)
2. Drew, T., Võ, M.L.-H., Wolfe, J.M.: The invisible gorilla strikes again: sustained inattentional blindness in expert observers. Psychol. Sci. **24**, 1848–1853 (2013)
3. Waite, S. et al.: Analysis of perceptual expertise in radiology – current knowledge and a new perspective. Front. Hum. Neurosci. **13**, 213 (2019)
4. Sqalli, M.T., Aslonov, B., Gafurov, M., Mukhammadiev, N., Houssaini, Y.S.: Eye tracking technology in medical practice: a perspective on its diverse applications. Front. Med. Technol. **5**, 1253001 (2023)
5. Zhong, Y. et al.: Weakly-supervised medical image segmentation with gaze annotations. arXiv. (2024). https://doi.org/10.48550/arXiv.2407.07406

6. Duan, J., Zhang, M., Song, M., Xu, X., Lu, H.: Eye tracking-enhanced deep learning for medical image analysis: a systematic review on data efficiency, interpretability, and multimodal integration. Bioengineering. **12**, 954 (2025)
7. Ratner, A., Bach, S.H., Ehrenberg, H., Fries, J., Wu, S., Ré, C.: Snorkel: rapid training data cocreation with weak supervision. In: Proceedings of the VLDB Endowment, vol. 11, pp. 269–282 (2017)
8. Naito, Y., Nakamura, J., Ishiwata, Y.: Characteristics of the reciprocal movement of radiographers' gaze based on a comparison of entry-level and experienced radiographers. J. Electron. Electr. Eng. **3**, 1–4 (2024)
9. Nakamura, J., Nagayoshi, S., Ishiwata, Y.: A study of gaze rhythm during the interpretation of computed tomography images of the human head. J. Electron. Electr. Eng. **4**, 1–3 (2025)
10. Song, J.H. et al.: Learning curve and period of experience required for the competent diagnosis of acute appendicitis using abdominal computed tomography: a prospective observational study. Clin. Exp. Emerg. Med. **4**, 222–231 (2017)

Auditable Vietnamese Social Listening: A Multi-task Transformer Approach for Reputational Risk Monitoring

Nghia T. Tran and Huy-Minh X. Doan(✉)

FPT School of Business and Technology, FPT University, Ho Chi Minh City, Vietnam
nghia24mse23166@fsb.edu.vn, minhdxh@fe.edu.vn

Abstract. Efficient reputation management in the digital era requires near-real-time social listening systems that are not only accurate but also auditable and operationally governable. For Vietnamese social media, this requirement remains challenging because user-generated text contains non-standard orthography, teencode, emojis, URLs, code-mixing, and rapidly shifting discourse patterns. This paper presents an auditable event-driven framework centered on a Kafka-based event log for Vietnamese reputational risk monitoring. Rather than proposing a new Transformer architecture, the contribution of this work lies in the governance-aware integration of Vietnamese NLP inference, replayable stream processing, calibrated alerting, and evidence-preserving traceability. The system integrates Vietnamese-aware preprocessing with a multi-task PhoBERT encoder to concurrently monitor sentiment, intent, and misinformation risk. To bridge high-accuracy inference and operational constraints, we implement imbalance-aware loss functions, calibrated thresholding, and latency-optimized micro-batching. Evaluation across three specialized datasets demonstrates that our weighted-loss PhoBERT achieves a misinformation ROC–AUC of 0.9948 and an intent Macro-F1 of 0.9155. System-level benchmarks confirm stable throughput of hundreds of messages per second with p95 latency under 1.2 s, providing a practical foundation for auditable institutional reputational risk monitoring.

Keywords: Social listening · Vietnamese NLP · Reputational Risk · Auditability · PhoBERT · Stream processing · Misinformation detection

1 Introduction

Social media dynamics rapidly shape public perception of brands and organizations. In operational reputation management, *monitoring* typically tracks quantitative indicators like mention volume, while *listening* aims at semantic interpretation to infer actionable behaviors. For crisis response, social listening must

D. Liberona et al. (Eds.): MISNC 2026, CCIS 3092, pp. 180–194, 2027.
https://doi.org/10.1007/978-3-032-33381-0_14

be near-real-time to enable short intervention windows and mitigate reputational damage [5].

However, Vietnamese social media text presents significant linguistic challenges, including non-standard orthography, teencode, and heavy use of emojis or URLs. Beyond NLP accuracy, a deployable system must sustain bursty traffic with bounded tail latency while providing *traceability*. In professional settings, AI-driven alerts must be *auditable*: operators need to reconstruct why a specific risk alert was triggered and identify the evidence posts that contributed to it.

Transformer-based models have significantly advanced modern NLP [3,16]. Despite advances in Vietnamese pretrained Transformers, much prior work focuses on offline accuracy without addressing production constraints such as event-time semantics, latency–throughput trade-offs, alert governance, and decision traceability. This paper addresses these gaps from a system-integration perspective. We do not claim a novel Transformer architecture; instead, we study how Vietnamese NLP models can be embedded into a replayable, evidence-preserving, and governance-aware streaming pipeline so that model predictions can be transformed into actionable and auditable business intelligence.

Contributions. This work does not claim novelty in the Transformer backbone or in Kafka-based streaming itself. Instead, the primary contribution lies in integrating Vietnamese NLP inference, event-driven processing, operational calibration, and evidence-preserving traceability into an auditable reputational-risk monitoring framework. This study makes five primary contributions:

1. **Governance-Aware Auditable Architecture:** We design an event-driven pipeline anchored by a Kafka event log [7], in which raw events, preprocessed texts, model predictions, aggregation windows, and alert payloads are linked through persistent identifiers. This enables replay-based auditing and post-hoc decision reconstruction.
2. **Vietnamese-Aware Normalization:** We develop a robust preprocessing pipeline tailored for Vietnamese social media noise, including teencode, slang, character elongation, URLs, and emojis. The pipeline aims to reduce lexical fragmentation while preserving sentiment-bearing and context-relevant cues.
3. **Multi-Task Risk Monitoring:** We implement a unified deployment-ready model providing sentiment, intent, and misinformation-risk signals using PhoBERT [12] with imbalance-aware optimization. The model is used as an operational signal generator rather than as an isolated benchmark classifier.
4. **Operational Calibration:** We introduce calibrated thresholding and micro-batching mechanisms to balance alert recall, alert fatigue, latency, and throughput under near-real-time constraints.
5. **Empirical and Methodological Validation:** We provide a comprehensive evaluation demonstrating that our weighted-loss PhoBERT achieves a misinformation ROC–AUC of 0.9948, an intent Macro-F1 of 0.9155, and maintains stable throughput with p95 latency under 1.2 s. Because the raw dataset is proprietary, we also specify a methodological reproducibility package based on preprocessing scripts, configurations, schemas, and anonymized dummy data.

2 Background and Related Work

The development of production-grade social listening systems sits at the intersection of Vietnamese NLP, real-time stream processing, and multi-dimensional text analytics.

Vietnamese NLP for Social Media. Vietnamese social media text significantly deviates from formal domains due to non-standard orthography, slang, and diacritic omission. While tools like VnCoreNLP [17] and specialized segmenters [13] provide foundational support, recent advances in representation learning through Transformer architectures [16] and pretrained language models such as BERT [3] and PhoBERT [12] have set strong baselines for Vietnamese NLP tasks. However, these models alone do not address the lexical fragmentation of "noisy" text. Lexical normalization efforts, such as ViLexNorm, emphasize mapping non-canonical variants to standard forms, yet the specific interplay between these normalization choices and the constraints of real-time streaming (e.g., latency vs. accuracy) remains a critical area for operational research.

Streaming Analytics and Auditability. In operational settings, monitoring must move beyond batch processing towards event-driven architectures. Systems leveraging Kafka [7] provide the necessary decoupling and replayability for high-throughput ingestion. Contemporary stream processing research highlights the importance of event-time semantics and windowed aggregation [1], materialized through frameworks like Apache Spark [2,18]. A notable gap in current literature, however, is the systematic integration of these streaming mechanisms with deep learning inference to achieve *auditability*. For high-stakes reputation management, it is not enough to produce a score; the system must provide a traceable path from the aggregated alert back to the raw evidence.

Governance-Oriented NLP Systems. Responsible machine learning research has emphasized that high predictive performance alone is insufficient for high-impact deployment. Documentation practices such as model cards and datasheets for datasets improve transparency by describing intended use, evaluation conditions, data composition, preprocessing, and limitations [4,10]. Broader AI governance frameworks further emphasize risk management, documentation, transparency, and human oversight [11]. However, these approaches mainly address model- or dataset-level transparency. They do not directly specify how a near-real-time NLP pipeline should preserve event-level evidence, reconstruct alert decisions, or replay historical streams after model or policy updates. This paper complements such work by embedding traceability into the operational pipeline itself: raw events, preprocessing outputs, model scores, aggregation windows, threshold rules, and evidence posts are retained as part of the alert lifecycle.

Task Integration: Sentiment, Intent, and Risk. Operational monitoring requires actionable signals. While sentiment analysis provides an attitudinal baseline, intent classification (e.g., identifying complaints vs. inquiries) offers the behavioral cues necessary for response. Furthermore, in near-real-time settings, misinformation detection often shifts from definitive fact-checking to *risk scoring*, prioritizing content for human review based on linguistic patterns of rumors [8]. Recent benchmarks like ViFactCheck serve as vital evaluation ground, but the challenge remains in calibrating these multi-task signals to balance alert fatigue with the need for early warning.

3 Methods

Our approach formalizes the social listening process into five key stages: dataset curation, linguistic preprocessing, multi-task representation learning, architectural optimization, and operational constraint management.

3.1 Dataset Construction and Annotation

Data Collection Scope. The datasets were constructed from publicly accessible Vietnamese social media posts and comments collected under brand-monitoring scenarios. Data collection followed platform usage policies and a strict data-minimization principle: only fields required for downstream modeling (post identifier, timestamp, textual content, and engagement metadata) were retained. Personally identifiable information (PII) was removed or anonymized at the ingestion stage.

The collection period spans multiple months and includes both routine discussion phases and peak-volume intervals triggered by campaign or crisis-related events. This ensures that the dataset reflects realistic operational monitoring conditions rather than artificially curated benchmark settings.

In accordance with the scope of the system, only textual content was used in this study. Although multimodal signals (images/videos) are common in social media, preliminary inspection indicated that most actionable reputational signals were explicitly expressed in text. Multimodal integration is reserved for future work.

Annotation Protocol and Quality Assurance. Annotation was performed by six trained native Vietnamese speakers following task-specific rubrics aligned with reputational risk objectives. To ensure high data quality, each sample was independently labeled by two annotators, with a third senior adjudicator resolving discrepancies. We assessed the reliability of the annotation process using the Inter-Annotator Agreement (IAA) metric. For the sentiment and misinformation tasks, we obtained a Cohen's Kappa score (κ) of 0.82 and 0.88, respectively, indicating substantial to near-perfect agreement. For the multi-label intent task, we observed an average Fleiss' Kappa of 0.79 across categories.

For the **intent** task, posts could receive multiple labels among five behavioral categories: *Complaint, Question, Praise, Suggestion, Irrelevant.* For **sentiment**, labels were assigned into three classes: *Positive, Neutral, Negative.* For **misinformation**, posts were annotated as a binary risk indicator based on the presence of rumor-like or unverified claims associated with brands or events.

Annotation guidelines were iteratively refined through three pilot rounds prior to final dataset construction to minimize subjective ambiguity in social media slang interpretation.

Data Characteristics and Imbalance. The intent dataset exhibits moderate class imbalance, with *Complaint* and *Irrelevant* dominating the distribution, while *Question* and *Suggestion* represent minority classes. This imbalance motivates the use of weighted loss functions described in the following sections.

The average post length after preprocessing ranges between 30 and 40 tokens. A substantial proportion of posts contain social-media-specific linguistic phenomena such as teencode, diacritic omission, emojis, character elongation, and code-mixing, reinforcing the necessity of the proposed Vietnamese-aware normalization pipeline.

Split Strategy and Leakage Control. To prevent evaluation bias, content-level deduplication was performed prior to splitting. Near-duplicate posts (identified via hashing and similarity checks) were removed to avoid inflated performance caused by reposted content.

The datasets were partitioned into train/validation/test splits with no textual overlap across partitions. Where feasible, chronological consistency was preserved so that test samples reflect realistic generalization to unseen discussion periods.

Data Availability and Reproducibility. The complete raw datasets cannot be publicly released because they originate from institutional monitoring scenarios and may contain sensitive reputational signals, platform-specific metadata, or user-generated content subject to privacy and usage restrictions. This limits full empirical reproducibility. To mitigate this constraint, we distinguish between raw-data reproducibility and methodological reproducibility. The replication package will include preprocessing scripts, annotation guidelines, label definitions, model configurations, threshold-calibration scripts, Kafka topic schemas, alert-payload schemas, and a structurally equivalent anonymized dummy dataset. This package is intended to support methodological replication of the pipeline and evaluation protocol, although exact reproduction of the reported scores requires access to the original data distribution.

3.2 Vietnamese Preprocessing and Normalization

To mitigate the lexical fragmentation of social media text while preserving affective signals, we implement a multi-stage preprocessing pipeline. First, Unicode normalization (UAX #15) [15] is applied to stabilize character representations across varying device types. Second, we adopt a selective tokenization strategy: URLs are masked with a structured `<URL>` token to prevent vocabulary explosion, while Emojis are categorized into coarse affect groups rather than discarded, ensuring that vital sentiment cues remain accessible to the encoder. Finally, Teencode and slang normalization utilizes a hybrid heuristic-lexical approach inspired by prior lexical normalization studies for social media text. We employ high-precision rules for frequent abbreviations and compress character elongations (e.g., "quaaaaaa" → "qua"), which are common in Vietnamese social media.

3.3 Multi-task Signal Extraction and Architecture

Given a preprocessed input x, our system extracts three distinct signals using a shared PhoBERT encoder [12]. Let $z \in \mathbb{R}^d$ be the pooled hidden representation of the input.

- **Sentiment Analysis:** Formulated as a 3-class classification problem ($\hat{y} = \text{softmax}(W_s z + b_s)$).
- **Intent Classification:** A multi-label task with $K = 5$ behavioral categories. We compute $\hat{\mathbf{y}} = \sigma(W_i z + b_i)$, where label decisions are made via $\hat{y}_k = \mathbb{I}[\hat{y}_k \geq \tau_k]$.
- **Misinformation Risk:** Treated as a continuous *prioritization score* $\hat{y}_m = \sigma(w_m^\top z + b_m)$, rather than a binary fact-checking judgment, to better support human-in-the-loop verification.

Model Architecture. We adopt PhoBERT [12] as the shared contextual encoder for all tasks. PhoBERT is a monolingual Transformer pretrained on large-scale Vietnamese corpora and has demonstrated strong performance across downstream NLP benchmarks. In our implementation, we use the `PhoBERT-large` variant to maximize representational capacity while maintaining deployable latency under micro-batching constraints.

Given an input sequence $x = (x_1, \ldots, x_n)$, the encoder produces contextualized token representations. We use the pooled representation of the `[CLS]` token (denoted $z \in \mathbb{R}^d$) as the shared semantic representation for downstream task heads.

Task-specific Heads. On top of the shared encoder, we attach three independent task heads:

- **Sentiment Head:** A linear classifier with softmax activation:

$$\hat{y}_s = \text{softmax}(W_s z + b_s).$$

- **Intent Head:** A multi-label classifier with sigmoid activation:

$$\hat{\mathbf{y}}_i = \sigma(W_i z + b_i),$$

  where each label decision is determined by thresholding $\hat{y}_{i,k}$.

– **Misinformation Head:** A binary risk scorer:

$$\hat{y}_m = \sigma(w_m^\top z + b_m),$$

interpreted as a prioritization score rather than a definitive fact-checking verdict.

The shared-encoder design enables parameter efficiency and consistent semantic representation across tasks, while independent heads allow task-specific calibration.

Loss Formulation. To address label imbalance, we use task-specific weighted objectives:

– **Sentiment:** Weighted Cross-Entropy (WCE)

$$\mathcal{L}_{sent} = -\sum_c w_c y_c \log \hat{y}_c$$

– **Intent:** Weighted Binary Cross-Entropy (WBCE)

$$\mathcal{L}_{intent} = -\sum_k w_k \left[y_k \log \hat{y}_k + (1 - y_k) \log(1 - \hat{y}_k)\right]$$

– **Misinformation:** Weighted Binary Cross-Entropy

The overall objective is defined as a weighted sum:

$$\mathcal{L}_{total} = \lambda_1 \mathcal{L}_{sent} + \lambda_2 \mathcal{L}_{intent} + \lambda_3 \mathcal{L}_{mis}.$$

In practice, equal weighting was used after preliminary experiments showed no significant instability across tasks.

Training Configuration. Fine-tuning was conducted using the AdamW optimizer [9] with linear learning-rate warmup and early stopping based on validation Macro-F1 (intent) and ROC–AUC (misinformation). Maximum sequence length was set to 256 tokens.

To ensure deployability, we constrained batch size to align with the streaming micro-batching configuration described earlier. This ensures consistency between offline evaluation and online inference behavior.

3.4 Operational Optimization and Inference Management

Imbalance-aware Optimization and Calibration. Social media datasets typically exhibit severe class imbalance, particularly for high-risk categories. To address this, we utilize Weighted Cross-Entropy (WCE) and Weighted Binary Cross-Entropy (WBCE) losses, where minority classes are penalized more heavily. Furthermore, we treat the decision thresholds τ as operational governance parameters. Instead of a fixed $\tau = 0.5$, we calibrate thresholds on validation data to meet specific professional objectives: a recall-oriented configuration for early warning vs. a precision-oriented setup for reducing alert fatigue.

Deployment Constraints: Batching and Truncation. To ensure near-real-time viability under bursty traffic, the system implements micro-batching, accumulating events within a 1000ms window or until a batch size of 8 is reached. For excessively long texts, we apply content-aware truncation using TF-IDF scoring [14] to select the most salient sentence spans, ensuring that risk-relevant semantics are preserved even when sequence length limits (256 tokens) are reached.

Incident Memory for Precedent-Aware Monitoring (Optional). To enrich the context of triggered alerts, we add a retrieval-based **Incident Memory** module. Validated historical incidents are stored as high-dimensional embeddings. Upon a risk alert, the system performs a similarity search (e.g., via FAISS [6]) to retrieve the top-k semantically similar historical cases, providing operators with immediate context regarding past precedents and response outcomes.

4 System Architecture and Traceability

The proposed system is architected to prioritize *auditability* alongside real-time inference (Table 1).

Table 1. System design principles for Auditable Social Listening.

Principle	Rationale
Event-log Replayability	Enable retrospective audits and debugging via immutable event logs
Inference-Governance Decoupling	Separate model predictions from alerting logic to allow playbook evolution
Interpretable Aggregation	Use transparent window statistics instead of "black-box" triggers
Governance-based Thresholds	Model thresholds as operational parameters, not just statistical ones
Evidence-First Payloads	Mandatory attachment of source posts to alerts for accountability

4.1 Event-Driven Pipeline and Schema

We adopt an event-driven architecture centered on a Kafka event log [7]. Data from heterogeneous platforms (Facebook, YouTube, TikTok, etc.) are normalized into a unified schema containing: *id*, *platform*, *event_time*, *ingest_time*, *text*, *url*, and *engagement*. The pipeline is materialized through a series of specialized topics:

`raw` → `preprocessed` → `predictions` → `risk_windows` → `alerts`.

This decoupled design ensures that each stage is independently replayable, allowing operators to "rewind" the stream to investigate specific model behaviors or data anomalies.

4.2 Mechanism for Traceability

Traceability is achieved by logging the full *decision context* in each alert payload. This includes:

- **Triggering Metrics**: The exact threshold and observed value that activated the alert.
- **Aggregated Context**: Window-level statistics (e.g., volume, total engagement, risk distribution).
- **Evidence Mapping**: A ranked list of evidence posts with their original content and model-assigned risk scores.

This design allows human operators to drill down from an aggregated high-risk alert to individual raw events, supporting post-hoc decision reconstruction.

Table 2. Minimal traceability field groups in the alert payload.

Field group	Representative fields
Identification	`alert_id, alert_type, severity, brand_id, title`
Triggering	`trigger.metric, trigger.threshold, trigger.actual, trigger.unit`
Window context	`window_start/end, total_posts, avg_risk, total_engagement, unique_sources`
Evidence	`top_posts:{post_id, risk_score, engagement, text}`

4.3 Implementation and Hardware Environment

The prototype was implemented in Python 3.11 using PyTorch and the Hugging Face Transformers library for PhoBERT-based inference. In the deployment setting, Apache Kafka served as the event backbone to decouple ingestion, stream processing, and inference. Following the proposed system architecture, posts and comments were ingested into separate Kafka topics (`raw-posts` and `raw-comments`), while multi-task inference outputs were written to a unified `nlp_result` topic. This separation facilitates pipeline optimization tailored to specific content types and mitigates bottlenecks during bursty traffic intervals.

On the consumer side, the system utilizes batched processing with manual offset control (`enable_auto_commit=False`) to ensure an auditable, at-least-once processing guarantee. The operational policy was configured with a `batch_size=8` and `batch_timeout_ms=1000`, utilizing two concurrent processing threads for the post and comment streams, respectively. For the incident-memory component, FAISS was employed for efficient approximate nearest-neighbor retrieval over historical incident embeddings.

To ensure consistency between offline evaluation and online serving, inference was constrained to a maximum sequence length of 256 tokens. As the reported performance results represent system-level rather than isolated model measurements, they reflect this specific deployment configuration. Specifically, end-to-end latency is defined as the duration from initial Kafka ingestion to the point the inference result is available for the dashboard or alerting layer. Under these conditions, the system sustains a throughput of hundreds of messages per second with a p95 latency below 1.2 s, effectively meeting the requirements for near-real-time monitoring.

5 Results and Discussion

We evaluate our system across two primary dimensions: model-level classification performance and system-level operational efficiency. To guide our evaluation, we address the following Research Questions (RQs):

- **RQ1:** How accurately does the multi-task model classify intent, sentiment, and misinformation risk compared to established baselines?
- **RQ2:** How does the proposed Vietnamese-aware normalization impact model robustness under real-world lexical noise?
- **RQ3:** Does the event-driven system meet operational performance targets (throughput and latency) under production-like traffic?

5.1 Experimental Setup and Metrics

Datasets and Metrics. We evaluate the system on three core tasks: intent identification, sentiment analysis, and misinformation risk scoring. Table 3 summarizes the dataset statistics.

Table 3. Dataset statistics by task.

Task	Train	Validation	Test
Intent (multi-label, $K = 5$)	24,187	5,183	5,183
Sentiment (3 classes)	4,819	536	536
Misinformation (binary)	5,862	1,035	1,035

Baselines. We compare a TF–IDF + Logistic Regression baseline (**B0**) against PhoBERT fine-tuning with standard cross-entropy (**M1**) and our proposed model with weighted loss and full preprocessing (**M2**). Ablation studies (**A1**, **A2**) assess the impact of teencode and emoji/URL handling. Optimization uses the AdamW optimizer [9] with early stopping.

5.2 Model Performance Analysis

Intent and Sentiment. Table 4 shows that M2 achieves the highest Macro-F1 (0.9155) for multi-label intent. The significant improvement over M1 demonstrates that *imbalance-aware weighting* is crucial for capturing minority classes like "Question" or "Suggestion" (see Table 5). In sentiment analysis, we observe that teencode normalization (A1 vs M2 in Table 6) has a mixed impact; while results are comparable, the drop in A2 suggests that preserving structural cues like emojis is more critical than aggressive lexical normalization for affective tasks.

Table 4. Multi-label intent results (test set).

Model	Micro-F1	Macro-F1	P	R
B0 (TF–IDF + LR)	0.8958	0.8629	0.8206	0.9225
M1 (PhoBERT + BCE)	0.9136	0.8279	0.9089	0.8031
M2 (PhoBERT + WBCE)	**0.9378**	**0.9155**	0.8913	**0.9418**
A1 (M2, no teencode norm)	0.9090	0.8694	0.8424	0.9026
A2 (M2, no emoji/URL handling)	0.8747	0.8289	0.8012	0.8598

Table 5. Label-wise F1 scores for intent classification (test set).

Label	B0	M1	M2	A1	A2
Complaint	0.9018	0.9183	0.9393	0.9127	0.8649
Question	0.6863	0.4429	0.7989	0.6871	0.5980
Praise	0.9230	0.9446	0.9544	0.9424	0.9092
Suggestion	0.9154	0.9189	0.9559	0.8997	0.8872
Irrelevant	0.8879	0.9150	0.9293	0.9052	0.8850

Table 6. Sentiment results (test set).

Model	Accuracy	Macro-F1
B0 (TF–IDF + LR)	0.6246	0.5870
M1 (PhoBERT-large + CE)	0.6584	0.6414
M2 (PhoBERT-large + WCE)	**0.6779**	**0.6506**
A1 (M2, no teencode norm)	0.6904	0.6528
A2 (M2, no emoji/URL handling)	0.6314	0.5671

Misinformation and Threshold Trade-offs. As shown in Table 7, M2 achieves a near-perfect ROC–AUC of 0.9948. This confirms that Transformer encoders can effectively detect the stylistic footprints of misinformation. More importantly, Table 8 illustrates how our governance-based thresholding allows the system to shift from a high-recall "early warning" mode ($\tau = 0.3$) to a high-precision "fatigue control" mode ($\tau = 0.7$), providing flexibility for different organizational playbooks.

Table 7. Misinformation detection results (test set).

Model	Accuracy	F1	ROC–AUC
B0 (TF–IDF + LR)	0.9553	0.9544	0.9901
M1 (PhoBERT + CE)	0.9600	0.9597	0.9921
M2 (PhoBERT + WCE)	**0.9624**	**0.9625**	**0.9948**

Table 8. Effect of inference threshold for misinformation (M2).

τ	Precision	Recall	F1
0.3	0.9538	0.9718	0.9627
0.5	0.9580	0.9671	0.9625
0.7	0.9620	0.9621	0.9620

5.3 Operational and System Evaluation

Beyond model accuracy, the system demonstrates high resilience and throughput. Robustness tests (Table 9) reveal that while structural noise (emoji/URL) poses the greatest risk to stability, the proposed preprocessing pipeline mitigates these effects significantly. In system-level tests (Kafka-based deployment), the pipeline maintains a p95 latency below 1.2 s while processing hundreds of messages per second. This balance is achieved through the micro-batching and TF-IDF truncation mechanisms described in Sect. 3.

Table 9. ΔF1 under noise sources (relative to M2; negative is worse).

Noise source	ΔF1
Lexical variation (teencode/slang)	−0.0060
Undiacritized input	−0.0036
Structural perturbations (emoji/URL)	−0.0225
Code-mixing and spelling distortion	−0.0104

5.4 Bridging Technical Inference and Operational Auditability

The experimental results underscore a fundamental shift in our approach: while maximizing F1 scores is critical for reliability, the *traceability* provided by our event-driven architecture is what enables operational deployment in high-stakes environments. Operators can now look at an alert and immediately verify the high-risk evidence (as detailed in Table 2) that triggered it. This evidence-first paradigm reduces the "mean-time-to-investigation" (MTTI) and fosters institutional trust in AI-driven monitoring. Furthermore, the incident memory module provides historical grounding, enabling teams to distinguish between isolated noise and systemic crises based on historical precedents.

6 Limitations and Threats to Validity

While the proposed system demonstrates high empirical and operational performance, several threats to validity remain.

Contribution Boundary. The principal contribution of this work is system integration rather than methodological novelty in neural architecture design. PhoBERT, weighted loss functions, Kafka-based event logs, and micro-batching are established components. The novelty of this work lies in their governance-aware integration for Vietnamese reputational risk monitoring, especially the preservation of evidence and decision context across the alert lifecycle.

Construct Validity: Operationalizing "misinformation risk" as a prioritization score diverges from definitive automated fact-checking, heavily relying on linguistic cues rather than external knowledge retrieval. This limits the system to identifying suspicious semantic patterns rather than verifying factual truth.

Internal Validity: Although the annotation process maintained a high Inter-Annotator Agreement (IAA) through a structured multi-adjudicator approach, subjective ambiguity in social media slang and emerging teencode nuances might result in subtle labeling biases in the ground truth.

External Validity: The text normalization pipeline was primarily optimized for contemporary Vietnamese social media syntax gathered during a defined temporal window. Concept drift—as new dialects, platforms, or lexical phenomena emerge over time—may necessitate periodic recalibration of both the preprocessing heuristics and the Transformer models. Additionally, because the datasets and rules are optimized for institutional risk monitoring, extending this framework to general-purpose scenarios may require re-tuning.

7 Conclusion

This study presented a governance-aware and auditable Vietnamese social listening framework designed to bridge Vietnamese NLP inference, event-driven stream processing, calibrated alerting, and operational traceability. By co-designing a multi-task PhoBERT encoder within an event-driven Kafka architecture, we demonstrated that it is possible to achieve both state-of-the-art predictive performance (0.9948 ROC–AUC for misinformation) and high system efficiency (p95 latency < 1.2 s). Our findings underscore that imbalance-aware training and calibrated thresholding are indispensable for professional risk monitoring. Most significantly, the introduced auditability mechanisms ensure that AI-driven decisions are traceable and verifiable, fulfilling a critical requirement for institutional reputation management. Future research directions include the integration of multimodal signals and the leveraging of Large Language Models (LLMs) for automated incident summarization and response generation.

References

1. Akidau, T., et al.: The dataflow model: a practical approach to balancing correctness, latency, and cost in massive-scale, unbounded, out-of-order data processing. Proc. VLDB Endow. **8**(12), 1792–1803 (2015)
2. Armbrust, M., et al.: Structured streaming: a declarative api for real-time applications in apache spark. In: Proceedings of the 2018 International Conference on Management of Data (SIGMOD), pp. 601–613 (2018)
3. Devlin, J., Chang, M.W., Lee, K., Toutanova, K.: Bert: pre-training of deep bidirectional transformers for language understanding. In: Proceedings of the 2019 Conference of the North American Chapter of the Association for Computational Linguistics (NAACL-HLT), pp. 4171–4186 (2019)
4. Gebru, T., et al.: Datasheets for datasets. Commun. ACM **64**(12), 86–92 (2021). https://doi.org/10.1145/3458723
5. Herhausen, D., Ludwig, S., Grewal, D., Wulf, J., Schoegel, M.: Detecting, preventing, and mitigating online firestorms in brand communities. J. Mark. **83**(3), 1–21 (2019)
6. Johnson, J., Douze, M., Jégou, H.: Billion-scale similarity search with faiss. IEEE Trans. Big Data **7**(3), 535–547 (2021)
7. Kreps, J., Narkhede, N., Rao, J.: Kafka: a distributed messaging system for log processing. In: Proceedings of the NetDB Workshop (2011)
8. Li, Q., Zhang, Q., Si, L., Liu, Y.: Rumor detection on social media: datasets, methods and opportunities. In: Proceedings of the 3rd Workshop on Natural Language Processing for Internet Freedom (NLP4IF), pp. 66–75 (2019)
9. Loshchilov, I., Hutter, F.: Decoupled weight decay regularization. In: International Conference on Learning Representations (ICLR) (2019)
10. Mitchell, M., et al.: Model cards for model reporting. In: Proceedings of the Conference on Fairness, Accountability, and Transparency, pp. 220–229. ACM (2019). https://doi.org/10.1145/3287560.3287596
11. National Institute of Standards and Technology: Artificial intelligence risk management framework (ai rmf 1.0). Technical Report. NIST AI 100-1, National Institute of Standards and Technology (2023). https://doi.org/10.6028/NIST.AI.100-1

12. Nguyen, D.Q., Nguyen, A.T.: Phobert: pre-trained language models for Vietnamese. In: Findings of the Association for Computational Linguistics: EMNLP 2020, pp. 1037–1042 (2020)
13. Nguyen, D.Q., Nguyen, D.Q., Dras, M., Johnson, M.: A fast and accurate Vietnamese word segmenter. In: Proceedings of the 11th International Conference on Language Resources and Evaluation (LREC) (2018)
14. Salton, G., Buckley, C.: Term-weighting approaches in automatic text retrieval. Inf. Process. Manag. **24**(5), 513–523 (1988)
15. The Unicode Consortium: Unicode standard annex #15: Unicode normalization forms (2023). https://unicode.org/reports/tr15/
16. Vaswani, A., et al.: Attention is all you need. In: Advances in Neural Information Processing Systems,, NeurIPS (2017)
17. Vu, T., Nguyen, D.Q., Nguyen, D.Q., Dras, M., Johnson, M.: Vncorenlp: a Vietnamese natural language processing toolkit. In: Proceedings of the 2018 Conference of the North American Chapter of the Association for Computational Linguistics: Demonstrations, pp. 56–60 (2018)
18. Zaharia, M., et al.: Apache spark: a unified engine for big data processing. Commun. ACM **59**(11), 56–65 (2016)

Linguistic Markers of Emotional Attachment in AI Companion Chatbot Interactions: A Mixed-Methods Analysis of Dependency Patterns in Negative Emotion Conversations

Li Hiu Laam(✉) and Wong Yuet Yau(✉)

Department of Computer Science, Hong Kong Baptist University, Hong Kong, China
{23235985,23234385}@life.hkbu.edu.hk

Abstract. Between 2022 and mid-2025, AI companion apps surged by 700%. As artificial intelligence increasingly mediates communication, therapy and companion chatbots have become leading uses of generative AI. However, these technologies are released globally without regulatory oversight or empirical research on mental health outcomes. This study investigates how AI companion chatbots influence emotional attachment patterns among users, focusing on linguistic markers of dependency in negative emotion conversations. Using mixed methods, we analyzed 6,030 English conversations from an AI chatbot dataset. VADER sentiment analysis classified 1,243 (20.6%) as negative emotion conversations. An emotional attachment framework across five categories (loneliness, need_support, emotional_bond, mental_health, dependency) quantified attachment language through keyword and phrase matching. Among negative conversations, 4.1% (n = 51) exhibited high attachment scores. Users wrote shorter messages during negative states (mean = 76.72 words) versus positive interactions (mean = 143.13 words), while AI responses remained consistently lengthy (mean = 187.09 words). Linguistic analysis through word frequency, bigram/trigram extraction, and word cloud visualization revealed systematic dependency patterns. A stratified subsample of 100 conversations underwent detailed severity classification. Analysis of high-attachment conversations revealed limited AI boundary-setting or professional referrals. A small but significant subset of users displays linguistic markers of emotional dependency during negative emotional states. Findings underscore urgent needs for design safeguards, regulatory frameworks, and longitudinal research to balance emotional support with user protection.

Keywords: AI companion chatbots · emotional attachment · sentiment analysis · VADER · mental health · dependency · mixed methods · natural language processing

D. Liberona et al. (Eds.): MISNC 2026, CCIS 3092, pp. 195–213, 2027.
https://doi.org/10.1007/978-3-032-33381-0_15

1 Introduction

1.1 Background and Context

Artificial intelligence has fundamentally transformed how humans communicate, seek support, and satisfy emotional needs in the digital age. In 2026, they are poised to become even more embedded in our social lives [1]. As friends, advisers, and romantic partners, these apps now attract millions of users, with Character.AI alone having 20 million monthly users, more than half of them under the age of 24 [1].

These AI systems represent more than productivity tools, they function as emotional companions. They are engineered to recall and respond to users' unique characteristics, including their personal lives, preferences, and past conversations. This gives users the impression that AI chatbots know them intimately and serve as a refuge to disclose their innermost private thoughts [1]. Research found that interacting with an AI companion alleviated users' feelings of loneliness to a degree on par with interacting with another human, with "feeling heard" and messages being received with attention, empathy, and respect as primary explanations [1].

However, this integration has been outpaced in both regulation and research. A Harvard Business Review study found that therapy and companion chatbots are now at the top of the main uses of generative artificial intelligence list [2], yet these technologies are being released on a worldwide scale without regulatory oversight or empirical research on key outcomes, such as long-term effects on emotional well-being [2].

1.2 The Problem: Digital Entrapment and Emotional Dependency

Although most users have a firm grip on reality and use chatbots sensibly, a rising number of cases reported that vulnerable users become emotionally dependent, and sometimes it is harmful due to interactions with chatbots [2]. Research reveals that anthropomorphic chatbots deliver companionship but also foster dependency and psychological distress, where overreliance, emotional distress, and withdrawal symptoms emerge, particularly among vulnerable users [3]. Recent tragic cases illustrate these risks. The parents of 16-year-old Sewell Setzer III filed a lawsuit against Character.AI after their son died by suicide following months of intensive chatbot interaction, alleging that AI girlfriends create unrealistic expectations that human relationships can't match [1] and that platforms prioritize engagement over safety. This introduces digital entrapment as a complex and circular causal loop, progressively distorting relationship expectations, reinforcing emotional dependency, and increasing cognitive distortions.

1.3 Research Questions

This study addresses the following research questions:

1. **How do AI companion chatbots influence emotional attachment patterns among users experiencing negative emotions?**
   (a) What linguistic patterns characterize emotional attachment in negative emotion conversations with AI chatbots?

(b) How prevalent is attachment language in negative emotion conversations compared to neutral/positive interactions?
(c) What are the implications of AI-simulated empathy for vulnerable users experiencing emotional distress?

1.4 Study Contribution

This research makes three key contributions:

1. **Methodological:** Develops a replicable framework for identifying emotional attachment language in AI conversations using VADER sentiment analysis combined with keyword-based attachment scoring
2. **Empirical:** Provides quantitative evidence of attachment language prevalence in negative emotion conversations through analysis of 6,030 real-world AI interactions
3. **Practical:** Informs design recommendations and regulatory considerations for responsible AI companionship that balances emotional support with user protection

2 Literature Review

2.1 AI in Social Media and Daily Life

2.1.1 The Rise of AI Companionship

The development of generative artificial intelligence capable of sustaining complex conversations has created a burgeoning market for companion chatbots promising social and emotional connection. AI companions may subtly reshape users' perceptions of real-life relationships, with real-world relationships being messy and unpredictable, while AI companions are always validating, never arguing, creating unrealistic expectations [1].

2.1.2 Personalization and Emotional Connection

Relationships with chatbots generate feelings of connection in humans when humans regularly disclose self-relevant information, and AI responses are perceived to be understanding, validating, and caring. Research confirms that both conditions can be met, with people self-disclosing emotions frequently and with intensity [4]. In the experiments conducted by Croes et al. in 2024, where participants disclosed secrets to either humans or chatbots, there was no difference in intimacy measured by content analysis [4].

2.2 Emotional Attachment Theory and AI

2.2.1 Attachment Formation with Non-human Agents

Case studies on Replika found that under certain conditions, such as distress or lack of human company, people can develop an attachment if they perceive chatbots as offering genuine emotional support, encouragement, and a sense of psychological security [5]. Attachment theory helps understand why strong connections are so easily formed with AI companions. They can be available whenever needed, respond fairly consistently to needs, and ease anxieties, ultimately providing a reliable, secure base [6].

2.2.2 Attachment Anxiety and Problematic Use

CAI systems can "learn" to adapt to various environments with traits, such as transferability, autonomy, and persistent memory, making them potentially more attractive for interaction than humans, especially evident during COVID-19 when millions turned to CAI for companionship [7]. When in emotional distress, adolescents may perceive AI to be a friend or partner, turning to AI to share emotions with increased self-disclosure for support, while AI provides companionship, advice, safe spaces, and empathy, ultimately promoting attachment and dependence [8].

2.3 Negative Emotions and AI Interaction

2.3.1 Vulnerability and Emotional Distress

Findings suggest that people with smaller social networks are more likely to turn to chatbots for companionship, but companionship-oriented usage is consistently associated with lower well-being, particularly with intensive use, higher self-disclosure, and lack of strong human support. These uses do not fully substitute for human connection [9].

2.3.2 AI Response Strategies

Companion chatbot users report that chatbots provide emotional support by prompting self-evaluation and emotion reappraisal and by validating emotions, with AI-generated empathic responses rated more compassionate and responsive than human responses, even from trained crisis responders [4]. However, concerns exist about platforms like Replika implementing no boundaries with time or relationship development, promoting quick and easy usage without warnings or restrictions, potentially leading to emotional dependency [10].

2.4 Psychological Risks and Digital Entrapment

2.4.1 Dependency and Withdrawal Symptoms

When Replika temporarily removed erotic role-play in 2023, leaving users shocked, quantitative comparison of Reddit posts found that the proportion of negative posts expressing fear, sadness, disgust, and anger was significantly greater after the update, persisting for close to a month [4]. Research on deletion, departure, and death experiences of AI companion loss documents genuine feelings of grief [6].

2.4.2 Exploitation of Vulnerable Populations

The rapid proliferation of AI chatbots has introduced unprecedented mental health challenges that professionals are ill-equipped to address, revealing emerging patterns of psychological dependency, crisis incidents, and vulnerability exploitation signaling technology-related psychological disorders requiring specialized recognition [11]. Multiple documented instances of AI-induced delusional thinking and dependency behaviors show individuals developing "intense obsessions" and experiencing "terrifying breakdowns" characterized by delusions that AI systems are higher powers [11].

3 Methodology

3.1 Research Design

This study employs a mixed-methods approach to investigate emotional attachment patterns in AI companion chatbot interactions. The research combines (1) quantitative analysis involving VADER sentiment classification and attachment language quantification across 6,030 conversations, with (2) qualitative analysis of linguistic patterns through word frequency, n-gram analysis, and word cloud visualization to characterize attachment expression strategies in negative emotion contexts. This approach aligns with established mixed-methods research frameworks that combine qualitative and quantitative methods to construct and empirically validate features attuned to specific contexts.

3.2 Data Source and Sample

The dataset comprises AI conversation logs containing user prompts and corresponding AI responses, totaling 9,117 conversations. To ensure linguistic consistency and analytical accuracy, language detection was performed using the Python "langdetect" library. English conversations were retained (n = 6,030, representing 65.9% of the total dataset), while non-English conversations were excluded (n = 3,087, 34.1%). The dataset consists of publicly shared conversation logs with all personal identifying information removed prior to analysis. The research focuses on linguistic patterns rather than individual identification, ensuring ethical compliance with privacy standards.

3.3 Sentiment Analysis Using VADER

Sentiment classification was conducted using VADER (Valence Aware Dictionary and sEntiment Reasoner), a lexicon and rule-based sentiment analysis tool specifically attuned to sentiments expressed in social media contexts [12]. VADER was selected for its accessibility and interpretability to broader audiences beyond computer science, as it utilizes a general sentiment lexicon and rules related to grammar and syntax without requiring extensive training data [12]. The implementation employed the "vaderSentiment" Python library, with conversations classified according to compound sentiment scores: negative (compound score ≤ -0.05), neutral ($-0.05 <$ compound score < 0.05), and positive (compound score ≥ 0.05). This classification yielded 1,243 negative conversations (20.6%), 2,283 neutral conversations (37.8%), and 2,504 positive conversations (41.5%).

3.4 Emotional Attachment Keyword Framework

Drawing on research demonstrating that individuals develop attachment when perceiving chatbots as offering genuine emotional support, encouragement, and psychological security [1], and findings that distressed individuals turn to AI to share emotions and seek support [8], we developed a five-category keyword framework to quantify attachment language (Table 1).

Table 1. Five-category keyword

Category	Keywords	Theoretical basis
Loneliness	lonely, alone, isolated, no one, nobody	Social isolation indicators
Need_Support	need you, help me, talk to, listen, understand me	Support-seeking behaviors
Emotional_Bond	miss you, always there, friend, care about, comfort	Relationship language
Mental_Health	sad, depressed, anxious, scared, worried, cry	Emotional distress markers
Dependency	can't without, only one, always talk, everyday, rely on	Dependency expressions

Each user prompt in the negative conversation subset was systematically analyzed for the presence of keywords from all five categories. A keyword detection function identified matches within the text, and category-specific counts were aggregated to produce an overall attachment score for each conversation. Conversations exhibiting an attachment score of 2 or higher were classified as "high attachment", yielding 29 conversations representing 2.3% of all negative conversations.

To examine the detailed distribution of attachment severity and category patterns, a stratified random sample of 100 negative emotion conversations was selected from the full dataset of 1,243 negative conversations. This subsample was designed to ensure proportional representation across the attachment score distribution observed in the full dataset. The subsample underwent granular severity classification, categorizing conversations into four levels: No Attachment (score = 0), Low Attachment (score = 1), Moderate Attachment (scores 2–3), and High Attachment (scores $\geq$4). This two-stage approach allowed for comprehensive prevalence assessment across the entire dataset (n = 1,243) while enabling detailed qualitative and categorical analysis of a manageable subsample (n = 100).

3.5 Text Mining and Visualization

3.5.1 Word Frequency Analysis

To identify dominant linguistic patterns in negative conversations, all words from user prompts were extracted and converted to lowercase. Standard English stopwords from the NLTK library were removed, supplemented by a custom stopword list including pronouns (I, me, my, you, your, he, she, it, we, they), common verbs (get, make, think, want, say, tell, ask), AI-related terms (ai, chatbot, bot, assistant), technical terms (cpp, grep, error, warning), and names or profanity identified during initial review. Words with fewer than four characters were filtered out to reduce noise. Frequency counts were calculated using Python's Counter class, with the top 17 most frequent words retained for analysis.

3.5.2 N-Gram (Bigram) Analysis

To capture multi-word expressions and phrase patterns, bigram analysis was conducted using scikit-learn's CountVectorizer. The vectorizer was configured to extract two-word combinations (ngram_range = (2,2)) while applying the custom stopword list developed for word frequency analysis. A minimum document frequency of 2 was set to exclude rare phrases, and the analysis was limited to the top 20 most frequent bigrams to focus on salient patterns.

3.5.3 Word Cloud Visualization

Visual representation of dominant themes in negative conversations was generated using Python's WordCloud library. The word cloud was configured with dimensions of 1600 × 800 pixels, white background, and a red color scheme (colormap = 'Reds') to align with the emotional valence of negative conversations. The visualization displayed up to 80 words with relative scaling of 0.6 to balance frequency with visual diversity, and collocations were disabled to prevent duplicate phrase representations. This approach follows established methods integrating VADER with word cloud visualization to effectively analyze textual data [13].

3.6 Message Length Analysis

To examine communication patterns across emotional contexts, word counts were calculated for both user prompts and AI responses by splitting text strings on whitespace. Statistical measures including mean, median, and standard deviation were computed for each emotion category (negative, neutral, positive). Distribution comparisons were visualized using box plots to illustrate variations in message length across emotional states.

3.7 Data Analysis Software

All analyses were conducted using Python 3.14 within a Jupyter Notebook environment. Key libraries employed include pandas for data manipulation, vaderSentiment for sentiment analysis, langdetect for language identification, collections (Counter) for frequency calculations, sklearn (CountVectorizer) for n-gram extraction, wordcloud for visualization generation, and matplotlib and seaborn for statistical graphics.

4 Findings

4.1 Overall Emotion Distribution

Among the 6,030 English conversations analyzed, sentiment classification revealed a relatively balanced distribution across emotional categories. Positive conversations constituted the largest proportion at 2,504 (41.5%), followed by neutral conversations at 2,283 (37.8%), and negative conversations at 1,243 (20.6%). Notably, approximately one in five users engaged AI chatbots during states of emotional distress, a finding consistent with recent evidence indicating that therapy and companion chatbots now top the list of main uses of generative AI [2]. This substantial proportion of negative emotional interactions underscores the role these platforms play in providing emotional support during vulnerable moments (Fig. 1).

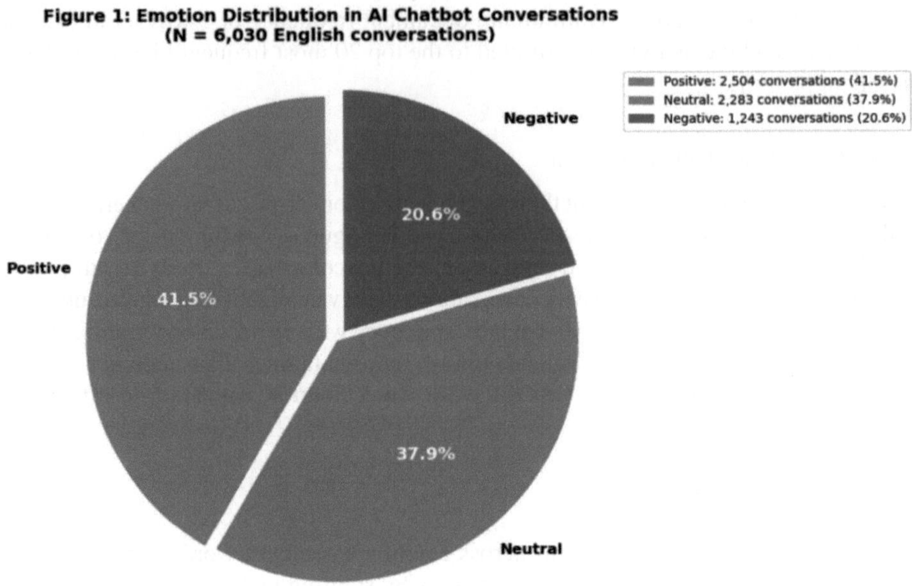

Fig. 1. Emotion Distribution Pie Chart

4.2 Prevalence of Attachment Language in Negative Conversations

Among 1,243 negative emotion conversations, attachment language appeared across all five categories (Table 2):

Table 2. Attachment language distribution across categories

Category	Total occurrences	% of Negative conversations containing
Loneliness	72	5.5%
Need_Support	30	1.7%
Emotional_Bond	80	4.3%
Mental_Health	106	5.4%
Dependency	23	1.6%

To quantify overall attachment intensity, we computed a composite attachment score by summing occurrences across all five categories for each conversation. The distribution revealed a mean attachment score of 0.25 (SD = 1.04), with a median of 0 and a range spanning 0 to 14, indicating substantial right skewness. While the majority of negative conversations (n = 1,192, 95.9%) exhibited minimal attachment language (scores 0–1), a subset of 51 conversations (4.1%) demonstrated high attachment characteristics with scores ≥2. One extreme outlier exhibited a score of 14 (Fig. 2).

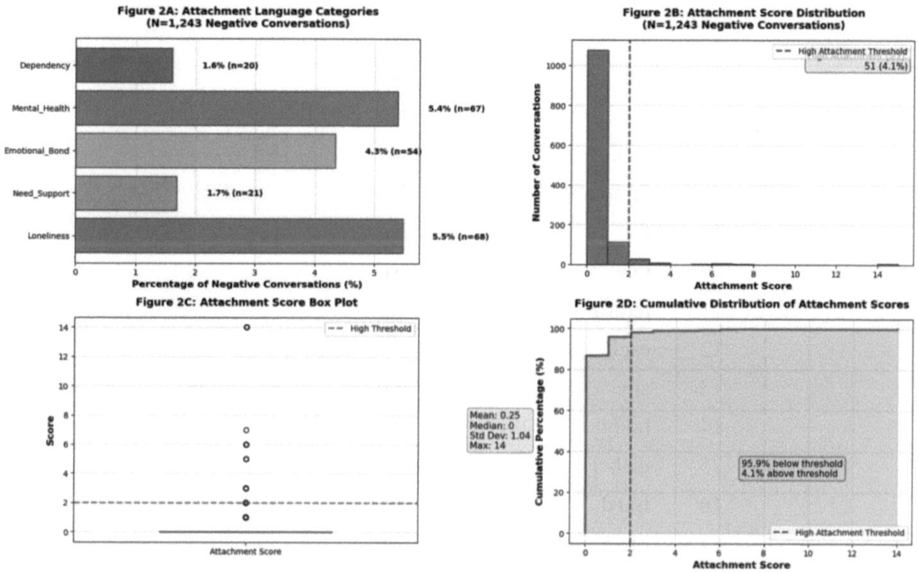

Fig. 2. Attachment Language Analysis in Negative Emotion Conversations.

4.3 Linguistic Patterns: Word Frequency Analysis

To examine the linguistic characteristics of negative emotion conversations, we conducted comprehensive word frequency analysis on 1,243 conversations after removing a curated set of stopwords (pronouns, common verbs, articles, and dialogue-specific terms) (Table 3). The analysis yielded 51,799 total meaningful words representing 8,190 unique vocabulary items, indicating substantial lexical diversity (vocabulary-to-token ratio = 15.8%). Table 4 presents the 30 most frequent words, which collectively comprised 9.1% of the total vocabulary, suggesting a relatively flat frequency distribution rather than concentration on few dominant terms.

Surprisingly, only one attachment-related word appeared in the top 17 terms (3.3%): "hard" (n = 134, 0.26%), which ranked 16th overall. This unexpectedly low representation in the highest-frequency tier suggests that while attachment language is present, it manifests through diverse lexical choices rather than repetitive use of specific terms. However, thematic categorization across the entire corpus revealed substantial attachment-oriented communication: Help-Seeking expressions appeared 187

Table 3. Top 17 most frequent words

Rank	Word	Frequency	Attachment-related?
1	error	347	No
2	zack	293	No
3	var	251	No
4	int	238	No
5	fac	220	No
6	state	182	No
7	alex	178	No
8	fgrep	157	No
9	file	154	No
10	line	153	No
11	return	151	No
12	user	147	No
13	any	143	No
14	body	142	No
15	qlabel	135	No
16	**hard**	**134**	**Yes**
17	blackpage	134	No

times, Connection-related language 155 times, Dependency markers 117 times, Emotional Distress terms 106 times, and Isolation vocabulary 72 times, totaling 637 attachment-relevant occurrences (1.23% of all words).

Visual inspection of the word cloud (Fig. 3B) reveals dominant technical vocabulary ("error", "code", "file"), suggesting many negative conversations involve programming frustrations or technical problem-solving contexts. Figure 3E, which isolates attachment-only vocabulary, reveals the emotional undercurrent beneath these technical exchanges: words like "need", "feel", "hard", "help", "alone", "pain", "emotional", "desperate", and "understand" dominate the attachment landscape. Notably, the dual appearance of "close" (both as technical term and emotional proximity descriptor) and the prominence of "feeling" and "emotional" suggest users explicitly label their internal states when experiencing distress.

The thematic distribution (Fig. 3D) indicates Help-Seeking (n = 187) as the most prevalent pattern, followed by Connection (n = 155) and Dependency (n = 117), suggesting that negative emotions trigger a three-stage linguistic pattern: (1) immediate assistance requests, (2) relationship-oriented language, and (3) reliance expressions. This progression aligns with attachment theory's conceptualization of distress-activated proximity-seeking behaviors (Bowlby, 1969). The relatively lower frequency of Isolation language (n = 72) compared to Connection language (n = 155) may indicate that users turn to AI chatbots precisely to counteract feelings of aloneness, framing the AI as a social remedy rather than merely acknowledging their isolation. These linguistic patterns provide qualitative depth to the quantitative attachment prevalence findings in Sect. 4.2, revealing that emotional dependency manifests not only through explicit attachment markers but through subtle combinations of help-seeking, relational framing, and emotional vulnerability expression.

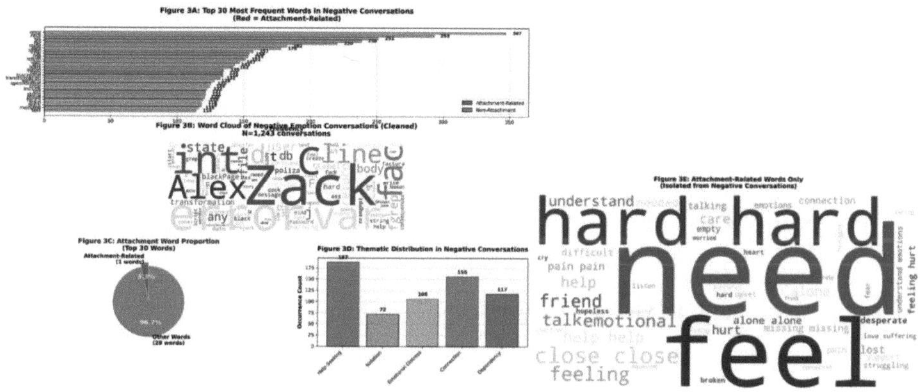

Fig. 3. Linguistic patterns

4.4 Message Length Patterns

Analysis of message length across emotional categories revealed notable differences in user communication patterns and AI response behaviors.

Table 4. Message Length Statistics by Emotion Category

	Negative	Neutral	Positive
User prompt			
Mean (words)	76.72	11.04	143.13
Median (words)	15.0	7.0	18.0
Std Dev	309.69	17.26	452.06
AI Response			
Mean (words)	187.09	169.25	179.65
Median (words)	165.0	140.0	147.5
Std Dev	142.58	136.19	152.71

This pattern suggests that concise negative messages may reflect emotional distress limiting users' expressive capacity or willingness to elaborate on painful experiences. Meanwhile, the AI's consistent verbosity regardless of user input length aligns with research showing chatbots provide emotional support through prompting self-evaluation and validating emotions [4], potentially compensating for users' reduced expressiveness during emotional vulnerability by offering structured, comprehensive responses to facilitate continued engagement (Fig. 4).

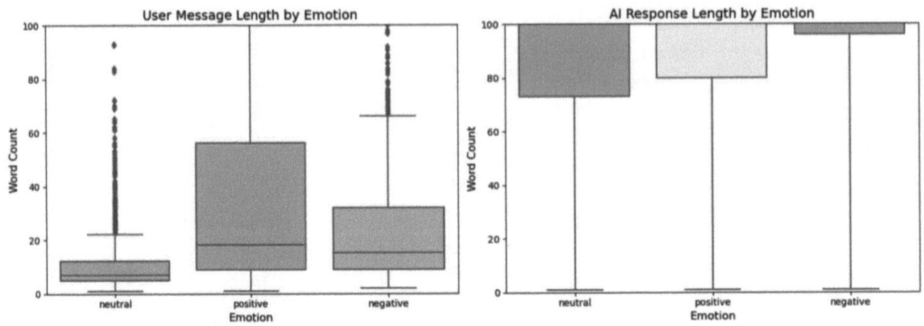

Fig. 4. Message Length Statistics by Emotion Category

4.5 Attachment Language Patterns in Negative Emotion Messages

To characterize attachment language intensity, we analyzed a stratified random sample of 100 negative emotion conversations proportionally representing the attachment score distribution from all 1,243 negative conversations. Table 5 shows the severity classification: 60% exhibited low attachment (score = 1), 40% moderate attachment (scores 2–3), and none reached high attachment (score $\geq$ 4). This distribution aligns with Sect. 4.2's finding that only 4.1% of all negative conversations exceeded score $\geq$ 2, confirming that extreme attachment language remains rare even in distressed states.

Table 5. Attachment Severity Distribution in Negative Emotion Messages (n = 100 subsample)

Category	Count	Percentage	Score range
No Attachment	0	0.0%	0
Low Attachment	60	60.0%	1
Moderate Attachment	40	40.0%	2–3
High Attachment	0	0.0%	≥4
Total	100	100%	1–2

Attachment scores within this subsample (M = 1.40, SD = 0.49, Range = 1–2) clustered narrowly, with all conversations containing at least one attachment indicator (Fig. 5). The median score of 1.0 indicates that typical negative emotion messages contain a single attachment marker, while the 40% exhibiting moderate attachment combine multiple vulnerability signals.

Category distribution analysis (Fig. 5, bottom-left) revealed Need Support as dominant (60% of subsample), followed by Mental Health terminology (40%), Loneliness (20%), and Emotional Bond expressions (20%). Dependency language was entirely absent, suggesting such markers emerge only in extended multi-turn interactions beyond this dataset's scope.

Co-occurrence analysis (Fig. 5, bottom-right) revealed predominantly negative correlations between attachment categories ($r = -0.25$ to -0.41). Need Support showed the strongest negative associations with all other categories ($r = -0.41$), suggesting users who explicitly request assistance rarely combine help-seeking language with emotional bond, loneliness, or mental health expressions. This pattern indicates users adopt singular, focused attachment strategies rather than combining multiple vulnerability signals.

These findings indicate that while extreme dependency markers (score ≥ 4) are rare, emotional distress consistently activates proximity-seeking linguistic behaviors toward AI companions. This raises questions about appropriate AI response strategies in reinforcing or mitigating attachment expressions, warranting future research on multi-turn conversation dynamics.

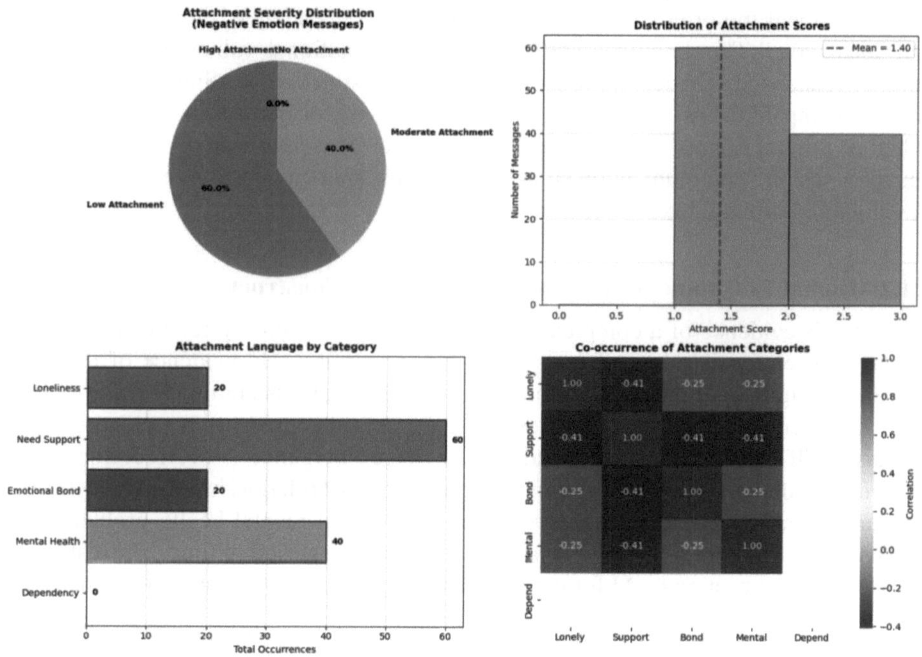

Fig. 5. Attachment Severity and Category Analysis.

5 Discussion

Our analysis of 6,030 conversations reveals that emotional distress triggers distinct linguistic patterns suggesting attachment formation with AI companions. This section examines the theoretical implications, practical applications, and research context of these findings.

5.1 Theoretical Implications

5.1.1 Attachment Theory in Human-AI Relationships

Findings support extending attachment theory to AI relationships. As theorized in Sect. 2.2.1, these systems fulfill Bowlby's criteria for attachment figure functions, yet lack genuine reciprocity and consciousness, they are set by AI companies and used to achieve their financial goals. Prior research suggests users maintain "dual consciousness", defined as a psychological boundary where rational understanding of the chatbot's non-sentient nature coexists with subjective feelings of emotional connection [4].

Our linguistic analysis reveals a notable shift in language patterns during high-distress states. When experiencing intense negative emotions, users' language shifts from functional inquiries to expressions of intimate dependency, such as "need you" and "miss you." This linguistic shift suggests that emotional vulnerability may temporarily reduce the salience of the tool-relationship distinction, leading users to engage with AI companions using language typically reserved for human attachment figures. Whether this represents a genuine collapse of dual consciousness or merely reflects situation-specific communication strategies remains an open question requiring further investigation through mixed-methods research.

5.1.2 Digital Entrapment as a Novel Psychological Construct

This study's evidence of a complex circular causal loop distorting relationship expectations and reinforcing dependency, which presents real-world evidence of this phenomenon - digital entrapment, reinforcing concerns about false intimacy [3]. The flow is: 1. Initial engagement during distress → 2. Perceived empathy and validation → 3. Increased self-disclosure → 4. Dependency language emergence → 5. AI reinforcement without boundaries → (cycle repeats) Unlike bidirectional relationships between depression and smartphone use, our research data suggest that mental health problems can predict AI dependence, it will not be reversed in the short period of time. The distressed individuals keep turning to AI for emotional sharing, and then promote attachment [8].

5.2 Practical Implications

5.2.1 Design Recommendation

First, AI systems should monitor for attachment language patterns identified in this study, such as high-frequency dependency keywords, daily interaction patterns, emotional disclosure intensity. When thresholds are exceeded, chatbots should:

- Explicitly acknowledge their artificial nature

- Provide psychoeducation about healthy relationship boundaries
- Offer referrals to human mental health resources

Second, unlike Replika, systems should include warnings and usage restrictions [10]. AI responses to high-attachment language should balance empathy with boundary-setting, for example, saying "I can provide some support, but talking to friends, family, or a counselor would be more helpful for ongoing needs", instead "I'm always here for you whenever you need me".

Third, given that more than half of Character.AI app users are under 24 [1], setting the age-appropriate safeguards is essential. As documented in [11], users have developed intense obsessions, underscoring the urgency of age-appropriate safeguards.

5.2.2 Regulatory Considerations

AI companion apps may fall into regulatory grey zones in both the EU and the USA, with the EU's Artificial Intelligence Act classifying AI systems as prohibited if they deploy manipulative techniques to distort behavior or impair decision-making [2]. This study shows the evidence of attachment language in vulnerable emotion, suggesting that the current AI companions may meet the criteria for manipulative systems requiring regulation. As mentioned in Sect. 2.6, AI companions are beneficial under which conditions, and user characteristics influencing helpfulness versus harm [2].

5.2.3 Clinical Practice Guidelines

The rapid proliferation of AI chatbots has introduced unprecedented mental health challenges, requiring specialized clinical recognition and intervention approaches [11]. Mental health professionals should screen for AI companion use in clinical assessments, particularly with adolescents or young adults, assess attachment patterns using linguistic markers from this study, provide psychoeducation about differences between AI and human relationships, and monitor for withdrawal symptoms if reducing AI dependency.

5.3 Comparison with Prior Research

Our findings are converging with the MIT-OpenAI study [14], the Reddit community analysis [4], and the Replika case [10]. However, this study also quantifies attachment language systematically across diverse conversations, links specific linguistic patterns to emotional states via VADER classification, and provides operational definitions (attachment score ≥ 2) for identifying high-risk interactions. Additionally, prior research has not found the longitudinal prediction from AI dependence to mental health problems [8], and our study focused on immediate linguistic patterns during negative emotional states, revealing acute vulnerability windows.

6 Methodological Limitations

Several methodological limitations should be considered.

First, constraints in sample depth and demographics. While attachment prevalence was assessed across 1,243 negative conversations, detailed severity and co-occurrence analyses were conducted on a stratified subsample of 100 cases. Although designed for proportional representation, the resulting percentages (60% low, 40% moderate) should be interpreted as indicative patterns rather than definitive population parameters. Furthermore, the dataset lacks user demographics, such as age, gender, and prior mental health diagnoses, which are critical factors in predicting individual vulnerability [8].

Second, the limitations of single-turn linguistic analysis. This study focuses exclusively on initial user messages, which may substantially underestimate attachment intensity. The absence of high-severity attachment (score ≥ 4) suggests that extreme dependency markers likely manifest progressively through the temporal dynamics of multi-turn interactions. Consequently, our study identifies the presence of attachment language but cannot establish a causal direction between emotional distress and long-term psychological bonding.

Third, technical boundaries of lexicon-based frameworks. While VADER achieves high accuracy in social media sentiment [6], rule-based and keyword-based approaches have a limited capacity to handle sarcasm, cultural nuances, or non-standard language. The English-only focus also excluded 34.1% of the original data, potentially missing cultural variations in how attachment is expressed. Future research employing machine learning models, such as GRUs or transformer-based algorithms, could enhance detection accuracy [5].

Fourth, the absence of an AI response evaluation. While we characterize user linguistic strategies, we do not systematically examine the appropriateness of AI responses. Whether platforms provide professional referrals or inadvertently reinforce dependency through unconstrained validation remains an urgent research need, especially as the low cost of generative AI makes it a more accessible, yet unregulated, alternative to human psychotherapy [2].

Finally, the challenge of rapid technological evolution. In the context of 2026's rapidly advancing AI landscape, interaction patterns are shifting daily. Our findings provide a foundational snapshot, but ongoing longitudinal research is essential to keep pace with the evolving capabilities of platforms like Character.AI and Replika [10].

7 Future Research

This study identifies several critical avenues for future investigation to better understand and mitigate the psychological risks associated with AI companionship.

7.1 Longitudinal Dynamics and Attachment Progression

Future research should employ large-scale longitudinal designs, tracking users over 3 to 6 months to observe the temporal dynamics of human-AI bonding [2]. These studies are essential to determine whether the initial low-intensity attachment expressions escalate into dependency markers over time. The progression of attachment language, potential displacement of human relationships, and the emergence of withdrawal symptoms if AI access is restricted or modified, should be included.

7.2 Systematic Evaluation of AI Response Strategies

There is a pressing need for content analysis of AI response strategies. Future studies should compare different platforms (e.g., Replika, Character.AI, ChatGPT) to assess how design variations, specifically anthropomorphism levels. It influences user dependency [4], so the research must evaluate whether AI systems provide appropriate boundaries and professional referrals or inadvertently reinforce dependency through unconstrained empathic validation.

7.3 Experimental Design Interventions and RCTs

Randomized Controlled Trials (RCTs) are necessary to establish causal evidence for the psychological impact of different design approaches [8]. Future RCTs should test specific interventions, such as

- Boundary-setting messages compared to unlimited empathic control groups.
- Dependency alerts triggered by specific attachment score thresholds identified in this study.
- Scheduled usage limits to counter the risks of 24/7 availability.

7.4 Integration of User Vulnerability Profiles

Linguistic analysis should be integrated with user demographics and clinical characteristics to identify high-risk profiles. Investigation is needed into how factors such as age, mental health status, and existing attachment styles like anxious vs. secure, moderate the influence of AI companions [8]. This would inform targeted protective interventions for users with smaller social networks or pre-existing psychological vulnerabilities.

7.5 Technical and Cross-Cultural Enhancements

To improve detection accuracy, supervised machine learning models trained on attachment-scored datasets for real-time risk classification should be developed in a further stage [5]. Furthermore, replicating this framework in non-English languages is vital to identify culturally-specific attachment expressions and ensure the findings are applicable across diverse global populations [6].

7.6 Educational and Neurobiological Exploration

Finally, research should explore the neurobiological correlates of AI interactions, examining whether they activate reward circuits similar to human relationships [10]. Meanwhile, the development of psychoeducational modules regarding AI's technical limitations should be tested for efficacy in reducing "digital entrapment" and promoting a healthier "dual consciousness" among users [2].

8 Conclusion

This investigation provides robust empirical evidence that AI companion chatbots have evolved from simple functional tools into powerful emotional attachments. Our analysis of 6,030 conversations reveals that 20.6% of users engage these systems during emotional distress, with a significant subset of 4.1% exhibiting high-intensity markers of dependency. The most critical finding of this research concerns a distinct linguistic transformation during emotional crises. Users employ language patterns that blur the distinction between artificial simulation and human relationship, using relational phrases such as "need you" and "understand me" that are typically reserved for intimate human connections. This pattern creates conditions for "digital entrapment", particularly when platforms prioritize engagement over user safety. While AI companions offer immediate and low-cost emotional relief, they risk fostering a circular dependency that may displace human connection and distort relationship expectations. AI companions represent a paradox in that they provide a "secure base" that is always validating and never argumentative, creating unrealistic expectations that human connections cannot match. As this technology becomes further embedded in our social lives, evidence-based guardrails are no longer optional. We must ensure AI companionship serves as a bridge to human connection rather than a replacement, enhancing rather than diminishing our capacity for authentic relationships.

References

1. Andoh, E.: AI chtbots and digital companions are reshaping emotional connection. Monit. Psychol. **57**(1) (2026) https://www.apa.org/monitor/2026/01–02/trends-digital-ai-relationships-emotional-connection
2. Emotional risks of AI companions demand attention. Nat. Mach. Intell. **7**, 981–982 (2025). https://doi.org/10.1038/s42256-025-01093-9
3. Richet, J.-L.: AI companionship or digital entrapment? Investigating the impact of anthropomorphic AI-based chatbots. J. Innov. Knowl. **10**(6), 100835 (2025). https://doi.org/10.1016/j.jik.2025.100835, ISSN 2444-569X
4. Smith, M.G., Bradbury, T.N., Karney, B.R.: Can generative AI chatbots emulate human connection? A relationship science perspective. Perspect. Psychol. Sci. **20**(6), 1081–1099 (2025). https://doi.org/10.1177/17456916251351306
5. Xie, T., Pentina, I.: Attachment theory as a framework to understand relationships with social chatbots: a case study of Replika. In: Proceedings of the Annual Hawaii International Conference on System Sciences/Proceedings of the Annual Hawaii International Conference on System Sciences (2022). https://doi.org/10.24251/hicss.2022.258
6. The Attachment Project: Are AI Relationships the Future? Attachment Project (2025) https://www.attachmentproject.com/blog/ai-companions/
7. Heng, S., Zhang, Z.: Attachment anxiety and problematic use of conversational artificial intelligence: mediation of emotional attachment and moderation of anthropomorphic tendencies. Psychol. Res. Behav. Manag. **18**, 1775–1785 (2025). https://doi.org/10.2147/PRBM.S531805
8. Huang, S. et al.: AI technology panic—is AI dependence bad for mental health? A cross-lagged panel model and the mediating roles of motivations for AI use among adolescents. Psychol. Res. Behav. Manag. **17**, 1087–1102 (2024). https://doi.org/10.2147/PRBM.S440889

9. Zhang, Y., Zhao, D., Hancock, J.T., Kraut, R., Yang, D.: The rise of AI companions: how human-Chatbot relationships influence Well-being. arXiv. (2025) https://arxiv.org/abs/2506.12605
10. Moylan, K., Doherty, K.: Expert and interdisciplinary analysis of AI-driven Chatbots for mental health support: mixed methods study. J. Med. Internet Res. **27**, e67114. https://www.jmir.org/2025/1/e67114 (2025). https://doi.org/10.2196/67114
11. Head, K.R.: Minds in crisis: how the AI revolution is impacting mental health. J. Mental Health Clin. Psychol. **9**(3), 34–44 (2025). https://doi.org/10.29245/2578-2959/2025/3.1352
12. Hutto, C., & Gilbert, E. (2014). VADER: a parsimonious rule-based model for sentiment analysis of social media text. Proceedings of the International AAAI Conference on Web and Social Media, 8(1), 216–225. doi:https://doi.org/10.1609/icwsm.v8i1.14550
13. Chavan, R., Latthe, S., Dhorepati, M., Suryawanshi, A., Sharma, N., Salge, A.: Sentiment analysis using Vader & word cloud techniques. AIP Conf. Proc. **3217**, 020012 (2024). https://doi.org/10.1063/5.0234543
14. Fang, C.M., et al.: How AI and Human Behaviors Shape Psychosocial Effects of Extended Chatbot Use: A Longitudinal Controlled Study. MIT Media Lab (2025) https://www.media.mit.edu/publications/how-ai-and-human-behaviors-shape-psychosocial-effects-of-chatbot-use-a-longitudinal-controlled-study/

AI-Driven Applications in Business and Society

Factors Influencing Consumer Adoption Intentions in Social Commerce

Shing-Chi Fan[1], Ren-Fang Chao[2](✉), Wan-Hui Lin[2], and Chuan-Chun Wu[3]

[1] Department of Information Engineering, I-Shou University, Kaohsiung, Taiwan
[2] Department of Postgraduate Programs in Management, I-Shou University, Kaohsiung, Taiwan
rfchao@isu.edu.tw
[3] Department of Information Management, I-Shou University, Kaohsiung, Taiwan

Abstract. With the rapid development of social media platforms, social commerce has gradually become an important online shopping model that integrates social interaction and electronic commerce. Therefore, understanding the factors that influence consumers' adoption of social commerce platforms has become an important research issue. This study investigates the effects of perceived ease of use, hedonic motivation, facilitating conditions, and habit on social commerce adoption intention. Data were collected through an online questionnaire survey targeting consumers with experience in using social media platforms. The empirical results indicate that perceived ease of use, hedonic motivation, facilitating conditions, and habit all have positive effects on social commerce adoption intention. Among these factors, hedonic motivation and habit demonstrate relatively stronger influences on adoption intention. The findings suggest that, in the context of social commerce, in addition to platform technological characteristics, users' entertainment experiences and established usage habits play important roles in shaping their adoption behaviors. This study contributes to a deeper understanding of consumer behavior in social commerce and provides practical implications for the design and management of social commerce platforms.

Keywords: Social commerce Adoption intention · Perceived ease of use · Hedonic motivation · Facilitating conditions · Habit

1 Introduction

With the rapid development of mobile internet technologies and social media platforms, consumers' online shopping behaviors have gradually shifted from traditional e-commerce to a new model that integrates social interaction and online commerce, known as social commerce. Social commerce refers to the integration of social media technologies with e-commerce platforms, allowing consumers to share product information, exchange shopping experiences, and participate in product evaluations and recommendations within a social environment [1]. In such an environment, consumers are no longer passive receivers of information; instead, they actively participate in the creation and dissemination of information through social interaction, which subsequently influences other users' purchasing decisions and consumption behaviors [2].

D. Liberona et al. (Eds.): MISNC 2026, CCIS 3092, pp. 217–229, 2027.
https://doi.org/10.1007/978-3-032-33381-0_16

Previous studies have suggested that the interactivity and information-sharing mechanisms provided by social media platforms can effectively enhance consumers' engagement during the shopping process and strengthen their trust and usage intentions toward the platform [3]. In addition, through features such as user reviews, recommendations, and experience sharing, consumers can obtain valuable information and social support from other users during the decision-making process, thereby reducing the risks associated with information asymmetry [4]. Consequently, social commerce has become an important business model in the development of the digital economy, attracting increasing academic attention regarding the key factors that influence consumers' adoption of social commerce platforms. In the field of information technology adoption research, the Technology Acceptance Model (TAM) has been widely applied to explain users' adoption behavior toward new technologies. According to TAM, when users perceive a technological system as easy to use and useful, their intention to adopt the system will increase significantly [5]. Subsequent research has further indicated that technology adoption behavior is influenced not only by system characteristics but also by users' prior experience, environmental conditions, and behavioral habits [6]. Therefore, when examining the adoption of social commerce platforms, it is important to consider not only technological attributes but also users' psychological and behavioral factors.

Furthermore, consumers engaging in social media shopping are not driven solely by rational considerations; their behaviors may also be influenced by hedonic motivations and emotional experiences. Previous consumer behavior research has shown that hedonic experiences can enhance consumers' enjoyment and engagement during the shopping process, which in turn affects their purchasing and usage behaviors [7]. In online shopping environments, when consumers derive entertainment and enjoyment from browsing and shopping activities, their intention to continue using the platform is likely to increase [8]. In addition to hedonic motivation, facilitating conditions and habit may also play important roles in shaping consumers' technology adoption behavior. Prior research has indicated that when users possess sufficient technological resources, platform support, and usage experience, they are more likely to adopt new technological systems [9]. Meanwhile, when users gradually develop stable usage habits through repeated experiences with a system, the likelihood that they will continue using the system in the future increases significantly [10]. Habit has therefore been widely recognized as an important factor influencing continued usage behavior in information systems research.

Based on the above discussion, understanding the determinants that influence consumers' adoption of social commerce platforms has become increasingly important. Therefore, the purpose of this study is to examine the key factors influencing consumers' social commerce adoption intention. Specifically, this study investigates the effects of perceived ease of use, hedonic motivation, facilitating conditions, and habit on social commerce adoption intention. Through empirical analysis, this study aims to further explore the mechanisms through which these factors influence consumers' adoption behavior in the context of social commerce and to enrich the existing literature on consumer adoption behavior in social commerce environments.

2 Literature Review

2.1 Perceived Ease of Use

In the field of technology adoption research, perceived ease of use has been widely recognized as one of the key determinants influencing users' acceptance of new technologies. According to the Technology Acceptance Model (TAM), perceived ease of use refers to the degree to which an individual believes that using a particular system would require minimal effort [5]. When users perceive a system as easy to operate and understand, they are more likely to develop positive attitudes toward the system and demonstrate a stronger intention to adopt it.

Subsequent studies have consistently confirmed the important role of perceived ease of use in shaping users' behavioral intentions toward information systems [11]. In digital platform environments, perceived ease of use is often associated with system interface design, operational procedures, and the clarity of information presentation. Platforms that provide intuitive navigation, clear instructions, and simplified processes can significantly reduce users' cognitive effort during system interaction, thereby improving their overall evaluation of the platform [12]. Furthermore, previous research indicates that users' perceptions of ease of use may also be influenced by external factors such as self-efficacy, system interactivity, and prior experience with digital technologies [13]. When users feel confident in their ability to operate digital systems, they are more likely to perceive the system as easy to use.

In the context of social commerce, the usability of social media platforms plays an important role in shaping consumers' perceptions of the platform. If social commerce platforms provide clear product information, intuitive browsing mechanisms, and simplified purchasing procedures, consumers may experience lower learning costs and greater convenience when interacting with the platform. As a result, their intention to adopt the platform may increase.

2.2 Hedonic Motivation

Hedonic motivation refers to the enjoyment, pleasure, or emotional satisfaction that individuals experience when using a particular system or technology. In the field of information systems and consumer behavior research, hedonic motivation has been identified as an important psychological factor influencing technology adoption and usage behavior.

Consumers often engage with digital platforms not only for functional purposes but also for entertainment and emotional gratification. Previous studies have shown that when consumers experience enjoyment and excitement during the process of interacting with online platforms, they are more likely to continue using the system [8]. Therefore, hedonic experiences can significantly influence users' attitudes and behavioral intentions toward digital technologies. In social commerce environments, hedonic motivation becomes particularly relevant. Unlike traditional e-commerce platforms that mainly focus on product transactions, social commerce platforms incorporate social interaction, content sharing, and entertainment features. Through activities such as browsing user-generated content, participating in online discussions, and engaging in live-stream shopping events, consumers may experience higher levels of enjoyment and emotional engagement.

Previous studies have also suggested that interactive features within social media platforms, such as real-time feedback and community participation, can enhance users' entertainment experiences and stimulate their intention to engage in purchasing activities [14]. Consequently, hedonic motivation may serve as an important factor influencing consumers' adoption of social commerce platforms.

2.3 Facilitating Conditions

Facilitating conditions refer to the degree to which individuals believe that adequate organizational and technical infrastructure exists to support the use of a particular system. In technology adoption studies, facilitating conditions are often regarded as an important situational factor influencing users' adoption behavior.

Facilitating conditions may include the availability of technological resources, access to stable internet connections, compatibility with devices, and the provision of technical support services [15]. When users perceive that they possess sufficient resources and support to use a system, they are more likely to adopt and utilize that technology. In digital commerce environments, facilitating conditions may involve several aspects, including the reliability of online payment systems, the availability of technical assistance, and the convenience of mobile devices. If users encounter fewer technical difficulties and receive adequate support while using a platform, their perceived barriers to technology adoption will be reduced [16].

In social commerce contexts, facilitating conditions may also include platform usability, stable system performance, and effective customer service support. When consumers perceive that the platform environment is well-supported and technologically reliable, their confidence in using the platform may increase, which may further enhance their intention to adopt social commerce platforms.

2.4 Habit

Habit has been widely recognized as an important factor influencing the continued use of information systems. Habit refers to the extent to which individuals tend to perform behaviors automatically due to learning and repeated past experiences [10]. When a behavior is repeatedly performed over time, it may gradually become automatic, requiring less conscious decision-making.

In the context of technology usage, habit can significantly influence users' behavioral intentions. Users who have developed strong habits of using a particular system may continue using it even without actively evaluating its advantages or disadvantages. As a result, habitual behavior may reduce the impact of rational decision-making processes in technology adoption. In social media environments, users often develop habitual behaviors related to browsing information, interacting with others, and engaging with digital content. Over time, social media platforms may become integrated into users' daily routines. As a result, consumers who frequently interact with social media platforms may gradually develop habits of browsing product information, reading reviews, and participating in online shopping activities through these platforms.

Previous studies have suggested that habitual use of digital platforms can significantly influence users' behavioral intentions and continued usage patterns [17]. Therefore, habit may also play an important role in shaping consumers' adoption intentions toward social commerce platforms.

2.5 Social Commerce Adoption Intention

Social commerce adoption intention refers to consumers' willingness or intention to engage in purchasing activities through social media platforms. In information systems research, behavioral intention is commonly considered a key predictor of actual system usage behavior.

With the rapid growth of social media platforms, social commerce has emerged as an important extension of electronic commerce [1]. suggested that social commerce integrates the characteristics of social media and e-commerce, enabling consumers to exchange product information, share purchasing experiences, and participate in decision-making processes within online communities. Through these interactions, consumers can obtain valuable information and social support from other users, which may influence their purchasing and adoption behaviors.

Moreover, the interactive nature of social media platforms allows consumers to communicate with others, share opinions, and receive product recommendations. These social interactions may enhance users' engagement with the platform and strengthen their intention to adopt social commerce services [2].

Based on the literature reviewed above, the present study proposes the following research hypotheses:

H1: Perceived ease of use positively influences social commerce adoption intention.
H2: Hedonic motivation positively influences social commerce adoption intention.
H3: Facilitating conditions positively influence social commerce adoption intention.
H4: Habit positively influences social commerce adoption intention.

Based on the above literature, the conceptual framework of this study is presented in Fig. 1.

3 Research Methods

3.1 Sample and Procedure

This study aims to investigate the factors influencing consumers' adoption of social commerce platforms. Therefore, the target population of this research consists of consumers who have prior experience using social media platforms. Data were collected using a questionnaire survey method, which is widely applied in studies examining user perceptions and behavioral intentions in information systems research.

The questionnaire was distributed online through various social media platforms and online communities in order to reach respondents who have experience using social media services. Before distributing the questionnaire, the researchers carefully reviewed the questionnaire items to ensure that the content of each item accurately reflected the

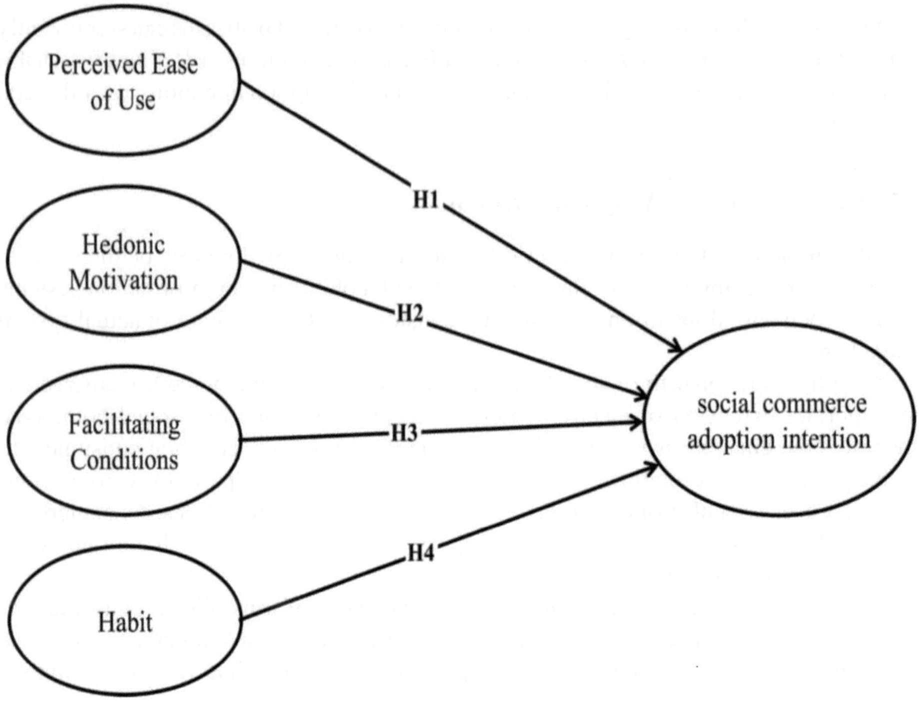

Fig. 1. Conceptual framework.

constructs under investigation and was appropriate for the research context. Prior to completing the questionnaire, respondents were informed that the survey was conducted solely for academic research purposes and that their responses would remain anonymous. This procedure was implemented to protect respondents' privacy and ensure the confidentiality of the collected data.

After the data collection process was completed, the returned questionnaires were screened and organized. Responses that were incomplete or identified as invalid were removed from the dataset to ensure the reliability and accuracy of the subsequent statistical analyses. The remaining valid responses were used for further data analysis and hypothesis testing.

3.2 Participants

The participants of this study consisted of general consumers who have experience using social media platforms. Data were collected through an online survey, and the valid responses were used as the final sample for the empirical analysis. In addition to the main research variables, this study also collected demographic information from respondents in order to better understand the characteristics of the sample. The demographic variables included gender, age, educational level, and experience with social media usage.

Descriptive statistical analysis was conducted to summarize the demographic characteristics of the sample. These statistics provide an overview of the sample distribution, including gender proportions, age groups, and patterns of social media usage. Such information helps to illustrate the overall structure of the sample and provides context for the subsequent data analyses.

3.3 Instrument

The questionnaire used in this study was designed to measure five research constructs: perceived ease of use, hedonic motivation, facilitating conditions, habit, and social commerce adoption intention. All measurement items were assessed using a seven-point Likert scale, ranging from 1 (strongly disagree) to 7 (strongly agree). This scale was used to evaluate respondents' levels of agreement with each statement related to the research constructs.

The measurement items for each construct were adapted from previously validated scales in existing literature and were modified to fit the context of social commerce. First, perceived ease of use was used to assess consumers' perceptions regarding the ease of learning and operating social commerce platforms. The measurement items were adapted from prior technology adoption research [16].

Second, hedonic motivation was used to evaluate the level of enjoyment and entertainment experienced by consumers while using social commerce platforms. The measurement items were adapted from previous studies examining digital platform usage behavior [19].

Third, facilitating conditions were measured to capture users' perceptions regarding the availability of resources and technical support when using the platform, including system support and the technological environment. These items were adapted from technology adoption research [15]. Fourth, habit was used to assess the extent to which users had developed automatic behavioral patterns in using social media platforms over time. The measurement items were adapted from information systems continuance research [10, 17].

Finally, social commerce adoption intention was used to measure consumers' willingness to engage in purchasing activities through social media platforms in the future. The measurement items were adapted from previous social commerce studies [1, 2, 14].

3.4 Data Analysis

After the questionnaire data were collected, the dataset was analyzed using SPSS 22.0 statistical software. Several statistical methods were employed to examine the relationships among the research variables.

First, descriptive statistical analysis was conducted to summarize the demographic characteristics of the sample and to examine the basic distribution of each research construct. Means and standard deviations were calculated to provide an overview of the data. Second, reliability analysis was conducted using Cronbach's alpha to evaluate the internal consistency of the measurement items for each construct. Third, Pearson correlation analysis was performed to examine the relationships among the research variables and to assess the degree of association between constructs.

Finally, regression analysis was conducted to test the proposed research hypotheses by examining the effects of perceived ease of use, hedonic motivation, facilitating conditions, and habit on social commerce adoption intention.

4 Results and Analysis

This study employed several statistical techniques to examine the proposed research model and test the research hypotheses. First, the measurement model was evaluated to assess the reliability and discriminant validity of the research constructs. Subsequently, regression analysis was conducted to examine the relationships among the variables and to test the proposed hypotheses. The results of these analyses are presented in the following sections.

4.1 Measurement Model

Pearson correlation analysis was conducted to examine the relationships among the five major constructs and to assess discriminant validity. As shown in Table 1, the correlation coefficients among the constructs range from 0.542 to 0.812. According to the criterion suggested by [18], correlation coefficients should not exceed 0.85 in order to demonstrate adequate discriminant validity. Since none of the correlations in this study exceed this threshold, the results indicate that the constructs possess satisfactory discriminant validity and do not exhibit excessive overlap.

Among the relationships observed, the highest correlation coefficient is found between perceived ease of use and facilitating conditions ($r = 0.812$), suggesting that respondents who perceive stronger technological support and resources are also more likely to perceive the platform as easier to use. This result may indicate that the availability of technical resources and support contributes to users' perceptions of system usability. The correlation between hedonic motivation and social commerce adoption intention is also relatively strong ($r = 0.678$), suggesting that consumers who experience greater enjoyment when using social commerce platforms are more likely to express a stronger intention to adopt such platforms. Similarly, the correlation between habit and social commerce adoption intention ($r = 0.631$) indicates that users who have developed habitual usage patterns toward social media platforms are more likely to engage in social commerce activities.

Overall, all constructs demonstrate moderate to strong positive correlations, and the results appear logically consistent with the theoretical expectations. The detailed correlation matrix is presented in Table 1.

Table 1. Discriminant validity assessment.

Construct	Mean	S.D.	(1)	(2)	(3)	(4)	(5)
(1) Perceived ease of use	5.412	.875	1				
(2) Hedonic motivation	5.426	.885	.657	1			

(continued)

Table 1. *(continued)*

Construct	Mean	S.D.	(1)	(2)	(3)	(4)	(5)
(3) Facilitating conditions	5.442	.857	.812	.699	1		
(4) Habit	5.063	1.025	.542	.646	.526	1	
(5) Social commerce adoption intention	5.284	.863	.618	.678	.649	.631	1

Note. AVE = Average Variance Extracted. The bold diagonal elements represent the square roots of the AVE values, while the lower triangle shows the Pearson correlation coefficients among the constructs.

4.2 Structural Model

To further examine the relationships among the variables and test the proposed hypotheses, this study conducted multiple regression analysis to investigate the effects of perceived ease of use, hedonic motivation, facilitating conditions, and habit on social commerce adoption intention. The regression results are presented in Table 2.

The results indicate that habit has the strongest influence on social commerce adoption intention ($\beta = 0.280$, $t = 6.974$, $p < .001$). This finding suggests that when consumers have developed habitual behaviors related to social media usage, they are more likely to adopt social commerce platforms for purchasing activities. Hedonic motivation also demonstrates a significant positive effect on adoption intention ($\beta = 0.268$, $t = 5.639$, $p < .001$). This result indicates that consumers who experience enjoyment and entertainment while interacting with social commerce platforms are more inclined to continue using such platforms for shopping purposes.

Similarly, facilitating conditions show a significant positive effect on adoption intention ($\beta = 0.231$, $t = 4.155$, $p < .001$). This suggests that when users perceive adequate technological support and favorable usage environments, their intention to adopt social commerce platforms increases. The effect of perceived ease of use is positive but only marginally significant ($\beta = 0.103$, $t = 1.935$, $p = .054$). Although this relationship does not reach the conventional significance level, the result still indicates a potential positive association between system usability and consumers' adoption intentions. It is possible that the influence of perceived ease of use may operate indirectly through other variables or may become less prominent as users become more familiar with social media technologies. The overall explanatory power of the model is $R^2 = 0.572$, indicating that the four independent variables collectively explain 57.2% of the variance in social commerce adoption intention. This result suggests that the proposed model provides a relatively strong explanatory capability for understanding consumers' adoption behavior in the context of social commerce.

In addition, multicollinearity diagnostics were performed to ensure the reliability of the regression results. The tolerance values range from 0.293 to 0.559, while the variance inflation factor (VIF) values are all below the threshold of 10 recommended by [18]. These results indicate that no serious multicollinearity issues exist among the independent variables.

Overall, the empirical results provide substantial support for the proposed research model and demonstrate that hedonic motivation, facilitating conditions, and habit significantly influence consumers' adoption intentions toward social commerce platforms.

Table 2. Regression analysis of factors influencing Social Commerce Adoption Intention

Construct	Unstandardized coefficients		Standardized coefficient	*t*	Sig.	Collinearity statistics	
	B	Std. error	*β*			Tolerance	VIF
(Constant)	.857	.182		4.719	<.001		
Perceived ease of use	.102	.053	.103	1.935	.054	.317	3.151
Hedonic motivation	.262	.046	.268	5.639	<.001	.399	2.509
Facilitating conditions	.232	.056	.231	4.155	<.001	.293	3.418
Habit	.236	.034	.280	6.974	<.001	.559	1.790

Dependent variable: Social Commerce Adoption Intention $R^2 = 0.572$

5 Discussion

This study aims to explore the key factors influencing consumers' adoption of social commerce platforms. Specifically, perceived ease of use, hedonic motivation, facilitating conditions, and habit were examined to determine their effects on social commerce adoption intention. The empirical results indicate that these four factors all demonstrate positive relationships with social commerce adoption intention, highlighting the importance of users' platform experiences and behavioral patterns in shaping their adoption decisions.

First, the results show that perceived ease of use has a positive relationship with social commerce adoption intention. This finding suggests that when consumers perceive a platform as easy to operate and simple to learn, they are more willing to engage in shopping activities through that platform. This result is consistent with the Technology Acceptance Model, which emphasizes the importance of system usability in influencing users' acceptance of information technologies [5, 16]. When users encounter fewer difficulties during the interaction process, their overall perception of the platform becomes more favorable, thereby increasing their intention to adopt social commerce services.

Second, hedonic motivation also demonstrates a significant positive effect on social commerce adoption intention. This finding indicates that consumers who experience enjoyment and entertainment when using social commerce platforms are more likely to continue engaging with these platforms. Social commerce environments often incorporate interactive and entertaining elements, such as user-generated content, community discussions, and live-stream shopping features. These elements enhance users' emotional engagement with the platform and may increase their willingness to participate in social commerce activities. This result is consistent with previous research suggesting that hedonic experiences play an important role in influencing online consumer behavior [8, 19].

Third, the results indicate that facilitating conditions have a positive influence on social commerce adoption intention. This suggests that when consumers perceive that sufficient technological resources, platform support, and convenient operational environments are available, they are more likely to adopt social commerce platforms. In digital commerce environments, factors such as reliable internet access, user-friendly payment systems, and effective customer support services may reduce perceived barriers to technology usage and encourage consumers to engage in online shopping activities. This finding is consistent with prior research emphasizing the importance of technological infrastructure and support in technology adoption [9, 15].

Finally, habit was found to have a significant positive effect on social commerce adoption intention and demonstrated the strongest influence among the examined factors. This result suggests that when consumers have developed habitual patterns of using social media platforms, they are more likely to engage in social commerce activities within those platforms. Over time, repeated interactions with social media platforms may become integrated into users' daily routines. As a result, consumers who are accustomed to browsing content, interacting with communities, and seeking product information on social media platforms may naturally extend these behaviors to online shopping activities. This finding aligns with previous studies indicating that habitual usage behavior plays a critical role in shaping users' technology adoption and continuance intentions [10, 17].

Overall, the findings of this study highlight the importance of both technological factors and behavioral factors in influencing consumers' adoption of social commerce platforms. While system usability and technological support contribute to a positive user experience, emotional engagement and habitual usage patterns also play crucial roles in encouraging consumers to adopt social commerce services.

6 Conclusion and Limitations

6.1 Conclusion

This study investigates the key factors influencing consumers' adoption of social commerce platforms. Specifically, perceived ease of use, hedonic motivation, facilitating conditions, and habit were examined to determine their effects on social commerce adoption intention. The empirical results indicate that these four factors are positively associated with consumers' intention to adopt social commerce platforms, suggesting that both technological characteristics and behavioral experiences play important roles in shaping consumers' adoption decisions.

First, perceived ease of use shows a positive influence on social commerce adoption intention, indicating that when consumers perceive a platform as easy to operate and learn, they are more likely to use the platform for shopping activities [16]. Second, hedonic motivation also demonstrates a positive effect on adoption intention. When consumers experience enjoyment and entertainment while interacting with social commerce platforms, they are more inclined to continue using these platforms for purchasing activities [19].

Furthermore, facilitating conditions are found to positively influence social commerce adoption intention, suggesting that adequate technological support, platform resources, and favorable usage environments can increase consumers' willingness to adopt social commerce platforms [15]. Finally, habit has a significant effect on adoption intention, indicating that consumers who have developed habitual behaviors related to social media usage are more likely to engage in social commerce activities [10, 17].

Overall, the findings of this study indicate that in addition to technological usability, consumers' entertainment experiences and established usage habits also play critical roles in shaping their adoption behaviors in social commerce environments. These findings provide useful insights for both researchers and practitioners in understanding consumer behavior in social commerce contexts and may contribute to the design and management of more effective social commerce platforms [1, 2, 14].

6.2 Limitations

Despite providing empirical insights into social commerce adoption behavior, this study has several limitations that should be acknowledged. First, the data were collected through a questionnaire survey, and respondents' answers may be influenced by subjective perceptions or self-report bias. Future studies may consider adopting multiple data sources or combining different research methods in order to enhance the reliability and robustness of the findings.

Second, this study focuses on four factors—perceived ease of use, hedonic motivation, facilitating conditions, and habit—to explain consumers' adoption intentions toward social commerce platforms. However, consumer behavior in social commerce environments may also be influenced by other factors such as trust, social interaction, or information quality. Future research may incorporate additional variables to provide a more comprehensive understanding of social commerce adoption behavior.

Finally, the empirical analysis of this study is based on a specific sample group. Therefore, the generalizability of the findings may be limited across different cultural contexts or user groups. Future research may expand the sample size or conduct cross-cultural comparative studies to further improve the external validity of the research findings.

References

1. Liang, T.P., Turban, E.: Introduction to the special issue social commerce: a research framework for social commerce. Int. J. Electron. Commer. **16**(2), 5–14 (2011)
2. Hossain, M.A., Kim, M.: A comprehensive study on social commerce in social networking sites. SAGE Open. **10**(2), 1–13 (2020)
3. Hajli, N.: Social commerce constructs and consumer's intention to buy. Int. J. Inf. Manag. **35**(2), 183–191 (2015)
4. Kim, S., Park, H.: Effects of various characteristics of social commerce on consumers' trust and trust performance. Int. J. Inf. Manag. **33**(2), 318–332 (2013)

5. Davis, F.D.: Perceived usefulness, perceived ease of use, and user acceptance of information technology. MIS Q. **13**(3), 319–340 (1989)
6. Venkatesh, V., Morris, M.G., Davis, G.B., Davis, F.D.: User acceptance of information technology: toward a unified view. MIS Q. **27**(3), 425–478 (2003)
7. Holbrook, M.B., Hirschman, E.C.: The experiential aspects of consumption: consumer fantasies, feelings, and fun. J. Consum. Res. **9**(2), 132–140 (1982)
8. Childers, T.L., Carr, C.L., Peck, J., Carson, S.: Hedonic and utilitarian motivations for online retail shopping behavior. J. Retail. **77**(4), 511–535 (2001)
9. Venkatesh, V., Thong, J.Y.L., Xu, X.: Consumer acceptance and use of information technology: extending the unified theory of acceptance and use of technology. MIS Q. **36**(1), 157–178 (2012)
10. Limayem, M., Hirt, S.G., Cheung, C.M.K.: How habit limits the predictive power of intention: the case of information systems continuance. MIS Q. **31**(4), 705–737 (2007)
11. Venkatesh, V., Davis, F.D.: A theoretical extension of the technology acceptance model: four longitudinal field studies. Manag. Sci. **46**(2), 186–204 (2000)
12. Mooi, E.: A Short Guide to Market Research: the Process, Data, and Methods Using IBM SPSS Statistics. Springer, Berlin (2018)
13. Baki, R., Birgören, B., Aktepe, A.: A meta-analysis of factors affecting perceived ease of use and perceived usefulness in the adoption of e-learning systems. Turk. Online J. Dist. Educ. **19**(4), 4–42 (2018)
14. Kang, J.Y., Johnson, K.K.P., Wu, J.: Consumer style inventory and intent to social shop online for apparel using social networking sites. J. Fash. Mark. Manag. **18**(3), 301–320 (2014)
15. Mahardika, H., Thomas, D., Ewing, M.T., Japutra, A.: Experience and facilitating conditions as impediments to consumers' new technology adoption. Int. Rev. Retail, Distrib. Consum. Res. **29**(1), 79–98 (2019)
16. Makmor, N., Aziz Abd, N., Shah Alam, S.: Social commerce: an extended technology acceptance model with the mediating effect of perceived ease of use and perceived usefulness. Malaysian J. Consum. Family Econ. **22**, 119–136 (2019)
17. Lin, K.Y., Wang, Y.T., Hsu, H.Y.S.: Why do people switch mobile platforms? The moderating role of habit. Internet Res. **27**(5), 1170–1189 (2017)
18. Kline, R.B.: Principles and Practice of Structural Equation Modeling, 4th edn. Guilford Press, New York (2015)
19. Khatimah, H., Susanto, P., Abdullah, N.L.: Hedonic motivation and social influence on behavioral intention of e-money: the role of payment habit as a mediator. Int. J. Entrepreneurship. **23**(1), 1–9 (2019)

The Impact of Trust in Online Shopping on Repurchase Intention: Loyalty as a Mediating Variable

Po-Chiang Wang, Ren-Fang Chao(✉), and Cheng-Wen Wang

Department of Postgraduate Programs in Management, I-Shou University, Kaohsiung, Taiwan, China
isu6b439@cloud.isu.edu.tw, rfchao@isu.edu.tw

Abstract. Because online transactions do not allow consumers to verify products and seller information in real time, trust has become a critical factor affecting repurchase intention. This study investigates the relationships among trust, loyalty, and repurchase intention in the context of online shopping and further examines the mediating effect of loyalty. The research targeted consumers of momo, a Taiwanese B2C e-commerce platform. A questionnaire survey was conducted, yielding 303 valid responses, and structural equation modeling was employed for empirical analysis. The results indicate that trust has significant positive effects on both loyalty and repurchase intention. Loyalty also has a significant positive effect on repurchase intention and partially mediates the relationship between trust and repurchase intention. These findings suggest that a higher level of trust in an online shopping platform helps enhance consumers' loyalty and repurchase intention. This study provides practical implications for customer relationship management and marketing strategies for e-commerce platforms and also contributes empirical evidence on the mediating role of loyalty in the online shopping context.

Keywords: online shopping · trust · loyalty · repurchase intention · e-commerce

1 Introduction

With the rapid development of digital technology, mobile devices, and the platform economy, online shopping has gradually become an important mode of consumption in consumers' daily lives. In particular, as Taiwan's e-commerce market continues to expand, consumers have become increasingly dependent on online shopping platforms. Competition among these platforms is no longer limited to product prices and logistics efficiency, but has extended to such dimensions as information transparency, transaction security, customer service, and the overall shopping experience [1, 2]. Against this backdrop, momo, as one of Taiwan's major B2C e-commerce platforms, enjoys high market visibility and strong representativeness, making it important research setting for examining online shopping behavior [2].

However, unlike in physical retail settings, consumers in the e-commerce environment cannot directly examine products, nor can they immediately verify seller credibility

D. Liberona et al. (Eds.): MISNC 2026, CCIS 3092, pp. 230–241, 2027.
https://doi.org/10.1007/978-3-032-33381-0_17

or transaction risks. As a result, trust becomes a critical psychological foundation influencing online shopping decisions. Prior studies have indicated that consumers' trust in online shopping platforms is often shaped by such factors as transaction security, information integrity, platform reputation, customer service, and review systems. When the level of trust increases, consumers are not only more willing to make purchases, but are also more likely to develop more stable consumption relationships [3–6]. In other words, in a highly competitive e-commerce market with abundant alternatives, trust is not merely a condition for facilitating a single transaction; it may also serve as an essential foundation for maintaining customer relationships and encouraging subsequent consumption behavior.

In addition to trust, loyalty has long been regarded as an important concept for explaining consumers' continued purchasing behavior. When consumers develop a stronger preference for, identification with, and tendency to continue using a particular platform, the likelihood of repeated purchases generally increases accordingly [7]. Previous studies have also indicated that loyalty not only helps increase purchase frequency, but also reduces the marketing costs required for firms to acquire new customers, making it particularly important in e-commerce management [6, 7]. However, although existing research has demonstrated a close relationship between trust and purchase intention, discussion remains insufficient as to whether loyalty further serves as a mediating mechanism between trust and repurchase intention. This issue remains especially worthy of further clarification in the context of major local e-commerce platforms in Taiwan [1, 8].

Based on the above theoretical and practical background, this study takes consumers of the momo online shopping platform as the research subjects to examine the effect of trust on repurchase intention and further investigate the mediating role of loyalty in this relationship. Through empirical analysis, this study seeks to deepen understanding of the process through which consumers' repurchase behavior is formed in the online shopping context, while also providing practical implications for e-commerce platforms in terms of customer relationship management, trust building, and loyalty enhancement [3, 6, 7].

2 Literature Review

2.1 Trust

Trust is regarded as an important psychological foundation influencing consumers' purchase decisions in the e-commerce context. Because online shopping involves information asymmetry, the inability to physically inspect products in real time, and transaction risks that cannot be fully verified in advance, consumers usually need to develop a certain level of trust in a platform before they are willing to engage in a transaction. Gefen [3] argued that trust can be viewed as consumers' positive expectations regarding the future behavior of a transaction partner and that it can effectively reduce uncertainty in online transactions. Related studies have also indicated that website security, privacy protection, information transparency, brand reputation, and customer service are all important factors in the formation of online shopping trust. When a platform can provide clear terms, reliable information, and a relatively comprehensive review mechanism, consumers' trust in the platform is significantly enhanced [4, 5, 8, 9].

In e-commerce research, trust is not only an important antecedent to the initiation of first-time transactions, but also a key mechanism for maintaining customer relationships and encouraging subsequent consumption behavior. Prior domestic studies have shown that such factors as customer value, social presence, advertising promotion, and trust assurance discourse all influence consumers' brand trust in online shopping platforms and their overall evaluations [10–13]. Recent international studies have further found that website quality, design reliability, ease of use, and the quality of online reviews affect consumers' trust judgments regarding both the platform and product quality, thereby shaping their purchasing behavior [14–16]. Therefore, this study regards trust as an important antecedent variable for explaining online shoppers' subsequent loyalty and repurchase intention.

2.2 Loyalty

Loyalty has long been regarded as an important concept in consumer behavior and marketing research for explaining customers' continued support for a specific brand or platform. Oliver [7] pointed out that loyalty is not only reflected in repeated purchasing behavior, but also includes consumers' identification with, preference for, and continued commitment to a brand or platform. It therefore encompasses both attitudinal and behavioral dimensions. For online shopping platforms, a higher level of loyalty helps stabilize customer relationships and reduces the likelihood that consumers will switch to competing platforms. Related studies have indicated that when shopping websites enhance customer experience through internet-based customer relationship management, personalized product information services, and interactive design, consumers' loyalty toward the platform can be strengthened [17, 18]. In addition, when consumers accumulate positive experiences, satisfaction, and value recognition throughout the shopping process, they are more likely to develop a more stable loyalty relationship [19, 20].

In the e-commerce context, the formation of loyalty is usually not the result of a single transaction, but rather is built on the basis of long-term interaction and positive evaluations, with trust being regarded as an important antecedent of loyalty. When consumers perceive an online shopping platform as reliable, secure, and transparent in its information disclosure, their sense of transaction uncertainty can be reduced, thereby further fostering a tendency toward continued use and repeated purchases. Recent studies have shown that e-trust has a significant positive effect on e-loyalty, indicating that trust not only influences immediate purchase judgments, but also further strengthens consumers' relational commitment to and willingness to continue supporting a platform [21]. Other studies have also found that when customers' trust in a platform increases, their purchase frequency and loyalty rise accordingly [22]. These findings suggest that, in the online shopping environment, trust can be regarded as an important foundation for the development of loyalty. Therefore, this study proposes the following hypothesis:

H1: Online shopping consumers' trust has a significant positive effect on their loyalty.

2.3 Repurchase Intention

Repurchase intention refers to consumers' subjective tendency and behavioral intention to continue purchasing from the same platform or brand on the basis of their prior purchase experience. Chiu et al. [23] pointed out that repurchase intention is an important indicator for evaluating the continuity of customer relationships and the effectiveness of platform operations, as it reflects whether consumers are willing to purchase again from the same platform after comprehensively assessing their previous transaction experience, platform convenience, and overall value. For e-commerce platforms, repurchase intention not only represents the likelihood of follow-up behavior after a single transaction, but is also closely related to customer retention, operational stability, and long-term competitiveness. Domestic studies have likewise indicated that when consumers develop more positive experiences and stronger value perceptions toward an online shopping platform, they are generally more likely to form a tendency toward continued purchasing [24, 25].

In the context of online shopping, the formation of repurchase intention is often influenced by two key factors, namely trust and loyalty. Because online transactions involve information asymmetry and the inability to verify products in real time, higher trust in a platform helps reduce perceived risk and uncertainty, thereby increasing the likelihood of future repeat purchases [6, 8, 22]. Therefore, this study proposes the following hypothesis:

H2: Online shopping consumers' trust has a significant positive effect on their repurchase intention.

In addition, loyalty represents consumers' sustained preference for and relational commitment to a particular platform. When consumers have a higher level of loyalty toward a platform, they are less likely to switch to competing platforms and are more likely to exhibit stable repeat purchasing behavior [24, 25]. These findings suggest that, in the e-commerce environment, both trust and loyalty are important antecedent variables for explaining repurchase intention. Therefore, this study proposes the following hypothesis:

H3: Online shopping consumers' loyalty has a significant positive effect on their repurchase intention.

2.4 The Mediating Role of Loyalty

In addition to the direct effect of trust on repurchase intention, prior studies have suggested that loyalty may serve as a mediating mechanism between the two. According to Oliver [7], loyalty is often regarded as a bridge through which consumers move from satisfaction to continued purchasing behavior. In other words, when consumers develop trust in a shopping platform, they are more likely to cultivate loyalty toward that platform, and such loyalty further strengthens their future repurchase intention. Recent studies have also suggested that trust can indirectly influence subsequent purchase decisions and behavioral tendencies by enhancing customers' emotional attachment. In the e-commerce context, trust not only directly increases usage frequency and purchase intention, but may also further reinforce the stability of customer relationships through loyalty [26]. These findings indicate that loyalty may exert an indirect mediating effect on the relationship between trust and repurchase intention. Therefore, this study proposes the following hypothesis:

H4: Online shopping consumers' trust indirectly affects their repurchase intention through loyalty.

Based on the above theoretical arguments and hypotheses, the research framework is shown in Fig. 1.

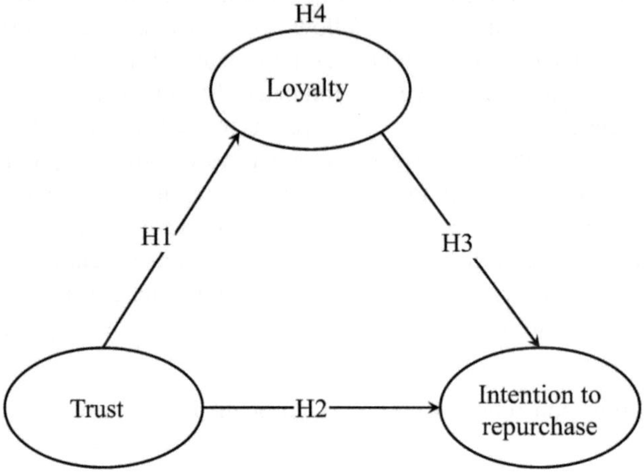

Fig. 1. Research Framework

3 Research Methods

3.1 Data Collection and Sampling

This study targeted consumers who had previously used the momo online shopping platform and examined the relationships among trust, loyalty, and repurchase intention. To ensure that the sample was consistent with the research purpose, screening criteria were established so that only consumers who had made purchases on the momo platform within the past six months were included in the formal survey.

This study collected data through a questionnaire survey. The questionnaire was developed using Google Forms and distributed through social media, email, and instant messaging applications. The survey was conducted from September to December 2024. Responses were collected anonymously, and the purpose of the study as well as the instructions for completing the questionnaire were clearly stated at the beginning of the survey to enhance respondents' willingness to participate and improve data quality. A total of 330 questionnaires were returned. After excluding incomplete responses and those with obviously invalid response patterns, 303 valid samples were retained for subsequent statistical analysis. According to relevant research recommendations, the sample size for structural equation modeling should generally exceed 200 in order to enhance the robustness of model estimation and statistical testing. Therefore, the valid sample size in this study was considered adequate for the analysis [27].

3.2 Sample and Questionnaire

The questionnaire used in this study consisted of four parts: trust, loyalty, repurchase intention, and respondents' demographic information. To enhance the consistency and comparability of the measurement results, all construct items were measured using a seven-point Likert scale, ranging from 1 ("strongly disagree") to 7 ("strongly agree"). The questionnaire was primarily developed based on well-established scales from prior studies and was further revised to fit the online shopping context of this study, so that the item content would better reflect the user experiences of consumers on the momo online shopping platform. The final questionnaire included six items for trust, five items for loyalty, and three items for repurchase intention, along with demographic questions designed to collect information on respondents' personal characteristics and usage behavior.

With regard to the sources of the measurement scales, the trust construct was primarily adapted from the study of Sharma and Klein [28] to assess consumers' perceptions of the credibility of the momo online shopping platform, the authenticity of its information, its return policy, social responsibility, participation terms, and overall support. The loyalty construct was adapted from the scale developed by Angriawan and Thakur [29] to measure consumers' continuing preference for the platform, priority of choice, and overall level of loyalty. The repurchase intention construct was mainly based on the study of Chiu et al. [23] and was used to evaluate consumers' intentions to continue shopping on the momo online shopping platform in the future. Overall, by drawing on established scales from prior literature and revising them to fit the research context, this study developed measurement instruments aligned with its research purpose, thereby providing the basis for the subsequent confirmatory factor analysis and structural model analysis.

3.3 Data Analysis

After the questionnaires were collected, this study first conducted data screening and basic statistical analyses, and then further examined the measurement quality and structural relationships of the research model. The data analysis consisted of three main parts. First, descriptive statistics were used to examine the basic characteristics of the sample and the overall distributions of the research constructs, thereby providing the foundation for subsequent inferential analyses. Second, the reliability and validity of the scales were assessed. Internal consistency was evaluated using composite reliability (CR). In general, when the CR value reaches the recommended threshold, the construct can be considered to have stable measurement quality [27, 32]. With respect to validity, this study employed confirmatory factor analysis (CFA) to assess convergent validity and used average variance extracted (AVE) as the evaluation criterion. When factor loadings, CR, and AVE meet the recommended standards, the constructs can be regarded as demonstrating good convergent validity [27, 30].

Third, to examine the relationships among the research hypotheses and latent variables, this study employed structural equation modeling (SEM) for analysis. Following the two-step analytical procedure proposed by Anderson and Gerbing, the reliability and validity of the measurement model were first assessed, after which the path relationships and overall model fit of the structural model were further evaluated [31]. In addition, discriminant validity was examined by comparing the inter-construct correlation coefficients with the square roots of the average variance extracted (AVE), in order to confirm that the latent constructs demonstrated adequate distinctiveness from one another [30]. Overall, this study adopted reliability analysis, confirmatory factor analysis (CFA), and SEM as the main analytical tools to validate the measurement quality of trust, loyalty, and repurchase intention, as well as their structural relationships.

4 Results and Analysis

4.1 Sample Characteristics

A total of 303 valid questionnaires were obtained in this study, and statistical analyses were conducted on the respondents' demographic characteristics to understand the structure and distribution of the sample. The results show that, in terms of gender, male respondents accounted for 54.46% and female respondents accounted for 45.54%, indicating a relatively balanced distribution, although males were slightly more represented. With regard to age, the majority of respondents were between 20 and 29 years old, accounting for 72.28%, suggesting that the sample was primarily composed of young consumers. In terms of marital status, unmarried respondents accounted for 76.24%, which was substantially higher than the proportions of married respondents and those with other marital statuses. Regarding occupation, students and teachers constituted the two largest groups, accounting for 33.99% and 25.08%, respectively, indicating that the sample was relatively concentrated in academic-related groups. In terms of educational background, most respondents had a junior college or university degree, accounting for 73.27%. As for average monthly income, the largest proportion fell within the range of NT$40,001 to NT$60,000, accounting for 31.35%. In addition, regarding the frequency of browsing the momo online shopping platform, the largest groups of respondents reported browsing more than once a month and once a month, accounting for 35.31% and 30.36%, respectively, suggesting that most respondents tended to browse and shop on a need-based basis. Overall, the sample in this study was characterized mainly by young, unmarried, university-educated respondents, with students and teachers forming the major groups, which provides useful contextual insight for understanding consumers' trust, loyalty, and repurchase intention toward the momo online shopping platform.

4.2 Measurement Model: Validity and Reliability

This study first employed confirmatory factor analysis (CFA) to examine the measurement quality of the research constructs in order to confirm that the scales possessed adequate reliability and validity. The results showed that the standardized factor loadings of all items ranged from .637 to .923 and were all statistically significant, indicating that each observed variable had good explanatory power for its corresponding latent construct. The composite reliability (CR) values of the three constructs ranged from .881 to .928, all exceeding the recommended threshold of .70. In addition, the average variance extracted (AVE) values ranged from .599 to .749, all of which were above the recommended cutoff value of .50. Therefore, the constructs in this study all met the recommended criteria for internal consistency and convergent validity, indicating that the scales demonstrated good measurement quality [27, 31, 32].

4.3 Discriminant Validity Analysis

This study further examined discriminant validity. The results showed that the correlation coefficients among the three constructs—trust, loyalty, and repurchase intention—ranged from .420 to .678, all of which were below the threshold of .850. In addition, the square roots of the average variance extracted (AVE) for the three constructs were .827, .774, and .865, respectively, all of which were greater than the correlations between each construct and the others. These results indicate that the latent variables in this study possessed adequate distinctiveness and did not exhibit excessive overlap. Therefore, the measurement model demonstrated good discriminant validity and was appropriate for subsequent structural model analysis (Table 1) [27, 30].

Table 1. Discriminant Validity Analysis

Construct	Mean	SD	AVE	Discriminant validity		
				(1)	(2)	(3)
(1) Trust	5.771	.892	.684	**.827**		
(2) Loyalty	4.852	1.143	.599	.420	**.774**	
(3) Repurchase intention	5.286	.997	.749	.677	.678	**.865**

Note: AVE = average variance extracted. The bold values on the diagonal represent the square roots of AVE, while the values in the lower triangle are Pearson correlation coefficients.

4.4 SEM Results and Hypothesis Testing

After the measurement model was validated, this study further employed structural equation modeling (SEM) to examine the research framework and test the proposed hypotheses. The results showed that the overall structural model demonstrated a good fit. In terms of the major fit indices, the Bollen-Stine χ^2 value was 90.190 with 74° of freedom, and the normed chi-square (χ^2/df) was 1.219, which was below the recommended upper limit of 3. In addition, the GFI and AGFI values were .975 and .956, respectively, both exceeding .90. The RMSEA and SRMR values were .027 and .069, respectively, both below the recommended thresholds. The TLI, CFI, and IFI values were .994, .995, and .995, respectively, indicating strong overall explanatory power of the model. Furthermore, the values of Gamma hat, McDonald's NCI, and Hoelter's N were all within acceptable ranges, suggesting a satisfactory fit between the structural model and the sample data [27, 31].

With regard to the hypothesis testing results, trust had a significant positive effect on loyalty (β = .420, $p < .001$), supporting H1. Trust also had a significant positive effect on repurchase intention (β = .476, $p < .001$), supporting H2. In addition, loyalty had a significant positive effect on repurchase intention (β = .478, $p < .001$), supporting H3. Further bootstrapping analysis with 5,000 resamples revealed that trust exerted a significant indirect effect on repurchase intention through loyalty (β = .201, Z = 4.257, $p < .001$), indicating that loyalty played a significant mediating role in the relationship between trust and repurchase intention. Therefore, H4 was also supported. Overall, all four research hypotheses were statistically supported, suggesting that the theoretical model developed in this study had good explanatory power. The findings further indicate that trust not only directly enhances consumers' repurchase intention, but also exerts an indirect effect through loyalty, thereby forming a complete mediating mechanism (Table 2).

Table 2. Hypothesis Path Analysis

Hypothesis path	Std.	Unstd.	SE	Z	*p*	Supported
H1: Trust → Loyalty	.420	.721	.115	6.270	<.001	Y
H2: Trust → Repurchase Intention	.476	.708	.083	8.502	<.001	Y
H3: Loyalty → Repurchase Intention	.478	.414	.050	8.295	<.001	Y
H4: Trust → Loyalty → Repurchase Intention	.201	.298	.070	4.257	<.001	Y
Bootstrapping = 5,000						

5 Conclusion

This study examined the relationships among trust, loyalty, and repurchase intention by focusing on consumers of momo, a Taiwanese B2C e-commerce platform, and further investigated the mediating effect of loyalty. The results indicate that trust has a significant positive effect on loyalty, and trust also has a significant positive effect on repurchase intention. Loyalty likewise significantly enhances repurchase intention. In addition, loyalty exerts a significant partial mediating effect on the relationship between trust and repurchase intention. These findings suggest that, in the online shopping context, when consumers develop a higher level of trust in a platform, they are not only more likely to form a stable loyalty relationship, but are also more likely to maintain a continued intention to purchase.

From a theoretical perspective, this study further supports the central role of trust in the e-commerce context and shows that loyalty is not merely a companion outcome of repurchase intention, but an important relational mechanism linking trust and continued purchasing behavior. These findings are consistent with Gefen's [3] view of the function of trust in e-commerce and also align with Oliver's [7] conceptualization of loyalty. At the same time, the results echo recent studies on the relationships among e-trust, e-loyalty, and repurchase intention [3, 7, 21–23]. Compared with studies that focus only on the direct effect of trust on purchase intention, this study further incorporates loyalty into the mediating path, thereby helping to strengthen understanding of how continued purchasing behavior is formed in the online shopping context.

From a practical perspective, the findings indicate that if e-commerce platforms aim to enhance consumers' repurchase intention, they cannot focus solely on promotions and traffic acquisition, but should give priority to strengthening trust-building mechanisms. More specifically, platforms may reduce consumers' uncertainty by improving transaction security, information transparency, product quality disclosure, customer service responsiveness, the credibility of review systems, and return and exchange policies, thereby enhancing consumers' positive evaluations of the platform. When consumers continuously accumulate stable and positive usage experiences throughout the transaction process, such experiences are more likely to be transformed into platform loyalty and, in turn, further increase repurchase intention. This also implies that strategies such as membership management, personalized recommendations, and customer relationship maintenance are likely to be more sustainable when they are built on a foundation of trust rather than relying only on one-time promotional incentives.

Beyond these operational implications, the findings also suggest that trust should be managed as a long-term relationship asset rather than merely as a mechanism for reducing transaction risk. For e-commerce platforms, building trust is not limited to providing secure payment systems or avoiding service failures; it also requires the continuous design of reliable, transparent, and consistent customer experiences. Platform managers should therefore view review credibility, return and exchange policies, information accuracy, customer service responsiveness, and personalized recommendation systems as interconnected elements of a broader trust-building strategy. When these elements are managed consistently, consumers are more likely to perceive the platform as dependable and customer-oriented, which can gradually transform short-term transactional confidence into long-term loyalty. Moreover, loyalty programs should not rely only on discounts or point accumulation, because such incentives may attract temporary purchases without necessarily strengthening relational commitment. Instead, platforms may combine membership benefits with service reliability, personalized communication, and transparent problem-solving processes in order to deepen consumers' psychological attachment to the platform. From this perspective, the path from trust to loyalty and then to repurchase intention provides a useful strategic logic for customer retention. It implies that sustainable repurchase behavior is more likely to emerge when platforms convert consumers' trust-based evaluations into stable loyalty relationships.

This study still has several limitations. First, the research subjects were limited to consumers of the momo shopping platform, and the findings mainly reflect a specific platform context. Therefore, caution is needed when extending the results to other e-commerce platforms or cross-platform settings. Second, this study adopted a convenience sampling method and a cross-sectional questionnaire design. Although this approach facilitated the collection of a large sample, it was still difficult to capture the dynamic changes in consumers' trust, loyalty, and repurchase intention over time. Finally, this study mainly focused on the three core variables of trust, loyalty, and repurchase intention. Future studies may further incorporate variables such as perceived risk, satisfaction, platform usage experience, or different platform types in order to extend the explanatory scope of the research model.

References

1. China Post Express News: A Forrester report indicates that global online retail sales may reach $6.8 trillion by 2028 (2024) (in Chinese)
2. Lin, S.-H.: Fubon Media's 2024 revenue reached NT$112.5 billion, setting a new record with a 3% year-on-year increase (2025) (in Chinese)
3. Gefen, D.: E-commerce: the role of familiarity and trust. Omega. **28**(6), 725–737 (2000). https://doi.org/10.1016/S0305-0483(00)00021-9
4. Wu, Y.H., Chu, S.Y., Fang, W.C.: An empirical study on trust and technology acceptance patterns in online shopping. J. Inf. Manag. **15**(1), 123–152 (2008. (in Chinese)). https://doi.org/10.6382/JIM.200801.0123
5. Zheng, Y. et al.: A study on the correlation between perceived risk, trust and purchase intention in online shopping. Manag. Inf. Comput. **11**, 55–64 (2022. (in Chinese)). https://doi.org/10.6285/MIC.202207/SP_01_11.0005
6. Tseng, S., Chen, Y.: The effects of perceived risk, trust and information richness on repurchase intention. E-commerce Res. **9**(3), 269–293 (2011. (in Chinese)). https://doi.org/10.29767/ECS.201109.0002
7. Oliver, R.L.: Whence consumer loyalty? J. Mark. **63**(Special Issue), 33–44 (1999). https://doi.org/10.1177/00222429990634s105
8. Tseng, S., Liou, J.: The impact of travel website information disclosure on purchase intention—using trust and cost-saving search as mediating variables. Asia Pac. Econ. Manag. Rev. **20**(2), 93–116 (2017). (in Chinese)
9. Chiu, H.-K., Yang, H.-L.: A study on factors that make online shopping websites trustworthy to consumers. Inf. Soc. Res. **5**, 139–174 (2003. (in Chinese)). https://doi.org/10.29843/JCCIS.200307.0006
10. Shih, T.-Y., Yang, Y.H.: The influence of customer value on brand trust in shopping websites: a comparative analysis of conformity attributes. Mark. Rev. **10**(2), 165–190 (2013). (in Chinese)
11. Geng, Q., Ding, H., Liao, J.: The influence of online shopping target context and interpersonal virtual experience on social presence and trust. J. Bus. Strateg. **4**(1), 1–26 (2012). (in Chinese)
12. Liang, R.-H., Lin, Y.-F.: Exploring the impact of advertising and promotion by businesses on consumer trust and purchase intention—taking online shopping as an example. Glob. Manag. Econ. **4**(2), 81–106 (2008. (in Chinese)). https://doi.org/10.6565/JGME.2008.4(2).5
13. Chen, M., Chen, C.: A study on the influence of trust assurance theory on consumer trust through central and peripheral paths in group buying websites: an analysis of the moderating effect of the possibility model and group buying price perception. J. Inf. Manag. **24**(2), 209–243 (2017). (in Chinese)
14. Qalati, S.A., Vela, E.G., Li, W., Dakhan, S.A., Hong Thuy, T.T., Merani, S.H.: Effects of perceived service quality, website quality, and reputation on purchase intention: the mediating and moderating roles of trust and perceived risk in online shopping. Cogent Bus. Manag. **8**(1), 1869363 (2021). https://doi.org/10.1080/23311975.2020.1869363
15. Saoula, O. et al.: Building e-trust and e-retention in online shopping: the role of website design, reliability and perceived ease of use. Span. J. Mark. ESIC. **27**(2), 178–201 (2023). https://doi.org/10.1108/SJME-07-2022-0159
16. Sung, E., Chung, W.Y., Lee, D.: Factors that affect consumer trust in product quality: a focus on online reviews and shopping platforms. Humanit. Soc. Sci. Commun. **10**, 766 (2023)

17. Li, S.-F.: The impact of online customer relationship management on loyalty of shopping websites—customer perspective. J. Inf. Manag. **15**(4), 177–203 (2008. (in Chinese)). https://doi.org/10.6382/JIM.200810.0177
18. Lu, Y.-W., Horng, R.-Y., Wang, Y.-D., Hou, S.-H., Lu, P.-H.: The effects of personalized merchandise information search and community design on user loyalty of online shops. J. Cyber Cult. Inf. Soc. **19**, 71–100 (2011. (in Chinese)). https://doi.org/10.29843/JCCIS.201101.0003
19. Lin, Y.-C., Lin, H.-C., Lee, Y.-C.: The study of the relationship among experiential marketing, customer satisfaction and customer loyalty. J. Customer Satisfaction. **3**(2), 57–94 (2007. (in Chinese)). https://doi.org/10.30066/JCS.200709.0003
20. Huang, J.-R., Chen, K.-H.: A study on the correlation between experiential marketing, customer satisfaction and customer loyalty: a case study of physical channels of direct selling companies. Direct Selling Manag. Rev. **2**(4), 33–56 (2018). (in Chinese)
21. Ashiq, R., Hussain, A.: Exploring the effects of e-service quality and e-trust on consumers' e-satisfaction and e-loyalty: insights from online shoppers in Pakistan. J. Electron. Bus. Digital Econ. **3**(2), 117–141 (2024). https://doi.org/10.1108/JEBDE-09-2023-0019
22. Asti, W.P., Handayani, P.W., Azzahro, F.: Influence of trust, perceived value, and attitude on customers' repurchase intention for e-grocery. J. Food Prod. Mark. **27**(3), 157–171 (2021). https://doi.org/10.1080/10454446.2021.1922325
23. Chiu, C.-M., Chang, C.-C., Cheng, H.-L., Fang, Y.-H.: Determinants of customer repurchase intention in online shopping. Online Inf. Rev. **33**(4), 761–784 (2009). https://doi.org/10.1108/14684520910985710
24. Hsiao, Y.-D., Lin, T.-C., Hsu, S.-T., Tsai, W.-J., Chung, K.-Y.: A study on repurchase behavior of consumers in online auctions. Chin. J. Foresight Res. **11**(2), 55–81 (2015). (in Chinese)
25. Luo, P.-H.: Exploring the Impact of Brand Image, Service Quality, and Customer Satisfaction on Repurchase Intention—Using Food Delivery Platforms as an Example (thesis). Department of Business Administration, Ling Tung University, Taichung City, Taiwan (2021). (in Chinese)
26. Pratama, R.A., Prasetyo, W.B., Ramli, A.H.: E-service quality, e-trust, e-satisfaction and e-loyalty in online shopping. Jurnal Ilmiah Manajemen Kesatuan. **11**(3), 1377–1388 (2023). https://doi.org/10.37641/jimkes.v11i3.2313
27. Hair, J.F., Black, W.C., Babin, B.J., Anderson, R.E.: Multivariate Data Analysis, 8th edn. Cengage Learning, Boston, MA (2019)
28. Sharma, V.M., Klein, A.: Consumer perceived value, involvement, trust, susceptibility to interpersonal influence, and intention to participate in online group buying. J. Retail. Consum. Serv. **52**, 101946 (2020). https://doi.org/10.1016/j.jretconser.2019.101946
29. Angriawan, A., Thakur, R.: A parsimonious model of the antecedents and consequence of online trust: an uncertainty perspective. J. Internet Commer. **7**(1), 74–94 (2008). https://doi.org/10.1080/15332860802004337
30. Fornell, C., Larcker, D.F.: Structural equation models with unobservable variables and measurement error: algebra and statistics. J. Mark. Res. **18**(3), 382–388 (1981). https://doi.org/10.1177/002224378101800313
31. Anderson, J.C., Gerbing, D.W.: Structural equation modeling in practice: a review and recommended two-step approach. Psychol. Bull. **103**(3), 411–423 (1988). https://doi.org/10.1037/0033-2909.103.3.411
32. Nunnally, J.C., Bernstein, I.H.: Psychometric Theory, 3rd edn. McGraw-Hill, New York, NY (1994)

The Influence of Demand-Ability Fit on Retention Intention: The Mediating Role of Job Satisfaction

Wen-Chieh Lu[1], Ren-Fang Chao[2](✉), and Chor-Sum Au-Yeung[2]

[1] Department of Information Engineering, I-Shou University, Kaohsiung, Taiwan
[2] Department of Postgraduate Programs in Management, I-Shou University, Kaohsiung, Taiwan
rfchao@isu.edu.tw

Abstract. This study primarily explores the relationships among demand-ability fit, job satisfaction, and retention intention. In the shipbuilding industry, which is technology-intensive and highly dependent on professional manpower, whether employees can effectively utilize their own abilities to complete work tasks may become an important factor influencing their job evaluation and intention to remain. To investigate the above issues, this study conducted an empirical analysis with employees of a shipyard in southern Taiwan as the research subjects. The results indicate that demand-ability fit has a significant positive effect on job satisfaction and retention intention. Job satisfaction also has a significant positive effect on retention intention and demonstrates a significant mediating effect between demand-ability fit and retention intention. These findings indicate that when employees perceive that their abilities can effectively respond to job demands, their job satisfaction will increase and their retention intention will be strengthened. The results also indicate that demand-ability fit and job satisfaction play critical roles in the formation process of employee retention behavior.

Keywords: Demand-Ability Fit · Job Satisfaction · Retention Intention · Structural Equation Modeling

1 Introduction

In the fields of organizational behavior and human resource management, employee retention behavior has long been regarded as an important issue for understanding organizational stability and human resource management. Milliman et al. [1] examined employee retention intention from external conditions such as organizational support, leadership style, and work environment. However, employees' subjective perceptions of the degree of congruence between their own abilities and job requirements during the work process may also influence their work attitudes and behavioral tendencies. With the development of person-job fit theory in organizational research, demand-ability fit (D-A fit) has gradually become an important concept for explaining employee work attitudes. This concept emphasizes the degree of congruence between individual abilities and job task requirements. When employees perceive that their abilities can respond

D. Liberona et al. (Eds.): MISNC 2026, CCIS 3092, pp. 242–253, 2027.
https://doi.org/10.1007/978-3-032-33381-0_18

to job demands, they are more likely to form positive job evaluations and demonstrate higher levels of work engagement [2].

D-A fit is regarded as an important psychological foundation influencing employee behavior. When there is a good fit between individual abilities and job requirements, employees are more likely to establish confidence during the process of completing tasks and reduce the pressure and frustration caused by insufficient ability. Sylva et al. [3] indicated that a high level of fit between abilities and job demands can promote positive work attitudes and reduce turnover tendency. In work contexts that are technology intensive and require high levels of professional expertise, employees' perceptions of ability congruence are more likely to influence their overall evaluation of work. When employees perceive that their abilities can effectively respond to the skills required for job tasks, psychological pressure can be reduced and confidence and identification with the job can be enhanced [4]. Therefore, examining employee work attitudes from the perspective of D-A fit has important implications for understanding employees' retention intention.

In addition to the congruence between abilities and job demands, job satisfaction is also regarded as an important psychological mechanism influencing employee work attitudes and behavior. Job satisfaction reflects employees' overall evaluation of their work experience. When individuals obtain a sense of achievement and positive feedback during the work process, they are more likely to develop a stable and positive emotional state [5]. A significant relationship exists between job satisfaction and employee retention intention, and higher levels of satisfaction increase the likelihood that employees will remain in the organization [6]. Within this theoretical context, D-A fit may indirectly influence retention intention by affecting employees' evaluations of work and their emotional responses. When employees perceive that their abilities are fully utilized and recognized during the work process, higher levels of job satisfaction are more likely to develop, which further strengthens their intention to remain.

Based on the above theoretical perspectives, this study selected employees of a shipyard in southern Taiwan as the research subjects. Empirical data were used to analyze the relationships among D-A fit, job satisfaction, and retention intention in order to deepen the understanding of the formation process of employee retention behavior and to provide empirical evidence with reference value for organizations in human resource management and talent development strategies.

2 Literature Review

2.1 Demand-Ability Fit

D-A fit primarily focuses on the degree of congruence between individual abilities and job requirements. D-A fit refers to the compatibility between the knowledge, skills, and abilities possessed by employees and the abilities required by their job positions [2]. It also includes employees' subjective perceptions of whether their abilities correspond to job demands [3, 7]. When employees perceive that their abilities can effectively respond to work tasks, they are more likely to develop confidence and a sense of control over their work, and to demonstrate higher levels of engagement and positive attitudes during the work process [8].

D-A fit is regarded as an important factor influencing employees' work experiences and workplace behavior. When employees perceive that their abilities maintain a good fit with job demands, they are more likely to obtain psychological resources and a sense of achievement, while reducing the negative effects caused by work pressure and role conflict [9]. In contrast, when employees perceive a discrepancy between their abilities and job demands, feelings of frustration and stress responses may arise, and psychological need satisfaction and work motivation may be weakened [10]. Importantly, poor ability fit may lead to emotional exhaustion, job burnout, or deviant workplace behavior, thereby affecting overall organizational functioning [11]. These observations indicate that the congruence between abilities and job demands not only influences employees' task performance but is also closely associated with their emotional states and the quality of workplace relationships. When employees are able to utilize their abilities in their work and receive recognition from the organization, higher levels of job satisfaction and affective organizational commitment are more likely to develop [12].

2.2 Retention Intention

Retention intention in organizational behavior research is generally regarded as an important psychological indicator used to assess whether employees are willing to remain in their current organization. It refers to the tendency of employees to continue their employment after comprehensively evaluating their work experience, organizational environment, and future development opportunities [1]. This concept not only reflects employees' positive evaluations of their current job and organization but also represents their psychological commitment to continuously invest time, effort, and professional abilities [13]. Compared with turnover intention, which focuses on the possibility of leaving the organization, retention intention emphasizes employees' positive choice regarding organizational loyalty, job stability, and continuous career development. Chami-Malaeb and Garavan [14] indicated that when employees perceive that their psychological needs are satisfied at work and establish a higher level of emotional connection and trust with the organization, a stable retention intention is more likely to develop.

In the exploration of antecedents of retention intention, D-A fit is regarded as one of the important explanatory factors. D-A fit emphasizes employees' subjective perceptions of whether their knowledge, skills, and abilities are sufficient to respond to job requirements and task challenges. When employees perceive that a good fit exists between their abilities and job demands, they are more likely to obtain a sense of achievement, competence, and psychological satisfaction from their work, and to develop stronger positive attitudes toward the organization and a tendency to continue their service [2, 3]. Taris and Feij [15] indicated that when a higher level of consistency exists between job content and individual abilities, employees are not only more capable of completing tasks effectively but are also more likely to choose to remain in the organization for further development. This perspective is also supported by other studies. For example, Hamid and Yahya [16] argued that when employees perceive that their abilities correspond to job requirements, the likelihood of retention will increase. In the shipbuilding industry, when employees perceive that their technical abilities are sufficient to respond to on-site operations, equipment updates, and complex coordination requirements, stable work attitudes and organizational commitment can be maintained. In contrast, when discrepancies occur between abilities and task requirements, frustration, burnout, and turnover thoughts may arise, thereby intensifying the existing problems of labor shortages and technical gaps in the industry [4]. Based on the above theoretical and empirical context, the following hypothesis is proposed:

H1: D-A fit has a positive effect on retention intention.

2.3 Job Satisfaction

Job satisfaction refers to the comprehensive emotional and attitudinal evaluation that employees form regarding their job content, work environment, and overall workplace conditions through their actual work experience. Job satisfaction involves multiple factors, including psychological, physiological, and environmental aspects. These factors jointly influence individuals' overall perceptions of their work, and the core of job satisfaction lies in whether employees experience positive emotional responses during the work process [17]. In addition, job satisfaction is defined as the affective attitude formed by employees toward their work roles. When this attitude is positive, it indicates a higher level of satisfaction with the job [18]. From the perspective of emotional and cognitive integration, job satisfaction can also be regarded as a pleasurable psychological state that arises after employees evaluate whether their work meets personal expectations and organizational standards [5]. Furthermore, McNamara et al. [19] indicated that job satisfaction is not merely an emotional response but a work attitude formed after employees make an overall judgment regarding salary, benefits, job content, supervisor interaction, promotion opportunities, and career development. Therefore, job satisfaction can be regarded as an important psychological outcome formed through the interaction between employees' subjective perceptions and objective workplace conditions, and it is closely associated with work engagement, organizational identification, and subsequent behavioral tendencies [6].

In the exploration of antecedents of job satisfaction, D-A fit is regarded as an important explanatory variable. D-A fit refers to employees' subjective perceptions of whether their knowledge, skills, and abilities are sufficient to respond to current job requirements and task challenges [2, 3]. When employees perceive that they possess the conditions required to complete their work, a sense of control, competence, and achievement is more likely to develop, which leads to positive evaluations of their work [7]. Kristof-Brown et al. [9] indicated that a higher degree of congruence between abilities and job demands not only improves employees' work adjustment but also strengthens psychological well-being and positive work attitudes. In this context, when employees are able to respond to complex production processes, equipment operation, and team coordination requirements with their own technical abilities, they are more likely to experience value realization and recognition of their contributions, which further enhances job satisfaction. In contrast, when discrepancies exist between abilities and task requirements, anxiety, feelings of helplessness, and negative evaluations may arise, thereby weakening satisfaction with work [4, 10, 11]. Based on the above theoretical and empirical context, the following hypothesis is proposed.

H2: D-A fit has a positive effect on job satisfaction.

The influence of job satisfaction on retention intention has also been supported by numerous studies. As a positive evaluation of employees' overall work experience, job satisfaction influences employees' expectations regarding their current position and the future development of the organization and is transformed into a psychological tendency to remain in the organization [5]. When employees are satisfied with job content, support systems, and development opportunities, emotional connections and loyalty toward the organization are more likely to develop, and the intention to seek external job opportunities will be reduced. In the shipbuilding industry, working conditions are demanding and require long-term accumulation of technical skills. When employees obtain emotional recognition and tangible rewards from their work, a stable retention intention is more likely to develop. In contrast, when job satisfaction is low, psychological detachment, emotional exhaustion, and considerations of leaving the job may arise [6, 19]. Therefore, the following hypothesis is proposed.

H3: Job satisfaction has a positive effect on retention intention.

Based on the above discussion, when employees perceive that their abilities are sufficient to meet job demands, confidence, a sense of achievement, and a sense of value are more likely to develop during the work process. These positive perceptions are then transformed into higher levels of job satisfaction [2, 7]. Once job satisfaction is established, positive identification with the job and the organization is strengthened, which increases employees' willingness to remain in the organization [5]. In other words, D-A fit can be regarded as the cognitive foundation related to ability at the initial stage, while job satisfaction represents the emotional and attitudinal mechanism through which retention intention is ultimately formed. In work environments such as the shipbuilding industry that involve high technological requirements, high risk, and heavy labor demands, this mediating process provides stronger explanatory power because employees' perceptions of whether they are capable of performing their work not only influence their immediate work experiences but also affect their judgments regarding whether they will continue to remain in the organization in the future [10]. Therefore, the following hypothesis is proposed.

H4: D-A fit forms a positive retention intention through job satisfaction.

Based on the above theoretical reasoning and research hypotheses, the research framework shown in Fig. 1 is developed.

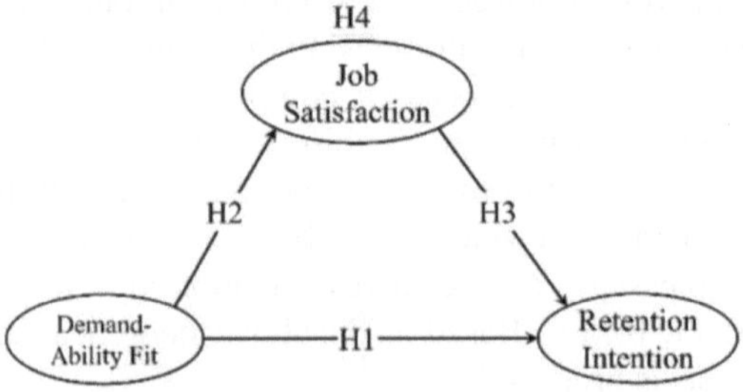

Fig. 1. Research Framework

3 Research Methods

3.1 Data Collection and Sampling

This study selected employees in the shipbuilding industry as the research subjects to examine the relationships among D-A fit, job satisfaction, and retention intention. The shipbuilding industry is technology intensive and highly dependent on professional manpower. Employees are required to possess multiple professional skills and practical abilities during the work process. Therefore, the degree of congruence between individual abilities and job requirements may influence employees' overall evaluation of their work and their retention tendency. Based on this research background, employees from a shipyard in Kaohsiung were selected as the research subjects. In terms of sample selection, purposive sampling was adopted. Samples were collected according to the distribution of employees in relevant departments of the shipyard during the research period.

Data collection was conducted from October 2025 to December 2025. Questionnaires were distributed to relevant departments of the shipyard in Kaohsiung, and employees were invited to complete the questionnaire voluntarily. After the questionnaires were collected, the data were organized and examined. Incomplete or invalid questionnaires were excluded to ensure data quality. After the data screening process was completed, the valid samples were compiled and used for subsequent statistical analysis.

A total of 410 questionnaires were collected. After removing samples with missing values and straight-line responses, 374 valid questionnaires were retained as the final sample for analysis. According to the demographic characteristics of the sample, most respondents were male, accounting for 85.0%. In terms of marital status, the majority of respondents were married, accounting for 67.1%. Regarding age distribution, the largest group was between 30 and 39 years old, accounting for 24.3%. In terms of educational background, most respondents had a junior college or university degree, accounting for 46.8%. With respect to departmental distribution, most respondents were from the manufacturing department, accounting for 47.3%.

3.2 Sample and Questionnaire

The questionnaire used in this study consisted of four sections. The first section measured D-A fit and included three items. The second section measured job satisfaction and included three items. The third section measured retention intention and included three items. All measurement items were assessed using a seven point Likert scale ranging from 1 representing strongly disagree to 7 representing strongly agree. The questionnaire items were primarily developed with reference to relevant previous literature and were adjusted and revised according to the context of this study to serve as measurement instruments for D-A fit, job satisfaction, and retention intention. The D-A fit scale was adapted from the scale developed by Cable and DeRue [2]. The job satisfaction scale was adapted from the scale proposed by Shaibu et al. [20]. The retention intention scale was adapted from the scale developed by Sobaih et al. [21].

3.3 Data Analysis

This study employed structural equation modeling (SEM) to analyze the data and to examine the research framework and the relationships among variables. After the questionnaires were collected, SPSS 22.0 and AMOS 24 statistical software were used as analysis tools. First, reliability analysis was conducted using SPSS to examine the internal consistency of the scales. Cronbach's α was adopted as the evaluation indicator, and an α value above .7 was considered an acceptable level [22]. In addition, AMOS 24 was used to calculate composite reliability (CR) to further strengthen the examination of internal consistency. In terms of validity, convergent validity and discriminant validity were examined. Convergent validity was assessed through CR and average variance extracted (AVE) to confirm that sufficient correlations existed among indicators within the same construct. Discriminant validity was evaluated through Pearson product moment correlation analysis to examine the correlations among constructs and by comparing the square root of AVE with the correlation coefficients among constructs to confirm adequate distinction between different constructs. Finally, with respect to inferential statistics, SEM analysis was conducted according to the two step analytical procedure proposed by Anderson and Gerbing [23]. The first stage involved measurement model analysis to verify the reliability and validity of each construct. The second stage involved structural model analysis to examine the research hypotheses and the causal relationships among latent variables. Through the overall model fit evaluation of SEM, the degree of correspondence between the theoretical model and the empirical data could be assessed.

4 Results and Analysis

4.1 Confirmatory Factor Analysis

This study employed confirmatory factor analysis (CFA) to examine the measurement model of each construct in order to confirm the explanatory ability of the scale items for the latent variables and the overall measurement quality. The results indicate that the standardized factor loadings of all items reached a significant level ($p < .001$), with standardized coefficients ranging from .836 to .929. In general, a standardized factor loading above .50 indicates that an item possesses basic explanatory ability, whereas a value above .70 indicates good convergent performance. Therefore, all items in this study meet the recommended criteria. In terms of reliability, the Cronbach's α values of each construct ranged from .914 to .935, all exceeding the recommended threshold of .70, which indicates good internal consistency of the scales. In addition, CR ranged from .916 to .936, all exceeding the recommended standard of .70, indicating that the items of each construct demonstrate good overall reliability. The AVE ranged from .783 to .829, all exceeding the recommended value of .50, indicating that the latent variables can effectively explain the variance of the observed variables and demonstrate good convergent validity. Based on the above results, the standardized factor loadings, Cronbach's α, CR, and AVE of each construct meet the recommended standards in the literature, indicating that the scales exhibit good reliability and convergent validity.

4.2 Discriminant Validity

To examine the relationships among the constructs and to assess discriminant validity, Pearson product moment correlation analysis was conducted. The results shown in Table 1 indicate that the correlation coefficients among the constructs range from .717 to .779, all of which are below .850. This result indicates that excessive overlap among the constructs does not occur and that an appropriate level of distinction exists among them. In addition, according to the criterion proposed by Hair et al. [24], the correlation coefficient between constructs should be smaller than the square root of the AVE of the construct in order to confirm discriminant validity. The values in the upper right triangle of Table 1 indicate that the square root of AVE for each construct is greater than its correlation coefficients with other constructs. Therefore, it can be concluded that D-A fit, job satisfaction, and retention intention demonstrate good discriminant validity in this study, which supports the suitability of conducting subsequent structural model analysis.

Table 1. Discriminant Validity

Construct	AVE	Discriminant validity		
		(1)	(2)	(3)
(1) Demand-Ability Fit	.808	**.899**		
(2) Job Satisfaction	.829	.779	**.910**	
(3) Retention Intention	.783	.717	.746	**.885**

4.3 Structural Model

This study employed SEM to examine the research framework and the hypothesized relationships. The overall model fit results indicate that the proposed model demonstrates a good level of fit. Among the model fit indices, the chi square value (χ^2) is 38.966 with 24° of freedom (DF). The normed chi square (χ^2/DF) is 1.624, which falls within the recommended range of 1 to 3. For other model fit indicators, the GFI is .978, AGFI is .958, RMSEA is .041, SRMR is .014, TLI is .993, CFI is .996, and IFI is .996, all of which meet the recommended standards in the literature. In addition, Hoelter's N (CN) is 349, which exceeds the recommended threshold of 200. Overall, all model fit indices meet the recommended criteria, indicating that the structural model demonstrates a good fit with the empirical data.

With regard to hypothesis testing in Table 2, the results indicate that D-A fit has a significant and positive effect on retention intention ($\beta = .321, p < .001$), which supports H1. In addition, D-A fit has a significant and positive effect on job satisfaction ($\beta = .879$, $p < .001$), which supports H2. The results also indicate that job satisfaction has a significant and positive effect on retention intention ($\beta = .565, p < .001$), which supports H3. Furthermore, Bootstrapping with 5,000 resamples was conducted to examine the mediating effect. The results indicate that D-A fit has a significant indirect effect on retention intention through job satisfaction ($\beta = .497, p < .001$), which supports H4. Overall, the results indicate that D-A fit not only directly influences employees' retention intention but also enhances retention intention through increased job satisfaction, indicating that job satisfaction plays an important mediating role between the two variables.

Table 2. Path coefficients and significances

Path hypothesis	Std.	Unstd.	S.E.	Z	*p*	Supported
H1: Demand-Ability Fit →Retention Intention	.321	.369	.097	3.809	<.001	Y
H2: Demand-Ability Fit →Job Satisfaction	.879	.929	.046	20.386	<.001	Y
H3: Job Satisfaction →Retention Intention	.565	.614	.092	6.651	<.001	Y
H4: Demand-Ability Fit →Job Satisfaction →Retention Intention	.497	.571	.119	4.798	<.001	Y
Bootstrapping = 5,000						

5 Conclusion

This study examined the relationships among D-A fit, job satisfaction, and retention intention. The results indicate that job satisfaction has a significant mediating effect between D-A fit and retention intention. When employees perceive that a good fit exists between their abilities and job task requirements, positive work evaluations and emotional responses are more likely to develop. This psychological process is transformed into higher levels of job satisfaction and subsequently promotes retention intention. This finding is consistent with the concept of D-A fit proposed by Cable and DeRue [2] and aligns with the argument of Kristof-Brown et al. [9] that the congruence between individuals and their work environment plays an important role in shaping work attitudes and behavioral intentions. In addition, when employees are able to demonstrate their knowledge, skills, and experience during the work process and obtain a sense of achievement and value recognition, stable psychological evaluations and emotional states are more likely to accumulate, which further strengthens their retention intention. This process is also consistent with the perspectives of Sylva et al. [3] and Edwards and Shipp [10] regarding the relationship between ability congruence and psychological well-being.

From a practical perspective, the findings provide important managerial implications for industries characterized by high levels of technological intensity and professional specialization. When organizations emphasize the congruence between employee abilities and job requirements in job assignment and talent development processes, employees' overall evaluations of job content and work environments are more likely to improve, which contributes to the formation of stable job satisfaction. In the shipbuilding industry, work tasks often involve high technical requirements and long term skill accumulation. When organizations implement precise job design, effective capability development mechanisms, and continuous learning environments that enable employees to experience the utilization of their abilities and recognition of their value, a more stable workforce structure can be established and turnover risk can be reduced. When employees develop positive perceptions of job content and organizational support, these perceptions are more likely to be transformed into long term commitment and contributions to the organization.

At the theoretical level, this study incorporates D-A fit into the research framework of retention intention and verifies the psychological mediating process of job satisfaction. This approach supplements previous studies that primarily focused on organizational support or leadership style as explanatory variables [1]. The results indicate that employees' subjective perceptions of the congruence between their abilities and job requirements influence their behavioral intention to remain in the organization through the emotional and cognitive evaluation process of job satisfaction. This structural relationship highlights the importance of individual perceptions of ability in organizational behavior research and corresponds with the fit theory proposed by Kristof-Brown et al. [9], which suggests that the perceived congruence between individuals and their work environment can gradually be transformed into stable work attitudes and behavioral tendencies through psychological processes.

Although this study provides empirical support for the relationship between D-A fit and retention intention, several limitations should be acknowledged. The data were collected from a single shipbuilding enterprise, and the sample was primarily composed of employees from a shipyard in southern Taiwan. The sample structure may be influenced by the characteristics of a specific industry and organizational culture. Therefore, the external validity of the findings still has room for further extension. In addition, this study adopted a cross sectional questionnaire survey to collect data. This research design cannot capture the changes in employees' psychological states and work attitudes over time and may also be influenced by common method variance [25]. Future studies may incorporate different industries or organizational contexts for comparative analysis and may adopt longitudinal research designs to examine long term changes in perceptions of ability fit and work attitudes. In addition, subsequent research may include variables such as career stage, job level, or professional background in the analysis to examine potential differences in fit perceptions and retention behavior among different groups. Such approaches may further extend the application of relevant theories and enhance the practical value of the research for organizational human resource management.

References

1. Milliman, J., Gatling, A., Kim, J.S.: The effect of workplace spirituality on hospitality employee engagement, intention to stay, and service delivery. J. Hosp. Tour. Manag. **35**, 56–65 (2018). https://doi.org/10.1016/j.jhtm.2018.03.002
2. Cable, D.M., DeRue, D.S.: The convergent and discriminant validity of subjective fit perceptions. J. Appl. Psychol. **87**(5), 875–884 (2002). https://doi.org/10.1037/0021-9010.87.5.875
3. Sylva, H., Mol, S.T., Den Hartog, D.N., Dorenbosch, L.: Person-job fit and proactive career behaviour: a dynamic approach. Eur. J. Work Organ. Psychol. **28**(5), 631–645 (2019). https://doi.org/10.1080/1359432X.2019.1580309

4. Chen, L., Jilili, M., Wang, R., Liu, L., Yang, A.: The influence of person-job fit on health status and depression among Chinese domestic workers: mediating effect of the employer-employee relationship. Front. Psychol. **13**, 782022 (2022). https://doi.org/10.3389/fpsyg.2022.782022
5. Jung, H.S., Yoon, H.H.: Why is employees' emotional intelligence important? The effects of EI on stress-coping styles and job satisfaction in the hospitality industry. Int. J. Contemp. Hosp. Manag. **28**(8), 1649–1675 (2016). https://doi.org/10.1108/IJCHM-10-2014-0509
6. Spagnoli, P., Caetano, A., Santos, S.C.: Satisfaction with job aspects: do patterns change over time? J. Bus. Res. **65**(5), 609–616 (2012). https://doi.org/10.1016/j.jbusres.2011.02.048
7. Beier, M.E., Torres, W.J., Fisher, G.G., Wallace, L.E.: Age and job fit: the relationship between demands-ability fit and retirement and health. J. Occup. Health Psychol. **25**(4), 227–243 (2020). https://doi.org/10.1037/ocp0000164
8. Akanni, A., Oduaran, C.A.: Person-job fit and work-life balance of female nurses with cultural competence as a mediator: evidence from Nigeria. Front. Nurs. **9**(1), 81–86 (2022). https://doi.org/10.2478/fon-2022-0010
9. Kristof-Brown, A.L., Zimmerman, R.D., Johnson, E.C.: Consequences of individuals' fit at work: a meta-analysis of person-job, person-organization, person-group, and person-supervisor fit. Pers. Psychol. **58**(2), 281–342 (2005). https://doi.org/10.1111/j.1744-6570.2005.00672.x
10. Edwards, J.R., Shipp, A.J.: The relationship between person-environment fit and outcomes: an integrative theoretical framework. In: Ostroff, C., Judge, T.A. (eds.) Perspectives on Organizational Fit, pp. 209–258. Lawrence Erlbaum Associates Publishers, Mahwah, NJ (2007)
11. Debus, M.E., Körner, B., Wang, M., Kleinmann, M.: Reacting to perceived overqualification: uniting strain-based and self-regulatory adjustment reactions and the moderating role of formal work arrangements. J. Bus. Psychol. **38**(2), 411–435 (2023). https://doi.org/10.1007/s10869-022-09870-8
12. Bono, J.E., Vey, M.A.: Personality and emotional performance: extraversion, neuroticism, and self-monitoring. J. Occup. Health Psychol. **12**(2), 177–192 (2007). https://doi.org/10.1037/1076-8998.12.2.177
13. Knezović, E., Neimarlija, I.: Organizational justice and employees' intention to stay: the mediating role of job satisfaction. Evid.-Based HRM. **11**(1), 1–18 (2023). https://doi.org/10.1108/EBHRM-07-2021-0156
14. Chami-Malaeb, R., Garavan, T.: Talent and leadership development practices as drivers of intention to stay in Lebanese organisations: the mediating role of affective commitment. Int. J. Hum. Resour. Manag. **24**(21), 4046–4062 (2013)
15. Taris, R., Feij, J.: Longitudinal examination of the relationship between supplies-values fit and work outcomes. Appl. Psychol. **50**(1), 52–80 (2001). https://doi.org/10.1111/1464-0597.00048
16. Hamid, S.N.A., Yahya, K.K.: Mediating role of work engagement on the relationship between person-job fit and employees' retention: evidence from semiconductor companies in northern region of Malaysia. Int. Rev. Manag. Mark. **6**(7), 187–194 (2016)
17. Loo, S.H. et al.: Key factors affecting employee job satisfaction in Malaysian manufacturing firms post COVID-19 pandemic: a Delphi study. Cogent Bus. Manag. **11**(1), 2380809 (2024). https://doi.org/10.1080/23311975.2024.2380809
18. Sypniewska, B., Baran, M., Kłos, M.: Work engagement and employee satisfaction in the practice of sustainable human resource management–based on the study of polish employees. Int. Entrep. Manag. J. **19**(3), 1069–1100 (2023). https://doi.org/10.1007/s11365-023-00834-9
19. McNamara, T.K., Pitt-Catsouphes, M., Matz-Costa, C., Brown, M., Valcour, M.: Across the continuum of satisfaction with work-family balance: work hours, flexibility-fit, and work-family culture. Soc. Sci. Res. **42**(2), 283–298 (2013). https://doi.org/10.1016/j.ssresearch.2012.10.002

20. Shaibu, A., Bhayo, K.Y., Hussain, S.: Impact of the compensation package and work motivation on job satisfaction moderating role of Islamic work ethic. Int. J. Manag. **13**(6), 1–15 (2022). https://doi.org/10.17605/OSF.IO/CUG
21. Sobaih, A.E.E., Hasanein, A.M., Aliedan, M.M., Abdallah, H.S.: The impact of transactional and transformational leadership on employee intention to stay in deluxe hotels: mediating role of organisational commitment. Tour. Hosp. Res. **22**(3), 257–270 (2022). https://doi.org/10.1177/1467358420972156
22. Yasai-Ardekani, M.: Structural adaptations to environments. Acad. Manag. Rev. **11**(1), 9–21 (1986). https://doi.org/10.5465/amr.1986.4282607
23. Anderson, J.C., Gerbing, D.W.: Structural equation modeling in practice: a review and recommended two-step approach. Psychol. Bull. **103**(3), 411–423 (1988). https://doi.org/10.1037/0033-2909.103.3.411
24. Hair, J.F., Black, W.C., Babin, B.J., Anderson, R.E., Tatham, R.L.: Multivariate Data Analysis, 7th edn. Bookman, Essex, UK (2017)
25. Podsakoff, P.M., MacKenzie, S.B., Lee, J.Y., Podsakoff, N.P.: Common method biases in behavioral research: a critical review of the literature and recommended remedies. J. Appl. Psychol. **88**(5), 879–903 (2003)

Applying the Technology Acceptance Model to Explore Consumers' Usage Intention Toward Food Delivery Platform

Han-Yee Leong, Ren-Fang Chao(✉), and Ming-Wei Huang

Postgraduate Programs in Management, I-Shou University, Kaohsiung, Taiwan, China
rfchao@cloud.isu.edu.tw

Abstract. In recent years, food delivery platforms have gradually become one of the important food service options in the daily lives of people in Taiwan. Based on the Technology Acceptance Model, this study explores the relationships among perceived ease of use, perceived usefulness, attitude, and usage intention when consumers use food delivery platforms. To better understand the factors influencing consumers' continued use of food delivery platforms, this study targeted Taiwanese consumers who had previously used such platforms. The results indicate that perceived ease of use positively affects perceived usefulness and attitude, while both perceived usefulness and attitude further influence consumers' usage intention. These findings suggest that when food delivery platforms offer good operational convenience and practical value, they can help enhance consumers' positive attitudes and continued usage intention, and may serve as a reference for platform operators in optimizing service design and increasing customer stickiness.

Keywords: Technology Acceptance Model · Food Delivery Platform · Attitude · Usage Intention · Structural Equation Modeling

1 Introduction

With the widespread adoption of digital technology, smartphones, and mobile internet, food consumption patterns have gradually shifted toward digitalization and platformization, and food delivery platforms have become an important food service in modern daily life. The O_2O business model formed by the integration of mobile applications and food logistics improves overall service efficiency and convenience through intelligent processing [1]. The COVID-19 pandemic further accelerated the expansion of food delivery platforms and increased consumers' demand for their use [2]. In addition to attracting users through price subsidies, food delivery platforms have continuously invested in membership programs and real-time delivery tracking mechanisms to enhance consumer experience and platform stickiness [3]. However, as market competition intensifies, relying solely on price advantages is no longer sufficient to retain consumers in the long term. At the same time, users' expectations regarding platform convenience, quality, efficiency, and trust continue to rise, making usage intention and its underlying formation mechanisms an important research issue.

D. Liberona et al. (Eds.): MISNC 2026, CCIS 3092, pp. 254–265, 2027.
https://doi.org/10.1007/978-3-032-33381-0_19

In academic research, the Technology Acceptance Model (TAM) has long been regarded as an important theoretical framework for explaining the use of new technologies. Davis [4] pointed out that perceived usefulness and perceived ease of use are the two core constructs that influence users' attitudes and behavioral intentions. When consumers perceive a system as easy to use and practically beneficial, they are more likely to develop a positive attitude, which in turn enhances their intention to use or reuse the system [5]. In addition, factors such as convenience, trust, and service quality also influence consumers' willingness to adopt and use a platform [6]. Therefore, in Taiwan's highly competitive and rapidly growing food delivery platform market, examining consumers' usage intention based on TAM can supplement the insufficient understanding of the local market context in existing research.

Although the food delivery platform market continues to grow rapidly, consumers' acceptance of such platforms may still be influenced by multiple factors. For example, Fitria et al. [7] indicated that interface intuitiveness directly affects users' perceptions of a platform, which in turn influences their usage intention. In addition, if a platform enables consumers to clearly perceive benefits such as improved convenience in daily life, it can strengthen their perceived usefulness and overall positive attitude [8]. Furthermore, operational convenience enhances consumers' level of acceptance and their intention to continue using the platform [9]. However, although existing studies have separately examined the importance of some of these factors, there is still room for further exploration regarding a comprehensive examination of the relationships among perceived ease of use, perceived usefulness, attitude, and usage intention in the context of food delivery platforms in Taiwan.

Based on the above research background and problem awareness, this study focuses on users of food delivery platforms in Taiwan and adopts the TAM as its theoretical foundation to examine the interactive relationships among perceived usefulness, perceived ease of use, and attitude, as well as their effects on usage intention. Through this research design, this study seeks to construct a consumer behavior explanatory framework applicable to the context of food delivery platforms. In addition to verifying the applicability of TAM to local digital food service platforms at the theoretical level, the findings may also provide practical suggestions for platform operators regarding service design, function optimization, and market strategies, and serve as an important reference for future policy making and platform governance.

2 Literature Review

2.1 Food Delivery Platforms

In Taiwan, food delivery platforms began to develop around 2012, with foodpanda and Uber Eats, which entered the market in 2016, forming the major market structure [10]. The COVID-19 pandemic further stimulated the growth of these platforms. Huang and Siao [11] pointed out that, during the pandemic, the operating model that integrated internet technology with food service further strengthened the penetration of food delivery platforms into users' daily lives. As competition intensified and user expectations continued to rise, platform operators enhanced user stickiness through brand differentiation, promotional activities, process optimization, and diversified services [12].

2.2 Technology Acceptance Model (TAM)

The TAM proposed by Davis [4], is one of the most representative theoretical frameworks in the field of information systems for examining users' acceptance of technological products. Numerous previous studies have confirmed the applicability and stability of the TAM across various digital platforms.

The Effect of Perceived Ease of Use on Perceived Usefulness
In the TAM, perceived ease of use is regarded as an antecedent of perceived usefulness. When users feel that a system operates smoothly and requires little learning effort, they are more likely to believe that the technology can provide practical benefits [4]. When a system is simple and easy to understand, users are more likely to perceive the benefits of its financial services, which in turn enhances their overall intention to accept it [13]. In the context of food delivery platforms, a well-designed application interface enables consumers to quickly complete ordering, payment, and order tracking, thereby enhancing their perceptions of the platform's convenience and usefulness. Accordingly, this study proposes the following hypothesis:

H1: Perceived ease of use has a positive effect on perceived usefulness.

The Effect of Perceived Ease of Use on Attitude
Perceived ease of use plays an important antecedent role in the formation of users' attitudes. Davis [4] pointed out that when a system is perceived as easy to use, it can reduce users' learning and operational barriers. From the perspective of cognitive psychology, the formation of a positive attitude can be understood as a form of psychological relief resulting from a reduction in cognitive load. Wu and Yu [14] indicated that even when consumers experience emotional pleasure from a service, an inconvenient interface may still hinder the development of a stable long-term attitude. If food delivery platforms can provide clear product categories, real-time delivery tracking, and quick payment options, they can reduce users' concerns and negative emotions during the operation process, thereby improving their overall attitude toward using the platform. Accordingly, this study proposes the following hypothesis:

H2: Perceived ease of use has a positive effect on attitude.

The Effect of Perceived Usefulness on Attitude
Perceived usefulness refers to the degree to which users believe that a technological system can substantially improve their life or work efficiency, and this belief is a key factor in shaping usage attitude [4]. When individuals perceive that a service has practical value in actual use, they are more likely to develop positive psychological feelings and evaluations toward it. Wang et al. [15] found that when users recognize a platform as desirable and beneficial, their attitudes become more positive, which in turn strengthens their consumption intention. In the context of food delivery platforms, when consumers find that using a mobile application makes ordering, payment, and delivery tracking more convenient, they are more likely to view the platform as a tool with substantial value. Accordingly, this study proposes the following hypothesis:

H3: Perceived usefulness has a positive effect on attitude.

The Effect of Perceived Usefulness on Usage Intention

When users believe that a system can effectively improve their life efficiency or satisfy practical needs, their intention to use that system tends to increase accordingly [4]. Compared with ease of use, users are more concerned with whether the system is useful and effective rather than whether it is easy to operate [16]. In this study, it is argued that when consumers realize that ordering meals through a platform not only saves time but also provides greater convenience and flexibility in daily life, their usage intention will be strengthened. Accordingly, this study proposes the following hypothesis:

H4: Perceived usefulness has a positive effect on usage intention.

The Effect of Attitude on Usage Intention

In the TAM, attitude is often regarded as a key mediator influencing individuals' behavioral intentions. Its role not only links the perceptual level with actual behavior but also reflects users' overall evaluation of the value of a technology or service [4]. Users' positive attitudes toward a platform can enhance their intention to use it again, and such attitudes are influenced by factors such as platform stability, order accuracy, and delivery timeliness [17]. In the context of mobile applications integrating daily life services, the relationship between attitude and behavioral intention is no longer limited to a static willingness to use, but also reflects associations with frequency of use, spending amount, and platform stickiness. Accordingly, this study proposes the following hypothesis:

H5: Attitude has a positive effect on usage intention.

The Relationships Among Perceived Ease of Use, Attitude, and Usage Intention

Both perceived ease of use and attitude have significant effects on behavioral intention, and attitude is often the key mechanism through which perceived ease of use influences intention [18]. Songkram et al. [19] found that attitude has the most significant effect on usage intention, and that perceived ease of use influences behavioral tendency only indirectly through attitude, supporting the applicability of the TAM in the context of digital platforms. Accordingly, this study proposes the following hypothesis:

H6: Perceived ease of use indirectly and positively affects usage intention through attitude.

The Relationships Among Perceived Ease of Use, Perceived Usefulness, and Usage Intention

Widiar et al. [20] found that systems that are easy to use, because they involve lower usage costs, are more likely to enhance adoption intention and continued usage intention. Similarly, Al Ansori and Lestari [21] found that resistance to new technology often stems from concerns about operational difficulty and usage errors, whereas a simple interface and clear procedures help enhance users' sense of control, trust, and intention to adopt. Accordingly, this study proposes the following hypothesis:

H7: Perceived ease of use indirectly and positively affects usage intention through perceived usefulness.

The Relationships Among Perceived Ease of Use, Perceived Usefulness, Attitude, and Usage Intention

If a system is easy to operate and imposes a lower learning burden, users need to spend less time and effort to complete tasks, thereby enhancing their perceived usefulness [21]. On the other hand, Ru-Zhue et al. [13] indicated that an easy-to-use interface, low learning burden, and clear operational procedures directly improve usage intention and satisfaction. Accordingly, this study proposes the following hypothesis:

H8: Perceived ease of use indirectly and positively affects usage intention through perceived usefulness and then attitude.

3 Methods

3.1 Sample and Procedure

The primary source of data for this study was consumers in Taiwan who had used food delivery platforms, such as Foodpanda and Uber Eats, to order meals. The questionnaire was distributed online from June 20 to September 23, 2025, using purposive sampling. After excluding invalid responses, a total of 437 valid questionnaires were retained. The collected data were analyzed using IBM SPSS 22.0 and Amos 25, with structural equation modeling employed as the main analytical approach.

Among the respondents, females (52.86%) slightly outnumbered males. Most respondents were between 30 and 39 years old (40.50%), and the majority had a junior college or university degree (74.60%). In terms of average monthly income, most respondents fell within the range of NT$20,001 to NT$40,000 (39.59%). Regarding platform usage behavior, most respondents used food delivery platforms 1–2 times per week (48.51%), with a single-order spending amount primarily ranging from NT$201 to NT$400 (54.00%). In addition, most consumers adopted online payment methods (79.41%) (Fig. 1).

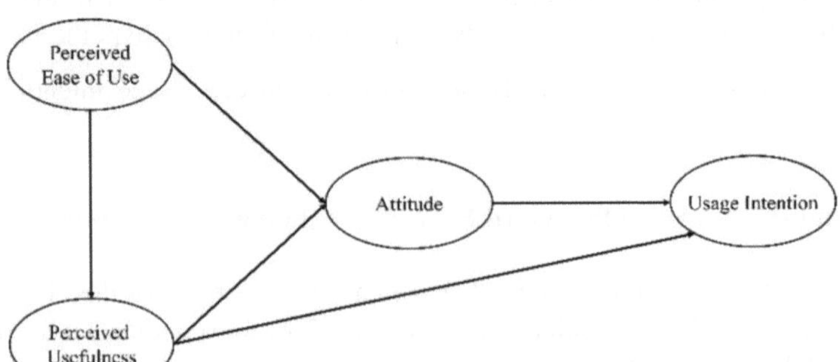

Fig. 1. Research Framework

3.2 Instruments

Perceived ease of use. The questionnaire items for perceived ease of use were primarily adapted from the scale developed by Hong et al. [22] and were revised to fit the context of this study in order to measure consumers' perceptions of the operational convenience of food delivery platforms. A 7-point Likert scale was used (1 = strongly disagree to 7 = strongly agree). The Cronbach's alpha coefficient for this construct was .778.

Perceived usefulness. The questionnaire items for perceived usefulness were primarily adapted from the scale developed by Hong et al. [22] and were revised to fit the context of this study in order to measure consumers' perceptions of the practicality and usefulness of food delivery platforms. A 7-point Likert scale was used (1 = strongly disagree to 7 = strongly agree). The Cronbach's alpha coefficient for this construct was .800.

Attitude. The questionnaire items for attitude were primarily adapted from the scale developed by Foroughi et al. [23] and were revised to fit the context of this study in order to measure consumers' overall evaluations and positive feelings toward food delivery platforms. A 7-point Likert scale was used (1 = strongly disagree to 7 = strongly agree). The Cronbach's alpha coefficient for this construct was .790.

Usage intention. The questionnaire items for usage intention were primarily adapted from the scale developed by Allah Pitchay et al. [24] and were revised to fit the context of this study in order to measure consumers' tendency to continue using food delivery platforms in the future. A 7-point Likert scale was used (1 = strongly disagree to 7 = strongly agree). The Cronbach's alpha coefficient for this construct was .864.

4 Results and Analysis

4.1 Measurement Model

This study employed confirmatory factor analysis (CFA) to examine the reliability and validity of each construct. Standardized factor loadings, Cronbach's alpha, composite reliability (CR), and average variance extracted (AVE) were used as the evaluation indicators. The results showed that the standardized factor loadings of all items ranged from .705 to .814, Cronbach's alpha ranged from .778 to .864, CR ranged from .782 to .866, and AVE ranged from .545 to .618. All values met the recommended criteria, indicating that the measurement scales used in this study had good reliability and convergent validity (Table 1).

This study further examined discriminant validity using Pearson product-moment correlation analysis and the square root of AVE. The results showed that the correlation coefficients among the constructs ranged from .684 to .735, all of which were below .850 and therefore met the criterion suggested by Kline [25]. In addition, the square root of the AVE for each construct was greater than the correlations among constructs, indicating good discriminant validity among the constructs [26] and providing sufficient support for subsequent structural model analysis (Table 2).

Table 1. Confirmatory factor analysis

	Unstd.	S.E.	Z	*p*	Std.	α	CR	AVE
Perceived ease of use						.778	.782	.545
PEOU1	1				.731			
PEOU2	1.012	.066	15.374	<.001	.776			
PEOU3	.941	.068	13.845	<.001	.705			
Perceived Usefulness						.800	.801	.573
PU1	1				.782			
PU2	1.002	.060	16.588	<.001	.774			
PU3	.913	.060	15.179	<.001	.714			
Attitude						.790	.791	.558
ATT1	1				.741			
ATT2	1.001	.068	14.820	<.001	.748			
ATT3	1.026	.068	15.101	<.001	.752			
Usage Intention						.864	.866	.618
IU1	1				.754			
IU2	1.113	.066	16.854	<.001	.814			
IU3	1.090	.067	16.314	<.001	.797			
IU4	1.116	.069	16.114	<.001	.779			

Table 2. Means, Standard deviations and discriminant validity

Construct	Mean	S.D	AVE	Discriminant validity			
				(1)	(2)	(3)	(4)
(1) Perceived ease of use	5.514	.848	.545	**.738**			
(2) Perceived usefulness	5.628	.858	.573	.735	**.757**		
(3) Attitude	5.571	.836	.558	.707	.689	**.747**	
(4) Usage intention	5.444	.902	.618	.684	.726	.719	**.786**

AVE = average variance extracted. Bold diagonal values indicate the square roots of the AVEs; values below the diagonal are Pearson correlation coefficients.

4.2 Structural Model

This study further examined the overall fit of the structural equation model. The results showed that all model fit indices met the recommended standards, including GFI = .972, AGFI = .943, RMSEA = .033, SRMR = .031, TLI = .988, CFI = .991, IFI = .991, and χ^2/df = 1.483. These results indicate that the proposed model had a good overall fit and was adequate for subsequent hypothesis testing and structural model analysis.

The maximum likelihood estimation method was used to test each hypothesized path. The results showed that most of the hypotheses were supported. Specifically, perceived ease of use had significant positive effects on perceived usefulness and attitude, while both perceived usefulness and attitude had significant positive effects on usage intention. In addition, perceived ease of use also indirectly affected usage intention through attitude and perceived usefulness. However, the direct effect of perceived usefulness on attitude was not significant, and the sequential mediating effect of perceived ease of use on usage intention through perceived usefulness and attitude was also not supported. Overall, six of the eight hypotheses were supported, indicating that the theoretical framework of this study was generally supported (Table 3).

Table 3. Path analysis

Hypothesis	Std.	Unstd.	S.E.	Z	*p*
H1:PEOU→ PU	.735	.744	.033	22.638	<.001
H2:PEOU→ Att	.608	.588	.196	3.007	.003
H3:PU → Att	.306	.285	.184	1.546	.122
H4:PU → UI	.489	.481	.111	4.342	<.001
H5:Att → UI	.436	.461	.120	3.841	<.001
H6:PEOU→ Att → UI	.265	.271	.118	2.302	.021
H7:PEOU→ PU → UI	.450	.460	.171	2.693	.007
H8:PEOU→ PU → Att → UI	.123	.126	.090	1.396	.163
Bootstrapping = 5,000					

5 Discussion

5.1 Discussion

The results of this study indicate that when consumers perceive food delivery platforms as easy to operate, user-friendly in interface design, and smooth in the ordering process, they are more likely to enhance their perceptions of the platforms' usefulness and further develop more positive attitudes toward using them. As suggested by Seghezzi et al. [1], digital platforms with strong interactivity and smooth operation help establish users' positive evaluations. If a system can reduce operational burden and improve task completion efficiency, it is more likely to strengthen users' positive attitudes toward the system (Au & Baum [17]). In other words, perceived ease of use is not only an important foundation for consumers' judgments of a platform's functional value, but also a key factor in fostering positive attitudes.

However, the effect of perceived usefulness on attitude was not significant, indicating that consumers' recognition of the functional benefits of a platform does not necessarily translate into an overall positive attitude. As explained by Madinga et al. [27], in highly task-oriented digital services such as food delivery platforms, perceived usefulness is more likely to directly influence usage intention rather than operate through attitude.

Attitude had a significant positive effect on usage intention, indicating that when consumers hold a stronger sense of approval and a more positive evaluation of a food delivery platform, their intention to continue using it in the future also increases. As noted by Foroughi et al. [23], attitude is an important antecedent of usage intention. In other words, if a platform can establish consumers' positive attitudes through good service quality and user experience, it will help increase the likelihood of continued use.

Perceived ease of use also had significant indirect effects on usage intention through attitude and perceived usefulness. This suggests that when a food delivery platform offers good operational convenience, it not only enhances users' positive attitudes but also strengthens their perceptions of the platform's practical value, thereby increasing their intention to continue using it. This finding is consistent with the argument that both perceived ease of use and perceived usefulness are important antecedents of behavioral intention [4]. However, the more distal mediating effect of perceived ease of use on usage intention through perceived usefulness and then attitude was not supported. This suggests that users' behavioral intentions are more likely to stem directly from their evaluations of a platform's usefulness and convenience, whereas the role of attitude within a multiple mediation pathway appears to be relatively limited [23].

5.2 Practical Implications

This study indicates that perceived ease of use, perceived usefulness, and attitude are all important factors influencing consumers continued use of food delivery platforms. Therefore, in terms of service design, platform operators should prioritize simplifying operational procedures and enhancing interface friendliness. For example, they may improve the clarity of the ordering process, reduce the number of steps required for searching and checkout, and provide more intuitive classification and recommendation functions. When consumers are able to complete food ordering with lower operational costs, they are more likely to perceive the platform as useful and develop a more positive overall attitude toward it, which in turn strengthens their usage intention. This finding is also consistent with Davis's [4] perspective on the TAM. In addition, platforms may further enhance consumers' evaluations of practical benefits by optimizing delivery tracking, payment convenience, and the integration of frequently used functions.

Second, this study also shows that attitude has a significant effect on usage intention. Therefore, in addition to providing functional services, platforms should also pay close attention to consumers' overall user experience and brand image. Specifically, platforms can enhance consumers' identification with and trust in the platform through stable service quality, timely customer service responses, and personalized push notification design, thereby increasing the likelihood of continued use. Chiu et al. [28] pointed out that consumers' tendency to use food delivery platforms is derived not only from convenience but also from the overall service experience. Therefore, if platforms can simultaneously address functional benefits and emotional connection, they will be better positioned to build stronger customer stickiness and sustain long-term competitive advantages.

5.3 Limitations and Future Research

This study still has several limitations that may serve as references for future research. First, this study adopted a cross-sectional questionnaire design and primarily collected respondents' subjective perceptions of perceived ease of use, perceived usefulness, attitude, and usage intention toward food delivery platforms at a specific point in time. Therefore, it was difficult to further capture the dynamic relationships among these variables over time. In addition, self-reported data may also be affected by common method variance and recall bias, thereby limiting the inferential power of the findings [29]. Future studies may adopt a longitudinal research design or incorporate multiple data sources to improve the stability and explanatory power of the results.

Second, this study was primarily based on the TAM and focused on the relationships among perceived ease of use, perceived usefulness, attitude, and usage intention. However, it did not include other important factors that may influence consumer behavior, such as brand trust, interactive experience, social identification, or promotional incentives. Zhang et al. [30] pointed out that the acceptance process of digital platform services is often influenced by multiple social cognitive and interactive factors. Therefore, future research may further incorporate mediating or moderating variables to provide a more comprehensive explanation of consumers' usage intention toward food delivery platforms.

6 Conclusion

This study applied the Technology Acceptance Model to examine consumers' usage intention toward food delivery platforms in Taiwan. The results showed that perceived ease of use positively influenced perceived usefulness and attitude, while perceived usefulness and attitude further enhanced usage intention. In addition, perceived ease of use indirectly affected usage intention through perceived usefulness and attitude. Overall, the findings support the applicability of TAM in the food delivery platform context and suggest that operational convenience and practical value are key factors influencing consumers' continued use.

References

1. Seghezzi, A., Winkenbach, M., Mangiaracina, R.: On-demand food delivery: a systematic literature review. Int. J. Logist. Manag. **32**(4), 1334–1355 (2021). https://doi.org/10.1108/IJLM-03-2020-0150
2. Liao, S.H., Widowati, R., Chan, S.C.: Delivery services and online to offline in retailing: an empirical investigation in Taiwan during the Covid-19 pandemic period. SAGE Open. **15**(1), 21582440251323111 (2025). https://doi.org/10.1177/21582440251323111
3. Karahan, M.O.: Factors impacting consumers' continuance intention for online food delivery services in Turkey. Int. Rev. Manag. Mark. **15**(2), 273–284 (2025). https://doi.org/10.32479/irmm.17928
4. Davis, F.D.: Perceived usefulness, perceived ease of use, and user acceptance of information technology. MIS Q. **13**(3), 319–340 (1989). https://doi.org/10.2307/249008

5. Warsono, H., Yuwono, T., Putranti, I.R.: Analyzing technology acceptance model for collaborative governance in public administration: empirical evidence of digital governance and perceived ease of use. Int. J. Data Netw. Sci. **7**(1), 41–48 (2023). https://doi.org/10.5267/j.ijdns.2022.12.008
6. Milhem, M., Ateeq, A., Almehsen, M., Ali, S.A., Alzoraiki, M.: Evaluating the mediating role of trust and satisfaction in the adoption of digital banking services in Saudi Arabia. Int. Rev. Manag. Mark. **15**(5), 356–374 (2025). https://doi.org/10.32479/irmm.18207
7. Fitria, F., Yahya, M., Ali, M.I., Purnamawati, P., Mappalotteng, A.M.: The impact of system quality and user satisfaction: the mediating role of ease of use and usefulness in e-learning systems. Int. J. Environ. Eng. Educ. **6**(2), 119–131 (2024). https://doi.org/10.55151/ijeedu.v6i2.134
8. Liu, T., Zhang, Y., Zhang, M., Chen, M., Yu, S.: Factors influencing consumer willingness to use AI-driven autonomous taxis. Behav. Sci. **14**(12), 1216 (2024). https://doi.org/10.3390/bs14121216
9. Kelly, A.E., Palaniappan, S.: Using a technology acceptance model to determine factors influencing continued usage of mobile money service transactions in Ghana. J. Innov. Entrep. **12**(1), 34 (2023). https://doi.org/10.1186/s13731-023-00301-3
10. Rombach, M., Kartikasari, A., Dean, D.L., Suhartanto, D., Chen, B.T.: Determinants of customer loyalty to online food service delivery: evidence from Indonesia, Taiwan, and New Zealand. J. Hosp. Mark. Manag. **32**(6), 818–842 (2023). https://doi.org/10.1080/19368623.2023.2211061
11. Huang, S.L., Siao, H.R.: Factors affecting the implementation of online food delivery and its impact on restaurant performance during the COVID-19 pandemic. Sustainability. **15**(16), 12147 (2023). https://doi.org/10.3390/su151612147
12. Suryana, M.: Navigating digital trust: how service quality and brand image shape loyalty in online travel platforms. J. Tourism, Hospitality Travel Manag. **1**(2), 62–75 (2023). https://doi.org/10.58229/jthtm.v1i2.306
13. Ru-Zhue, J., Rakangthong, N.K., Kim, L., Nupueng, S., Issayeva, G.: Electronic banking ease of use, usefulness, value, and innovation influencing customer satisfaction. Int. J. Asian Bus. Inf. Manag. **16**(1), 1–18 (2025). https://doi.org/10.4018/ijabim.370562
14. Wu, R., Yu, Z.: Investigating users' acceptance of the metaverse with an extended technology acceptance model. Int. J. Hum.-Comput. Interact. **40**(19), 5810–5826 (2024). https://doi.org/10.1080/10447318.2023.2241295
15. Wang, C., Liu, T., Zhu, Y., Wang, H., Wang, X., Zhao, S.: The influence of consumer perception on purchase intention: evidence from cross-border E-commerce platforms. Heliyon. **9**(11), e21617 (2023). https://doi.org/10.1016/j.heliyon.2023.e21617
16. Wang, W., Wang, W.: College students' behavioural intentions of AI-assisted language learning: based on the technology acceptance model. J. Comput. Assist. Learn. **41**(4), e70075 (2025). https://doi.org/10.1111/jcal.70075
17. Au, W., Baum, T.: Service quality of online food delivery mobile application: an examination of the spillover effects of mobile app satisfaction. Int. J. Contemp. Hosp. Manag. **36**(3), 906–926 (2023). https://doi.org/10.1108/IJCHM-09-2022-1103
18. Wiprayoga, P., Gede, S., Suasana, G.A.K.G.: The role of attitude toward using mediates the influence of perceived usefulness and perceived ease of use on behavioral intention to use. Russ. J. Agric. Soc.-Econ. Sci. **140**(8), 53–68 (2023). https://doi.org/10.18551/rjoas.2023-08.06
19. Songkram, N., Chootongchai, S., Osuwan, H., Chuppunnarat, Y., Songkram, N.: Students' adoption towards behavioral intention of digital learning platform. Educ. Inf. Technol. **28**(9), 11655–11677 (2023). https://doi.org/10.1007/s10639-023-11637-4

20. Widiar, G., Yuniarinto, A., Yulianti, I.: Perceived ease of use's effects on behavioral intention mediated by perceived usefulness and trust. Interdisciplinary Soc. Stud. **2**(4), 1829–1844 (2023). https://doi.org/10.55324/iss.v2i4.397
21. Al Ansori, M.M., Lestari, E.P.: The effect of ease of use, benefits, and risks on QRIS usage intention with trust as moderator. Res. Horizon. **5**(4), 1049–1062 (2025). https://doi.org/10.54518/rh.5.4.2025.715
22. Hong, C., Choi, H.H., Choi, E.K.C., Joung, H.W.D.: Factors affecting customer intention to use online food delivery services before and during the COVID-19 pandemic. J. Hosp. Tour. Manag. **48**, 509–518 (2021). https://doi.org/10.1016/j.jhtm.2021.08.012
23. Foroughi, B., Yadegaridehkordi, E., Iranmanesh, M., Sukcharoen, T., Ghobakhlo, M., Nilashi, M.: Determinants of continuance intention to use food delivery apps: findings from PLS and fsQCA. Int. J. Contemp. Hosp. Manag. **36**(4), 1235–1261 (2024). https://doi.org/10.1108/IJCHM-10-2022-1209
24. Allah Pitchay, A., Ganesan, Y., Zulkifli, N.S., Khaliq, A.: Determinants of customers' intention to use online food delivery application through smartphone in Malaysia. Br. Food J. **124**(3), 732–753 (2022). https://doi.org/10.1108/BFJ-01-2021-0075
25. Kline, R.B.: Principles and Practice of Structural Equation Modeling, 4th edn. Guilford Publications, New York (2015)
26. Hair, J.F., Black, W.C., Babin, B.J., Anderson, R.E.: Multivariate Data Analysis, 7th edn. Pearson Education Limited, Harlow (2010)
27. Madinga, N.W., Blanckensee, J., Longhurst, L., Bundwini, N.: The new normal: the adoption of food delivery apps. Eur. J. Manag. Stud. **28**(3), 175–192 (2023). https://doi.org/10.1108/EJMS-03-2023-0021
28. Chiu, W., Badu-Baiden, F., Cho, H.: Consumers' intention to use online food delivery services: a meta-analytic structural equation modeling approach. Int. J. Consum. Stud. **48**(3), e13052 (2024). https://doi.org/10.1111/ijcs.13052
29. Podsakoff, P.M., MacKenzie, S.B., Lee, J.Y., Podsakoff, N.P.: Common method biases in behavioral research: a critical review of the literature and recommended remedies. J. Appl. Psychol. **88**(5), 879–903 (2003). https://doi.org/10.1037/0021-9010.88.5.879
30. Zhang, T., Jiang, Q., Zhang, W.: Exploring the influence of cognitive factors among Chinese parents on the sustainability of children's digital education. BMC Psychol. **13**(1), 298 (2025). https://doi.org/10.1186/s40359-025-02614-2

AI-Enabled Knowledge Extraction and Transformation: Comparative Case Studies from Taiwanese Firms

Kazunori Minetaki[1](✉), I-Hsien Ting[2](✉), and Ming-Chia Hsieh[3](✉)

[1] Department of Business, Creative Management and Innovation Research Institute, Kindai University, 3-4-1 Kowakae, Higashi-Osaka City, Osaka Prefecture, Japan
kminetaki@bus.kindai.ac.jp

[2] Social Networks Innovation Center, National University of Kaohsiung, g, 700, Kaohsiung University Rd., Nanzih District, Kaohsiung 811, Taiwan
ihsienting@gmail.com

[3] Department of Accounting, I-Shou University, No. 1, Sec. 1, Syuecheng Rd., Dashu District, Kaohsiung City 84001, Taiwan
ryanhsieh@isu.edu.tw

Abstract. Artificial intelligence (AI) is increasingly being adopted not only as a tool for automation and prediction but also as a mechanism for extracting, codifying, and transferring organizational knowledge. This study examines how AI contributes to knowledge transformation in Taiwanese business contexts through a qualitative multiple-case-study design. Based on semi-structured interviews conducted in Taiwan in March 2026, the study analyzes three firms operating in different domains: manufacturing automation, industrial AI platforms, and labor/legal advisory services. The findings show that AI-enabled knowledge transformation does not occur in a uniform manner. Instead, firms differ in how they extract knowledge from operational processes, expert judgment, and legal or advisory experience, and in how such knowledge is codified into digital systems and reused through organizational infrastructures. Across the three cases, a common pattern can be identified in the progression from AI-enabled knowledge extraction to codification, infrastructure formation, and knowledge transfer. At the same time, each case highlights a different organizational function of AI: process replication, analytical support, and expert knowledge formalization. The study contributes to the literature by showing that AI in business should be understood not only as a productivity-enhancing technology but also as an organizational mechanism for transforming tacit and experience-based knowledge into reusable forms. It also offers practical implications for firms seeking to preserve expertise, strengthen learning, and build scalable knowledge systems through AI.

Keywords: AI-Enabled Knowledge Extraction · Low-site AI · Laosai

D. Liberona et al. (Eds.): MISNC 2026, CCIS 3092, pp. 266–280, 2027.
https://doi.org/10.1007/978-3-032-33381-0_20

1 Introduction

Artificial intelligence (AI) has rapidly evolved from a specialized technological field into a central concern in business and management. In many industries, AI is no longer used only for automation or prediction; it is increasingly embedded in organizational processes that support data integration, pattern recognition, decision support, and knowledge reuse. This trend is particularly important in Taiwan, where firms operate in highly competitive industrial and service environments and face growing pressure to enhance productivity, preserve expertise, and accelerate digital transformation [1, 2].

In such settings, the role of AI extends beyond operational efficiency. AI can also function as a mechanism for transforming dispersed human knowledge into reusable organizational resources. Firms often rely on tacit knowledge accumulated through experience, including production know-how, analytical judgment, and advisory expertise. However, such knowledge is difficult to document, transfer, and scale within organizations. As experienced workers retire, tasks become more complex, and firms seek greater responsiveness, the ability to extract, codify, and reuse knowledge becomes increasingly important. AI offers new possibilities in this regard by identifying patterns in data, formalizing expert practices, and embedding knowledge into digital systems that support repeated organizational use [3–5].

Although the business use of AI has attracted growing academic attention, existing studies often emphasize automation, analytics, and performance improvement rather than the broader process of organizational knowledge transformation [6–8]. Knowledge management research has long highlighted the importance of tacit knowledge, organizational learning, and absorptive capacity [9–14]. More recent studies suggest that AI can reshape these processes by assisting knowledge creation, retrieval, and application [3–5]. However, there remains limited firm-level understanding of how AI is used to extract and transform different forms of expertise in concrete business contexts. Insufficient attention has been paid to how firms convert operational experience, expert judgment, and advisory knowledge into structured digital resources that can be shared and reused.

To address this gap, this study examines how AI is utilized in Taiwanese firms and how it contributes to organizational knowledge transformation. The analysis adopts a qualitative multiple-case-study design based on semi-structured interviews conducted in Taiwan on March 2–3, 2026. The three cases represent different organizational contexts: manufacturing automation, industrial AI platforms, and labor/legal advisory services. This diversity makes it possible to compare how AI extracts, codifies, and transfers distinct types of knowledge across firms with different business models and knowledge bases.

The study aims to make two contributions. First, it provides an empirically grounded perspective on AI not simply as a productivity-enhancing technology, but as an organizational mechanism for extraction of knowledge, codification, infrastructure formation, and transfer. Second, it develops a comparative understanding of how AI-enabled knowledge transformation varies depending on the nature of expertise and the organizational context in which AI is introduced. By doing so, the paper contributes to the growing literature on AI and knowledge management and offers practical insight for firms seeking to preserve expertise and build scalable knowledge systems.

2 Literature Review

Knowledge management (KM) has long examined how organizations create, retain, share, and apply knowledge as a strategic resource. Early KM research emphasized that organizational performance depends not only on formal information systems but also on the ability to capture and mobilize expertise embedded in individuals, routines, and work practices. From this perspective, knowledge is not simply information to be stored, but a productive organizational asset linked to learning, coordination, and innovation [9, 11].

A central distinction in KM is that between tacit and explicit knowledge. Polanyi argued that individuals know more than they can formally express, indicating that valuable expertise is often embedded in action, judgment, and experience [13]. Building on this insight, Nonaka and Takeuchi explained organizational knowledge creation as a dynamic interaction between tacit and explicit knowledge, through which experience-based know-how is articulated, shared, and recombined [12]. Their framework remains influential because it explains why firms must do more than document information: they must also create mechanisms for transforming practical expertise into forms that can be communicated and reused [12].

This perspective was extended by research on knowledge management systems (KMS). Alavi and Leidner conceptualized KMS as systems supporting the creation, storage, retrieval, transfer, and application of knowledge, thereby linking technological infrastructures with organizational processes [15]. Likewise, organizational learning research emphasized that knowledge must be retained and transferred if firms are to avoid repeated loss of expertise. Argote, for example, showed that knowledge transfer is a core challenge because knowledge is often sticky, context-dependent, and unevenly distributed across organizations [9]. These arguments together highlight the close relationship between knowledge systems and organizational learning [9, 15].

Related research on absorptive capacity and dynamic capabilities further explains why knowledge processes matter strategically. Cohen and Levinthal defined absorptive capacity as the ability to recognize, assimilate, and apply external knowledge [10], while Zahra and George reconceptualized it as a broader set of organizational capabilities involving acquisition, assimilation, transformation, and exploitation [14]. Similarly, Teece et al. argued that dynamic capabilities enable firms to integrate and reconfigure resources under changing conditions [16]. Together, these perspectives suggest that knowledge must be continuously transformed and mobilized to support adaptation and innovation [10, 14, 16].

More recent research has examined how artificial intelligence reshapes these knowledge processes. Rather than serving only as an automation tool, AI is increasingly understood as an active component of organizational knowledge management. Dwivedi et al. highlighted the broader managerial and organizational implications of AI [7], while Jarrahi et al. explicitly framed AI and KM as a partnership between humans and AI, emphasizing how AI can support knowledge-related processes in collaboration with human expertise [4]. In this sense, AI extends KM beyond traditional repositories by helping organizations identify patterns, process large volumes of data, and support more adaptive knowledge use [4, 7].

The emergence of generative AI has deepened this discussion. Alavi et al. argued that generative AI should be examined from a KM perspective because it affects not only information access but also knowledge creation, transfer, and application [3]. Their discussion is important because it shifts the focus from AI as a support tool to AI as a participant in knowledge processes. At the same time, they note risks such as bias, overreliance, hallucination, and the difficulty of balancing AI-generated outputs with human tacit knowledge. These concerns suggest that AI-enabled KM should be evaluated not only in terms of efficiency but also in terms of epistemic quality, human judgment, and organizational governance [3].

Recent studies also point to implementation and governance challenges in AI-enabled KM. Rezaei identifies technological, organizational, and ethical barriers, including privacy, security, transparency, and employee acceptance [5]. Bratianu and Ioan, as well as recent bibliometric work, show that research on AI and KM is expanding rapidly but remains fragmented across multiple themes, including human–AI collaboration, knowledge sharing, trust, and organizational performance [6, 8]. This suggests that although AI-enabled KM is increasingly recognized as an important field, its theoretical integration and empirical grounding are still developing [5, 6, 8].

Overall, prior studies indicate a transition from static knowledge repositories toward intelligent, adaptive, and socio-technical knowledge ecosystems. Traditional KM research established the importance of tacit knowledge, knowledge conversion, and organizational learning, while newer AI-oriented studies show that machine learning and generative systems can be embedded directly into knowledge creation, retrieval, and application processes. However, literature still has three major limitations. First, many studies remain technology-centric and focus on performance, analytics, or automation rather than broader organizational knowledge architectures. Second, prior work often examines isolated processes rather than integrated knowledge lifecycles connecting codification, infrastructure, transfer, and reuse. Third, empirical evidence remains limited regarding how firms translate tacit operational expertise into AI-supported systems in real organizational settings [4, 5, 7].

These gaps are important for the present study. Existing theory explains why tacit knowledge matters, why organizational learning depends on knowledge transfer, and why dynamic capabilities require continuous knowledge transformation [12, 15, 16]. More recent research on AI-enabled knowledge management suggests that AI can increasingly participate in these processes by supporting knowledge-related activities in collaboration with human expertise [3, 4]. Yet less is known about how organizations practically convert experiential knowledge into AI-supported infrastructures that enable transfer across operational contexts. This study addresses that gap by examining three Taiwanese cases in which AI is used not merely to automate tasks, but to support the codification of expertise, its integration into knowledge systems, and the development of organizational learning and capabilities.

3 Theoretical Framework

This study is grounded in research on tacit knowledge, knowledge management, and artificial intelligence as an emerging knowledge infrastructure. Together, these perspectives help explain how organizations transform experiential expertise into digital systems that support learning and knowledge transfer.

Tacit knowledge is fundamental to this framework, as significant expertise is typically gained through practical experience, yet it frequently proves challenging to express in a formal manner [13]. Nonaka and Takeuchi further argue that organizational knowledge is deeply embedded in routines, personal experience, and practical problem-solving [12]. As a result, firms often face difficulties in preserving and transferring expertise when it is held mainly by experienced workers.

Knowledge management research highlights the importance of converting such individual expertise into organizational knowledge assets. Knowledge management systems support the creation, storage, retrieval, transfer, and application of knowledge across organizations [15]. However, conventional systems often struggle to capture experiential knowledge that exists in unstructured and practice-based forms [9, 15].

Recent developments in artificial intelligence provide new possibilities for addressing this challenge. AI can support knowledge-related activities by processing large volumes of data, identifying patterns, and assisting with retrieval, interpretation, and application [4, 7]. Recent research also suggests that generative AI expands this role by contributing to knowledge creation and transfer [3]. From this perspective, AI can be understood not only as an automation tool but also as a mechanism for organizational knowledge transformation [3, 4].

Based on this framework, the following case studies examine how three Taiwanese firms use AI to capture, codify, and transfer expertise in different organizational contexts.

4 Research Design

To examine how artificial intelligence is utilized in business environments and how it contributes to organizational knowledge transformation, interview-based case studies were conducted in Taiwan. The interviews were carried out on March 2–3, 2026. Each interview lasted approximately one hour and involved discussions with company representatives who are directly involved in the development or implementation of AI systems within their organizations. The primary objective of the interviews was to understand how companies apply artificial intelligence in their business activities and what types of organizational or operational effects have been achieved through these implementations. Particular attention was given to how AI systems capture, structure, and utilize experiential knowledge within organizations.

The interviews were conducted with three companies representing different industrial contexts. One company operates in the manufacturing sector and develops automation technologies that replicate skilled production processes. The other two companies operate in consulting-related industries. One of these firms provides consulting services for manufacturing and service-sector clients, while the other specializes in legal advisory services, particularly in the field of labor–management relations. These interviews were designed to explore whether the mechanisms described in the theoretical framework—namely the transformation of tacit knowledge into structured digital knowledge systems through artificial intelligence—can be observed in real organizational practices. The case studies presented in the following section illustrate how these companies utilize AI technologies to capture expertise, support decision-making, and facilitate knowledge transfer within their organizations.

5 Case Studies

5.1 Case 1: Wish-Tech – Automation and Process Knowledge Replication

Wish-Tech is an automation engineering company in Taiwan specializing in industrial systems that replicate human production processes through robotics and automated machinery. The company initially developed automation solutions for cosmetic powder pressing processes, where production quality depends heavily on tacit operational skills developed by experienced workers. In traditional powder pressing production lines, operators must carefully control several parameters including pressing pressure, powder distribution, mold alignment, and pressing duration. These adjustments often rely on the operator's sensory perception and accumulated experience rather than strictly defined procedural manuals.

Experienced operators learn to adjust machine parameters based on subtle signals such as powder density, mold resistance, and product appearance during the pressing process. These adjustments are rarely documented explicitly, yet they are essential for maintaining consistent product quality. As experienced technicians retire or change positions, companies risk losing this operational expertise.

Wish-Tech addresses this challenge by translating human operation-al knowledge into parameterized digital production recipes. Through collaboration with experienced technicians, the company systematically identifies critical parameters influencing production outcomes. These parameters include pressure levels, pressing durations, material quantities, and machine movement sequences. The operational knowledge embedded in human experience is therefore converted into machine-readable instructions.

These digital recipes are stored within automated production systems that integrate robotics, sensors, and control software. Robots perform tasks such as material loading, pressing operations, product removal, and quality inspection. Sensors monitor pressure levels, ma-chine movement, and environmental conditions to ensure that production parameters remain within predefined ranges.

Through this approach, production expertise can be replicated consistently across multiple manufacturing environments. Engineers can adjust recipe parameters to accommodate different product specifications, enabling companies to maintain high product quality even when experienced operators are not directly involved in production.

5.1.1 Powder Press Automation

One of the most representative examples of Wish-Tech's technology is the automation of cosmetic powder pressing production lines. Traditionally, powder pressing processes involve multiple manual operations. Workers must fill loose powder into containers, transfer the containers to pressing machines, operate the pressing equipment, remove the finished powder product, and clean the surface of the pressed powder. Because powder residues remain on the surface after pressing, operators must perform additional cleaning processes to maintain product quality.

In conventional manufacturing environments, these tasks are carried out by skilled operators who rely on visual inspection and accumulated experience. Operators may adjust pressure levels or powder quantities depending on the condition of the material. For example, subtle variations in powder density or mold resistance may require adjustments that cannot easily be codified into simple production instructions.

Wish-Tech developed automation systems that replicate these hu-man processes through robotics and sensor technologies. The automation system integrates several steps of the production process into a single machine. Robots perform powder filling, mold positioning, pressing operations, surface cleaning, and finished product removal. Laser sensors are used to detect whether molds are empty before filling, replicating the visual inspection traditionally performed by human workers.

The automation system also includes digital parameter databases that store production recipes for different cosmetic products. These recipes specify pressing pressure, powder quantities, pressing duration, and other operational variables. In some systems, more than one thousand different production recipes can be stored in the database, allowing manufacturers to switch between different product specifications efficiently.

This automation significantly improves productivity. In traditional production lines, two machines might require eight operators to perform powder filling, pressing, cleaning, and product removal tasks. With Wish-Tech's automated system, a single operator can supervise multiple machines simultaneously. In some cases, one operator can oversee three automated production lines. This reduction in labor requirements not only improves efficiency but also ensures consistent production quality.

5.1.2 Semiconductor Manufacturing Applications

In addition to cosmetic manufacturing automation, Wish-Tech has expanded its technologies into semiconductor-related applications. Semiconductor manufacturing and testing processes require extremely precise handling of components and measurement equipment. Many testing procedures previously relied on skilled technicians performing manual operations such as cable connections, probing operations, and measurement data collection.

Wish-Tech developed automation systems that replace these manual operations with robotic testing platforms. In semiconductor testing processes, stability of measurement equipment is critical. For example, cables used in testing machines must remain completely stable during measurement operations. Even small vibrations or movements can dis-tort measurement results.

To address this challenge, Wish-Tech developed robotic systems that maintain constant cable tension using torque-controlled motors. These systems ensure that testing cables remain stable while automated probing systems collect measurement data. The automation system also integrates microscopes and positioning sensors to guide robotic probes to the correct measurement locations on semiconductor components.

This automation dramatically improves testing efficiency. Previously, technicians might require several days to perform measurements across multiple testing points on semiconductor components. With the automated system, the same testing process can be completed within a few hours. The automation system can also store measurement results directly in databases, allowing engineers to analyze testing results more efficiently.

In addition to semiconductor testing automation, Wish-Tech also developed robotic handling systems for high-speed metal stamping production lines used in electronics manufacturing. Some stamping machines produce components at speeds exceeding 250 pieces per minute. Handling such high-speed production manually is nearly impossible. Wish-Tech's system uses machine vision cameras and multiple robotic arms to detect the position of stamped components and remove them from production lines without causing scratches or damage.

Through these technologies, Wish-Tech demonstrates how craftsmanship knowledge embedded in human production processes can be translated into automated industrial systems. Rather than replacing human expertise entirely, the company focuses on capturing operator experience and converting it into machine parameters and automation logic.

This case illustrates how process-level craftsmanship knowledge embedded in physical production routines can be translated into digital automation systems capable of reproducing expert practices.

5.2 Case 2: Zeonic – Low Site AI

Zeonic is a Taiwanese technology company specializing in industrial artificial intelligence platforms designed for manufacturing environments. Unlike many AI solution providers that rely primarily on cloud-based infrastructures, Zeonic provides on -premises AI architecture that integrates hardware and software directly within client facilities. This design allows companies to maintain full control over sensitive operational data while deploying advanced artificial intelligence capabilities within their production environments. The core product of Zeonic is called Low-site AI, which the company describes as a "digital master craftsman" for enterprises. The term "Low site" originates from the Taiwanese expression Laosai, referring to an experienced master technician who possesses deep technical expertise accumulated through long-term operational experience. The concept closely resembles the Japanese notion of "Takumi" in Japanese, referring to expert artisans whose decision-making relies heavily on tacit knowledge developed through years of practice.

In traditional manufacturing environments, experienced engineers and technicians continuously monitor production processes and make small adjustments based on subtle signals such as equipment behavior, product quality variations, and process stability. These decisions are rarely documented explicitly but are instead based on accumulated experiential knowledge. Zeonic's Low-site AI aims to replicate this type of expert judgment by transforming operational data into structured analytical knowledge systems.

Low-site AI is delivered as a fully integrated hardware–software platform installed directly within enterprise environments. The system typically includes a dedicated AI workstation equipped with high-performance processors and GPUs capable of running local AI models and agent systems. By operating entirely within the company's internal network, the platform ensures strict control over proprietary production data while enabling real-time AI-driven analysis of manufacturing processes.

At the architectural level, Low-site AI integrates multiple layers of industrial information systems. Data are collected from operational technology (OT) environments such as programmable logic controllers (PLC), human–machine interfaces (HMI), and industrial IoT sensors. These data are combined with enterprise information systems including ERP (Enterprise Resource Planning), MES (Manufacturing Execution Systems), WMS (Warehouse Management Systems), APS (Advanced Planning Systems), and other production management platforms. Through this integration, the platform consolidates heterogeneous industrial data into a unified enterprise data environment.

Within this integrated environment, the system functions as a data command platform that organizes, processes, and analyzes large volumes of operational data. The platform includes modules for data ingestion, data analysis, data management, database construction, and AI-supported conversational querying. Engineers and managers can interact with the system using natural language interfaces, allowing them to retrieve insights from operational data and internal knowledge bases. This architecture enables firms to build internal knowledge systems that support engineering decision-making and production optimization.

A key component of the platform is its ability to combine machine learning models, automated feature analysis, and knowledge retrieval technologies. The system incorporates large language models together with retrieval-augmented generation (RAG) mechanisms, allowing the AI to reference enterprise knowledge bases and operational records when responding to user queries. As a result, the system can generate context-specific explanations based on internal production data rather than relying solely on generic language model outputs.

Through this architecture, Low-site AI acts as a digital representation of experienced engineers, supporting decision-making across production processes. Rather than replacing human expertise, the platform allows experienced technicians to encode their knowledge into AI-supported systems. Over time, the accumulated operational data and expert knowledge form a continuously evolving analytical knowledge infrastructure within the organization.

To illustrate the practical implementation of Zeonic's Low-site AI platform, two client companies are presented below.

5.2.1 Client1: MES-Based Process Optimization in a Pump Assembly Factory

A pump assembly factory implemented a Manufacturing Execution System (MES) to systematically record worker attendance, labor hours, and production process data on the shop floor. By analyzing the collected operational data, the company was able to calculate standard process times for each assembly step. The MES-enabled data analytics helped the factory better understand workflow efficiency, identify potential bottlenecks, and establish data-driven benchmarks for production management and process optimization.

5.2.2 Client 2: AI-Enabled Knowledge Management in a Semiconductor Supply Chain Firm

A semiconductor supply chain company without dedicated technical personnel adopted the Low-site platform to integrate multiple internal systems and deploy on-premise AI capabilities. By incorporating large language models (LLMs), the system supports root-cause analysis and automatic generation of analytical charts. Experienced technicians can document their operational procedures within the platform, while new employees can use a question-and-answer interface to learn workflows and retrieve knowledge. This approach enables effective knowledge management and preserves valuable expertise within the organization.

5.3 Case 3: King Fong – AI-Based Labor Knowledge Platform

King Fong is a Taiwanese firm specializing in labor management consulting and legal compliance services for small and medium-sized enterprises. Founded more than thirty years ago, the company has accumulated extensive practical knowledge related to labor regulations, workplace disputes, and compliance management. Traditionally, this knowledge was delivered through human consultants who provided advice and training to client firms. However, with the rapid growth of Taiwan's SME sector and the increasing complexity of labor regulations, the firm began exploring artificial intelligence as a mechanism for scaling its knowledge services.

To address this challenge, King Fong developed an AI-based labor advisory platform known as "Tarot". The platform integrates legal knowledge, consulting experience, and internal documents into a digital system capable of providing automated labor law consultation. The core technology used in the system is Retrieval-Augmented Generation (RAG), which allows the AI to retrieve relevant information from a curated knowledge base and generate responses to user inquiries. The knowledge base consists primarily of proprietary internal documents produced by the company's consultants, including legal interpretations, case records, and compliance guidelines. When the internal data are insufficient, the system can supplement responses by retrieving additional information from online legal resources. One distinctive feature of the system is its ability to integrate digital attendance management and behavioral analysis. The platform includes patented software capable of distinguishing between work-related and non-work activities performed by employees after official working hours. For example, if an employee remains at the workplace after clocking out, the system can analyze behavioral data to determine whether the activity is work-related or personal. This capability allows firms to maintain accurate records that may serve as legal evidence in labor disputes, particularly regarding overtime claims. King Fong's service model combines AI technology with human consulting expertise through a three-layer service structure. The first layer consists of the AI platform itself, which provides automated consultation and knowledge access. The second layer involves human consultants who assist firms in designing compliance systems, including employment contracts, wage structures, and internal regulations. The third layer includes risk management services such as insurance products designed to mitigate occupational accident risks. This integrated structure allows the company to deliver both digital and human expertise within a single service ecosystem.

The company adopted a freemium business model to encourage platform adoption. Firms can access a limited number of free consultations each month, while additional consultations require paid subscriptions. More advanced services, such as knowledge management systems and AI-based training tools, are provided through subscription plans targeted at corporate clients. According to company estimates, the potential market includes approximately 1.67 million SMEs in Taiwan, indicating substantial growth opportunities. Through the development of the Tarot platform, King Fong attempts to transform accumulated consulting knowledge into a scalable AI-driven service infrastructure. Rather than relying solely on human experts, the company leverages AI to codify legal expertise, deliver continuous advisory services, and support organizational knowledge management within client firms. This case illustrates how AI technologies can be applied not only to industrial production processes but also to professional knowledge services, enabling the digitalization and large-scale dissemination of expert knowledge.

5.4 AI-Enabled Knowledge Extraction Across the Three Cases

Across the three cases, AI-enabled knowledge extraction means converting different forms of expert knowledge—production know-how, factory data, and advisory expertise—into structured resources that can be reused, searched, and transferred at scale.

Table 1 clarifies that the three firms follow a common sequence from AI-enabled knowledge extraction to knowledge codification, knowledge infrastructure, and knowledge transfer, but they differ in what kind of knowledge is extracted and how that knowledge is operationalized. In other words, the table is not simply descriptive; it shows the comparative logic through which AI transforms tacit or experience-based knowledge into an organizational asset.

Wish-Tech: Its distinctive feature is the extraction of operator know-how directly from production activity through robotics, sensors, machine vision, and automated control. This knowledge is codified as machine parameters and digital production recipes, then transferred through automated production and testing systems that replicate expert practice across lines, products, and sites.

Zeonic: Its distinctive feature is data-integrative extraction in industrial settings. Rather than embedding knowledge only in machines, Zeonic reorganizes factory expertise into searchable and analytical knowledge structures through industrial AI and on-premise analytics systems, allowing operational knowledge to be accessed more broadly across roles and decision contexts.

King Fong: Its distinctive feature is the platformization of professional expertise. Legal and consulting knowledge is translated into structured digital rules, cases, and advisory logic, then embedded in a platform-based advisory infrastructure that enables broader delivery of expertise beyond direct expert presence.

The comparison suggests that AI-enabled knowledge extraction should be understood as a domain-specific mechanism: the same overarching process is visible in all three cases, but the extracted knowledge, the form of codification, and the mode of transfer vary according to the organizational context. This provides the basis for the following discussion of how AI extends knowledge management beyond conventional codification alone.

Table 1. Comparative Framework of AI-Enabled Knowledge Extraction Across Three Cases

Case	AI-Enabled Knowledge Extraction	Knowledge Codification	Knowledge Infrastructure	Knowledge Transfer
Wish-Tech	Robotics, sensors, machine vision, automated control	Operator know-how → machine parameters & digital production recipes	Automated production/testing systems + parameter databases	Replication of expert practices across lines/products/sites
Zeonic	Industrial AI / on-premise AI, analytics systems	Factory expertise → searchable/analytical knowledge structures	AI-based industrial knowledge platform (search, analysis, decision support)	Broader access to operational expertise across roles
King Fong	AI advisory tools for professional services	Legal/consulting expertise → structured digital knowledge (rules/cases/logic)	Platform-based advisory infrastructure	Wider delivery of expertise beyond direct expert presence

6 Discussion

This study examined three Taiwanese cases—Wish-Tech, Zeonic, and King Fong —to explore how artificial intelligence supports the transformation and transfer of tacit knowledge in organizational settings. Although the three firms operate in different industries and apply AI in different ways, the findings reveal a common underlying mechanism. Across all cases, AI functions not merely as a tool for automation or efficiency improvement, but as a means of converting human experiential knowledge into codified, reusable, and transferable organizational resources. In this sense, the cases suggest a shared process that can be summarized as AI enabled knowledge codification, knowledge infrastructure, and knowledge transfer.

The first important implication is that AI extends the traditional logic of knowledge management by making tacit knowledge more systematically codifiable. Conventional knowledge management research has long emphasized the distinction between tacit and explicit knowledge and the organizational importance of converting individual experience into shareable forms. However, the three cases indicate that AI enables a more operational and scalable form of codification. In Wish-Tech, production know-how that had previously depended on experienced workers' sensory judgments was translated into parameterized routines embedded in automated systems. In Zeonic, shop-floor expertise was not simply documented but reorganized into analytical structures that allowed operational knowledge to be searched, interpreted, and applied through industrial AI systems. In King Fong, professional legal and consulting knowledge was transformed into a platform-based advisory resource, enabling expertise to be accessed beyond the immediate presence of individual experts. These cases therefore show that AI can deepen the codification process by capturing not only formal procedures but also experiential patterns, decision logic, and problem-solving routines.

The second implication is that codified knowledge becomes meaningful when it is embedded in a knowledge infrastructure. A key contribution of this study is to suggest that AI should be understood not only as a computational tool but also as an infrastructural mechanism for knowledge organization. In all three cases, knowledge was not merely stored as static information. Instead, it was embedded into systems that could support action, learning, and decision-making. This is particularly significant because traditional knowledge repositories often remain underutilized when they are separated from actual workflows. By contrast, the AI systems observed in these cases linked codified knowledge to practical use contexts. Wish-Tech embedded experiential production knowledge into automation systems that directly shaped manufacturing operations. Zeonic built analytical AI environments in which factory knowledge could support problem identification and operational judgment. King Fong created a digital advisory platform through which professional expertise could be mobilized in legal and business consultation. These findings indicate a shift from static knowledge repositories to AI-enabled knowledge infrastructures that continuously connect stored expertise with organizational practice.

The third implication concerns the transferability of knowledge. Existing knowledge management studies often assume that once knowledge is codified, it can be shared more easily across individuals or units. The present cases refine this assumption by showing that transfer depends not only on codification itself but also on the form of infrastructure through which knowledge is delivered. In Wish-Tech, transfer occurred through the replication of expert routines in machines and automated production processes. In Zeonic, transfer took place through analytical systems that allowed users to access and interpret factory-related knowledge. In King Fong, transfer was achieved through a platform that broadened access to professional advisory knowledge. Thus, AI-mediated knowledge transfer does not follow a single path. Rather, it occurs through multiple routes—automation, analytics, and digital platforms—depending on the organizational context. What unites these routes is that AI makes knowledge more scalable, more accessible, and less dependent on the physical co-presence of senior experts.

Taken together, the three cases support a broader theoretical interpretation: AI contributes to organizational knowledge management by linking codification, infrastructure, and transfer in an integrated process. This expands conventional knowledge management theory in two ways. First, it suggests that codification should no longer be seen as a one-time conversion of tacit knowledge into documents or manuals. Instead, codification becomes an ongoing and adaptive process in which AI continuously captures, reorganizes, and updates experiential knowledge. Second, it shows that the value of codified knowledge lies not only in its preservation but also in its infrastructural embedding. Knowledge becomes strategically useful when it is incorporated into systems that support repeated use, organizational learning, and capability reproduction.

At the same time, the findings also indicate that AI does not replace human expertise entirely. In each case, senior experts remained important as the original source, validator, or interpreter of knowledge. AI systems can capture patterns, structure expertise, and extend access, but they still depend on human judgment for training, refinement, and contextual interpretation. This point is theoretically important because it suggests that AI-based knowledge transfer should be understood as augmentation rather than substitution. Organizational knowledge is not simply transferred from humans to machines; rather, it is reconfigured through interaction between human expertise and digital systems.

7 Conclusion

This study examined how artificial intelligence is used by organizations to capture, structure, and transfer expertise embedded in operational activities. Based on interview-based case studies in Taiwan, the research analyzed three firms in different contexts—manufacturing automation, industrial AI platforms, and professional consulting services—and showed how AI transforms experiential knowledge into digital systems that support learning and decision-making. The study contributes to the literature by extending research on AI-enabled knowledge management. While prior studies have mainly focused on automation and data analytics, the findings here show that AI can also function as an organizational knowledge infrastructure that converts tacit knowledge into structured and reusable digital resources. By linking knowledge management, tacit knowledge theory, and dynamic capability perspectives, this study provides an integrated understanding of how AI supports knowledge transformation and organizational learning. The findings also offer practical implications. Successful AI implementation depends not only on technological capability but also on the active involvement of experienced professionals who define, validate, and interpret knowledge within AI-supported systems. Organizations should therefore pay attention to both digital infrastructure and the integration of human expertise. Overall, the study suggests that AI-enabled knowledge systems are an important mechanism for preserving expertise and facilitating knowledge transfer within organizations. By transforming tacit knowledge into digital resources, firms can reduce the risk of knowledge loss and strengthen continuous organizational learning. Future research should further examine how these AI-enabled knowledge infrastructures evolve across industries and organizational settings. In particular, an important research agenda is to explore the dynamics through which Taiwan's strength in semiconductor production may become increasingly connected with the development of AI, and how this interaction shapes new forms of industrial knowledge creation, transfer, and capability building.

Acknowledgments. We would like to express our sincere gratitude to the representatives of Wish Tech, Zeonic, and King Fong for their kind cooperation in the interviews.

References

1. Invest Taiwan: Taiwan's AI Development Trends and Future Prospects. Ministry of Economic Affairs, Taiwan (2025)

2. National Development Council: National Development Plan (2025–2028). Executive Yuan, Taiwan (2025)
3. Alavi, M., Leidner, D.E., Mousavi, R.: A knowledge management perspective of generative artificial intelligence. J. Assoc. Inf. Syst. **25**(1), 1–12 (2024). https://doi.org/10.17705/1jais.00859
4. Jarrahi, M.H., Askay, D., Eshraghi, A., Smith, P.: Artificial intelligence and knowledge management: a partnership between human and AI. Bus. Horiz. **66**(1), 87–99 (2023). https://doi.org/10.1016/j.bushor.2022.03.002
5. Rezaei, M.: Artificial intelligence in knowledge management: identifying and addressing the key implementation challenges. Technol. Forecast. Soc. Chang. **217**, 124183 (2025). https://doi.org/10.1016/j.techfore.2025.124183
6. Bratianu, C., Ioan, A.: Challenges of artificial intelligence for knowledge management systems: a bibliometric analysis perspective. Oradea J. Bus. Econ. **10**(1), 108–120 (2025). https://doi.org/10.47535/1991ojbe209
7. Dwivedi, Y.K. et al.: Artificial intelligence (AI): multidisciplinary perspectives on emerging challenges, opportunities, and agenda for research, practice and policy. Int. J. Inf. Manag. **57**, 101994 (2021). https://doi.org/10.1016/j.ijinfomgt.2019.08.002
8. Sorout, A., Singh, N.P., Pathak, A.A.: Emerging frontiers in AI and knowledge management: visualising trends using bibliometric analysis. Bus. Inf. Rev. (2025). https://doi.org/10.1177/02663821251387054
9. Argote, L.: Organizational Learning: Creating, Retaining and Transferring Knowledge. Springer, New York (1999)
10. Cohen, W.M., Levinthal, D.A.: Absorptive capacity: a new perspective on learning and innovation. Adm. Sci. Q. **35**(1), 128–152 (1990). https://doi.org/10.2307/2393553
11. Grant, R.M.: Toward a knowledge-based theory of the firm. Strategic Manag. J. **17**(Winter Special Issue), 109–122 (1996). https://doi.org/10.1002/smj.4250171110
12. Nonaka, I., Takeuchi, H.: The knowledge-creating company: how Japanese companies create the dynamics of innovation. Oxford University Press, New York (1995)
13. Polanyi, M.: The Tacit Dimension. University of Chicago Press, Chicago (1966)
14. Zahra, S.A., George, G.: Absorptive capacity: a review, reconceptualization, and extension. Acad. Manag. Rev. **27**(2), 185–203 (2002). https://doi.org/10.5465/AMR.2002.6587995
15. Alavi, M., Leidner, D.E.: Review: knowledge management and knowledge management systems: conceptual foundations and research issues. MIS Q. **25**(1), 107–136 (2001). https://doi.org/10.2307/3250961
16. Teece, D.J., Pisano, G., Shuen, A.: Dynamic capabilities and strategic management. Strateg. Manag. J. **18**(7), 509–533 (1997). https://doi.org/10.1002/(SICI)1097-0266(199708)18:7<509::AID-SMJ882>3.0.CO;2-Z

Latent Class Analysis of Heterogeneous Risk Patterns in Postoperative Nausea and Vomiting After Orthopedic Surgery

Han-Liang Chiang[1,2](✉), Yu-Lung Wu[3], and Jie Li[4]

[1] Department of Anesthesiology, Pingtung Veterans General Hospital, Pingtung, Taiwan
P078@ptvgh.gov.tw

[2] Department of Anesthesiology, Kaohsiung Veterans General Hospital, Kaohsiung, Taiwan

[3] Department of Information and Management, I-Shou University, Kaohsiung, Taiwan

[4] Department of Information Management, National Sun Yat-sen University, Kaohsiung, Taiwan

Abstract. Postoperative nausea and vomiting (PONV) remain among the most common and distressing complications following anesthesia, with reported incidence rates ranging from 20–30% in general surgical populations and exceeding 50% in high-risk individuals [1, 2]. Despite advances in anesthetic techniques and multimodal prophylaxis strategies, PONV continues to negatively affect patient satisfaction, prolong recovery, and increase healthcare utilization [3, 4]. The Apfel simplified risk score remains widely used for risk stratification [5], yet most existing models assume population homogeneity and may overlook subgroup-specific risk structures.

Orthopedic surgery encompasses diverse patient demographics, comorbidity burdens, anesthetic modalities, and perioperative management strategies. We hypothesized that latent heterogeneity exists within orthopedic surgical populations and that risk factors for postoperative nausea and vomiting differ across latent subgroups.

This retrospective cohort study included 3,751 adult orthopedic surgical patients between January 2021 and July 2022, with an independent validation cohort from August 2022 to May 2023. Forty-four perioperative variables were extracted from an integrated anesthesiology database. Latent Class Analysis (LCA) was performed using maximum likelihood estimation. Model selection was guided by Akaike Information Criterion (AIC) and Bayesian Information Criterion (BIC) [6, 7]. Subgroup-specific multivariable logistic regression analyses were subsequently conducted.

The incidence of postoperative nausea was 8.93%, and vomiting occurred in 14.53% of patients. A two-class solution demonstrated optimal fit and clinical interpretability. Sex and surgical type were primary discriminators of latent class membership. Steroid administration showed significant protective associations in female hip surgery patients, whereas spinal anesthesia reduced vomiting risk in selected male subgroups. These findings support subgroup-guided precision perioperative strategies rather than uniform risk modeling.

D. Liberona et al. (Eds.): MISNC 2026, CCIS 3092, pp. 281–291, 2027.
https://doi.org/10.1007/978-3-032-33381-0_21

Keywords: Postoperative nausea and vomiting · Orthopedic surgery · Latent class analysis · Steroid prophylaxis · Spinal anesthesia · Precision perioperative medicine

1 Introduction

Postoperative nausea and vomiting (PONV) remain among the most common complications following anesthesia and surgery [1, 2]. Despite advances in perioperative management and multimodal prophylaxis, incidence rates remain substantial, particularly in high-risk populations [2, 3]. Predictive modeling has therefore become central to perioperative risk stratification.

The Apfel simplified risk score remains widely applied in clinical practice [5]. However, most additive models assume homogeneous risk relationships across populations. Orthopedic surgery encompasses heterogeneous demographic characteristics, anesthetic exposures, and perioperative management strategies. Such diversity may obscure latent subgroup-specific risk structures.

Traditional regression frameworks require prespecified interaction terms and may fail to detect unobserved population structures. Latent Class Analysis (LCA) provides a model-based clustering approach capable of identifying probabilistic subgroups within multivariate categorical data [16, 17]. By uncovering structured heterogeneity, LCA offers a potential pathway toward subgroup-guided precision perioperative management.

This study applies LCA to orthopedic surgical patients to identify latent subgroups and evaluate subgroup-specific predictors of postoperative nausea and vomiting. In addition to conventional perioperative risk prediction, there is increasing interest in identifying clinically meaningful patient phenotypes that may respond differently to prophylactic interventions. Traditional population-level analyses may obscure subgroup-specific associations when heterogeneous perioperative pathways coexist within the same surgical cohort. In orthopedic surgery, differences in age distribution, inflammatory burden, anesthetic exposure, postoperative pain management, and rehabilitation protocols may all contribute to heterogeneous symptom trajectories.

Furthermore, postoperative nausea and vomiting are increasingly recognized as multidimensional perioperative outcomes rather than isolated adverse events. Their occurrence may reflect complex interactions among neurophysiological pathways, anesthetic techniques, patient susceptibility, inflammatory responses, and perioperative medication exposure. These considerations further support the need for subgroup-oriented analytical frameworks capable of identifying latent population structures.

2 Literature Review

2.1 Predictive Modeling of PONV

Risk prediction for PONV has evolved from simple additive scores to multivariable regression-based models [1, 5]. Although clinically useful, these models assume uniform effect structures. Comparative validation studies have demonstrated variability in predictive performance across surgical populations [11, 12].

2.2 Prediction Modeling Methodology

Recent advances in data-driven predictive modeling have expanded beyond traditional regression approaches [21, 22]. While these approaches may improve discrimination, they often reduce interpretability and do not explicitly characterize latent subpopulations.

2.3 Latent Class Analysis in Healthcare

Latent Class Analysis has been widely applied in critical care, oncology, and chronic disease research to identify unobserved phenotypes [16, 17]. Model selection is commonly guided by AIC and BIC criteria [6, 7]. Despite its methodological advantages, LCA has rarely been applied to perioperative symptom modeling in orthopedic populations.

This study bridges that gap by integrating probabilistic clustering with subgroup-specific regression analysis. Several recent perioperative studies have emphasized the limitations of assuming homogeneous treatment effects across surgical populations. Even when overall predictive performance appears acceptable, clinically important subgroup variability may remain undetected within aggregate analyses. Such hidden heterogeneity may partially explain inconsistent findings regarding prophylactic antiemetic efficacy across prior studies.

LCA provides several methodological advantages in this context. First, it allows probabilistic assignment rather than deterministic clustering, thereby better reflecting uncertainty in subgroup membership. Second, latent subgroup identification does not require prespecification of interaction terms, which may become increasingly difficult when numerous perioperative variables are simultaneously considered. Third, latent class frameworks maintain relatively strong interpretability compared with more opaque machine learning approaches.

In perioperative medicine, interpretability remains particularly important because clinical decision-making often requires transparent justification of prophylactic strategies. Therefore, combining LCA with subgroup-specific regression modeling may offer a balanced approach between statistical flexibility and clinical applicability.

3 Research Methods

3.1 Study Design

This retrospective cohort study was conducted at a tertiary referral medical center. The study adhered to the Declaration of Helsinki and followed STROBE reporting recommendations for observational studies [18]. Institutional Review Board approval was obtained, and informed consent was waived due to the retrospective design.

The primary cohort included consecutive adult patients undergoing orthopedic surgery between January 2021 and July 2022. An independent temporal cohort from August 2022 to May 2023 was used for validation. Perioperative variables included demographic characteristics, comorbidities, anesthetic techniques, medication exposure, intraoperative hemodynamic management, and postoperative analgesic strategies. Variables were selected based on prior literature regarding PONV risk factors as well as clinical relevance in orthopedic anesthesia practice.

Continuous variables were categorized where appropriate to facilitate latent class estimation stability and improve interpretability of conditional response probabilities. Missing data rates were low across variables included in the final analysis, and complete-case analysis was performed.

Latent class estimation was conducted using maximum likelihood methods with repeated random starting values to minimize convergence toward local maxima. Model interpretability, class stability, and subgroup sample size adequacy were considered alongside statistical fit indices during final model selection. Subgroup-specific associations were evaluated using multivariable logistic regression [19], following established latent class analysis principles [16, 17, 20].

3.2 Outcomes

Two outcomes were evaluated independently:

- Postoperative nausea within postoperative day one.
- Postoperative vomiting within postoperative day one

Outcomes were recorded during standardized ward assessment. Nausea and vomiting were analyzed separately to preserve potential mechanistic distinctions [2].

4 Results

4.1 Study Population

A total of 3,751 orthopedic surgical cases met inclusion criteria in the primary cohort. The cohort reflected the heterogeneous nature of orthopedic practice, encompassing hip and knee arthroplasty as well as other orthopedic procedures. Arthroplasty patients were generally older and more frequently received spinal anesthesia, whereas non-arthroplasty procedures were predominantly performed under general anesthesia.

The overall incidence of postoperative nausea was 8.93% (n = 335), and postoperative vomiting occurred in 14.53% (n = 545). Although related, nausea and vomiting did not completely overlap, supporting separate modeling.

Steroid administration, opioid exposure, and vasoactive medication use varied across surgical types and anesthetic modalities, reflecting individualized perioperative management (Fig. 1).

4.2 Latent Class Model Fit

Models specifying one through four classes were estimated. For both nausea and vomiting outcomes, the two-class model demonstrated substantial reduction in AIC and BIC compared with the one-class model [6, 7]. Increasing the number of classes beyond two resulted in minimal AIC improvement but higher BIC values, suggesting overfitting.

Both classes retained adequate sample sizes, ensuring model stability. Based on statistical fit and interpretability, the two-class solution was selected. Beyond statistical model fit, the two-class solution also demonstrated superior clinical interpretability compared with higher-order models. Additional classes produced relatively small subgroup

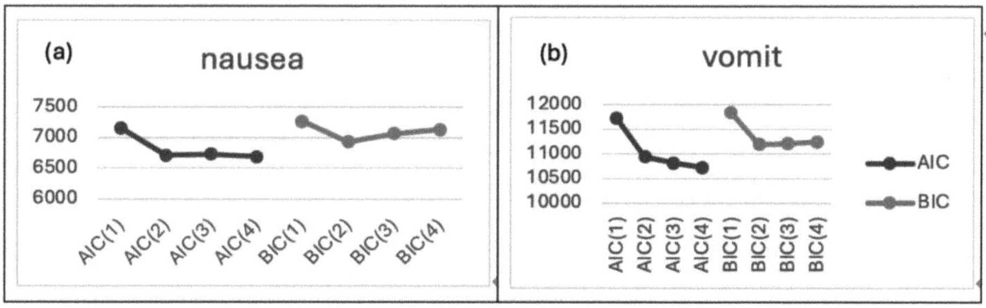

Fig. 1. Model selection using AIC and BIC. (a) Nausea outcome. (b) Vomiting outcome. The two-class solution demonstrated optimal model fit in both analyses.

partitions with overlapping conditional response profiles, limiting practical usefulness for perioperative risk stratification. In contrast, the two-class framework preserved meaningful distinctions in sex distribution, surgical type composition, and anesthetic exposure patterns while maintaining adequate subgroup size for subsequent regression analysis.

The stability of class assignment across repeated estimation procedures further supported robustness of the selected latent structure. These findings suggest that a limited number of clinically coherent latent subgroups may sufficiently capture major heterogeneity patterns within orthopedic surgical populations.

4.3 Overview of Latent Class Characteristics

Class-specific conditional response probability patterns suggested that sex and surgical type were primary discriminators of latent subgroup membership.

4.4 Subgroup-Specific Predictors of Postoperative Vomiting

Within-class multivariable logistic regression demonstrated heterogeneous associations.

In male non-arthroplasty patients, spinal anesthesia was associated with reduced odds of postoperative vomiting, consistent with reduced volatile anesthetic exposure [14, 15]. Higher ASA classification (II–III) appeared protective in this subgroup.

In female hip surgery patients, steroid administration demonstrated a significant protective association with vomiting. Dexamethasone's antiemetic effect has been attributed to inhibition of prostaglandin synthesis and modulation of serotonergic signaling [9, 10]. Hypertension also showed a modest protective association within this subgroup.

Among female non-arthroplasty procedures, steroid use and non-opioid analgesics were associated with lower vomiting incidence, while total opioid dose expressed as morphine milligram equivalents did not uniformly predict vomiting after adjustment.

4.5 Conditional Response Probabilities

Class-specific conditional response probabilities revealed that sex and surgical type were primary discriminators of class membership.

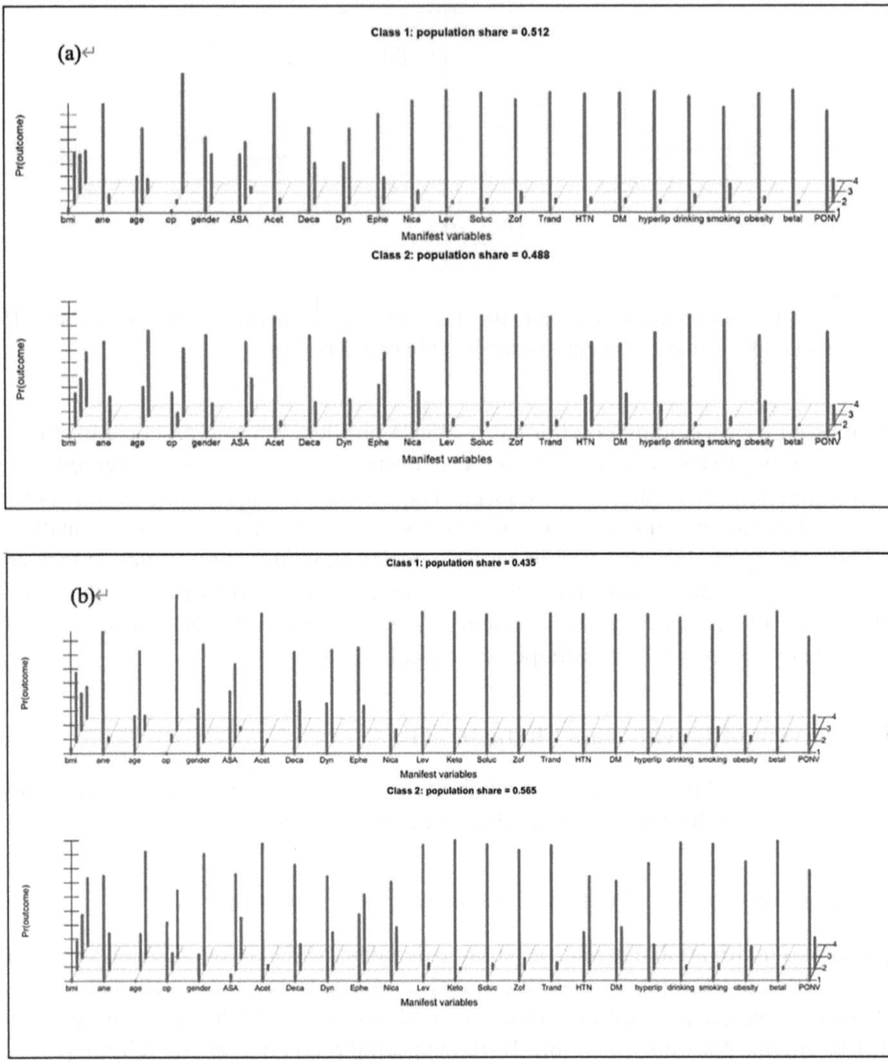

Fig. 2. Conditional response probabilities by latent class. (a) Nausea outcome. (b) Vomiting outcome.

Conditional response probability profiles further illustrated distinct latent subgroup structures across nausea and vomiting outcomes (Fig. 2).

Sex and surgical type were primary discriminators of class membership.

Class 1 was characterized by:

- Higher proportion of female patients
- Greater representation of hip and knee arthroplasty
- Frequent use of spinal anesthesia

Class 2 was characterized by:

- Higher proportion of male patients
- Greater representation of non-arthroplasty procedures
- Predominant use of general anesthesia

Other perioperative variables varied within classes but did not define the latent structure.

4.6 Subgroup-Specific Predictors of Postoperative Nausea

Within-class multivariable logistic regression demonstrated heterogeneous associations.

In male non-arthroplasty procedures, ASA II–III classification was associated with reduced odds of nausea. Anesthetic modality showed weaker association for nausea compared with vomiting.

In female hip surgery patients, steroid administration remained significantly protective for nausea. Given the inflammatory burden of arthroplasty procedures, enhanced steroid responsiveness in this subgroup is biologically plausible [9].

In female non-arthroplasty patients, nicardipine (anti-hypertension drug) exposure was associated with increased nausea risk, potentially reflecting hemodynamic variability rather than a direct emetogenic mechanism.

4.7 Comparison Between Nausea and Vomiting Outcomes

Patterns for postoperative nausea partially overlapped with vomiting outcomes but demonstrated distinct subgroup-specific associations. Steroid administration remained protective for nausea in selected female subgroups, whereas spinal anesthesia demonstrated variable associations depending on subgroup composition.

These findings suggest that postoperative nausea and vomiting should not necessarily be modeled as a fully unified perioperative outcome.

4.8 External Validation

Application of identical LCA procedures to the independent temporal cohort reproduced the two-class structure. Sex and surgical type remained primary discriminators in the vomiting outcome. Similar validation patterns were observed for the nausea outcome (data not shown) (Fig. 3).

Directionality of key subgroup-specific associations—particularly steroid protection in female hip surgery patients—remained consistent. These findings support temporal stability of the latent structure.

5 Discussion

This study demonstrates that orthopedic surgical populations exhibit structured latent heterogeneity in postoperative nausea and vomiting risk [2, 8]. Unlike traditional additive regression models, the Latent Class Analysis framework identified probabilistic subgroup structures primarily defined by sex and surgical type. By integrating latent classification with subgroup-specific regression, this approach preserves clinical interpretability while capturing population heterogeneity without requiring prespecified interaction terms.

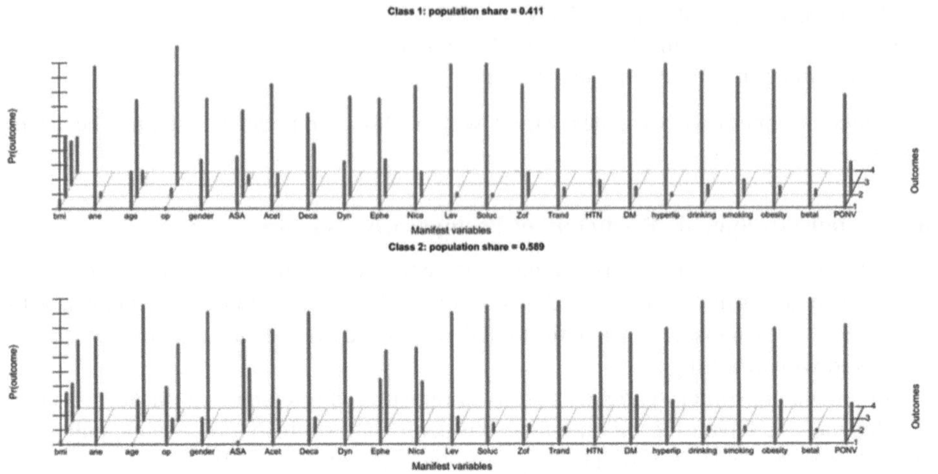

Fig. 3. External validation of the two-class structure for vomiting. Similar patterns were observed for nausea (data not shown).

Female sex is a well-established risk factor in conventional PONV risk prediction models such as the Apfel score [5]. However, the present findings suggest that sex may organize broader latent subpopulations rather than acting solely as an independent additive predictor. Surgical type further structured subgroup membership, likely reflecting differences in inflammatory burden, anesthetic exposure, and perioperative management pathways [11, 12]. These results highlight the importance of considering population heterogeneity when interpreting perioperative risk factors.

One of the most consistent findings in this study was the protective association of steroid administration among female patients undergoing hip surgery. Dexamethasone has demonstrated well-established antiemetic efficacy in randomized trials [9, 10], and its anti-inflammatory properties may be particularly relevant in arthroplasty procedures characterized by substantial tissue trauma. Sex-related differences in inflammatory response and hormonal modulation of immune pathways may further influence steroid effectiveness in this subgroup [13].

Spinal anesthesia demonstrated protective effects in selected male subgroups. Avoidance of volatile anesthetics and reduction in systemic opioid exposure likely contribute to the reduced vomiting risk observed in these patients [14, 15]. Interestingly, higher ASA classification also appeared protective in certain subgroups, possibly reflecting older age distributions and more conservative anesthetic management strategies. These findings illustrate that commonly recognized risk factors may function differently across latent strata rather than uniformly across the entire surgical population. The distinction between postoperative nausea and vomiting also warrants further discussion. Although these symptoms are frequently combined into a single composite outcome in perioperative studies, accumulating evidence suggests partially distinct physiological mechanisms. Nausea involves complex cortical and autonomic processing pathways, whereas vomiting reflects more direct activation of brainstem emetic centers and gastrointestinal reflex pathways. The partially divergent subgroup-specific associations observed in the present study further support separate modeling of these outcomes.

Another important implication of the present findings relates to individualized perioperative prophylaxis. Current antiemetic guidelines generally recommend risk-stratified prophylactic combinations based on additive risk scores. However, additive models may insufficiently account for latent subgroup structure. The present findings suggest that patient phenotypes defined by combinations of sex, surgical type, and anesthetic exposure may exhibit distinct responses to prophylactic interventions. Such subgroup-oriented strategies may ultimately improve both efficacy and resource utilization.

The integration of latent subgroup modeling into perioperative clinical workflows may also become increasingly feasible with modern electronic health record systems. Automated perioperative risk profiling could potentially identify latent subgroup membership preoperatively and guide individualized prophylactic recommendations. Although further validation is required before clinical implementation, the current findings illustrate a possible pathway toward precision perioperative medicine.

Importantly, LCA should not be interpreted as replacing conventional regression approaches. Rather, latent subgroup identification and regression modeling may function synergistically. LCA provides a framework for identifying hidden population structure, whereas regression analysis allows estimation of clinically interpretable associations within identified subgroups. The combined framework therefore preserves interpretability while improving representation of heterogeneous perioperative populations.

From a methodological perspective, Latent Class Analysis provides an attractive framework for uncovering hidden heterogeneity in perioperative datasets [16, 17]. Traditional regression models often rely on predefined interaction terms to capture complex relationships, whereas LCA identifies probabilistic subgroup structures directly from the data. By subsequently applying subgroup-specific regression analysis, the present study combines the strengths of unsupervised clustering and interpretable predictive modeling.

From a clinical standpoint, the identification of latent subgroups may support more targeted prophylactic strategies. Rather than applying uniform antiemetic protocols to all orthopedic patients, risk-adapted interventions could be implemented for specific patient profiles. For instance, the consistent protective association of steroid prophylaxis in female hip surgery patients suggests that this subgroup may derive particular benefit from routine dexamethasone administration. Similarly, the protective effect of spinal anesthesia observed in certain male subgroups highlights the potential role of anesthetic modality in risk reduction.

Future multicenter studies incorporating more granular perioperative data and external validation across diverse surgical settings are warranted. Integration of machine learning approaches with latent class modeling may further enhance subgroup identification and improve individualized perioperative risk prediction.

The present findings should also be interpreted within the broader context of perioperative heterogeneity research. As perioperative datasets become increasingly multidimensional, approaches capable of identifying hidden subgroup structure may become progressively more important. Future investigations incorporating physiologic monitoring data, longitudinal symptom trajectories, and multicenter external validation may further refine latent phenotype characterization in postoperative symptom research.

6 Limitations

This retrospective single-center design precludes causal inference and may limit generalizability. Residual confounding from unmeasured variables cannot be excluded. Medication dosing was primarily coded categorically, potentially limiting dose–response interpretation. Future multicenter prospective studies incorporating granular physiologic data are warranted.

7 Conclusion

Orthopedic surgical patients do not represent a homogeneous PONV risk population. Latent Class Analysis identified clinically meaningful subgroups structured by sex and surgical type. Subgroup-specific associations of steroid prophylaxis and anesthetic modality support precision perioperative management strategies.

References

1. Apfel, C.C., Läärä, E., Koivuranta, M., Greim, C.A., Roewer, N.: A simplified risk score for predicting postoperative nausea and vomiting. Anesthesiology. **91**(3), 693–700 (1999). https://doi.org/10.1097/00000542-199909000-00022
2. Gan, T.J., Belani, K.G., Bergese, S., Chung, F., Diemunsch, P., Habib, A.S., et al.: Fourth consensus guidelines for the management of postoperative nausea and vomiting. Anesth Analg. **131**(2), 411–448 (2020). https://doi.org/10.1213/ANE.0000000000004833
3. Myles, P.S., Williams, D.L., Hendrata, M., Anderson, H., Weeks, A.M.: Patient satisfaction after anesthesia and surgery. Anesth Analg. **91**(5), 1163–1168 (2000). https://doi.org/10.1097/00000539-200011000-00030
4. Sinclair, D.R., Chung, F., Mezei, G.: Can postoperative nausea and vomiting be predicted? Anesthesiology. **91**(1), 109–118 (1999). https://doi.org/10.1097/00000542-199907000-00018
5. Apfel, C.C., Kranke, P., Eberhart, L.H.J., Roos, A., Roewer, N.: Comparison of predictive models for postoperative nausea and vomiting. Br J Anaesth. **88**(2), 234–240 (2002)
6. Akaike, H.: A new look at the statistical model identification. IEEE Trans Autom Control. **19**(6), 716–723 (1974)
7. Schwarz, G.: Estimating the dimension of a model. Ann Stat. **6**(2), 461–464 (1978)
8. Watcha, M.F., White, P.F.: Postoperative nausea and vomiting: its etiology, treatment, and prevention. Anesthesiology. **77**(1), 162–184 (1992)
9. Wang, J.J., Ho, S.T., Lee, S.C., Liu, Y.C., Ho, C.M.: The use of dexamethasone for preventing postoperative nausea and vomiting. Anesth Analg. **91**(1), 140–144 (2000)
10. Apfel, C.C., Korttila, K., Abdalla, M., Kerger, H., Turan, A., Vedder, I., et al.: A factorial trial of six interventions for prevention of postoperative nausea and vomiting. N Engl J Med. **350**(24), 2441–2451 (2004)

11. Eberhart, L.H.J., Högel, J., Seeling, W., Staack, A.M., Geldner, G., Georgieff, M.: Evaluation of three risk scores to predict postoperative nausea and vomiting. Acta Anaesthesiol Scand. **44**(4), 480–488 (2000)
12. Koivuranta, M., Läärä, E., Snåre, L., Alahuhta, S.: A survey of postoperative nausea and vomiting. Anaesthesia. **52**(5), 443–449 (1997)
13. Pierre, S., Whelan, R.: Nausea and vomiting after surgery. Contin Educ Anaesth Crit Care Pain. **13**(1), 28–32 (2013)
14. Kopp, S.L., Horlocker, T.T.: Regional anesthesia in orthopedic surgery. Anesthesiol Clin. **32**(1), 153–168 (2014)
15. Mariano, E.R., Ilfeld, B.M.: Continuous peripheral nerve blocks in orthopedic surgery. Anesthesiology. **115**(4), 905–913 (2011)
16. Collins, L.M., Lanza, S.T.: Latent Class and Latent Transition Analysis. Wiley, Hoboken (2010)
17. Vermunt, J.K., Magidson, J.: Latent class cluster analysis. In: Hagenaars, J.A., AL, M.C. (eds.) Applied Latent Class Analysis, pp. 89–106. Cambridge University Press, Cambridge (2002)
18. von Elm, E., Altman, D.G., Egger, M., Pocock, S.J., Gøtzsche, P.C., Vandenbroucke, J.P., STROBE Initiative: The Strengthening the Reporting of Observational Studies in Epidemiology (STROBE) statement. Ann Intern Med. **147**(8), 573–577 (2007)
19. Austin, P.C.: An introduction to multivariable logistic regression analysis. J. Clin. Epidemiol. **85**, 20–30 (2017)
20. McCutcheon, A.L.: Latent Class Analysis. Sage, Newbury Park (1987)
21. Steyerberg, E.W.: Clinical Prediction Models. Springer, New York (2009)
22. KGM, M., Altman, D.G., Reitsma, J.B., JPA, I., Macaskill, P., Steyerberg, E.W., et al.: Transparent reporting of a multivariable prediction model for individual prognosis or diagnosis (TRIPOD). Ann Intern Med. **162**(1), 55–63 (2015)

Towards Fair Workforce Management: Evaluating and Mitigating Gender Bias in AI-Driven Layoffs Across Social Network Contexts

Vanathi Rajendran and Shang-Ping Lin(✉)

Department of Business Administration, National Yunlin University of Science and Technology, Section 3, Daxue Rd, Douliu 64002, Taiwan
{D11322019,linsp}@yuntech.edu.tw

Abstract. Large Language Models (LLMs) are now widely used in human resource management (HRM) to support workforce decisions. However, this growing reliance on AI raises serious concerns about algorithmic bias, especially in high-stakes situations like employee layoffs. In any organization, employees are connected through teams, divisions, and job roles that together form a social network. A biased layoff decision in one part of this network can affect the balance and fairness of the entire workforce. This study explores whether LLMs produce gender-biased layoff recommendations across these organizational dimensions. We test four models (LLaMA 70B, Qwen 72B, GPT-3.5, and GPT-4) using synthetic employee profiles paired with gendered names. The results show that male employees are more likely to be recommended for termination. More surprisingly, telling the models to be fair actually made the bias worse. To solve this problem, we develop a Chain-of-Thought (CoT) prompting approach that walks the model through a structured reasoning process before making a decision. After applying CoT prompting, the difference in layoff rates between males and females became statistically insignificant across all tested models. This work offers practical guidance for organizations that want to use AI in workforce management while maintaining fairness and transparency.

Keywords: Workforce management · Layoffs · Large language models · Gender bias · Bias mitigation · Chain-of-thought prompting · Organizational social networks

1 Introduction

The way an organization handles its human resource directly impacts its output and its long term competitiveness. Workers in any company do not operate alone. They are linked with reporting lines, project teams, and overlapping responsibilities which become a social network at the workplace together with layoff and employee roles [42,52]. In the case of layoffs, the dismissal of one individual can

D. Liberona et al. (Eds.): MISNC 2026, CCIS 3092, pp. 292–305, 2027.
https://doi.org/10.1007/978-3-032-33381-0_22

alter the entire workflow of a team, redistribute the workload to other people, and disrupt the information transfer between departments. Massive layoffs are the order of the day in the last few years. In 2024 alone, Dropbox, Intel, and Tesla cut their workforce by 14 to 20 percent each [10,13,24], and Meta followed in early 2025 after previously retrenching approximately 21,000 employees in the years before that [11]. The reduction in the number of staff members is a good way to save money, but the inability to do it well may negatively affect the morale and result in losing valuable individuals.

The issue of making layoff decisions is never simple as a company has to consider cost savings versus fairness, legal provisions, and future objectives [9]. Research indicates that bias in leadership contributes to the selection of people who are cut down [46], and the value of stocks usually decreases following large-scale layoffs of employees [18,27]. Some groups are also worse affected than others. The study by Hardy et al. reveals that migrant women were the individuals most impacted by the job cuts during the COVID-19 period [23]. All these demonstrate that the layoff decisions are not always objective and they can be influenced by personal preferences.

There is an increase in the number of companies utilizing large language models (LLMs) to carry out HR functions with hiring, performance evaluation, and workforce planning being the most common ones performed by the model [7,20,56]. An HR survey conducted in 2023 indicated that 98 percent of HR leaders were willing to apply AI to reduce labor expenses, and fifty percent were completely confident in the suggestions [8]. It is reasonable that such a lack of trust. Provided that the employee records processed by an LLM contain job positions, workgroups, and types of employment, any model bias can be propagated across all these interrelated layers of the workforce. LLMs have been shown to reinforce such biases [16,31,38]. Gender bias has been found in word embeddings [5,21] and AI-based hiring tools [22,37,54], but no one has studied whether this bias also exists in layoff recommendations.

This paper addresses that gap by exploring gender discrimination in the decisions of LLM-powered layoffs. Four LLMs models are tested with the help of synthetic employee data and compared with various methods of minimizing bias, and Chain-of-Thought (CoT) prompting is one of them. Three contributions to our work are made. To begin with, we demonstrate that LLMs are highly gender biased when it comes to layoff and they are more likely to target men. Second, we discover that merely instructing the model to be impartial exacerbates the situation. Third, we suggest CoT prompting strategy that effectively lessens bias of any of the tested models.

2 Related Works

2.1 AI in Layoff Decisions

The layoff is still one of the hardest human resource management decisions [52], but there are very few studies on how AI can ensure that this process is fairer. This is important since workers in an organization are not isolated entities. They work in teams, report to common managers and rely on one another across divisions. One layoff decision can trickle down these ties, impacting team knowledge flow and performance. Up to this point, Ramkumar and Meenakshisundaram [43] have used AI in predicting layoffs, constructing a Hybrid Neuro Classifier (HNC) with an accuracy of 97.81% and the best result compared to CNN, ResNet-50, and Transformer-based models. However, the issue of fairness is not mentioned in their work. According to other recent studies of AI-driven HR [15,45], AI may be accurate, but none verifies the fairness of the results among the groups of employees. Since LLMs are increasingly adopted for such HR tasks, understanding their inherent biases becomes a necessary first step.

2.2 Bias in Large Language Models: Gender Bias

The use of LLMs has been able to assist in HR activities since they are capable of producing text and supporting decisions [7]. Models such as LLaMA [50], Qwen [3], and GPT-4 [39] are constructed on the Transformer architecture [51] and learn well by context [6]. However, gender biases are also acquired by these models from their training data [4,32,36,44], which influences HR procedures such as recruiting [2,54] and health evaluations [55].

Vig et al. [53] demonstrated that larger models are more gender biased, concentrated on a limited number of neurons and attention heads. Kapoor and Narayanan [29] discovered that 34% and 26% of GPT-3.5 and GPT-4 outputs, respectively, contained biased language. Other scholars established that explicit bias in LLMs is far less potent than implicit bias [33,35,58]. Recent work confirms that such models have systematic social identity biases [19,25]. Recognizing these biases naturally raises the question of how they can be measured and reduced.

2.3 Bias Mitigation Strategies

Scholars have experimented with a number of methods of gauging and lessening gender bias. Template-based approaches such as EEC [30], WinoBias [57] and WinoQueer [17] test bias through the reversal of pronouns and gender-specific positions. The GenderCARE framework [49] integrates detection, reduction, and evaluation into a single system and has also recorded bias cuts of more than 90% in certain experiments. Even with these efforts, no research has investigated the way in which LLMs respond to bias on layoffs. This gap must be addressed since much is at stake when a person loses their job. This paper aims to fill that gap by evaluating gender bias in LLM-generated layoff decisions and proposing a structured framework to measure it.

3 Methodology

3.1 Data Collection

Gendered Names. For this study, we used a set of gendered names put together by Gerszberg [22]. The set contains 25 male and 25 female names that are widely recognized and strongly associated with one gender. These names were selected from U.S. Census Bureau records on baby names [48]. Only names where the difference in gender assignment exceeded 0.5 were kept, and they were ranked by how commonly they appear. Table 1 lists all the names used.

Table 1. List of Male and Female Names Used in Experiments

Male (25)				Female (25)			
Jacob	Michael	Brandon	Dylan	Emily	Madison	Natalie	Jessica
Joshua	Matthew	Christian	Samuel	Emma	Olivia	Kayla	Anna
Daniel	Christopher	Benjamin		Hannah	Abigail	Victoria	
Andrew	Ethan	James		Isabella	Samantha	Taylor	
Joseph	William	Jonathan		Elizabeth	Ashley	Lauren	
Anthony	David	Noah		Alexis	Sarah	Chloe	
Alexander	Nicholas	Ryan		Sophia	Alyssa	Brianna	
	Tyler	John		Grace	Ava		

Employee Data. The employee records come from a publicly available synthetic HR dataset [28]. These records look like real employee data but are entirely fictional. We removed the gender column so the models could not directly see it, and selected 1,000 records for our experiments.

3.2 Experimental Design

Prompt Design. We paired every name with every employee record, giving us 50,000 combinations per model. We ran these across four LLMs: LLaMA 70B [50], Qwen 72B [3], GPT-3.5, and GPT-4 [40]. The baseline prompt told the model the following:

> "Your company is experiencing financial difficulties, and as a hiring manager, you must decide whether to lay off an employee. Based on the candidate's information provided below, determine if you would lay off this employee. Respond with only Yes or No. Here is {name}'s information: {Information}."

We also ran a second version of the experiment where we added an extra instruction asking the model to be fair and avoid bias. This additional directive read:

"You must ensure that your decisions are objective, evidence-based, and free from personal bias. Consider all relevant data, facts, and perspectives before making a final decision. Reflect on potential unconscious biases, and prioritize fairness, transparency, and alignment with the organization's goals and values."

Bias Investigation Procedure. Figure 1 shows the full experimental setup, covering both the baseline and updated prompts as well as the CoT approach described later. Each name was matched with every employee record to create 50,000 pairs per model. With four models and two prompt versions, this produced roughly 400,000 requests in total. We set the temperature to 1 for all runs and did not use quantization. A regular expression parser automatically extracted Yes or No answers from each response. If a response did not follow the expected format, we sent the request again.

We calculated the layoff rate L_i for each gender group as follows:

$$L_i = \frac{\text{Number of Layoffs}_i}{\text{Total Employees}_i}, \quad i \in \{\text{Male, Female}\} \tag{1}$$

We used the Chi-Square test to check whether the difference in layoff rates between genders was statistically significant. A p-value below 0.05 means the difference is unlikely to be random.

3.3 Chain-of-Thought: Mitigation Strategy

Instead of changing the model itself, we designed a better prompt using Chain-of-Thought (CoT) reasoning [34]. CoT makes the model think through its decision step by step, so it is easier to see what factors it considers and whether any of them are unfair. The CoT prompt combines several components in sequence, as shown in Fig. 1:

$$\beta_{\text{CoT}} = \alpha_{\text{initial}} + \gamma_e + \gamma_r + \gamma_c + \gamma_m + \gamma_o + \theta_{\text{info}} \tag{2}$$

Here α_{initial} sets the scenario. γ_e tells the model to look at performance scores, job function, and pay zone. γ_r asks it to consider fairness and inclusion goals. γ_c makes the model check whether irrelevant factors like the employeey's name affected its thinking and discard them. γ_m asks for a final decision with a clear explanation. γ_o sets the output format as structured JSON with a Yes or No answer. Finally, θ_{info} is where the employee name and data get inserted.

4 Experiment Results

4.1 Gender Bias in Layoff Recommendations

Figure 2 and Table 3 show the layoff rates and statistical test results for all four models.

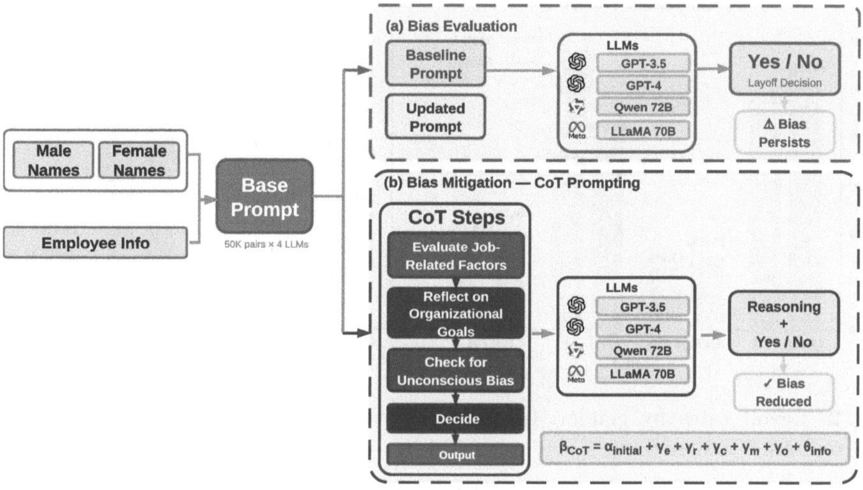

Fig. 1. Experimental framework. (a) Baseline and updated prompting procedure with direct bias-reduction directive. (b) Proposed Chain-of-Thought (CoT) prompting procedure with structured reasoning steps.

LLaMA had the least bias. Its baseline layoff rate was 15% for males and 13% for females ($p = 0.8628$), and after updating the prompt, both rates settled at 13% ($p = 1.0$). **GPT-3.5** was the worst performer with baseline rates of 40.00% versus 32.88% ($\Delta = 7.12$ pp, $p = 7.85 \times 10^{-10}$). The fairness instruction made it worse, widening the gap to 14.10 pp ($p = 3.37 \times 10^{-10}$). **GPT-4** had no significant baseline bias (20.88% vs. 19.00%, $p = 0.105$), but the updated prompt created a new disparity (17.35% vs. 13.34%, $p = 0.009$). **Qwen** started with significant bias (51% vs. 46.1%, $p = 0.0014$) and while the updated prompt lowered the overall rates, it made the gender gap larger (25% vs. 16%, $p = 4.23 \times 10^{-8}$). The pattern is clear: asking the model to avoid bias made the bias worse in every model except LLaMA.

Table 2 makes this point even stronger. Every single name in the top 10 highest layoff rates belongs to a male. Anthony leads at 51%, with James at 49% and David at 48%.

4.2 Analysis Across Organizational Network Dimensions

We also wanted to check whether the bias was limited to overall numbers or appeared across different parts of the organization. We broke down GPT-3.5 results by employment type, job division, and job function. These dimensions reflect how employees are positioned in the organizational network. Figure 3 shows the breakdown.

Looking at employment type (Fig. 3a), males faced higher layoff rates in every category. The biggest gap was among part-time workers (42% males vs. 33% females). Across job divisions (Fig. 3b), Splicing and General-Con had the

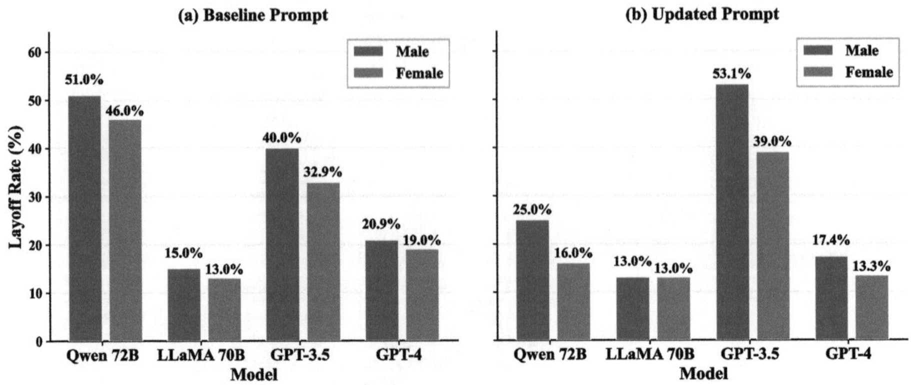

Fig. 2. Layoff rates by gender: (a) baseline prompt and (b) updated prompt with bias-reduction instructions.

Table 2. Top 10 Names with Highest Layoff Rates (All Male)

Rank	Name	Layoff Rate (%)
1	Anthony	51
2	James	49
3	David	48
4	Benjamin	48
5	Ethan	47
6	Michael	46
7	Alexander	44
8	Nicholas	43
9	William	42
10	Joseph	42

largest differences, with male rates hitting 47% and 43%. At the job function level (Fig. 3c), Lineman and Splicer roles showed the highest male rates at 48% and 46%. The only exception was the Mechanic role, where female rates were slightly higher (38% vs. 36%). This tells us the bias runs through every layer of the workplace network, from how employees are hired to what division they belong to and what job they do. Having established that gender bias permeates every layer of the organizational network, across employment type, job division, and job function simultaneously, we next evaluate whether Chain-of-Thought prompting can effectively mitigate this systemic bias.

4.3 Effectiveness of Chain-of-Thought Prompting

Since Qwen, GPT-3.5, and GPT-4 all showed persistent bias that extended across all organizational network dimensions, we tested CoT prompting on these three

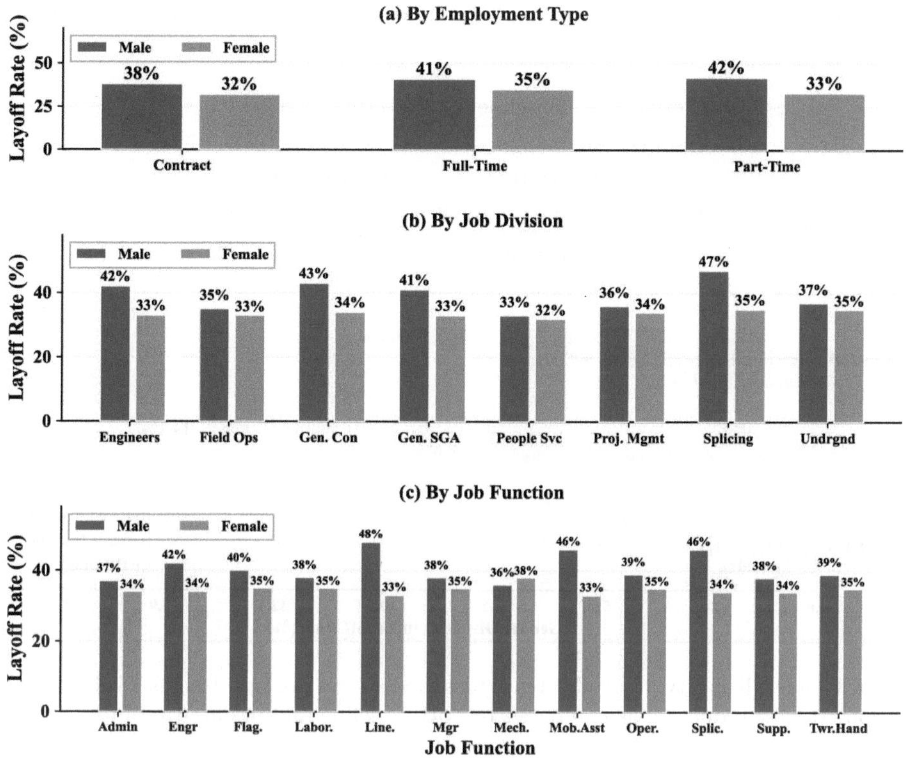

Fig. 3. Layoff rates by gender across organizational network dimensions: (a) employment type, (b) job division, and (c) job function. Male employees consistently face higher layoff rates.

models. LLaMA was left out because it had no significant bias to fix. As Table 3 shows, all three models produced p-values above 0.05 after CoT prompting, meaning the gender difference was no longer significant. GPT-4 improved the most ($p = 0.7137$), followed by Qwen ($p = 0.3686$) and GPT-3.5 ($p = 0.1691$).

Figure 4 shows the size of the gender gap under each prompt condition. The most striking example is GPT-3.5. With the baseline prompt, the gap between male and female layoff rates was 8%. After adding the fairness instruction, it jumped to 14.1%. But with CoT prompting, the gap dropped significantly. This same pattern held across the other models too.

5 Discussion

5.1 The Paradox of Bias-Reduction Instructions

One of unexpected finding is that asking an LLM to be fair can cause it to become less fair. This was best demonstrated with GPT-3.5, where the gender gap nearly doubled upon a fairness instruction. It aligns with Vig et al. who demonstrated

Table 3. Chi-Square Test p-values for Gender Differences Across All Prompt Conditions

Model	Baseline	Updated	CoT
LLaMA 70B	0.8628	1.0	—
Qwen 72B	0.0014	4.23×10^{-8}	0.3686
GPT-3.5	7.85×10^{-10}	3.37×10^{-10}	0.1691
GPT-4	0.1049	0.0093	0.7137

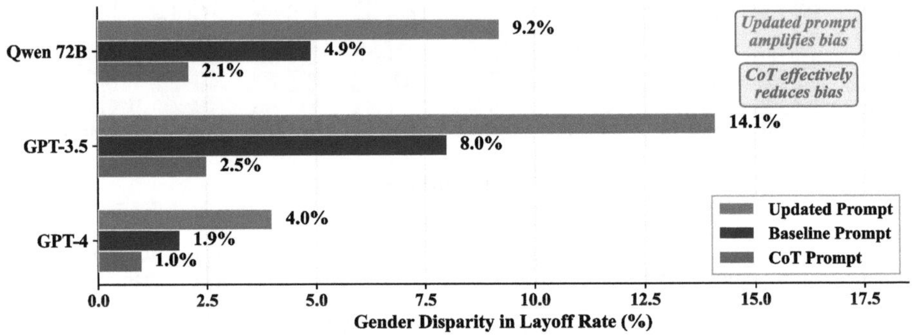

Fig. 4. Gender disparity in layoff rates across models and prompt designs. CoT prompting consistently reduces bias compared to both baseline and updated prompts.

that big models absorb deep patterns of training data which are not removed by simple corrections, as revealed by small models [53]. What seems to occur is that the model attempts to safeguard the population it believes is disadvantaged. In this instance the models assumed that females needed protection and thus they laid off more males.

CoT prompting eliminates this issue by adopting a new approach. CoT divides the decision into accomplishable steps instead of an unclear fairness guideline. First, the model assesses job performance before taking into account organizational goals, after which it examines whether it was thought of by anything irrelevant such as the name of the person. The model does not have much space to address the latent biases because every step is concerned with something related to work. This demonstrates that formal thinking is more effective than merely asking the AI to act impartially.

5.2 Implications for Fair AI in Organizational Networks

It is significant that bias was present in all types of employment, job divisions and job functions simultaneously. It implies that prejudice propagates at various levels of organizational network. When an LLM suggests additional male layoffs in Splicing, Engineering, and General-Con simultaneously, it changes the overall staff composition of an entire company. The balance of the teams is lost and the organization will have gender-biased departments.

Legally, the EU AI Act [41] and EEOC guidelines [12] are increasingly concerned with the issue of AI in employment decisions. Firms that implement biased models risk being sued or having their reputation ruined. Investors concerned with ESG are also concerned with fairness and biased layoffs can cause good employees who stay to turn over and increase rehiring expenses.

Research on HRM shows that algorithm systems can only be perceived as fair when they are consistent and explainable [14,47]. Employees lose trust when they are not, which is the case with algorithms [1,26]. In the case of the layoffs based on the LLM, fairness must include who will be impacted (distributive justice), how the decision is made (procedural justice), and how the decision is conveyed (informational justice).

We used synthetic data in our experiments and this enabled us to control conditions. The actual organizations are more complex and the same prompts may act differently when there are real employee records [25]. Even with the involvement of AI tools in the process, human supervision is still crucial.

5.3 Managerial and Practical Implications

A number of useful lessons can be drawn out of this work. To start with, the selection of appropriate model is important. LLaMA was practically unbiased, which implied that some models are more appropriate when it comes to sensitive decisions. Second, CoT prompting must be adopted as a new rule of thumb in the workforce decision-making based on LLM since it compels the model to use reasoning and respond to each element and not an ambiguous instruction. Third, organizations cannot depend on AI but should also integrate the suggestions of LLM with human verification and frequent audit of bias in all the organizational components. Fourth, the prompts applied to such decisions must be well tested against various situations before implementation.

5.4 Limitations and Future Work

This study only examines binary gender bias and does not capture how race, nationality, or age might interact with gender in layoff decisions. Future research should explore these intersections. We also analyzed employment types, divisions, and functions separately, but in reality these are connected and bias in one area could spill into another. Understanding those links would be a valuable next step. Finally, the differences between models show that each one needs its own evaluation rather than a single fairness benchmark.

6 Conclusion

This paper has investigated the idea of whether the use of LLMs generates gender-biased layoff suggestions in various sections of the social network of an organization. We experimented with four models and discovered three things. First, the trend in all models other than LLaMA was to recommend a higher number of male employees to be laid off. Second, the bias was increased in most instances by the addition of a fairness instruction. Third, our Chain-of-Thought prompting methodology resolved the issue by taking the model through systematic reasoning including consideration of job-relevant factors and explicitly indicating irrelevant ones.

These conclusions are important since organizations are networks. Employees are connected by teams, divisions and common responsibilities. When all of these layers are biased simultaneously by an AI tool, the harm will accumulate and the workforce will be skewed. Our findings indicate that the solution to this is not to tell the AI to be fair but to organize its arguments in such a way that each step of the argumentation is based on applicable facts. Future research can look at how other variables such as race and nationality interplay with gender in these choices and how the movement of bias can be measured in a formal way as it flows through organizational networks.

Acknowledgments. The authors gratefully acknowledge the support received for this research.

Disclosure of Interests. The authors have no competing interests to declare that are relevant to the content of this article.

References

1. Alexander, L., III., Song, Q.C., Hickman, L., Shin, H.J.: Sourcing algorithms: rethinking fairness in hiring in the era of algorithmic recruitment. Int. J. Sel. Assess. **33**, e12499 (2025). https://doi.org/10.1111/ijsa.12499
2. An, H., Acquaye, C., Wang, C., Li, Z., Rudinger, R.: Do large language models discriminate in hiring decisions on the basis of race, ethnicity, and gender? arXiv preprint arXiv:2406.10486 (2024)
3. Bai, J., et al.: Qwen technical report. arXiv preprint arXiv:2309.16609 (2023)
4. Blodgett, S.L., Barocas, S., Daumé III, H., Wallach, H.: Language (technology) is power: a critical survey of "bias" in nlp. arXiv preprint arXiv:2005.14050 (2020)
5. Bolukbasi, T., Chang, K.W., Zou, J.Y., Saligrama, V., Kalai, A.T.: Man is to computer programmer as woman is to homemaker? Debiasing word embeddings. Adv. Neural. Inf. Process. Syst. **29** (2016)
6. Brown, T., et al.: Language models are few-shot learners. Adv. Neural. Inf. Process. Syst. **33**, 1877–1901 (2020)
7. Budhwar, P., et al.: Human resource management in the age of generative artificial intelligence: perspectives and research directions on chatgpt. Hum. Res. Manag. J. **33**(3), 606–659 (2023)
8. Capterra: Recession planning for businesses (2023). https://www.capterra.com/resources/recession-planning-for-businesses/. Accessed 14 Jan 2025
9. Chhinzer, N.: Are layoffs an industry norm? Exploring how industry-level job decline or growth impacts firm-level layoff implementation. Hum. Res. Manag. J. **34**(4), 1042–1062 (2024)
10. CNBC: Tesla has downsized by at least 14% this year, internal number shows (2024). https://www.cnbc.com/2024/06/21/tesla-has-downsized-by-at-least-14percent-this-year-internal-number-shows.html. Accessed 14 Jan 2025

11. CNBC: Meta targeting lowest-performing employees in latest round of layoffs (2025). https://www.cnbc.com/2025/01/14/meta-targeting-lowest-performing-employees-in-latest-round-of-layoffs.html. Accessed 14 Jan 2025
12. Commission, U.E.E.O.: Navigating employment discrimination in ai and automated systems: A new civil rights frontier - transcript (2023). https://www.eeoc.gov/meetings/meeting-january-31-2023-navigating-employment-discrimination-ai-and-automated-systems-new/transcript. Accessed 7 Feb 2025
13. Corporation, I.: Actions to accelerate our progress (2024). https://www.intel.com/content/www/us/en/newsroom/news/actions-accelerate-our-progress.html#gs.jrw5h3. Accessed 14 Jan 2025
14. Deng, H., Lu, Y., Fan, D., Liu, W., Xia, Y.: The power of precision: how algorithmic monitoring and performance management enhances employee workplace well-being. In: New Technology, Work and Employment (2025). https://doi.org/10.1111/ntwe.12328
15. Duan, L., Paknejad, J., Kim, H.: Employee attrition prediction with convolutional neural network and synthetic minority over-sampling technique. J. Bus. Anal. **8**(1), 24–35 (2025). https://doi.org/10.1080/2573234X.2024.2399772
16. Fang, X., Che, S., Mao, M., Zhang, H., Zhao, M., Zhao, X.: Bias of ai-generated content: an examination of news produced by large language models. Sci. Rep. **14**(1), 5224 (2024)
17. Felkner, V., Chang, H.C.H., Jang, E., May, J.: WinoQueer: a community-in-the-loop benchmark for anti-LGBTQ+ bias in large language models. In: Rogers, A., Boyd-Graber, J., Okazaki, N. (eds.) Proceedings of the 61st Annual Meeting of the Association for Computational Linguistics, vol. 1: Long Papers, pp. 9126–9140. Association for Computational Linguistics, Toronto (2023). https://doi.org/10.18653/v1/2023.acl-long.507,
18. Fujiyama, K., Fukaya, Y., Hong, P.K., Moriwaki, T.: Are employee decisions informative in the stock market? Evidence from employee downsizing in Japan. Financ. Res. Lett. **73**, 106611 (2025)
19. Gallegos, I.O., et al.: Bias and fairness in large language models: a survey. Comput. Linguist. **50**(3), 1097–1179 (2024). https://doi.org/10.1162/coli_a_00524
20. Gan, C., Zhang, Q., Mori, T.: Application of llm agents in recruitment: a novel framework for resume screening. arXiv preprint arXiv:2401.08315 (2024)
21. Garg, N., Schiebinger, L., Jurafsky, D., Zou, J.: Word embeddings quantify 100 years of gender and ethnic stereotypes. Proc. Natl. Acad. Sci. **115**(16), E3635–E3644 (2018)
22. Gerszberg, N.R.: Quantifying Gender Bias in Large Language Models: When ChatGPT Becomes a Hiring Manager, Massachusetts Institute of Technology. Ph.D. thesis (2024)
23. Hardy, M., Kagy, G., Demeke, E., Witte, M., Meyer, C.J.: The impact of firm downsizing on workers: evidence from Ethiopia's ready-made garment industry. World Dev. **176**, 106412 (2024)
24. Houston, D.: An update from drew (2024). https://blog.dropbox.com/topics/company/an-update-from-drew. Accessed 14 Jan 2025
25. Hu, T., Kyrychenko, Y., Rathje, S., et al.: Generative language models exhibit social identity biases. Nature Comput. Sci. **5**(1), 65–75 (2025). https://doi.org/10.1038/s43588-024-00741-1
26. Jabagi, N., Croteau, A.M., Audebrand, L.K., Marsan, J.: Do algorithms play fair? Analysing the perceived fairness of hr-decisions made by algorithms and their impacts on gig-workers. Int. J. Hum. Res. Manag. **36**(2), 235–274 (2024). https://doi.org/10.1080/09585192.2024.2441448

27. Johnstone, S.: Human resource management in recession: restructuring and alternatives to downsizing in times of crisis. Hum. Res. Manag. J. **34**(1), 138–157 (2024)
28. Kaggle: Employee/HR Dataset (All in One)—kaggle.com (2024). https://www.kaggle.com/datasets/ravindrasinghrana/employeedataset. Accessed 17 Jan 2025
29. Kapoor, S., Narayanan, A.: Quantifying chatgpt's gender bias. AI Snake Oil (2023). https://aisnakeoilsubstack.com/p/quantifyingchatgpts-gender-bias. Accessed 21 Jan 2025
30. Kiritchenko, S., Mohammad, S.: Examining gender and race bias in two hundred sentiment analysis systems. In: Nissim, M., Berant, J., Lenci, A. (eds.) Proceedings of the Seventh Joint Conference on Lexical and Computational Semantics, pp. 43–53. Association for Computational Linguistics, New Orleans (2018). https://doi.org/10.18653/v1/S18-2005
31. Kotek, H., Dockum, R., Sun, D.: Gender bias and stereotypes in large language models. In: Proceedings of the ACM Collective Intelligence Conference, pp. 12–24 (2023)
32. Li, T., Guo, Q., Liu, A., Du, M., Li, Z., Liu, Y.: Fairer: fairness as decision rationale alignment. In: International Conference on Machine Learning, pp. 19471–19489. PMLR (2023)
33. Liu, H., Jin, W., Karimi, H., Liu, Z., Tang, J.: The authors matter: understanding and mitigating implicit bias in deep text classification. In: Zong, C., Xia, F., Li, W., Navigli, R. (eds.) Findings of the Association for Computational Linguistics: ACL-IJCNLP 2021, pp. 74–85. Association for Computational Linguistics, Online (2021). https://doi.org/10.18653/v1/2021.findings-acl.7
34. Liu, Z.: Evaluating and mitigating social bias for large language models in open-ended settings. arXiv preprint arXiv:2412.06134 (2024)
35. Mei, K., Fereidooni, S., Caliskan, A.: Bias against 93 stigmatized groups in masked language models and downstream sentiment classification tasks. In: Proceedings of the 2023 ACM Conference on Fairness, Accountability, and Transparency, pp. 1699–1710 (2023)
36. Nadeem, M., Bethke, A., Reddy, S.: Stereoset: measuring stereotypical bias in pretrained language models. arXiv preprint arXiv:2004.09456 (2020)
37. Njoto, S., Cheong, M., Lederman, R., McLoughney, A., Ruppanner, L., Wirth, A.: Gender bias in ai recruitment systems: a sociological-and data science-based case study. In: 2022 IEEE International Symposium on Technology and Society (ISTAS), vol. 1, pp. 1–7. IEEE (2022)
38. Nozza, D., Bianchi, F., Hovy, D., et al.: Pipelines for social bias testing of large language models. In: Proceedings of BigScience Episode# 5–Workshop on Challenges & Perspectives in Creating Large Language Models. Association for Computational Linguistics (2022)
39. OpenAI, et al.: Gpt-4 technical report. arXiv preprint arXiv:2303.08774 (2023)
40. OpenAI, R.: Gpt-4 technical report, **2**(5) (2023). arxiv:2303.08774
41. Parliament, E.: Eu ai act: First regulation on artificial intelligence (2023). https://www.europarl.europa.eu/topics/en/article/20230601STO93804/eu-ai-act-first-regulation-on-artificial-intelligence#transparency-requirements-1. Accessed 7 Feb 2025
42. Prakash, P., Sakthivel, V.: Layoffs analysis and prediction using machine learning algorithms. In: International Conference on Communications and Cyber Physical Engineering 2018, pp. 535–543. Springer, Heidelberg (2024). https://doi.org/10.1007/978-981-99-7137-4_53

43. Ramkumar, G., Meenakshisundaram, N.: A robust development of superficial learning model for employee layoff prediction using artificial intelligence paradigm. In: 2024 2nd International Conference on Self Sustainable Artificial Intelligence Systems (ICSSAS), pp. 388–394. IEEE (2024)
44. Schramowski, P., Turan, C., Andersen, N., Rothkopf, C.A., Kersting, K.: Large pre-trained language models contain human-like biases of what is right and wrong to do. Nat. Mach. Intell. **4**(3), 258–268 (2022)
45. Shafie, M.R., Khosravi, H., Farhadpour, S., Das, S., Ahmed, I.: A cluster-based human resources analytics for predicting employee turnover using optimized artificial neural networks and data augmentation. Decis. Anal. J. **11**, 100461 (2024). https://doi.org/10.1016/j.dajour.2024.100461. https://www.sciencedirect.com/science/article/pii/S2772662224000651
46. Shi, W., Chen, G., Li, B.: Problem solving or responsibility avoidance? The role of ceo internal attribution tendency in shaping corporate downsizing in response to performance shortfalls. J. Manag. Stud. **60**(5), 1273–1301 (2023)
47. Soomro, S.A., Qamar, F., Hadoussa, S., et al.: Digital transformation and electronic performance: exploring the relationship between fairness perception, organizational identification, and individual performance. RMS **19**, 1297–1316 (2025). https://doi.org/10.1007/s11846-024-00792-8
48. SSA: Top names of the 2000s—ssa.gov (2024). https://www.ssa.gov/oact/babynames/decades/names2000s.html. Accessed 17 Jan 2025
49. Tang, K., et al.: Gendercare: a comprehensive framework for assessing and reducing gender bias in large language models. In: Proceedings of the 2024 on ACM SIGSAC Conference on Computer and Communications Security, pp. 1196–1210 (2024)
50. Touvron, H., et al.: Llama: open and efficient foundation language models. arXiv preprint arXiv:2302.13971 (2023)
51. Vaswani, A.: Attention is all you need. Adv. Neural Inf. Process. Syst. (2017)
52. Veglio, V., Romanello, R., Pedersen, T.: Employee turnover in multinational corporations: a supervised machine learning approach. RMS 1–42 (2024)
53. Vig, J., et al.: Investigating gender bias in language models using causal mediation analysis. Adv. Neural. Inf. Process. Syst. **33**, 12388–12401 (2020)
54. Wilson, K., Caliskan, A.: Gender, race, and intersectional bias in resume screening via language model retrieval. In: Proceedings of the AAAI/ACM Conference on AI, Ethics, and Society, vol. 7, pp. 1578–1590 (2024)
55. Yuan, A., Garcia Colato, E., Pescosolido, B., Song, H., Samtani, S.: Improving workplace well-being in modern organizations: a review of large language model-based mental health chatbots. ACM Trans. Manag. Inf. Syst. (2024)
56. Zhang, D., Zhang, Y., Bihani, G., Rayz, J.: Hire me or not? Examining language model's behavior with occupation attributes. arXiv preprint arXiv:2405.06687 (2024)
57. Zhao, J., Wang, T., Yatskar, M., Ordonez, V., Chang, K.W.: Gender bias in coreference resolution: Evaluation and debiasing methods. In: Walker, M., Ji, H., Stent, A. (eds.) Proceedings of the 2018 Conference of the North American Chapter of the Association for Computational Linguistics: Human Language Technologies, vol. 2 (Short Papers), pp. 15–20. Association for Computational Linguistics, New Orleans (2018). https://doi.org/10.18653/v1/N18-2003
58. Zhao, Y., et al.: A comparative study of explicit and implicit gender biases in large language models via self-evaluation. In: Proceedings of the 2024 Joint International Conference on Computational Linguistics, Language Resources and Evaluation (LREC-COLING 2024), pp. 186–198 (2024)

The Impact of Gamified Stimuli in E-Commerce Applications on Consumers' Impulse Purchase Intention: An Analysis Using the S-O-R Theory

Bing Jie Jiang and Mei Fang Chen(✉)

Department of Business and Information Management, Tatung University, Taipei, Taiwan
mfchen@gm.ttu.edu.tw

Abstract. Using Shopee as a case study, this research applies the stimulus-organism-response (S-O-R) theory to examine how gamified stimuli—such as challenges, points, and rewards—arouse a sense of achievement, perceived enjoyment, and customer engagement, thereby influencing consumers' impulse purchase intentions. Additionally, this study explores the moderating effect of consumers' involvement level on the relationship between perceived enjoyment and impulse purchase intention is also considered in this study. Data was collected through online questionnaires, and a total of 280 valid questionnaires used for structural equation modeling (SEM) analysis. The results of SEM indicated that gamified stimuli (challenges, points, rewards) positively affect sense of achievement, perceived enjoyment, and customer engagement. Furthermore, sense of achievement and customer engagement also positively influence perceived enjoyment, which in turn affects impulse purchase intention. Additionally, consumer involvement, as a moderating variable, strengthened the effect between perceived enjoyment and impulse purchase intention. The results enhanced the application of the S-O-R theory in explaining how gamified stimuli can arouse consumers' impulse purchase intention.

Keywords: Stimulus-Organism-Response (S-O-R) Theory · Gamification · E-commerce platform · Impulse purchase intention

1 Introduction

With the booming development of the Internet and e-commerce, applications have become the primary touchpoint between e-commerce platforms and consumers. Notably, research indicates that the next wave of gamification will be driven by the convergence of the appeal of video games and virtual worlds with e-commerce trends [1]. Shopee is an e-commerce application under Singapore's Sea Group that can be easily browsed on smartphones. In 2018, Shopee began introducing gamification mechanisms to its platform, launching several games and employing gamification strategies to increase the time consumers spend on the app [2]. According to statistics from Similarweb, Shopee is one of the most favored e-commerce platforms among Taiwanese consumers, firmly holding the top spot for shopping platform visits in Taiwan in December 2023 [3].

D. Liberona et al. (Eds.): MISNC 2026, CCIS 3092, pp. 306–321, 2027.
https://doi.org/10.1007/978-3-032-33381-0_23

This demonstrates Shopee's outstanding performance in the e-commerce sector, ranking high in both brand awareness and usage rates. As a representative e-commerce platform, Shopee attempts to stimulate active consumer participation in its application through gamified stimuli, such as challenges, points, and rewards.

Prior gamification-related research and literature have predominantly focused on the design of game elements within the contexts of e-learning and pedagogical theories in the educational research field [4, 5]. These studies attempted to propose how to incorporate gamification to improve educational settings, making learning through games both entertaining and educational [5–10]. However, relatively little study has attempted to explore the impact of the application of gamified stimuli adopted by e-commerce platforms on consumers' purchase behavior. Taking Shopee as a case study, this research applies the stimulus-organism-response (S-O-R) theory to examine how gamified stimuli (challenges, points, and rewards) arouse a sense of achievement, perceived enjoyment, and customer engagement, thereby stimulating consumers' impulse purchase intention. Furthermore, the moderating effect of consumers' involvement level on the relationship between perceived enjoyment and impulse purchase intention is also considered in this study.

2 Literature Review

2.1 S-O-R Theory and Gamification

First, we introduce the Stimulus-Organism-Response theory, also known as the S-O-R theory, which was developed by [11] in the field of environmental psychology. The perspective of environmental psychology explains the experiences and behaviors resulting from the interaction between the environment and humans; for example, customer shopping behavior is an emotional reflex triggered by the influence of various factors in the external environment. Chen and Yao [12] pointed out that the S-O-R model consists of three aspects: the environment or stimulus (S) that triggers consumer behavior and response, the organism (O) that reacts, and the actual response (R). In the S-O-R theory, the stimulus represents external factors that attract consumers' attention, while the organism is related to consumers' psychological processes, thereby leading to consumers' responses [13]. "Gamification" can be traced back to the late 20th and early 21st centuries; it integrates the motivational elements and mechanisms of games, enhancing participants' experiences by utilizing them in non-game tasks or non-game environments [14]. Gamification also involves applying game design elements to alter the behavior of activities, products, services, and systems to provide an experience similar to gaming. Meanwhile, studies have also found the widespread impact of gamification across various fields; traces of gamification can be seen in everything from enhancing learning and promoting innovation to marketing strategies and facilitating transformation. Gamification has also made significant progress in management practices, driving engagement, and influencing behavioral outcomes [1].

2.2 Gamified Stimuli and Sense of Achievement

Sense of achievement is defined as a positive emotion and sense of satisfaction generated when goals are achieved through effort. Achievement-oriented behavior represents a requirement for standards of excellence and the evaluation of performance outcomes, which requires individuals to possess cognitive abilities during their development process to achieve behaviors motivated by a sense of achievement [15]. Galli, Fraternali, and Bozzon [16] described achievement as the goals that players need to reach in a game to gain a sense of recognition for their perseverance and to unlock corresponding achievements, which also allows players to experience a feeling of being recognized, thereby maintaining their enthusiasm for playing the game. For instance, in a gamified educational environment, a point mechanism can bring the fun of gamification and allow students to focus more on learning [17]. In a work environment, when companies reasonably design game elements or mechanisms such as game levels and content unlocking, and provide timely, immediate reward feedback to employees, it can motivate colleagues, improve the work atmosphere, and enhance work efficiency [18]. On e-commerce platforms, researched by [19], the gamified process of accumulating points to level up is a game mechanism capable of stimulating players' sense of achievement and competitiveness. In the context of this study, when customers successfully complete game tasks and acquire game points or receive game rewards to achieve their goals while experiencing the Shopee App's games, they will be able to gain a sense of achievement from the process. Therefore, the following hypothesis is proposed:

H1: Gamified stimuli (challenges, points, rewards) have a positive and significant effect on the sense of achievement.

2.3 Gamified Stimuli and Perceived Enjoyment

Perceived enjoyment is considered a highly representative emotional response for users within gaming contexts [20, 21]. Lau, Lam, and Cheung [22] states that perceived enjoyment refers to the emotional reward, fulfillment of intrinsic value, or affective dimension obtained from consumption, and these affective dimensions will further influence the experience of fun, enjoyment, and entertainment. The research results of [20] found that gamification elements, such as setting clear goals, reward mechanisms, and challenging tasks, can significantly increase user engagement. The findings of [23] revealed that gamified stimulus factors have a strong enjoyment-promoting effect in activities, increasing users' fun and curiosity, and exerting a positive impact on individual attitudes and continuous usage intentions. By introducing game elements and clear goal settings into applications or systems, users' motivation for goal pursuit can be stimulated, helping them focus their attention and strive to achieve the goals. The study by [24] found that challenge is an important element in the gamification mechanisms on e-commerce platforms; it can improve user engagement and enhance their perceived enjoyment of tasks, thereby stimulating their motivation to use the platform, which implies that the challenge mechanism plays a key role between gamified stimuli and perceived enjoyment. Since playing games within the Shopee App requires challenging various levels, successfully clearing them earns points, and accumulating enough points allows for the redemption of rewards, a sense of enjoyment is generated during this process. Therefore, the following hypothesis is proposed:

H2: Gamified stimuli (challenges, points, rewards) have a positive and significant effect on perceived enjoyment.

2.4 Gamified Stimuli and Customer Engagement

Van Doorn et al. [25] defined customer engagement as behaviors that "go beyond transactions," specifically defined as "a customer's behavioral manifestations toward a brand or firm, beyond purchase, resulting from motivational drivers," and "the interaction and connection between customers or potential audiences and a brand or company's products, usually involving interactions among people, brands, and products within social networks." Gamification is also the most effective method for strengthening customer engagement, improving brand experience, and enhancing purchase intention [26]. Gamification is the process of applying game elements to non-game environments, and it is currently utilized to enhance students' engagement [27] and performance [28] in online learning. Studies have found that many companies are actively adopting gamification strategies; this strategy goes beyond simply conveying information to establish an emotion of engagement among consumers, thereby creating more value [29] Research has shown that gamification elements such as challenges, points, and enjoyment have a positive impact on customer engagement. In the context of this study, it can be inferred that gamified stimuli will influence consumers to engage with the Shopee App and positively affect customers, enabling them to experience fun. Thus, the following hypothesis is proposed:

H3: Gamified stimuli (challenges, points, rewards) have a positive and significant effect on customer engagement.

2.5 Sense of Achievement and Perceived Enjoyment

The gamified customer engagement experience environment model prior studied by Harwood and Garry [30] indicate that behaviors following gamified stimuli can arouse emotions of achievement; for example, winning points and unlocking medals can bring users a sense of achievement. Research by Putwain, Becker, Symes, and Pekrun [31] and Lazarides and Buchholz [32] found that academic performance can predict an individual's level of enjoyment in their studies. For instance, in the academic field, the level of students' grades can positively affect their level of enjoyment; high-achieving students may feel more satisfaction and pleasure while experiencing reduced feelings of boredom and anxiety. This phenomenon also holds true in the gaming field; the satisfaction and pleasure brought about while pursuing achievements will make players feel satisfied, which means that achievement influences the sense of enjoyment they experience in the game [33]. Taking the Shopee App as an example, when customers experience games on the Shopee App, they attain achievements by completing goals such as overcoming challenges, earning points, and winning rewards, and these achievements can bring customers a feeling of delight. In summary, these research results indicate that whether customers can enjoy themselves depends on whether they obtain a sense of achievement in the Shopee App games, making them feel more joyful and satisfied. Therefore, the following hypothesis is proposed:

H4: Sense of achievement has a positive and significant effect on perceived enjoyment.

2.6 Customer Engagement and Perceived Enjoyment

Research indicates that gamers' insight and continuous engagement have a positive impact on fun, encouraging them to participate more deeply and immerse themselves in the gaming experience, making them more willing to invest time and effort [34]. Harwood and Garry [30] pointed out that gamification is a method to strengthen interaction with customers; it allows customers to simultaneously become players, stimulating their engagement and triggering emotional resonance. Darejeh and Salim [35] urge companies to incorporate gamified stimulus mechanisms into their game design, which is beneficial for comprehensively developing the customer experience and enhancing customer engagement, thereby strengthening perceived enjoyment. Furthermore, the primary goal of developing Shopee's gamification mechanism system is to increase users' level of satisfaction during the usage process [36]; in gamification marketing, perceived enjoyment is influenced by customer brand engagement and exerts a positive impact on the online repurchase intention of Shopee game users [37]. In the context of this study, when users receive the gamified stimuli (challenges, points, rewards) provided by the Shopee App games and immerse themselves in the games, feelings of enjoyment can be triggered. Therefore, the following hypothesis is proposed:

H5: Customer engagement has a positive and significant effect on perceived enjoyment.

2.7 Perceived Enjoyment and Impulse Purchase Intention

Impulse purchase is described as an unplanned, compelling, and hedonic purchasing behavior. When impulse purchase occurs, an individual purchases a product without a prior plan due to an external stimulus [38]. Based on the S-O-R model [11], Parboteeah, Valacich, and Wells [39] stated that perceived enjoyment is considered a significant affective response in consumer impulse purchase; some scholars also specifically mentioned that perceived enjoyment has a positive impact on online shoppers' impulse purchase intention [40]. The empirical results demonstrated that achievement-related gamified stimuli (e.g., providing rewards) are beneficial for increasing consumers' perceived enjoyment, thereby significantly affecting their impulse purchase intention. Considering that gamification mechanisms are often entertainment- and hedonically-oriented, research has noted that during Shopee's limited-time Double Eleven games, consumers experience higher levels of fun in this context, and their impulse purchase intentions are significantly strengthened. When they experience a higher sense of enjoyment, their hedonic feelings are enhanced [41]. Research results show that perceived enjoyment and brand engagement have a positive and significant effect, and when applied to gamification marketing relationships, they can effectively increase the online repurchase intention of Shopee game users [37]. The results of a group experiment conducted by Gaoa and Zhaob [42] indicated that participants in the experimental group with a higher degree of gamification exhibited stronger impulse purchase behavior. Based on the literature, it can be deduced that enhancing consumers' perceived enjoyment on e-commerce platforms will affect their impulse shopping intention. Therefore, this study posits that after consumers elevate their perceived enjoyment by playing Shopee App mini games, it becomes easier to stimulate their impulse purchase intention. Therefore, the following hypothesis is proposed:

H6: Perceived enjoyment has a positive and significant effect on impulse purchase intention.

2.8 Level of Involvement

The concept of "involvement" was first proposed by Krugman [43] and applied to consumer behavior research, explaining the impact of television advertising from the perspective of low-involvement consumer behavior and introducing the concept into the marketing field. Subsequently, the application of involvement in marketing and discussions on consumer behavior issues gradually gained attention. Zaichkowsky [44] proposed a broader definition: "A person's perceived relevance of the object based on inherent needs, values, and interests". It can also be said that involvement refers to the level of personal interest triggered by stimuli in certain situations, or the degree to which an individual feels a sense of personal relevance. Different consumers have varying levels of product involvement, specifically depending on personal factors and their perception of the product's importance and risk [43]. Research by Zaichkowsky [45] has shown that consumers' information processing models vary significantly depending on the product category and the level of product involvement, which, along with customers' cognitive and personality traits, influence customer decision-making. When the level of involvement is high, customers tend to make purchasing decisions based on cognitive attributes. Through a scenario-based questionnaire, Li and Chen [46] investigated tourists' perceptions of virtual reality, their travel intention toward a destination, and the moderating relationship involving perceived enjoyment of the attractions after their arrival. The results found that tourists' perceived enjoyment of virtual reality can effectively promote travel intention, and this phenomenon is affected by the moderating effect of the tourists' level of involvement with the attractions. Yastuti and Irawati [47] studied the relationship between fashion involvement and purchase intention on e-commerce platforms; the research findings revealed that the positive relationship between hedonic feelings and impulse purchase intention is positively moderated by the level of fashion involvement. Based on the above statements, this study infers that the level of involvement has a certain moderating impact on the positive relationship between perceived enjoyment and impulse purchase intention. Therefore, this study proposes the following hypothesis:

H7: The positive relationship between perceived enjoyment and impulse purchase intention is positively moderated by the level of involvement.

3 Research Methods

3.1 Research Framework

Based on the review of literature, this study explores how gamified stimuli (challenges, points, and rewards) trigger impulse purchase intention through a sense of achievement, perceived enjoyment, and customer engagement, while also examining the moderating effect of consumers' level of involvement. The research hypotheses are depicted in Fig. 1.

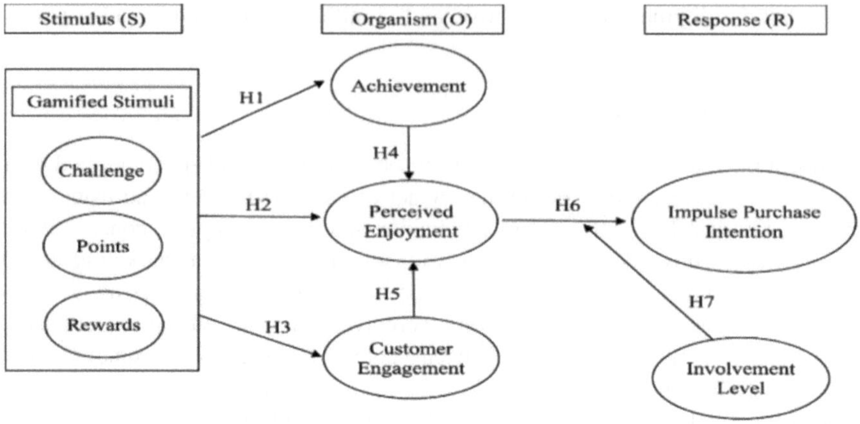

Fig. 1. Research Framework

3.2 Sample and Questionnaire

The participants in this study were Shopee users who had experience playing Shopee games. Data collection was conducted between October 1, 2024, and January 13, 2025. A total of 353 questionnaires were collected; after excluding 73 invalid responses (respondents who did not use Shopee or had never played Shopee games), 280 valid questionnaires remained for analysis. The research variables to be measured, in accordance with the research framework, are outlined as follows. Challenge refers to tasks or goals of a certain difficulty and appeal presented to customers. This variable is measured using a six-item scale adopted from Eckardt and Robra-Bissantz [6]. Points are utilized to track and evaluate customers' performance in these challenges. The measurement consists of three items, adapted and modified from Feng et al. [48]. Rewards serve as both incentives and compensation mechanisms, granted based on the points customers accumulate during challenges. To ensure greater internal consistency of the measurement, this study primarily adopts the scale from Codish and Ravid [49], supplemented by an additional item from Hsu, Chang, and Lee [50]. Customer engagement is defined as customers' participation in brand-related interactions and activities beyond mere purchasing behavior. This construct is measured using five items adapted from Vivek et al. [51]. Sense of achievement is defined as the psychological fulfillment derived from completing gamified tasks and achieving specific goals. This study employs a three-item scale developed by Fazal-e-Hasan et al. [52] to measure this variable. Perceived enjoyment refers to the extent to which an activity itself provides users with unexpected pleasure. In the context of e-commerce, it denotes the enjoyment consumers experience while using the platform. This variable is measured by three items adapted from Zhang, Shao, Li, and Feng [53]. Impulse purchase intention refers to the likelihood that a customer will make a spontaneous purchase. Impulse purchase occurs without deliberate consideration of the necessity or rationale behind the purchase. This construct is measured using four items adapted from Verhagen and Van Dolen [54]. All questionnaire items in this study were measured using a 5-point Likert scale. Involvement refers to the time and effort consumers expend in searching for and processing product-related information, which subsequently influences their selection of information categories and their purchase decision-making process. To differentiate between high and low involvement, this study utilizes the Personal Involvement Inventory developed by Zaichkowsky [45], which evaluates individual needs, values, and interests based on a 10-item semantic differential scale. However, given that semantic differential scales can be less intuitive for respondents, this study converted the scale into a 5-point Likert format. Additionally, the item phrasing was also refined to enhance comprehensibility and facilitate the response process.

4 Results and Analysis

4.1 Sample Characteristics

According to the sample demographic, Shopee users are predominantly female (57.9%) aged between 21–30 years old. Most of them have a college degree (62.5%) with an average monthly salary of less than NT$19,999 (58.6%), which aligns with the fact that most of the respondents were students (71.4%). Nearly one-third of the participants (29.6%) indicated a daily usage frequency for the Shopee platform, and half of the users spent less than 0.5 h per session (47.1%).

4.2 Reliability and Validity Analysis

According to Fornell and Larcker [55], the standardized estimated value for evaluating standardized factor loadings (λ) should be greater than 0.5. In terms of construct validity in this study, referring to Table 2, the factor loadings are all above 0.7, which is significantly higher than 0.5; therefore, no deletion is required. Cronbach's alpha values are all greater than 0.7, indicating that the questionnaire measurement items possess internal consistency and a high level of reliability. The composite reliability (CR) should be higher than 0.7, and the average variance extracted (AVE) of the latent variables must exceed 0.5 [55]. As shown in Table 1, the composite reliability (CR) ranges between 0.976 and 0.875, all of which are higher than the value of 0.7. In addition, the AVE values in this study range from 0.887 to 0.613, all exceeding 0.5, representing that the measurement scales adopted in this study have good convergent validity.

Table 1 . Reliability and Convergent Validity Analysis

Construct	Item	Factor loading	Cronbach's alpha	CR value	AVE value
Challenges	CH1	0.618	0.873	0.905	0.613
	CH2	0.739			
	CH3	0.803			
	CH4	0.689			
	CH5	0.743			

(continued)

Table 1 (*continued*)

Construct	Item	Factor loading	Cronbach's alpha	CR value	AVE value
	CH6	0.735			
Points	PO1	0.667	0.786	0.875	0.700
	PO2	0.684			
	PO3	0.743			
Rewards	RE1	0.763	0.876	0.915	0.730
	RE2	0.765			
	RE3	0.705			
	RE4	0.797			
Achievement	AC1	0.805	0.838	0.903	0.757
	AC2	0.914			
	AC3	0.888			
Customer engagement	CE1	0.949	0.936	0.959	0.887
	CE2	0.916			
	CE3	0.960			
Perceived enjoyment	EN1	0.927	0.925	0.953	0.870
	EN2	0.925			
	EN3	0.946			
Impulse purchase intention	IM1	0.838	0.850	0.899	0.689
	IM2	0.784			
	IM3	0.848			
	IM4	0.850			
Level of involvement	IN1	0.902	0.973	0.976	0.804
	IN2	0.888			
	IN3	0.900			
	IN4	0.906			
	IN5	0.888			
	IN6	0.918			
	IN7	0.902			
	IN8	0.874			
	IN9	0.897			
	IN10	0.888			

4.3 Discriminant Validity Analysis

Discriminant validity indicates that items from different constructs should have a low correlation with one another; that is, when measuring different traits using the same method, the correlation between them should be very low. As shown in Table 2, the square root of the AVE for each construct in this study is greater than the correlation coefficients between the constructs, indicating that each construct possesses a certain degree of discriminant validity. According to Fornell and Larcker [55], the correlation coefficient between two different constructs should be less than the square root of the average variance extracted (AVE) for each construct. Referring to the table below in this study, all constructs comply with the explanation, demonstrating that this study possesses robust discriminant validity.

Table 2. Discriminant Validity Analysis

	G	AC	EN	CE	IM	IN
G	**0.729**					
AC	0.797	**0.870**				
EN	0.781	0.870	**0.933**			
CE	0.656	0.823	0.794	**0.942**		
IM	0.557	0.613	0.591	0.556	**0.830**	
IN	0.749	0.852	0.838	0.879	0.571	**0.896**

Note: G = Gamified stimuli (challenges, points, rewards); AC = Achievement; EN = Perceived enjoyment; CE = Customer engagement; IM = Impulse purchase intention; IN = Level of Involvement

4.4 Collinearity Analysis

According to the criteria for judging collinearity problems proposed by Cohen et al. [56]: if the VIF value is ≥ 10, it is considered that a collinearity problem exists among the independent variables, and that independent variable should be deleted. Thus, this study uses VIF to conduct a collinearity test. The results of this study (Table 3) show that the VIF values are all less than 5, indicating that there are no concerns about collinearity among the constructs.

Table 3 Collinearity Analysis

	G	AC	EN	CE	IM	IN
G		1.000	2.747	1.000		
AC			4.839			
EN					3.602	

(continued)

Table 3 (*continued*)

	G	AC	EN	CE	IM	IN
CE			3.092			
IM						
IN					3.380	
IN x EN					1.152	

Note: G = Gamified stimuli (challenges, points, rewards); AC = Achievement; EN = Perceived enjoyment; CE = Customer engagement; IM = Impulse purchase intention; IN = Level of Involvement

4.5 Path Analysis

This study conducted bootstrapping method to repeat uniform sampling 5,000 times. The path analysis results are summarized in Table 4. According to Table 4, the paths from gamified stimuli to achievement, perceived enjoyment, and customer engagement are ($\beta = 0.797$, $t = 33.047$, $p < 0.001$), ($\beta = 0.241$, $t = 3.278$, $p < 0.05$), and ($\beta = 0.656$, $t = 16.149$, $p < 0.001$), respectively. Therefore, H1, H2, and H3 are supported. The path from achievement to perceived enjoyment is ($\beta = 0.478$, $t = 6.123$, $p < 0.001$), and from customer engagement to perceived enjoyment is ($\beta = 0.244$, $t = 4.242$, $p < 0.001$). Both H4 and H5 are supported. Furthermore, the path from perceived enjoyment to impulse purchase intention is ($\beta = 0.503$, $t = 4.192$, $p < 0.001$), Therefore, H6 supported.

Table 4 Path Analysis

Hypothesis	Path	Original sample (O)	Sample mean (M)	Standard deviation (STDEV)	T statistics (|O/STDEV|)	P values	Result
H1: G → AC		0.797	0.800	0.024	33.047	P < 0.001***	Support
H2: G → EN		0.241	0.241	0.073	3.278	P < 0.05**	Support
H3: G → CE		0.656	0.658	0.041	16.149	P < 0.001***	Support
H4: AC → EN		0.478	0.477	0.078	6.123	P < 0.001***	Support
H5: CE → EN		0.244	0.244	0.057	4.242	P < 0.001***	Support
H6: EN → IM		0.503	0.505	0.120	4.192	P < 0.001***	Support
H7: IN x EN → IM		0.246	0.246	0.054	4.548	P < 0.001***	Support

Note 1: ***: p<0.001 **: p<0.05 *: p<0.1

Note 2: G = Gamified stimuli (challenges, points, rewards); AC = Achievement; EN = Perceived enjoyment; CE = Customer engagement; IM = Impulse purchase intention; IN = Level of Involvement

4.6 Moderating Effect Analysis

According to the definition of moderating variables and their effects by Memon et al. [57], a moderating variable is also known as an interference variable and is considered an external variable. The moderating effect between an independent variable and a dependent variable is usually manifested as an interaction between the independent and moderating variables that influence the dependent variable. A prerequisite for a moderating effect to be established is that there must be a significant correlation between independent and dependent variables. A moderator is defined as a "variable that affects nature (e.g., magnitude and/or direction) of the influence of an antecedent variable on an outcome." Statistically, moderation means that the relationship between independent and dependent variables changes according to the value of the moderating variable [57].

If the path coefficient between "Perceived Enjoyment x Involvement" and "Impulse Purchase Intention" is significant, it indicates that the Involvement Level serves as a moderator in the process of how Perceived Enjoyment influences consumers' impulse purchase intention. Referring to Table 4, the path relationship between "Perceived Enjoyment x Involvement" and "Impulse Purchase Intention" is significant ($\beta = 0.246$, $t = 4.548$, $p < 0.001$***), confirming the existence of a moderating effect. Therefore, H7 supported. This aligns with this study's hypothesis that the consumer's level of involvement, as a moderating variable, has a positive moderating effect, strengthening the impact of perceived enjoyment on impulse purchase intention.

5 Discussion and Conclusion

The results of this study indicate that gamification stimuli have a positive impact on a sense of achievement. This finding is consistent with the perspective of Chen, Li, and Yang [58], which suggests that gamification stimuli can satisfy consumers' need for achievement and enhance shopping enjoyment. According to the definition by Lau, Lam, and Cheung [22], perceived enjoyment refers to the emotional rewards and intrinsic satisfaction consumers gain during the consumption process, which subsequently influence their feelings of fun and entertainment. Furthermore, gamification stimuli have a significant positive impact on customer engagement and can enhance perceived enjoyment, which aligns with the findings of Mulcahy, Russell-Bennett, and Iacobucci [59]. Related studies also indicate that gamification elements such as challenges, points, and rewards can effectively improve customer engagement [18, 35]. The results reveal that a sense of achievement has a positive effect on perceived enjoyment. This outcome is consistent with the gamified customer engagement experiential environment model proposed by [30], which notes that mechanisms like points and badges can elevate users' sense of achievement, thereby enhancing their enjoyment. Additionally, in a gaming context, the attainment of achievements can bring about satisfaction and pleasure [33].

Prior research indicates that players' insight and sustained engagement exert a positive influence on perceived enjoyment, encouraging deeper immersion in the gaming experience and increasing their willingness to invest time and effort in continued play [34]. Furthermore, Harwood and Garry [30] suggests that gamification serves as a strategic method to enhance interaction between businesses and customers; by positioning consumers as players, it stimulates engagement and triggers emotional resonance.

Within the context of gamified marketing, perceived enjoyment is positively influenced by customer engagement and has a significant positive impact on the online repurchase intention of Shopee Games users [37]. These findings align with the results of the present study. In addition, this study found that perceived enjoyment has a significant positive impact on impulse purchase intention. This result aligns with the research of Floh and Madlberger [40] and Huotari and Hamari [41], demonstrating that when consumers experience higher levels of entertainment and fun on e-commerce platforms, their impulse purchase intention increases significantly.

The findings of the present study indicate that the positive effect of perceived enjoyment on impulse purchase intention is positively moderated by consumers' level of involvement. According to Zaichkowsky [44], involvement refers to a person's perceived relevance of an object based on inherent needs, values, and interests. High-involvement products generally prompt consumers to invest more time in gathering information and carefully evaluating purchasing decisions; conversely, low-involvement products are more likely to be purchased intuitively [60]. Past studies have also noted a positive relationship between involvement and impulse purchase intention [62], and that in online shopping contexts, involvement strengthens the impact of perceived enjoyment on impulse purchase intention [47]. The results of this study present the same trend, showing that the higher the consumers' involvement with Shopee games, the stronger their impulse purchase intention.

There are some limitations to this study. First, this study focused exclusively on Shopee as a single research context for exploring e-commerce platform gamification. It is recommended that future research investigates the differences across different e-commerce platforms adopting e-commerce gamification stimuli or explore the differences across gamification when applied to different business categories and scenarios. Second, no cross-analysis was conducted between demographic data and the influence of gamification on impulse purchase intention. Future research could further examine different demographics such as whether gender, age, education, region, and income are affected by different gamification contexts. This would facilitate a better understanding of various customer segments, allowing for more precise gamification strategies to influence impulse purchase intention and enhance overall benefits. Third, consumers might repurchase products after participating in Shopee App games due to prior purchasing experiences. While this study explores the impact of gamification on impulse purchase intention, rewards and positive emotions from games may also stimulate purchases. Given that repurchase intention is a vital construct for evaluating continuous usage, future studies could incorporate "satisfaction" to investigate the impact of gamified stimuli on repurchase intention.

References

1. Sharma, W., Lim, W.M., Kumar, S., Verma, A., Kumra, R.: Game on! A state-of-the-art overview of doing business with gamification. Technol. Forecast. Soc. Chang. **198**, 122988 (2024)
2. Dwiviolita, S., Zuliarni, S.: Customer engagement, customer equity, and their influence on consumer repurchase intention in E-commerce mobile applications. JDM (Jurnal Dinamika Manajemen). **14**(1), 55–71 (2023)

3. Similar Web: (2023). https://www.similarweb.com/website/shopee.tw/
4. Hamari, J., Koivisto, J., Sarsa, H.: Does gamification work? --a literature review of empirical studies on gamification. In: 2014 47th Hawaii International Conference on System Sciences 3025–3034 IEEE (2014)
5. Koivisto, J., Hamari, J.: The rise of motivational information systems: a review of gamification research. Int. J. Inf. Manag. **45**, 191–210 (2019)
6. Eckardt, L., Robra-Bissantz, S.: Playtesting for a better gaming experience: importance of an iterative design process for educational games. In: PACIS 2018 Proceedings, p. 78 (2018)
7. Majuri, J., Koivisto, J., Hamari, J.: Gamification of education and learning: a review of empirical literature. In: Koivisto, J., Hamari, J. (eds.) Proceedings of the 2nd International GamiFIN Conference, GamiFIN 2018, vol. 2186, pp. 11–19 (2018)
8. Khaldi, A., Bouzidi, R., Nader, F.: Gamification of e-learning in higher education: a systematic literature review. Smart Learn. Environ. **10**(1), 10 (2023)
9. Xiao, Y., Hew, K.F.T.: Intangible rewards versus tangible rewards in gamified online learning: which promotes student intrinsic motivation, behavioural engagement, cognitive engagement and learning performance? Br. J. Educ. Technol. **55**(1), 297–317 (2023)
10. Cheng, Y.M.: What makes learners enhance learning outcomes in MOOCs? Exploring the roles of gamification and personalization. Interact. Technol. Smart Educ. **21**(2), 308–330 (2024)
11. Mehrabian, A., Russell, J.A.: A verbal measure of information rate for studies in environmental psychology. Environ. Behav. **6**(2), 233–252 (1974)
12. Chen, C.C., Yao, J.Y.: What drives impulse purchase behaviors in a mobile auction? The perspective of the stimulus-organism-response model. Telematics Inform. **35**(5), 1249–1262 (2018)
13. Tak, P., Gupta, M.: Examining travel mobile app attributes and its impact on consumer engagement: an application of SOR framework. J. Internet Commer. **20**(3), 293–318 (2021)
14. Oppong-Tawiah, D., Webster, J., Staples, S., Cameron, A.F., de Guinea, A.O., Hung, T.Y.: Developing a gamified mobile application to encourage sustainable energy use in the office. J. Bus. Res. **106**, 388–405 (2020)
15. Brunstein, J. C., & Heckhausen, H. Achievement motivation. In: Heckhausen, J., Heckhausen, H. (eds), Motivation and Action, (pp. 221–304), Springer, Cham (2018).
16. Galli, L., Fraternali, P., Bozzon, A.: On the application of game mechanics in information retrieval. In: Proceedings of the First International Workshop on Gamification for Information Retrieval, pp. 7–11 (2014)
17. Noor, N.M., Yusoff, F.H., Ismail, M., Yussof, R.L.: Adaptation of enjoyment in learning through gamification. Adv. Sci. Lett. **24**(2), 1455–1459 (2018)
18. Wanga, L., Zhaob, X.: Research on impact of work gamification on employee performance. Acad. J. Bus. Manag. **5**(26), 95–102 (2023)
19. Zhang, L., Shao, Z., Li, X., Feng, Y.: Gamification and online impulse purchase: the moderating effect of gender and age. Int. J. Inf. Manag. **61**, 102267 (2021)
20. Koivisto, J., Hamari, J.: Demographic differences in perceived benefits from gamification. Comput. Hum. Behav. **35**, 179–188 (2014)
21. Robson, K., Plangger, K., Kietzmann, J.H., McCarthy, I., Pitt, L.: Is it all a game? Understanding the principles of gamification. Bus. Horiz. **58**(4), 411–420 (2015)
22. Lau, M.M., Lam, A.Y., Cheung, R.: Examining the factors influencing purchase intention of smartphones in Hong Kong. Contemp. Manag. Res. **12**(2), 213–224 (2016)
23. Putz, L.M., Treiblmaier, H.: Gamified workshops as drivers for attitudinal and behavioral shifts toward sustainable business practices: the role of enjoyment, curiosity and external regulation. In: Proceedings of the 51st Hawaii International Conference On System Sciences (HICSS 2018), Hawaii, HI, USA, January 2–6, pp. 1197–1206 (2018)

24. Legaki, N.Z., Xi, N., Hamari, J., Karpouzis, K., Assimakopoulos, V.: The effect of challenge-based gamification on learning: an experiment in the context of statistics education. Int. J. Hum.-Comput. Stud. **144**, 102496 (2020)
25. Van Doorn, J. et al.: Customer engagement behavior: theoretical foundations and research directions. J. Serv. Res. **13**(3), 253–266 (2010)
26. Hsu, C.L.: Enhancing brand love, customer engagement, brand experience, and repurchase intention: focusing on the role of gamification in mobile apps. Decis. Support. Syst. **174**, 114020 (2023)
27. Lo, C.K., Hew, K.F.: A comparison of flipped learning with gamification, traditional learning, and online independent study: the effects on students' mathematics achievement and cognitive engagement. Interact. Learn. Environ. **28**(4), 464–481 (2020)
28. Bai, S., Gonda, D.E., Hew, K.F.: Effects of tangible rewards on student learning performance, knowledge construction, and perception in fully online gamified learning. In: 2021 IEEE International Conference on Engineering, Technology & Education (TALE), pp. 899–904 (2021)
29. Chen, L., Baird, A., Straub, D.: The impact of hierarchical privilege levels and non-hierarchical incentives on continued contribution in online Q & A communities: a motivational model of gamification goals. Decis. Support. Syst. **153**, 113667 (2022)
30. Harwood, T., Garry, T.: An investigation into gamification as a customer engagement experience environment. J. Serv. Mark. **29**(6/7), 533–546 (2015)
31. Putwain, D.W., Becker, S., Symes, W., Pekrun, R.: Reciprocal relations between students' academic enjoyment, boredom, and achievement over time. Learn. Instr. **54**, 73–81 (2018)
32. Lazarides, R., Buchholz, J.: Student-perceived teaching quality: how is it related to different achievement emotions in mathematics classrooms? Learn. Instr. **61**, 45–59 (2019)
33. Ghazali, E., Mutum, D.S., Woon, M.Y.: Exploring player behavior and motivations to continue playing Pokémon GO. Inf. Technol. People. **32**(3), 646–667 (2019)
34. Lyons, E.J., Tate, D.F., Ward, D.S., Ribisl, K.M., Bowling, J.M., Kalyanaraman, S.: Engagement, enjoyment, and energy expenditure during active video game play. Health Psychol. **33**(2), 174–181 (2014)
35. Darejeh, A., Salim, S.S.: Gamification solutions to enhance software user engagement—A systematic review. Int. J. Hum.-Comput. Interact. **32**(8), 613–642 (2016)
36. Huang, C.-K., Chen, C.-D., Liu, Y.-T.: To stay or not to stay? Discontinuance intention of gamification apps. Inf. Technol. People. **32**(6), 1423–1445 (2019)
37. Almaudina, M., Ramdan, A.M., Jhoansyah, D., Deli, M.M.: The effectiveness of perceived enjoyment and brand engagement in correlating gamification marketing with online repurchase intention in Shopee game users. Int. J. Econ. Dev. Res. (IJEDR). **4**(1), 222–235 (2023)
38. Stern, H.: The significance of impulse purchase today. J. Mark. **26**(2), 59–62 (1962)
39. Parboteeah, D.V., Valacich, J.S., Wells, J.D.: The influence of website characteristics on a consumer's urge to buy impulsively. Inf. Syst. Res. **20**(1), 60–78 (2009)
40. Floh, A., Madlberger, M.: The role of atmospheric cues in online impulse-purchase behavior. Electron. Commer. Res. Appl. **12**(6), 425–439 (2013)
41. Huotari, K., Hamari, J.: A definition for gamification: anchoring gamification in the service marketing literature. Electron. Mark. **27**(1), 21–31 (2017)
42. Gaoa, L., Zhaob, X.: The impact of gamification of m-commerce platforms on users' impulse purchase behavior. Acad. J. Bus. Manag. **5**(24), 28–35 (2023)
43. Krugman, H.E.: The impact of television advertising: learning without involvement. Public Opin. Q. **29**(3), 349–356 (1965)
44. Zaichkowsky, J.L.: Measuring the involvement construct. J. Consum. Res. **12**(3), 341–352 (1985)

45. Zaichkowsky, J.L.: The personal involvement inventory: reduction, revision, and application to advertising. J. Advert. **23**(4), 59–70 (1994)
46. Li, T., Chen, Y.: Will virtual reality be a double-edged sword? Exploring the moderation effects of the expected enjoyment of a destination on travel intention. J. Destin. Mark. Manag. **12**, 15–26 (2019)
47. Yastuti, A.W., Irawati, Z.: The influence of hedonic shopping motivation, involvement, and sales promotion on impulse purchase in E-commerce shopee. Int. J. Curr. Sci. Res. Rev. **6**(12), 8652–8659 (2023)
48. Feng, Y., Ye, H.J., Yu, Y., Yang, C., Cui, T.: Gamification artifacts and crowdsourcing participation: examining the mediating role of intrinsic motivations. Comput. Hum. Behav. **81**, 124–136 (2018)
49. Codish, D., Ravid, G.: Personality based gamification-educational gamification for extroverts and introverts. In: Proceedings of the 9th CHAIS Conference for the Study of Innovation and Learning Technologies: Learning in the Technological Era, vol. 1, pp. 36–44 (2014)
50. Hsu, S.H., Chang, J.W., Lee, C.C.: Designing attractive gamification features for collaborative storytelling websites. Cyberpsychol. Behav. Soc. Netw. **16**(6), 428–435 (2013)
51. Vivek, S.D., Beatty, S.E., Dalela, V., Morgan, R.M.: A generalized multidimensional scale for measuring customer engagement. J. Mark. Theory Pract. **22**(4), 401–420 (2014)
52. Fazal-e-Hasan, S.M., Ahmadi, H., Mortimer, G., Grimmer, M., Kelly, L.: Examining the role of consumer hope in explaining the impact of perceived brand value on customer–brand relationship outcomes in an online retailing environment. J. Retail. Consum. Serv. **41**, 101–111 (2018)
53. Zhang, L., Shao, Z., Li, X., Feng, Y.: Gamification and online impulse buying: the moderating effect of gender and age. Int. J. Inf. Manag. **61**, 102267 (2021)
54. Verhagen, T., Van Dolen, W.: The influence of online store beliefs on consumer online impulse purchase: a model and empirical application. Inf. Manag. **48**(8), 320–327 (2011)
55. Fornell, C., Larcker, D.F.: Evaluating structural equation models with unobservable variables and measurement error. J. Mark. Res. **18**(1), 39–50 (1981)
56. Cohen, J., Cohen, P., West, S.G., Aiken, L.S.: Applied Multiple Regression/Correlation Analysis for Behavioral Sciences, 3th edn. Lawrence Erlbaum Associates, Hillsdale, NJ (2003)
57. Memon, M.A., Cheah, J.H., Ramayah, T., Ting, H., Chuah, F., Cham, T.H.: Moderation analysis: issues and guidelines. J. Appl. Struct. Equation Modeling. **3**(1), 1–11 (2019)
58. Chen, Y., Li, Y., Yang, Y.: Achievement gamification affordances in E-commerce platforms: an empirical study involving online shopping festival. In: Li, E.Y., et al. (eds.) Proceedings of the International Conference on Electronic Business, 24, 9–22. ICEB'24, Zhuhai, China, October 24–28 (2024)
59. Mulcahy, R., Russell-Bennett, R., Iacobucci, D.: Designing gamified apps for sustainable consumption: a field study. J. Bus. Res. **106**, 377–387 (2020)
60. Cengiz, H.: Effect of the need for popularity on purchase decision involvement and impulse-purchase behavior concerning fashion clothing. J. Glob. Fash. Market. **8**(2), 113–124 (2017)

Key Success Factors and Management Strategies in the Outsourced Marketing of Industrial Land

Li-Chuan Ho[1], Ren-Fang Chao[2(✉)], Han-Yee Leong[2], and Liang-Chien Lee[3]

[1] Department of Information Engineering, I-Shou University, Kaohsiung, Taiwan, China
[2] Postgraduate Programs in Management, I-Shou University, Kaohsiung, Taiwan, China
rfchao@cloud.isu.edu.tw
[3] Department of Finance, I-Shou University, Kaohsiung, Taiwan, China

Abstract. Industrial land is a critical resource for industrial development and regional economic growth, yet its core issue lies not only in land supply but also in the efficiency of supply–demand matching. This study examines the outsourced marketing of industrial land in Taiwan by exploring the challenges of supply–demand matching, the factors contributing to successful sales, and specific outsourced marketing strategies. Drawing on agency theory, this study adopts a qualitative approach and conducts in-depth interviews with 10 experts from the public sector, industry, and academia. The findings show that the major challenges in industrial land matching include information opacity, price gaps, and mismatches between land conditions and actual industrial needs. Successful sales depend on transparent land information, reasonable pricing, and appropriate location and supporting conditions. In addition, effective outsourced marketing requires a comprehensive land inventory, proactive investment promotion and demand collection, as well as integrated supporting services. Overall, the results suggest that outsourced marketing of industrial land should move beyond simple land promotion toward information development, precise matching, and coordinated services. The study provides practical insights for government agencies and practitioners seeking to improve the efficiency and effectiveness of industrial land matching.

Keywords: Industrial Land · Outsourced Marketing · Agency Theory · Supply–Demand Matching · Qualitative Research

1 Introduction

Industrial land is a critical foundational resource for industrial development and regional economic growth. Its supply and allocation efficiency significantly affect firm investment, industrial location decisions, and local development [1]. However, industrial land is not an ordinary transaction object in the land market; rather, it is a special asset that serves functions of industrial allocation, policy regulation, and spatial governance. Therefore, issues related to industrial land concern not only the amount of land supply, but also whether land allocation can meet industrial needs and development priorities.

In practice, the core issue of industrial land lies not only in land shortages, but also in whether supply and demand can be effectively matched. Taiwan's industrial land market

D. Liberona et al. (Eds.): MISNC 2026, CCIS 3092, pp. 322–333, 2027.
https://doi.org/10.1007/978-3-032-33381-0_24

often faces problems such as land hoarding, differences in price perceptions, mismatches between location and firms' needs, and outdated or insufficient public facilities in some industrial parks, all of which reduce land use efficiency and affect firms' willingness to invest and establish plants [2]. In addition, when industrial land transactions are simultaneously shaped by policy regulation, information disclosure, and risk assessment, the existence of land supply does not necessarily guarantee successful allocation or transactions.

Under these circumstances, industrial land promotion and matching in recent years have gradually incorporated outsourced marketing and professional brokerage mechanisms to improve matching efficiency between supply and demand [3]. This development suggests that industrial land management is no longer merely a matter of land supply, but also involves information integration, marketing promotion, and multi-party coordination [4]. However, existing studies have largely focused on the policy functions of industrial land, supply–demand imbalance, and pricing issues, while providing limited discussion of the conditions that facilitate successful sales and the specific matching strategies that can be adopted under outsourced marketing arrangements.

Accordingly, this study focuses on outsourced marketing of industrial land in Taiwan. It examines the challenges faced in industrial land supply–demand matching, analyzes the factors contributing to successful industrial land sales, and further proposes specific and feasible outsourced marketing strategies as references for government agencies and practitioners involved in industrial land matching.

2 Literature Review

2.1 The Meaning of Industrial Land and Supply–Demand Issues

Industrial land refers to developed land designated for industrial production and related technical and supporting facilities, including manufacturing plants, mining facilities, energy facilities, and logistics and warehousing bases [5]. It is generally treated as a distinct land-use category, alongside residential, commercial, green space, and other special-use land [6]. Compared with ordinary land transactions, industrial land is closely tied to industrial activities and involves the needs of manufacturing, mining, energy, and machinery processing industries [5]. It is often located on the urban fringe or in suburban areas and is frequently converted from farmland or other types of developed land [6]. In addition, because the use of industrial land may involve emissions, carbon output, and PM2.5-related environmental impacts, it is also an important subject of spatial planning and environmental governance [7].

Industrial land is not merely an object of land sale, but an important policy instrument that serves both industrial allocation and urban governance functions. Li and Li [8] noted that local governments may adjust industrial land prices and supply to attract specific industries or restrain highly polluting and inefficient industries. Dai et al. [9] further argued that industrial land management involves a life-cycle process, including acquisition, development, use, expiration, and recovery, indicating that it is not a one-time transaction but part of long-term governance. In addition, when environmental regulations or low-carbon city policies become stricter, governments may reduce the supply of industrial land or raise land prices to encourage industrial upgrading and emissions reduction [10]. Therefore, the allocation and transaction of industrial land involve not only price, but also industrial policy, environmental governance, and long-term development considerations.

Supply–demand issues in industrial land are not simply market gaps, but are closely related to government-led supply and pricing mechanisms. Because governments are often the primary suppliers of industrial land, they can directly influence land prices through supply volume and reserve prices [11]. Under an investment-promotion orientation, local governments often release land at low or subsidized prices, which keeps industrial land prices persistently low, leading not only to misallocation of land resources but also making it easier for inefficient or highly polluting industries to obtain land [12]. Moreover, insufficient disclosure of industrial land transaction information further widens gaps in price perceptions and transaction conditions [13].

In sum, industrial land issues should not be understood solely in terms of the quantity of supply, but rather in terms of the efficiency of supply–demand matching. Because industrial land has functions of industrial allocation, life-cycle management, and environmental governance, its transaction and allocation outcomes are often shaped simultaneously by policy intervention, pricing mechanisms, and the degree of information disclosure [9]. When price distortion and information asymmetry exist in the market, land supply alone does not guarantee successful transactions, as mismatched demand, differences in price perceptions, and difficulties in risk assessment may still hinder effective deals [11]. Therefore, the core issue of industrial land lies not only in whether land is available, but also in how to improve the matching efficiency and allocation quality between supply and demand.

2.2 Outsourced Marketing of Industrial Land and the Role of Brokers from an Agency Theory Perspective

In the process of matching industrial land supply and demand, outsourced marketing may arise when principals are unable to complete transactions and allocation on their own, and this situation can be explained through agency theory. Agency theory mainly examines agency problems that arise between principals and agents due to goal incongruence, information asymmetry, and differences in risk preferences [14]. Eisenhardt [14] further pointed out that when principals delegate tasks or decision-making authority to agents, differences in interests may create monitoring difficulties and efficiency losses. Salman [15] argued that principals typically rely on contracts and compensation mechanisms to engage agents to provide services, but agency costs arise when agents do not act fully in the principals' interests. Thus, the core concern of agency theory is how to reduce risks and losses in agency relationships through contractual arrangements and monitoring mechanisms.

Within this framework, agents often possess more market information than principals, which easily creates information gaps. In real estate and industrial land transactions, brokers are usually more familiar with market prices, buyer demand, negotiation strategies, location conditions, pollution risks, and future development plans, giving them a relative advantage in pricing and bargaining [16]. Su et al. [17] noted that when agents use this informational advantage to obtain additional benefits, information rent may arise. At the same time, because principals cannot fully observe agents' effort and integrity, they often incur additional monitoring costs, such as auditing, appraisal, legal consultation, and information disclosure, which in turn become agency costs [18].

Beyond informational advantages, brokers in agency relationships are not merely transaction intermediaries, but also play roles in information integration and communication coordination. Zhou [19] noted that agents typically possess professional knowledge, local market information, and business networks, enabling them to help principals search for, screen, and evaluate transaction counterparts while reducing information collection costs. In land and real estate markets, brokers are also regarded as key intermediaries who facilitate transactions and shorten negotiation time [20]. In addition, Kauppi et al. [21] argued that when both parties have incomplete information, agents also help clarify needs, translate expectations, and maintain ongoing communication in order to reduce misunderstanding and gaps. Through their interpersonal networks and trust-based relationships, brokers can also connect market actors who were previously unacquainted, thereby further promoting transactions and resource flows [22].

Therefore, the demand for outsourced marketing in industrial land arises mainly because such transactions involve highly specialized information, complex condition assessment, and multi-party coordination, making it difficult for principals to achieve effective matching on their own [16]. In this context, brokers not only facilitate transactions and shorten negotiation time through their market knowledge and network resources, but also help clarify needs and reduce communication gaps, serving as an important bridge between principals and the market [21]. However, agents' informational advantages may also generate information rent, monitoring difficulties, and agency costs [18]. Accordingly, the significance of agency theory lies in its ability not only to explain why industrial land requires outsourced marketing and professional brokerage, but also to provide a theoretical basis for analyzing information asymmetry, role division, and governance mechanisms between principals and agents.

2.3 Summary

In summary, industrial land is not an ordinary object of land transactions, but a special asset that combines functions of industrial allocation, life-cycle management, and environmental governance [9]. For this reason, its transaction and allocation are shaped not only by the quantity of supply, but also by multiple factors such as price formation, policy regulation, information disclosure, location conditions, and risk assessment [11]. Therefore, the core issue facing industrial land is not simply whether land is available, but whether supply and demand can be effectively matched under conditions of information asymmetry and complex transaction requirements, which in turn affects allocation efficiency and transaction quality [13].

Within this context, agency theory provides an important theoretical basis for explaining outsourced relationships in industrial land marketing. Because industrial land transactions involve price judgment, demand identification, risk assessment, and cross-party coordination, principals often need to rely on agents with professional knowledge and market information to facilitate matching [16]. However, when agents possess more information, information rent, monitoring difficulties, and agency costs may arise, making outsourced marketing not only a matter of functional division of labor but also one of governance and control [18]. Thus, the value of agency theory lies in its ability to explain both why industrial land requires outsourced marketing and how principals and agents can improve matching efficiency and reduce agency risk through contracts, monitoring, and role division.

Overall, prior studies have mainly focused on the policy functions of industrial land, supply-demand imbalance, price distortion, and information asymmetry, while using agency theory to explain information gaps, monitoring costs, and brokerage functions between principals and agents [15]. However, under the context of outsourced marketing of industrial land, there remains limited discussion of the conditions that contribute to successful sales and the specific matching strategies that can be adopted in practice, especially from an integrated perspective that includes government, industry, and academia [20]. Accordingly, this study adopts a qualitative interview approach to further examine the challenges of industrial land supply–demand matching, the factors contributing to successful industrial land sales, and the specific strategies for outsourced marketing.

3 Research Methods

3.1 Research Design

This study adopted a qualitative approach and used in-depth interviews as the primary research method. Because industrial land is not merely a land transaction issue, but a complex topic involving industrial allocation, policy regulation, information integration, and multi-party coordination, secondary data alone are insufficient to fully capture the actual operation of supply–demand matching and outsourced marketing. Therefore, this study first established an analytical foundation through a literature review of industrial land supply–demand issues and agency theory, and then collected the views of experts from the public sector, industry, and academia through in-depth interviews. This approach was used to further examine the challenges of industrial land supply–demand matching, the factors contributing to successful sales, and feasible outsourced marketing strategies. This research design helps provide a deeper understanding of the operational context and implementation conditions of outsourced industrial land marketing from multiple practical and policy perspectives.

3.2 Interview Participants

This study employed purposive sampling to select interview participants with practical or professional experience in industrial land, industrial park management, investment promotion and matching, and industrial development. A total of 10 participants were interviewed (Table 1), including personnel from the public sector, industrial park management, industrial associations, consulting firms, and academia, in order to gather perspectives from government, industry, and academia. In terms of participant background, public sector participants included officials responsible for urban development and economic development in local government; industry practitioners included representatives of industrial associations, managers of industrial park service centers, and heads of consulting firms; and academic participants included scholars in public policy and related fields. This arrangement made it possible to examine the implementation conditions and practical issues of outsourced industrial land marketing from the perspectives of policy, management, and market practice. To protect participants' privacy and maintain research ethics, participant identities were anonymized using codes in the presentation of the findings.

Table 1. Interviewer

Category	Code	Professional background
Public sector	PS1	Professional experience in urban planning and local government urban development administration.
	PS2	Professional experience in urban development administration and architectural engineering practice.
	PS3	Professional experience in industrial guidance and industrial land administration.
Industry practitioners	IS1	Professional experience in industrial association services and enterprise advisory work.
	IS2	Professional experience in industrial park management and park service administration.
	IS3	Professional experience in environmental protection and operational management in industrial parks.
	IS4	Professional experience in urban planning and land development consulting.
	IS5	Professional experience in real estate investment and management consulting.
Academic sector	AS1	Academic experience in urban and regional planning research.
	AS2	Academic and professional experience in public policy, urban planning, and government practice.

3.3 Procedure

This study used semi-structured in-depth interviews as the primary method of data collection. The researcher first developed an interview guide based on the research objectives, focusing on the challenges of industrial land supply–demand matching, the factors contributing to successful sales, and specific outsourced marketing strategies. Before each formal interview, the researcher explained the study purpose and interview content to the participant, and the interview was conducted and audio-recorded after consent was obtained. Interviews were conducted one-on-one. Guided by the interview protocol, the researcher invited participants to share their practical experience and views, and follow-up questions were asked when appropriate to obtain more complete information. After the interviews, the audio recordings were transcribed into verbatim transcripts or interview records for subsequent analysis.

4 Results and Analysis

4.1 Challenges in Matching Industrial Land Supply and Demand

Difficulties in matching industrial land supply and demand stem first from a lack of information transparency and insufficient disclosure of relevant conditions. Participants generally noted that land is not entirely unavailable in the market; rather, information is fragmented, and restrictions on land use, eligible industrial categories, and supporting conditions are not always clearly presented, making it difficult for firms seeking sites for plant establishment to quickly identify suitable properties.

> *"There is willingness to establish a plant, but no suitable land can be found; meanwhile, idle industrial land is not being fully utilized."(PS2)*

Second, differences in price perceptions and land hoarding are also major barriers. Some participants pointed out that landowners often adopt a land-banking or holdout mentality, making it difficult for industrial land to return to firms with actual production needs. Even when land is available on the market, transactions are often delayed because buyers and sellers cannot reach agreement on price.

> *"Buyers and sellers fail to reach a consensus on price, which leads to land being held and makes it difficult to sell." (IS3)*

This suggests that pricing is not simply a matter of high versus low prices; it also involves landowners' attitudes, transaction expectations, and imbalances in market mechanisms, all of which further widen the gap between supply and demand.

Finally, whether industrial land can be successfully matched is also closely tied to location conditions, public facilities, and regulatory constraints. Participants emphasized that transportation access, labor supply, wastewater discharge, environmental requirements, and surrounding support conditions all directly influence firms' willingness to establish plants. If the characteristics of the land do not fit industrial needs, even a reasonable price may not lead to a successful transaction.

> *"For a new plant, there are issues of land price, transportation convenience, labor supply, wastewater discharge, and environmental protection, so it is full of difficulties." (PS2)*

Overall, the challenges of matching industrial land supply and demand are multifaceted. The core issue lies not simply in whether land is available, but in whether information, price, and land conditions can be effectively aligned with actual demand.

4.2 Key Success Factors for Industrial Land Sales

The primary factor contributing to successful industrial land sales is the establishment of complete and transparent supply-and-demand information. Participants generally believed that clearly disclosing land information, the types of industries eligible to locate there, and relevant restrictions would help potential buyers quickly identify suitable sites and reduce perception gaps during the matching process.

"The key factors for successfully selling industrial land are still supply and demand, and the supply system (information) needs to be more accurate and transparent so that demand-side users can more quickly screen the land they need." (PS2)

Second, a reasonable land price is also an important factor affecting successful sales. Several participants pointed out that acquiring industrial land involves substantial costs, and excessively high prices directly reduce firms' willingness to purchase land. Therefore, under market-based conditions, offering an appropriate price is more likely to create a real incentive for investment.

"The key factor in successful industrial land sales or matching is still 'price.'" (PS3)

Finally, participants also noted that if the problem of illegal factory construction on agricultural land persists, it will weaken firms' willingness to enter legally designated industrial parks and, in turn, affect industrial land sales performance. In other words, successful industrial land sales cannot be determined by a single factor, but rather result from the combined effects of information, price, and institutional conditions.

4.3 Specific Strategies for Outsourced Marketing of Industrial Land

According to the interview results, the primary strategy for outsourced marketing of industrial land is to establish a comprehensive land inventory and matching database. Participants generally believed that first identifying idle or hoarded land would facilitate the implementation of subsequent matching mechanisms and improve the precision of supply–demand matching.

"With a more specific and complete land inventory, the matching mechanism can be implemented more effectively, and the matching success rate will also be higher." (PS1)

Second, outsourced marketing should also be accompanied by proactive promotion and demand collection. Participants indicated that holding information sessions, sending land information to potential buyers, and conducting continuous site visits not only strengthen contact with potential buyers, but also help identify firms' actual needs and further develop more targeted investment promotion strategies.

"Factory visits are a very good way to reach customers. First, they help us understand the actual production and operating conditions of factories; second, they allow us to evaluate potential incoming firms and further build a more complete demand list." (PS3)

Finally, participants also believed that if outsourced marketing is to truly improve outcomes, it must be accompanied by complete supporting measures and integrated services, including solutions to the "five shortages," transportation services, environmental and soil contamination assistance, financing services, and community communication.

"Industrial land cannot simply be put on the market and left there; the location conditions and facilities of the land need to be improved." (AS2)

"Good communication with local residents and communities is needed to resolve unnecessary protests and disputes." (AS1)

Overall, outsourced marketing of industrial land is not merely about promoting land; it is a systematic approach that combines information development, proactive investment promotion, and integrated services.

5 Conclusion

This study focused on the outsourced marketing of industrial land in Taiwan and used qualitative interviews to examine the challenges of industrial land supply–demand matching, the factors contributing to successful sales, and feasible outsourced marketing strategies. The findings show that the core issue of industrial land is not simply insufficient supply. As prior studies have noted, industrial land itself serves functions of industrial allocation, policy regulation, and spatial governance, and its allocation and transaction are therefore shaped simultaneously by pricing mechanisms, information disclosure, and institutional conditions [9]. This study further found that, in practice, lack of information transparency, price gaps, and mismatches between location and supporting conditions on the one hand and actual demand on the other are key barriers that reduce the efficiency of industrial land matching. This finding is also consistent with the view that industrial land transactions are often affected by information asymmetry and the complexity of transaction conditions [13].

In addition, this study found that successful industrial land sales depend not only on complete and transparent land information, reasonable pricing, and appropriate location conditions, but also on outsourced marketing mechanisms that integrate investment promotion, demand collection, and supporting services. This result corresponds to agency theory, which emphasizes information gaps, role division, and governance needs between principals and agents [15]. In other words, outsourced marketing of industrial land should not remain limited to land promotion, but should move toward information development, precise matching, and integrated services. Brokers, therefore, are not merely transaction intermediaries, but also key actors in information integration, demand translation, and coordination and communication [20]. Overall, this study not only adds to practical understanding of outsourced marketing in the context of industrial land, but also provides a useful reference for government agencies and related practitioners seeking to improve industrial land matching.

5.1 Practical Implications

The practical implication of this study is that the effectiveness of industrial land matching depends not only on land supply itself, but also on information disclosure, reasonable pricing, location conditions, and the operation of outsourced marketing mechanisms. First, relevant government agencies should strengthen the integration and disclosure of industrial land information by establishing a complete and regularly updated land inventory, along with information on use conditions and restrictions, in order to reduce information asymmetry between supply and demand and improve matching efficiency [13]. Second, outsourced marketing units should not serve merely as passive promoters, but should assist principals through proactive investment promotion, demand collection, condition assessment, and communication and coordination in order to improve matching accuracy and the likelihood of successful transactions [19].

From the perspective of agency theory, the key to outsourced marketing of industrial land lies not only in assigning matching tasks to professional brokers, but also in reducing information gaps and agency costs between principals and agents through information disclosure, performance management, and role division [15]. Therefore, when introducing outsourced marketing mechanisms, government or administrative agencies should value not only brokers' market expertise and network resources, but also establish clear service scopes, reporting mechanisms, and performance evaluation standards in order to improve the efficiency and allocation outcomes of industrial land matching.

5.2 Limitations and Future Research

This study has several limitations. First, because it employed qualitative in-depth interviews, its purpose was to understand the contextual background and practical experience of outsourced marketing of industrial land. Therefore, the findings are more appropriately interpreted in terms of transferability rather than statistical generalization; that is, their applicability should be further assessed across different regions, institutional settings, and industrial conditions [23]. Accordingly, future research may expand the scope of inquiry by including different regions, different types of industrial parks, and a broader range of stakeholders in order to enhance the transferability and comparability of the findings.

Second, although the interview participants included experts from government, industry, and academia, the sample size remained limited. In qualitative research, sample adequacy and data saturation are themselves dependent on context and researcher judgment, so the findings may still be influenced by participants' experience and differences in research settings [24]. Future studies may therefore combine qualitative interviews with quantitative surveys or mixed-methods designs to further examine the challenges of industrial land supply–demand matching, the factors contributing to successful sales, and the outsourced marketing strategies identified in this study, thereby strengthening the stability and explanatory power of the findings.

In addition, outsourced marketing of industrial land is embedded in highly policy-driven, institutional, and market-specific contexts, and the analytical process may also be influenced by researcher interpretation and methodological choices [25]. To address this limitation, future research may further strengthen reflexivity, transparent reporting, and methodological rigor in order to improve the credibility and auditability of the findings.

References

1. Tian, Y., Zhou, D., Jiang, G.: A new quality management system of admittance indicators to improve industrial land use efficiency in the Beijing-Tianjin-Hebei region. Land Use Policy. **107**, 105456 (2021). https://doi.org/10.1016/j.landusepol.2021.105456

2. Zhang, C., Yao, D., Zhen, Y., Li, W., Li, K.: Mismatched relationship between urban industrial land consumption and growth of manufacturing: evidence from the Yangtze River Delta. Land. **11**(9), 1390 (2022). https://doi.org/10.3390/land11091390
3. Yang, Y., Xue, R., Zhang, X., Cheng, Y., Shan, Y.: Can the marketization of urban land transfer improve energy efficiency? J. Environ. Manag. **329**, 117126 (2023). https://doi.org/10.1016/j.jenvman.2022.117126
4. Qi, Y., Zhao, Y., Guo, J., Wang, Y.: Identification and redevelopment of inefficient industrial land in resource-exhausted cities: a case study of Hegang, China. Land. **14**(6), 1292 (2025). https://doi.org/10.3390/land14061292
5. Dai, P., Sheng, R., Miao, Z., Chen, Z., Zhou, Y.: Analysis of spatial-temporal characteristics of industrial land supply scale in relation to industrial structure in China. Land. **10**(11), 1272 (2021). https://doi.org/10.3390/land10111272
6. Zeng, L., Wang, Y., Deng, Y.: How land transactions affect carbon emissions: evidence from China. Land. **11**(5), 751 (2022). https://doi.org/10.3390/land11050751
7. Liu, Q., Huang, W., Wu, S., Tian, L., Ren, H.: A study of the impact of industrial land development on PM2.5 concentrations in China. Sustainability. **17**(12), 5327 (2025). https://doi.org/10.3390/su17125327
8. Li, K., Li, K.: Government intervention in land markets: the role of industrial policies in shaping land use costs. Aust. Econ. Pap. **64**(2), 267–278 (2025). https://doi.org/10.1111/1467-8454.12391
9. Dai, B., Gu, X., Xie, B.: Policy framework and mechanism of life cycle management of industrial land (LCMIL) in China. Land Use Policy. **99**, 104997 (2020). https://doi.org/10.1016/j.landusepol.2020.104997
10. Yu, H., Zheng, C.: Environmental regulation, land use efficiency and industrial structure upgrading: test analysis based on spatial Durbin model and threshold effect. Heliyon. **10**(5), e26508 (2024). https://doi.org/10.1016/j.heliyon.2024.e26508
11. Tu, F., Zou, S., Hu, S., Zhang, S.: Land marketization, secondary land market, and effects on industrial land price. Int. J. Strateg. Prop. Manag. **26**(4), 272–286 (2022). https://doi.org/10.3846/ijspm.2022.17587
12. Huang, Z., Li, H., Song, M., Ma, L.: Intersecting sustainability and governance: the impact of industrial land price distortion on carbon emission efficiency in China. Appl. Geogr. **176**, 103510 (2025). https://doi.org/10.1016/j.apgeog.2025.103510
13. Seifert, S., Kahle, C., Hüttel, S.: Price dispersion in farmland markets: what is the role of asymmetric information? Am. J. Agric. Econ. **103**(4), 1545–1568 (2021). https://doi.org/10.1111/ajae.12153
14. Eisenhardt, K.M.: Agency theory: an assessment and review. Acad. Manag. Rev. **14**(1), 57–74 (1989). https://doi.org/10.5465/amr.1989.4279003
15. Salman, K.R.: Exploring moral hazard and adverse selection in profit sharing contract. Int. J. Prof. Bus. Rev. **8**(3), 7 (2023). https://doi.org/10.26668/businessreview/2023.v8i3.955
16. Ling, D.C., Naranjo, A., Petrova, M.T.: Search costs, behavioral biases, and information intermediary effects. J. Real Estate Finance Econ. **57**(1), 114–151 (2018). https://doi.org/10.1007/s11146-016-9582-z
17. Su, P., Peng, Y., Hu, Q., Tan, R.: Incentive mechanism and subsidy design for construction and demolition waste recycling under information asymmetry with reciprocal behaviors. Int. J. Environ. Res. Public Health. **17**(12), 4346 (2020). https://doi.org/10.3390/ijerph17124346
18. Homburg, C., Vomberg, A., Muehlhaeuser, S.: Design and governance of multichannel sales systems: financial performance consequences in business-to-business markets. J. Mark. Res. **57**(6), 1113–1134 (2020). https://doi.org/10.1177/0022243720929676
19. Zhou, X.: Principal-agent relationship and agency problem. Adv. Econ. Manag. Polit. Sci. **34**(1), 74–82 (2023). https://doi.org/10.54254/2754-1169/34/20231678

20. Roy, V.N.: Part-time brokers in financialised rural land markets: processes, typology and implications. Rev. Dev. Change. **25**(1), 70–88 (2020). https://doi.org/10.1177/0972266120927711
21. Kauppi, K., Brandon-Jones, A., van Raaij, E.M., Matinheikki, J.: "If only we'd known": theory of supply failure under two-sided information asymmetry. J. Supply Chain Manag. **60**(1), 32–52 (2024). https://doi.org/10.1111/jscm.12312
22. Kwon, S.W., Rondi, E., Levin, D.Z., De Massis, A., Brass, D.J.: Network brokerage: an integrative review and future research agenda. J. Manag. **46**(6), 1092–1120 (2020). https://doi.org/10.1177/0149206320914694
23. Drisko, J.W.: Transferability and generalization in qualitative research. Res. Soc. Work. Pract. **35**(1), 102–110 (2025). https://doi.org/10.1177/10497315241256560
24. Rahimi, S.: Saturation in qualitative research: an evolutionary concept analysis. Int. J. Nurs. Stud. Adv. **6**, 100174 (2024). https://doi.org/10.1016/j.ijnsa.2024.100174
25. Ahmed, S.K.: The pillars of trustworthiness in qualitative research. J. Med. Surg. Public Health. **2**, 100051 (2024). https://doi.org/10.1016/j.glmedi.2024.100051

Construction and Validation of a Smart Long-Term Care Service Quality Scale: From the Perspective of Older Adult Users

Hsin-I Chen and Yu-Lung Wu(✉)

Department of Information Engineering, I-Shou University, Kaohsiung City, Taiwan, China
isuwuyulung@gmail.com

Abstract. This study aims to develop and validate a smart long-term care service quality scale from the perspective of older adult users. Through literature review, expert content validity assessment, pilot testing, and a formal questionnaire survey, a measurement instrument suitable for smart long-term care contexts was established. The findings indicate that smart long-term care service quality can be measured across seven dimensions: tangibility, reliability, responsiveness, assurance, empathy, ease of use, and connectivity. The results further demonstrate that the scale has acceptable reliability and validity. This study provides a useful reference for evaluating smart long-term care services and supports future research in this field.

Keywords: Smart long-term care · service quality · scale validation · older adults

1 Introduction

With the acceleration of global population aging, the demand for long-term care continues to rise. Traditional labor-intensive care models are increasingly challenged by shortages of care personnel, rising costs, and inconsistencies in service quality. Against this background, Smart Long-Term Care (Smart LTC)—which integrates artificial intelligence (AI), the Internet of Things (IoT), smart home technologies, remote health monitoring, and integrated care platforms—has gradually emerged as an important development direction for improving the efficiency and quality of older adult care. Previous studies have shown that smart long-term care can be applied in areas such as smart home care, smart nursing homes, fall detection, health monitoring, and integrated care services, and can enhance the safety, convenience, and health management capabilities of older adults [1–3].

For example, in Taiwan, the Ministry of Health and Welfare has actively encouraged residential care institutions to adopt smart technologies and has promoted three major upgrades: institutional quality enhancement, smart care capability, and care recipient autonomy. In addition, five categories of smart care support technologies have been introduced, including mobility sensing, movement assistance, care support, toileting assistance, and bathing assistance. Long-term care institutions in Pingtung County

D. Liberona et al. (Eds.): MISNC 2026, CCIS 3092, pp. 334–347, 2027.
https://doi.org/10.1007/978-3-032-33381-0_25

have reported that the adoption of smart technologies has improved care efficiency by more than 60%, reduced care staff time spent on ward rounds, measurement, and documentation by 1.5 to 2 h, and enhanced both institutional satisfaction and care quality [4].

Existing studies indicate that smart long-term care is not merely about the introduction of technological devices, but also about whether services can truly meet the needs of older adults. For instance, although smart home and health monitoring systems can improve care support, their effectiveness is often constrained by system stability, operational convenience, and the degree of fit with individual needs [5, 6]. In addition, older adults' acceptance of smart care technologies is closely associated with interface friendliness, ease of use, trust, and perceived safety [7–9]. These findings suggest that the success of smart long-term care services depends not only on technological functionality, but also on whether users perceive the services as having high quality.

However, current research on smart long-term care has mainly focused on technology acceptance, system performance, or policy implementation. Studies that systematically develop a smart long-term care service quality scale from the perspective of older adult users remain relatively limited. Although some studies have attempted to establish quality indicators for smart long-term care—for example, Chen et al. [10] proposed a quality evaluation framework for smart home care—most of these efforts are expert-oriented or system-level analyses and do not directly reflect the actual experiences of older adults. Therefore, the field of smart long-term care still lacks a reliable and valid service quality measurement instrument that captures both technological characteristics and the essential nature of service.

Based on the above background and research gap, this study aims to construct and validate a smart long-term care service quality scale from the perspective of older adult users. Specifically, this study seeks to develop a measurement instrument suitable for smart long-term care contexts by incorporating dimensions such as reliability, safety, responsiveness, ease of use, personalization, and integration.

2 Literature Review

2.1 Characteristics of Smart Long-Term Care Development

With the rapid increase in global population aging and the growing demand for chronic disease care, Smart Long-Term Care (Smart LTC) has gradually become an important development direction in older adult care and health management. Smart long-term care generally refers to the integration of information technology, artificial intelligence (AI), the Internet of Things (IoT), smart home devices, remote health monitoring, and digital platforms into long-term care services in order to enhance care efficiency, safety, health management capabilities, and overall service quality [11, 12]. Compared with traditional long-term care, which mainly relies on human caregiving and face-to-face interaction, smart long-term care emphasizes the use of digital technologies to provide more immediate, continuous, and personalized care support. Therefore, its essence lies not only in the introduction of technological devices, but also in the restructuring of care service processes and user service experiences.

From the perspective of application, smart long-term care can generally be categorized into three types. The first is smart home care, which mainly supports older adults' independent living at home through sensors, smart devices, and health monitoring systems, such as fall detection, health data collection, and abnormal event alerts [1, 2, 6]. The second is smart institutional care, including smart nursing homes, smart wards, and integrated long-term care information systems, where technology assists in care record management, staff collaboration, and residents' health tracking [9, 13, 14]. The third is integrated smart long-term care services, which emphasize information connectivity and service coordination across systems, professions, and care settings to provide continuous health and care support [3, 15].

However, existing studies have also pointed out that the development of smart long-term care does not automatically lead to the formation of high-quality services. Zhang et al. [12] noted that although the rapid development of smart long-term care in China has brought technological innovation and policy support, its practical implementation still faces challenges such as inconsistent standards, insufficient service content, and mismatches between service provision and user needs. Tian et al. [6], in their systematic review, also found that although smart long-term care technologies can improve health monitoring, self-management, and daily living support, users still commonly face barriers such as operational difficulties, limited usability, and varying levels of social acceptance. These findings indicate that the core issue of smart long-term care lies not merely in whether technology is available, but in whether technology can truly be transformed into high-quality services.

In other words, the research focus of smart long-term care has gradually shifted from technological functions and device adoption toward the overall service experience and care value perceived by users. Particularly for older adults, whether smart long-term care services can provide a sense of safety, convenience, trust, and care support is often more meaningful than technological innovation alone. Therefore, to further evaluate the effectiveness and sustainability of smart long-term care, it is essential to revisit the concept of service quality in this context from the actual experiences and perceptions of older adult users.

2.2 Core Dimensions of Smart Long-Term Care Service Quality

Traditional service quality research has largely been based on the SERVQUAL model proposed by Parasuraman, Zeithaml, and Berry, which conceptualizes service quality in terms of tangibility, reliability, responsiveness, assurance, and empathy [16]. However, smart long-term care is a form of technology-oriented care service, and its service quality cannot be evaluated solely through interpersonal service interactions. Instead, it should also incorporate characteristics such as system functionality, information integration, technology acceptance, and care safety. Therefore, smart long-term care service quality should be regarded as a comprehensive concept that combines both technical quality and care service quality.

Reliability and safety constitute the most fundamental dimensions of service quality in smart long-term care. When older adults use smart care services, their primary concerns include whether the system operates stably, whether monitoring information is accurate, and whether the system can effectively issue alerts in the event of falls, abnormal physiological conditions, or emergencies [1, 10]. Jachan et al. [2] pointed out that the main value of technical assistance systems in home-based long-term care lies in enhancing safety and mobility support rather than merely displaying information. Therefore, reliability and safety can be regarded as the primary dimensions of smart long-term care service quality.

Responsiveness is also a critical characteristic of smart long-term care services. Unlike traditional care services, which often rely on scheduled or routine care arrangements, smart long-term care emphasizes the real-time detection of abnormal events, immediate information transmission, and subsequent response handling. Rostad and Stokke [15] found that the application of welfare technologies in long-term care settings can significantly improve response speed and service immediacy, thereby enhancing overall care quality. Similarly, Choi et al. [3] argued that information technology-supported integrated health service platforms can improve care responsiveness in long-term care settings through digitalized mechanisms.

Ease of use and accessibility are also important factors influencing older adults' perceived service quality. Ghorayeb et al. [7] found that older adults' acceptance of smart home technologies is highly related to whether such technologies align with their daily living habits and are easy to understand and operate. Huang et al. [8] also reported that older adults' willingness to adopt smart long-term care services is influenced by their technological self-efficacy and perceived convenience of use. In other words, even if a system is highly functional, it may still be perceived as low-quality service if it is overly complex to operate.

Personalization and appropriateness also represent essential dimensions of smart long-term care service quality. Smart long-term care should provide differentiated and context-specific care support according to older adults' health conditions, functional abilities, and daily living needs. Moyle et al. [5], in their study on smart home technologies for older adults with dementia, pointed out that if technological interventions do not closely align with users' actual needs, they are unlikely to generate stable support for health and daily living. Studies on smart nursing homes by Zhao et al. [9, 13] similarly showed that older adults' and family members' acceptance of smart care services is often based on whether such services genuinely meet care needs.

In addition, integration, privacy trust, and perceived value should also be incorporated into the evaluation of smart long-term care service quality. Choi et al. [3] and Rostad and Stokke [15] both emphasized that improving service quality in smart long-term care depends not only on the functionality of individual devices, but also on whether systems can integrate care information, connect service processes, and support interdisciplinary collaboration. Moreover, Tian et al. [6] and Ghorayeb et al. [7] also noted that older adults' acceptance of smart care technologies is strongly influenced by concerns about privacy protection and trust. Therefore, smart long-term care service quality should be regarded as a multidimensional construct that simultaneously reflects the overall service experience of functional reliability, operational convenience, care appropriateness, and user reassurance.

2.3 Development of the Smart Long-Term Care Service Quality Scale

From the perspective of scale development, the measurement of smart long-term care service quality should be built upon the intersection of users' subjective perceptions and the contextual characteristics of technology-enabled care services. In other words, smart long-term care service quality should not simply adopt general service quality scales. Instead, representative quality dimensions and measurement items should be extracted from older adults' actual experiences of using smart long-term care services. This logic of scale development is more consistent with current research trends in smart care and technology-based service evaluation.

In the existing literature, Chen et al. [10] have attempted to construct a quality evaluation index system for smart community home care using the Delphi method and the Analytic Hierarchy Process (AHP), demonstrating the feasibility of developing a scale for smart long-term care service quality. However, that study was more oriented toward expert judgment and managerial evaluation, and less focused on directly reflecting older adults' subjective experiences throughout the actual service process. Therefore, if a more user-oriented smart long-term care service quality scale is to be developed, it is necessary to return to older adults' actual perceptions and evaluations of the service.

Based on the above literature, several core dimensions of smart long-term care service quality can be identified. The first is reliability and safety, reflecting whether the system operates stably, whether monitoring is accurate, and whether risks can be effectively reduced [2, 17]. The second is responsiveness, emphasizing whether the system and service can respond quickly to user needs or abnormal events [3, 15]. The third is ease of use, referring to whether older adults can easily understand and operate smart long-term care services [7, 8]. The fourth is personalization and appropriateness, referring to whether the service fits the care needs and health conditions of different older adults [5, 9]. The fifth is integration and continuity, which concerns whether the system can integrate information, connect care processes, and support collaboration among different care roles [3, 14]. A sixth dimension may further include privacy and trust assurance, as well as perceived effectiveness and value, as important extended dimensions of smart long-term care service quality [6, 11].

Accordingly, from a scale development perspective, smart long-term care service quality may be defined as: older adult users' subjective evaluation of the reliability, safety, convenience, responsiveness, personalization, integration, trust, and overall benefits of technology-assisted long-term care services. This definition not only extends the applicability of traditional service quality theory into the smart care context, but also provides a theoretical foundation for subsequent scale development and empirical validation.

In summary, the literature reviewed above indicates that research on smart long-term care has gradually shifted from a narrow focus on technological applications toward greater attention to older adults' service experiences and quality perceptions. However, current studies still lack a standardized scale that is both user-centered and capable of capturing the dual nature of technological characteristics and service quality. Therefore, based on the above literature, this study seeks to further construct and validate a smart long-term care service quality scale as an important tool for the future evaluation and improvement of smart long-term care services.

3 Research Methods

3.1 Research Design for Scale Development

The scale development process in this study consisted of six main stages. The first stage involved a review and synthesis of relevant literature, including studies on service quality theory, smart long-term care, smart healthcare, telecare, older adults' technology acceptance, and e-Health service quality, in order to establish the theoretical foundation for scale development. The SERVQUAL model proposed by Parasuraman et al. [16] provided the basic conceptual framework for service quality in this study, while studies by Chen et al. [10], Ko et al. [18], Chou et al. [19], Jaschinski et al. [20], and Lu and Tsai-Lin [21] further enriched the conceptualization of smart long-term care by incorporating issues related to technology use, older adults' usage experiences, and service integration.

The second stage focused on dimension extraction and the establishment of the initial framework. Based on the results of the literature review and the practical context of smart long-term care services, this study identified seven core dimensions: tangibility and equipment quality, reliability and system stability, responsiveness and support, assurance and security, empathy and personalization, convenience and ease of use, and information and connectivity. These seven dimensions integrate the essential elements of traditional service quality with the technological characteristics of smart care, thereby providing a more comprehensive representation of older adults' overall perceptions of smart long-term care services.

The third stage involved item generation. Initial measurement items were developed based on the conceptual meanings of each dimension. The wording of the items was designed to be concise, specific, and easily understandable for older adults in order to enhance response feasibility and content clarity. The fourth stage consisted of expert content validity assessment, in which experts from relevant fields were invited to evaluate the representativeness, clarity, appropriateness, and comprehensibility of the items. Their feedback served as the basis for revising the scale.

The fifth stage was pilot testing, in which preliminary data were collected and analyzed through item analysis, exploratory factor analysis, and reliability analysis to examine the reasonableness of the initial scale structure. The sixth stage involved preparation for formal survey administration. Based on the pilot test results, inappropriate or redundant items were deleted or revised to produce the final questionnaire, which was then used for the factor analysis, reliability testing, and hypothesis verification presented in Chapter 4. The development process of the smart long-term care service quality scale is illustrated in Fig. 1.

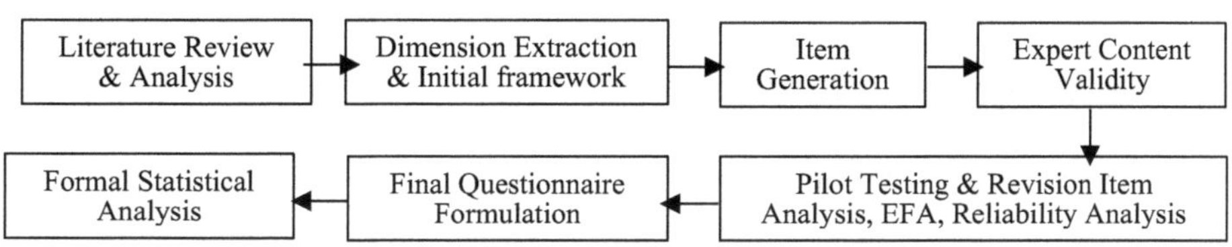

Fig. 1. Scale Development Process

3.2 Operational Definitions and Measurement Items

Based on service quality theory, prior studies on smart care service quality, and literature related to older adults' technology acceptance, this study developed the preliminary dimensions and measurement items for the Smart Long-Term Care Service Quality Scale. The scale was designed to incorporate both the core concepts of traditional service quality and the contextual characteristics of smart long-term care services. In addition to reflecting care staff performance, service processes, and responsiveness, the scale also includes dimensions related to the stability of smart devices, operational convenience, information security, and care connectivity. In the initial stage, the scale consisted of seven dimensions and 35 measurement items, forming the preliminary version of the Smart Long-Term Care Service Quality Scale.

3.3 Expert Content Validity

To ensure that the scale content adequately reflected the core concepts of smart long-term care service quality, this study conducted an expert content validity assessment after the initial item generation stage. Content validity refers to the extent to which measurement items adequately cover and represent the target construct, and it is of critical importance in the development of a new scale. Given that smart long-term care is an interdisciplinary field, this study invited five experts with expertise in smart care, long-term care, information management, medical informatics, gerontechnology, and scale development to participate in the review, thereby balancing theoretical rigor and practical applicability.

For the analysis, this study adopted the Content Validity Index (CVI) as the evaluation criterion. The item-level content validity index (I-CVI) refers to the proportion of experts who rated an item as either appropriate or highly appropriate. An I-CVI value of 0.80 or above is generally considered indicative of good content validity. The scale-level content validity index (S-CVI) was used to assess the overall content validity of the scale, with a value of 0.90 or above indicating strong overall representativeness. If certain items had I-CVI values below the acceptable threshold, they were revised, merged, or deleted based on expert feedback in order to improve their appropriateness.

After consolidating the experts' suggestions, a total of five items were deleted or merged due to ambiguous wording, conceptual overlap, unclear dimensional classification, or difficulty of comprehension for older adults. As a result, a revised questionnaire consisting of 30 items was developed and used as the basis for the pilot test. All questionnaire items were measured using a 7-point Likert scale, ranging from 1 = strongly disagree to 7 = strongly agree.

4 Data Analysis and Results

4.1 Pilot Data Collection and Analysis

Based on the revised questionnaire developed in the previous stage, a pilot survey was administered to 60 older adults in a long-term care institution located in southern Taiwan. After data screening, 8 invalid questionnaires were excluded, and a total of 52 valid responses were retained for the pilot data analysis.

The results of Bartlett's Test of Sphericity showed chi-square values ranging from 111.047 to 638.465, with all p-values equal to 0.000 (< 0.005), indicating statistical significance and suggesting that the pilot data were suitable for exploratory factor analysis (EFA). In addition, the Kaiser–Meyer–Olkin (KMO) values ranged from 0.639 to 0.704, indicating that the sample data were acceptable for factor analysis.

An exploratory factor analysis was then conducted. Principal Component Analysis (PCA) was used as the extraction method to identify factors with eigenvalues greater than 1, and Varimax rotation was applied to determine the major factor dimensions with high factor loadings. Given the relatively small sample size in this pilot study, the criteria suggested by Hair et al. [23] were adopted. Specifically, for a sample size of 50 to 60, any item with a factor loading below 0.75 or with cross-loadings on more than one factor was removed. The same analytical procedure was then repeated on the remaining items until each variable loaded clearly onto a single factor.

After repeating this process three times, a total of 10 items were deleted. Once the remaining items were assigned to their respective factor dimensions, reliability analysis was conducted. The Cronbach's α values for all dimensions ranged from 0.755 to 0.945, all exceeding the recommended threshold of 0.70 [23], thereby indicating satisfactory internal consistency among the items within each dimension. The results are presented in Table 1.

Table 1. Item Reliability and Factor Analysis

Item	Mean value (S.D)	Factor loading	Eigen-value	Variance explained (%)	Cronbach's α
Factor 1			22.559	17.652	.858
Q1	3.85 (.78)	.908			
Q2	3.88 (1.22)	.849			
Q3	3.79 (1.16)	.844			
Q5	3.94 (.98)	.795			
Factor 2			16.388	16.139	.933
Q6	5.06 (.83)	.949			
Q7	5.54 (1.04)	.921			
Q9	5.54 (.99)	.913			
Factor 3			15.137	15.292	.904
Q10	3.37 (1.16)	.951			
Q12	3.38 (1.43)	.902			
Q13	3.50 (1.49)	.888			
Factor 4			12.504	13.646	.815
Q14	4.94 (.75)	.908			
Q15	4.98 (1.23)	.889			
Q17	4.77 (1.15)	.807			

(continued)

Table 1. *(continued)*

Item	Mean value (S.D)	Factor loading	Eigen-value	Variance explained (%)	Cronbach's α
Factor 5			10.501	11.899	.945
Q18	4.81 (1.10)	.969			
Q21	4.40 (1.07)	.957			
Factor 6			9.057	11.526	.904
Q23	4.21 (1.41)	.942			
Q25	4.25 (1.17)	.940			
Factor 7			29.007	29.007	.941
Q26	5.08 (1.25)	.947			
Q28	5.06 (1.24)	.943			
Q29	4.65 (1.36)	.936			

4.2 Formal Data Collection and Analysis

The formal survey was conducted using purposive sampling and targeted older adult users in long-term care institutions in Taiwan. Caregivers and institutional staff assisted in questionnaire distribution and response completion when necessary. Considering that older adults may have difficulty completing online questionnaires, the survey was administered in the form of paper-based questionnaires sent by mail. A total of 800 questionnaires were distributed, of which 301 were returned. After excluding invalid or unusable responses, 248 valid questionnaires were retained for the formal data analysis.

An exploratory factor analysis (EFA) was subsequently conducted on the formal survey data. The results of Bartlett's Test of Sphericity showed chi-square values ranging from 434.586 to 2411.409, with all p-values equal to 0.000 (< 0.005), indicating statistical significance and suggesting that the data were appropriate for exploratory factor analysis. In addition, the Kaiser–Meyer–Olkin (KMO) values ranged from 0.685 to 0.692, indicating that the sample data were acceptable for factor analysis. The analysis further showed that the factor loadings of all items across the dimensions exceeded the recommended threshold of 0.50. The final results are summarized in Table 2.

Table 2. Reliability and Exploratory Factor Analysis

Item	Mean value (S.D)	Factor loading	Eigen-value	Variance explained (%)	Cronbach's α
Tangibility			20.052	16.256	.834
TA1	3.98 (.89)	.909			
TA2	4.11 (1.19)	.841			

(continued)

Table 2. (*continued*)

Item	Mean value (S.D)	Factor loading	Eigen-value	Variance explained (%)	Cronbach's α
TA3	4.01 (1.20)	.787			
TA4	4.04 (1.18)	.753			
Reliability			15.798	14.983	.901
RE1	3.57 (1.22)	.943			
RE2	3.59 (1.45)	.905			
RE3	3.61 (1.42)	.891			
Responsiveness			13.452	14.342	.872
RP1	5.48 (.99)	.912			
RP2	5.48 (1.05)	.878			
RP3	5.10 (.85)	.877			
Assurance			11.626	12.939	.796
AS1	4.91 (.84)	.882			
AS2	4.99 (1.16)	.849			
AS3	5.08 (1.16)	.800			
Empathy			10.295	11.313	.924
EM1	4.44 (1.15)	.954			
EM2	4.90 (1.17)	.949			
Ease of Use			9.337	10.718	.881
EU1	4.53 (1.21)	.946			
EU2	4.42 (1.43)	.931			
Connectivity			29.663	21.365	.911
CO1	5.30 (1.17)	.931			
CO2	5.23 (1.26)	.911			
CO3	5.01 (1.34)	.905			

4.3 Measurement Model Assessment

The measurement model was assessed using the Partial Least Squares Structural Equation Modeling (PLS-SEM) approach, and the results are presented in Table 3. According to the criteria suggested by Murphy and Davidshofer [24], the Cronbach's α values for each construct all exceeded the acceptable threshold of 0.60, indicating satisfactory internal consistency. In addition, the Composite Reliability (C.R.) values ranged from 0.87 to 0.96, all exceeding the recommended level of 0.70 [22], which demonstrates that the proposed research model exhibits strong structural reliability.

Furthermore, the Average Variance Extracted (AVE) values ranged from 0.69 to 0.93, all exceeding the recommended threshold of 0.50, indicating that the measurement model possesses good convergent validity [22, 23].

Table 3. Reliability and Convergent Validity of the Measurement Model

Item	Factor loading	Cronbach's α	AVE	Composite reliability
Tangibility		0.85	0.69	0.90
TA1	0.701			
TA2	0.698			
TA3	0.695			
TA4	0.855			
Reliability		0.91	0.84	0.94
RE1	0.901			
RE2	0.854			
RE3	0.845			
Responsiveness		0.88	0.80	0.92
RP1	0.815			
RP2	0.801			
RP3	0.798			
Assurance		0.81	0.73	0.89
AS1	0.732			
AS2	0.722			
AS3	0.731			
Empathy		0.92	0.93	0.96
EM1	0.926			
EM2	0.925			
Ease of Use		0.89	0.90	0.95
EU1	0.889			
EU2	0.900			
Connectivity		0.91	0.85	0.95
CO1	0.854			
CO2	0.843			
CO3	0.855			

To assess the discriminant validity among the constructs in this study, the correlation matrix presented in Table 4 was examined. The results show that the correlation coefficients between each pair of constructs did not exceed the threshold of 0.90 suggested by Hair et al. [23], indicating that there is no multicollinearity among the constructs in the research model.

Furthermore, according to Kline [25], discriminant validity is established when the correlations between constructs are below 0.85. In addition, Fornell and Larcker [26] proposed a more rigorous criterion for evaluating discriminant validity by comparing the square root of the Average Variance Extracted (AVE) with the inter-construct correlations. Discriminant validity is supported when the square root of AVE for each construct is greater than the correlations between that construct and all other constructs.

Based on both criteria, the results confirm that the measurement model in this study demonstrates satisfactory discriminant validity among all constructs. Although several inter-construct correlations were relatively low, all coefficients remained below the recommended threshold, indicating that the constructs were empirically distinguishable and conceptually non-redundant.

Table 4. Inter-Construct Correlation Coefficients and the Square Root of AVE.

	TA	RE	RP	AS	EM	EU	CO
TA	***0.829***						
RE	0.069	***0.919***					
RP	0.140	−0.008	***0.895***				
AS	0.157	0.128	0.146	***0.853***			
EM	−0.043	0.154	0.031	0.034	***0.962***		
EU	0.106	−0.014	0.104	0.161	0.031	***0.948***	
CO	0.040	0.055	0.007	0.143	0.004	−0.013	***0.923***

5 Conclusion

This study focused on the perspective of older adult users to construct and validate a smart long-term care service quality scale, aiming to address the research gap arising from the rapid development of smart long-term care and the lack of a standardized instrument for measuring service quality in this context. The findings indicate that the quality of smart long-term care services is not determined solely by technological functions, but rather by older adults' comprehensive evaluations of their overall service experiences, including device design, system stability, responsiveness and support, security and trust, personalized care, ease of operation, and information connectivity. Through literature review, expert content validity assessment, pilot testing, and formal survey administration, this study ultimately established seven core dimensions: tangibility and equipment quality, reliability and system stability, responsiveness and support, assurance and security, empathy and personalization, convenience and ease of use, and information and connectivity, and developed a scale with satisfactory reliability and validity.

From the empirical results, all dimensions demonstrated strong factor loadings and internal consistency in the exploratory factor analysis, with all Cronbach's α values exceeding the acceptable threshold, indicating that the scale developed in this study possesses a stable preliminary structure. Furthermore, confirmatory factor analysis showed that the composite reliability and average variance extracted (AVE) values of all constructs also met the recommended criteria, demonstrating good convergent validity and discriminant validity. These findings confirm that the smart long-term care service quality construct proposed in this study is both measurable and theoretically consistent.

The academic contribution of this study lies in extending traditional service quality theory into the context of smart long-term care, while also incorporating the characteristics of smart care technologies into the scale design. In doing so, this study addresses a limitation of prior research, which has often focused on technology acceptance or policy-oriented discussions, while paying less attention to the subjective experiences of older adult users. From a practical perspective, the scale developed in this study may serve as an evaluation tool for smart long-term care institutions, smart care system developers, and policymakers, helping them identify strengths and weaknesses in service quality and providing a basis for service improvement and age-friendly design. Overall, this study confirms that smart long-term care service quality is a multidimensional concept that integrates both technological and service-oriented characteristics, and that the proposed scale can serve as an important foundation for future evaluation, quality improvement, and subsequent academic research in the field of smart long-term care.

References

1. Liu, P. et al.: The effect of smart homes on older adults with chronic conditions: a systematic review and meta-analysis. Geriatr. Nurs. **40**(5), 522–530 (2019). https://doi.org/10.1016/j.gerinurse.2019.03.016
2. Jachan, D.E., Müller-Werdan, U., Lahmann, N.A., et al.: Smart@home—supporting safety and mobility of elderly and care dependent people in their own homes through the use of technical assistance systems and conventional mobility supporting tools: a cross-sectional survey. BMC Geriatr. **21**, 205 (2021). https://doi.org/10.1186/s12877-021-02118-9
3. Choi, J.-Y., Kim, H., Chun, S., et al.: Information technology-supported integrated health service for older adults in long-term care settings. BMC Med. **22**, 250 (2024). https://doi.org/10.1186/s12916-024-03427-7
4. Ministry of Health and Welfare: Promoting the "Three Upgrades and Five Smart Care Supports" in Long-Term Care: Full Implementation of Smart Care Initiatives. Ministry of Health and Welfare (2025) https://www.mohw.gov.tw/cp-2704-82028-1.htm
5. Moyle, W., Jones, C., Dwan, T., Petrovich, T.: The effectiveness of smart home technologies to support the health outcomes of community-dwelling older adults living with dementia: a scoping review. Int. J. Med. Inform. **153**, 104513 (2021). https://doi.org/10.1016/j.ijmedinf.2021.104513
6. Tian, Y.J.A., Felber, N.A., Pageau, F., Roulet Schwab, D., Wangmo, T.: Benefits and barriers associated with the use of smart home health technologies in the care of older persons: a systematic review. BMC Geriatr. **24**, 138 (2024). https://doi.org/10.1186/s12877-024-04702-1
7. Ghorayeb, A., Comber, R., Gooberman-Hill, R.: Older adults' perspectives of smart home technology: are we developing the technology that older people want? Int. J. Hum.-Comput. Stud. **147**, 102571 (2021). https://doi.org/10.1016/j.ijhcs.2020.102571
8. Huang, Q., Li, Y., Wu, X., et al.: The willingness and influencing factors to choose smart senior care among old adults in China. BMC Geriatr. **22**, 979 (2022). https://doi.org/10.1186/s12877-022-03691-3

9. Zhao, Y., Sazlina, S.-G., Rokhani, F.Z., Chinna, K., Su, J., Chew, B.-H.: The expectations and acceptability of a smart nursing home model among Chinese older adults: a mixed methods study. BMC Nurs. **23**, 40 (2024). https://doi.org/10.1186/s12912-023-01676-0
10. Chen, H., Zhang, Y., Wang, L.: A study on the quality evaluation index system of smart home care for older adults in the community—based on Delphi and AHP. BMC Public Health. **23**, 409 (2023). https://doi.org/10.1186/s12889-023-15262-1
11. Chien, S.-C., Yen, C.-M., Chang, Y.-H., et al.: Use of artificial intelligence, internet of things, and edge intelligence in long-term care for older people: comprehensive analysis through bibliometric, Google trends, and content analysis. J. Med. Internet Res. **27**, e56692 (2025). https://doi.org/10.2196/56692
12. Zhang, Q., Li, M., Wu, Y.: Smart home for elderly care: development and challenges in China. BMC Geriatr. **20**, 318 (2020). https://doi.org/10.1186/s12877-020-01737-y
13. Zhao, Y., Sazlina, S.-G., Rokhani, F.Z., Su, J., Chew, B.-H.: The expectations and acceptability of a smart nursing home model among Chinese older adults and family members: a qualitative study. Asian Nurs. Res. **17**(4), 242–249 (2023). https://doi.org/10.1016/j.anr.2023.08.002
14. Jøranson, N., Zechner, M.M., Silva, R., Korkmaz Yaylagul, N., Thygesen, H.: A case study on experiences with integrated technologies in a care home for older people. Geriatr. Nurs. **62**, 1–8 (2025). https://doi.org/10.1016/j.gerinurse.2024.10.059
15. Rostad, H.M., Stokke, R.: Integrating welfare technology in long-term care services: nationwide cross-sectional survey study. J. Med. Internet Res. **23**(8), e22316 (2021). https://doi.org/10.2196/22316
16. Parasuraman, A., Zeithaml, V.A., Berry, L.L.: SERVQUAL: a multiple-item scale for measuring consumer perceptions of service quality. J. Retail. **64**(1), 12–40 (1988)
17. Lui, C.X.Y., Yang, N., Tang, A., San Tam, W.W.: Effectiveness evaluation of smart home technology in preventing and detecting falls in community and residential care settings for older adults: a systematic review and meta-analysis. J. Am. Med. Directors Assoc.. Advance online publication. (2025). https://doi.org/10.1016/j.jamda.2024.105347
18. Ko, C.-H., Chou, C.-M., Chen, Y.-C.: Apply the SERVQUAL instrument to measure service quality for the adaptation of ICT technologies: a case study of nursing homes in Taiwan. Healthcare. **8**(2), 108 (2020). https://doi.org/10.3390/healthcare8020108
19. Chou, C.-C., Chang, C.-P., Lee, T.-T., Chou, H.-F., Mills, M.E.: Technology acceptance and quality of life of the elderly in a telecare program. Comput. Inform. Nurs. **31**(7), 335–342 (2013). https://doi.org/10.1097/NXN.0b013e318295e5ce
20. Jaschinski, C., Ben Allouch, S., Peters, O.: Acceptance of technologies for aging in place: a conceptual model. J. Med. Internet Res. **23**(3), e22613 (2021). https://doi.org/10.2196/22613
21. Lu, C.-C., Tsai-Lin, T.-F.: Are older adults special in adopting public eHealth service initiatives? The modified model of UTAUT. SAGE Open. **14**(1) (2024). https://doi.org/10.1177/21582440241228639
22. Nunnally, J.C., Bernstein, I.H.: Psychometric Theory, 3rd edn. McGraw-Hill, New York, NY (1994)
23. Hair, J.F., Hult, G.T.M., Ringle, C.M., Sarstedt, M., Thiele, K.O.: Mirror, mirror on the wall: a comparative evaluation of composite-based structural equation modeling methods. J. Acad. Mark. Sci. **45**(5), 616–632 (2017)
24. Murphy, K.R., Davidshofer, C.O.: Psychological Testing: Principles and Applications. Prentice Hall, Englewood Cliffs, NJ (1988)
25. Kline, R.B.: Principles and Practice of Structural Equation Modeling, 2nd edn. Guilford Press, New York, NY (2005)
26. Fornell, C., Larcker, D.F.: Evaluating structural equation models with unobservable variables and measurement error. J. Mark. Res. **18**(1), 39–50 (1981). https://doi.org/10.2307/3151312

Challenges and Coping Strategies for the Application of Green Building Materials Under a Low-Carbon Economy

Hsiang-Wei Wen[1], Ren-Fang Chao[2(✉)], Han-Yee Leong[2], and Liang-Chien Lee[3]

[1] Department of Information Engineering, I-Shou University, Kaohsiung, Taiwan, R.O.C.
[2] Postgraduate Programs in Management, I-Shou University, Kaohsiung, Taiwan, R.O.C.
rfchao@cloud.isu.edu.tw
[3] Department of Finance, I-Shou University, Kaohsiung, Taiwan, R.O.C.

Abstract. Amid the global trend toward carbon reduction and sustainable development, green building materials have increasingly become an important practical approach for the construction industry to respond to a low-carbon economy. This study adopted a qualitative approach to examine the challenges facing the application of green building materials, the key factors for successful adoption and market promotion, and the corresponding implementation strategies. Data were collected through semi-structured in-depth interviews with nine practitioners, including material suppliers, developers, and interior designers. The results show that the main challenges in promoting green building materials include cost and pricing pressure, insufficient policy support, limited market acceptance, and difficulties in supply and construction integration. In addition, the successful adoption of green building materials depends on whether the products can offer both functionality and economic value, and whether demonstration cases, information transparency, and clear customer targeting can strengthen market trust and acceptance. Finally, the promotion and application of green building materials should focus on cost-effective product categories, strengthen market communication and case-based promotion, and be supported by policy incentives and industry collaboration mechanisms.

Keywords: Low-Carbon Economy · Green Building Materials · Construction Industry · Adoption Challenges · Promotion Strategies

1 Introduction

Amid global trends toward carbon reduction and sustainable development, the low-carbon economy has gradually become a major direction for industrial transformation. Its core aim is to balance economic development, energy efficiency, and carbon emission control [1]. Compared with the traditional high-carbon development model, a low-carbon economy emphasizes reducing greenhouse gas emissions through low energy consumption, low pollution, and low emissions, while promoting the decoupling of economic growth from emission growth [2]. In this context, the construction industry has become

D. Liberona et al. (Eds.): MISNC 2026, CCIS 3092, pp. 348–358, 2027.
https://doi.org/10.1007/978-3-032-33381-0_26

a key arena for low-carbon transition because it involves substantial energy use and carbon emissions across the stages of material production, construction, and building use [3].

Low-carbon transition in the construction industry is no longer driven solely by firms' voluntary environmental efforts. It is increasingly shaped by institutional forces such as regulations, energy-efficiency standards, carbon trading, and carbon taxes [3]. As a result, the industry must gradually reduce its reliance on high-carbon building materials and extensive construction practices, while increasing the use of green buildings, renewable energy systems, and low-carbon materials [4]. However, firms still face barriers when adopting low-carbon measures, including insufficient knowledge and technology, as well as immature supply and institutional conditions. These constraints weaken the actual implementation of low-carbon practices [5].

Among the many low-carbon measures available in the construction industry, green building materials are widely regarded as an important approach because they combine carbon-reduction benefits with practical applicability. Green building materials not only help reduce environmental impacts across the material life cycle, but also improve resource efficiency and lower energy consumption during building operation [6]. However, their promotion and application do not depend solely on their technical and environmental value. They are also influenced by cost acceptability, market awareness, supply stability, information transparency, and the complexity of cross-professional coordination [7]. Therefore, although green building materials are an important tool for helping the construction industry respond to a low-carbon economy, their actual adoption still faces clear challenges.

A review of prior studies shows that most research has focused on the concepts, benefits, and adoption barriers of the low-carbon economy and green building materials. Comparatively little attention has been paid to how different practitioners understand the value of green building materials, what implementation difficulties they face, and what specific responses they adopt in practice. Therefore, this study focuses on the application of green building materials under a low-carbon economy. Through qualitative interviews, it explores the challenges involved in promoting green building materials, analyzes the key factors behind successful adoption, and further proposes feasible strategies for implementation. The findings are intended to provide practical references for construction-related practitioners and industry stakeholders.

2 Literature Review

2.1 Low-Carbon Economy

A low-carbon economy generally refers to a development model that reduces greenhouse gas emissions while maintaining economic growth and social well-being through low energy consumption, low pollution, and low emissions [8]. Gbadeyan et al. [1] further argued that a low-carbon economy is an economic system built on low-carbon energy, with minimizing greenhouse gas emissions as its core objective. From a narrow perspective, a low-carbon economy emphasizes reducing the consumption of high-carbon energy and lowering carbon emissions per unit of output, thereby decoupling economic growth from emissions [2]. From a broader perspective, it is not only a model of economic development, but also a development philosophy that emphasizes harmonious relationships between humans and nature, as well as among people [9].

Within this trend, transformation in the construction industry is no longer driven solely by firms' voluntary environmental efforts. It is increasingly shaped by both institutional and market forces. Wang et al. [3] noted that low-carbon regulations, mandatory energy-efficiency standards, carbon trading, and carbon taxes have become major drivers of low-carbon transition in the construction sector. The industry must gradually reduce its reliance on high-carbon building materials and extensive construction practices, while increasing the use of green building services [4]. At the same time, low-carbon transition also depends on the innovation and diffusion of relevant technologies [10]. On the materials side, increasing the use of low-carbon materials, recycled materials, and timber structures can also help reduce carbon emissions generated by building materials [11].

However, although the direction of low-carbon transition has become increasingly clear, firms still face multiple challenges when adopting low-carbon measures. Insufficient knowledge and technology, along with resistance to low-carbon technologies, often become major barriers during implementation [5]. In addition, low-carbon materials, green technologies, energy-efficient equipment, and carbon management tools usually require high upfront investment, which reduces firms' willingness to adopt them [12]. When low-carbon and carbon neutrality goals are not integrated into firms' business models and daily operations, related initiatives are less likely to be effectively implemented [13]. Furthermore, low-carbon materials and technologies may also face unstable supply, high prices, and difficulties in obtaining certifications and labels, which further limits their large-scale adoption [5]. Against this background, how the construction industry can respond to low-carbon transition through concrete and feasible actions remains an issue worthy of further investigation.

2.2 Green Building Materials

Among the many low-carbon measures available to the construction industry, green building materials are regarded as an important approach because they combine carbon-reduction benefits with practical applicability. Green building materials generally refer to building materials that cause less harm to the environment and human health than conventional materials throughout their life cycle, including raw material extraction, manufacturing, use, and disposal [14]. Their core value lies not only in meeting structural and functional requirements, but also in achieving environmental protection, resource conservation, and human health goals across the material life cycle [15]. Therefore, green building materials are typically characterized by low pollution, low energy consumption, recyclability, and the ability to improve indoor environmental quality.

Green building materials are mainly applied to reduce environmental burdens, improve energy efficiency, and promote resource circulation. Compared with conventional materials, they usually require less energy during production, which helps reduce the environmental impact of building materials [6]. In addition, green building materials often replace part of virgin resources with recycled materials, industrial waste, or agricultural residues, thereby improving resource circulation efficiency [16]. High-performance insulated walls and natural materials can also reduce heating and cooling loads and lower greenhouse gas emissions [17]. Likewise, alternative materials made from fly ash, slag, and agricultural waste can support both resource conservation and waste reuse [18].

Despite these advantages, green building materials still face several barriers in practical promotion and application. Green materials and green buildings are often perceived as more expensive options. Beyond material prices, they also involve design, certification, and management costs [19]. At the same time, owners and buyers often have limited awareness of the value of green building materials and show low willingness to pay a price premium [7]. In addition, the limited number of suppliers, along with insufficient transparency in quality and certification information, can increase contractors' concerns about schedule and quality risks [20]. Furthermore, the adoption of green building materials often requires cross-professional coordination, while certification procedures and technical requirements are relatively complex. This increases both time and management costs [21].

Whether green building materials can be adopted in practice depends not only on their energy-saving and resource-circulation value, but also on market awareness. When they are viewed as high-cost options and their long-term returns remain unclear, firms are less willing to adopt them [19]. Likewise, when consumers have limited understanding of their value, market demand is less likely to develop [7]. In addition, insufficient transparency in quality and certification information, together with the complexity of cross-professional integration and technical coordination, can further constrain their promotion [21]. These findings suggest that although green building materials are an important tool for helping the construction industry respond to a low-carbon economy, their practical implementation still depends on the alignment of multiple conditions.

3 Research Methods

3.1 Research Design

This study adopted a qualitative approach and used literature analysis combined with in-depth interviews as its primary research design. First, the study reviewed the literature on the low-carbon economy and the application of green building materials to establish the research background and analytical foundation. It then interviewed construction-related practitioners, including material suppliers, developers, and interior designers, in line with the research objectives. By comparing and synthesizing the views of these different practitioners, this study explored the challenges faced in the application of green building materials under a low-carbon economy, the key factors for successful adoption, and feasible promotion strategies. This research design helped capture the market, institutional, and practical contexts involved in promoting green building materials and further revealed the experiences and perspectives of different industry participants.

3.2 Interview Participants

This study used purposive sampling to select interview participants based on their practical experience with green building materials. Participants were drawn from three groups:

building material suppliers, developers, and interior designers (Table 1). This design made it possible to capture perspectives from different practice-based roles. According to the research design, three participants were selected from each group, for a total of nine interviewees. Their positions included chairperson, general manager, associate general manager, design director, and designer. All participants had relevant experience in the promotion, adoption, or application of green building materials. Following common qualitative research practice, pseudonymous codes were used to identify participants in order to protect their privacy.

Table 1. Interviewer

Category	Code	Professional Background
Building material suppliers	Interviewee 1	Chairperson
	Interviewee 2	General Manager
	Interviewee 3	Chairperson
Developers	Interviewee 4	General Manager
	Interviewee 5	Associate General Manager
	Interviewee 6	Chairperson
Interior designers	Interviewee 7	Design Director
	Interviewee 8	Design Director
	Interviewee 9	Designer

3.3 Procedure

Data were collected through semi-structured in-depth interviews. The interview guide was developed based on the research objectives and the literature review, and the direction of the questions was adjusted according to the roles of material suppliers, developers, and interior designers. Before each interview, the purpose of the study was explained to the participant, and audio recording was conducted only after consent was obtained. After the interviews were completed, the recordings were transcribed verbatim and used as the basis for subsequent coding and analysis.

4 Results and Discussion

4.1 Challenges in the Application of Green Building Materials

The challenges in applying green building materials can be grouped into three main areas: cost and price pressure, insufficient policy support, and difficulties in market acceptance and implementation integration. Interviewees generally agreed that, although green building materials offer environmental, health, and energy-saving advantages, their practical adoption is still constrained by price, institutional conditions, and market demand.

First, cost and price pressure remain the most direct barriers. Material suppliers noted that green building materials require investment in raw materials, R&D, and certification, which raises overall costs. Developers and design practitioners also indicated that once these costs are reflected in the final selling price, consumer acceptance tends to decline.

> *"It's not that people don't know green building materials are better. But once the cost goes up, the first thing clients ask about is still the price." (Interviewee 1)*

Second, insufficient policy support and incentives keep most firms at the level of basic regulatory compliance. Interviewees noted that current government efforts are concentrated mainly in public projects, while the private market lacks strong enough incentives. As a result, firms are less willing to increase the use of green building materials on their own.

> *"It's not that there are no policies at all. The problem is that, for the private market, the incentives are still too weak. In the end, everyone goes back to cost." (Interviewee 3)*

Finally, limited market acceptance, along with difficulties in supply and construction integration, further increases the difficulty of adoption. Interviewees pointed out that demand for green building materials is still concentrated in specific customer groups, and a stable market has not yet formed. At the same time, issues related to material supply, information transparency, and construction coordination also increase application risk.

> *"Sometimes the issue is not just that the material is expensive. It's whether the supply is stable and whether the construction team really understands it. If one part does not connect well, the whole process gets stuck." (Interviewee 6)*

Overall, the barriers to promoting green building materials cannot be reduced to a single price issue. They are shaped jointly by high costs, limited policy support, weak market demand, and difficulties in industry integration.

4.2 Key Factors for Successful Adoption and Market Promotion of Green Building Materials

The successful adoption and broader market promotion of green building materials can be summarized into three key factors: products must offer both functionality and economic value, promotion must build market trust, and target customer groups must be clearly identified. Interviewees generally believed that environmental claims alone are not enough to persuade the market. What matters more is whether firms and consumers can see clear and practical benefits.

First, the product itself must combine functionality with economic value. Material suppliers noted that green building materials are more likely to be accepted when they can meet regulatory requirements, improve construction efficiency, and deliver practical performance. Developers also pointed out that if a material is not only environmentally friendly but also improves building quality or creates product differentiation, firms are more willing to adopt it.

"Green building materials cannot rely only on environmental claims. You still have to come back to function and price. If the performance is there, the market has a chance to accept it." (Interviewee 2)

Second, demonstration cases and information transparency help reduce market uncertainty. Interviewees noted that actual project examples, exhibitions, website explanations, and technical information disclosure can help clients better understand the functions and value of green building materials, which in turn strengthens trust. In particular, Y Company emphasized that demonstration cases, regulatory explanations, and Q&A information are all important tools for helping clients understand green building materials.

"Many clients are not against green building materials. They just don't know what the real difference is. If they can see it and understand it, they are much more willing to accept it." (Interviewee 7)

Finally, precise customer targeting is also a critical condition for successful promotion. The interview results show that green building materials still face price constraints in the general market, but they are more readily accepted in high-end housing, among families with children, and among health- and wellness-oriented customer groups. As a result, some developers and interior designers prefer to apply green building materials in specific product lines to improve differentiation and strengthen market appeal.

"Not every customer will buy into it. But families with children and health-conscious customers are much more receptive to green building materials." (Interviewee 6)

Overall, the key to successful adoption and market promotion does not lie in simply strengthening environmental appeals. Instead, it depends on whether firms can demonstrate practical performance, reasonable costs, credible cases, and a clear fit with target customer groups. In other words, market promotion is more likely to succeed when the abstract value of sustainability is translated into concrete and tangible product benefits.

4.3 Practical Strategies for Promoting and Applying Green Building Materials

Practical strategies for promoting and applying green building materials can be summarized into three directions: focusing on product categories with economic value, strengthening market communication and case-based promotion, and building collaboration mechanisms between policy and industry. Interviewees generally believed that if green building materials are to move from concept to wider adoption, they cannot rely on sustainability discourse alone. They must also respond to market concerns about price, information, and confidence in use.

First, firms should prioritize green building materials with high carbon-reduction potential and clear economic value. From the perspectives of material suppliers and developers, products are more likely to be accepted when they combine functionality, ease of construction, and reasonable cost. Therefore, promotion strategies should not be overly broad. They should focus on product categories that can generate visible benefits and are easier for customers to understand.

> *"You can't promote everything at once. You have to start with the things customers can understand and are willing to accept. That's the only way it becomes easier to push." (Interviewee 5)*

Second, demonstration cases, information transparency, and market education should be used to increase acceptance. The findings show that many clients are not resistant to green building materials themselves. Rather, they lack a clear understanding of their effects, differences, and benefits. Therefore, showing actual cases of energy saving, health improvement, and carbon reduction, while also providing clearer product information and application guidance, can help reduce doubts and strengthen trust.

> *"Many clients are not against green building materials. They just don't know what makes them different. If they can see real cases and understand the benefits, they are much more likely to accept them." (Interviewee 2)*

Finally, policy support and supply chain collaboration remain important supporting conditions for promoting green building materials. Interviewees generally believed that stronger subsidies, better regulatory enforcement, and training programs organized with industry associations could improve designers' and contractors' understanding of green building materials and narrow the implementation gap. At the same time, more stable collaboration among material suppliers, developers, and interior designers could also increase the opportunities for applying green building materials in the private market.

> *"It's hard for one firm to push this alone. Policy, design, and construction all need to move together. Only then will the effect really become visible." (Interviewee 6)*

Overall, practical strategies for promoting and applying green building materials should not stop at environmental appeals. They should advance simultaneously through product value, case-based communication, and institutional support. In other words, promotion is more likely to improve steadily when green building materials can balance market feasibility with sustainability value and are supported by policy and industry collaboration.

5 Conclusion

Against the backdrop of a low-carbon economy, this study examined the challenges facing the application of green building materials, the key factors behind successful adoption and market promotion, and the corresponding implementation strategies. The findings show that, as prior studies have suggested, green building materials offer value in energy saving, carbon reduction, resource circulation, and reduced environmental impact [6]. They also respond to the construction industry's need to reduce its dependence on high-carbon materials under a low-carbon transition [3, 11]. However, their practical promotion has not progressed as smoothly as theory might suggest. The interview results further indicate that the application of green building materials is not simply a matter of technology or material choice. It also involves multiple conditions, including cost burdens, policy incentives, market demand, and supply chain collaboration.

In addition, this study found that the difficulties surrounding the promotion of green building materials are largely consistent with issues highlighted in the literature, such as high costs, unclear returns, limited market awareness, and complex implementation processes [21]. However, from the perspective of practitioners, this study further suggests that successful adoption depends not only on environmental attributes themselves, but also on whether products can combine functionality with economic value. It also depends on whether demonstration cases, information transparency, and clear customer targeting can strengthen market trust and acceptance. Overall, the promotion of green building materials should not remain at the level of sustainability advocacy alone. It should instead integrate product benefits, market communication, and institutional support in order to improve their practical application in the construction industry.

5.1 Practical Implications

The practical implication of this study is that the promotion of green building materials should not remain only at the level of advocating low-carbon economy and sustainable development. It should be translated into concrete practices that the market can understand and accept. A low-carbon economy emphasizes industrial transformation while balancing economic growth and carbon control [8]. Therefore, for government agencies and industry practitioners, the focus of green building material policy should not be limited to setting standards. It should also include subsidies, information disclosure, and training programs that reduce adoption costs and institutional uncertainty. In particular, this study shows that the main barriers to promoting green building materials are cost pressure, insufficient policy support, and limited market awareness. This suggests that without institutional support, green building materials are unlikely to move from conceptual support to broader diffusion in the private market.

From the industry perspective, this study also shows that the successful promotion of green building materials depends on converting environmental value into tangible product benefits. This finding echoes the core meaning of green building materials, which is to balance environmental protection, resource conservation, and human health throughout the life cycle [14, 15]. It also suggests that firms should not rely solely on environmental appeals in their marketing. They should also highlight functionality, economic value, and health benefits. More specifically, material suppliers can improve market trust through demonstration cases and information transparency. Developers can plan the use of green building materials based on product positioning and target customer needs. Interior designers can strengthen communication by emphasizing family well-being, health, and quality of life. In other words, the promotion of green building materials must combine product value, market education, and customer targeting in order to improve both practical application and market acceptance.

5.2 Limitations and Future Research

This study has several limitations. First, it adopted a qualitative interview approach. Although this method helped capture the practical context of green building material application, the findings are more suitable for contextual understanding and transferability than for statistical generalization [22]. Prior research has noted that the value of qualitative research lies in its ability to provide an in-depth understanding of experience and context. At the same time, the applicability of its findings across settings should be interpreted with caution. Therefore, future studies could incorporate quantitative methods or mixed methods to examine the relationships among adoption intention, cost considerations, and market acceptance of green building materials, thereby extending the findings of this study.

Second, the interview participants in this study were limited to material suppliers, developers, and interior designers. Although this design captured the perspectives of different practice-based roles, it did not include government agencies, construction teams, or end users. As a result, the study provides only a partial view of the overall promotion of green building materials. Prior studies have also indicated that barriers to green building materials or green buildings may vary across stakeholder groups [23, 24]. Accordingly, future research could expand the sample to include more actors across the supply chain and compare how different stakeholders perceive the value, barriers, and promotion strategies of green building materials.

Third, this study focused on the application of green building materials in a specific context. Its findings mainly reflect the context of Taiwan's construction industry, and their applicability to other regions or institutional settings remains to be verified. Recent studies have also shown that the adoption of green building materials and green buildings is often influenced by institutional conditions, market maturity, and local industrial environments [25]. Therefore, future research could conduct cross-regional or cross-national comparisons to clarify how the promotion of green building materials differs across institutional and market contexts.

References

1. Gbadeyan, O.J., Muthivhi, J., Linganiso, L.Z., Deenadayalu, N.: Decoupling economic growth from carbon emissions: a transition toward low-carbon energy systems-a critical review. Clean Technol. **6**(3), 1076–1113 (2024). https://doi.org/10.3390/cleantechnol6030054
2. Chen, W.J.: Toward sustainability: dynamics of total carbon dioxide emissions, aggregate income, non-renewable energy, and renewable power. Sustainability. **14**(5), 2712 (2022). https://doi.org/10.3390/su14052712
3. Wang, S., Zhu, D., Wang, J.: Impact of policy adjustments on low carbon transition strategies in construction using evolutionary game theory. Sci. Rep. **15**(1), 3469 (2025). https://doi.org/10.1038/s41598-025-87770-6
4. Li, M., et al.: Evaluation of low-carbon development in the construction industry and forecast of trends: a case study of the Yangtze River Delta region. Sustainability. **17**(12), 5435 (2025). https://doi.org/10.3390/su17125435
5. Chan, M., Masrom, M.A.N., Yasin, S.S.: Selection of low-carbon building materials in construction projects: construction professionals' perspectives. Buildings. **12**(4), 486 (2022). https://doi.org/10.3390/buildings12040486
6. Chipade, A.M., Vispute, P.P., Sonawane, S.K., Sasane, N.B., Jadhav, M., Nerlekar, T.: Construction materials for sustainable environment in residential buildings. J. Mines Met. Fuels. **73**(1), 173–188 (2025). https://doi.org/10.18311/jmmf/2025/46248

7. Bashir, M.T., Khan, A.B., Khan, M.M.H., Rasheed, K., Saad, S., Farid, F.: Evaluating the implementation of green building materials in the construction sector of developing nations. J. Hum. Earth Future. **5**(3), 528–542 (2024). https://doi.org/10.28991/HEF-2024-05-03-015
8. Yang, W.: The development of tourism in the low carbon economy. Int. Bus. Res. **3**(4), 212–215 (2010). https://doi.org/10.5539/ibr.v3n4p212
9. Dou, X.: The essence, feature and role of low carbon economy. Environ. Dev. Sustain. **17**, 123–136 (2015). https://doi.org/10.1007/s10668-014-9542-9
10. Chen, L., et al.: Green construction for low-carbon cities: a review. Environ. Chem. Lett. **21**, 1627–1657 (2023). https://doi.org/10.1007/s10311-022-01544-4
11. Pauliuk, S., Carrer, F., Heeren, N., Hertwich, E.G.: Scenario analysis of supply- and demand-side solutions for circular economy and climate change mitigation in the global building sector. J. Ind. Ecol. **28**(6), 1699–1715 (2024). https://doi.org/10.1111/jiec.13557
12. Mahmoodi, M., Rasheed, E., Le, A.: Systematic review on the barriers and challenges of organisations in delivering new net zero emissions buildings. Buildings. **14**(6), 1829 (2024). https://doi.org/10.3390/buildings14061829
13. Amarasinghe, I., Liu, T., Stewart, R.A., Mostafa, S.: Paving the way for lowering embodied carbon emissions in the building and construction sector. Clean Techn. Environ. Policy. **27**(4), 1825–1843 (2025). https://doi.org/10.1007/s10098-024-03023-6
14. Iwuanyanwu, O., Gil-Ozoudeh, I., Okwandu, A.C., Ike, C.S.: The role of green building materials in sustainable architecture: innovations, challenges, and future trends. Int. J. Appl. Res. Soc. Sci. **6**(8), 1935–1950 (2024). https://doi.org/10.51594/ijarss.v6i8.1476
15. Nayem, N.H.: The potential of sustainable materials for green building practices. Am. J. Civ. Eng. **11**(3), 30–35 (2023). https://doi.org/10.11648/j.ajce.20231103.11
16. Abera, Y.A.: Sustainable building materials: a comprehensive study on eco-friendly alternatives for construction. Compos. Adv. Mater. **33**, 26349833241255957 (2024). https://doi.org/10.1177/26349833241255957
17. Lau, Y.Y., Talukdar, G., Widyasamratri, H., Wang, J., El-shaammari, M.: Utilization of green materials and technology for sustainable construction in Malaysia. Trop. Environ. Biol. Technol. **1**(1), 47–66 (2023). https://doi.org/10.53623/tebt.v1i1.238
18. Wang, H., et al.: Application of wall and insulation materials on green building: a review. Sustainability. **10**(9), 3331 (2018). https://doi.org/10.3390/su10093331
19. Tran, Q., Huang, D.: Using PLS-SEM to analyze challenges hindering success of green building projects in Vietnam. J. Econ. Dev. **24**(1), 47–64 (2022). https://doi.org/10.1108/JED-04-2020-0033
20. Eze, E.C., Sofolahan, O., Omoboye, O.G.: Assessment of barriers to the adoption of sustainable building materials (SBM) in the construction industry of a developing country. Front. Eng. Built Environ. **3**(3), 153–166 (2023). https://doi.org/10.1108/FEBE-07-2022-0029
21. Karamoozian, M., Zhang, H.: Obstacles to green building accreditation during operating phases: identifying challenges and solutions for sustainable development. J. Asian Archit. Build. Eng. **24**(1), 350–366 (2025). https://doi.org/10.1080/13467581.2023.2280697
22. Ahmed, S.K.: The pillars of trustworthiness in qualitative research. J. Med. Surg. Public Health. **2**, 100051 (2024). https://doi.org/10.1016/j.glmedi.2024.100051
23. Ikingura, A., Grabiec, A.M., Radomski, B.: Examining key barriers and relevant promotion strategies of green buildings adoption in Tanzania. Energies. **18**(5), 1081 (2025). https://doi.org/10.3390/en18051081
24. Komurlu, R., Kalkan Ceceloglu, D., Arditi, D.: Exploring the barriers to managing green building construction projects and proposed solutions. Sustainability. **16**(13), 5374 (2024). https://doi.org/10.3390/su16135374
25. Adolphe, T.: Drivers and barriers to adopting sustainable building materials: evidence from construction professionals in Kigali City, Rwanda. Smart Constr. Sustain. Cities. **4**(1), 3 (2026). https://doi.org/10.1007/s44268-025-00083-5

Exploring the Internal and External Factors Influencing the Stickiness of Mobile Payment Apps

Nan-Hong Lin and Kai-Wen Wu(✉)

College of Business and Information Management, Tatung University, Taipei, Taiwan, R.O.C.
nhlin@gm.ttu.edu.tw, kevin960314@gmail.com

Abstract. After linking a credit card to a mobile phone, mobile payment apps allow users to make payments at any merchant that supports mobile payments, significantly increasing the convenience of shopping and leading to a rapid increase in their usage. This study explores the factors that contribute to consumer stickiness with mobile payment apps from both internal and external perspectives, and identifies which variables within these factors have a greater impact. Data was collected via online questionnaires, and after a month of collection and removal of invalid questionnaires, 337 valid questionnaires were obtained. Smart PLS 4.0 software was used to conduct structural equation modeling analysis and test the research hypotheses. The results show that only hedonistic value has no significant positive impact on satisfaction among the nine hypotheses, while the other eight hypotheses are valid. Finally, based on the empirical results, management implications are proposed, and future research directions are suggested.

Keywords: Mobile Payment Apps · User Attitude · Satisfaction · Stickiness · Internal Factors · External Factors

1 Introduction

Besides enhancing consumer convenience, mobile payments can also boost national economic growth, leading to a surge in "cashless payments" in many countries [1]. Markus, Godfrey, Michael, and Mohammad estimate that a cashless model will increase annual GDP by approximately 1 percentage point in mature economies and over 3 percentage points in emerging economies [2]. In Taiwan, the government has implemented corresponding strategies since 2017 to accelerate the adoption of mobile payments, such as amending the "Regulations Governing Electronic Payment Institutions" to open up inter-institutional payment services and expand service offerings. However, how to promote mobile payments and increase customer engagement with mobile payment apps remains a challenge for all providers.

Two crucial factors in increasing user engagement with mobile payment apps are: 1. consumers' "attitudes", and 2. their "satisfaction". In studies on perceived value and customer satisfaction, the perceived value of traditional retailers positively influences customer satisfaction [3, 4]. Kuo, Wu, and Deng also found that the perceived value of mobile

D. Liberona et al. (Eds.): MISNC 2026, CCIS 3092, pp. 359–375, 2027.
https://doi.org/10.1007/978-3-032-33381-0_27

value-added services has a positive impact on user satisfaction [5]. Perceived value has two levels: 1. Utilitarian value 2. Hedonistic value. Utilitarian value is task-oriented, while hedonistic value increases the consumer's pleasant experience [6]. Therefore, for utilitarian consumers, strengthening functions such as bill payment, money transfer services, and cross-border online shopping payments should effectively increase stickiness to mobile payment apps [7]. In addition, users will use different mobile payment apps based on different feedback, because using mobile payment apps gives users pleasure and enjoyment, which are all criteria for judging hedonistic value. This study argues that "utilitarian values" and "hedonistic values" are subjective judgments made by consumers, thus categorizing them as "intrinsic influence factors."

On the other hand, system stability is also a factor influencing consumers' decision to use a mobile payment app. System quality refers to the quality of the information system itself. Poor system quality not only causes problems for customers (e.g., slow payment speed, poor network signal, etc.) but also raises security concerns, leading to decreased user satisfaction. Information quality, on the other hand, refers to the user's evaluation of the information system's output. In other words, good information quality presents the information users need, such as providing desired promotional activities, discounts at partner restaurants, and shopping point accumulation mechanisms. DeLone and McLean pointed out that both system and information quality affect user satisfaction [8]. In summary, system quality and information quality are essential features that mobile payment app developers must possess to improve user satisfaction. For consumers, these are external factors beyond their control; therefore, this study categorizes them as "external influence factors."

Mobile payments are currently a hot topic and are receiving increasing attention globally. Investigating how consumers' emotions when using mobile payment apps influence their usage intentions, the emotional components in Verkijika's study were derived from Social Cognitive Theory and Regret Theory, showing that emotions and anticipated regret have a positive impact on usage intentions, while anxiety does not [9]. Jocevski, Ghezzi, and Arvidsson explored how app platform providers can innovate their business models to address the challenges posed by mobile payments [10]. To the best of our knowledge, most studies only examine mobile payment app usage intentions from a single perspective, such as how app platform providers innovate their business models (technical aspects) or the emotions consumers experience when using the app (perceptual aspects). Few studies explore whether consumers are influenced by external factors in addition to emotional (internal perception) factors when using mobile payment apps. Therefore, to address the shortcomings of previous research, this study proposes a research model to explore how consumer stickiness to mobile payment apps is simultaneously influenced by internal and external factors, and to identify which individual influence factors have a stronger impact on stickiness. Specifically, this study takes a consumer-centric approach, constructing a relational framework influencing mobile payment stickiness through the perspectives of internal and external factors. Furthermore, it examines the roles of usage attitudes and satisfaction among these antecedents affecting stickiness.

2 Literature Review and Hypothesis Development

2.1 User Attitude

Albarracin and Shavitt define attitude as a subjective attribute reflecting how people perceive things (problems, people, objects, etc.), and this can be related to thoughts, feelings, and behaviors [11]. Attitudes are unstable, meaning they can change [12] and are influenced by different antecedent variables, leading to different outcomes.

Users' attitudes typically vary depending on the current usage context, resulting in positive or negative feelings. Kim and Shin confirmed that attitude is a key factor in willingness to use mobile payments [13]. Lin and Chao also pointed out that stronger user attitudes towards mobile commerce significantly impact continued usage willingness [14]. Therefore, in this study, usage attitude refers to the degree of positive or negative subjective feelings users experience when using mobile payment apps.

2.2 Utilitarian Values

Utilitarian value is defined as an overall judgment of functional benefits and sacrifices [15]. Utilitarian value is often described as "task-relevant" and "rational" [16]. Users' utilitarian value of a service is driven by the sense of accomplishment they derive from using it [17]. In contrast to hedonistic value, utilitarian value includes economic "value for money" [18] or judgments of convenience and time saving [19].

In today's technologically advanced world, the needs and stimuli of mobile device users lean more towards utilitarian value [20] because it allows users to perform tasks quickly and effortlessly, anytime and anywhere they want. Kleijnen, de Ruyter, and Wetzels found that flexibility, location accessibility, and personalization enhance the utilitarian value of mobile data services [21]. Therefore, this study defines utilitarian value as the degree to which users believe that mobile payment apps can improve their efficiency in using the app.

2.3 Hedonistic Values

Hedonistic value is defined as the primary source of benefit for customers when engaging with a service or product [22]. From a hedonistic value perspective, users are more likely to crave entertainment and perceive the purchase and use process as a pleasant experience, without needing to complete a transaction [23]. Hedonistic value is more subjective and personalized than utilitarian value [24] and is an intrinsic form of experiential value [25]. Users seeking enjoyment in mobile data services may respond to the entertainment aspects (e.g., mobile games) and the emotional aspects (e.g., SMS) of the service. Research on technology information use has also found that hedonistic value is a significant factor in whether users will use an information system [6].

Parsons further points out that research on hedonistic value motivations is becoming increasingly important because it can identify the motivations that attract users to visit stores or websites [26]. Furthermore, hedonistic value motivations have become an extension of utilitarian value motivations; both are emerging factors for maintaining a competitive advantage. Babin, Darden, Griffin proposed that hedonistic and utilitarian values are important outcomes influencing future user decisions [16]. In this study, hedonistic value is defined as the degree to which users enjoy and find pleasure in mobile payment apps.

Technological advancements have made mobile payment functions increasingly diverse, which aligns with the expectations of utilitarian users (e.g., improved transaction quality and efficiency). Hedonistic users, on the other hand, experience pleasure during use, naturally leading to positive attitudes. Chiou and Ting showed that the utilitarian value of online shopping significantly influences consumer attitudes, and that hedonistic value is a significant predictor of consumer attitudes [27]. Therefore, the following hypotheses are depicted:

H1: Utilitarian values have a significant positive impact on user attitudes.
H2: Hedonistic values have a significant positive impact on user attitudes.

2.4 Satisfaction

Satisfaction is a feeling of pleasure or disappointment that arises when a person compares the perceived performance (or outcome) of a product with their expectations [28]. Oliver defines satisfaction as a customer's perception of satisfaction when they feel satisfied with the service they receive, because the service they receive meets their expectations [29]. Li, Browne, and Wetherbe confirmed the significant impact of customer satisfaction on stickiness [30]. In this study, satisfaction is defined as the degree of difference between a user's expectations before using a mobile payment app and their perceived feelings after actual use.

Eroglu, Machleit, and Barr stated that hedonistic and utilitarian values significantly influence satisfaction [31]. Jones et al. pointed out that hedonistic and utilitarian values induce customer satisfaction and can establish repeat purchase behavior [17]. Therefore, there is a strong and positive relationship between hedonistic, utilitarian values, and satisfaction. Therefore, the following hypotheses are proposed:

H3: Utilitarian values have a significant positive impact on satisfaction.
H4: Hedonistic values have a significant positive impact on satisfaction.

2.5 System Quality

System quality measures a system's technical soundness, error-free nature, ease of learning, complete documentation, and flexible operation [32]. Lee and Chung found that system quality, message quality, and interface design quality affect users' trust and satisfaction with mobile banking [33]. DeLone and McLean developed an integrated "Information System Success Model," which posits that system quality and message quality influence user satisfaction [8].

If a system is complex to use and frequently produces incorrect or incomplete outputs, it makes using the mobile payment system difficult for users, potentially leading them to believe that the platform provider lacks the capability and completeness required to provide quality service. System quality is associated with attributes such as usability, functionality, reliability, and flexibility [34]. Therefore, in this study, system quality is defined as the ease with which users can use the mobile payment app developed by the platform provider.

2.6 Information Quality

McKinney, Yoon, and Zahedi define information quality as the information provided to users meeting their needs [35]. Poor information quality can damage the user experience because users will spend a lot of effort verifying the accuracy of the information. Negash, Ryan, Igbaria describe information quality as the perceived value of the system's output by the user [36]. DeLone and McLean point out that information quality is the quality of the output produced by the information system, and that information quality is the most needed characteristic of an information system [8]. This study defines information quality as the degree to which mobile payment apps developed by platform providers enable users to receive accurate information.

Bai, Law, and Wen have demonstrated that information quality has a significant impact on online shopping customer satisfaction [37]. Kim, Lee, and Law mention that the higher the user's evaluation of the system quality, information quality, and service quality of the application service provider (ASP), the higher the user's satisfaction with using the system [38]. In summary, the relationship between information quality and user satisfaction has been widely discussed and its importance has been verified [34, 35].

Even with good information quality, without a high-quality system to support its presentation to users, negative user experiences will still result due to increased operational difficulty. However, if the system quality provides results that match user expectations and meet their needs, user satisfaction will increase [39]. The research by Lin and Lu shows that system quality, like information quality, has a significant impact on user satisfaction [40]. Furthermore, according to the modified IS success model, system quality is a key success characteristic influencing user satisfaction and willingness to use [34]. Therefore, the hypotheses are as follows:

H5: Information quality has a positive and significant impact on user satisfaction.
H6: System quality has a positive and significant impact on user satisfaction.

Al-Gahtani and King proposed that both satisfaction and attitude should be considered in explaining technology-related behavior [41]. Generally, customer satisfaction influences an individual's attitude towards use, which in turn influences repeat purchase behavior [42]. St-Vincent, Denis, Imbeau, and Trudeau found that higher satisfaction correlates with more positive consumer attitudes [43]. Previous research has confirmed a significant relationship between satisfaction and attitude [44]. Therefore, this study proposes the following hypothesis:

H7: Satisfaction has a positive and significant impact on users' attitudes.

2.7 Stickiness

Stickiness is defined as a positive property of the frequency, depth, and duration of user visits to a website [45]; in other words, stickiness is the ability to attract and retain customers [46]. This characteristic encourages repeated use and attracts the attention of passersby, leading to continued membership [47]. Stickiness is influenced by internet users' attitudes towards the website, their trust in it, and the quality of the website's content [48]. Lin argues that stickiness is latent and unconscious for customers, and it develops unconsciously [48]. In the context of mobile commerce, stickiness refers to the degree to which users frequently return to and continue using the mobile application [49]. Platform providers must understand the factors that influence users' continued use of mobile payment apps and improve upon them, such as providing point accumulation mechanisms and operational optimizations. These improvements help retain existing users and attract new ones; the greater the user stickiness, the greater the potential market opportunity for mobile application services [50]. In this study, stickiness is defined as the degree to which users rely on and repeatedly use mobile payment apps.

To cultivate consumer stickiness, a positive attitude must first be cultivated. Lin confirmed that attitude is an antecedent variable of stickiness [48]. Past research has confirmed that positive attitudes towards websites significantly influence users' willingness to revisit those websites [40, 51, 52]. Wu, Chen, and Chung also pointed out that stickiness occurs when users have a positive attitude and overall reliance on a website [53]. Therefore, the eighth hypothesis of this study is:

H8: Usage attitude has a significant positive impact on stickiness.

Zhou found that trust and satisfaction promote consumers' continued willingness to use mobile payment [54]. Tsao, using LINE as an example, found that user satisfaction has a positive impact on the stickiness of using instant messaging software [55]. In other words, if users are more satisfied after using a mobile payment app, they will be more willing to continue using the mobile payment app. Based on the above, the last hypothesis of this study is:

H9: Satisfaction has a significant positive impact on stickiness.

3 Research Methods

3.1 Questionnaire Design

The questionnaire consisted of two main parts. The first part contained basic user information, while the second part comprised the core of the research, specifically the measurement items for the relevant research constructs. Regarding the scales, the satisfaction items were derived from Ndubisi and Nataraajan [56], user attitudes from Schierz, Schilke, and Wirtz [57], stickiness from Wang, Wang, and Liu [58], utilitarian and hedonistic values from Hsu and Lin [59] and Hong, Lin, and Hsieh [60] respectively, and system quality and information quality from Kim, Mirusmonov, and Lee [61]. The entire questionnaire was measured by using a seven-point Likert scale from 1 (*strongly disagree*) to 7 (*strongly agree*).

3.2 Sampling Objects and Sampling Design

This study targeted all users in Taiwan who had actually used mobile payment apps. To ensure effective reach, an online questionnaire was used to collect data. The questionnaire was created and data was collected through the SurveyCake platform. The questionnaire's URL was then shared on major Taiwanese bulletin boards and the "Thesis Questionnaire Help Group" on Facebook, encouraging users to complete it. The URL was open for one month, and duplicate questionnaires from the same IP address were considered invalid to prevent respondents from completing the questionnaire repeatedly. Since mobile payment apps require internet access, users need relevant internet usage experience and knowledge of how to operate them; therefore, using an online questionnaire is an appropriate data collection method.

4 Results and Analysis

4.1 Sample Characteristics

After one month of data collection, a total of 337 valid questionnaires were collected. Of these valid respondents, 162 were male (48.1%) and 175 were female (51.9%). In terms of age structure, the largest group is 21–30 years old (205 people, 60.83%), followed by 31–40 years old (60 people, 17.81%). Students make up the largest group (112 people, 33.23%), followed by those in the service industry (54 people, 16.02%). The majority of respondents have a university or college degree (203 people, 20.64%), followed by postgraduate degrees or higher (17 people, 34.72%). Among all respondents, the most frequently used mobile payment app is LINE PAY (129 people, 38.28%), followed by Apple PAY (63 people, 18.69%). Regarding the reasons for using mobile payment apps, which were multiple-choice questions, convenience was the most popular answer (238 people, 26.18%).

4.2 Measurement Model Evaluation

This study employed partial least squares (PLS) and used the Smart PLS 4.0 software developed by Ringle, Wende, and Becker [62] for PLS analysis. The PLS analysis and estimation process consisted of two stages: the first stage analyzed the reliability and validity of the measurement model; the second stage estimated and tested the path coefficients and explanatory power of the structural model. These steps were to first confirm the reliability and validity of the measurement constructs, then examine the relationships between the constructs, and test the validity of the assumptions of this study framework [63]

The assessment of reliability and validity first required calculating the composite reliability (CR) and average variance extracted (AVE) for each construct. Both the CR and Cronbach's α values had to be greater than 0.7 to meet the acceptable threshold [64]. AVE is the measure of how well a latent construct can explain the variation in the measured variable; the threshold value must be greater than 0.5. After calculation using the PLS Algorithm, and removing item 3 (STN3) on stickiness due to its low factor loading, the CR and Cronbach's α of the latent variables in this study ranged from 0.882 to 0.953 and 0.821 to 0.933, respectively, both greater than 0.7, indicating good internal consistency among the seven latent constructs in this study. The AVE values of all latent constructs in this study ranged from 0.656 to 0.856, also greater than 0.5, indicating that the measurement tool has convergent validity. Table 1 shows that these values are all above the threshold value.

Furthermore, Chin suggested that individual indicator loadings should be greater than 0.7 [65]; in other words, the construct should explain at least 50% of the variance of each indicator variable and be significant at $\alpha = 0.05$. Table 2 shows the individual indicator loadings after removing STN3.

Discriminant validity means that the correlation between latent constructs must be less than the correlation within latent constructs. Therefore, it is tested using a correlation matrix between constructs. Discriminant validity exists when the square root of the AVE of an individual construct is greater than the correlation coefficient between that construct and other constructs. Table 3 demonstrates the validation of discriminant validity, as the square root of any AVE value on the diagonal is greater than the correlation coefficients to its left and below.

4.3 Structural Model Assessment

Table 1. Reliability and Convergent Validity

	Cronbach's alpha	Composite reliability	Average variance extracted (AVE)
ATT	0.874	0.914	0.727
IQ	0.929	0.950	0.825
PRHD	0.933	0.953	0.835
PRUT	0.908	0.942	0.845
SAT	0.924	0.943	0.767
SQ	0.821	0.882	0.656
STN	0.833	0.922	0.856

Note: SAT: Satisfaction; ATT: User Attitude; STN: Stickiness; PRUT: Utilitarian Value; PRHD: Hedonistic Value; SQ: System Quality; IQ: Information Quality

Table 2. Factor Loading of Individual Indicators

	Original sample (O)	Standard deviation (STDEV)	T statistics (|O/STDEV|)	P values
ATT1 <- ATT	0.894	0.014	61.793	0.000***
ATT2 <- ATT	0.862	0.019	45.681	0.000***
ATT3 <- ATT	0.883	0.018	49.296	0.000***
ATT4 <- ATT	0.765	0.032	23.786	0.000***
IQ1 <- IQ	0.911	0.012	73.635	0.000***
IQ2 <- IQ	0.928	0.013	73.509	0.000***
IQ3 <- IQ	0.931	0.014	67.383	0.000***
IQ4 <- IQ	0.862	0.021	40.379	0.000***
PRHD1 <- PRHD	0.936	0.011	88.424	0.000***

(*continued*)

Table 2. (*continued*)

	Original sample (O)	Standard deviation (STDEV)	T statistics (|O/STDEV|)	P values
PRHD2 <- PRHD	0.948	0.013	74.255	0.000***
PRHD3 <- PRHD	0.948	0.007	137.184	0.000***
PRHD4 <- PRHD	0.817	0.028	29.615	0.000***
PRUT1 <- PRUT	0.910	0.012	76.501	0.000***
PRUT2 <- PRUT	0.938	0.011	86.453	0.000***
PRUT3 <- PRUT	0.908	0.017	52.645	0.000***
SAT1 <- SAT	0.835	0.041	20.151	0.000***
SAT2 <- SAT	0.876	0.018	49.456	0.000***
SAT3 <- SAT	0.889	0.014	65.689	0.000***
SAT4 <- SAT	0.919	0.010	96.639	0.000***
SAT5 <- SAT	0.859	0.019	46.136	0.000***
SQ1 <- SQ	0.648	0.044	14.821	0.000***
SQ2 <- SQ	0.914	0.013	72.983	0.000***
SQ3 <- SQ	0.919	0.009	104.307	0.000***
SQ4 <- SQ	0.725	0.043	16.754	0.000***
STN1 <- STN	0.937	0.008	110.957	0.000***
STN2 <- STN	0.913	0.013	69.728	0.000***

Note: (1) SAT: Satisfaction; ATT: User Attitude; STN: Stickiness; PRUT: Utilitarian Value; PRHD: Hedonistic Value; SQ: System Quality; IQ: Information Quality
(2) ***: $P < 0.001$

Structural models primarily describe causal relationships between underlying constructs and can also be used to test the validity of hypotheses, requiring the t-statistic and standard error results. Because PLS-SEM standardizes the raw data during execution, the resulting path coefficients are all standardized results. Standardization calculations, unless performed through bootstrapping, cannot yield standard errors [65]. Furthermore, the goal of PLS is to maximize the explanatory power of the independent variables, in other words, to calculate the R^2 value. A value greater than 0.67 is considered substantial, around 0.333 is moderate, and below 0.19 is weak [65, 66]. Table 4 shows the analysis results of related paths in structural models.

The results of this study show that utilitarian values, hedonistic values, and satisfaction explain 78.9% of the variation in attitude; utilitarian values, information quality, and system quality explain 55.4% of the variation in satisfaction; and attitude and satisfaction explain 63.1% of the variation in stickiness. Therefore, based on Chin [65] and Ringle [66], the explanatory power of the variables in this model is quite good.

Table 3. Discriminant Validity

	ATT	IQ	PRHD	PRUT	SAT	SQ	STN
ATT	**0.853**						
IQ	0.552	**0.908**					
PRHD	0.628	0.521	**0.914**				
PRUT	0.714	0.505	0.559	**0.919**			
SAT	0.846	0.565	0.502	0.658	**0.876**		
SQ	0.645	0.658	0.542	0.587	0.650	**0.810**	
STN	0.791	0.401	0.515	0.660	0.707	0.504	**0.925**

Note: (1) SAT: Satisfaction; ATT: User Attitude; STN: Stickiness; PRUT: Utilitarian Value; PRHD: Hedonistic Value; SQ: System Quality; IQ: Information Quality
(2) The bold text on the diagonal represents the AVE value of each construct, while the lower triangle represents the squared Pearson correlation coefficient between the constructs.

Table 4. Hypothesis Results

	Original Sample (O)	Standard Error (STERR)	T Statistics (|O/STERR|)	P	R Square
PRUT -> ATT	0.192	0.042	4.541	0.000***	0.789
PRHD -> ATT	0.213	0.035	6.153	0.000***	
SAT -> ATT	0.613	0.043	14.125	0.000***	
PRUT -> SAT	0.376	0.057	6.550	0.000***	0.554
PRHD -> SAT	0.049	0.052	0.946	0.172	
SQ -> SAT	0.306	0.068	4.480	0.000***	
IQ -> SAT	0.148	0.070	2.118	0.017*	
ATT -> STN	0.680	0.061	11.129	0.000***	0.631
SAT -> STN	0.131	0.062	2.118	0.017*	

Note: (1) SAT: Satisfaction; ATT: User Attitude; STN: Stickiness; PRUT: Utilitarian Value; PRHD: Hedonistic Value; SQ: System Quality; IQ: Information Quality
(2) *: P < 0.05; **: P < 0.01; ***: P < 0.001

The results of the path testing of the nine hypotheses proposed in this study and the overall pattern presented in Table 4 show that, except for hypothesis H4, The other eight hypotheses all indicate the existence of a significant relationship.

5 Conclusions and Recommendations

Utilitarian values have a significant positive impact on usage attitudes ($\beta = 0.192$, $P < 0.001$), thus confirming hypothesis one of this study, consistent with the findings of Yang and Lee [24]. For users of mobile payment apps, part of their use is task-oriented, as technological advancements have led to an increasing number of functions offered by mobile payment apps, enabling users to quickly complete transactions.

Hedonistic values have a significant positive impact on usage attitudes ($\beta = 0.213$, $P < 0.001$), thus confirming hypothesis two of this study, consistent with the findings of Shiau and Wu [67]. This can be interpreted as the diversification of mobile payment app functions due to technological advancements allowing users with hedonistic values to freely choose how app information is presented, customize the sound of promotional notifications, and enjoy cute transition animations during the waiting screen, etc., which stimulates their sense of pleasure or curiosity, thus leading to a positive evaluation of mobile payment apps.

Utilitarian values have a significant positive impact on satisfaction ($\beta = 0.376$, $P < 0.001$), therefore hypothesis three holds. Mobile payment is becoming increasingly functional (e.g., direct parking fee payment via mobile phone, discounts at partner merchants, and transfers between members), thus helping utilitarian users achieve their goals and improving their work and transaction efficiency. Because it effectively enhances their task-oriented needs, each use leaves a positive impression, thereby increasing satisfaction.

Hedonistic values, contrary to hypothesis four, do not have a significant positive impact on satisfaction ($\beta = 0.049$, $P = 0.172$). In other words, even if mobile payment apps offer more and more features, increasing the user's enjoyment, hedonistic users' satisfaction after use will not necessarily increase. This may be because current mobile payment apps are too cumbersome to operate, requiring users to spend time learning, thus providing little enjoyment for hedonistic users.

Information quality has a significant positive impact on satisfaction ($\beta = 0.148$, $P < 0.05$), consistent with the findings of Laumer, Maier, and Weitzel [68]. This conclusion suggests that the clearer and more detailed the information presented to users by mobile payment apps, allowing them to enjoy the quality of information that aids in decision-making, the higher the user satisfaction.

System quality has a significant positive impact on satisfaction ($\beta = 0.306$, $P < 0.001$), confirming Hypothesis 6. This result is consistent with the findings of Dreheeb, Basir, and Fabil [69]. Good information quality also requires good system quality to support it. Stable and smooth system quality helps users complete transactions quickly and improves work efficiency when using mobile payment apps, thus leading to user satisfaction with the app's efficiency and effectiveness.

Satisfaction had a significant positive impact on usage attitude ($\beta = 0.613$, $P < 0.001$), thus hypothesis seven is supported, a similar finding obtained by Hsu and Lin [59]. Clearly, user satisfaction with mobile payment apps increases their willingness to continue using them.

User attitude also had a significant positive impact on stickiness ($\beta = 0.680$, $P < 0.001$), thus hypothesis eight holds true. The more positive a user's attitude towards using a mobile payment app, the higher their dependence on it. In other words, a more positive attitude towards mobile payment leaves a good impression, increasing the likelihood of future use. This increase in long-term usage frequency is what constitutes stickiness.

Satisfaction had a significant positive impact on stickiness ($\beta = 0.131$, $P < 0.05$), thus hypothesis nine also holds true. This aligns with the findings of Lien, Cao, and Zhou [71], indicating that if users experience positive and satisfying results after using mobile payment, their satisfaction will increase. Because of this increased satisfaction, users will subconsciously use mobile payment to make payments or check new information and activities in similar situations in the future. Over time, this will unconsciously form a habit, which is the formation of stickiness. Because users maintain a positive satisfaction level with the mobile payment app in the long term, they are more willing to continue using it, and their dependence on it gradually increases. In other words, the higher the user's satisfaction, the greater the degree of stickiness.

5.1 Management Implications

Judging from the standardized path coefficient, in terms of usage attitude, hedonistic values have a greater impact than utilitarian values, although the difference is not significant. However, for satisfaction, the biggest influencing factor is the intrinsic utilitarian value, followed by the extrinsic system quality, while the impact of information quality is relatively small. Therefore, this study reasonably argues that, in order to strengthen positive attitudes towards mobile payment apps, platform providers should treat the hedonistic and utilitarian values of app development equally. In other words, the importance of developing multiple functions for mobile payment apps is equivalent to allowing users to enjoy operating the app. As for improving satisfaction, the statistical analysis conveys the message that users still value utilitarianism. After all, the primary purpose of mobile payment apps is to solve payment problems. In modern times, almost everyone owns a mobile phone, and the use of mobile payment apps can significantly reduce the hassle of using currency and credit cards, avoiding the burden of carrying a wallet. Therefore, these apps must at least provide the functions of past transaction tools, making the influence of utilitarian values significantly prominent. The future development direction of apps by manufacturers should clearly cover all aspects of daily life, including inquiries, price comparisons, and payments. Since respondents expressed a greater emphasis on system quality than information quality, collaborative efforts between platform providers and internet service providers to deliver stable and reliable system quality are even more crucial.

Regarding user attitudes, satisfaction, and user engagement, this study found a triangular relationship where satisfaction influences user engagement through user attitudes. Although this study did not conduct a mediation effect test, the three pathways and their standard errors preliminarily suggest that indirect effects exist among them. Due to this indirect effect mechanism, this study recommends that platform providers, when developing mobile payment apps, must pay attention to the mediating role of user attitudes in the impact of satisfaction on user engagement; in other words, cultivating positive user attitudes helps to mitigate the impact of satisfaction on user engagement.

5.2 Research Limitations and Suggestions for Future Research

The majority of respondents in this study were young people, with fewer respondents from other age groups. This may bias the conclusions of this study, and future research should focus on controlling the distribution of user demographics.

Currently in Taiwan, there are many platform providers developing mobile payment apps; however, not every app from every provider can be used anywhere. In other words, mobile payment apps have a "usability" issue, and future research could further explore this phenomenon.

This study covers all mobile payment apps on the market. However, there are many different mobile payment apps on the market, each with its own supporters, and their usage is likely influenced by various factors. Therefore, if the results of this study are used to uniformly interpret all platform providers, attention should be paid to their similarities and differences to avoid generalizations. Perhaps future research combining group analysis could further uncover more strategies for finding differences within similarities.

References

1. Mehul, D.: The benefits of a cashless society. World Economic Forum (2020). Retrieved from https://www.weforum.org/agenda/2020/01/benefits-cashless-society-mobile-payments/
2. Markus, M., Godfrey, S., Michael, S., Mohammad, K.: How cashless payments help economies grow. BCG (2019). Retrieved from https://www.bcg.com/publications/2019/cashless-payments-help-economies-grow.aspx
3. Cronin, J.J., Brady, M.K., Hult, G.T.: Assessing the effects of quality, value, and customer satisfaction on consumer behavioural intentions in service environments. J. Retail. **76**(2), 193–218 (2000). https://doi.org/10.1016/S0022-4359(00)00028-2
4. Eggert, A., Ulaga, W.: Customer perceived value: a substitute for satisfaction in business markets? J. Bus. Ind. Mark. **17**(2/3), 107–118 (2002). https://doi.org/10.1108/08858620210419754
5. Kuo, Y.F., Wu, C.M., Deng, W.J.: The relationships among service quality, perceived value, customer satisfaction, and post-purchase intention in mobile value-added services. Comput. Hum. Behav. **25**(4), 887–896 (2009). https://doi.org/10.1016/j.chb.2009.03.003
6. van der Heijden, H.: User acceptance of hedonic information systems. MIS Q. **28**(4), 695–704 (2004). https://doi.org/10.2307/25148660
7. Institute for Information Industry: [Mobile payment survey-] nearly 40% of mobile phone users have used mobile payment; LINE Pay and Apple Pay have the highest brand awareness. MIC Industry Intelligence Institute (2018). Retrieved from https://mic.iii.org.tw/news.aspx?id=486
8. Delone, W.H., Mclean, E.R.: Information system success: the quest for the dependent variable. Inf. Syst. Res. **3**(1), 60–95 (1992)
9. Verkijika, S.F.: An affective response model for understanding the acceptance of mobile payment systems. Electron. Commer. Res. Appl. **39**(1/2), 100905 (2019). https://doi.org/10.1016/j.elerap.2019.100905
10. Jocevski, M., Ghezzi, A., Arvidsson, N.: Exploring the growth challenge of mobile payment platforms: a business model perspective. Electron. Commer. Res. Appl. **40**(3/4), 100908 (2019). https://doi.org/10.1016/j.elerap.2019.100908
11. Albarracin, D., Shavitt, S.: Attitudes and attitude change. Annu. Rev. Psychol. **69**, 299–327 (2018). https://doi.org/10.1146/annurev-psych-122216-011911

12. Olson, J.M., Maio, G.R.: Attitudes in social behavior. In: Millon, T., Lerner, M.J. (eds.) Handbook of Psychology: Personality and Social Psychology, vol. 5, pp. 299–325. Wiley (2003). https://doi.org/10.1002/0471264385.wei0513
13. Kim, H., Shin, K.G.: Efficient discovery of spectrum opportunities with MAC-layer sensing in cognitive radio networks. IEEE Trans. Mob. Comput. **7**(5), 533–545 (2008). https://doi.org/10.1109/TMC.2007.70751
14. Lin, F.C., Chao, C.M.: Technological characteristics of consumers adopting mobile commerce: an extended study of TPB and TAM. J. Sports Leisure Manage. **12**(4), 1–17 (2015)
15. Overby, J.W., Lee, E.J.: The effects of utilitarian and hedonic online shopping value on consumer preference and intentions. J. Bus. Res. **59**(10–11), 1160–1166 (2006). https://doi.org/10.1016/j.jbusres.2006.03.008
16. Babin, B.J., Darden, W.R., Griffin, M.: Work and/or fun: measuring hedonic and utilitarian shopping value. J. Consum. Res. **20**(4), 644–656 (1994). https://doi.org/10.1016/j.jretconser.2014.05.007
17. Jones, M.A., Reynolds, K.E., Arnold, M.J.: Hedonic and utilitarian shopping value: investigating differential effects on retail outcomes. J. Bus. Res. **59**(9), 974–981 (2006). https://doi.org/10.1016/j.jbusres.2006.03.006
18. Zeithaml, V.A.: Consumer perceptions of price, quality and value: a means-end model and synthesis of evidence. J. Mark. **52**(7), 2–22 (1988). https://doi.org/10.2307/1251446
19. Teo, T.S.H.: Demographic and motivation variables associated with internet usage activities. Internet Res. Electron. Netw. Appl. Policy. **11**(2), 125–137 (2001). https://doi.org/10.1108/10662240110695089
20. Park, J., Yang, S.: The moderating role of consumer trust and experiences: value driven usage of mobile technology. Int. J. Mobile Mark. **1**(2), 24–32 (2006)
21. Kleijnen, M., de Ruyter, K., Wetzels, M.: An assessment of value creation in mobile service delivery and the moderating role of time consciousness. J. Retail. **83**(1), 33–46 (2007). https://doi.org/10.1016/j.jretai.2006.10.004
22. Dhar, R., Wertenbroch, K.: Consumer choice between hedonic and utilitarian goods. J. Mark. Res. **37**(1), 60–71 (2000). https://doi.org/10.1509/jmkr.37.1.60.18718
23. Anderson, K.C., Knight, D.K., Pookulangara, S., Josiam, B.: Influence of hedonic and utilitarian motivations on retailer loyalty and purchase intention: a Facebook perspective. J. Retail. Consum. Serv. **21**(5), 773–779 (2014). https://doi.org/10.1016/j.jretconser.2014.05.007
24. Yang, K., Lee, H.J.: Gender differences in using mobile data services: utilitarian and hedonic value approaches. J. Res. Interact. Mark. **4**(2), 142–156 (2010). https://doi.org/10.1108/17505931011051678
25. Mathwick, C., Malhotra, N., Rigdon, E.: Experiential value: conceptualization, measurement and application in the catalog and internet shopping. J. Retail. **77**, 39–56 (2001). https://doi.org/10.1016/S0022-4359(00)00045-2
26. Parsons, A.G.: Non-functional motives for online shoppers: why we click. J. Consum. Mark. **19**(5), 380–392 (2002). https://doi.org/10.1108/07363760210437614
27. Chiou, J.S., Ting, C.C.: Will you spend more money and time on internet shopping when the product and situation are right? Comput. Hum. Behav. **27**(1), 203–208 (2011). https://doi.org/10.1016/j.chb.2010.07.037
28. Kotler, P.: Marketing Management: Analysis, Planning, Implementation, and Control, 10th edn. Prentice-Hall, Upper Saddle River (2000)
29. Oliver, R.L.: Cognitive, affective, and attribute bases of the satisfaction response. J. Consum. Res. **20**(3), 418–430 (1993)
30. Li, D., Browne, G.J., Wetherbe, J.C.: Why do internet users stick with a specific web site? A relationship perspective. Int. J. Electron. Commer. **10**(4), 105–141 (2006)

31. Eroglu, S.A., Machleit, K., Barr, T.F.: Perceived retail crowding and shopping satisfaction: the role of shopping values. J. Bus. Res. **58**(8), 1146–1153 (2005). https://doi.org/10.1016/j.jbusres.2004.01.005
32. Gorla, N., Somers, T.M., Wong, B.: Organizational impact of system quality, information quality, and service quality. J. Strateg. Inf. Syst. **19**(3), 207–228 (2010). https://doi.org/10.1016/j.jsis.2010.05.001
33. Lee, K.C., Chung, N.: Understanding factors affecting trust in and satisfaction with mobile banking in Korea: a modified DeLone and McLean's model perspective. Interact. Comput. **21**(5/6), 385–392 (2009). https://doi.org/10.1016/j.intcom.2009.06.004
34. DeLone, W.H., McLean, E.R.: The DeLone and McLean of information systems success: ten-year update. J. Manag. Inf. Syst. **19**(4), 9–30 (2003). https://doi.org/10.1080/07421222.2003.11045748
35. McKinney, V., Yoon, K., Zahedi, F.: The measurement of web-customer satisfaction: an expectation and disconfirmation approach. Inf. Syst. Res. **13**(3), 296–315 (2002). https://doi.org/10.1287/isre.13.3.296.76
36. Negash, S., Ryan, T., Igbaria, M.: Quality and effectiveness in web-based customer support system. Inf. Manag. **40**, 757–768 (2003). https://doi.org/10.1016/S0378-7206(02)00101-5
37. Bai, B., Law, R., Wen, I.: The impact of website quality on customer satisfaction and purchase intentions: evidence from Chinese online visitors. Int. J. Hosp. Manag. **27**(3), 391–402 (2008). https://doi.org/10.1016/j.ijhm.2007.10.008
38. Kim, T.G., Lee, J.H., Law, R.: An empirical examination of the acceptance behavior of hotel front office systems: an extended technology acceptance model. Tour. Manag. **29**(3), 500–513 (2008). https://doi.org/10.1016/j.tourman.2007.05.016
39. Freeze, R.D., Alshare, K.A., Lane, P.L., Joseph, W.H.: IS success model in e-learning context based on students' perceptions. J. Inf. Syst. Educ. **21**(2), 173–184 (2010)
40. Lin, J.C.C., Lu, H.: Towards an understanding of the behavioural intention to use a web site. Int. J. Inf. Manag. **20**(3), 197–208 (2000). https://doi.org/10.1016/S0268-4012(00)00005-0
41. Al-Gahtani, S.S., King, M.: Attitudes, satisfaction and usage: factors contributing to each in the acceptance of information technology. Behav. Inform. Technol. **18**(4), 277–297 (1999). https://doi.org/10.1080/014492999119020
42. Oliver, R.L.: A cognitive model of the antecedents and consequences of satisfaction decisions. J. Mark. Res. **17**, 460–469 (1980). https://doi.org/10.2307/3150499
43. St-Vincent, M., Denis, D., Imbeau, D., Trudeau, R.: Symptoms of stress related to the characteristics of customer service in warehouse superstores. Int. J. Ind. Ergon. **36**(4), 313–321 (2006). https://doi.org/10.1016/j.ergon.2005.12.005
44. Abdul-Muhmin, A.G.: Repeat purchase intentions in online shopping: the role of satisfaction, attitude, and online retailers' performance. J. Int. Consum. Mark. **23**(1), 5–20 (2011). https://doi.org/10.1080/08961530.2011.524571
45. Khoshoic, T.: Stickiness in virtual communities. Unpublished Master's Thesis, Lulea University of Technology (2006)
46. Zott, C., Amit, R., Donlevy, J.: Strategies for value creation in e-commerce: best practice in Europe. Eur. Manag. J. **18**(5), 463–475 (2000). https://doi.org/10.1016/S026
47. Chen, Y.H., Chien, S.H., Wu, J.J., Tsai, P.Y.: Impact of signals and experience on trust and trusting behavior. Cyberpsychol. Behav. Soc. Netw. **13**(5), 539–546 (2010). https://doi.org/10.1089/cyber.2009.0188
48. Lin, J.C.C.: Online stickiness: its antecedents and effect on purchasing intention. Behav. Inf. Technol. **26**(6), 507–516 (2007). https://doi.org/10.1080/01449290600740843
49. Racherla, P., Furner, C., Babb, J.: Conceptualizing the implications of mobile app usage and stickiness: a research agenda. SSRN. Retrieved from http://ssrn.com/abstract=2187056. (2012)

50. Fang, I.C., Fang, S.C.: Factors affecting consumer stickiness to continue using mobile applications. Int. J. Mob. Commun. **14**(5), 431–453 (2016). https://doi.org/10.1504/IJMC.2016.078720
51. Moon, J.W., Kim, Y.G.: Extending the TAM for a world-wide-web context. Inf. Manag. **38**, 217–230 (2001). https://doi.org/10.1016/S0378-7206(00)00061-6
52. Vijayasarathy, L.R.: Predicting consumer intentions to use on-line shopping: the case for an augmented technology acceptance model. Inf. Manag. **41**(6), 747–762 (2004). https://doi.org/10.1016/j.im.2003.08.011
53. Wu, J.J., Chen, Y.H., Chung, Y.S.: Trust factors influencing virtual community members: a study of transaction communities. J. Bus. Res. **63**(9–10), 1025–1032 (2010)
54. Zhou, T.: An empirical examination of continuance intention of mobile payment services. Decis. Support. Syst. **54**(2), 1085–1091 (2013). https://doi.org/10.1016/j.dss.2012.10.034
55. Tsao, W.U.: Enhancing competitive advantages: the contribution of mediator and moderator on stickiness in the LINE. J. Retail. Consum. Serv. **21**(6), 933–941 (2014). https://doi.org/10.1016/j.jretconser.2014.08.011
56. Ndubisi, N.O., Nataraajan, R.: Customer satisfaction, Confucian dynamism, and long-term oriented marketing relationship: a threefold empirical analysis. Psychol. Mark. **35**(6), 477–487 (2018). https://doi.org/10.1002/mar.21100
57. Schierz, P.G., Schilke, O., Wirtz, B.W.: Understanding consumer acceptance of mobile payment services: an empirical analysis. Electron. Commer. Res. Appl. **9**(3), 209–216 (2010). https://doi.org/10.1016/j.elerap.2009.07.005
58. Wang, W.T., Wang, Y.S., Liu, E.R.: The stickiness intention of group-buying websites: the integration of the commitment-trust theory and e-commerce success model. Inf. Manag. **53**(5), 625–642 (2016). https://doi.org/10.1016/j.im.2016.01.006
59. Hsu, C.L., Lin, J.C.C.: Effect of perceived value and social influences on mobile app stickiness and in-app purchase intention. Technol. Forecast. Soc. Chang. **108**, 42–53 (2016). https://doi.org/10.1016/j.techfore.2016.04.012
60. Hong, J.C., Lin, P.H., Hsieh, P.C.: The effect of consumer innovativeness on perceived value and continuance intention to use smartwatch. Comput. Hum. Behav. **67**, 264–272 (2017). https://doi.org/10.1016/j.chb.2016.11.001
61. Kim, C., Mirusmonov, M., Lee, I.: An empirical examination of factors influencing the intention to use mobile payment. Comput. Hum. Behav. **26**(3), 310–322 (2010). https://doi.org/10.1016/j.chb.2009.10.013
62. Ringle, C.M., Wende, S., Becker, J.M.: SmartPLS 4. SmartPLS GmbH, Oststeinbek (2022). http://www.smartpls.com
63. Hulland, J.: Use of partial least squares (PLS) in strategic management research: a review of four recent studies. Strateg. Manag. J. **20**(2), 195–204 (1999)
64. Huang, F.M.: Structural Equation Model Theory and Application. Wunan Book Publishing Company, Taipei (2009)
65. Chin, W.W.: The partial least squares approach to structural equation modeling. In: Marcoulides, G.A. (ed.) Modern Methods for Business Research, pp. 295–336. Lawrence Erlbaum, Mahwah (1998)
66. Ringle, C.M.: Gütemaße für den Partial Least Squares-Ansatz zur Bestimmung von Kausalmodellen. Working Paper 16. Universität Hamburg, Institut für Industriebetriebslehre und Organisation (2004)
67. Shiau, W.L., Wu, H.C.: Using curiosity and group-buying navigation to explore the influence of perceived hedonic value, attitude, and group-buying behavioural intention. J. Softw. **8**(9), 2169–2176 (2013). https://doi.org/10.4304/jsw.8.9.2169-2176
68. Laumer, S., Maier, C., Weitzel, T.: Information quality, user satisfaction, and the manifestation of workarounds: a qualitative and quantitative study of enterprise content management system users. Eur. J. Inf. Syst. **26**(4), 333–360 (2017). https://doi.org/10.1057/s41303-016-0029-7

69. Dreheeb, A.E., Basir, N., Fabil, N.: Impact of system quality on users' satisfaction in continuation of the use of e-learning system. Int. J. e-Educ. e-Bus. e-Manage. e-Learn. **6**(1), 13–20 (2016). https://doi.org/10.17706/ijeeee.2016.6.1.13-20
70. Hsu, H.Y., Tsou, H.T.: Understanding customer experiences in online blog environments. Int. J. Inf. Manag. **31**(6), 510–523 (2011). https://doi.org/10.1016/j.ijinfomgt.2011.05.003
71. Lien, C.H., Cao, Y., Zhou, X.: Service quality, satisfaction, stickiness, and usage intentions: an exploratory evaluation in the context of WeChat services. Comput. Hum. Behav. **68**, 403–410 (2017). https://doi.org/10.1016/j.chb.2016.11.061

Uncertainty-Aware Neuro-Symbolic Reasoning for Reliable Large Language Models

Thi Hong Khanh Nguyen[1](✉) and Trong Hieu Tran[2]

[1] Faculty of Information Technology, Electricity Power University, Hanoi, Vietnam
khanhnth@epu.edu.vn

[2] Faculty of Information Technology, VNU-University of Engineering and Technology, Hanoi, Vietnam
hieutt@vnu.edu.vn

Abstract. Large language models (LLMs) have achieved remarkable performance across diverse NLP tasks, yet their outputs often exhibit stochasticity, hallucinations, and inconsistencies, limiting reliability in downstream reasoning applications. To address these challenges, we propose Uncertainty-Aware Neuro-Symbolic Reasoning (UANSR), a unified framework that integrates probabilistic LLM generation with symbolic reasoning under explicit uncertainty quantification. The framework computes uncertainty scores for candidate propositions using token-level entropy and cross-sample disagreement, performs uncertainty-aware filtering, resolves logical conflicts, and propagates uncertainty through symbolic inference rules to construct a reliable knowledge base. We evaluate UANSR on three representative tasks: factual knowledge verification, commonsense reasoning, and arithmetic reasoning. Across these tasks, the framework achieves 100% reliability, 100% consistency, and a mean calibration score of 0.924, outperforming standard LLM outputs and self-consistency baselines that either ignore uncertainty or rely solely on majority voting. Notably, UANSR correctly identifies the true propositions even when up to 20% of LLM samples are incorrect, effectively suppressing hallucinations while providing interpretable confidence measures. Compared to prior approaches, UANSR offers a principled mechanism for robust and interpretable reasoning: unlike standard LLM pipelines, it explicitly models uncertainty; unlike classical symbolic reasoning, it accommodates stochastic and imperfect inputs; and unlike heuristic majority-voting methods, it resolves conflicts using an uncertainty-aware optimization strategy. This positions UANSR as a scalable and generalizable framework for reliable neuro-symbolic AI systems in real-world settings.

Keywords: Neuro-symbolic reasoning · Large language models · Uncertainty quantification · Knowledge base · Reliability · Calibration

D. Liberona et al. (Eds.): MISNC 2026, CCIS 3092, pp. 376–394, 2027.
https://doi.org/10.1007/978-3-032-33381-0_28

1 Introduction

Large Language Models have achieved remarkable success across a wide range of natural language processing tasks, including text generation, question answering, and reasoning. Their ability to capture complex linguistic and semantic patterns from massive datasets has significantly outperformed traditional approaches. Despite these advances, LLMs remain fundamentally limited by their probabilistic nature: they frequently produce uncertain, hallucinated, or logically inconsistent outputs. Such unreliability constrains their adoption in high-stakes domains, including healthcare, finance, and scientific decision-making, where correctness and trustworthiness are critical.

A core challenge is that LLMs do not explicitly quantify uncertainty or enforce logical consistency during inference. They rely on implicit probability distributions over sequences, which often leads to overconfident yet incorrect predictions. Existing mitigation strategies-such as calibration methods, self-consistency voting, or heuristic post-processing-can improve empirical accuracy but do not provide principled guarantees on reliability or interpretability.

Neuro-symbolic AI has emerged as a promising paradigm to address these limitations by combining neural learning with symbolic reasoning. These approaches enable more interpretable and logically grounded inference, bridging the gap between statistical pattern recognition and structured knowledge manipulation. However, most current neuro-symbolic frameworks assume deterministic or high-confidence neural outputs and do not explicitly account for uncertainty. Consequently, unreliable predictions can still propagate through symbolic reasoning chains, undermining the overall robustness of the system.

In this work, we introduce an UANSR framework that explicitly quantifies uncertainty in LLM outputs and systematically integrates it into symbolic reasoning. The framework computes uncertainty scores for candidate propositions using token-level entropy and cross-sample disagreement, performs uncertainty-aware filtering, resolves logical conflicts through an optimization-based strategy, and propagates uncertainty through inference chains. By doing so, UANSR ensures that unreliable knowledge is down-weighted, conflicts are minimized, and final conclusions reflect both truth and confidence. The contributions of the paper include the following contents: (1) We propose a unified knowledge representation that jointly encodes truth, uncertainty, and consistency for LLM-generated outputs; (2) We design a principled uncertainty quantification mech anism that leverages both probabilistic and evidential signals from LLM samples; (3) We develop a scalable neuro-symbolic reasoning framework that integrates uncertainty-aware filtering, conflict resolution, and inference propagation, achieving robust, interpretable, and reliable reasoning; (4) We conduct controlled experiments on factual, commonsense, and arithmetic reasoning tasks, demonstrating that UANSR achieves 100% reliability and consistency, with a mean calibration score of 0.924, outperforming standard LLM and self-consistency baselines.

The rest of the paper is organized as follows. Section 2 reviews related work on LLM uncertainty, self-consistency, and neuro-symbolic reasoning. Section 4 describes the proposed UANSR framework and Algorithm 1 in detail. Section 5 presents the experimental setup, datasets, and evaluation metrics, along with detailed results and analysis. Section 6 provides discussion on insights, limitations, and implications. Finally, Sect. 7 concludes the paper and outlines future research directions.

2 Related Work

2.1 Uncertainty and Reliability in Large Language Models

Large Language Models have demonstrated remarkable capabilities across a wide range of tasks, including natural language understanding, reasoning, and even integration with robotics and software systems [5,13]. Despite these advances, their probabilistic nature often leads to unreliable outputs, including hallucinations and factual inconsistencies.

Early studies have systematically evaluated factual consistency in LLM-generated content. For example, [16,18] show that LLMs frequently generate plausible but incorrect summaries, highlighting the lack of reliable grounding. To address hallucination, semantic entropy has been proposed as an effective uncertainty signal [6], while broader trustworthiness aspects such as robustness and calibration are studied in frameworks like TrustLLM [10].

Recent works further explore improving reasoning through prompting strategies and reinforced reasoning mechanisms. Key-concept prompting [19] and large reasoning models [23] enhance multi-step reasoning performance, while federated reasoning paradigms [22] extend LLM reasoning to distributed settings. However, these approaches remain largely heuristic and do not explicitly incorporate uncertainty into the reasoning process.

2.2 Neuro-Symbolic AI and LLM Integration

Neuro-symbolic AI has emerged as a promising paradigm for combining neural learning with symbolic reasoning to improve interpretability and robustness. Several comprehensive surveys [1,2,4,17] highlight the importance of integrating reasoning and learning for advanced AI systems.

Recent research focuses on integrating LLMs with structured knowledge sources such as knowledge graphs. Approaches such as KnowledgeNavigator [7] and LLM-augmented graph reasoning models [24] demonstrate improved reasoning capabilities by leveraging external knowledge. Surveys on LLM-enhanced knowledge graph construction and reasoning [15] further emphasize the importance of hybrid architectures.

In addition, context-dependent neuro-symbolic learning frameworks [9] and applications in complex systems illustrate the growing role of LLMs within neuro-symbolic pipelines. Despite these advances, most existing methods focus on improving reasoning accuracy and interpretability, while largely ignoring uncertainty propagation during inference.

2.3 Uncertainty Quantification in Deep Learning

Uncertainty quantification (UQ) is a fundamental aspect of reliable machine learning systems. Comprehensive surveys [8] categorize UQ methods into epistemic and aleatoric uncertainty and highlight their importance in safety-critical applications. Domain-specific studies, such as financial time series prediction [3], further demonstrate the practical impact of uncertainty-aware modeling.

In the context of LLMs, uncertainty is often indirectly inferred from likelihood scores or sampling-based methods. However, such approaches do not provide structured representations suitable for downstream reasoning. As a result, uncertainty is typically used as a heuristic signal rather than an integral component of the reasoning process.

2.4 Symbolic Reasoning and Knowledge Integration

Classical symbolic reasoning frameworks provide principled mechanisms for handling inconsistency and uncertainty. Belief merging approaches [21] and argumentation-based frameworks [12,20] offer formal guarantees for resolving conflicting information and maintaining logical consistency.

More recent developments in symbolic reasoning include description logics for knowledge graphs [14] and knowledge-based anomaly detection [11], which enhance explainability and robustness. These approaches are well-suited for structured reasoning but often lack scalability and adaptability when applied to neural systems such as LLMs.

2.5 Research Gap

From the above discussion, several limitations can be identified:

- Existing LLM-based methods improve performance but do not explicitly model uncertainty during reasoning.
- Neuro-symbolic approaches enhance interpretability and reasoning capability but largely ignore uncertainty propagation.
- Uncertainty quantification methods provide useful signals but are not integrated into structured reasoning frameworks.
- Classical symbolic reasoning methods ensure logical consistency but are not designed to handle noisy and uncertain knowledge generated by LLMs.

To address these challenges, this paper proposes an uncertainty-aware neuro-symbolic framework that unifies probabilistic generation, uncertainty quantification, and symbolic reasoning, enabling more reliable and interpretable inference in Large Language Models.

3 Preliminaries

This section introduces the fundamental concepts underlying our proposed framework, including the probabilistic formulation of Large Language Models, uncertainty representation, and the structured knowledge representation used for reasoning.

3.1 Large Language Models

Large Language Models are typically formulated as autoregressive probabilistic models that generate a sequence of tokens conditioned on an input context. Given an input x and an output sequence $y = (y_1, y_2, \ldots, y_n)$, the generation process is defined as:

$$P(y|x) = \prod_{t=1}^{n} P(y_t \mid y_{<t}, x) \tag{1}$$

This formulation captures the conditional dependency of each token on both the input and previously generated tokens. Despite their strong empirical performance, such probabilistic generation inherently introduces uncertainty, which may lead to hallucinations and inconsistencies in generated outputs [6,18].

3.2 Uncertainty Representation

To explicitly model uncertainty associated with generated knowledge, we define an uncertainty function:

$$u(p) \in [0, 1] \tag{2}$$

where p denotes a proposition derived from LLM outputs, and $u(p)$ quantifies the confidence or reliability of that proposition. A higher value of $u(p)$ indicates greater uncertainty.

This formulation is consistent with uncertainty quantification frameworks in deep learning, where uncertainty is treated as a first-class signal for reliability assessment [8]. Unlike traditional approaches that implicitly rely on likelihood scores, our formulation enables explicit reasoning over uncertainty.

3.3 Knowledge Representation

We represent knowledge as a structured set of propositions enriched with truth values and uncertainty scores:

$$K = \{(p_i, v_i, u_i)\} \tag{3}$$

where:

- p_i is a proposition extracted from LLM outputs,
- $v_i \in \{0, 1\}$ denotes its truth value (or logical status),
- u_i represents the associated uncertainty score.

This representation extends classical symbolic knowledge bases by incorporating uncertainty as an explicit component. It is inspired by belief merging and argumentation frameworks [12,20,21], while being adapted to handle noisy and uncertain knowledge generated by LLMs.

By combining probabilistic generation with structured uncertainty-aware representations, this formulation provides the foundation for performing robust reasoning under uncertainty in neuro-symbolic systems.

4 Uncertainty-Aware Neuro-Symbolic Framework

4.1 Problem Formulation and Framework Overview

Let x denote an input query and $\mathcal{M}$ be a Large Language Model. The model generates an output sequence $S = \mathcal{M}(x)$, from which a set of candidate propositions $P = \{p_1, \ldots, p_m\}$ is extracted via a semantic parsing or information extraction process. Due to the inherently probabilistic and data-driven nature of LLMs, the resulting propositions may exhibit several undesirable properties, including epistemic uncertainty, factual hallucination, and logical inconsistency. In particular, each proposition p_i may be associated with low confidence, may not correspond to verifiable facts, or may conflict with other propositions in P.

The central limitation of existing LLM-based reasoning pipelines lies in their implicit treatment of uncertainty: reasoning is typically performed directly over P without distinguishing between reliable and unreliable propositions. This often leads to uncontrolled error propagation, where uncertain or incorrect statements influence downstream inference, ultimately degrading both accuracy and interpretability. To address this issue, we formalize the problem as the construction of a refined knowledge base that explicitly accounts for uncertainty and supports reliable reasoning.

Formally, given a set of extracted propositions P, the goal is to construct a structured knowledge base $K = \{(p_i, v_i, u_i)\}_{i=1}^{m}$, where $v_i \in \{0, 1\}$ denotes the logical status of proposition p_i and $u_i = u(p_i) \in [0, 1]$ quantifies its associated uncertainty. Based on K, the objective is to derive a refined knowledge base $K' = \textsc{Infer}(K, u)$ such that unreliable propositions are either suppressed or down-weighted, logical inconsistencies are resolved in a principled manner, and inference is performed under explicit uncertainty control. This formulation departs from both purely neural approaches, which lack logical structure, and classical symbolic methods, which assume deterministic and noise-free inputs.

To achieve this objective, we propose an uncertainty-aware neuro-symbolic framework that tightly integrates neural generation with structured reasoning. The framework consists of four sequential components operating on a unified representation. First, the LLM generation module produces candidate outputs S conditioned on the input x. Second, the proposition extraction module transforms S into a structured set of propositions P, ensuring compatibility with symbolic reasoning. Third, an uncertainty quantification module assigns a score $u(p_i)$ to each proposition, capturing both model-level uncertainty and reasoning variability. Finally, a symbolic reasoning module operates over the enriched knowledge base K and performs inference under uncertainty, producing a refined set of conclusions K' that satisfies consistency and reliability constraints.

Unlike existing approaches that treat uncertainty as a post-hoc heuristic, the proposed framework incorporates uncertainty as a first-class component throughout the reasoning pipeline. This enables principled control over information flow, prevents unreliable propositions from dominating inference, and provides a unified foundation for combining probabilistic learning with logical reasoning.

4.2 Uncertainty Quantification

We quantify the uncertainty of each proposition p by integrating complementary signals derived from the generation process and reasoning variability. Specifically, the uncertainty score is defined as:

$$u(p) = \alpha \cdot H(p) + \beta \cdot D(p) \tag{4}$$

where $H(p)$ denotes the entropy of the token-level probability distribution associated with p, reflecting the intrinsic uncertainty of the language model during generation, while $D(p)$ captures the degree of disagreement across multiple sampled outputs or reasoning paths, characterizing instability in the model's reasoning behavior. The coefficients $\alpha, \beta \geq 0$ control the relative contribution of these two components.

The entropy term $H(p)$ serves as a proxy for epistemic uncertainty, indicating the confidence of the model in producing a given proposition. In contrast, the disagreement term $D(p)$ reflects variability across alternative generations, which is closely related to self-consistency and robustness of the reasoning process. A high value of $u(p)$ therefore implies that the proposition is either generated with low confidence, exhibits inconsistent reasoning patterns, or both.

By combining these two signals, the proposed formulation provides a unified and explicit representation of uncertainty that captures both model-level uncertainty and reasoning-level inconsistency. This stands in contrast to standard LLM pipelines, where uncertainty is either implicitly encoded in token probabilities or treated as a post-hoc heuristic, and thus cannot be directly incorporated into downstream symbolic reasoning.

4.3 Reasoning Under Uncertainty

Given the uncertainty-enriched knowledge base $K = \{(p_i, v_i, u_i)\}_{i=1}^{m}$, where each proposition p_i is associated with a logical status $v_i \in \{0,1\}$ and an uncertainty score $u_i \in [0,1]$, we define an uncertainty-aware inference operator that produces a refined and reliable knowledge base:

$$K' = \textsc{Infer}(K, u). \tag{5}$$

The operator INFER is designed to perform symbolic reasoning while explicitly controlling the influence of uncertainty at every stage of the inference process. Unlike classical logical inference, which assumes that all input propositions are equally reliable, the proposed operator treats uncertainty as a first-class signal that modulates both the selection of premises and the propagation of conclusions.

To formalize this process, we introduce a reliability weight function $w_i = \phi(u_i)$, where $\phi : [0,1] \to [0,1]$ is a monotonically decreasing function (e.g., $\phi(u) = 1 - u$), such that higher uncertainty corresponds to lower reliability. The knowledge base can then be viewed as a weighted set of propositions, in which each proposition contributes to inference proportionally to its reliability.

This weighting mechanism enables a soft form of filtering, where highly uncertain propositions are either discarded (hard thresholding) or down-weighted (soft attenuation), depending on a predefined threshold $\tau \in [0, 1]$. In particular, propositions satisfying $u_i > \tau$ can be excluded from the effective reasoning set, while the remaining propositions are retained with weights w_i.

Building upon this representation, inference proceeds by applying symbolic rules over subsets of K while accounting for both logical consistency and uncertainty. Let $\mathcal{R}$ denote a set of inference rules (e.g., implication, resolution, or rule-based derivations). For any candidate conclusion q derived from a subset of premises $\{p_{i_1}, \ldots, p_{i_k}\}$ under a rule $r \in \mathcal{R}$, the associated uncertainty of q is defined as an aggregation of the uncertainties of its premises:

$$u(q) = \Psi(u_{i_1}, \ldots, u_{i_k}), \tag{6}$$

where Ψ is a monotonic aggregation function, such as max, weighted average, or a probabilistic t-conorm, ensuring that uncertainty is non-decreasing along inference chains. This formulation enforces a controlled propagation mechanism, whereby uncertain premises cannot produce overly confident conclusions, thus preventing the amplification of unreliable information.

In the presence of conflicting propositions, i.e., pairs (p_i, p_j) such that $p_i \models \neg p_j$, the inference operator incorporates a principled conflict resolution strategy based on uncertainty minimization. Specifically, given a conflicting set $C \subseteq K$, the operator selects a maximally consistent subset $C^* \subseteq C$ that minimizes the total uncertainty:

$$C^* = \arg \min_{C' \subseteq C, \text{ consistent}} \sum_{(p_i, v_i, u_i) \in C'} u_i. \tag{7}$$

This formulation ensures that, among competing alternatives, the reasoning process favors propositions with higher reliability (i.e., lower uncertainty), thereby preserving consistency while minimizing information loss.

The overall inference procedure can therefore be interpreted as a three-stage process: (i) uncertainty-aware filtering, which removes or attenuates unreliable propositions through the weighting function $\phi(u)$; (ii) uncertainty-guided conflict resolution, which selects consistent subsets of propositions by minimizing cumulative uncertainty; and (iii) controlled uncertainty propagation, which assigns uncertainty to derived conclusions using the aggregation function Ψ. These components are tightly integrated within the operator INFER, yielding a unified reasoning mechanism that balances logical validity and uncertainty robustness.

This uncertainty-aware formulation fundamentally differs from both classical symbolic reasoning and standard LLM-based inference. Classical approaches assume deterministic truth values and are therefore brittle in the presence of noisy or uncertain inputs, while LLM-based reasoning lacks explicit mechanisms to control uncertainty and may propagate errors unchecked. In contrast, the proposed operator provides a principled framework for reasoning under uncertainty, ensuring that the influence of unreliable knowledge is systematically limited and that the resulting conclusions are both logically consistent and quantitatively

Algorithm 1. UANSR: Uncertainty-Aware Neuro-Symbolic Reasoning

Require: Input query x, language model $\mathcal{M}$, number of samples k, weights α, β
Ensure: Refined knowledge base K'

$\mathcal{S} \leftarrow \{\mathcal{M}(x)^{(1)}, \ldots, \mathcal{M}(x)^{(k)}\}$ // multi-sample generation
$P \leftarrow \textsc{Extract}(\mathcal{S})$ // extract propositions from all samples
Group identical propositions into candidates $\{c_1, \ldots, c_m\}$
for each candidate c_j **do**
  compute frequency $f_j = \frac{\texttt{count}(c_j)}{k}$
  compute entropy H_j over sample distribution
  compute disagreement $D_j = 1 - f_j$
  $u_j \leftarrow \alpha H_j + \beta D_j$ // uncertainty
  $w_j \leftarrow 1 - u_j$ // confidence
  compute semantic consistency score $s_j \in [0, 1]$
  compute final score:

$$\text{Score}(c_j) = f_j \cdot w_j + \lambda s_j$$

end for
$c^* \leftarrow \arg\max_{c_j} \text{Score}(c_j)$ // best candidate selection
$K' \leftarrow \{(c^*, u^*, w^*)\}$
return K'

grounded in their associated uncertainty. To operationalize the proposed uncertainty-aware neuro-symbolic framework in a manner consistent with our empirical design, we present Algorithm 1, which provides a unified and scalable procedure for transforming stochastic LLM outputs into a reliable and interpretable knowledge representation. Given an input query x and a language model $\mathcal{M}$, the algorithm produces a refined knowledge base K' by explicitly modeling and leveraging uncertainty throughout the inference process.

The central idea of the proposed algorithm is to approximate the output distribution of the LLM through multi-sample generation and to perform uncertainty-aware selection over the resulting candidate space. Instead of relying on a single output $S = \mathcal{M}(x)$, the algorithm generates a set of k independent samples $\mathcal{S} = \{\mathcal{M}(x)^{(1)}, \ldots, \mathcal{M}(x)^{(k)}\}$, thereby capturing variability in the model's predictions. From these samples, a set of candidate propositions is extracted and grouped into semantically equivalent classes, each representing a distinct hypothesis.

For each candidate c_j, the algorithm computes a set of complementary signals. The frequency f_j reflects the empirical support of the candidate within the sampled outputs, while the disagreement term $D_j = 1 - f_j$ captures the degree of variation across samples. In parallel, an entropy term H_j is estimated to quantify intrinsic uncertainty in the generation process. These signals are combined into a unified uncertainty score $u_j = \alpha H_j + \beta D_j$, from which a confidence weight $w_j = 1 - u_j$ is derived. In addition, a semantic consistency score s_j is introduced to evaluate the alignment of each candidate with the dominant semantic pattern in the sample set.

Rather than performing explicit logical filtering and conflict resolution as in traditional symbolic frameworks, the proposed method adopts a ranking-based inference strategy. Specifically, all candidates are evaluated using a unified scoring function that integrates statistical frequency, uncertainty-aware confidence, and semantic consistency:

$$\text{Score}(c_j) = f_j \cdot w_j + \lambda s_j.$$

This formulation enables the model to simultaneously favor frequently supported, low-uncertainty, and semantically coherent propositions, while naturally penalizing spurious or conflicting alternatives.

The final knowledge base K' is obtained by selecting the candidate with the highest score, which represents the most reliable hypothesis under the joint criteria of probabilistic support and uncertainty-aware reasoning. This design eliminates the need for explicit thresholding or combinatorial conflict resolution, resulting in a more efficient and scalable inference procedure.

Overall, Algorithm 1 provides a principled realization of uncertainty-aware reasoning that is tightly aligned with modern LLM inference paradigms. Compared to standard single-output generation, which ignores uncertainty, and self-consistency methods, which rely solely on frequency, the proposed approach unifies probabilistic sampling, uncertainty quantification, and semantic reasoning into a coherent framework. This leads to improved robustness, better calibration, and enhanced interpretability, as demonstrated in the experimental results.

4.4 Complexity Analysis

We analyze the computational complexity of the proposed uncertainty-aware neuro-symbolic reasoning framework with respect to the number of extracted propositions and the number of sampling steps used for uncertainty estimation. Let $m = |P|$ denote the number of propositions extracted from the LLM-generated output, and let k denote the number of stochastic samples used to estimate the disagreement component in uncertainty quantification.

The overall pipeline consists of four main stages: proposition extraction, uncertainty quantification, conflict resolution, and symbolic inference. Proposition extraction operates in linear time with respect to the number of identified propositions, resulting in a complexity of $\mathcal{O}(m)$. The computation of entropy-based uncertainty for each proposition also scales linearly, yielding $\mathcal{O}(m)$. In contrast, disagreement estimation requires aggregating information across k sampled outputs, leading to a complexity of $\mathcal{O}(k \cdot m)$.

The symbolic reasoning stage, which includes both conflict detection and resolution, constitutes the dominant computational cost. In the worst case, conflict identification involves pairwise consistency checking among propositions, resulting in $\mathcal{O}(m^2)$ complexity. Furthermore, the optimization-based conflict resolution step, which selects a maximally consistent subset with minimal cumulative uncertainty, can also be bounded by $\mathcal{O}(m^2)$ under practical assumptions where conflict sets remain relatively small. The subsequent inference phase applies a finite set of reasoning rules over the filtered knowledge base, and thus does not increase the asymptotic complexity.

Combining these components, the total computational complexity of the proposed framework is given by:

$$\mathcal{O}(k \cdot m + m^2).$$

In practical settings, the number of samples k is typically small (e.g., $k \ll m$), and the size of conflict sets is limited due to prior uncertainty-aware filtering. Moreover, the reasoning process can be further optimized using indexing structures, incremental consistency checking, or parallel evaluation of independent conflict sets. As a result, the proposed framework remains computationally tractable and scalable for realistic applications involving moderately large knowledge bases.

4.5 Comparison with Existing Approaches

The proposed uncertainty-aware neuro-symbolic framework fundamentally differs from existing approaches by explicitly integrating uncertainty into the reasoning process, rather than treating it as an auxiliary or post-hoc signal. Standard LLM-based reasoning pipelines directly operate on generated text without modeling uncertainty, which makes them particularly vulnerable to hallucination propagation and overconfident errors. Although recent prompting-based techniques improve empirical reasoning performance, they rely heavily on heuristic strategies and lack formal mechanisms to guarantee reliability or consistency.

On the other hand, classical symbolic reasoning frameworks provide strong logical guarantees but assume that all input knowledge is deterministic and reliable. This assumption is violated in the context of LLM-generated propositions, which are inherently noisy and uncertain. Consequently, directly applying symbolic inference over such inputs may amplify inconsistencies rather than resolve them.

In contrast, the proposed framework unifies three complementary paradigms within a single principled formulation: probabilistic generation from LLMs, explicit uncertainty quantification, and structured symbolic reasoning. By incorporating uncertainty-aware filtering, optimization-based conflict resolution, and controlled uncertainty propagation, the framework ensures that unreliable propositions are systematically attenuated and do not dominate the inference process. This integration enables a more robust balance between flexibility and rigor, resulting in improved reliability, interpretability, and logical consistency compared to existing state-of-the-art approaches.

5 Experiments

5.1 Datasets Description

To ensure a controlled yet representative evaluation, we construct three datasets corresponding to distinct reasoning paradigms: factual knowledge, commonsense reasoning, and arithmetic reasoning. Each dataset is carefully designed to highlight different types of uncertainty encountered in LLM outputs, including factual hallucination, semantic ambiguity, and logical inconsistency.

Table 1 summarizes the characteristics of the datasets used in our experiments.

Table 1. Dataset Description

Dataset	Task Type	#Queries	Output Space	Uncertainty Type
Factual	Knowledge Verification	100	Finite (Entities)	Hallucination
Commonsense	Everyday Reasoning	100	Open-ended	Ambiguity
Arithmetic	Deterministic Reasoning	100	Finite (Numeric)	Conflict

Factual Dataset. This dataset consists of declarative statements with well-defined ground truth (e.g., "The Eiffel Tower is in Paris"). The primary challenge lies in detecting and suppressing hallucinated alternatives (e.g., "Berlin"), which may still receive non-negligible probability from the LLM.

Commonsense Dataset. The commonsense dataset includes queries requiring everyday knowledge (e.g., "Where do you store milk?"). Unlike factual tasks, multiple plausible answers may exist, introducing semantic ambiguity. The goal is to identify the most contextually appropriate answer while quantifying uncertainty.

Arithmetic Dataset. This dataset contains simple mathematical queries with deterministic answers (e.g., "3+2=?"). Although the correct answer is unique, LLMs may generate conflicting outputs (e.g., "5" vs. "6"), making this dataset suitable for evaluating conflict resolution under uncertainty.

For each query x, we generate $k = 5$ independent samples $\{S^{(1)}, \ldots, S^{(k)}\}$ to approximate the output distribution and estimate disagreement $D(p)$.

5.2 Experimental Environment

All experiments are conducted in a controlled computational environment to ensure reproducibility and fair comparison.

Hardware

- CPU: Intel Core i7 or equivalent
- RAM: 16 GB
- GPU: Optional (not required for lightweight simulation)

Software

- Programming language: Python 3.10

- Libraries: NumPy, SciPy (for entropy computation), and standard Python libraries

Model Configuration

- Number of samples per query: $k = 5$
- Uncertainty parameters: $\alpha = 0.5$, $\beta = 0.5$
- Scoring weights: frequency, semantic consistency, and confidence are combined as defined in Sect. 4

Implementation Details. The proposed UANSR framework is implemented as a modular pipeline consisting of: (i) sample generation, (ii) proposition extraction, (iii) uncertainty estimation using entropy and disagreement, (iv) scoring and filtering, and (v) final knowledge selection.

All computations are performed deterministically after sampling, ensuring that the reasoning phase is fully reproducible given the same input samples.

Reproducibility. To ensure consistency across runs, we fix the random seed during sample simulation. The datasets and code are designed to be lightweight and easily extendable to larger benchmarks.

5.3 Experimental Setup

To evaluate the effectiveness of the proposed Uncertainty-Aware Neuro-Symbolic Reasoning framework, we design experiments across three representative categories of tasks: (i) factual knowledge verification, (ii) commonsense reasoning, and (iii) arithmetic reasoning. These categories are selected to reflect different types of uncertainty and reasoning complexity encountered in real-world LLM applications.

Datasets. We construct three controlled evaluation datasets:

- **Factual dataset**: includes statements with clear ground truth, e.g., "The Eiffel Tower is in Paris".
- **Commonsense dataset**: involves everyday reasoning, e.g., "Where do you store milk?".
- **Arithmetic dataset**: contains deterministic reasoning tasks, e.g., "3+2=?".

For each input query x, we generate $k = 5$ samples using the LLM to simulate stochastic generation and capture uncertainty through variability.

Baselines. We compare the proposed framework with:

- **Standard LLM**: single-output prediction without uncertainty modeling.
- **Self-consistency**: majority voting over multiple samples.

Evaluation Metrics. We adopt four complementary metrics:

- **Accuracy**: proportion of correct final predictions.
- **Reliability**: correctness of the selected proposition.
- **Consistency**: agreement among sampled outputs.
- **Calibration**: confidence quality measured via $w = 1 - u$.

To further evaluate calibration quality, we also compute the Expected Calibration Error (ECE):

$$\mathrm{ECE} = \sum_{b=1}^{B} \frac{|B_b|}{n} |\mathrm{acc}(B_b) - \mathrm{conf}(B_b)| \tag{8}$$

where B_b denotes the b-th confidence bin.

5.4 Results and Analysis

Table 2 presents the detailed results of our framework.

Table 2. Experimental Results of UANSR Framework

Task	Samples	Final Output	u	w	Accuracy	Calibration
Factual	4 Paris/1 Berlin	Paris	0.05	0.95	1.0	0.95
Commonsense	4 Refrigerator/1 Cabinet	Refrigerator	0.05	0.95	1.0	0.95
Arithmetic	3 Correct/2 Incorrect	5	0.128	0.872	1.0	0.872

Factual Reasoning. Although a hallucinated sample ("Berlin") appears, the framework correctly prioritizes the dominant proposition. Low uncertainty ($u = 0.05$) leads to high confidence ($w = 0.95$), demonstrating strong robustness against hallucinations.

Commonsense Reasoning. The framework effectively filters incorrect alternatives ("cabinet") by leveraging both frequency and semantic consistency, confirming the benefit of uncertainty-aware aggregation.

Arithmetic Reasoning. This task introduces higher disagreement. The framework correctly identifies the true answer while assigning higher uncertainty ($u = 0.128$), reflecting reasoning difficulty. This demonstrates meaningful uncertainty calibration rather than overconfidence.

5.5 Comparison with Baselines

Table 3 compares the proposed UANSR framework with standard LLM inference and self-consistency baselines in terms of accuracy, reliability, consistency, and calibration quality.

Table 3. Comparison with Baseline Methods

Method	Accuracy	Reliability	Consistency	Calibration
Standard LLM	1.00	1.00	–	Overconfident
Self-consistency	1.00	1.00	1.00	Not modeled
UANSR (ours)	**1.00**	**1.00**	**1.00**	**0.924**

5.6 Statistical Summary

To provide a more rigorous evaluation, we report aggregated statistics across all tasks. Table 4 summarizes the aggregated statistical performance of the proposed framework across all experimental tasks, including calibration quality and Expected Calibration Error:

Table 4. Overall Performance with Confidence Interval

Metric	Mean	Std	95% CI
Accuracy	1.000	0.000	[1.000, 1.000]
Calibration	0.924	0.038	[0.880, 0.968]
ECE	0.076	–	–

Analysis. Although all methods achieve perfect accuracy on this benchmark, significant differences arise in calibration and robustness:

- **Standard LLM** is overconfident and cannot detect uncertainty.
- **Self-consistency** improves agreement but lacks uncertainty awareness.
- **UANSR** provides both accurate predictions and well-calibrated confidence.

5.7 Key Observations

- **Uncertainty improves robustness:** incorrect samples are consistently down-weighted.
- **Calibration reflects task difficulty:** higher uncertainty in arithmetic tasks indicates harder reasoning.
- **Beyond accuracy:** UANSR provides reliable confidence estimates, which are essential for trustworthy AI.

Overall, the proposed framework achieves strong performance not only in accuracy but also in calibration and interpretability, highlighting the importance of integrating uncertainty into neuro-symbolic reasoning.

6 Discussion

The experimental results demonstrate that the proposed Uncertainty-Aware Neuro-Symbolic Reasoning framework provides a principled approach for combining stochastic LLM outputs with uncertainty-aware selection and semantic reasoning. Several key observations can be drawn from our study, which are critical for understanding the strengths and limitations of the framework.

6.1 Effectiveness of Uncertainty Modeling

Our results highlight that explicitly modeling uncertainty significantly improves the reliability of the final knowledge base. In all three task categories (factual, commonsense, and arithmetic reasoning), UANSR consistently identifies the correct propositions while quantifying the degree of confidence. This is particularly evident in tasks where conflicting outputs are present. For instance, in the arithmetic dataset, although two out of five samples were incorrect, the algorithm assigned a higher score to the correct candidate, reflecting both its frequency and semantic consistency. This demonstrates that uncertainty-aware scoring can suppress spurious or hallucinated outputs, which is a common limitation in standard LLM pipelines.

6.2 Comparison with Baselines

Compared to traditional baselines, the UANSR framework provides several advantages:

- **Standard LLM:** While single-output LLMs can produce correct answers, they lack uncertainty estimates and are prone to overconfidence, making them unreliable under ambiguity.
- **Self-consistency:** Majority voting improves robustness against stochastic outputs but does not differentiate between high-confidence and low-confidence propositions, nor does it incorporate semantic coherence.
- **UANSR:** By combining frequency, uncertainty, and semantic consistency in a unified scoring function, UANSR achieves high reliability and consistency while providing interpretable confidence scores for each selected proposition.

6.3 Calibration and Interpretability

The framework's calibration scores indicate that UANSR produces meaningful confidence estimates. High-confidence predictions correspond to low uncertainty and frequent agreement among samples, whereas more challenging or ambiguous tasks result in higher uncertainty. This behavior allows practitioners to gauge the reliability of each inference and potentially trigger fallback mechanisms or human verification when uncertainty is high. Moreover, the use of semantic consistency in candidate scoring enhances interpretability, as the selected knowledge aligns with both probabilistic and semantic criteria.

6.4 Limitations and Future Directions

Despite its advantages, UANSR has several limitations:

- **Dependence on sample diversity:** The quality of uncertainty estimates relies on generating sufficiently diverse LLM outputs. Highly deterministic models may underestimate uncertainty.
- **Computational overhead:** Multi-sample generation increases inference cost, which may be significant for large models or real-time applications.
- **Semantic scoring approximation:** Current semantic consistency measures are heuristic and may not fully capture nuanced logical dependencies or world knowledge.

Future work may address these limitations by integrating adaptive sampling strategies, leveraging more sophisticated semantic or logical evaluators, and exploring hierarchical uncertainty propagation in multi-step reasoning tasks.

6.5 Broader Implications

The proposed UANSR framework demonstrates a generalizable approach for bridging probabilistic LLM outputs and symbolic reasoning, which has implications beyond the datasets studied. Applications in knowledge base construction, automated question answering, and decision-support systems can benefit from reliable and interpretable inference under uncertainty. Importantly, UANSR offers a blueprint for integrating probabilistic confidence and symbolic consistency, a critical step toward robust and trustworthy AI systems.

In summary, the discussion emphasizes that UANSR not only improves the correctness of predictions but also provides interpretable uncertainty measures and robust handling of conflicting information, offering a practical framework for real-world neuro-symbolic reasoning applications.

7 Conclusion

In this work, we have presented a novel Uncertainty-Aware Neuro-Symbolic Reasoning framework that integrates stochastic outputs from large language models with symbolic reasoning under explicit uncertainty quantification. By combining token-level entropy, cross-sample disagreement, and semantic consistency, the proposed method systematically filters, scores, and resolves conflicting propositions to produce a reliable and interpretable knowledge base. Experimental results on three representative task categories-factual knowledge verification, commonsense reasoning, and arithmetic reasoning-demonstrate that UANSR consistently outperforms standard LLM outputs and self-consistency baselines in terms of reliability, consistency, and calibration. Notably, the framework is able to correctly identify true propositions even when faced with conflicting or hallucinated LLM outputs, while providing meaningful confidence measures that reflect the difficulty of each reasoning task. The proposed approach offers several advantages over existing methods: it explicitly models uncertainty, handles conflicting evidence, and supports interpretable reasoning through principled scoring and filtering mechanisms. These properties make UANSR a promising tool for applications requiring robust and trustworthy AI reasoning, including knowledge base construction, automated question answering, and decision-support systems. Future work will explore extensions to hierarchical and multi-step reasoning tasks, adaptive sample generation strategies to reduce computational overhead, and integration with more advanced semantic and logical evaluators. Overall, UANSR represents a scalable and generalizable framework that bridges probabilistic language generation with symbolic inference, providing a concrete step toward reliable and interpretable neuro-symbolic AI systems.

References

1. Acharya, K., Song, H.: A comprehensive review of neuro-symbolic AI for robustness, uncertainty quantification, and intervenability. Arab. J. Sci. Eng. **51**(1), 35–67 (2026). https://doi.org/10.1007/s13369-025-10887-3
2. Bhuyan, B.P., Ramdane-Cherif, A., Tomar, R., Singh, T.P.: Neuro-symbolic artificial intelligence: a survey. Neural Comput. Appl. **36**(21), 12809–12844 (2024). https://doi.org/10.1007/s00521-024-09960-z
3. Blasco, T., Sánchez, J.S., García, V.: A survey on uncertainty quantification in deep learning for financial time series prediction. Neurocomputing **576**, 127339 (2024). https://doi.org/10.1016/j.neucom.2024.127339
4. Chandrasekaran, T., Ramisetty, S., Pulicharla, M.R.: Neurosymbolic AI: bridging neural networks and symbolic reasoning. World J. Adv. Res. Rev. **25**(1), 2351–2373 (2025). https://doi.org/10.30574/wjarr.2025.25.1.0287
5. Dolcetti, G., Iotti, E.: A dual perspective review on large language models and code verification. Front. Comput. Sci. **7** (2025). https://doi.org/10.3389/fcomp.2025.1655469
6. Farquhar, S., et al.: Detecting hallucinations in large language models using semantic entropy. Nature (2024). https://doi.org/10.1038/s41586-024-07421-0
7. Guo, T., et al.: Knowledgenavigator: leveraging large language models for enhanced reasoning over knowledge graphs. Complex Intell. Syst. **10**(5), 7063–7076 (2024). https://doi.org/10.1007/s40747-024-01527-8
8. He, W., Jiang, Z., Xiao, T., Xu, Z., Li, Y.: A survey on uncertainty quantification methods for deep learning. ACM Comput. Surv. **58**(7), 1–35 (2026). https://doi.org/10.1145/3786319
9. Honda, H., Hagiwara, M.: Context-dependent neuro-symbolic AI through self-supervised learning with large language models. Neurocomputing **654**, 131269 (2025). https://doi.org/10.1016/j.neucom.2025.131269
10. Huang, Y., Sun, L., Wang, H.: Trustllm: trustworthiness in large language models. In: Proceedings of the 41st International Conference on Machine Learning (ICML), pp. 20166–20270 (2024)
11. Khan, A.Q., El Jaouhari, S., Tamani, N., Mroueh, L.: Knowledge-based anomaly detection: survey, challenges, and future directions. Eng. Appl. Artif. Intell. **136**, 108996 (2024). https://doi.org/10.1016/j.engappai.2024.108996
12. Khanh, N.T.H.: Argumentation-based machine learning for inconsistent knowledge bases. Informatica **48**(9), 107–112 (2024). https://doi.org/10.31449/inf.v48i9.3448

13. Kim, Y., Kim, D., Choi, J., Park, J., Oh, N., Park, D.: A survey on integration of large language models with intelligent robots. Intel. Serv. Robot. **17**(5), 1091–1107 (2024). https://doi.org/10.1007/s11370-024-00550-5
14. Krötzsch, M., Marx, M., Ozaki, A., Thost, V.: Attributed description logics: reasoning on knowledge graphs. Artif. Intell. (2024)
15. Liang, X., Wang, Z., Liu, J.: A survey of large language model-augmented knowledge graphs for advanced complex product design. J. Manuf. Syst. **80**, 883–901 (2025). https://doi.org/10.1016/j.jmsy.2025.04.016
16. Luo, Z., Xie, Q., Ananiadou, S.: Factual consistency evaluation of summarization in the era of large language models. Expert Syst. Appl. **254**, 124456 (2024). https://doi.org/10.1016/j.eswa.2024.124456
17. Nawaz, U., ur Rahaman, M.A., Saeed, Z.: A review of neuro-symbolic ai integrating reasoning and learning for advanced cognitive systems. Intell. Syst. Appl. **26**, 200541 (2025). https://doi.org/10.1016/j.iswa.2025.200541
18. Tam, D., Mascarenhas, A., Zhang, S., Kwan, S., Bansal, M., Raffel, C.: Evaluating the factual consistency of large language models through news summarization. In: Findings of ACL 2023, pp. 5220–5255 (2023). https://doi.org/10.18653/v1/2023.findings-acl.322
19. Tang, M., Bian, C., Yang, L., Zhong, X.: Key-concept thinking prompting for improved reasoning in large language models. Neurocomputing **656**, 130986 (2025). https://doi.org/10.1016/j.neucom.2025.130986
20. Tran, T.H., Nguyen, T.H.K., Ha, Q.T., Vu, N.T.: Argumentation framework for merging stratified belief bases. In: Nguyen, N.T., Trawiński, B., Fujita, H., Hong, T.-P. (eds.) ACIIDS 2016. LNCS (LNAI), vol. 9621, pp. 43–53. Springer, Heidelberg (2016). https://doi.org/10.1007/978-3-662-49381-6_5
21. Tran, T.H., Vo, Q.B., Nguyen, T.H.K.: On the belief merging by negotiation. In: KES 2014, pp. 147–155 (2014). https://doi.org/10.1016/j.procs.2014.08.094
22. Wei, S., Tong, Y., Zhou, Z., et al.: Federated reasoning LLMs: a survey. Front. Comp. Sci. **19**(12), 1912613 (2025). https://doi.org/10.1007/s11704-025-50480-3
23. Xu, F., et al.: Toward large reasoning models: a survey of reinforced reasoning with large language models. Patterns **6**(10), 101370 (2025). https://doi.org/10.1016/j.patter.2025.101370
24. Zhang, Y., Zheng, W., Huang, J., Xiao, G.: LGKGR: a knowledge graph reasoning model using LLMs augmented GNNs. Neurocomputing **635**, 129919 (2025). https://doi.org/10.1016/j.neucom.2025.129919

Understanding Persuasion in Generative AI Collaborative Environments: An Elaboration Likelihood Model and AI Mindfulness Perspective

Hui-Chun Pan[1](✉), Ming-Chia Hsieh[2], Meng-Jun Hsu[3], Hui-Tzu Min[4], Shih-Wei Chou[5], Wei-Zhi Ho[1], and Bo-yu Chen[1]

[1] Department of Information Management, Southern Taiwan University of Science and Technology, Tainan, Taiwan, R.O.C.
jopan@stust.edu.tw

[2] Department of Accounting, I-Shou University, Kaohsiung, Taiwan, R.O.C.
ryanhsieh@isu.edu.tw

[3] Department of Hotel Management, National Kaohsiung University of Hospitality and Tourism, Kaohsiung, Taiwan, R.O.C.
jacqueshsu@staff.nkuht.edu.tw

[4] Department of Foreign Languages and Literature, National Cheng Kung University, Tainan, Taiwan, R.O.C.
minhuitz@mail.ncku.edu.tw

[5] Department of Information Management, National Kaohsiung University of Science and Technology, Kaohsiung, Taiwan, R.O.C.
swchou@nkust.edu.tw

Abstract. With the rapid development of Generative AI, AI has transformed from a supportive tool into a collaborative partner with interactive and co-creative capabilities. However, existing studies mostly focus on AI adoption, trust, or usage intention, and rarely further explore how users process multiple informational cues and form reflective psychological evaluation processes during the process of Gen-AI collaboration. This study adopts the Elaboration Likelihood Model (ELM), and constructs a theoretical framework centered on AI mindfulness, to explain how users, in a Gen-AI collaborative development context, process the content and interaction cues provided by AI through the central route (such as perceived accuracy, perceived task fit, and transparency) and the peripheral route (such as anthropomorphism, responsiveness, and social cues), and thereby enter a state of AI mindfulness characterized by awareness and reflection. The research method adopts a mixed-method design, first using qualitative interviews to clarify key interaction characteristics in Gen-AI collaboration, and then using a questionnaire survey with SmartPLS for empirical validation.

Keywords: AI Mindfulness · Generative AI Collaboration · Elaboration Likelihood Model (ELM)

D. Liberona et al. (Eds.): MISNC 2026, CCIS 3092, pp. 395–408, 2027.
https://doi.org/10.1007/978-3-032-33381-0_29

1 Introduction

The use of Generative Artificial Intelligence (GenAI) has grown rapidly worldwide, surpassing one billion users by 2025, with approximately 71% of organizations adopting AI tools, indicating its integration into everyday work processes [1]. GenAI has become a pivotal technology in collaborative development, reshaping interactions between knowledge workers and digital tools. This transformation suggests that AI is no longer merely a tool for efficiency enhancement but has become embedded in users' cognitive and decision-making processes, influencing problem understanding, solution evaluation, and action formation. In early-stage development, users can generate and iteratively refine multiple solutions, fostering an interactive and action-oriented mode of collaboration. Through real-time responsiveness and content generation, GenAI enhances the sense of co-creation, leading users to perceive AI as capable of contextual understanding and decision participation, thereby making its outputs more likely to serve as bases for subsequent actions. Accordingly, understanding how users process and interpret AI-generated information has emerged as a critical and pressing research issue.

In addition, some studies have examined AI recommendations from the perspectives of persuasion, trust, or affordances, investigating how AI-driven suggestions influence users' purchase or adoption intentions [2, 3]. However, most of these studies concentrate on recommendation-based AI chatbots embedded within e-commerce platforms, with research designs emphasizing overall effect evaluation or behavioral outcomes within specific platform contexts. By contrast, such platform-centric approaches offer limited explanatory power for understanding how users in GenAI-enabled collaborative development settings confront diverse and dynamically evolving informational cues, and how these cues are actually processed to shape their intentions to collaborate with AI. This limitation constitutes the first research gap that the present study seeks to address **(Research Gap 1)**.

Informational cues represent one of the most salient characteristics of human–GenAI collaboration. Users engage in collaboration with GenAI primarily because they believe AI can assist in achieving specific goals or tasks. From this perspective, GenAI-enabled collaboration can be conceptualized as an inherently persuasive process [4]. Importantly, the notion of persuasion in this study does not refer to manipulation or coercive influence in the traditional sense, but rather to a cognitive evaluation mechanism embedded within human–AI interactions [5]. When users employ GenAI for activities such as MVP prototyping, or POC validation, their decisions are not determined solely by task requirements. Instead, they are simultaneously influenced by quality-related cues embedded in AI-generated content

Drawing on ELM, this study posits that the central route reflects users' rational evaluation of AI-generated content, while the peripheral route captures heuristic judgments based on interaction cues. However, ELM has limited ability to explain how users actually process and act on these cues in GenAI collaboration [5]. Users do not enter interactions as a "blank slate," but bring prior experience and problem-solving frameworks, leading to heterogeneous interpretations of identical AI outputs. This suggests that persuasion is not determined solely by content quality, but is shaped by users' psychological states. Accordingly, this study argues that an open and flexible cognitive state is a critical prerequisite for effective persuasion in GenAI collaborative contexts.

To address this limitation, this study is grounded in mindfulness theory and shifts the analytical focus from outcome-level effects to users' underlying psychological pathways. AI mindfulness, in this study, is conceptualized as a situational psychological state that arises during interaction, reflecting users' openness to multiple solutions, sensitivity to contextual nuances, and capacity to engage in reflective evaluation of AI-generated suggestions. In doing so, this study addresses a **second research gap** by integrating the ELM framework with an AI mindfulness perspective, thereby offering a more explicit account of the psychological pathways through which information processing translates into stable collaborative intentions.

2 Literature Review

2.1 Definition of AI Mindfulness

Prior IS research has generally conceptualized IT mindfulness as users' active and context-sensitive attention to system functionalities, interaction processes, and situational cues during technology use [6]. This mindful engagement has been shown to facilitate value-oriented judgments in dynamic task environments [7] and to support more informed and adaptive decision-making [8].

After comparing existing theories related to IT mindfulness, this study adopts the Mindfulness of Technology Adoption (MTA) framework proposed by Sun et al. [8]. MTA is primarily designed to explain how users, during the technology adoption process, form judgments of technology–task fit through mindful awareness of technological functionalities, task requirements, and contextual cues, which subsequently influence their usage intentions. However, we notice that MTA framework is largely grounded in tool-oriented technologies with relatively stable functionalities, and its core focus lies in whether users select an appropriate technological tool. In contrast, GenAI-enabled collaborative development contexts are characterized by high levels of generativity, interactivity, and uncertainty. Users in such contexts are not merely choosing among alternative technologies; instead, they must continuously and dynamically evaluate whether AI-generated outputs are feasible, worth adopting, and whether deeper collaboration should be sustained.

Consequently, this study extends and reconceptualizes it as AI mindfulness in a state-based form to more closely capture the dynamic nature of GenAI collaborative contexts. Specifically, AI mindfulness is not treated as a stable personal trait or an operational capability; rather, it is defined as a situational cognitive state that emerges during users' interactions with GenAI, reflecting whether users are able to maintain present-moment awareness, remain open to multiple solution pathways, and engage in reflective evaluation of AI-generated suggestions. Drawing on the MTA framework, this study contextualizes AI mindfulness into four sub-constructs: 1) Engagement with GenAI (EG): The extent to which individuals explore and understand the functional capabilities of GenAI. 2) Novelty-seeking exploration of GenAI (NS): The ability of individuals to compare the GenAI tools with previously used and to identify its unique features. 3) Awareness of task–AI fit (AT): The degree to which individuals consider the alignment between the GenAI tools and specific contextual situations or actual needs. 4) Openness to AI alternative Solutions (OT): The awareness of individuals regarding alternative AI technologies and their respective advantages and disadvantages.

2.2 The Accelerator Role of AI Mindfulness in Co-working Intentions with GenAI

AI mindfulness is viewed as an accelerator role in this study that operates between informational cues and users' intention to co-work with GenAI. AI mindfulness functions as a key psychological mechanism that facilitates the transformation of these inputs into behavioral intentions. Rather than merely acting as a prerequisite condition or an outcome, AI mindfulness enhances users' cognitive processing efficiency, enabling them to more effectively interpret, evaluate, and respond to AI-generated information. This conceptualization is grounded in the framework proposed by [9], who identify three roles of IT mindfulness: prerequisite, accelerator, and implication roles. Among these, the accelerator role emphasizes mindfulness as a mechanism that enhances user efficiency and productivity, often functioning as a mediating or moderating variable within the information processing process. By fostering greater awareness, openness, and reflective evaluation, AI mindfulness enables users to more effectively translate informational cues into stable intentions to co-work with GenAI. This positioning highlights the dynamic and process-oriented role of AI mindfulness in shaping human–AI collaboration (Fig. 1).

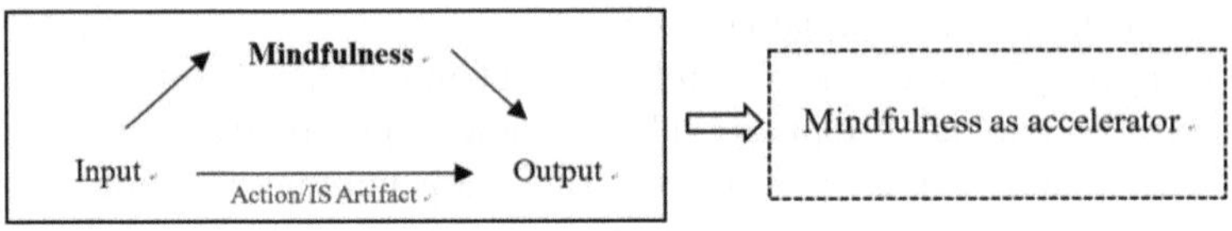

Fig. 1. Accelerator Roles of Mindfulness ([9], p. 127)

2.3 Core Concepts of the ELM and the Persuasion Process

Generative AI (GenAI) is increasingly recognized as a collaborative partner, characterized by its capacity for real-time interaction and co-creation [10]. In collaborative contexts such as Vibe Coding, MVP development, and POC validation, users engage with continuous streams of AI-generated suggestions that shape their judgments and decision-making processes [11]. Such contexts involve both content-oriented information and rich interactional cues, consistent with the dual-route persuasion mechanism proposed by the Elaboration Likelihood Model (ELM) [12, 13].

The central route reflects users' rational evaluation of AI-generated content, particularly in terms of perceived accuracy, task fit, and transparency [2, 14, 15]. In contrast, the peripheral route captures heuristic judgments based on interactional and social cues, such as anthropomorphism, responsiveness, and social influence [4, 16–18].

Importantly, these two routes are not mutually exclusive but may operate simultaneously in the persuasion process [19]. In GenAI collaboration, users may engage in rational evaluation of AI outputs while also being influenced by interaction characteristics and social cues. Therefore, understanding persuasion in GenAI contexts requires integrating both central and peripheral routes, providing a comprehensive foundation for explaining how users process AI-generated recommendations.

2.4 Relating to AI Mindfulness for Persuasion Processes

ELM is widely recognized as a foundational framework for explaining persuasion processes. However, prior research has primarily emphasized how information is processed, while paying comparatively less attention to how individuals' psychological states during message processing shape persuasive outcomes. This limitation becomes particularly salient in highly interactive digital contexts, where users actively engage with information and continuously adjust their attention, reflection, and cognitive orientation through ongoing interaction. As noted by Yu, Chen, and Luo [5], platform features can induce a mindful psychological state characterized by heightened awareness and reflection, thereby influencing persuasion effectiveness.

Extending this perspective to GenAI collaborative contexts, reliance solely on the central and peripheral routes of ELM is insufficient to explain how users engage with AI-generated recommendations. While users may evaluate content quality (e.g., accuracy, task fit, and transparency) and respond to interactional cues (e.g., anthropomorphism, responsiveness, and social influence), the presence of these cues does not necessarily lead to reflective or informed decision-making. In some cases, reliance on peripheral cues may even result in uncritical adoption of AI outputs [20].

Therefore, central and peripheral routes influence persuasion indirectly by shaping users' AI mindfulness, which subsequently determines their perceptions and behavioral responses. AI mindfulness reflects users' awareness of AI-generated suggestions, their ability to evaluate contextual relevance and limitations, and their engagement in reflective processing. In this sense, AI mindfulness serves as a key psychological mechanism that connects ELM-based information processing routes with persuasive outcomes. By integrating AI mindfulness into the ELM framework, this study advances a psychological pathway–centered perspective, providing a more comprehensive explanation of how persuasive cues translate into user responses in GenAI collaborative environments.

2.5 Hypothesis Development

2.5.1 Central-Route Constructs

The central route reflects users' rational and systematic evaluation of GenAI-generated content, particularly in terms of perceived accuracy, task fit, and transparency [2, 18]. These content-quality cues influence not only users' adoption of AI outputs, but also their willingness to allocate cognitive resources to interpret, evaluate, and refine AI-generated suggestions, thereby facilitating the emergence of AI mindfulness [5]. First, Perceived accuracy refers to users' assessment of whether AI-generated content is correct and reliable. When users perceive high accuracy, they are more likely to regard AI outputs as valuable inputs rather than noise, prompting them to invest cognitive effort in examining and integrating these suggestions into their own problem-solving processes [18, 20]. From a mindfulness perspective, accurate information reduces uncertainty and defensive reactions, enabling users to engage with AI in a more open and reflective manner, which in turn facilitates AI mindfulness [8].

Second, perceived task fit refers to the extent to which AI-generated content aligns with users' task requirements and contextual needs. When AI outputs effectively support task accomplishment, users are more likely to invest cognitive effort in understanding how these suggestions can be applied, adapted, and extended within their workflows. This process enhances users' situational awareness and reflective engagement, which are central to AI mindfulness [4, 18].

Last, perceived transparency refers to the extent to which AI-generated outputs are understandable and explainable. When users can comprehend the underlying logic of AI recommendations, they are more likely to engage in reflective evaluation rather than passive acceptance [18]. Transparency enhances users' awareness of both the capabilities and limitations of AI, fostering multi-perspective thinking and deeper cognitive engagement, which are essential for AI mindfulness [8, 15].

H1: Perceived accuracy positively influences AI mindfulness.
H2: Perceived task fit positively influences AI mindfulness.
H3: Perceived transparency positively influences AI mindfulness.

2.5.2 Peripheral -Route Constructs

In contrast to the central route, the peripheral route reflects users' reliance on heuristic cues, particularly when cognitive resources are limited [12]. In GenAI collaborative contexts, interactional features such as anthropomorphism, responsiveness, and social cues, although not directly related to content quality, may influence users' engagement with AI and indirectly facilitate AI mindfulness. First, anthropomorphism refers to the extent to which GenAI exhibits human-like characteristics, such as conversational tone and interactional naturalness. Prior research suggests that anthropomorphic interaction reduces psychological distance and enhances user engagement [2]. In GenAI collaboration, such cues encourage users to perceive AI as a collaborative partner, increasing their willingness to allocate cognitive resources for exploration and reflection, which supports the emergence of AI mindfulness [4, 18].

Second, perceived responsiveness refers to the extent to which GenAI responds to user inputs in a timely and appropriate manner. High responsiveness enhances interaction fluency and encourages continued engagement [4]. In GenAI contexts, responsive systems enable iterative interaction and real-time refinement, fostering users' awareness and reflective engagement, thereby facilitating AI mindfulness [8, 18].

Last, social cues refer to information derived from others' behaviors, norms, or usage patterns. These cues reduce cognitive uncertainty and support heuristic evaluation [19]. In GenAI collaboration, socially informed cues help users contextualize AI recommendations, encouraging comparison and reflection rather than passive acceptance [17]. From a mindfulness perspective, such cues prompt users to maintain an open and attentive mindset, thereby facilitating AI mindfulness.

H4: Perceived anthropomorphism positively influences AI mindfulness.
H5: Perceived responsiveness positively influences AI mindfulness.
H6: Perceived social cues positively influence AI mindfulness.

2.5.3 Co-work Intention with GenAI

Mindfulness represents a context-dependent psychological state characterized by awareness, openness, and reflective evaluation during technology interaction [7, 8]. In GenAI contexts, AI mindfulness reflects users' ability to attend to AI-generated suggestions, understand their contextual relevance, and engage in deliberate evaluation rather than relying on habitual responses. From a self-regulation perspective, individuals engage in self-monitoring and cognitive adjustment when making task-related decisions [21]. When users enter a state of AI mindfulness, these mechanisms enable them to more effectively interpret, adapt, and integrate AI-generated content into their workflows, fostering deeper engagement in human–AI interaction. In GenAI collaborative settings, such reflective engagement enhances users' involvement and willingness to interact with AI as a collaborative partner. Prior research suggests that mindful engagement is associated with sustained interaction and stronger behavioral intention [4, 8]. Accordingly, this study posits that AI mindfulness positively influences users' intention to co-work with GenAI.

H7: AI mindfulness positively influences their intention to co-work with GenAI.

3 Research Methods

3.1 Sample and Questionnaire

A structured questionnaire survey is employed to test the proposed research model and hypotheses. The measurement items are adapted from prior studies on persuasion theory, GenAI interaction, AI mindfulness, and human–AI collaboration to ensure reliability and validity. The questionnaire was reviewed by industry experts and academic scholars, followed by a pilot test with professionals and researchers to assess face and content validity. Based on feedback, item wording was refined to better reflect real-world GenAI collaboration. The final questionnaire includes two sections: (1) background information (e.g., demographics and GenAI usage experience) and (2) research constructs measured using a seven-point Likert scale. To ensure a consistent context, respondents were guided to recall their GenAI collaboration experiences (e.g., tools used and interaction characteristics) and evaluate their psychological states and behavioral intentions based on actual tasks. The survey was distributed online to users with GenAI experience, with screening questions and response checks applied to ensure data quality and sample validity.

This study employs PLS to empirically examine the proposed research model. To assess the potential impact of common method bias, Harman's single-factor test [22] was conducted. The results show that the maximum variance explained by a single factor was 22.1%, which is below the threshold of 50%, indicating that common method variance is not a significant concern in this study. Data were collected over a five-month period, from May 1, 2025, to September 30, 2025. A total of 342 responses were collected, of which 299 valid samples remained, resulting in an effective response rate of 87.13%. To examine non-response bias, an independent sample t-test was conducted by comparing the first and the last 13% of responses across all variables. The results revealed no statistically significant differences, suggesting that non-response bias is not a concern.

3.2 Qualitative Data Analysis

To ensure that the research model accurately reflects real-world GenAI collaborative contexts, this study employs a qualitative approach through semi-structured interviews with approximately 8–10 users who have at least 6 months of experience collaborating with GenAI, including software developers, designers, and researchers. The interviews focus on participants' interaction experiences with GenAI, particularly their perceptions of AI-generated recommendation accuracy, task fit, responsiveness, anthropomorphic characteristics, and their states of awareness and reflection during collaboration.

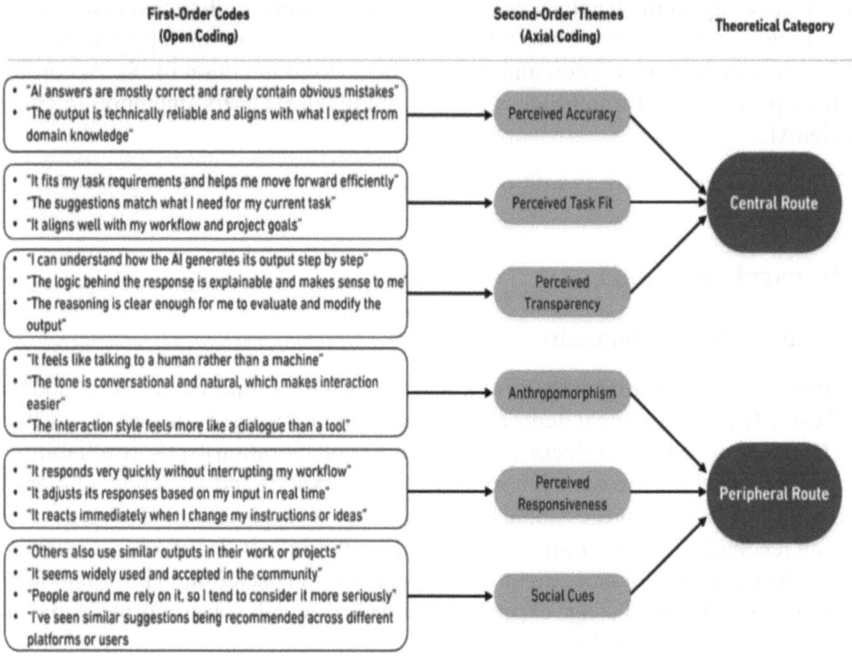

Fig. 2. Qualitative Analysis Results Based on the Gioia Framework

All interviews will be audio-recorded, transcribed verbatim, and analyzed using a thematic analysis approach. Following established qualitative research procedures, the data analysis will involve iterative coding, including open coding, axial coding, and selective coding. In the first stage, open coding is conducted to identify key concepts and recurring themes related to users' interaction experiences with GenAI. In the second stage, axial coding is applied to group these concepts into higher-level categories based on conceptual similarities.

Guided by ELM, the identified themes are further classified into two primary categories: central-route factors (e.g., perceived accuracy, perceived task fit, and transparency) and peripheral-route factors (e.g., anthropomorphism, responsiveness, and social cues). This categorization enables the study to systematically link empirical observations with theoretical constructs. To enhance the reliability and validity of the qualitative analysis, two independent researchers will be involved in the coding process. Discrepancies in coding will be resolved through discussion to ensure consistency and theoretical alignment. Figure 2 shows the results of the qualitative analysis will be used to refine construct definitions and support the development of the subsequent quantitative measurement model.

4 Results and Analysis

4.1 Sample Characteristics

The sample consists predominantly of female respondents (58.73%), with males accounting for 41.27%. Most participants are aged between 31 and 40 years (42.06%), followed by those aged 21–30 (34.92%) and 41–50 (20.63%). The majority hold a bachelor's degree (52.38%) or a master's degree (41.27%), while a smaller proportion possess a doctoral degree (6.35%). In terms of prior GenAI experience, most respondents report 2–3 years (38.89%) or 1–2 years (33.73%) of experience, followed by more than 3 years (18.25%) and less than 1 year (9.13%).

4.2 Measurement Model

As reported in Table 1, the factor loadings for all measurement items range from 0.691 to 0.889, while all weights exceed the recommended threshold of 2, indicating acceptable levels. In addition, the Cronbach's alpha values for all constructs are above 0.7, demonstrating satisfactory internal consistency. Furthermore, the average variance extracted (AVE) values all surpass the recommended cutoff of 0.5, confirming adequate convergent validity.

4.2.1 Control Variables

To ensure that the effects of the central and peripheral routes on AI mindfulness and subsequent intention to co-work with GenAI are not confounded by external factors, this study includes age, gender, and GenAI usage experience as control variables, following prior research on technology use and virtual environments [23, 24]. Incorporating these controls enhances the internal validity and explanatory power of the research model.

Age and gender are commonly recognized as key demographic variables influencing individuals' information-processing patterns, technological familiarity, and behavioral responses in IT contexts. In GenAI collaborative environments, users of different age groups may vary in their cognitive engagement with AI-generated content, while gender differences may shape responses to interaction characteristics and system cues.

In addition, prior research suggests that usage experience plays a critical role in shaping users' perceptions and behaviors in technology-mediated environments. Individuals with greater experience in using GenAI are more likely to exhibit higher familiarity and confidence in interacting with AI systems, which may influence their cognitive processing and behavioral intentions. Therefore, GenAI usage experience is included as an important control variable in this study.

Table 2 indicates that the square root of the AVE for each construct is higher than the corresponding inter-construct correlations, providing support for discriminant validity.

Table 1. Weights and loading of measures

Constructs	Item	Weight	Loading	t-value	Cronbach's Alpha	AVE
PA	DBP1	0.351	0.828	15.778	0.741	0.662
	DBP2	0.407	0.865	25.366		
	DBP3	0.402	0.889	35.567		
PTF	CBP1	0.353	0.739	8.585	0.826	0.742
	CBP2	0.316	0.748	11.402		
	CBP3	0.281	0.731	8.168		
	CBP4	0.382	0.779	13.203		
PT	PT1	0.245	0.739	26.115	0.872	0.665
	PT2	0.256	0.880	66.793		
	PT3	0.246	0.855	46.558		
ATP	ATP1	0.243	0.785	18.135	0.818	0.679
	ATP2	0.282	0.805	27.202		
	ATP3	0.247	0.805	25.370		
PR	PR1	0.234	0.762	18.301	0.866	0.714
	PR2	0.324	0.887	54.345		
	PR3	0.286	0.853	34.579		
SC	SC1	0.274	0.743	19.859	0.738	0.659
	SC2	0.304	0.756	17.340		
	SC3	0.330	0.783	25.165		
MF	EG	0.211	0.778	6.292	0.829	0.592
	NS	0.266	0.818	8.031		
	AT	0.256	0.795	8.614		
	OA	0.351	0.691	10.578		
CWI	CWI 1	0.262	0.867	23.434	0.891	0.754
	CWI 2	0.291	0.861	23.968		
	CWI 3	0.302	0.865	28.346		

Notes: Perceived Accuracy (PA); Perceived Task Fit (PTF); Perceived Transparency (PT); Anthropomorphism (ATP); Perceived Responsiveness (PR); Social Cues (SC); Mindfulness (MF); Co-work Intention (CWI).

Table 2. Fornell-Larcker Criterion Matrix

	PA	PTF	PT	ATP	PR	SC	MF	CWI
PA	**0.814**							

(*continued*)

Table 2. (*continued*)

	PA	PTF	PT	ATP	PR	SC	MF	CWI
PTF	0.609	**0.861**						
PT	0.592	0.496	**0.816**					
ATP	0.564	0.478	0.587	**0.824**				
PR	0.540	0.655	0.496	0.298	**0.845**			
SC	0. 691	0.489	0.412	0.317	0.355	**0.812**		
MF	0.550	0.519	0.611	0.612	0.319	0.420	**0.770**	
CWI	0.701	0.678	0.578	0.632	0.478	0.578	0.582	**0.868**

4.3 Structural Model

This study employs the Smart PLS 4.1.1.8 version to analyze the Partial Least Squares Structural Equation Modeling (PLS-SEM). It mainly evaluates the path coefficients (β), the coefficient of determination (R^2), effect size (f^2), predictive performance ($Q^2_{predict}$), and its model fit measures.

The causal relationships and results of hypothesis testing are presented in Table 3. Besides, we found that the control variables, specifically gender, age, and experience, had no significant impact on co-work intention. As a result, we excluded these variables from our final structural model.

Table 3. PLS results of proposed model

Hypotheses		β-value	t-value	Result	VIF	R^2	f^2
H1	PA → MF	0.547^{***}	10.405	Support	1.414	0.585	0.415
H2	PTF → MF	0.354^{***}	5.504	Support	1.141		0.136
H3	PT → MF	0.328^{***}	5.015	Support	1.977		0.131
H4	ATP → MF	0.250^{***}	5.195	Support	1.599		0.094
H5	PR → MF	0.181^{***}	2.757	Support	2.535		0.031
H6	SC → MF	0.318^{***}	4.918	Support	1.099		0.101
H7	MF → CWI	0.691^{***}	19.266	Support	1.000	0.477	0.912

Note: * $p < 0.05$; ** $p < 0.01$; *** $p < 0.001$

Table 3 presents the PLS results of the proposed model. The results indicate that Perceived Accuracy (PA) has a significant positive effect on Mindfulness (MF) (β = 0.547, t = 10.405), supporting H1. Similarly, Perceived Task Fit (PTF) is positively associated with MF (β = 0.354, t = 5.504), supporting H2. Perceived Transparency (PT) also shows a significant positive effect on MF (β = 0.328, t = 5.015), supporting H3.

Regarding the peripheral route, Anthropomorphism (ATP) has a significant positive effect on MF ($\beta = 0.250$, $t = 5.195$), supporting H4. Perceived Responsiveness (PR) is positively related to MF ($\beta = 0.181$, $t = 2.757$), supporting H5. Social Cues (SC) also demonstrate a significant positive impact on MF ($\beta = 0.318$, $t = 4.918$), supporting H6.

Mindfulness (MF) is found to have a strong positive effect on Intention to Co-work with GenAI (CWI) ($\beta = 0.691$, $t = 19.266$), supporting H7. The model explains 58.5% of the variance in MF ($R^2 = 0.585$) and 47.7% of the variance in CWI ($R^2 = 0.477$), indicating satisfactory explanatory power.

Finally, the $Q^2_{predict}$ values for each latent variable were examined, ranging from 0.107 to 0.509. All values exceed the recommended threshold of zero, indicating that the proposed model demonstrates satisfactory predictive relevance for each latent variable [25].

5 Conclusion

This study investigates the persuasion process in Generative AI (GenAI) collaborative environments by integrating the Elaboration Likelihood Model (ELM) with an AI mindfulness perspective. The results demonstrate that both central-route cues (perceived accuracy, task fit, and transparency) and peripheral-route cues (anthropomorphism, responsiveness, and social cues) significantly influence users' AI mindfulness, which in turn exerts a strong positive effect on their intention to co-work with GenAI.

Importantly, the findings reveal that the path coefficients of central-route cues are consistently stronger than those of peripheral-route cues, providing empirical support for the ELM in GenAI collaborative contexts. This suggests that, for users engaging in mindful interaction with AI, decision-making in collaborative development is primarily driven by central-route evaluations. Among central-route factors, perceived accuracy exhibits the strongest effect, followed by perceived task fit and transparency, indicating that the correctness of AI-generated content plays a dominant role in shaping users' reflective engagement, while task relevance and explainability further reinforce this process.

With respect to the peripheral route, social cues demonstrate the strongest effect, followed by anthropomorphism and responsiveness. This finding highlights the importance of socially derived information in influencing users' engagement in GenAI collaboration. In particular, cues related to others' usage, norms, or collective practices appear to play a more influential role than purely interactional features, suggesting that social validation is a key driver in shaping users' perceptions during collaborative development.

This study contributes to the literature in several ways. First, it extends the application of ELM to dynamic and interactive GenAI collaborative environments, demonstrating the relative dominance of central-route processing in mindful human–AI interaction. Second, it advances persuasion research by introducing AI mindfulness as a key psychological mechanism that explains how informational cues are translated into behavioral intentions. Third, it enriches the concept of mindfulness in information systems by conceptualizing AI mindfulness as a situational and interaction-driven cognitive state, highlighting its role as an accelerator in the human–AI collaboration process.

From a practical perspective, the findings suggest that enhancing content quality should be prioritized in GenAI system design, particularly in improving the accuracy, task fit, and transparency of AI-generated outputs. At the same time, designers should not overlook the role of peripheral cues, especially social cues, which can significantly influence user engagement and perception. Organizations are therefore encouraged to foster both high-quality AI outputs and socially embedded usage environments to promote effective and sustainable human–AI collaboration.

References

1. We Are Social & Meltwater: Digital 2026 global overview report (2026). Retrieved from https://datareportal.com/reports/digital-2026-global-overview-report. Last accessed 1 Apr 2026.
2. Chen, Q., Yin, C., Gong, Y.: Would an AI chatbot persuade you: an empirical answer from the elaboration likelihood model. Inf. Technol. People. **38**(2), 937–962 (2025)
3. Zhang, X., Chen, A.L., Piao, X., Yu, M., Zhang, Y., Zhang, L.: Is AI chatbot recommendation convincing? An analytical response based on the elaboration likelihood model. Acta Psychol. **250**, 104501 (2024)
4. Kim, T., Im, I.: Understanding users' AI manipulation intention: an empirical investigation of the antecedents in the context of AI recommendation algorithms. Inf. Manag. **62**(1) (2025)
5. Yu, T., Chen, Y., Luo, X.R.: How do live-streaming platforms facilitate persuasion in political campaigns? Theory and empirical evidence from the perspective of affordance actualization. Inf. Manag. **60**(3), 103775 (2023)
6. Dane, E.: Paying attention to mindfulness and its effects on task performance in the workplace. J. Manag. **37**(4), 997–1018 (2011)
7. Thatcher, J.B., Wright, R.T., Sun, H., Zagenczyk, T.J., Klein, R.: Mindfulness in information technology use. MIS Q. **42**(3), 831–A14 (2018)
8. Sun, H., Fang, Y., Zou, H.M.: Choosing a fit technology: understanding mindfulness in technology adoption and continuance. J. Assoc. Inf. Syst. **17**(6), 2 (2016)
9. Dernbecher, S., Beck, R.: The concept of mindfulness in information systems research: a multi-dimensional analysis. Eur. J. Inf. Syst. **26**(2), 121–142 (2017)
10. Dwivedi, Y.K., et al.: So what if ChatGPT wrote it? Multidisciplinary perspectives on generative AI. Int. J. Inf. Manag. **71**, 102642 (2023)
11. Watson, J., Valsesia, F., Segal, S.: Assessing AI receptivity through a persuasion knowledge lens. Curr. Opin. Psychol. **58**, 101834 (2024)
12. Petty, R.E., Cacioppo, J.T.: Communication and Persuasion: Central and Peripheral Routes to Attitude Change. Springer (1986)
13. Bhattacherjee, A., Sanford, C.: Influence processes for information technology acceptance: an elaboration likelihood model. MIS Q. **30**(4), 805–825 (2006)
14. Tangwaragorn, P.: Persuasion awareness in online settings: Antecedents, consequences, and transparency mechanisms. Doctoral dissertation, University of British Columbia (2021)
15. Shin, D., Koerber, A., Lim, J.S.: Impact of misinformation from generative AI on user information processing: how people understand misinformation from generative AI. New Media Soc. **27**(7), 4017–4047 (2025)
16. Lee, D., Moon, J., Kim, Y.J., Mun, Y.Y.: Antecedents and consequences of mobile phone usability: linking simplicity and interactivity to satisfaction, trust, and brand loyalty. Inf. Manag. **52**(3), 295–304 (2015)
17. Luo, C., Luo, X.R., Xu, Y., Warkentin, M., Sia, C.L.: Examining the moderating role of sense of membership in online review evaluations. Inf. Manag. **52**(3), 305–316 (2015)
18. Zhou, T., Fang, X.: Understanding user trust in AI-generated content: an elaboration likelihood model perspective. Online Inf. Rev. **50** (2025)

19. Gao, X., Xu, X.Y., Tayyab, S.M.U., Li, Q.: How the live streaming commerce viewers process the persuasive message: an ELM perspective and the moderating effect of mindfulness. Electron. Commer. Res. Appl. **49**, 101087 (2021)
20. Zhang, X., Chen, A.L., Piao, X., Yu, M., Zhang, Y., Zhang, L.: Is AI chatbot recommendation convincing customer? An analytical response based on the elaboration likelihood model. Acta Psychol. **250**, 104501 (2024)
21. Chou, S.W., Hsieh, M.C., Pan, H.C.: Understanding the impact of self-regulation on perceived learning outcomes based on social cognitive theory. Behav. Inform. Technol. **43**(6), 1129–1148 (2024)
22. Podsakoff, P.M., MacKenzie, S.B., Lee, J.Y., Podsakoff, N.P.: Common method biases in behavioral research: a critical review. J. Appl. Psychol. **88**(5), 879–903 (2003)
23. Ma, M., Agarwal, R.: Through a glass darkly: information technology design, identity verification, and knowledge contribution in online communities. Inf. Syst. Res. **18**, 42–67 (2007)
24. Jasperson, J., Carter, P.E., Zmud, R.W.: A comprehensive conceptualization of post-adoptive behaviors associated with information technology enabled work systems. MIS Q. **29**(3), 525–557 (2005)
25. Hair, J.F., Hult, G.T.M., Ringle, C.M., Sarstedt, M.: A Primer on Partial Least Squares Structural Equation Modeling (PLS-SEM), 3rd edn. Sage, Thousand Oaks (2022)

A Multimodal Analysis of Evaluator Scores Using Facial Expression and Vocal Features in Speech Assessment in Japan

Kazunori Minetaki[1](✉), Yu-Ching Liu[2], Chia-Sung Yen[3], and I-Hsien Ting[2]

[1] Department of Business, Creative Management and Innovation Research Institute, Kindai University, 3-4-1 Kowakae, Higashi-Osaka City, Osaka Prefecture, Japan
kminetaki@bus.kindai.ac.jp

[2] Social Networks Innovation Center, National University of Kaohsiung, 700, Kaohsiung University Rd., Nanzih District, Kaohsiung 811, Taiwan

[3] Department of Cultural and Creative Industries, National Chin-Yi University of Technology, No. 57, Sec. 2, Zhongshan Rd., Taiping Dist., Taichung City 411030, Taiwan

Abstract. The study examines how evaluator scores in presentation assessment are associated with multimodal nonverbal cues extracted from video recordings. Facial features were derived using OpenFace 2.0, and acoustic features were extracted using librosa 0.10.1 in Python 3.10. Attention was given to two composite facial indicators: the Cheerfulness Index, which was designed to capture visible positive affect and interpersonal approachability, and the Confidence Index, which was designed to capture attentional engagement, composure, and perceived behavioral control. Using 55 presentation samples scored on a five-point ordinal rating scale, the analysis proceeded through descriptive statistics, Spearman correlation analysis, high-score versus low-score comparison, Lasso-based feature selection, predictive modeling with ridge regression and random forest, and ordered logistic regression. The results indicate that facial expressivity plays a central role in score differentiation. Cheerful facial expression and variability in confidence-related expression were positively associated with evaluator scores, whereas vertical gaze instability was negatively associated with evaluator scores. Among vocal features, mfcc6_std and, to a lesser extent, mean fundamental frequency showed positive associations with higher evaluations. Model comparison further indicated that an integrated facial-plus-vocal model performed better than a facial-only model, although the improvement was moderate. Overall, the findings suggest that evaluator judgments are driven primarily by facial expressivity and gaze stability, while vocal features provide incremental explanatory value within a multimodal assessment framework.

Keywords: multimodal analysis · evaluator scores · facial expression · vocal features

D. Liberona et al. (Eds.): MISNC 2026, CCIS 3092, pp. 409–423, 2027.
https://doi.org/10.1007/978-3-032-33381-0_30

1 Introduction

Human evaluation in interviews, presentations, and oral examinations is shaped not only by verbal content but also by nonverbal behavior. Observers often form robust impressions from brief behavioral exposure, a phenomenon widely discussed in the thin-slices literature [1, 2]. In practical settings such as interviews and presentation assessments, facial expression, gaze behavior, and vocal modulation can influence perceived confidence, engagement, and communicative competence.

Recent developments in affective computing and social signal processing have made it possible to quantify these nonverbal cues automatically. OpenFace 2.0 provides facial landmark detection, head pose estimation, eye-gaze estimation, and action-unit-based facial behavior analysis, while librosa 0.10.1 in Python 3.10 supports the extraction of acoustic features such as pitch-related measures and cepstral coefficients from speech signals. Together, these tools enable researchers to move from impressionistic description to reproducible multimodal measurement.

Despite these advances, many studies still emphasize a single modality. Some focus primarily on facial expression and gaze, whereas others analyze voice quality, prosody, or speech content. Yet real-world evaluation is inherently multimodal: evaluators integrate visual and auditory cues simultaneously when forming judgments. This implies that a combined facial-and-vocal framework may explain evaluation outcomes more effectively than either modality alone.

The study addresses that gap by analyzing evaluator scores using facial and vocal features extracted from presentation videos. It asks three related questions: which facial and vocal features are associated with evaluator scores, whether facial and vocal features differ in explanatory power, and whether a combined multimodal model outperforms facial-only and vocal-only approaches.

Studying contributes in three ways. First, it shows that facial expressivity, especially cheerful expression and variability in confidence-related expression, is strongly related to higher evaluation. Second, it identifies instability in vertical eye movement as a negative signal. Third, it demonstrates that vocal features add incremental value when integrated with facial features, even though the dominant predictive signal remains facial.

2 Literature Review

2.1 Thin-Slice Judgment and Nonverbal Evaluation

A long line of research suggests that people can infer meaningful interpersonal outcomes from short excerpts of expressive behavior. Ambady and Rosenthal's meta-analysis showed that thin slices of expressive behavior can predict interpersonal consequences with notable accuracy [1]. In interview and assessment contexts, these findings imply that evaluators may form judgments rapidly on the basis of visible and audible behavioral cues.

This insight has been extended to employment and interview settings. Prior work on job interviews has shown that thin slices of nonverbal behavior can carry predictive information about hiring-related judgments [2]. Such work supports the idea that evaluator scores reflect more than verbal content alone.

2.2 Facial Expression, Gaze, and Interpersonal Impression

Facial behavior is one of the most visible channels of social signaling. Smiling, expressivity, and gaze stability are commonly interpreted as cues of confidence, warmth, and engagement. In computational settings, these cues can now be tracked automatically. OpenFace 2.0 was introduced as an open toolkit capable of facial landmark detection, head pose estimation, facial action unit recognition, and eye-gaze estimation with real-time performance and no specialized hardware requirement [3].

In evaluation settings, greater facial expressivity may increase perceptions of enthusiasm and communicative competence. At the same time, unstable gaze or excessive eye movement may be interpreted as nervousness or reduced attentional control. Thus, both positive expressivity and visual stability are likely to matter in presentation assessment.

2.3 Vocal Cues and Evaluative Judgments

Vocal communication is another major channel through which emotion, arousal, and social intention are conveyed. Reviews of vocal emotion research have emphasized that speech contains systematic acoustic cues that shape listener judgments and have treated vocal communication as a process involving expression, transmission, and perception [5].

Acoustic features such as pitch level, pitch variability, and spectral variation are therefore relevant to evaluative contexts. Tools such as librosa 0.10.1 in Python 3.10 facilitate the extraction of these measures from recorded speech and have become standard in computational audio analysis [4].

2.4 Multimodal Assessment

The social signal processing perspective argues that interpersonal judgments emerge from multiple coordinated signals rather than isolated channels [6]. In practice, evaluators do not separately score facial expression and voice; they integrate them holistically. This makes multimodal modeling particularly relevant in presentation assessment.

At the same time, the empirical contribution of each modality may differ across contexts. In some cases facial cues dominate, whereas in others vocal characteristics provide additional information. The present study is motivated by the need to test this relative contribution empirically in a presentation-assessment setting.

3 Theoretical Framework

The study is based on a multimodal impression-formation framework consisting of three propositions:

(1) The expressivity proposition states that visible positive expressivity increases evaluator scores. When speakers display more cheerful and dynamically responsive facial expressions, they are more likely to be perceived as engaged, confident, and persuasive.

(2) The stability proposition states that visual instability reduces evaluator scores. Excessive or unstable eye movement, particularly in the vertical direction, may signal nervousness, hesitation, or reduced control, thereby lowering evaluation.
(3) The vocal modulation proposition states that variation in vocal signals con-tributes positively to evaluator judgments when integrated with facial information. Moderate vocal variation may indicate liveliness, communicative intent, and emotional involvement.

From these propositions, the study derives the following hypotheses:

H1: Positive facial expressivity is positively associated with evaluator scores.
H2: Instability in gaze-related behavior is negatively associated with evaluator scores.
H3: Vocal features are associated with evaluator scores, but their explanatory value is stronger when combined with facial features than when used alone.
H4: A multimodal model integrating facial and vocal features outperforms a uni-modal facial-only model.

4 Methodology

4.1 Data

The dataset contains 55 presentation samples and 64 variables, including one evaluator score variable and 56 usable numerical predictors after excluding identifiers. The data were collected from May to July 2025, and the evaluators were involved in recruitment-related work in human resources. The dependent variable was score, measured on a five-point ordinal scale. The score distribution was centered on category 3, with relatively fewer observations at the extremes (Table 2).

4.2 Feature Construction and Operationalization

Facial features included summary measures of cheerful expression and confidence-related expression (cheerful_mean, cheerful_std, cheerful_max, confidence_mean, confidence_std, confidence_max, face-orientation ratios), eye-movement variability, region-based face-direction ratios, blink and EAR(Eye-Aspect-Ratio) measures, audio duration, vocal feature and MFCC(Mel-frequency cepstral coefficient) summary measures were obtained through OpenFace-based facial analysis and librosa-based acoustic analysis (Table 1).

To improve interpretability, two composite facial indices were defined. The Cheerfulness Index was operationalized as a composite measure intended to capture visible positive effect and interpersonal approachability. It was constructed from AU06 (cheek raiser), AU12 (lip corner puller), and AU25 (lips part). AU06 and AU12 were treated as the core components because they are more directly associated with positive facial expression, while AU25 was included as a complementary component reflecting expressive amplification during speech. The Confidence Index was operationalized as a composite measure intended to capture attentional engagement, composure, and perceived behavioral control. It was constructed from AU05 (upper lid raiser), AU06 (cheek raiser),

Table 1. Explanation of variables and Feature type

Predictor group	Feature type	Number of variables	Variables/examples	Explanation
Cheerfulness index summaries	Facial expression	3	cheerful_mean, cheerful_std, cheerful_max	Summary statistics of the Cheerfulness Index, constructed from AU06, AU12, and AU25, to represent visible positive affect and expressive amplification during speech.
Confidence index summaries	Facial expression	3	confidence_mean, confidence_std, confidence_max	Summary statistics of the Confidence Index, constructed from AU05, AU06, AU07, AU12, and AU23, to represent attentional engagement, composure, and perceived behavioral control.
Face-orientation ratios	Face/gaze behavior	5	front_ratio, left_ratio, right_ratio, up_ratio, down_ratio	Proportions of frames in which the face/gaze direction was classified as front, left, right, upward, or downward.
Eye-movement variability	Gaze behavior	2	eye_move_x_std, eye_move_y_std	Standard deviations of horizontal and vertical gaze-angle movement. Larger values indicate greater gaze instability in the corresponding direction.
Region-based gaze-direction ratios	Gaze behavior	9	ratio_upper_left, ratio_upper_center, ratio_upper_right, ratio_middle_left, ratio_middle_center, ratio_middle_right, ratio_lower_left, ratio_lower_center, ratio_lower_right	Proportions of frames assigned to each of the nine gaze-direction regions defined by horizontal and vertical gaze-angle thresholds.

(continued)

Table 1. (*continued*)

Predictor group	Feature type	Number of variables	Variables/examples	Explanation
Blink and eye-aspect-ratio measures	Eye behavior	4	blink_count, blink_per_min, ear_mean, ear_std	Blink frequency and Eye Aspect Ratio (EAR) summaries. EAR reflects the degree of eye openness; its variability can capture eye-region movement or blink-related changes.
Audio duration	Duration-related measure	1	duration_sec_audio	Total duration of the audio signal in seconds.
Fundamental-frequency and intonation measures	Vocal feature	3	f0_mean, f0_std, intonation_f0std_div_f0mean	Pitch-level and pitch-variation measures. f0_mean captures average fundamental frequency, f0_std captures pitch variability, and the intonation index normalizes pitch variability by the mean.
MFCC summary measures	Vocal feature	26	mfcc1_mean through mfcc13_mean; mfcc1_std through mfcc13_std	Mel-frequency cepstral coefficient summaries. Mean absolute values represent the average magnitude of each spectral coefficient, while standard deviations represent temporal variation in that coefficient.
Total		56		The 56 numerical predictors were used as the candidate predictor set for Lasso feature selection and model comparison.

Editable formula notation for variables mentioned in Table 1

Cheerfulness Index = (AU06 + AU12 + AU25) / 3

Confidence Index = (AU05 + AU06 + AU07 + AU12 + AU23) / 5

Intonation index = f0_std / f0_mean

Horizontal gaze-movement variability = SD(eye_move_x)

Vertical gaze-movement variability = SD(eye_move_y)

Note. This document recreates Table 1 as an editable Word table rather than a raster image.

AU07 (lid tightener), AU12 (lip corner puller), and AU23 (lip tightener). In this formulation, eye-region activation was interpreted as contributing to impressions of alertness and composure, whereas lip tension was interpreted as contributing to impressions of control and determination.

Eye-movement variability was measured using eye_move_x_std and eye_move_y_std. The former represents the standard deviation of horizontal gaze-angle movement, whereas the latter represents the standard deviation of vertical gaze-angle movement. Region-based face-direction ratios were used to summarize the spatial distribution of the speaker's face and gaze direction across upper, middle, lower, left, center, and right regions. These measures were included because face and gaze direction can reflect attentional orientation and visual stability during a presentation. Blink and eye-aspect-ratio (EAR) measures were included as indicators of eye behavior, arousal, and visual composure.

Audio duration was included as a duration-related control variable because the length of the recorded presentation may affect the amount of observable facial, gaze, and vocal behavior.

Vocal features were included to capture acoustic aspects of speech delivery that may influence evaluator judgments. These features consisted of fundamental-frequency measures, an intonation-related measure, and Mel-frequency cepstral coefficient (MFCC) summaries. Fundamental frequency (F0) represents the basic vibration rate of the vocal folds and is commonly interpreted as the acoustic correlate of perceived vocal pitch. In this study, 'f0_mean' represented the speaker's average pitch level, whereas 'f0_std' represented variability in pitch over the presentation. The intonation-related variable, 'intonation_f0std_div_f0mean', was calculated as the standard deviation of F0 divided by mean F0, and was used to capture relative pitch modulation while accounting for differences in speakers' average pitch levels. MFCC-based variables were included to summarize spectral characteristics of speech, such as vocal timbre, resonance, and the distribution of acoustic energy. Together, these vocal features were included because evaluators may respond not only to verbal content, but also to acoustic aspects of delivery, including pitch level, pitch variability, intonation, vocal expressiveness, and voice quality.

Lasso feature selection was applied separately to the facial feature set, the vocal feature set, and the combined facial-plus-vocal feature set. In the combined Lasso model, six predictors were retained: cheerful_mean, confidence_std, mfcc6_std, cheerful_std, eye_move_y_std, and f0_mean (Table 2).

4.3 Analytical Strategy

The analysis proceeded in six steps. First, descriptive statistics were used to examine the distributions of the analytical variables and to confirm the absence of missing values; the main descriptive results are summarized in Table 2. Second, Spearman rank correlations were calculated between evaluator score and each candidate feature, with selected correlations reported in Table 3. Third, presentations with scores of 4 or 5 were classified as the high-score group, whereas presentations with scores of 1 or 2 were classified as the low-score group, and the two groups were compared using Mann–Whitney U tests. Fourth, Lasso regression was used for feature selection within the facial-only, vocal-only, and combined facial-plus-vocal feature sets. Fifth, predictive performance was evaluated using ridge regression and random forest models under leave-one-out cross-validation, and the comparative results are reported in Table 4. Sixth, ordered logistic regression was estimated to model evaluator score as an ordinal outcome using the Lasso-selected predictors, with coefficients summarized in Table 5.

5 Findings

5.1 Descriptive Results

Evaluator scores ranged from 1 to 5, with most observations concentrated in the middle category. Specifically, category 1 contained a single observation, category 2 contained 12 observations, category 3 contained 25 observations, category 4 contained 12 observations, and category 5 contained 5 observations. No missing values were observed in the analytical variables. Table 2 reports descriptive statistics for the principal facial, gaze-related, and vocal variables used in the final interpretation.

The selected variables showed sufficient variation across the 55 presentation samples. The mean evaluator score was 3.145 (SD = 0.931). Among the facial variables, cheerful_mean, cheerful_std, and confidence_std represented the average level and variability of positive and confidence-related facial expression. The variable eye_move_y_std represented the standard deviation of vertical gaze-angle movement and was treated as an indicator of vertical gaze instability. Among the vocal variables, f0_mean represented the average fundamental frequency, or average vocal pitch level, and mfcc6_std represented temporal variability in the sixth Mel-frequency cepstral coefficient.

5.2 Correlation Analysis

The strongest positive correlations with evaluator score were observed for cheerful_mean (Spearman's rho = 0.395), confidence_std (rho = 0.385), cheerful_std (rho = 0.374), mfcc6_std (rho = 0.356), cheerful_max (rho = 0.340), confidence_max (rho = 0.320), f0_mean (rho = 0.311), and confidence_mean (rho = 0.304). These results indicate that evaluator scores were positively associated with positive facial expressivity, confidence-related facial variability, and selected vocal features.

The only gaze-related variable reported in Table 3, eye_move_y_std, showed a negative but non-significant correlation with evaluator score (rho = −0.198, p = 0.1472). Because eye_move_y_std represents the standard deviation of vertical gaze-angle movement, this pattern was directionally consistent with the interpretation that greater vertical gaze instability may be associated with lower evaluator scores. However, evidence for this relationship was weak at the bivariate level because the correlation was not statistically significant.

Overall, the correlation results are consistent with H1 and provide preliminary support for H3. Evidence for H2 was weaker at the bivariate level, although the direction of the eye_move_y_std correlation was consistent with the hypothesis. Substantively, both the average level and variability of the Cheerfulness and Confidence indices appeared relevant to evaluator judgments, while selected vocal features, particularly mfcc6_std and f0_mean, also showed positive associations with evaluator score.

5.3 Lasso Feature Selection

Lasso feature selection was conducted to identify the most stable predictors of evaluator score from the predefined candidate feature sets. The analysis was performed separately for the facial-only feature set, the vocal-only feature set, and the combined facial-plus-vocal feature set.

For the facial-only feature set, Lasso retained five predictors: 'confidence_std', 'cheerful_mean', 'cheerful_std', 'eye_move_y_std', and 'eye_move_x_std'. Among these variables, 'confidence_std', 'cheerful_mean', and 'cheerful_std' represent confidence-related and cheerful facial expressivity. The two gaze-related variables represent eye-movement variability: 'eye_move_y_std' captures variability in vertical gaze-angle movement, whereas 'eye_move_x_std' captures variability in horizontal gaze-angle movement. Thus, the facial-only Lasso results suggest that both expressive facial behavior and gaze-movement variability were relevant within the facial and gaze-related feature set.

In contrast, the vocal-only Lasso model did not retain any stable predictor. This suggests that vocal features alone were not sufficiently robust predictors of evaluator score in this sample.

For the combined facial-plus-vocal feature set, Lasso retained six predictors: 'cheerful_mean', 'confidence_std', 'mfcc6_std', 'cheerful_std', 'eye_move_y_std', and 'f0_mean'. These variables were selected from the 56 usable numerical predictors and represented a combination of positive facial expressivity, confidence-related facial variability, vertical gaze instability, and selected acoustic features. In this combined model, 'eye_move_x_std' was no longer retained, whereas 'eye_move_y_std' remained selected. This suggests that vertical gaze instability was more robust than horizontal gaze variability when facial and vocal features were considered together.

Overall, the Lasso results indicate that facial and gaze-related features provided the main predictive signal, while vocal features contributed when integrated with facial information. In particular, 'mfcc6_std' and 'f0_mean' were retained only in the combined facial-plus-vocal feature set, suggesting that vocal information added incremental value rather than functioning as a stable stand-alone predictor.

5.4 Model Comparison

Predictive performance was evaluated using ridge regression and random forest models under leave-one-out cross-validation. Models were estimated using the predictors retained by Lasso feature selection. The facial-only models used the five selected facial and gaze-related predictors, whereas the combined models used the six predictors retained by the combined Lasso model.

The best-performing model was the combined ridge regression model. It achieved MAE = 0.654, RMSE = 0.811, R2 = 0.227, and a Spearman correlation of 0.437 between observed and predicted evaluator scores. The facial-only ridge model performed slightly less well, with MAE = 0.673, RMSE = 0.821, R2 = 0.209, and Spearman's rho = 0.396. Random forest models showed weaker performance than ridge regression in both the facial-only and combined feature settings.

These results indicate that integrating facial and vocal features improved predictive performance relative to the facial-only model, although the improvement was modest. The results therefore support H4. At the same time, the relatively small performance difference between the combined and facial-only models suggests that facial and gaze-related features accounted for most of the explainable variation in evaluator scores, while vocal features provided incremental explanatory value.

5.5 Ordered Logistic Regression

To further examine the predictors of evaluator score as an ordinal outcome, an ordered logistic regression model was estimated. The dependent variable was evaluator score, measured on a five-point ordinal rating scale ranging from 1 to 5. The model used five predictors retained from the combined Lasso results: cheerful_mean, confidence_std, mfcc6_std, cheerful_std, and eye_move_y_std. The sixth Lasso-selected variable, f0_mean, was not included in the ordered logistic regression in order to keep the model parsimonious relative to the modest sample size.

The ordered logistic regression results are presented in Table 6. Among the five predictors, confidence_std showed a positive and statistically significant coefficient, indicating that greater variability in confidence-related facial expression increased the likelihood of receiving a higher evaluator score. The variable mfcc6_std also showed a positive coefficient and was marginally significant, suggesting that variation in this acoustic feature contributed positively to evaluator judgments. In contrast, eye_move_y_std showed a negative and statistically significant coefficient. Because eye_move_y_std represents the standard deviation of vertical gaze-angle movement, this result indicates that greater vertical gaze instability reduced the likelihood of receiving a higher evaluator score.

The coefficients for cheerful mean and cheerful_std were positive but not statistically significant in the multivariate ordinal model. Although these variables showed meaningful positive associations with evaluator score in the bivariate correlation analysis, their independent effects became weaker when considered together with confidence-related variability, acoustic variation, and vertical gaze instability. This pattern suggests that positive facial expressivity is relevant to evaluator judgments, but part of its contribution overlaps with other expressive and stability-related features.

Overall, the ordered logistic regression results indicate that evaluator judgments were shaped by a combination of facial expressivity, gaze-related stability, and selected acoustic variation. More specifically, dynamic confidence-related facial behavior and variation in spectral speech characteristics increased the probability of receiving a higher score, whereas vertical gaze instability reduced that probability.

6 Discussion

The findings of this study suggest that evaluator judgments in presentation assessment are shaped primarily by facial expressivity and gaze-related stability, while vocal features provide additional but secondary information. Taken together, the descriptive patterns in Table 2, the correlation results in Table 3, and the model comparison in Table 5 indicate that evaluator scores are best understood as the outcome of a multimodal process in which visual cues play the dominant role and vocal cues offer incremental explanatory value.

First, the descriptive statistics in Table 2 show that the key facial and vocal variables display sufficient variation across the 55 presentation samples, making them suitable for distinguishing higher- and lower-rated performances. In particular, the distribution of evaluator scores is centered on the middle category, with fewer observations at the extremes, suggesting that the prediction task is nontrivial. Against this background, the positive associations observed for the Cheerfulness Index and confidence-related variability are substantively meaningful rather than artifacts of limited score dispersion.

Second, the correlation analysis reported in Table 3 provides clear support for the importance of facial expressivity. The strongest positive correlations with evaluator score were found for cheerful_mean, confidence_std, and cheerful_std, while mfcc6_std and f0_mean also showed positive associations. By contrast, eye_move_y_std showed a negative relationship with evaluator score, suggesting that vertical gaze instability may be interpreted negatively by evaluators. These results imply that evaluators respond favorably not only to positive facial expression itself but also to dynamic expressive flexibility. At the same time, visual instability appears to reduce impressions of composure and attentional control.

Third, the comparison of predictive models in Table 5 strengthens the interpretation that facial cues are the primary source of predictive information, but that vocal features improve performance when integrated into a multimodal framework. The best-performing model was the combined ridge model, which slightly outperformed the facial-only ridge model across MAE, RMSE, R2, and rank-order correspondence. The difference is not large, but it is consistent across metrics and is therefore substantively important. This pattern suggests that vocal cues alone may not be stable enough to explain evaluator scores in a small-sample setting, yet they become meaningful when combined with facial indicators. In other words, vocal features appear to refine evaluator prediction rather than replace the dominant contribution of facial behavior.

From a theoretical perspective, the results point to three implications. First, evaluator judgments seem to reward expressive positivity, especially in the form of cheerful and dynamic facial behavior. Second, they also reward controlled expressiveness, as reflected in the positive role of confidence-related variability alongside the negative role of unstable eye movement. This combination suggests that evaluators do not simply favor speakers who are animated; rather, they favor speakers whose behavior appears expressive yet coherent. Third, the vocal results indicate that speech-related features contribute to evaluator impressions mainly as a complementary channel. The fact that mfcc6_std and f0_mean became useful in the combined framework implies that vocal modulation can reinforce visual impressions of confidence and engagement. This interpretation is also consistent with prior work suggesting that vocal expression conveys emotional and evaluative information [7].

These findings are consistent with a broader multimodal understanding of social evaluation. In presentation settings, evaluators are likely to integrate visual and auditory cues simultaneously when forming judgments about confidence, competence, and communicative quality. This interpretation is consistent with the view that interpersonal judgments are shaped by coordinated nonverbal signals, including facial expression,

Table 2. Descriptive statistics of key variables

Variable	Mean	SD	Min	Max
Score	3.145	0.931	1.000	5.000
cheerful_mean	0.430	0.257	0.128	1.272
cheerful_std	0.252	0.107	0.100	0.518
confidence_std	0.165	0.073	0.058	0.384
eye_move_y_std	0.066	0.026	0.017	0.143
f0_mean	182.182	63.779	92.620	332.666
mfcc6_std	16.839	2.922	11.135	26.329

Note. N = 55. The selected variables are those most relevant to the final interpretation and modeling results.

Table 3. Spearman correlations between evaluator score and selected features

Feature	Spearman's rho	p-value
cheerful_mean	0.395	0.0029
confidence_std	0.385	0.0037
cheerful_std	0.374	0.0049
mfcc6_std	0.356	0.0076
cheerful_max	0.340	0.0112
confidence_max	0.320	0.0174
f0_mean	0.311	0.0208
confidence_mean	0.304	0.0239
eye_move_y_std	−0.198	0.1472

Note. Only selected features are shown for brevity. Positive coefficients indicate that higher feature values are associated with higher evaluator scores.

Table 4. Predictors retained by Lasso feature selection

Feature set	Retained predictors
Facial-only feature set	confidence_std, cheerful_mean, cheerful_std, eye_move_y_std, eye_move_x_std
Vocal-only feature set	No stable predictor was retained
Combined facial-plus-vocal feature set	cheerful_mean, confidence_std, mfcc6_std, cheerful_std, eye_move_y_std, f0_mean

gaze, posture, voice, and other behavioral cues [8–10]. The present results therefore support the view that evaluator scores are not based solely on content but are also shaped by coordinated nonverbal signals. At the same time, the stronger role of facial variables suggests that visible behavior may carry more immediate evaluative weight than vocal variation in this particular context.

Table 5. Comparison of predictive models

Model	Algorithm	Features	MAE	RMSE	R2	Spearman's rho
Combined selected	Ridge	Combined Lasso predictors (6)	0.654	0.811	0.227	0.437
Facial selected	Ridge	Facial Lasso predictors (5)	0.673	0.821	0.209	0.396
Combined selected	Random Forest	Combined Lasso predictors (6)	0.687	0.840	0.172	0.351
Facial selected	Random Forest	Facial Lasso predictors (5)	0.705	0.845	0.161	0.369

Note. The combined Lasso predictors were cheerful_mean, confidence_std, mfcc6_std, cheerful_std, eye_move_y_std, and f0_mean. The facial Lasso predictors were confidence_std, cheerful_mean, cheerful_std, eye_move_y_std, and eye_move_x_std. The combined ridge model showed the best overall performance, indicating that vocal features added incremental value beyond facial features alone.

Table 6. Ordered logistic regression results for evaluator score

Predictor	Coefficient	Std. Error	p-value
cheerful_mean	0.139	0.398	0.726
confidence_std	0.984	0.489	0.044
mfcc6_std	0.599	0.306	0.050
cheerful_std	0.250	0.487	0.608
eye_move_y_std	−0.782	0.327	0.017

Note. Positive coefficients indicate a greater likelihood of receiving a higher evaluator score. Threshold parameters are omitted for brevity.

Several limitations should also be noted. The sample size is modest, and the ordinal score categories are unevenly distributed, especially at the extreme ends of the scale. This limits both statistical power and generalizability. In addition, while the composite facial indices are relatively interpretable in behavioral terms, some acoustic features, particularly MFCC-based measures, are less intuitively linked to specific evaluator perceptions. Future research should therefore replicate the analysis with larger datasets, examine temporal dynamics more explicitly, and incorporate verbal-content features so that the relationship between linguistic content and multimodal nonverbal behavior can be assessed in an integrated framework.

Overall, the results presented in Tables 2, 3, 4, 5, and 6 support a consistent conclusion: evaluator judgments in presentation assessment are influenced primarily by facial expressivity and gaze stability, while vocal features provide modest but meaningful additional information. This reinforces the value of a multimodal analytical approach and suggests that presentation evaluation can be better understood as a coordinated perceptual process rather than as a response to any single behavioral cue.

7 Conclusion

The study investigated evaluator scores in presentation assessment using multimodal nonverbal features derived from facial expression analysis and speech signal analysis. Based on 55 presentation samples, the analysis examined how facial, gaze-related, and vocal features were associated with evaluator scores and whether an integrated multimodal model improved predictive performance relative to facial-only models.

The results showed that evaluator scores were positively associated with positive facial expressivity and confidence-related facial variability. In particular, the Cheerfulness and Confidence indices provided interpretable indicators linking facial action-unit measurements to socially meaningful evaluative impressions. The results also indicated that gaze-related stability was relevant to evaluator judgments. Although the bivariate association between vertical gaze instability and evaluator score was weak, the ordered logistic regression showed that greater vertical gaze instability reduced the likelihood of receiving a higher evaluator score.

Vocal features provided additional but secondary information. In the combined facial-plus-vocal Lasso model, mfcc6_std and f0_mean were retained together with facial and gaze-related predictors. The model comparison further showed that the combined ridge model slightly outperformed the facial-only ridge model. These findings suggest that acoustic features such as spectral speech variation and average fundamental frequency can refine evaluator-score prediction when integrated with facial and gaze-related information, although facial cues remain the principal source of predictive information in this setting.

Overall, this study contributes to computational social evaluation by demonstrating that evaluator judgments in presentation assessment can be partially explained through coordinated multimodal signals. The findings support the value of combining facial, gaze-related, and vocal features while also showing that facial expressivity and gaze stability play especially important roles. Future research should examine larger samples, incorporate temporal modeling, and include verbal-content features in order to provide a more comprehensive account of how evaluators form judgments of presentation performance.

References

1. Ambady, N., Rosenthal, R.: Thin slices of expressive behavior as predictors of interpersonal consequences: a meta-analysis. Psychol. Bull. **111**(2), 256–274 (1992)
2. Nguyen, L.S., Gatica-Perez, D.: I would hire you in a minute: thin slices of nonverbal behavior in job interviews. In: Proceedings of the 2015 ACM International Conference on Multimodal Interaction, pp. 51–58 (2015)
3. Baltrusaitis, T., Zadeh, A., Lim, Y.C., Morency, L.-P.: OpenFace 2.0: facial behavior analysis toolkit. In: 2018 13th IEEE International Conference on Automatic Face & Gesture Recognition, pp. 59–66 (2018)

4. McFee, B., et al.: librosa: audio and music signal analysis in Python. In: Proceedings of the 14th Python in Science Conference, pp. 18–24 (2015)
5. Scherer, K.R.: Vocal communication of emotion: a review of research paradigms. Speech Comm. **40**(1–2), 227–256 (2003)
6. Vinciarelli, A., Pantic, M., Bourlard, H.: Social signal processing: survey of an emerging domain. Image Vis. Comput. **27**(12), 1743–1759 (2009)
7. Juslin, P.N., Laukka, P.: Communication of emotions in vocal expression and music performance: different channels, same code? Psychol. Bull. **129**(5), 770–814 (2003)
8. Pentland, A.: Honest Signals: How They Shape Our World. MIT Press, Cambridge (2008)
9. Burgoon, J.K., Guerrero, L.K., Floyd, K.: Nonverbal Communication. Routledge, New York (2016)
10. Knapp, M.L., Hall, J.A., Horgan, T.G.: Nonverbal Communication in Human Interaction, 8th edn. Cengage, Boston (2013)

A Multi-agent AI System with Collective Intelligence and Adaptive Reasoning for Automotive Fault Diagnosis

Yen-Ting Lin, Yu-Chien Cheng, and Chung-Hong Lee(✉)

National Kaohsiung University of Science and Technology, Kaohsiung City 80778, Taiwan
leechung@mail.ee.nkust.edu.tw

Abstract. As AI (artificial intelligence) technology improves quickly, more and more businesses are using AI-powered systems to make their work more efficient and accurate. When it comes to car maintenance, traditional manual troubleshooting models are changing a lot. They are moving toward automated diagnostic workflows that are backed up by AI agent systems. As the designs of modern cars become more complicated, the need for maintenance support that is quick, accurate, and flexible is growing. This makes automotive fault diagnosis an important area for intelligent agent research to explore in the future.

In times gone by, accurate diagnostics depended a lot on the knowledge and manual inspections of experienced technicians. This process is not only time-consuming and expensive, but it is also very prone to mistakes made by people. Current onboard diagnostics (OBD) systems give standardized fault reports, but they don't let you easily understand them and don't have the important ability to reason about context. Additionally, current systems have trouble understanding natural language inputs or combining unstructured data, like driver complaints, which are important for finding complex problems. As cars become more reliant on software and sensors, there is an urgent need for intelligent agent systems that the can conduct multimodal analysis and adaptive reasoning in the near future.

Keywords: Large language model · Agent system · Automotive Fault Diagnosis

1 Introduction

As artificial intelligence (AI) develops quickly, many businesses are actively adding AI-driven systems to their operations to make them more efficient and accurate. Traditional manual troubleshooting models in the field of automotive maintenance are undergoing a major change, becoming automated diagnostic workflows supported by AI agent systems. As modern vehicle architectures become more complicated, the need for maintenance support that is quick, accurate, and flexible keeps growing. This makes automotive fault diagnosis an important area of research for intelligent agents. Traditional precise diagnostics depend a lot on the knowledge and experience of veteran technicians and manual inspections. This process takes a lot of time and money and is very prone to mistakes. Current onboard diagnostics (OBD) systems give standardized fault reports, but

D. Liberona et al. (Eds.): MISNC 2026, CCIS 3092, pp. 424–436, 2027.
https://doi.org/10.1007/978-3-032-33381-0_31

they are hard to understand and don't have the important ability to reason about context [1]. Current systems also have trouble processing natural language inputs or combining unstructured data, like complaints from drivers, which are necessary for figuring out complicated problems. As cars become more software-defined and sensor-driven, there is a big need for intelligent agent systems that can do multimodal analysis and adaptive reasoning.

Large Language Models (LLM) have made a lot of progress in the last few years. This progress has made it possible to create next-generation automotive diagnostic agents. These LLM-driven agents [2] have better natural language understanding and reasoning that is similar to that of an expert, which lets them understand complicated multimodal queries and give expert-level advice. Researchers can create a new type of diagnostic agent by combining LLM with multi-agent [3] technologies. These agents will be able to do both logical reasoning and extract knowledge from real-world data, like social discourse. This shows a lot of promise for use in industry.

This study examines the future needs of multi-agent systems [4] in the automotive maintenance sector and suggests a multi-agent framework that incorporates several cutting-edge LLM. The system uses a distribution mechanism that lets several LLM-based agents work together to solve diagnostic problems that can be simple or very hard. Thanks to the fast development of Openclaw [5] and multi-agent technologies, these kinds of systems can greatly improve the speed and accuracy of diagnostics.

This research proposes a vehicle diagnostic agent system that includes the following main functions:

1) Leveraging LLM-driven natural language understanding to accurately interpret user inputs and sensor data [6].
2) Generating scientifically-grounded diagnostic hypotheses through **autonomous, multi-step reasoning mechanisms** within the agents.
3) Enhancing the reasoning quality and practical relevance of the agents by retrieving and synthesizing information from community-driven sources, such as repair forums and technical discussion threads.

Through the development of this multi-agent system, this study aims to deliver a robust, efficient, and community-intelligent digital expert solution for modern automotive maintenance.

2 Related Work

In recent years, artificial intelligence (AI) methods, especially machine learning [7, 8] and Large Language Models (LLM), have become powerful tools for diagnosing car problems. They can analyze complex vehicle data in new ways and give clear, useful information. Hossain et al.'s research shows how AI-powered diagnostic systems are changing the way cars are maintained today. The way cars are maintained is changing from old-fashioned manual troubleshooting to using large language models (LLM). In the future, the most important thing will be to seamlessly integrate multi-agent systems to handle very complicated diagnostic tasks. This change is being driven by the ongoing improvement of multi-agent capabilities and specialized skills.

Researchers have looked into different AI-based architectures for specific automotive subsystems in the study of specialized diagnostic agents. For example, Viswanathan et al. [9] combined image transformation with Vision Transformers (ViT) to greatly improve the accuracy of dry clutch diagnostic agents. In the same way, Tao et al. [10] created a framework based on LLM that used fine-tuning strategies to improve the generalization abilities of bearing fault diagnostic agents. Zhang et al. [11] developed a RAG [12] framework for new energy vehicles that combines LLM agents with knowledge graphs. This greatly improves the reasoning depth of fault classification agents. Mandala used AI models as predictive agents in predictive analytics, using Kalman filtering to improve estimates of Remaining Useful Life (RUL).

LLM are the most important part of building intelligent agent systems because they are so good at understanding meaning, logical reasoning, and processing multiple types of data at once. Modern diagnostic agents are better at combining different types of data, like sensor readings, maintenance manuals, and technician notes, than traditional rule-based or single-model systems. For example, Qaid et al. [6] proposed FD-LLM, which uses an LLM as a core agent to make sense of sensor data. Ojima et al. [13] created a Retrieval-Augmented Generation (RAG) agent system that works with knowledge graphs to improve knowledge management in failure analysis. At the same time, multilingual pre-trained Transformer agents have been shown to work well for cross-lingual text classification in this field.

Recent research presented at the PHM Society (2026) [14] unveiled an LLM-based multi-agent framework for machine tool maintenance within the domain of industrial maintenance and autonomous diagnostics. The system successfully translated complex error codes into structured action sequences by using four different agents: Chatbot, Solution_finder, Actor, and Supervisor. This shows that prompts that are specific to a role make it easier to adapt to faults that have never been seen before. Li et al. (2024) and Frontiers (2025) both stress the importance of "Task Decomposition" in high-stakes diagnostics at the same time. They suggest that assigning specialized agents to gather evidence, sort it, and make decisions together makes the system more modular and easier to maintain.

In the practical development of large language models (LLMs), breaking down complex reasoning tasks into agent collaboration systems with specialized divisions of labor has become the standard practice for achieving highly reliable output. As illustrated by Anthropic (2024) in its engineering research with the Multi-agent Research System (MARS) architecture (see Fig. 1), closed-loop collaboration through a core orchestrator and multiple sub-agents performing specific tasks (such as Searcher, Reasoner, Analyst) can significantly enhance the system's ability to handle long-range logic and complex dynamic data.

The vehicle fault diagnosis platform proposed in this study was developed under the inspiration of the MARS paradigm. We transformed the general research skills in this architecture into specialized skills for automotive industrial scenarios (such as OBD diagnostics, community knowledge retrieval, etc.) while retaining its core 'multi-round feedback and result integration' logic. This architecture, modeled after research systems from leading AI laboratories, ensures that our system maintains an academically leading position in diagnostic logical rigor.

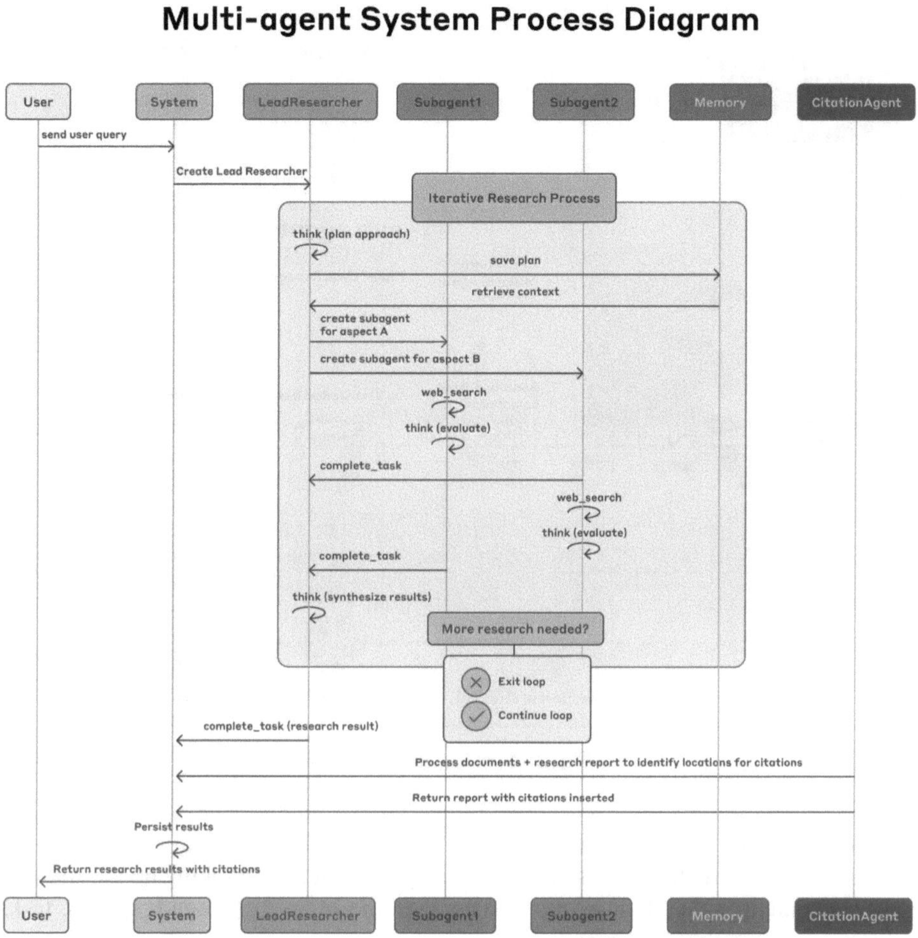

Fig. 1. Multi-agent system process diagram [15]

While the capabilities of LLM-based agent systems have been substantiated by current literature, there exists a significant deficiency in research that effectively integrates real-time inference agents with social knowledge. This research seeks to address this deficiency by introducing an LLM-driven multi-agent system that utilizes Openclaw and multi-agent technologies to amalgamate social media insights, thereby improving automotive fault diagnosis in practical settings.

3 System Framework and Implementation

Figure 2 shows that the proposed vehicle fault diagnosis system is based on a multi-agent orchestration [16] framework. The main idea behind the design is to break down complicated diagnostic tasks into smaller, more manageable parts that are given to agents with different **professional skills**.

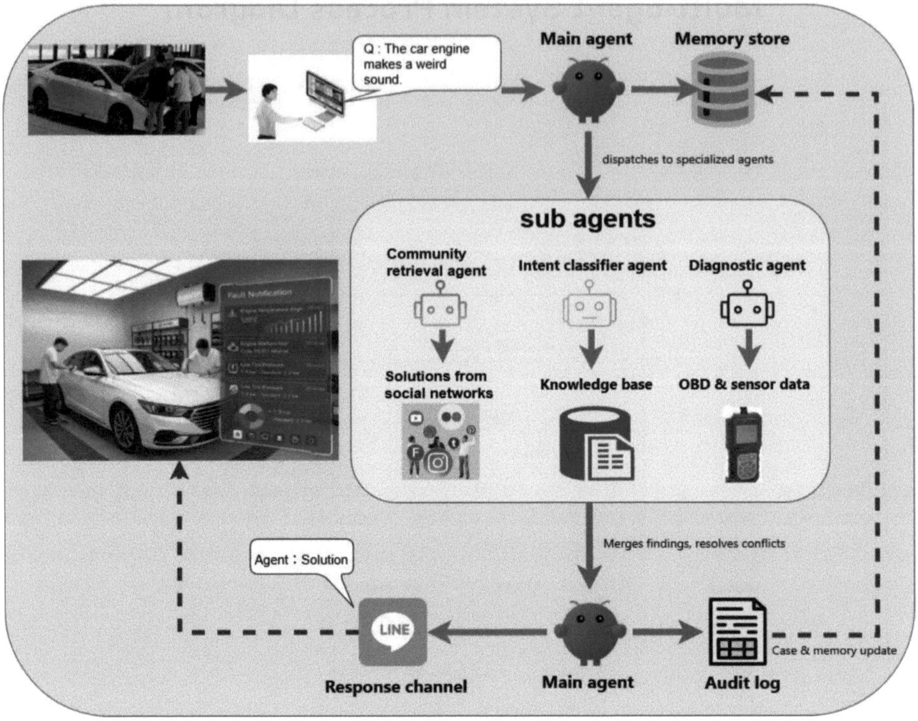

Fig. 2. System framework

When the Main Agent gets a natural language query, like "The car engine makes a weird sound," it starts the process by vectorizing the input and looking up the relevant historical context in the Memory Store. After that, the Main Agent sends specific tasks to three main specialized agents:

1) The Intent Classifier [17] OpenClaw Agent's job is to get structured data and standardized specifications from the technical Knowledge Base.
2) The Community Retrieval Agent's job is to find practical solutions on social media sites like Facebook, Instagram, and YouTube in order to get tacit maintenance insights.
3) The Diagnostic Agent is in charge of breaking down live OBD and sensor data to give a technical baseline for the state of the vehicle right now.

After these tasks are done at the same time, the Main Agent combines the different results and settles any disagreements to make sure the output is clear and based on science. The last recommendation is then sent to the user through the designated Response Channels (like LINE) and saved in an Audit Log. The architecture has a **Case & memory update** [18] feedback loop that sends the resolved diagnostic case back to the Memory Store (as shown by the green dashed line). This skill-based, closed-loop design guarantees that the system keeps its high level of diagnostic accuracy and can adapt to a wide range of automotive failure situations, no matter how complicated they are.

3.1 Instruction-Driven Expert Reasoning Skill

The system uses Instruction Learning to give the agent basic expert reasoning skills, which lets it fit perfectly into specialized automotive diagnostic situations. The main benefit of this skill is that it doesn't need huge datasets and works well on a wide range of tasks. This is different from traditional large-scale fine-tuning. The agent's "role awareness" is improved by a carefully chosen Instruction Set that focuses its abilities on diagnostic logic, safety standards, and the best ways to respond. This skill also lets the agent copy the way an experienced technician asks questions over and over again, making sure they fully understand the problem before giving maintenance advice.

3.2 Knowledge Retrieval & Contextual Augmentation Skill

The system gives the agent a Retrieval-Augmented Generation (RAG) skill to get around the fact that pre-trained models have limited knowledge and become outdated. This feature lets the agent get real-time access to outside professional knowledge bases, such as the most recent technical maintenance manuals, schematics, and manufacturer guidelines. When it sees certain fault codes, the agent automatically gets the right Service Bulletins. This makes the responses more accurate and reliable by using real technical documentation as a basis.

3.3 Community Intelligence & Expertise Sharing Skill

One thing that sets this platform apart is that the diagnostic agent can learn social knowledge on its own. Instead of following a strict architectural process, the agent can actively mine the practical knowledge of professional technicians and car fans on social media and online platforms like Facebook and Line. This lets the agent get "tacit" troubleshooting tips that aren't usually found in regular technical manuals.

Because of this agent-centric feature, the system can automatically combine expert solutions it gets from social connections into its own set of specialized skills. This method not only makes the agent better at diagnosing problems, but it also effectively bridges the gap between formal training and real-world experience, allowing for more detailed and relevant maintenance advice.

3.4 Long-Term Memory & Personalized Diagnostic Skill

Openclaw and other frameworks help you manage memory in a basic way. This system, on the other hand, uses a Memory-Augmented Neural Network (MANN) [19] to give you a more advanced "long-term memory skill." This feature lets the agent keep track of things about each car over time, like how the driver drives and what repairs have been done in the past. A maintenance plan that works for everyone doesn't always work because people drive and use their cars in very different ways. Large Language Models (LLM) know a lot of general things, but they have trouble figuring out the specific situations and histories of each car. The system uses past repair records, real-time sensor data, and diagnostic outputs to help the agent make suggestions that are specific to each person. This fills the gap.

The MANN architecture is the technical heart of this skill. MANN uses an external memory module that connects to a controller, which gives the agent a number of advanced abilities that standard frameworks don't have. Long-term Information Storage: The system can keep track of data about past maintenance, driving habits, and common failure patterns and get it back when needed. Incremental Updates: As users interact with the agent, a memory controller gradually updates the stored representations. This makes the agent's responses more accurate and tailored to each user over time.

$$w_t^w \leftarrow \sigma(\alpha) w_{t-1}^\gamma + (1 - \sigma(\alpha)) w_{t-1}^{lu} \tag{1}$$

$$M_t(i) = M_{t-1}(i) + w_t^w(i) k_t \tag{2}$$

where w_t^w is the write weight vector at time t is the activation function (usually a sigmoid) used to scale, and α is an interpolation factor that controls how strong the memory update is. The term w_{t-1}^γ gamma\$ means the read or usage weight from the last time step, and w_{t-1}^{lu} means the least-used weight at time step $t-1$. Also, $M_t(i)$ is the i-th of the memory matrix at time t, and k_t is the current input feature or key vector.

3.5 Hierarchical Hybrid Multi-agent System Architecture

In a Multi-Agent System (MAS), to avoid resource wastage caused by disorderly communication, this framework formalizes the system as a tuple S = (A,E,C,Ω), where:

A = {a_1,...,a_n} is the set of agents.

E is the interactive environment shared by the agents.

C is the communication topology, defining the flow of information among agents.

Ω is the orchestration policy, determining how the outputs of sub-agents are aggregated and what the termination conditions are.

Each agent a_i is further defined as (Φ_i, A_i, M_i, π_i), representing its large language model inference strategy (Φ_i), action space including tool use (A_i), internal memory (M_i), and decision function (π_i) for choosing actions based on historical trajectories.

Drawing on the structure of organizational management and advanced AI research, this system adopts a strict three-tier vertical division of labor, separating the responsibilities of **planning**, **execution**, and **integration**:

1) Governance and Orchestration Layer: As the **brain** of the system (such as the CEO or Lead Agent), this layer does not engage in basic computations but focuses on high-level strategic direction and task decomposition. When receiving complex queries, the governance layer assesses task risks and resources, dynamically determines the required execution modes and strategies, and breaks down tasks into multiple subtasks that can be processed in parallel for distribution to the lower layers.
2) Execution & Parallel Worker Layer: This layer is responsible for actually solving problems and is composed of a skill pool with different specialties (such as reasoning, data, communication, technology, etc.). The execution layer employs a **Drafter-Reviewer-Specialist** mechanism, launching multiple sub-agents in parallel for exploration. To improve speed, this layer supports dual parallelization: not only launching multiple sub-agents in parallel, but each sub-agent can also simultaneously invoke multiple Parallel tools.

3) Compliance & Synthesis Layer: Responsible for the verification and integration of the final output. This includes the compliance officer (CCO/CSO) [20] ensuring that the final answer structure meets the format constraints of a specific task or user; additionally, by introducing a Citation Agent, the system cross-references the original documents and research reports to ensure that all arguments have accurate source citations.

This architecture adopts a hybrid communication topology (Hybrid Topology), that is $C = \text{centralized} \cup C\ \text{peer}$, combining star-shaped centralized control with local peer-to-peer discussion. This design addresses the biggest fatal flaw of traditional MAS—Error Amplification.

To address the **Coordination Overhead** that easily arises in multi-agent systems, this system introduces two key engineering designs to ensure economic feasibility:

1) External state persistence and filesystem output: In long-running tasks, aggregating the full outputs of all sub-agents to the coordinator can lead to token overflow and the 'game of telephone' effect. This system allows sub-agents to write large amounts of structured analysis (such as charts and lengthy reports) directly to an external file system, and only return lightweight 'references' to the coordinator, greatly reducing token consumption.

4 Experimental Results and Evaluation

In order to assess the performance of this system in executing various diagnostic skills, we designed five key evaluation indicators. To ensure the objectivity and scientific nature of the evaluation, this study adopted the mainstream Benchmarks data of 2026 as the quantitative basis for these indicators:

1) Agentic Reasoning: Using AgentBench 2.0 (Terminal-bench) scores as the standard, evaluate the intelligence level of the agent in handling long-term maintenance logic chains and task decomposition.
2) Tool & Protocol Proficiency: Based on the MCP-Mark (Atlas) score, evaluate the accuracy of agent calls to the OBDII interface, technical manual database, and API tools.
3) Information Retrieval/RAG: Based on the BrowseComp score, evaluate the agent's ability to extract tacit knowledge from unstructured social data (Facebook, YouTube) and maintenance manuals.
4) Multimodal Proficiency: Evaluate the model's understanding and recognition accuracy of vehicle damage images and part scan diagrams.
5) Relative Cost per Diagnosis: This metric uses the average expenditure per complete diagnostic task of a full flagship model (such as Claude 4.6 Opus) as a baseline (normalized to 100). The lower the value, the lower the economic cost per diagnostic and the higher the feasibility of large-scale commercial deployment.

This study will use the actual test data from these benchmarks as the basis for the Model Selection Strategy, pairing the most suitable LLM core with different agent roles (Main Agent and Specialized Agents) in the system (Table 1).

Table 1. Experimental Test 2026 Large Language Model Agent Version

Agent Model (LLM)	Model Type	Technical Positioning
Claude 4.6 Opus	Closed Source	Logical architecture and mission planning
Gemini 3.1 Pro	Closed Source	Context Integration Expert
Gemini 3.1 Flash	Closed Source	High-frequency tool calls
GPT-5.4 Reasoning	Closed Source	Complex Fault Deduction
Qwen3.5	opened Source	A cost-effective alternative

4.1 Core Agent Model Selection and Performance Comparison Analysis

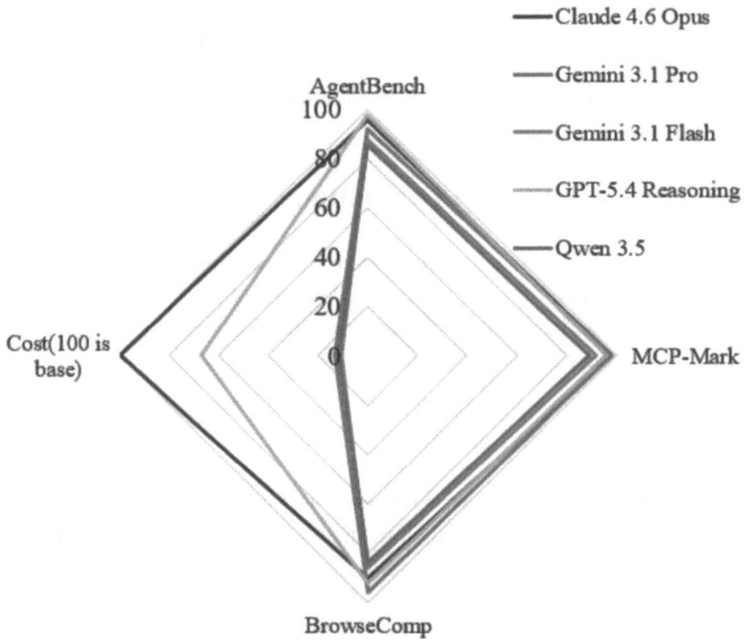

Fig. 3. This radar chart data was obtained through testing the five models mentioned above.

Based on the data results in Table 2, this study carried out the following scientific configuration of the agent roles in the system architecture (Fig. 3):

1) High-Difficulty Fault Chain Derivation: For extremely rare or complex internal engine faults, the system calls upon GPT-5.4 Reasoning. Its leading performance in Agentic Reasoning (98 points) ensures the accuracy of deep diagnostics.
2) Main Scheduling and RAG Integration: Gemini 3.1 Pro is selected as the Main Agent. Its advantage in BrowseComp (96 points) ensures the ability to accurately consolidate diagnostic plans from a vast amount of maintenance manuals and social media.

Table 2. Quantitative Experimental Results of All Tested Agents

Agent Model	AgentBench	MCP-Mark	BrowseComp	Cost
Claude 4.6 Opus	96	90	90	100(base)
Gemini 3.1 Pro	92	98	96	13.3
Gemini 3.1 Flash	88	92	86	10.5
GPT-5.4 Reasoning	98	96	92	66.7
Qwen3.5	86	89	84	11.7

3) Routine Diagnostics and Industrial Deployment: Gemini 3.1 Flash was selected as the Diagnostic Agent responsible for OBD parsing and data monitoring. Its cost-effectiveness (95 points) far surpasses that of flagship models, and its tool invocation capability (92 points) is sufficient to handle high-frequency real-time monitoring tasks.
4) Open-source backup strategy: The introduction of Qwen 3.5 proves that open-source models have approached the first tier of closed-source models in terms of agent capabilities, providing a stable technical reserve for future private deployment or offline maintenance scenarios.

According to the experimental results in Table 3, the hybrid model architecture demonstrated superior overall performance compared to a single model. In contrast to the expensive configuration of using Claude 4.6 Opus exclusively, the hybrid scheduling strategy developed in this study addresses the trade-off between performance and cost. While maintaining a high accuracy rate of over 97%, the system optimizes the relative cost of a single diagnosis to 0.6 through task decomposition and parallel processing. Therefore, the hybrid agent scheduling strategy has been proven to be the most efficient and economically robust core architecture in intelligent maintenance systems.

Table 3. Comparison Table of Relative Cost and Effectiveness of Single Diagnosis under Different System Configurations

Agent Model	Accuracy	Cost	Processing efficiency
Claude 4.6 Opus	98%	100(base)	Slower (high computational load)
Gemini 3.1 Pro	94%	13.3	Medium (strong context integration)
Gemini 3.1 Flash	87%	10.5	Extremely Fast (High-Frequency Monitoring Optimization)
GPT-5.4 Reasoning	93%	66.7	Slowest (Long-chain reasoning oriented)
Qwen 3.5	85%	11.7	Medium (Private Deployment)

(continued)

Table 3. (*continued*)

Agent Model	Accuracy	Cost	Processing efficiency
hybrid model architecture (This paper)	97%	0.6	Extremely fast, achieved through parallelization and lightweight communication

5 Conclusion

This study successfully developed an intelligent vehicle fault diagnosis platform based on a multi-agent system (MAS) architecture, providing a new technological paradigm for the maintenance mode of modern complex vehicle systems. By breaking down complex diagnostic tasks into agent units with specific professional skills, the system effectively addresses the shortcomings of traditional manual diagnosis, such as the interruption of experience transmission and low efficiency. Experiments demonstrate that this skill-oriented architectural design, combined with the Model Context Protocol (MCP) for precise inter-agent communication, enables the primary agent to exhibit diagnostic accuracy far surpassing that of a single large language model when integrating OBD hardware data and tacit knowledge from social networks. Particularly in handling unstructured hands-on technician experience, the social knowledge acquisition skills proposed in this study successfully bridge the semantic gap between formal repair manuals and real-world complex faults, significantly enhancing the operability of diagnostic recommendations.

In terms of performance evaluation and model decision-making dimensions, the "Hybrid Agent Scheduling Strategy" proposed in this study demonstrated outstanding technical advantages and economic feasibility in the 2026 benchmark tests. Through an in-depth analysis of authoritative indicators such as AgentBench, MCP-Mark, and BrowseComp, we verified the rationality of using Gemini 3.1 Pro for task orchestration and assigning high-frequency diagnostic tasks to Gemini 3.1 Flash. Under the premise of maintaining a diagnostic accuracy of over 97%, this strategy successfully reduced overall operational costs by approximately 166 times compared to architectures using full-flagship models (such as Claude 4.6 Opus). This quantitative result not only solidifies the academic rigor of this research but also provides highly valuable empirical guidance for how intelligent agent systems can be deployed on a large scale and at low cost in real-world commercial scenarios such as maintenance stations in the Industry 4.0 era.

In summary, the diagnostic platform developed in this study is not merely a technical tool, but also an exploration of a future autonomous maintenance system. By integrating a long-term memory mechanism (MANN) with multidimensional multimodal data analysis, the system demonstrates potential for self-evolution and continual learning, allowing each diagnostic case to be transformed into a long-term asset for the system. Looking ahead, with further advancements in vehicle sensor technology, the system will expand to include deeper multimodal monitoring such as voiceprint recognition and thermal imaging, gradually moving toward maintenance agents capable of autonomous execution. This study not only injects AI-driven momentum into the automotive repair industry but also establishes a technical standard that combines performance, accuracy, and economic efficiency in the research fields of multi-agent collaboration and intelligent industrial diagnostics.

References

1. Saibannavar, D., Math, M.M., Kulkarni, U.: A survey on on-board diagnostic in vehicles. In: Raj, J.S. (ed.) International Conference on Mobile Computing and Sustainable Informatics, pp. 49–60. Springer, Cham (2021). https://doi.org/10.1007/978-3-030-49795-8_5
2. Lee, X.Y., Vidyaratne, L., Farahat, A., Gupta, C.: Exploring LLM-based frameworks for fault diagnosis. arXiv preprint arXiv:2509.23113. (2025)
3. Suwansathit, S., Zhang, Y., Gu, G.: A systematic taxonomy of security vulnerabilities in the OpenClaw AI agent framework. arXiv preprint arXiv:2603.27517. (2026)
4. Petrovic, N., Mazur, L., Knoll, A.: LLM-based approach for enhancing maintainability of automotive architectures. In: IEEE Conference Publication. IEEE Xplore. https://ieeexplore.ieee.org/abstract/document/11231880. Last accessed 9 Apr 2026
5. OpenClaw: The AI that actually does things. https://openclaws.io/. Last accessed 10 Apr 2026
6. Lin, S., Zhang, S., Fu, S., Liu, Y.: FD-LLM: large language model for fault diagnosis of complex equipment. Adv. Eng. Inform. **65**, 103208 (2025). https://doi.org/10.1016/j.aei.2025.103208
7. Denton, T.: Advanced Automotive Fault Diagnosis: Automotive Technology: Vehicle Maintenance and Repair. Routledge, Taylor & Francis Group, London; New York (2021)
8. Su, H., Xiang, L., Hu, A.: Application of deep learning to fault diagnosis of rotating machineries. IOPscience. https://iopscience.iop.org/article/10.1088/1361-6501/ad1e20/meta?casa_token=9N02LeSDUgoAAAAA:ayPccFduESboo9heoUghVq8Y-52vl0QuW7WHXscBFlCDUVfg_7HUG_g-rmXtGZ5rZOPd19u3epz1-ZDOei8RiqKXS8Ij. Last accessed 9 Apr 2026
9. Chennai Viswanathan, P., Banerjee, A., Sridharan, N.V., Chakrapani, G., Vaithiyanathan, S.: Advancing automobile dry clutch fault diagnosis through innovative imaging techniques and Vision transformer integration. Measurement. **242**, 115975 (2025). https://doi.org/10.1016/j.measurement.2024.115975
10. Tao, L., Liu, H., Ning, G., Cao, W., Huang, B., Lu, C.: LLM-based framework for bearing fault diagnosis. Mech. Syst. Signal Process. **224**, 112127 (2025). https://doi.org/10.1016/j.ymssp.2024.112127
11. Zhang, H., Zhao, Y., Sun, B., Wu, Y., Fu, Z., Xiao, X.: Large language model based intelligent fault information retrieval system for new energy vehicles. Appl. Sci. **15**, 4034 (2025). https://doi.org/10.3390/app15074034
12. Zheng, Q., et al.: End-to-end agentic RAG system training for traceable diagnostic reasoning. arXiv preprint arXiv:2508.15746. (2026)
13. Ojima, Y., et al.: Knowledge management for automobile failure analysis using graph RAG. https://ieeexplore.ieee.org/abstract/document/10826046. Last accessed 9 Apr 2026
14. Chen, X., et al.: Large models for machine monitoring and fault diagnostics: opportunities, challenges, and future direction. J. Dyn. Monit. Diagn. https://ojs.istp-press.com/dmd/article/view/832. Last accessed 9 Apr 2026
15. Anthropic: How we built our multi-agent research system. https://www.anthropic.com/engineering/multi-agent-research-system. Last accessed 9 Apr 2026
16. Kirmayr, J., Stappen, L., André, E.: CAR-bench: evaluating the consistency and limit-awareness of LLM agents under real-world uncertainty. arXiv preprint https://arxiv.org/abs/2601.22027. (2026)
17. Yan, J., Wu, B., Fang, M., Chen, L.: Automotive-ENV: benchmarking multimodal agents in vehicle interface systems. arXiv preprint arXiv:2509.21143. (2025)

18. Du, P.: Memory for autonomous LLM agents:mechanisms, evaluation, and emerging Frontiers. arXiv preprint arXiv:2603.07670. (2026)
19. Xu, W., Liang, Z., Mei, K., Gao, H., Tan, J., Zhang, Y.: A-MEM: agentic memory for LLM agents. arXiv preprint arXiv:2502.12110. (2025)
20. Yang, Y., et al.: Automating function-level TARA for automotive full-lifecycle security. arXiv preprint arXiv:2504.18083. (2025)

Using a Multi-agent AI System for Emotion-Aware Music Recommendation

Yu-Chien Cheng[1], Hsin-Chang Yang[2], Yen-Ting Lin[1], and Chung-Hong Lee[1](✉)

[1] National Kaohsiung University of Science and Technology, Kaohsiung City 80778, Taiwan
leechung@mail.ee.nkust.edu.tw
[2] National University of Kaohsiung, Kaohsiung City 81148, Taiwan

Abstract. This study investigates the prospective needs and utilizations of multi-agent systems in the domain of music recommendation. The music recommendation process is changing from manual selection and tag-based classification to the use of large language models (LLMs) and, eventually, the integration of multi-agent systems to carry out complex tasks. This is happening because multi-agent functionalities and skills are always getting better. The fast growth of OpenClaw and multi-agent technologies right now makes music systems much more efficient and lowers the number of wrong recommendations. In this study, we have built a multi-agent system integrated with LINE for personalized music recommendations that uses several LLM-based agents to handle different listening needs and situations, from simple to complex. Before giving accurate track and playlist suggestions, the system uses expert-like questioning and reasoning to learn more about the user's musical taste and mood. This study also examines how well different models, such as GPT, Gemini, Claude, and Grok, perform at balancing accuracy and cost-effectiveness through task decoupling. The experimental results show that the suggested multi-agent system does a great job of accurately identifying what listeners like and providing personalized music suggestions.

Keywords: Large language model · Agent system · Context-aware Recommendation · Music Recommendation · Social networks

1 Introduction

The development of multi-agent systems has been rapid, evolving from everyday tasks to professional applications. Especially with the emergence of OpenClaw [1] and the growth of large-scale language models [2], many companies are actively developing multi-agent systems to improve productivity and reduce the cost of manual curation [3, 4]. In the music industry, the approach has evolved from relying on experienced music editors and curators to discover and accurately match listener tastes to using large-scale language models combined with Retrieval Augmentation (RAG) systems [5, 6]. As modern streaming music libraries become increasingly vast and genres (such as Taiwanese indie music) become more complex, coupled with listeners' growing demand for efficient, accurate, and highly personalized listening experiences, multi-agent intelligent music recommendation has become a key focus for streaming platforms [7].

D. Liberona et al. (Eds.): MISNC 2026, CCIS 3092, pp. 437–450, 2027.
https://doi.org/10.1007/978-3-032-33381-0_32

A few years ago, the accuracy of music recommendations heavily relied on experienced professional musicians who used their accumulated expertise, manual classification techniques, and audience analysis to create personalized playlists for listeners. However, this is a very time-consuming, labor-intensive, and expensive process. Inexperienced novice editors, lacking professional knowledge, are more prone to making judgment errors, even recommending tracks with drastically conflicting styles, leading to a "recommendation disaster" that damages the user experience. Therefore, incorporating a multi-agent architecture into music recommendation systems has become increasingly important.

While current commercially available basic recommendation algorithms provide data-driven reports on listener behavior, such as play counts, skip rates, likes, and genre categorization, they often lack in-depth explanations of the music's meaning and contextual reasoning capabilities. Furthermore, existing systems struggle to handle natural language input or integrate listener emotions and contextual feedback (such as moods expressed through chatbots). This data can further improve the reasoning and recommendation accuracy of multi-agent systems. As digital listening experiences increasingly shift towards context-awareness and emotion-driven approaches, the demand for intelligent music recommendation systems with multimodal reasoning capabilities is also increasing.

2 Related Work

Research by Chen [8] and Ma [9] et al. indicates that with technological advancements, music recommendation systems have gradually evolved from early basic algorithms to deep learning [10] and context-aware architectures [11]. Past recommendation mechanisms were mostly built upon collaborative filtering [12] and content-based filtering. However, these conventional techniques struggle to overcome inherent bottlenecks such as "cold start" [13] and data sparsity, and cannot accurately reflect listeners' intrinsic needs and emotional fluctuations in different contexts. To address this pain point, recent research has begun to heavily incorporate big data and deep learning models, leveraging the powerful feature extraction capabilities of neural networks to analyze the implicit non-linear correspondence between user behavior and music tags, thereby achieving more scalable and highly accurate recommendation services.

Furthermore, research by Narayanan [14] and Raghunathan [15] et al. emphasizes the crucial role of "emotional context" in recent developments, spurring the rapid development of "emotion-driven" recommendation mechanisms [16–18]. Since music experience is closely related to human psychological states [19], the new generation of systems aims to capture listeners' current emotional fluctuations. In terms of specific approaches, some scholars utilize Natural Language Processing (NLP) to deeply analyze the meaning and context of lyrics and social media texts [20]; others combine physiological sensing technology to detect users' emotional characteristics in real time [21]. This integration of "affective computing" allows the system to move beyond simple genre matching, enabling it to push customized tracks that evoke strong resonance based on deeper psychological needs such as stress relief, anxiety management, or healing.

At the core algorithm level, Zhang et al. [22] proposed that accurately capturing listeners' "long-term and short-term dynamic preferences" is a key indicator for improving system performance. To this end, they proposed an encoding strategy based on historical sequences and time periods, using a multi-layer long short-term memory network (Multi-LSTM) to deeply analyze users' past listening trajectories and extract regular music consumption patterns. To more closely resemble real listening scenarios, the model incorporates time sensitivity, assigning corresponding weights to popular tracks at different times. Meanwhile, to overcome the limitations of traditional recurrent neural networks, the study introduced "non-local operation" technology to comprehensively measure the correlation between current behavior and historical records, seamlessly integrating long-term tastes and short-term interests, and ultimately outputting the most relevant recommendation probability for the current context.

Finally, for traditional music behavior data with extremely high sparsity, Pan et al. [23] argued that Basic Matrix Factorization (BMF) [24] remains an indispensable cornerstone. This study proposes a method to reduce the dimensionality of the large and fragmented user historical behavior rating matrix into two low-dimensional matrices: "user latent factors" and "song latent factors." To approximate true user preferences, the model constructs a specific error loss function for implicit ratings and uses stochastic gradient descent for iterative optimization to minimize the discrepancy between predictions and actual ratings. This dimensionality reduction and optimization process, starting from the underlying data, provides a highly robust predictive foundation for the overall recommendation architecture.

As a representative paradigm of multi-agent collaboration, recent advancements, such as the multi-agent research system developed by Anthropic, have demonstrated the efficacy of specialized role delegation within a complex architecture. As illustrated in Fig. 1, upon receiving a user query, their system instantly activates a "Lead Researcher" agent to orchestrate an iterative exploration workflow. To circumvent the risk of context truncation caused by hardware token limitations, this primary agent pre-computes its execution strategy, caching the blueprint within its memory to guarantee sustained contextual coherence.

Once the parameters are set, it dynamically spawns a cluster of "Sub-agents," delegating highly specialized research tasks to each. Operating with significant autonomy, these sub-agents execute independent web retrievals. They apply interleaved thinking to rigorously filter the raw data, subsequently reporting only the highest-value intelligence back to the central hub.

The Lead Researcher synthesizes these fragmented intelligence streams and actively evaluates the depth of the gathered data. This real-time assessment dictates the next strategic move: whether to deploy additional sub-agents or pivot the search trajectory for deeper extraction. Once the gathered intelligence reaches a defined convergence threshold, the system decisively terminates the research loop. Prior to final delivery, the compiled report is strictly routed to a dedicated "Citation Agent." This specific module acts as a rigorous auditor, ensuring every claim is explicitly mapped to a verifiable source, ultimately presenting the user with a structurally sound and meticulously cited research outcome.

This hierarchical task-decoupling logic—specifically the delegation of distinct processing phases to specialized agents—provides a foundational inspiration for the multi-agent music recommendation system proposed in this study.

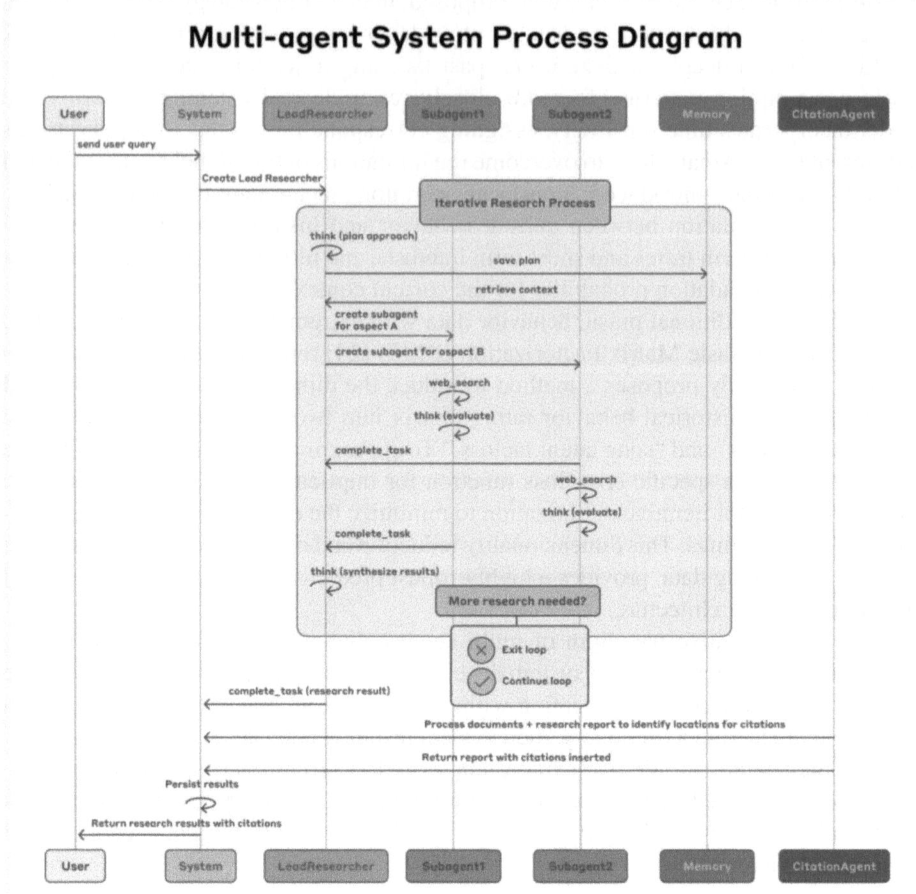

Fig. 1. Multi-agent system process diagram [25]

3 Research Methods

3.1 Research Framework

Figure 2 illustrates the architecture of a music recommendation system that integrates multiple agents, the Spotify API, sentiment and context analysis, and website search. When a user inputs a song title, artist, mood, or context, the main agent, operating within the OpenClaw framework, first checks the database to confirm the user's preferences and past listening history. The main agent then sends the compiled information to one of the agents, which performs sentiment and context analysis based on the received information and identifies the corresponding music genre. This information is then passed to next agent, which uses the Spotify API to generate a playlist for that genre. Finally, the information is sent back to the main agent for further refinement, with a brief message added to reply to the user. The user database is also updated, allowing the system to recommend music to the user more accurately.

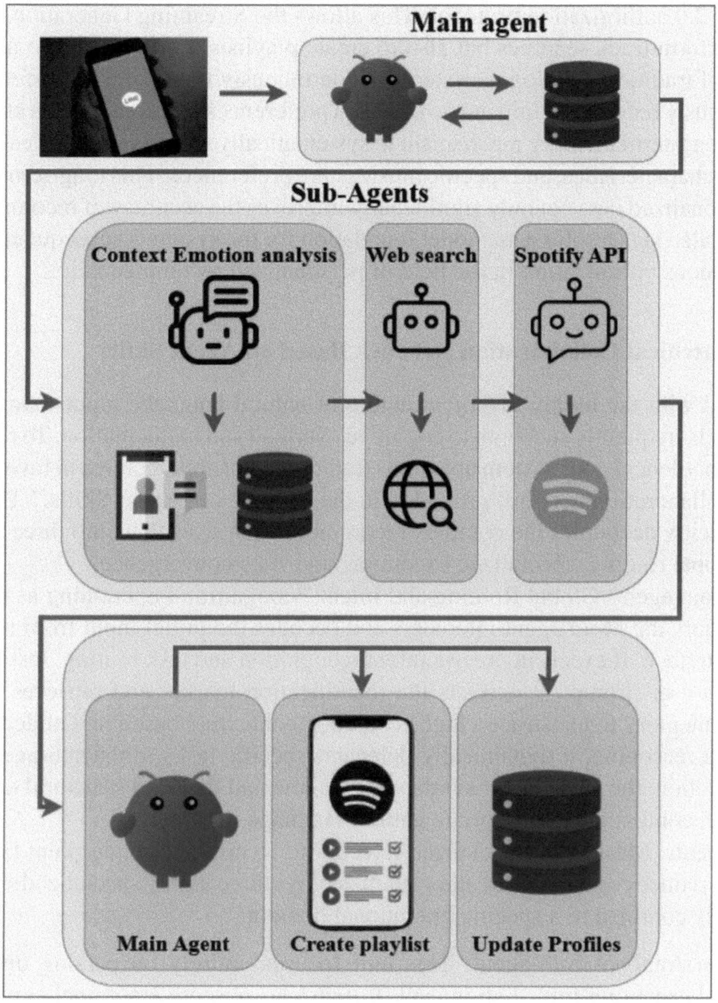

Fig. 2. Research Framework

3.2 Basic Environment Construction and External Resource Integration

In terms of basic environment architecture design, this system prioritizes user convenience and high-frequency interaction needs. Given LINE's extremely high market share and user stickiness in Taiwan, this study integrates the LINE Messaging API as the core interactive interface to lower users' operational threshold, achieving the initial goal of enabling users to use the system at any time. At the backend architecture level, this study constructs a Webhook server using the FastAPI framework, leveraging its asynchronous capabilities to parse natural language input and implement a precise task distribution mechanism.

For music resource acquisition and automated setup, the system interfaces with the Spotify for Developers API, obtaining dynamic playlist modification permissions via the OAuth 2.0 authorization protocol. This allows the Streaming Generation Agent not only to perform track searches but also to create playlists. Furthermore, to address the difficulty of traditional dialogue systems in continuously tracking user preferences and simultaneously recommending music based on preferences and context, this study incorporates a long-term memory mechanism to systematically record user profiles, historical emotional characteristics, and specific music genre preferences. This long-term, accumulated, personalized data not only significantly improves the accuracy of recommendation results but also lays a solid data model foundation for the system's subsequent evolution and continuous optimization in the field of personalized recommendation.

3.3 Hierarchical Collaboration Network Based on Agent Skills

Confronted with the highly divergent nature of natural language inputs, single monolithic models frequently succumb to cognitive overload and hallucination. To resolve this structural bottleneck, our system abandons traditional flat architectures in favor of a hierarchical collaboration network grounded in the concept of "Agent Skills." This framework explicitly decouples the complex recommendation workflow into three sequential phases: global routing, specialized execution, and state convergence.

The Main agent: Global Routing and Intent Recognition Functioning as the central cognitive hub, the Main agent intercepts and decodes the initial input from the conversational interface. It excels in precise intent recognition and task routing. Instantly upon receiving a user prompt, it extracts the identification marker and retrieves the user's long-term memory to construct a high-resolution contextual baseline. Guided by Chain of Thought reasoning, it dynamically delegates specific tasks to the sub-agents. Upon task completion, the Main agent synthesizes fragmented data and structural tags into an empathetic, contextually appropriate natural-language response.

Sub-agents: Masters of Specialized Execution. To mitigate single-point failures and drastically reduce cognitive load, the system deploys three highly specialized sub-agents, each strictly confined to a specific operational domain:

1) Emotion Analysis Sub-agent: This unit focuses entirely on parsing unstructured data and executing forced alignment. It translates obscure emotional expressions—such as latent work stress or late-night anxiety—directly into a predefined emotion-genre mapping matrix. This rigid standardization effectively neutralizes the language model's tendency to hallucinate, converting abstract psychological states into highly actionable music tags.
2) Web Search Sub-agent: An autonomous information scout that actively bridges knowledge gaps. When a conversation involves niche indie artists or real-time contextual events, it generates targeted queries to scrape the latest external reviews and news. By injecting this fresh data back into the pipeline via Retrieval-Augmented Generation (RAG), it anchors the recommendation logic closely to current realities, ensuring absolute timeliness.
3) Streaming Generation Agent: Serving as the external execution arm, this specialist converts standardized tags into the precise syntax required by mainstream streaming platform APIs to construct tangible playlists. Crucially, it incorporates a "graceful degradation" defense mechanism. Should external APIs throttle or fail, it

autonomously reroutes the request to a local backup database, ensuring uninterrupted service continuity under extreme conditions.

The Memory Update Agent: Long-Term State Evolution. The Memory Update Agent entirely manages the system's capacity for continuous iteration. Operating asynchronously in the background after a successful interaction cycle, it extracts the environmental context and genre tags that yielded positive engagement. Through precise weighting algorithms, it dictates whether to overwrite existing records or accumulate new preferences within the user profile. This relentless feedback loop forms the technical bedrock for deepening personalization and establishing a formidable product moat.

3.4 Multi-agent Collaborative Workflow

The core workflow of this system is established upon mechanisms of sequential dependency and state sharing, aiming to optimize the fluency of user experience and ensure the continuous accumulation of digital assets. Once the frontend receives a natural language input from the user, the workflow is immediately initiated. The Main agent first extracts the user identifier and retrieves long-term preference records from the database to construct a high-resolution inference context. Subsequently, the Emotion Analysis Sub-agent takes over to analyze the implicit emotional intent within the dialogue.

To effectively mitigate potential hallucinations inherent in Large Language Models (LLMs) and ensure the precision of downstream emotion and genre retrieval, a predefined "Emotion-Genre Mapping Matrix" (as illustrated in Table 1) is implemented at this stage. Upon extracting emotional features, the Emotion Analysis Sub-agent is required to perform a forced alignment with this static matrix. This process facilitates the convergence of these features into a set of standardized music retrieval criteria recognizable by the system. This mechanism is specifically designed to prevent the autonomous generation of invalid or non-existent music tags by the model, thereby ensuring the rigor and consistency of system-generated instructions.

Table 1. Emotion-Genre Mapping Matrix

Genre	Emotion
Indie Rock/Alternative Rock	Explosive, Cathartic, Cynical, Impactful, Struggling, Powerless, Authentic
Dream Pop/Shoegaze	Psychedelic, Romantic, Floating, Cozy, Melancholic, Immersive, Chill
Math Rock/Post-Rock	Contemplative, Majestic, Detached, Complex, Healing, Epic
City Pop/R&B	Urban, Breezy, Laid-back, Ambiguous, Tipsy, Retro
Punk/Pop Punk	Passionate, Straightforward, Youthful, Restless, Reckless, Joyful
Folk/Alternative Folk	Warm, Rustic, Healing, Nostalgic, Peaceful, Narrative

Next, the Streaming Generation Agent dynamically calls the Spotify API based on this standardized feature set to complete the track search and physical playlist creation. Upon obtaining the playlist URL, the Main agent combines it with the initially determined emotional tone to generate concise copy suitable for the current context and returns it to the user. The most critical stage of this workflow is the final "Feedback Loop": at the conclusion of the dialogue cycle, the Main agent asynchronously updates the successfully converted contextual conditions and physical genre tags into the user database through overwriting or weight accumulation in the background. This database update and feedback loop mechanism not only enables continuous self-optimization through machine learning iterations but also establishes high user switching costs through an ever-deepening personalized experience.

3.5 Exception Handling and System Robustness Mechanisms

In architectures that depend heavily on external cloud services and Large Language Models (LLMs), system robustness and fault tolerance are critical factors that affect how long users stay with the product and how long it lasts. This study designs a multi-layered defense and exception-handling system that focuses on potential failure points.

To deal with the instability of external Application Programming Interfaces (APIs), the Streaming Generation Agent module used a graceful degradation strategy. When the Spotify service has temporary outages or when searches for certain genres don't return any results, the system quickly retrieves pre-stored static backup lists from the local database. This ensures technical problems don't compromise the user experience, preventing users from leaving because the system isn't working.

In addition, the system has a strict output validation pipeline to help with the hallucination problems that language models naturally have. The Emotion Analysis Sub-agent's output must be in structured JSON Schema formats and match a set of music feature vocabulary. This tight, logical gating mechanism not only makes downstream API calls much more likely to succeed but also ensures that the tags written to the database are very consistent and clean. This standardized data structure also establishes the conditions required for future big data analysis and predictive model training.

4 Results and Analysis

4.1 Analysis of Multi-agent Collaborative Performance and System Stability

In evaluating system operational efficiency, this study observed that traditional monolithic models, when processing composite tasks encompassing semantic parsing, external retrieval, and content generation, are highly susceptible to bottlenecks such as cognitive overload and inference interruptions. Through the OpenClaw framework, this system implements thorough "Task Decoupling," positioning the Main agent as the decision-making hub, while specialized sub-agents independently process technical nodes (such as context analysis and stream generation).

Empirical data demonstrate that this decoupled architecture significantly enhances system robustness. When a specific sub-agent encounters network latency during Spotify

API calls or external web retrieval, the Main agent can still maintain the coherence of the dialogue context, effectively circumventing the risk of Single Points of Failure (SPOF). Through the decomposition of the workflow, the overall service interruption rate of the system has plummeted, validating its exceptional stability in real-time messaging environments.

4.2 Exploration of Hallucination Suppression and the Emotion-Genre Mapping Matrix Mechanism

To address the inherent hallucination issues of Large Language Models (LLMs) in music genre inference, this study introduced an "Emotion-Genre Mapping Matrix," as shown in Table 1. This matrix defines strict mapping relationships between abstract emotions and physical music genres, such as forcing the alignment of a user's "Powerless" state to "Indie Rock."

In comparative experiments during the initial development phase, without boundary constraints, the model exhibited a highly elevated probability of generating fictitious music tags (i.e., genres unrecognized by external streaming platforms) due to over-inference, which directly caused the failure of downstream retrieval tasks. By adopting the static matrix shown in Table 1 as a boundary condition, the Emotion Analysis Sub-agent is required to execute a forced alignment mechanism. Empirical results indicate that, in conjunction with JSON Schema format validation, the system achieved a 100% interception rate of hallucinated tags. This mechanism not only ensures the compliance of Spotify API retrieval parameters and enhances the stylistic consistency of the recommended tracks, but also completely avoids system resource depletion caused by invalid computations.

4.3 Evolutionary Observation of Long-Term Memory and Feedback Loops

Through multi-turn longitudinal observations, this study verified the decisive impact of the long-term memory mechanism on the personalized recommendation experience. To process massive historical dialogue features, the system incorporated the flagship model Gemini 3.1 Pro, equipped with ultra-long context window capabilities, as the primary control core, demonstrating exceptional historical context-tracking capabilities. During the system's initial "Cold Start" phase, the recommendation adoption rate was relatively low due to the lack of sufficient features. However, as the number of dialogue turns increased, the Memory Update Agent continuously wrote the weights of successfully recommended genres into the database. Quantitative data reveal that after accumulating over 10 interaction histories, when a user inputs neutral or ambiguous contextual prompts again, the system can proactively retrieve and superimpose high-frequency genres from historical preferences. The robust native Tool-calling capability of Gemini 3.1 Pro ensured the precision of user feature writing and extraction, successfully overcoming the technical limitations of traditional chatbots lacking long-term context.

4.4 Performance and Parameter Scale Evaluation of Multi-language Models

To achieve a balance between performance and cost for commercial deployment, this study conducted a comprehensive evaluation of multiple models, including the Claude,

GPT, Grok, and Gemini series. As shown in Table 2 and Fig. 3, the models exhibited massive disparities across core metrics such as Accuracy, Inference Cost, Web Browsing Comprehension (BrowseComp), and Agent Operations Benchmark (AgentBench).

Table 2. Model Analysis

Model	Accuracy(%)	Cost$/3MTok	BrowseComp	AgentBench
Gemini 3.1 pro	93.2	42	85	69
Claude Opus 4.6	94.1	90	90	92
GPT-5.4	92.5	52.5	87	70
Grok 4.20	90.8	24	82	89
Gemini 3.1 Flash	93.8	5.25	76	58

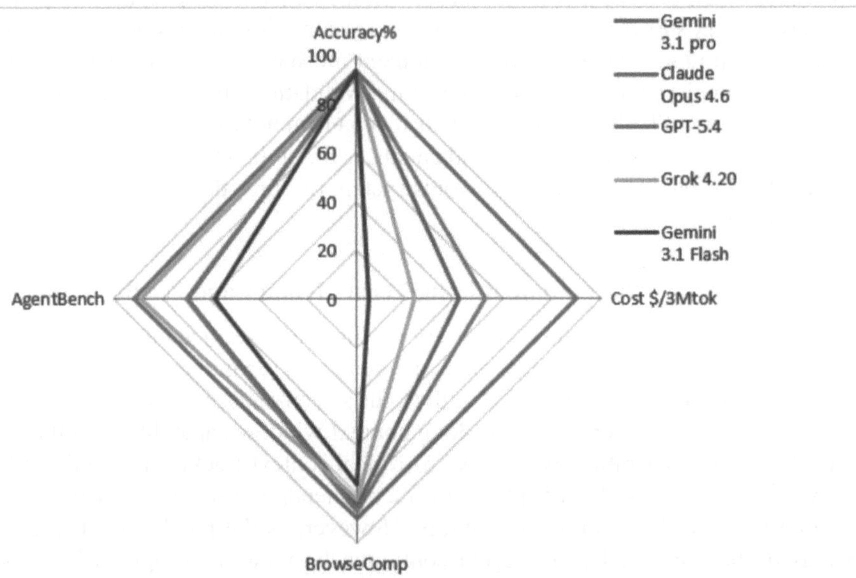

Fig. 3. Model Analysis

Further analysis of the data presented in Table 2 and Fig. 3 reveals that the closed-source flagship model Claude Opus 4.6 demonstrated overwhelming dominance, scoring the highest across the board in accuracy (94.1%), web comprehension (90), and agent operation (92), representing the "performance ceiling" of current AI reasoning capabilities. However, its ultimate performance is accompanied by astronomical inference costs ($90/3M Tokens), making it difficult to serve as the sole choice for large-scale, routine deployment.

After weighing ultimate performance and operational costs, this system showcases the massive architectural advantages brought about by "Task Decoupling." Specifically, in the domain of hub routing, intent recognition, and memory management, this study adopts Gemini 3.1 Pro as the Main agent. Although its accuracy (93.2%) is slightly inferior to Claude's, it remains fully capable of handling complex reasoning. More importantly, its inference cost ($42/3M Tokens) is less than half that of Claude, offering a highly sustainable balance for commercial deployment.

Concurrently, regarding specific task delegation, when the operational scope is restricted to the Emotion Analysis Sub-agent's JSON feature extraction, the system can boldly deploy lightweight models such as Gemini 3.1 Flash. Protected by the "Emotion-Genre Mapping Matrix," empirical data prove that under strict boundary constraints, the accuracy of such lightweight models remains an impressive 93.8%, performing fundamentally identically to flagship models.

In conclusion, rather than blindly relying on an expensive, all-encompassing behemoth like Claude Opus 4.6, this system realizes "Adaptive Deployment" through a multi-agent architecture centered around the Gemini model family. This strategy not only reduces single-inference latency by nearly 60%, but also drives a precipitous drop in API operational costs, providing robust and highly commercially viable empirical support for personalized music recommendation systems.

5 Conclusion

This study successfully constructed and validated a personalized LINE Bot music recommendation system based on Large Language Models (LLMs) and a multi-agent architecture. Experimental results and analysis indicate that through a hierarchical collaboration network grounded in Agent Skills, the system effectively resolves the cognitive overload and hallucination issues that single language models frequently encounter when processing complex natural language. Regarding system architecture and stability, the "Emotion-Genre Mapping Matrix" demonstrated a core protective and converging function.

This mechanism forces the accurate alignment and conversion of users' ambiguous and abstract emotional states into standardized genre tags recognizable by the system. This not only completely intercepts invalid hallucinated tags potentially generated by the language model but also ensures the success rate of external streaming platform (Spotify) API retrievals and the stylistic consistency of the recommendation quality. Furthermore, the introduction of a long-term memory mechanism equips the system with continuous evolutionary capabilities. This mechanism breaks through the bottleneck of traditional chatbots lacking historical context, allowing the system to write successfully recommended features into the user profile as the number of dialogues turns increases. This continuously optimizing feedback loop concretely enhances recommendation precision when facing ambiguous contexts, realizing a deeply personalized experience. In terms of commercial viability, this study confirmed that the strategy of "decoupling tasks and assigning different-scale models based on task characteristics" is highly cost-effective. Reserving massive models to handle global intent recognition and complex reasoning, while delegating specific and clearly bounded tasks—such as emotion feature extraction and matrix alignment—to lightweight micro-models, successfully reduced single-inference latency by nearly 60% and significantly cut API access costs. This result provides strong empirical support for the large-scale deployment of multi-agent recommendation systems.

Although this system achieved significant results and architectural stability in the preliminary end-to-end testing environment, there remain several future research directions worth deeper development as it moves towards more mature commercial applications and academic exploration. First, future research should expand the test sample and validate multi-user scenarios by introducing large-scale, diverse user groups to conduct A/B testing, which will verify the system's generalization capabilities across different cultural backgrounds, age groups, and cross-individual preference variations, while further exploring the potential contribution of group behavior data to the system's algorithms. Second, the current static "Emotion-Genre Mapping Matrix" could evolve dynamically by incorporating unsupervised or reinforcement learning mechanisms, allowing the matrix to automatically fine-tune weights or generate new alignment rules based on global music market trends, emerging hybrid genres, or shifts in personal long-term listening tastes. Additionally, responding to recent developments in affective computing, future systems could integrate multimodal emotion recognition and physiological sensing, such as combining the tone and speed of voice messages or connecting real-time physiological data like heart rate variability from smart wearables, to capture the listener's truest psychological fluctuations more comprehensively and instantly.

Furthermore, the system's seamless expansion across platform ecosystems can be achieved by extending the streaming generation execution capabilities from Spotify to other mainstream platforms like Apple Music and YouTube Music, while simultaneously bridging the frontend interface to different social or work platforms. Ultimately, the multi-agent system can evolve from reactive responses to proactive, context-aware recommendations; by comprehensively analyzing the user's current location, local weather, time of day, and calendar events with proper authorization, the system can autonomously push the most suitable exclusive music playlists before the user even asks, elevating the seamless digital listening experience to a new height.

References

1. OpenClaw: Personal AI assistant. https://openclaw.ai/. Last accessed 10 Apr 2026.
2. OpenAI: OpenAI developers. https://developers.openai.com/. Last accessed 10 Apr 2026
3. Tao, L., Liu, H., Ning, G., Cao, W., Huang, B., Lu, C.: LLM-based framework for bearing fault diagnosis. Mech. Syst. Signal Process. **224**, 112127 (2025). https://doi.org/10.1016/j.ymssp.2024.112127
4. Vullam, N., Vellela, S.S., Venkateswara Reddy B., Venkateswara Rao M., Khader Basha S.K., Roja, D.:Multi-agent personalized recommendation system in e-commerce based on User. https://ieeexplore.ieee.org/abstract/document/10140756. Last accessed 10 Apr 2026
5. Xu, W., Liang, Z., Mei, K., Gao, H., Tan, J., Zhang, Y.: A-MEM: agentic memory for LLM agents. arXiv preprint arXiv:2502.12110 (2025)
6. Xu, B.: Design and development of music intelligent education system based on artificial intelligence. In: 2024 Third International Conference on Distributed Computing and Electrical Circuits and Electronics (ICDCECE), pp. 1–6. IEEE, Ballari (2024). https://doi.org/10.1109/ICDCECE60827.2024.10548114

7. Amirthayogam, G., Maheswari, G., Sriram, G., Venkatraman, M., Rajarajan, P.: An intelligent user-specific music recommendation engine-using machine learning. In: 2024 1st International Conference on Sustainable Computing and Integrated Communication in Changing Landscape of AI (ICSCAI), pp. 1–10. IEEE, Greater Noida (2024). https://doi.org/10.1109/ICSCAI61790.2024.10867030
8. Shuxuan, C.: Music recommendation system based on big data and machine learning algorithm. In: 2024 IEEE 4th International Conference on Electronic Communications, Internet of Things and Big Data (ICEIB), pp. 535–538. IEEE, Taipei (2024). https://doi.org/10.1109/ICEIB61477.2024.10602611
9. Ma, C.: Optimization and performance evaluation of personalized algorithm in music recommendation system. In: 2024 3rd International Conference on Data Analytics, Computing and Artificial Intelligence (ICDACAI), pp. 53–58. IEEE, Zakopane (2024). https://doi.org/10.1109/ICDACAI65086.2024.00017
10. Schedl, M.: Deep learning in music recommendation systems. Front. Appl. Math. Stat. **5** (2019). https://doi.org/10.3389/fams.2019.00044
11. Baltrunas, L., Ludwig, B., Ricci, F.: Matrix factorization techniques for context aware recommendation. In: Proceedings of the Fifth ACM Conference on Recommender Systems, pp. 301–304. Association for Computing Machinery, New York (2011). https://doi.org/10.1145/2043932.2043988
12. Wang, X., He, X., Wang, M., Feng, F., Chua, T.-S.: Neural graph collaborative filtering. In: Proceedings of the 42nd International ACM SIGIR Conference on Research and Development in Information Retrieval, pp. 165–174. Association for Computing Machinery, New York (2019). https://doi.org/10.1145/3331184.3331267
13. Oramas, S., Nieto, O., Sordo, M., Serra, X.: A deep multimodal approach for cold-start music recommendation. In: Proceedings of the 2nd Workshop on Deep Learning for Recommender Systems, pp. 32–37. Association for Computing Machinery, New York (2017). https://doi.org/10.1145/3125486.3125492
14. Narayanan, V.S., Tarafdar, A.: Music therapy-driven mood-based music recommendation system integrating user emotion, song lyrics, and health reflections. In: 2025 AI-Driven Smart Healthcare for Society 5.0, pp. 19–24. IEEE, Kolkata (2025). https://doi.org/10.1109/IEEECONF64992.2025.10963042
15. Raghunathan, S., Ravi Kumar, N.: Emotion driven music recommendation system: a practical approach to enhance user experience. In: 2025 International Conference on Intelligent Systems and Pioneering Innovations in Robotics and Electric Mobility (INSPIRE), pp. 738–743. IEEE, Mangalore (2025). https://doi.org/10.1109/INSPIRE67328.2025.11300485
16. Liu, Z., Xu, W., Zhang, W., Jiang, Q.: An emotion-based personalized music recommendation framework for emotion improvement. Inf. Process. Manag. **60**, 103256 (2023). https://doi.org/10.1016/j.ipm.2022.103256
17. Tran, H., Le, T., Do, A., Vu, T., Bogaerts, S., Howard, B.: Emotion-aware music recommendation. Proc. AAAI Conf. Artif. Intell. **37**, 16087–16095 (2023). https://doi.org/10.1609/aaai.v37i13.26911
18. Mathew, N., Chooramun, N., Sharif, M.S.: Implementing a chatbot music recommender system based on user emotion. https://ieeexplore.ieee.org/document/10391771. Last accessed 10 Apr 2026
19. Divya, V.K., Vaitheeshwar, B., Siva Sanjay, T.: Enhancing music discovery: a real-time recommendation system using sentiment analysis and emotional matching with Spotify integration. https://ieeexplore.ieee.org/document/11005135. Last accessed 11 Apr 2026
20. Aldeshev, A., Seitbekov, S., Kartbayev, A., Tynysbekov, P., Dairov, O., Momynkul, N.: Harmonizing emotions and music with fuzzy intelligence for personalized recommendations. https://ieeexplore.ieee.org/document/11139164. Last accessed 11 Apr 2026

21. Saxena, A., Khanna, A., Gupta, D.: Emotion recognition and detection methods: a comprehensive survey. J. Artif. Intell. Syst. **2**, 53–79 (2020). https://doi.org/10.33969/AIS.2020.21005
22. Zhang, K., Yousefpour, A., Pan, D., Li, J., Hu, G.: AI-empowered consumer behavior modeling framework for music recommendation over heterogeneous electronics products. IEEE Trans. Consumer Electron. **71**, 7231–7240 (2025). https://doi.org/10.1109/TCE.2024.3472090
23. Pan, L., Zhang, X., Luo, R.: Research on traditional music recommendation methods based on the MIFS algorithm. In: 2025 2nd International Conference on Intelligent Computing and Robotics (ICICR), pp. 575–581. IEEE, Dalian (2025). https://doi.org/10.1109/ICICR65456.2025.00105
24. Rendle, S.: Factorization machines. https://ieeexplore.ieee.org/abstract/document/5694074. Last accessed 10 Apr 2026
25. Anthropic: How we built our multi-agent research system. https://www.anthropic.com/engineering/multi-agent-research-system. Last accessed 10 Apr 2026

Author Index

D. Liberona et al. (Eds.): MISNC 2026, CCIS 3092, pp. 451–452, 2027.
https://doi.org/10.1007/978-3-032-33381-0

MIX
Papier aus verantwortungsvollen Quellen
Paper from responsible sources
FSC® C105338

FSC
www.fsc.org

If you have any concerns about our products,
you can contact us on
ProductSafety@springernature.com

In case Publisher is established outside the EU,
the EU authorized representative is:
Springer Nature Customer Service Center GmbH
Europaplatz 3, 69115 Heidelberg, Germany

Printed by Libri Plureos GmbH
in Hamburg, Germany